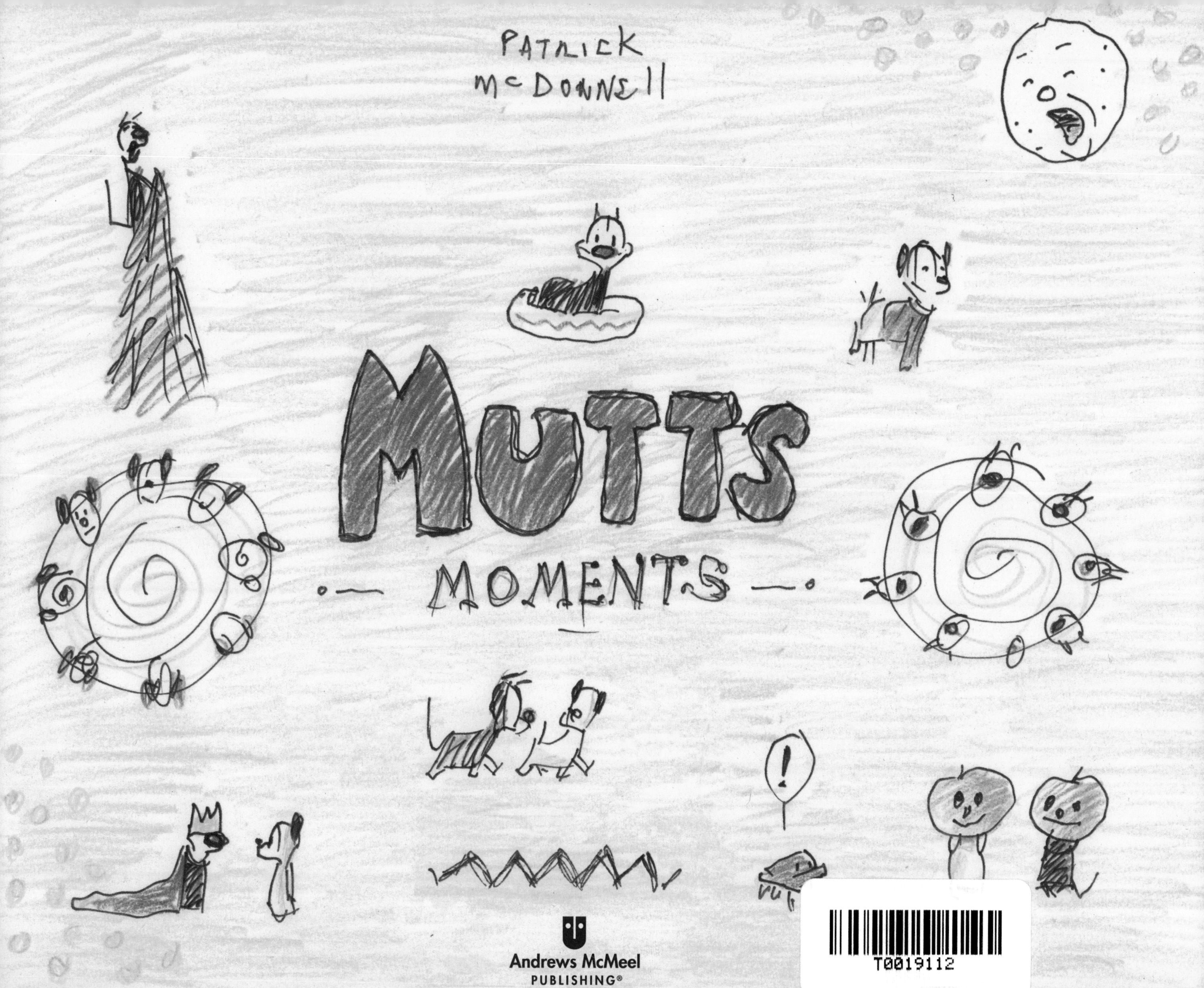
PATRICK McDONNELL
MUTTS
MOMENTS

Andrews McMeel
PUBLISHING®

Other Books by Patrick McDonnell

Mutts	*Everyday Mutts*	*Playtime*
Cats and Dogs: Mutts II	*Animal Friendly*	*Year of Yesh*
More Shtuff: Mutts III	*Call of the Wild*	*#LoveMutts*
Yesh!: Mutts IV	*Stop and Smell the Roses*	*You've Got Those Wild Eyes Again, Mooch*
Our Mutts: Five	*Earl & Mooch*	*Mutts Sundays*
A Little Look-See: Mutts VI	*Our Little Kat King*	*Hot Dogs, Hot Cats*
What Now: Mutts VII	*Bonk!*	*Sunday Mornings*
I Want to Be the Kitty: Mutts VIII	*A Shtinky Little Christmas*	*Sunday Afternoons*
Dog-Eared: Mutts IX	*Cat Crazy*	*Sunday Evenings*
Who Let the Cat Out: Mutts X	*Living the Dream*	*Mutts Go Green*

Mutts is distributed internationally by King Features Syndicate, Inc. For information, write to King Features Syndicate, Inc., 300 West Fifty-Seventh Street, New York, New York 10019, or visit www.KingFeatures.com.

21 22 23 24 25 POA 10 9 8 7 6 5 4 3 2 1

ISBN: 978-1-5248-6978-6

Library of Congress Control Number: 2021935207

Cover design: Nicole Tramontana

Printed on recycled paper.

Mutts can be found on the Internet at **www.mutts.com**.

ATTENTION: SCHOOLS AND BUSINESSES

Andrews McMeel books are available at quantity discounts with bulk purchase for educational, business, or sales promotional use. For information, please e-mail the Andrews McMeel Publishing Special Sales Department: specialsales@amuniversal.com.

MUTTS
MOMENTS

"Always say 'yes' to the present moment." *-Eckhart Tolle*

"Yesh!" *-Mooch*

I've always felt the comic strip is a perfect medium for capturing the simple, precious, fleeting moments of life. And that our family dogs and cats are natural conduits for taking us out of our troubled minds and bringing us to the present moment. With *MUTTS,* I try to celebrate both.

This collection is from the twenty-fifth anniversary year of my daily strip. *Twenty-five years.* That's a lot of moments. Thank you for sharing them with me.

There are two Sunday comics included in this book (on pages 58 and 59) that were inked by legendary Marvel comic book artist Joe Sinnott. Joe was the preeminent inker for Jack Kirby's run of the *Fantastic Four* in the 1960s. What a thrill and honor to have my pencils graced with his brushwork.

So cuddle up on the couch with your very best friend and this latest collection. And enjoy the moment.

—PATRICK

And now we welcome the new year,
full of things that have never been.

~ Rainer Maria Rilke

4

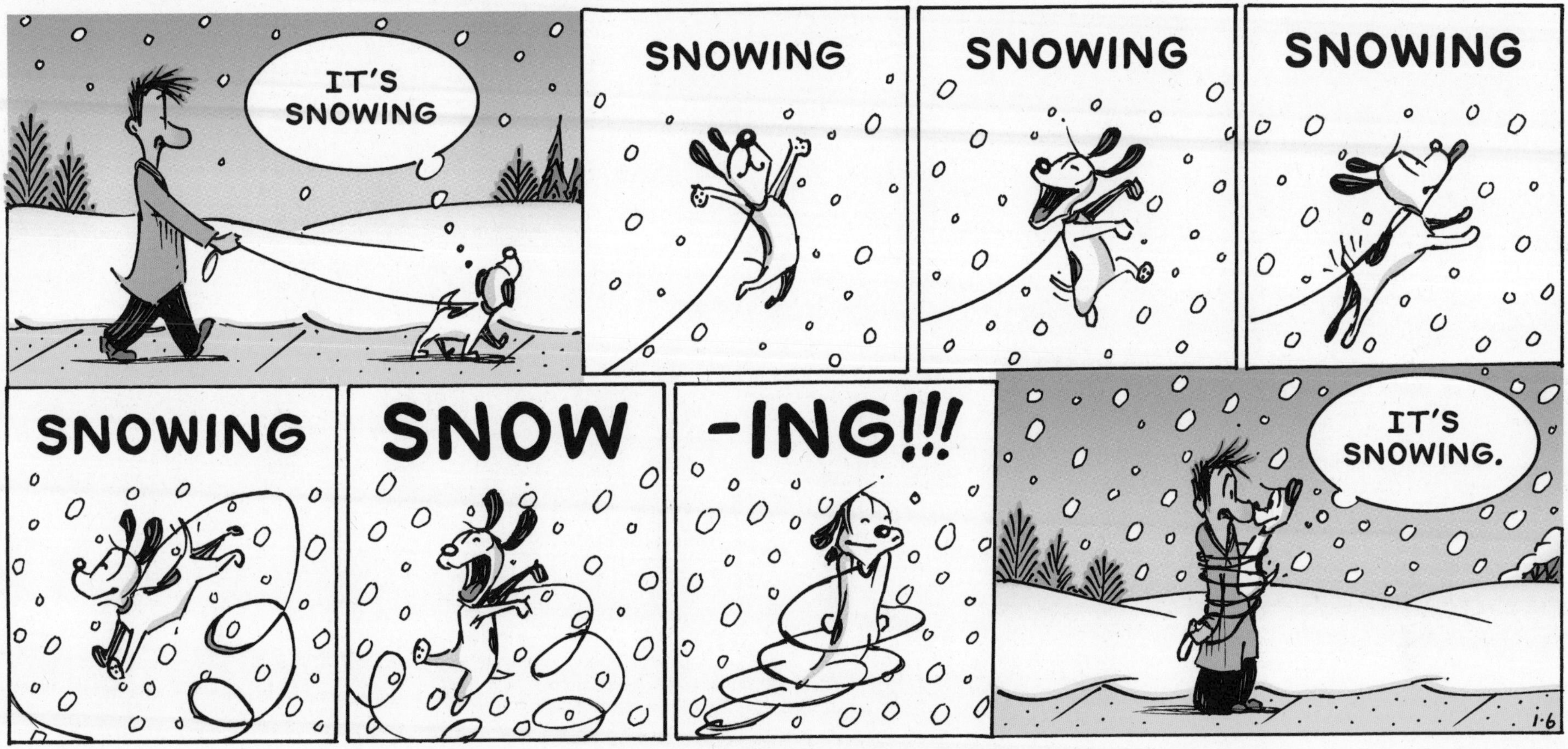

IT'S SNOWING
SNOWING
SNOWING
SNOWING
SNOWING
SNOW
-ING!!!
IT'S SNOWING.
1·6

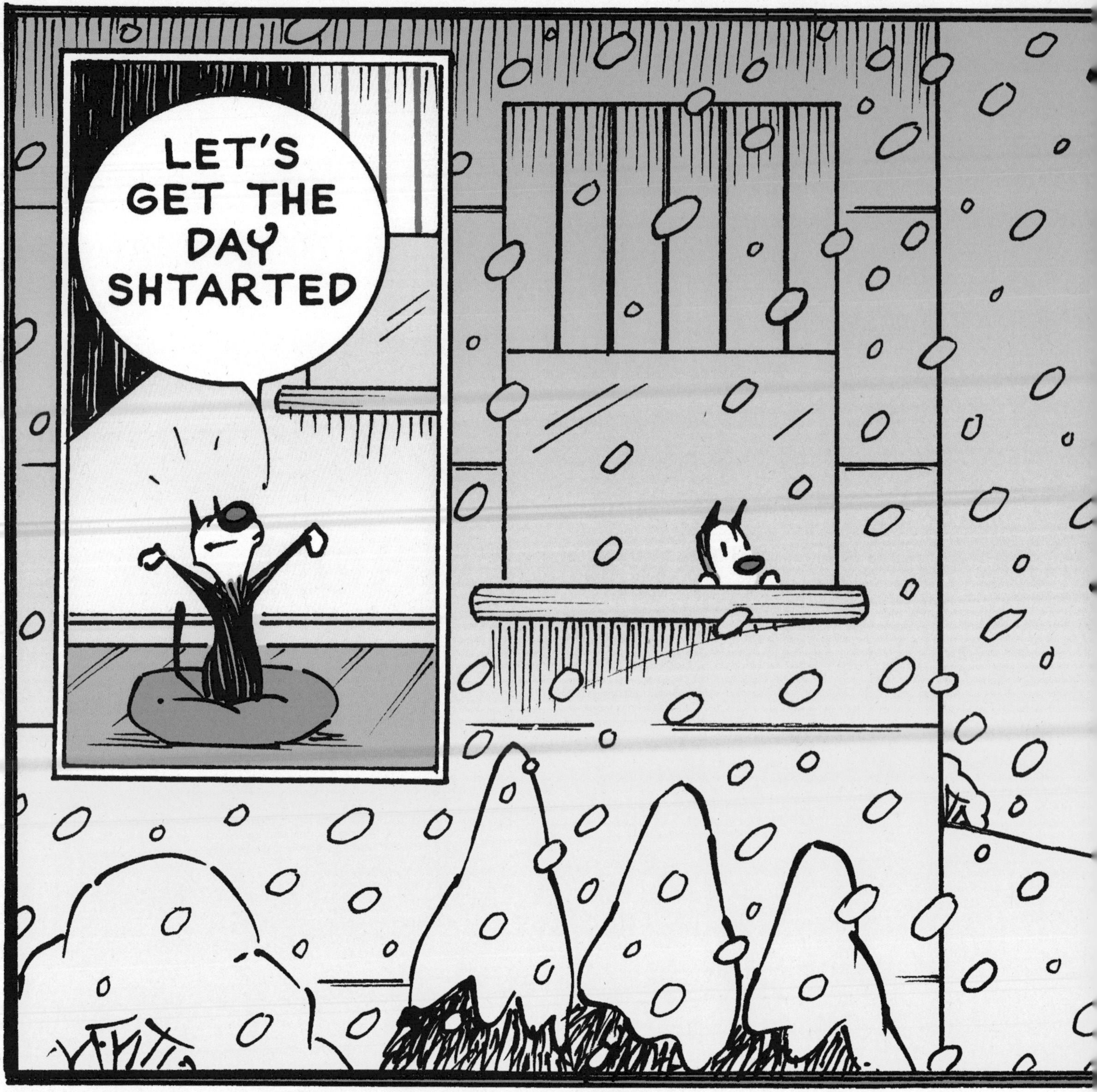
LET'S GET THE DAY SHTARTED

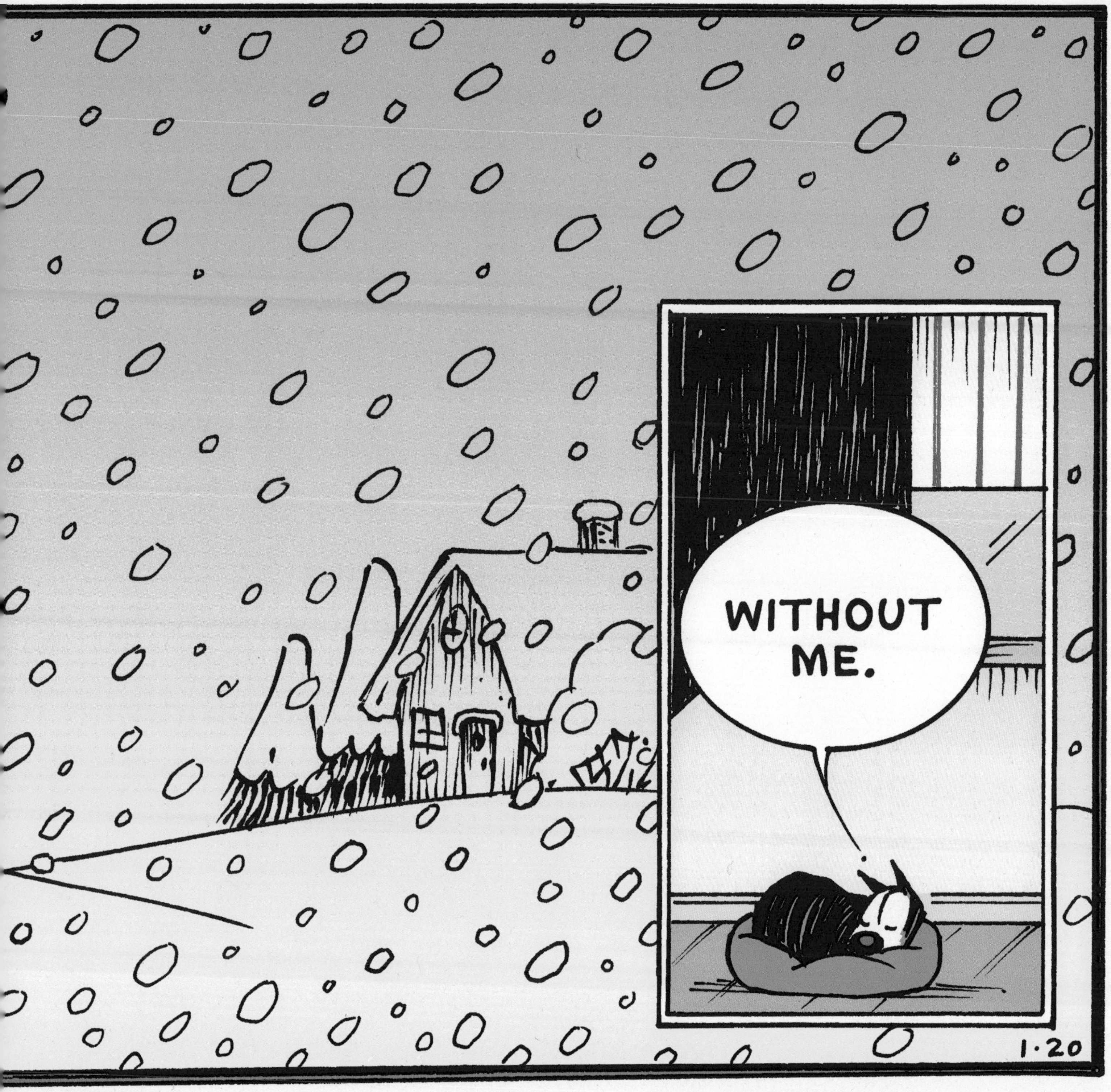
WITHOUT ME.
1·20

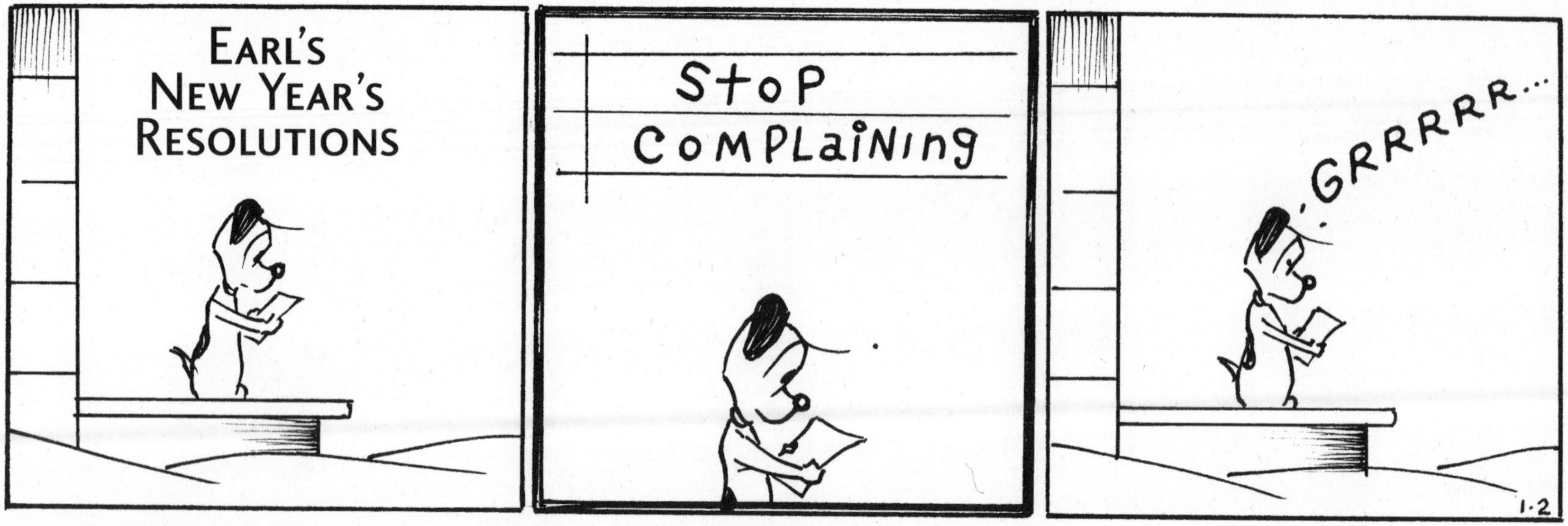
EARL'S NEW YEAR'S RESOLUTIONS
STOP COMPLAINING
GRRRRR...
1·2

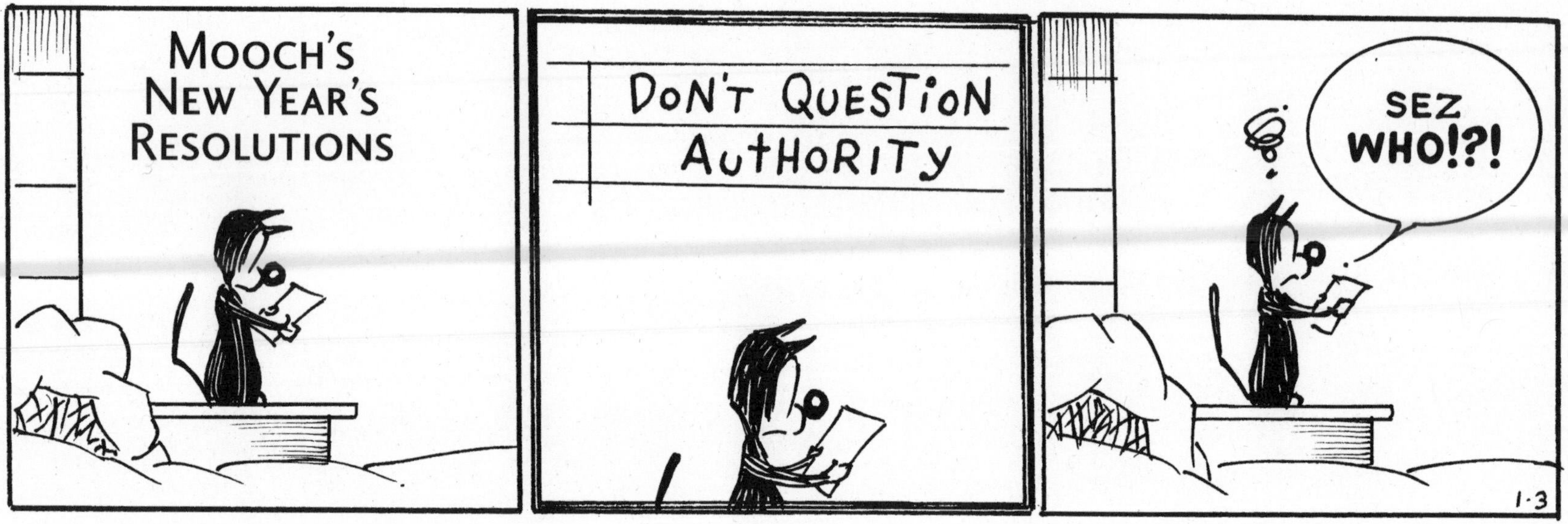
MOOCH'S NEW YEAR'S RESOLUTIONS
DON'T QUESTION AUTHORITY
SEZ WHO!?!
1·3

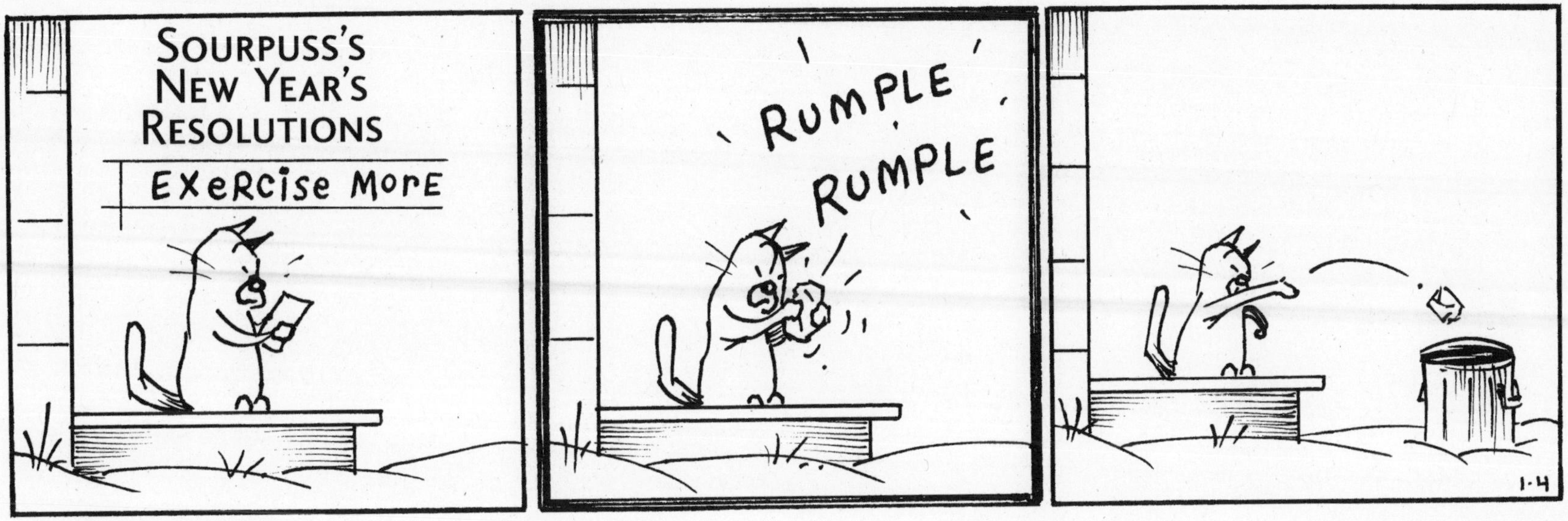
SOURPUSS'S NEW YEAR'S RESOLUTIONS
EXERCISE MORE
RUMPLE
RUMPLE
1·4

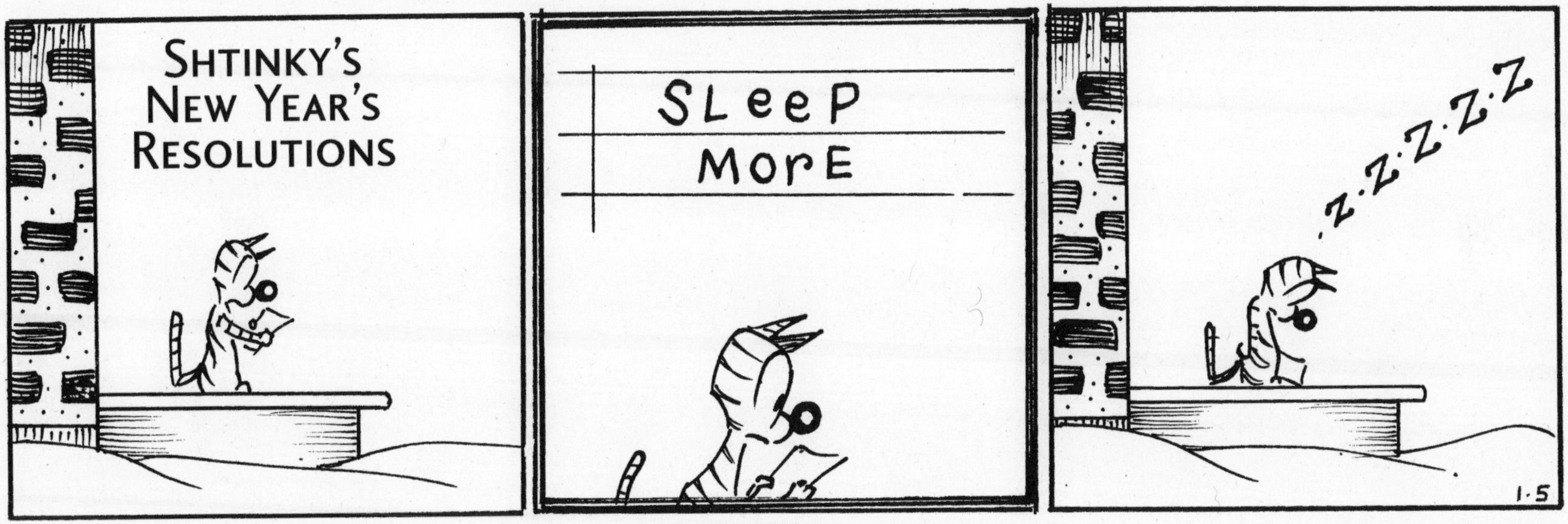
SHTINKY'S NEW YEAR'S RESOLUTIONS
SLEEP MORE
Z·Z·Z·Z·Z·Z
1·5

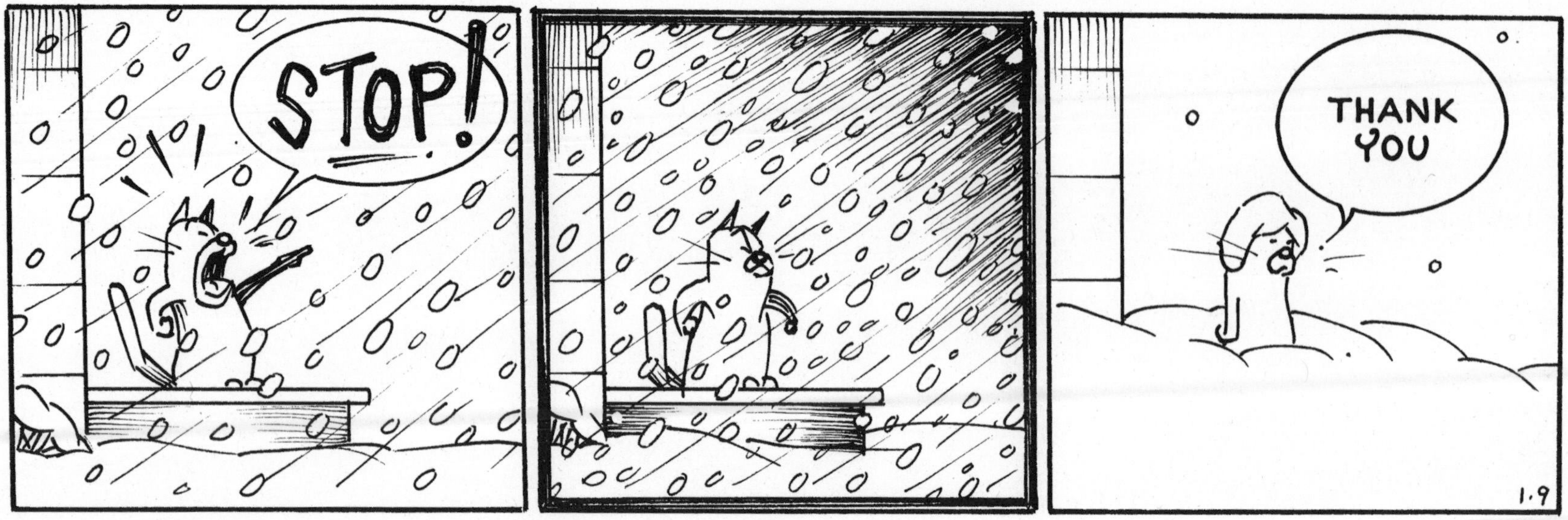
STOP!
THANK YOU
1·9

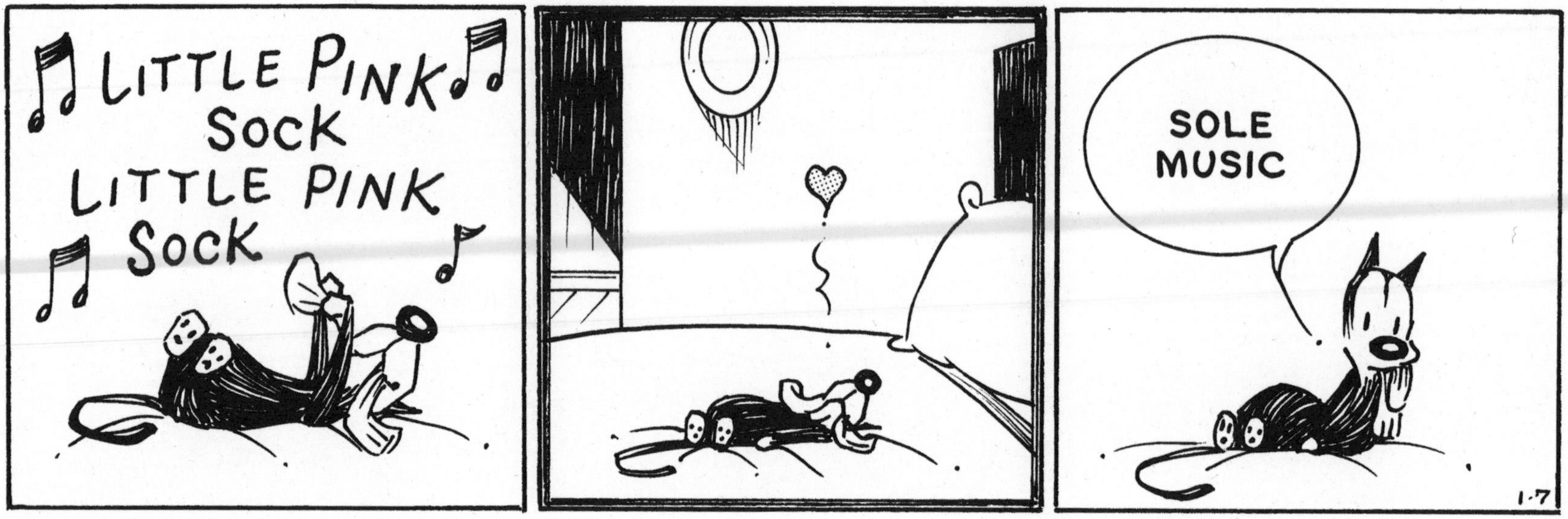
LITTLE PINK SOCK LITTLE PINK SOCK
SOLE MUSIC
1·7

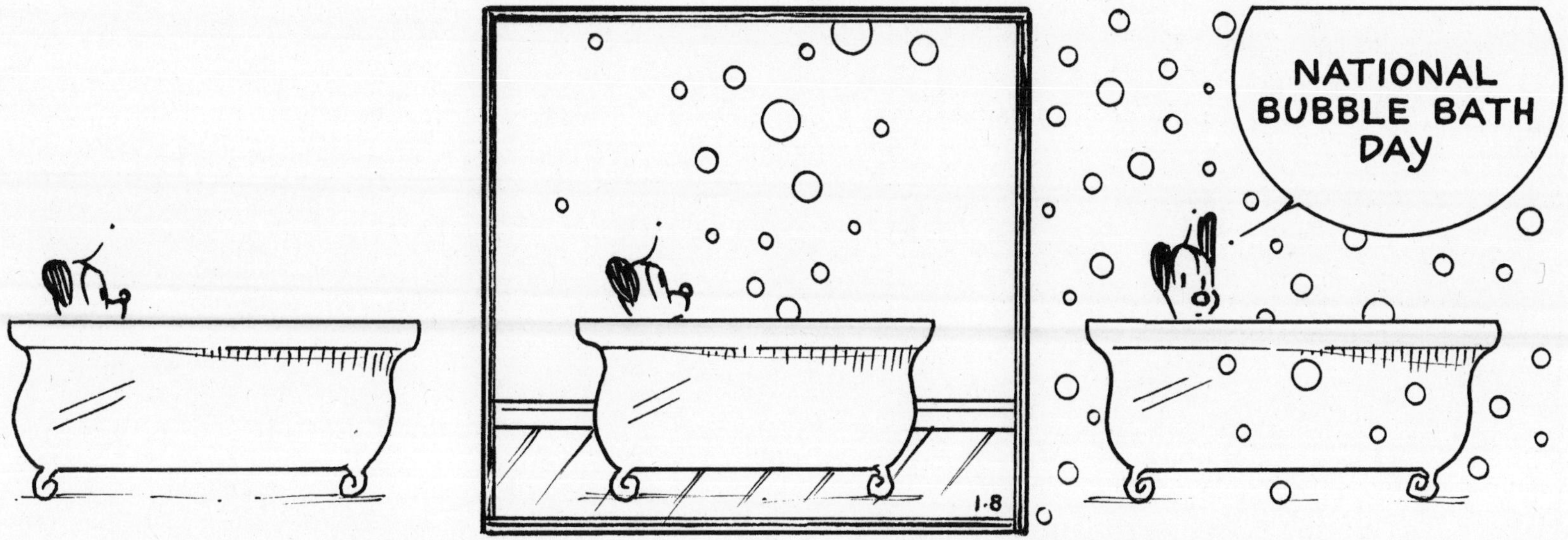
NATIONAL BUBBLE BATH DAY
1·8

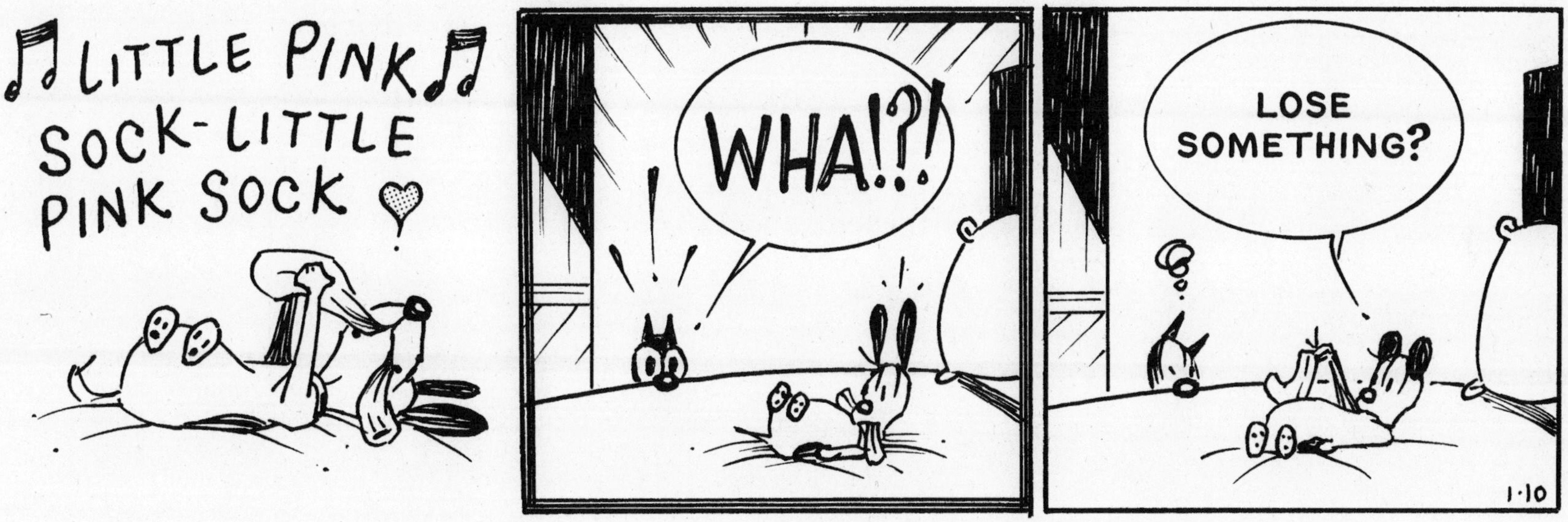
LITTLE PINK SOCK-LITTLE PINK SOCK
WHA!?!
LOSE SOMETHING?
1·10

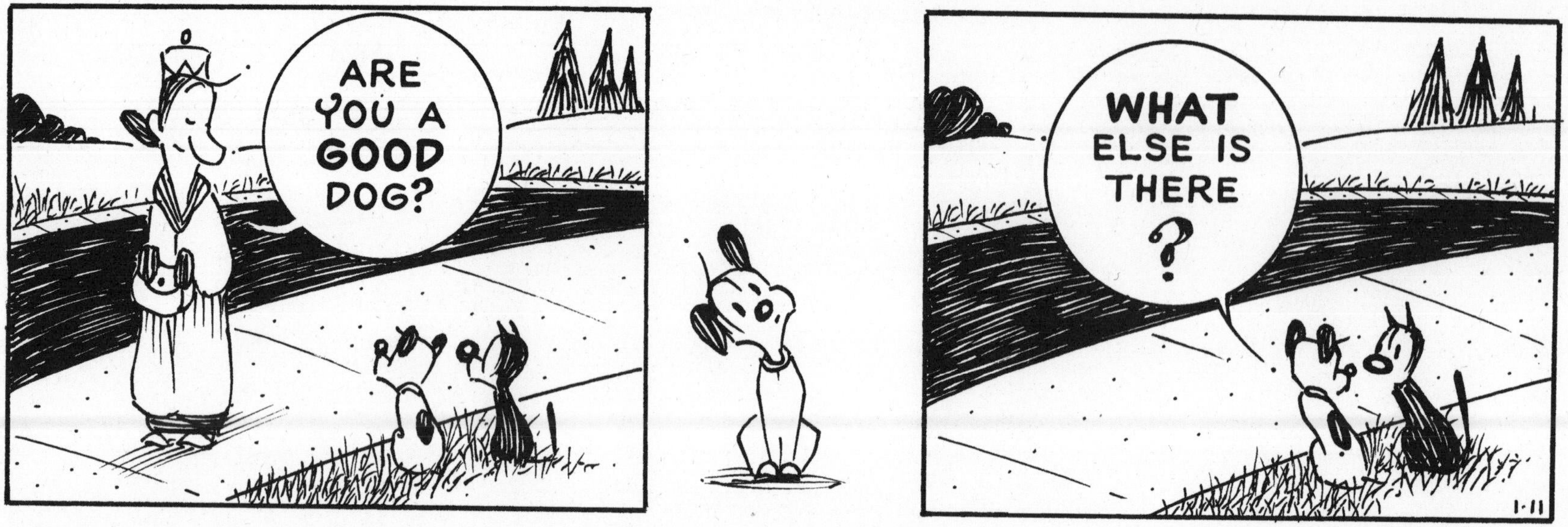
ARE YOU A GOOD DOG?
WHAT ELSE IS THERE ?
1·11

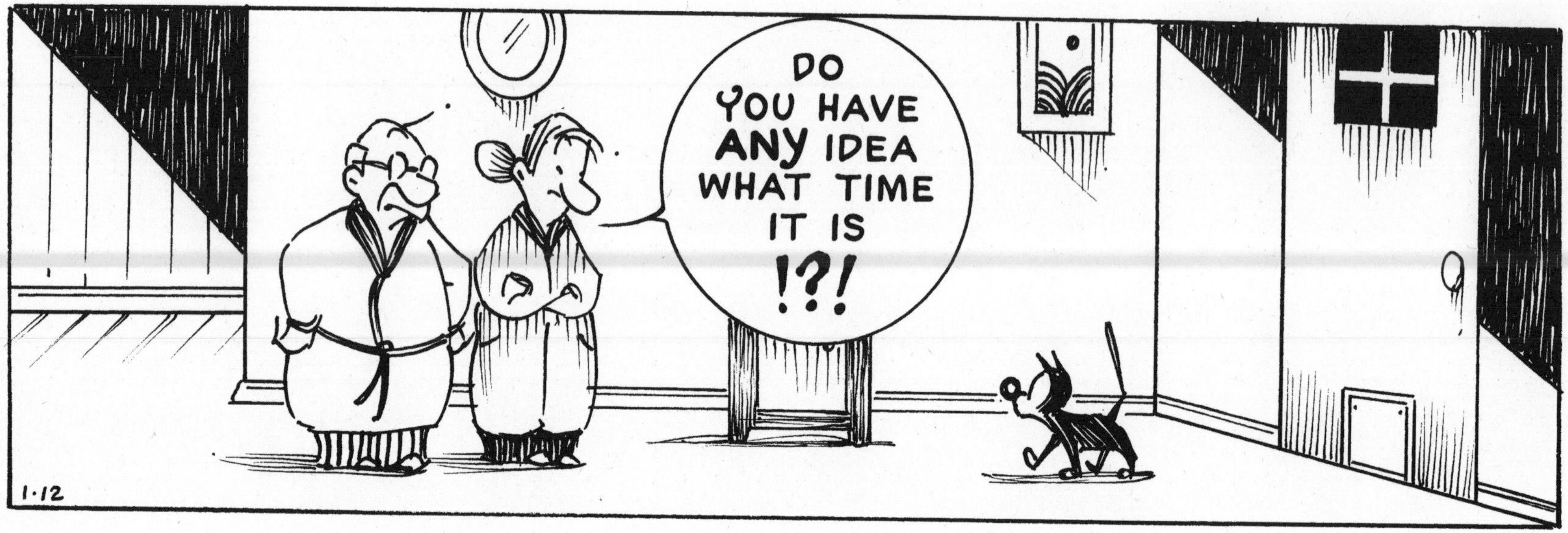
DO YOU HAVE ANY IDEA WHAT TIME IT IS !?!
1·12

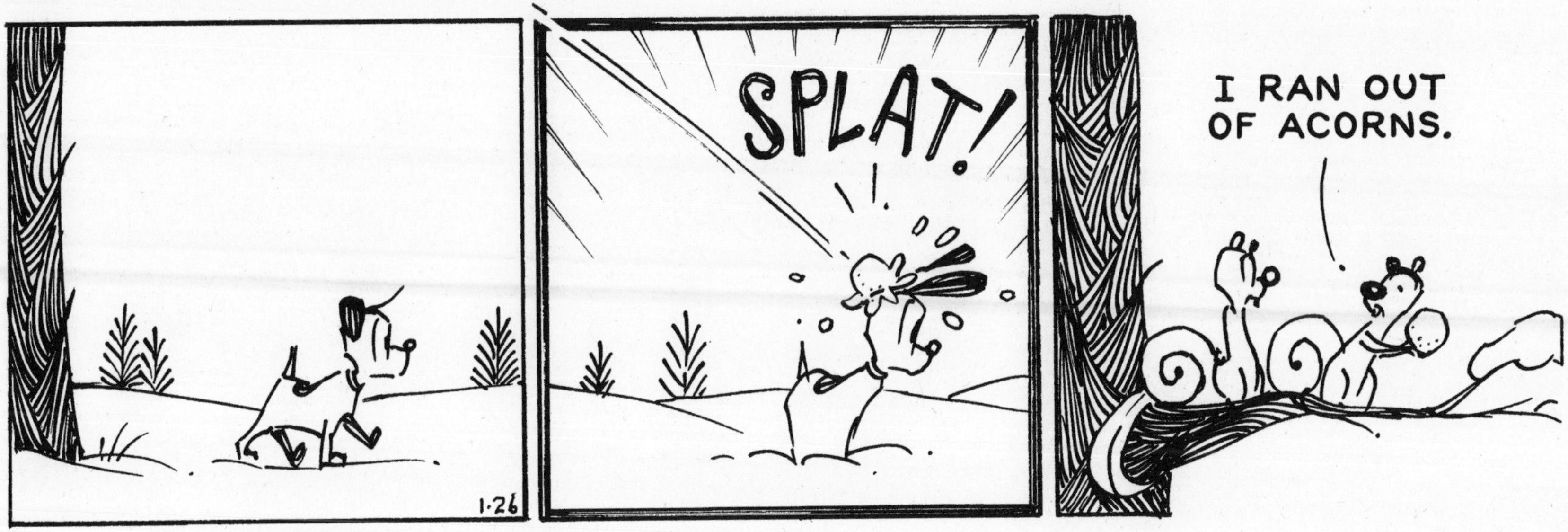
1·26
SPLAT!
I RAN OUT OF ACORNS.

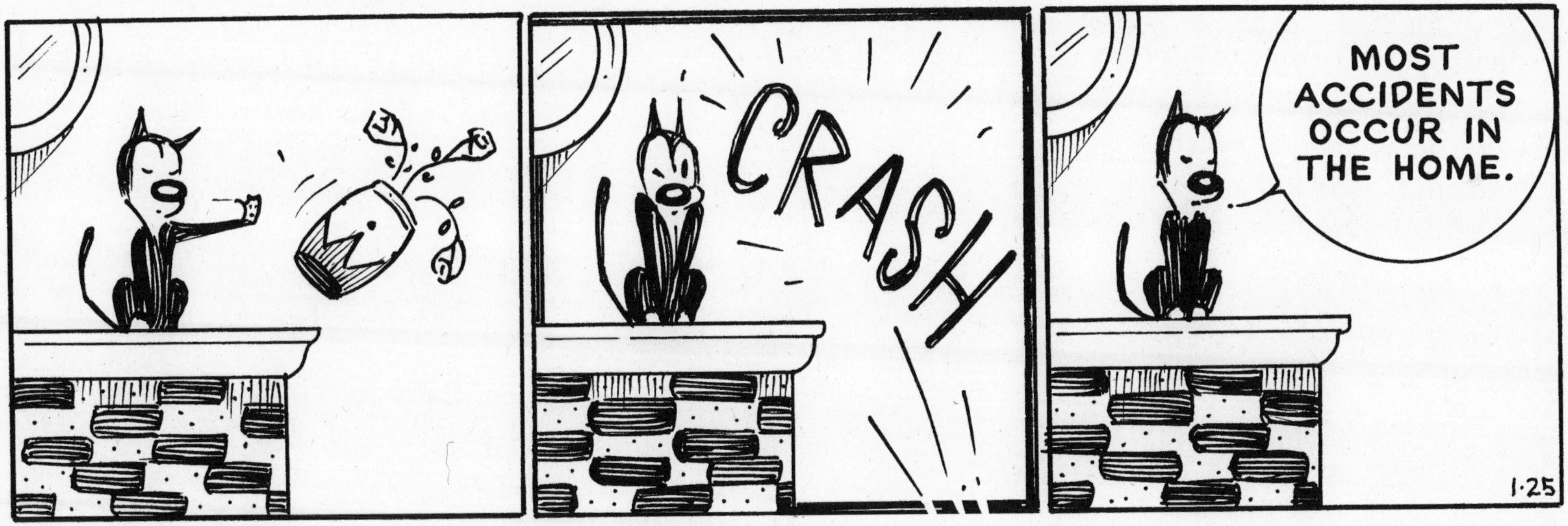
CRASH
MOST ACCIDENTS OCCUR IN THE HOME.
1·25

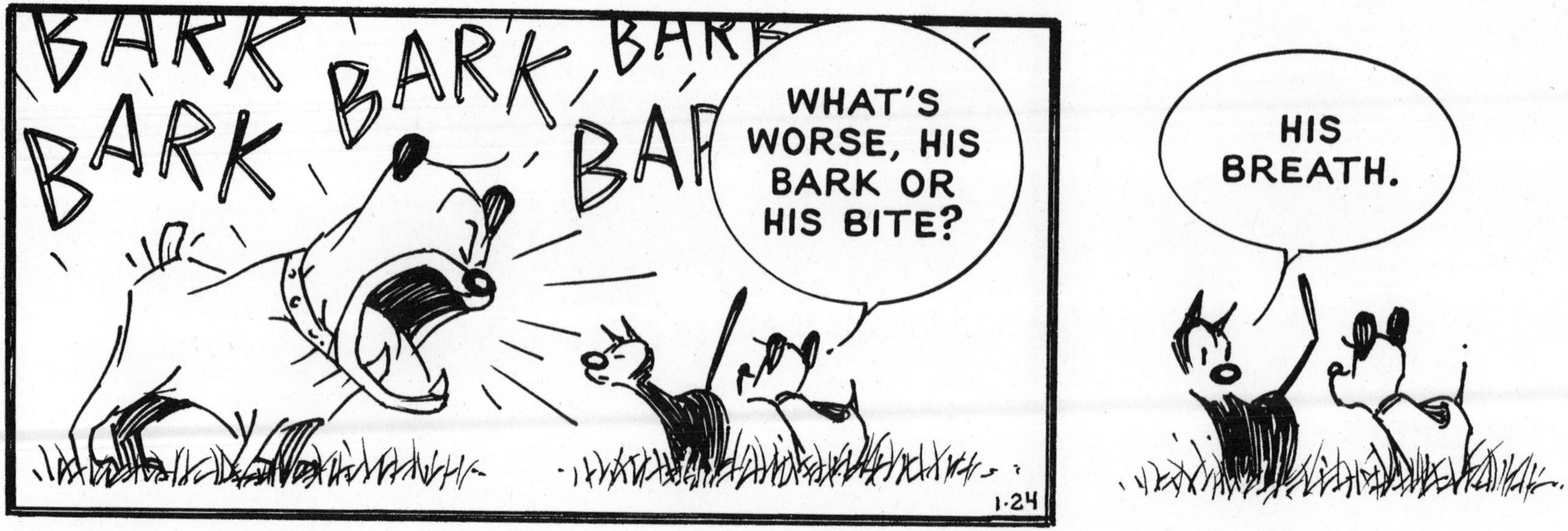
BARK
BARK
BARK
BAR
WHAT'S WORSE, HIS BARK OR HIS BITE?
HIS BREATH.
1·24

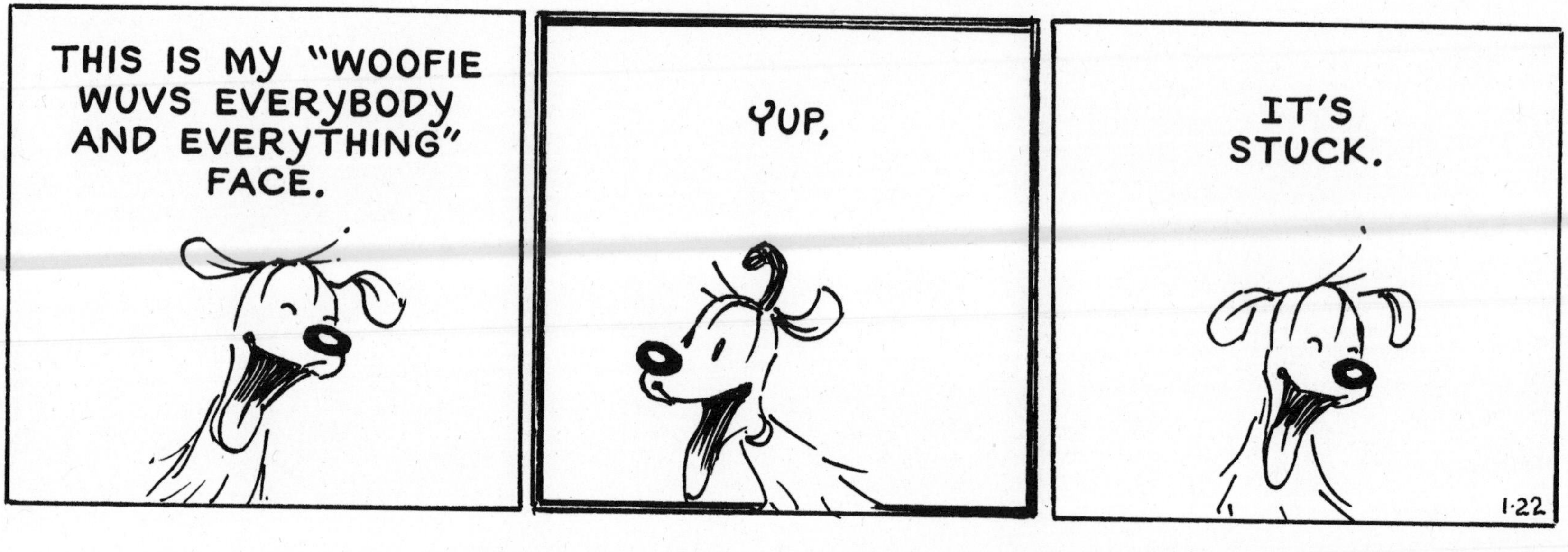
THIS IS MY "WOOFIE WUVS EVERYBODY AND EVERYTHING" FACE.
YUP.
IT'S STUCK.
1·22

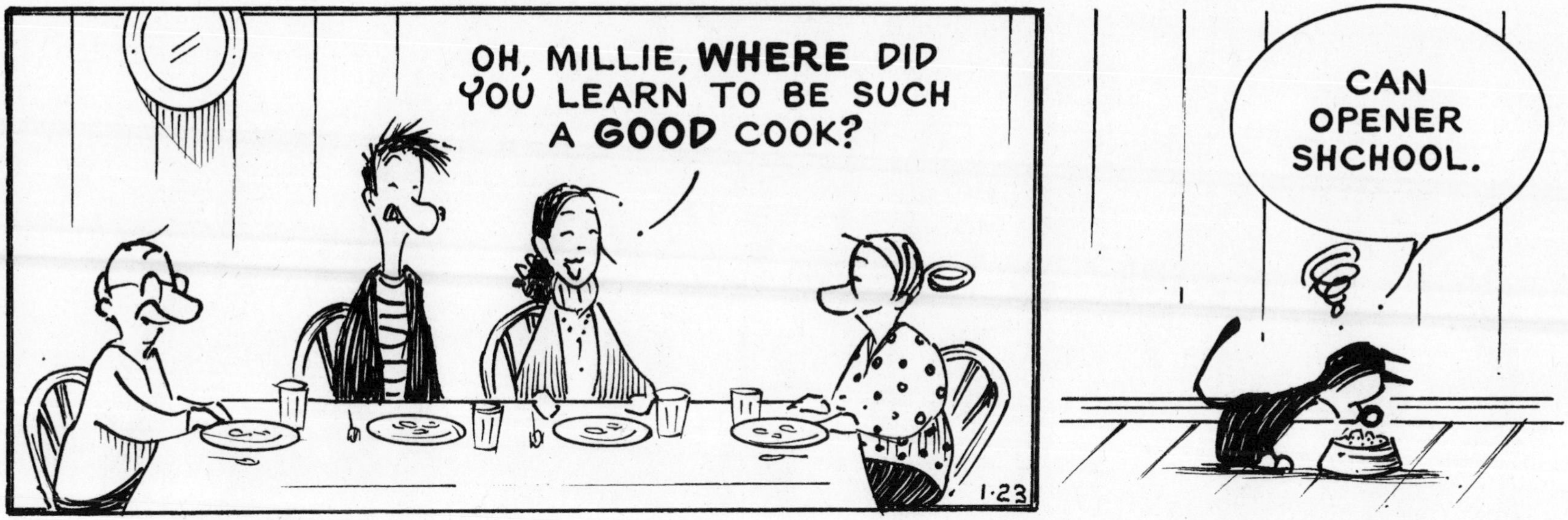
OH, MILLIE, WHERE DID YOU LEARN TO BE SUCH A GOOD COOK?
CAN OPENER SHCHOOL.
1·23

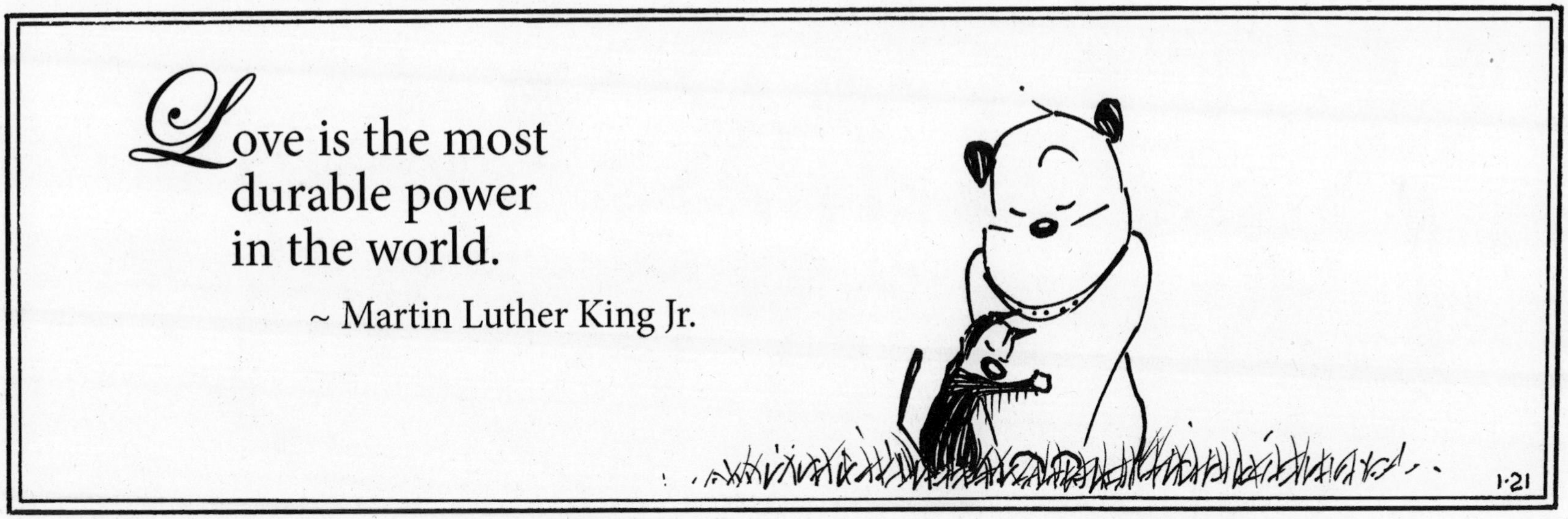
Love is the most durable power in the world.
~ Martin Luther King Jr.
1·21

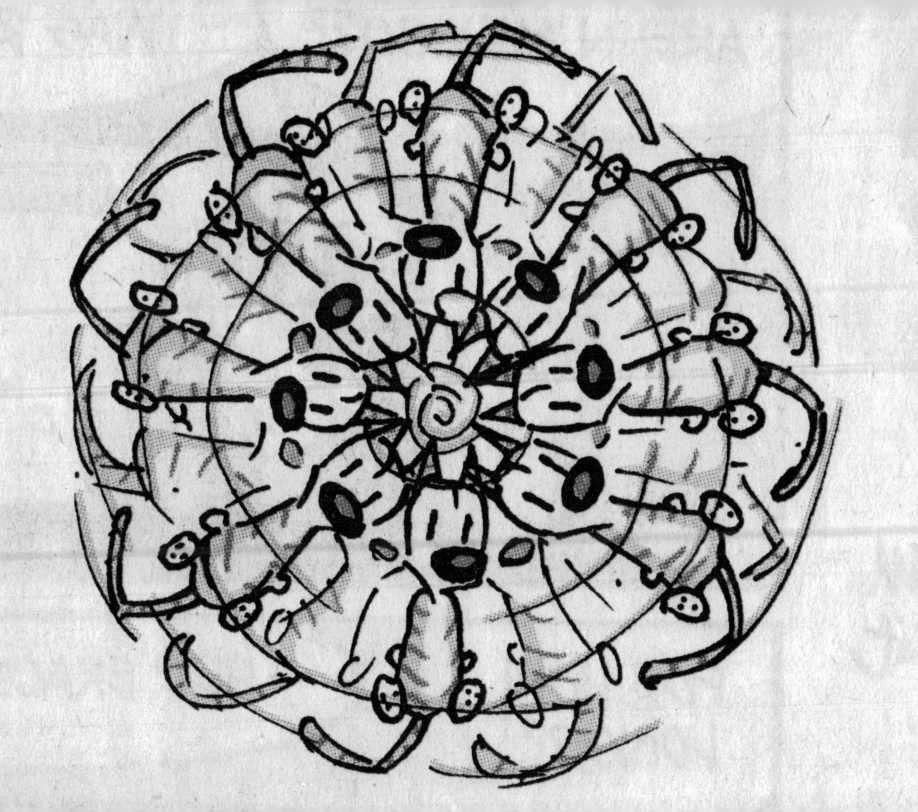

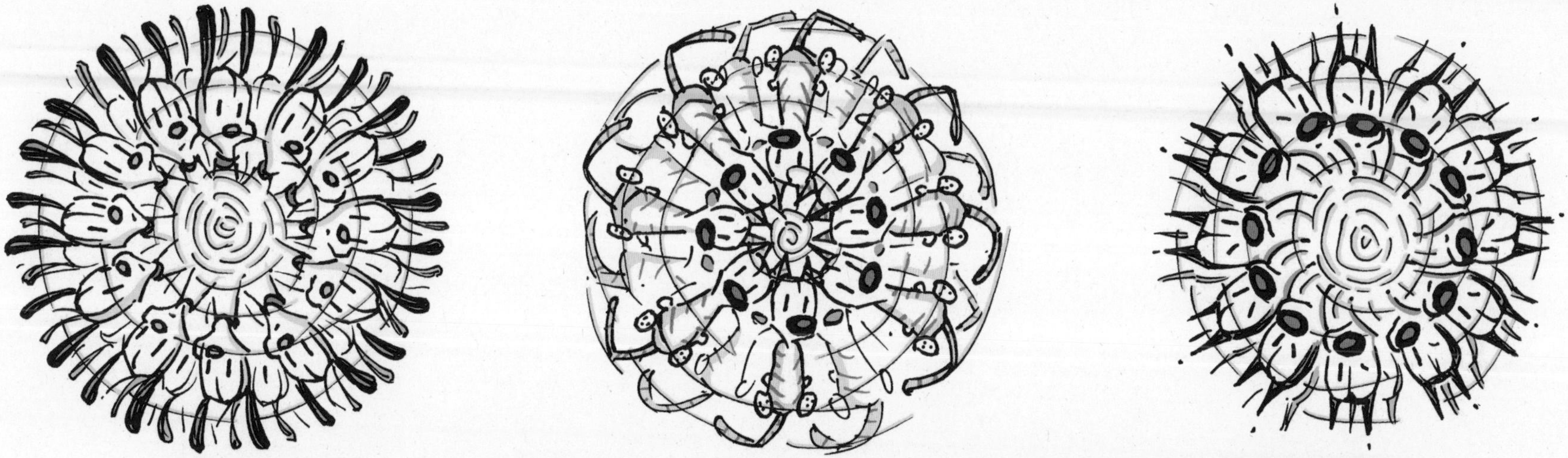

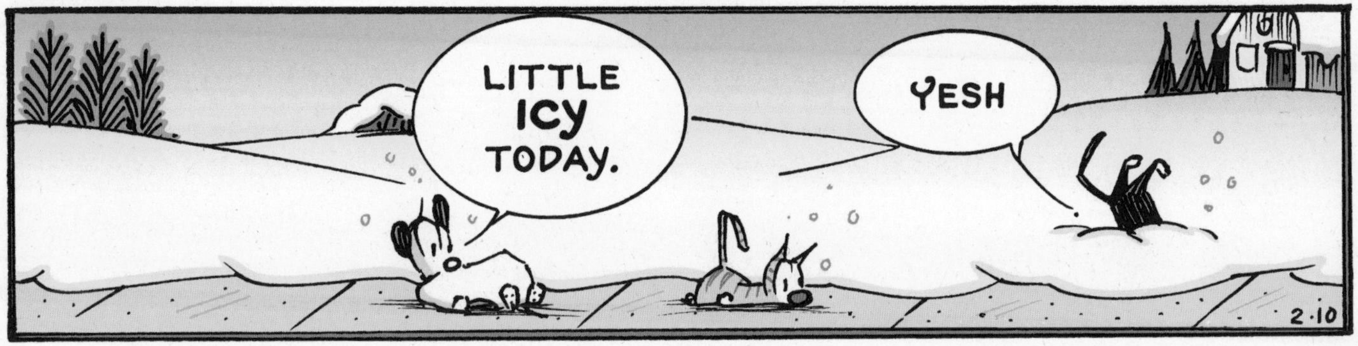
LITTLE ICY TODAY.
YESH
2·10

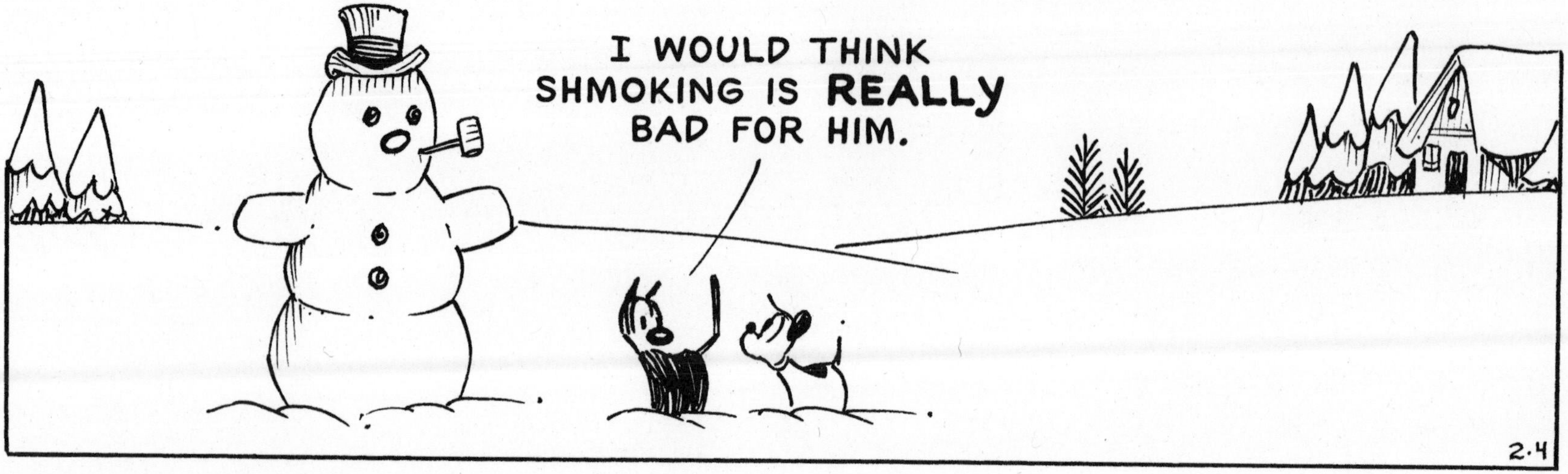
I WOULD THINK SHMOKING IS REALLY BAD FOR HIM.
2·4

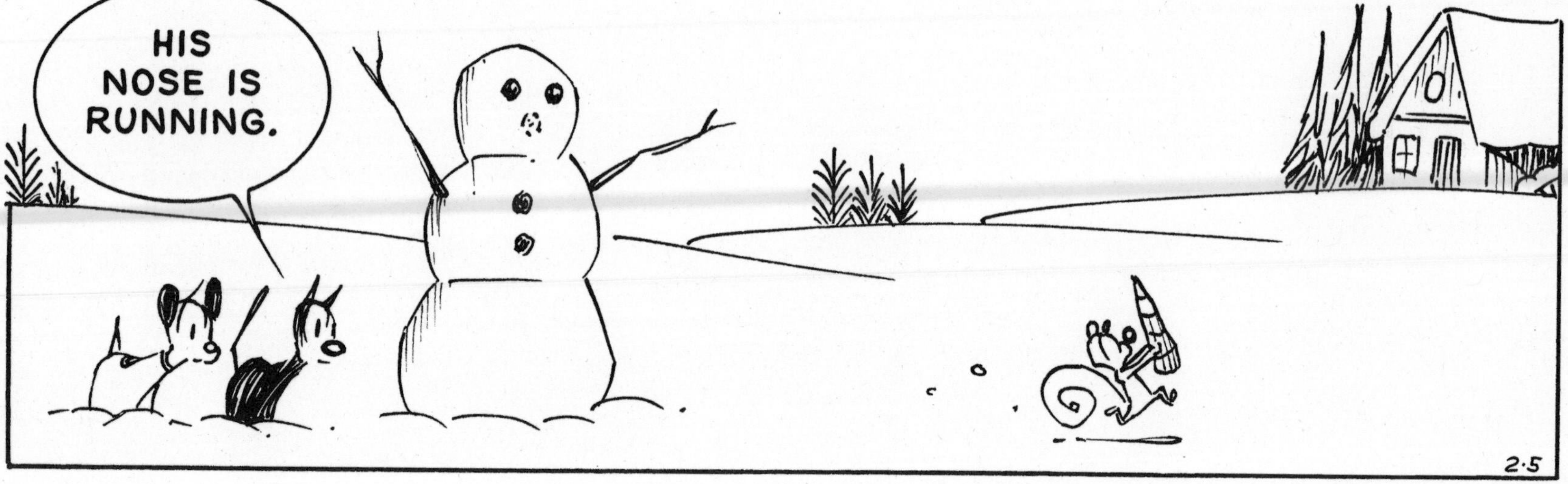
HIS NOSE IS RUNNING.
2·5

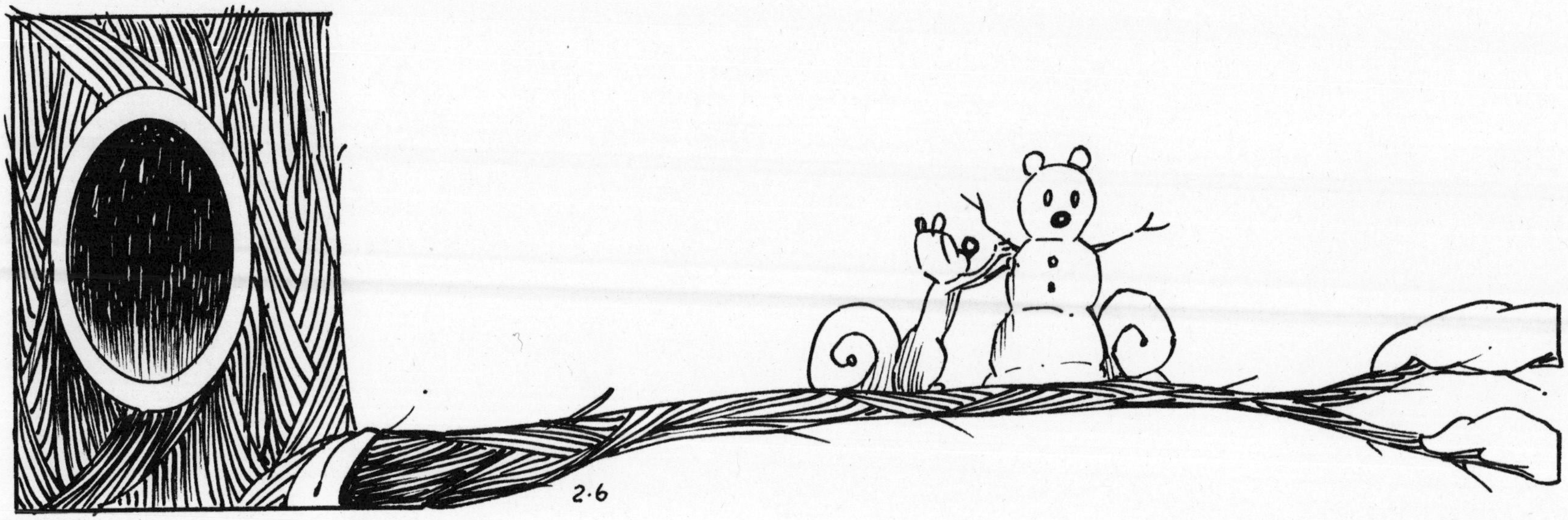
2·6

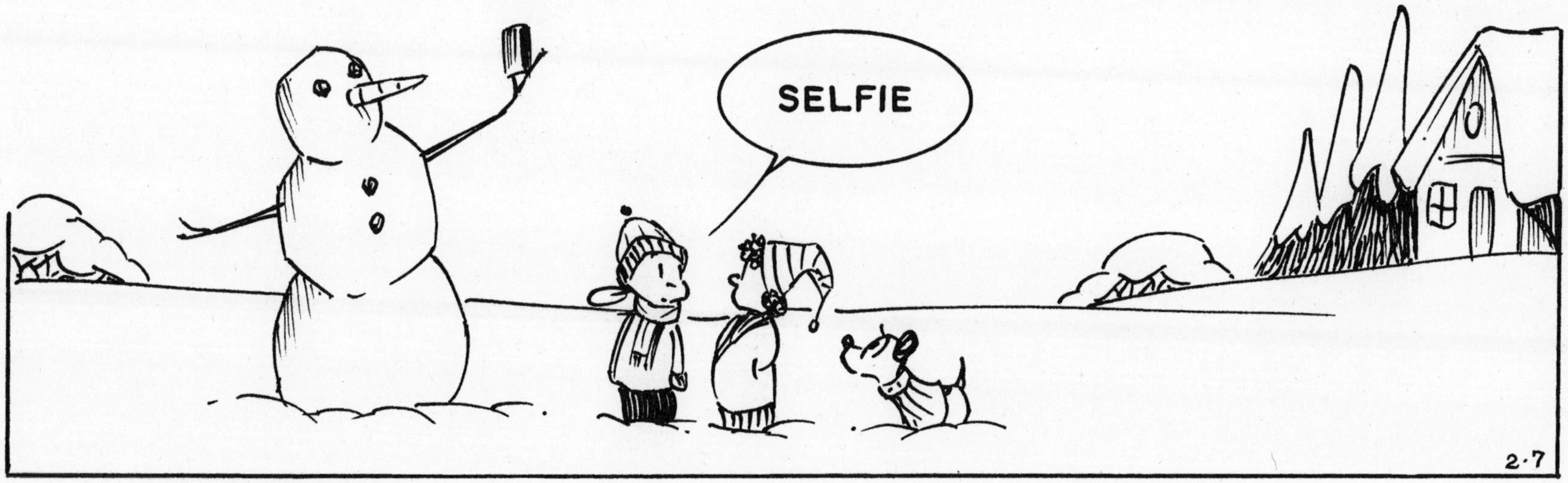
SELFIE
2·7

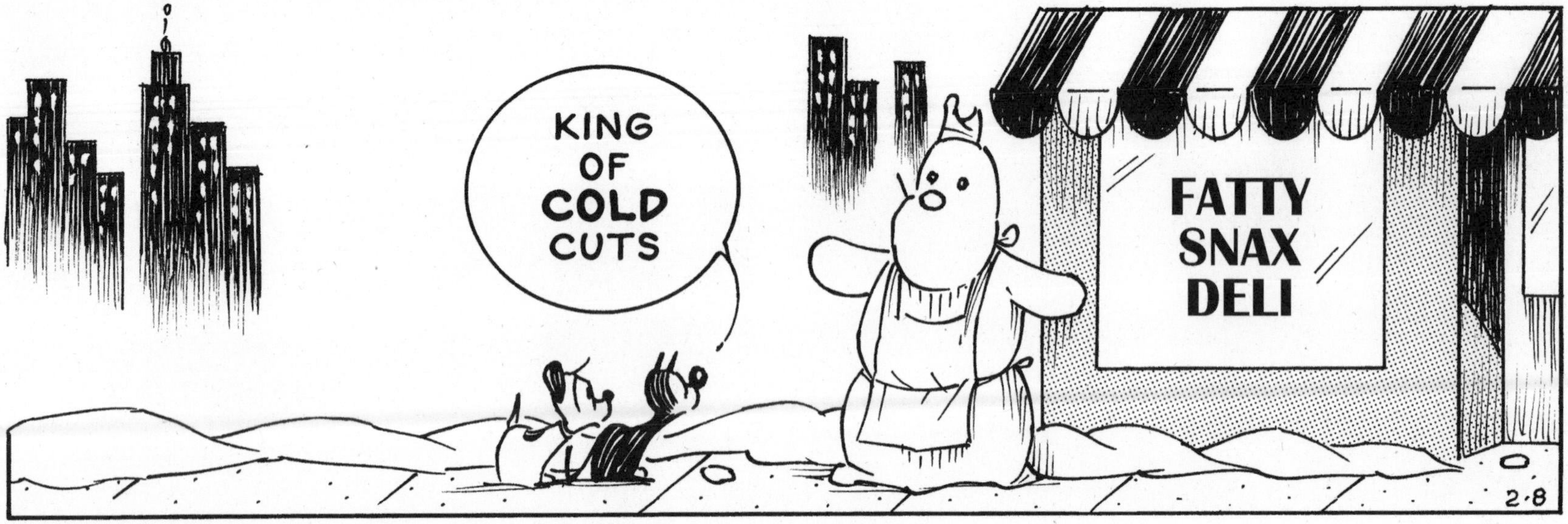
KING OF COLD CUTS
FATTY SNAX DELI
2·8

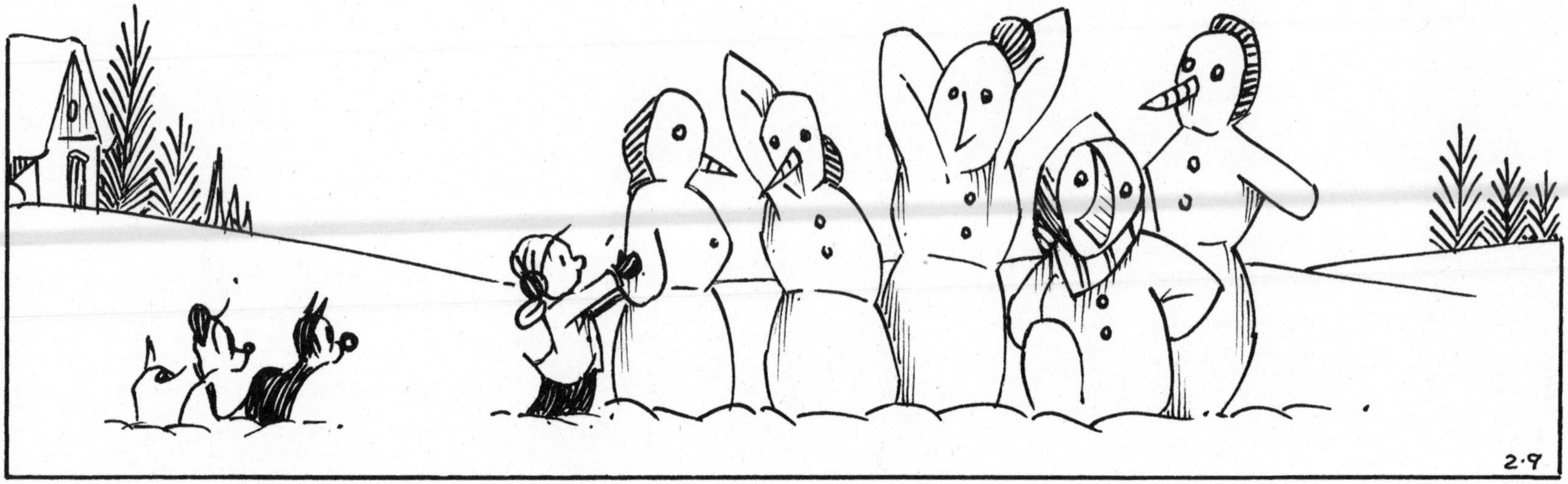
2·9

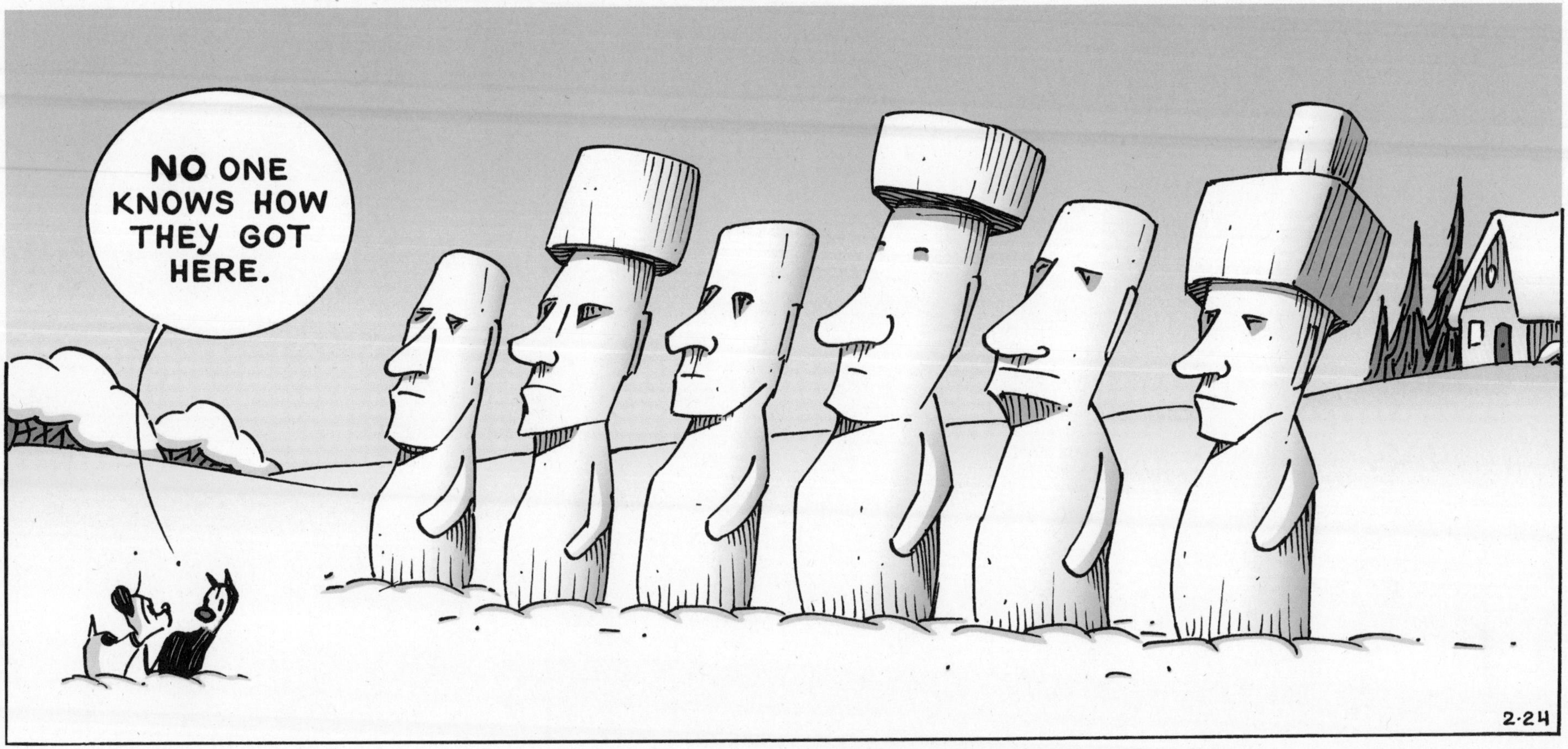
NO ONE KNOWS HOW THEY GOT HERE.
2-24

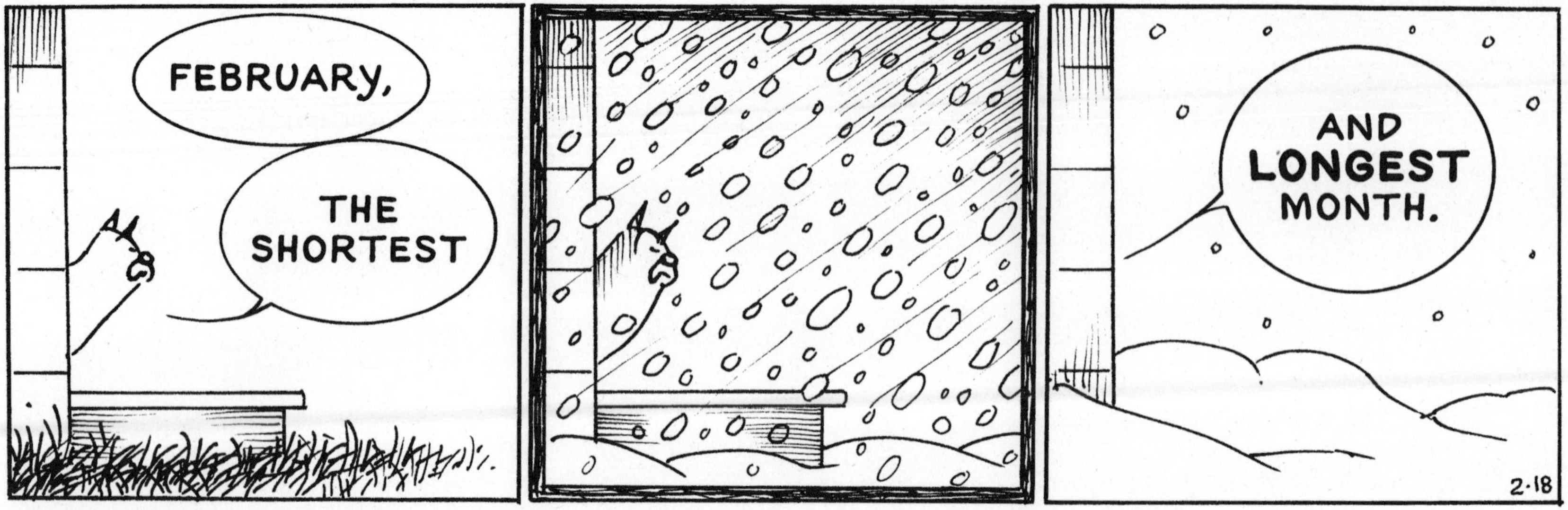
FEBRUARY,
THE SHORTEST
AND LONGEST MONTH.
2·18

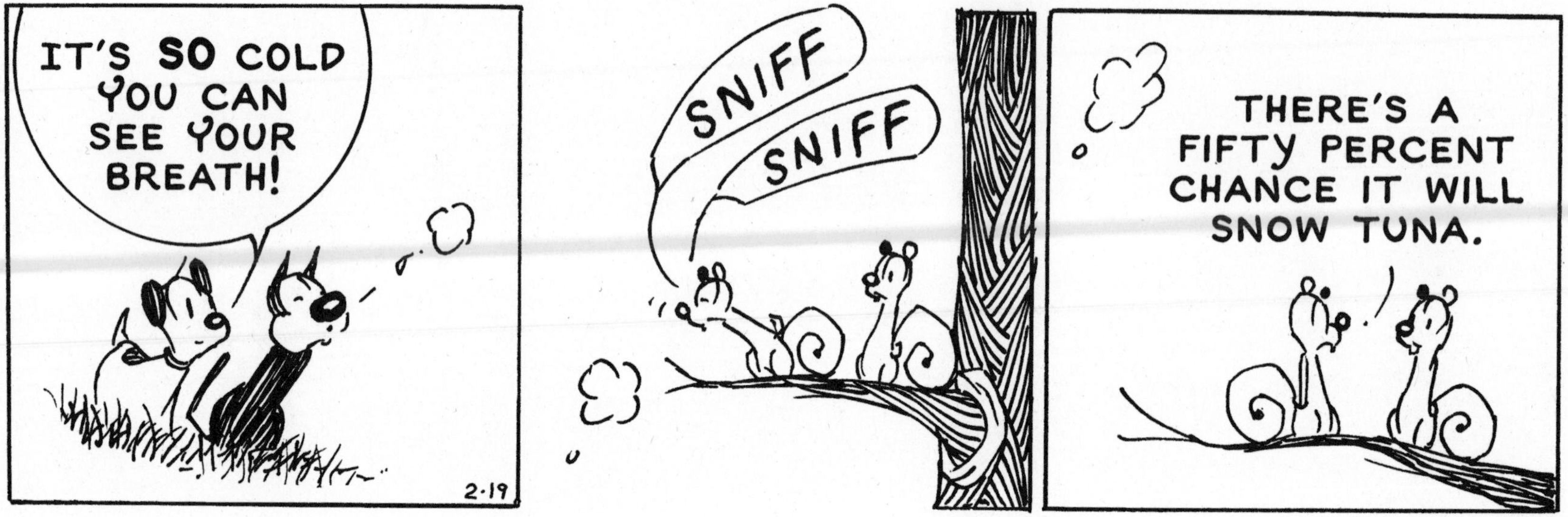
IT'S SO COLD YOU CAN SEE YOUR BREATH!
2·19
SNIFF
SNIFF
THERE'S A FIFTY PERCENT CHANCE IT WILL SNOW TUNA.

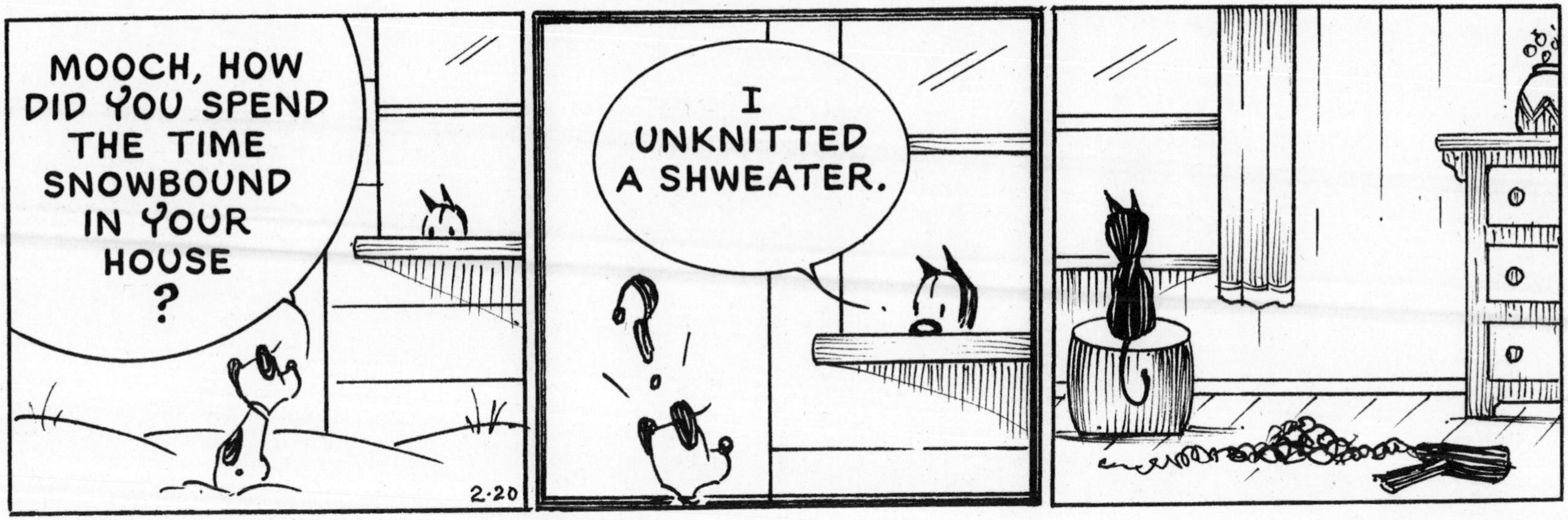
MOOCH, HOW DID YOU SPEND THE TIME SNOWBOUND IN YOUR HOUSE ?
2·20
I UNKNITTED A SHWEATER.

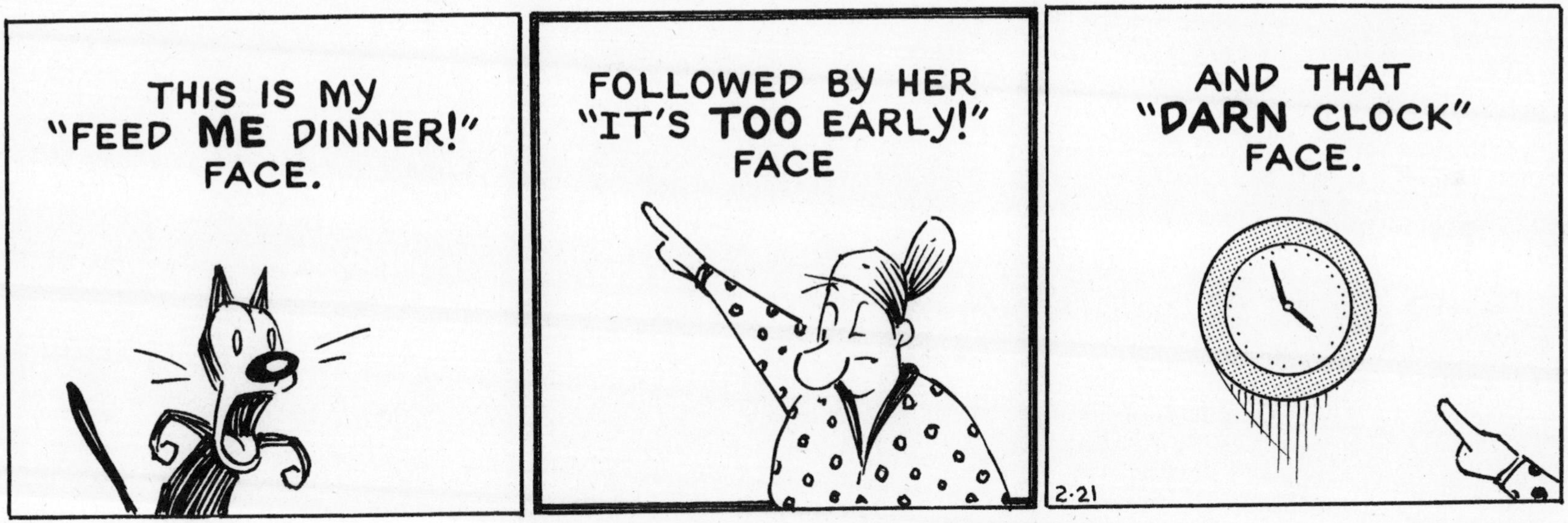
THIS IS MY "FEED ME DINNER!" FACE.
FOLLOWED BY HER "IT'S TOO EARLY!" FACE
AND THAT "DARN CLOCK" FACE.
2·21

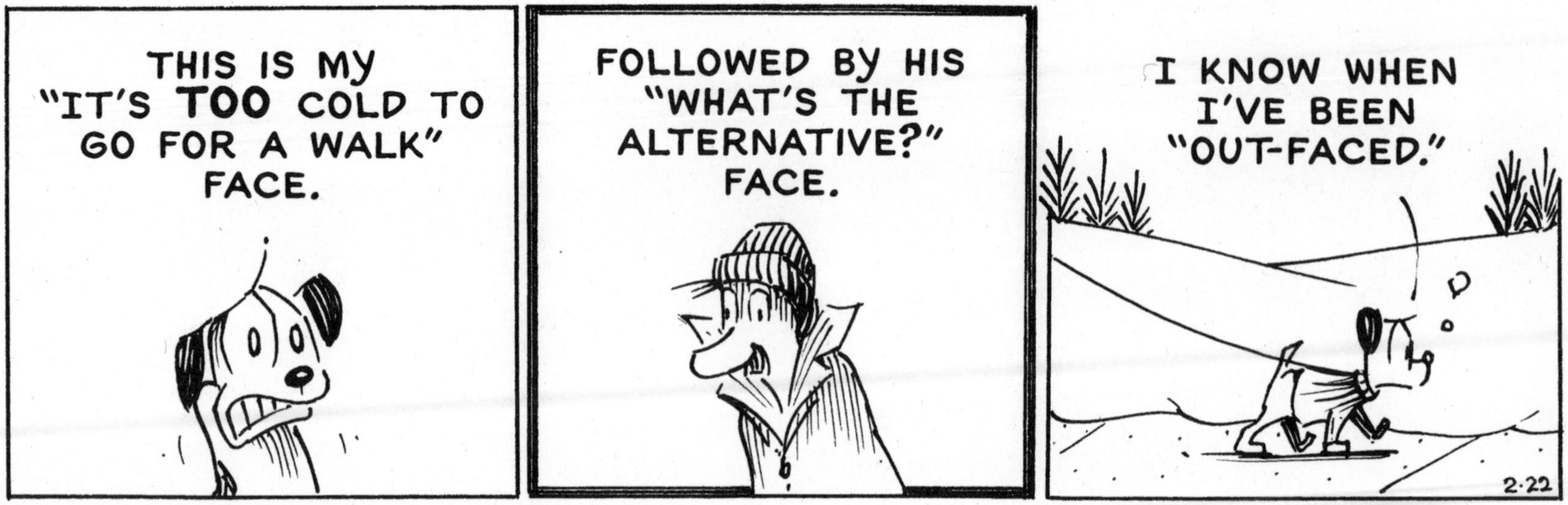
THIS IS MY "IT'S **TOO** COLD TO GO FOR A WALK" FACE.
FOLLOWED BY HIS "WHAT'S THE ALTERNATIVE?" FACE.
I KNOW WHEN I'VE BEEN "OUT-FACED."
2-22

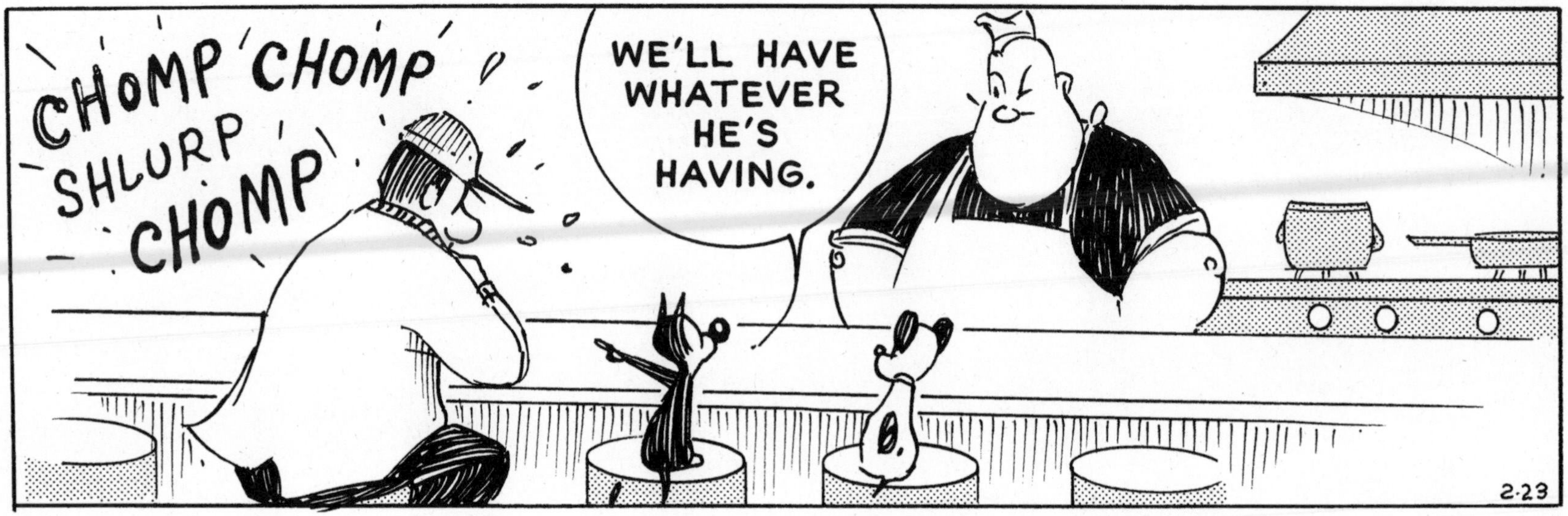
CHOMP CHOMP
SHLURP
CHOMP
WE'LL HAVE WHATEVER HE'S HAVING.
2-23

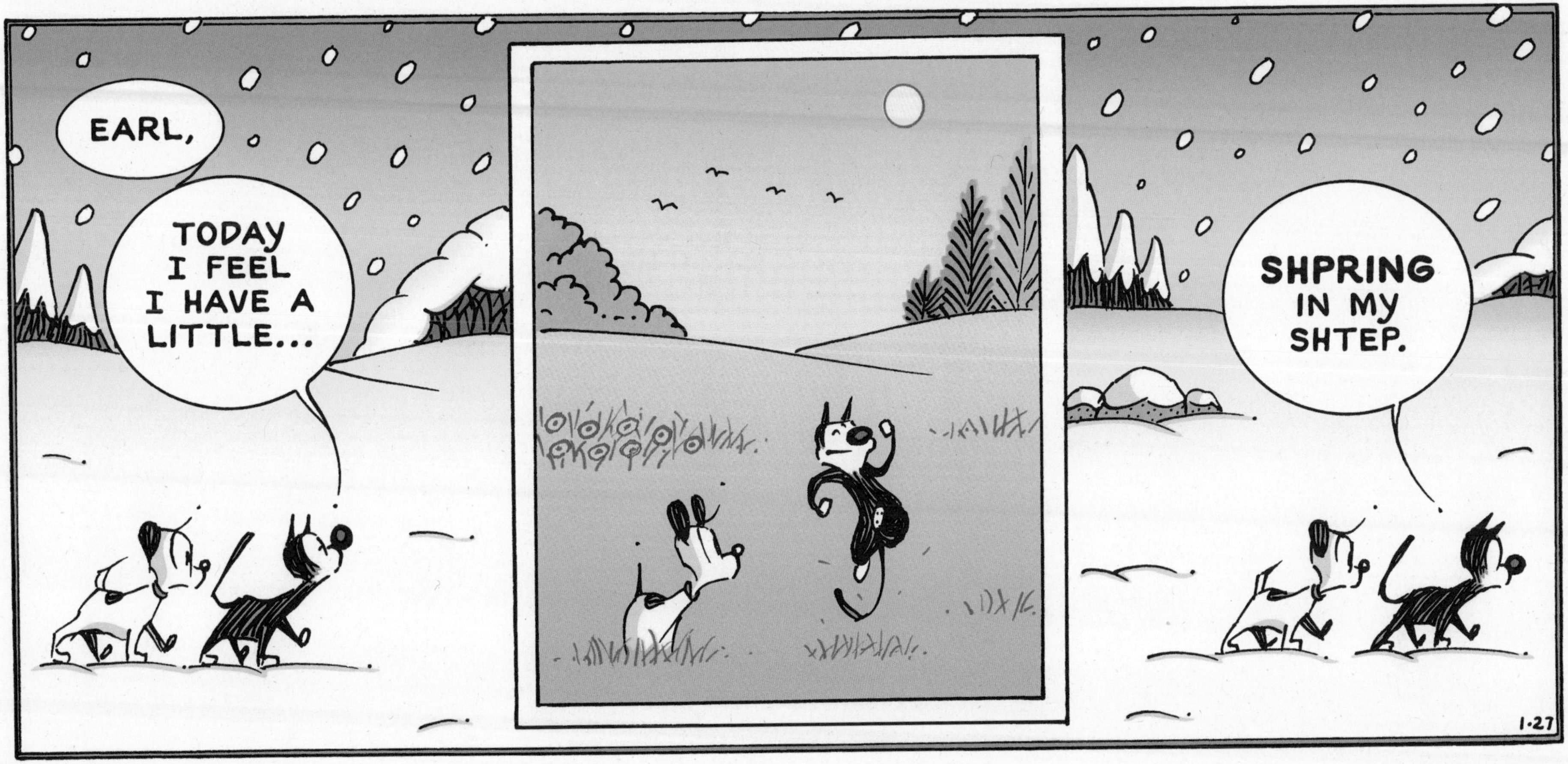
EARL,
TODAY I FEEL I HAVE A LITTLE...
SHPRING IN MY SHTEP.
1-27

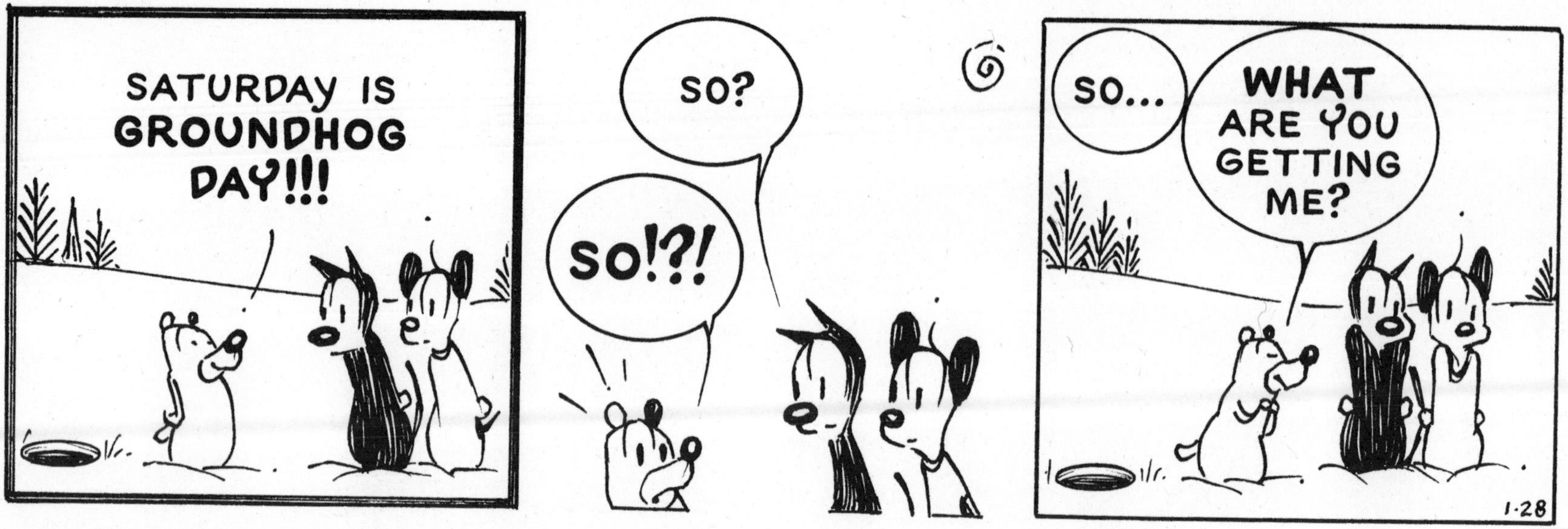
SATURDAY IS GROUNDHOG DAY!!!
SO?
SO!?!
SO...
WHAT ARE YOU GETTING ME?
1·28

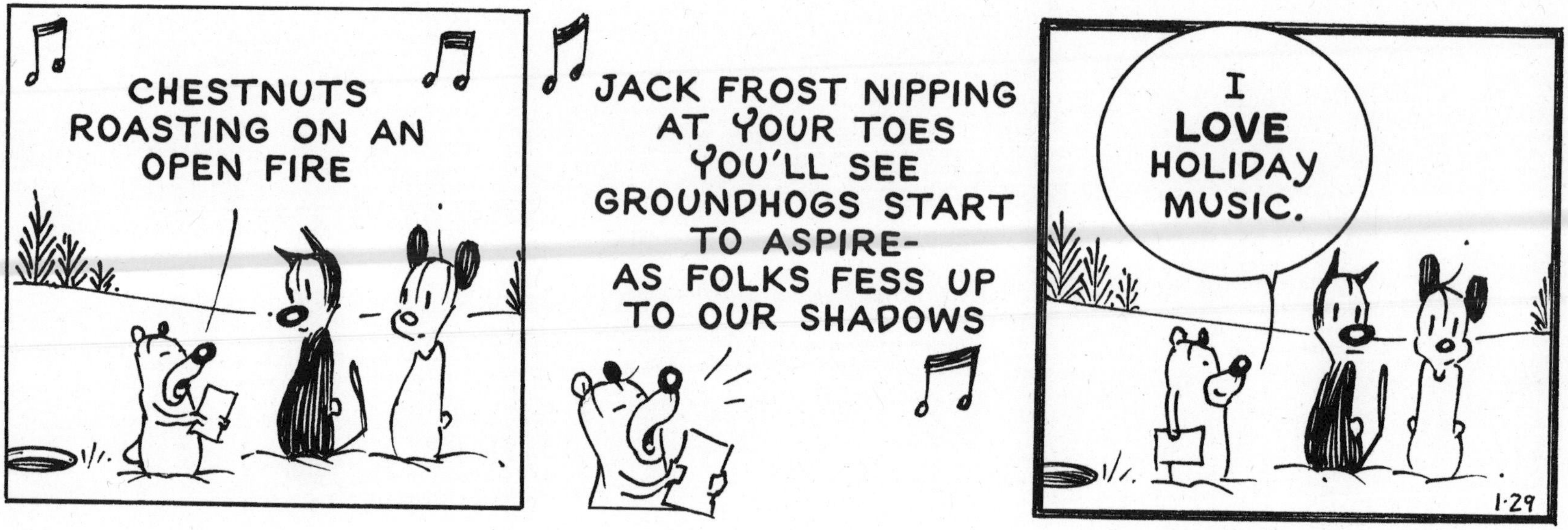
CHESTNUTS ROASTING ON AN OPEN FIRE
JACK FROST NIPPING AT YOUR TOES YOU'LL SEE GROUNDHOGS START TO ASPIRE- AS FOLKS FESS UP TO OUR SHADOWS
I LOVE HOLIDAY MUSIC.
1·29

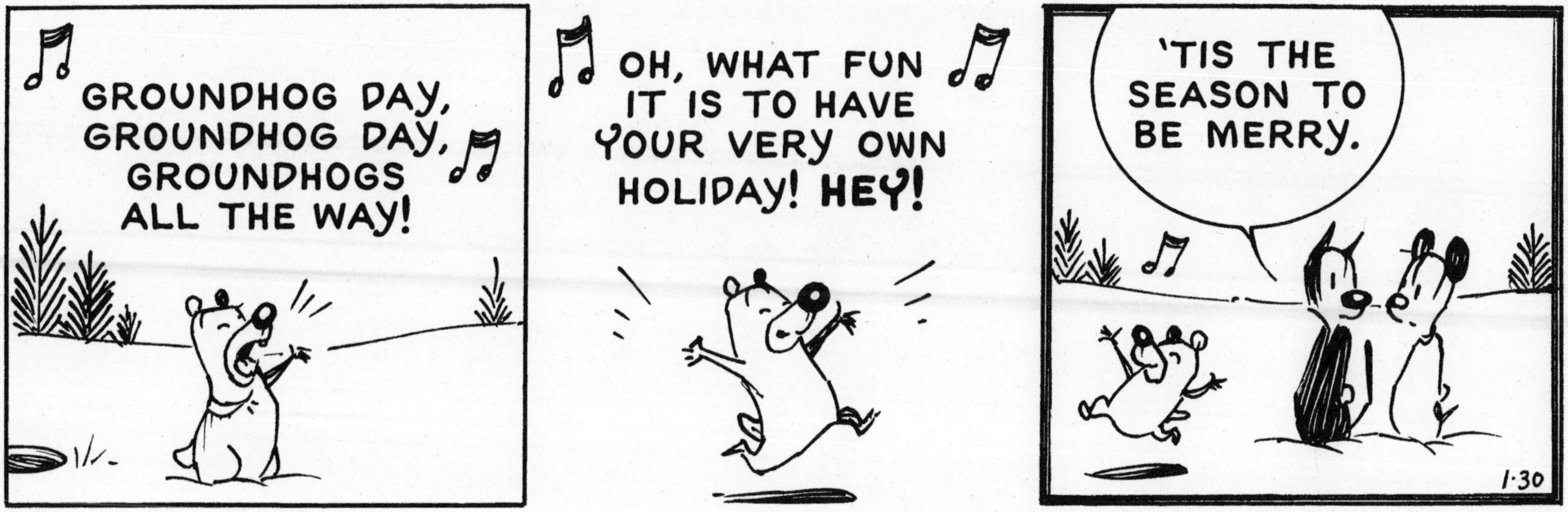
GROUNDHOG DAY, GROUNDHOG DAY, GROUNDHOGS ALL THE WAY!
OH, WHAT FUN IT IS TO HAVE YOUR VERY OWN HOLIDAY! **HEY!**
'TIS THE SEASON TO BE MERRY.
1·30

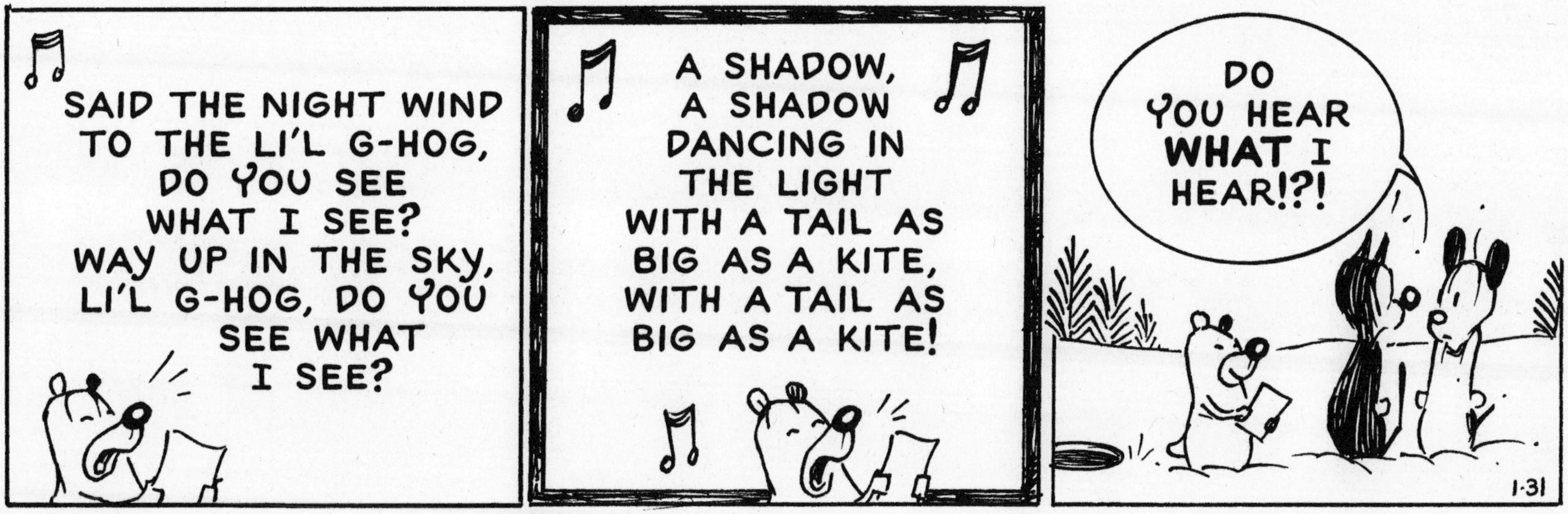
SAID THE NIGHT WIND TO THE LI'L G-HOG, DO YOU SEE WHAT I SEE? WAY UP IN THE SKY, LI'L G-HOG, DO YOU SEE WHAT I SEE?
A SHADOW, A SHADOW DANCING IN THE LIGHT WITH A TAIL AS BIG AS A KITE, WITH A TAIL AS BIG AS A KITE!
DO YOU HEAR **WHAT** I HEAR!?!
1·31

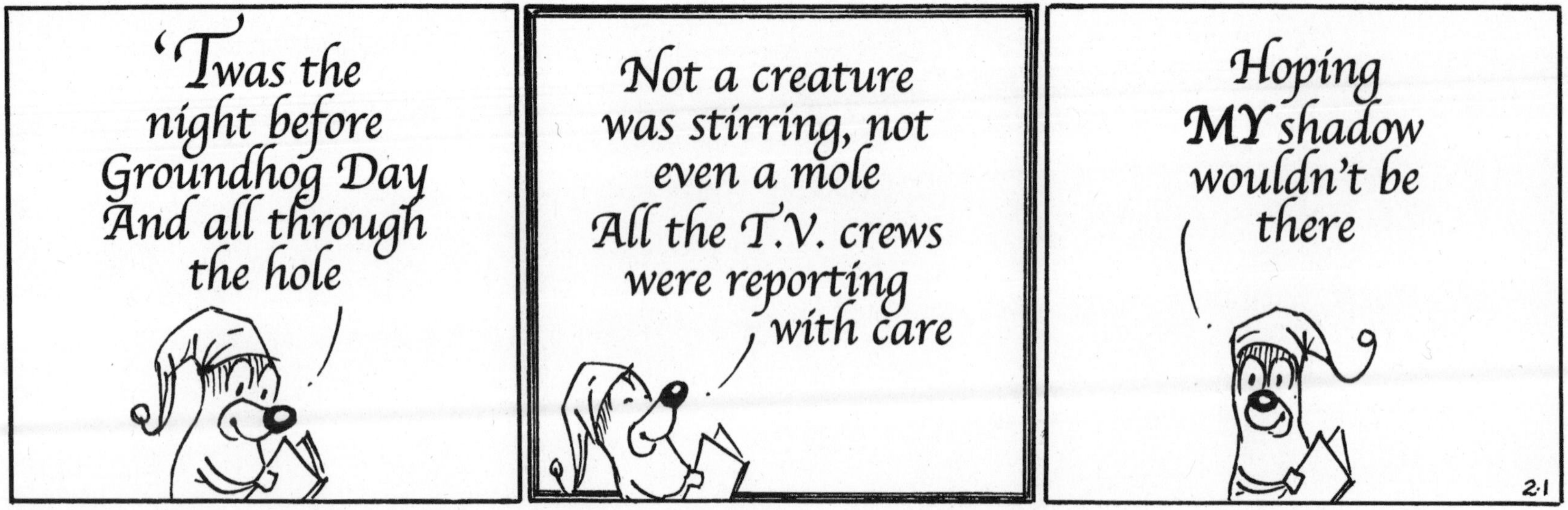
'Twas the night before Groundhog Day And all through the hole
Not a creature was stirring, not even a mole All the T.V. crews were reporting with care
Hoping MY shadow wouldn't be there
2·1

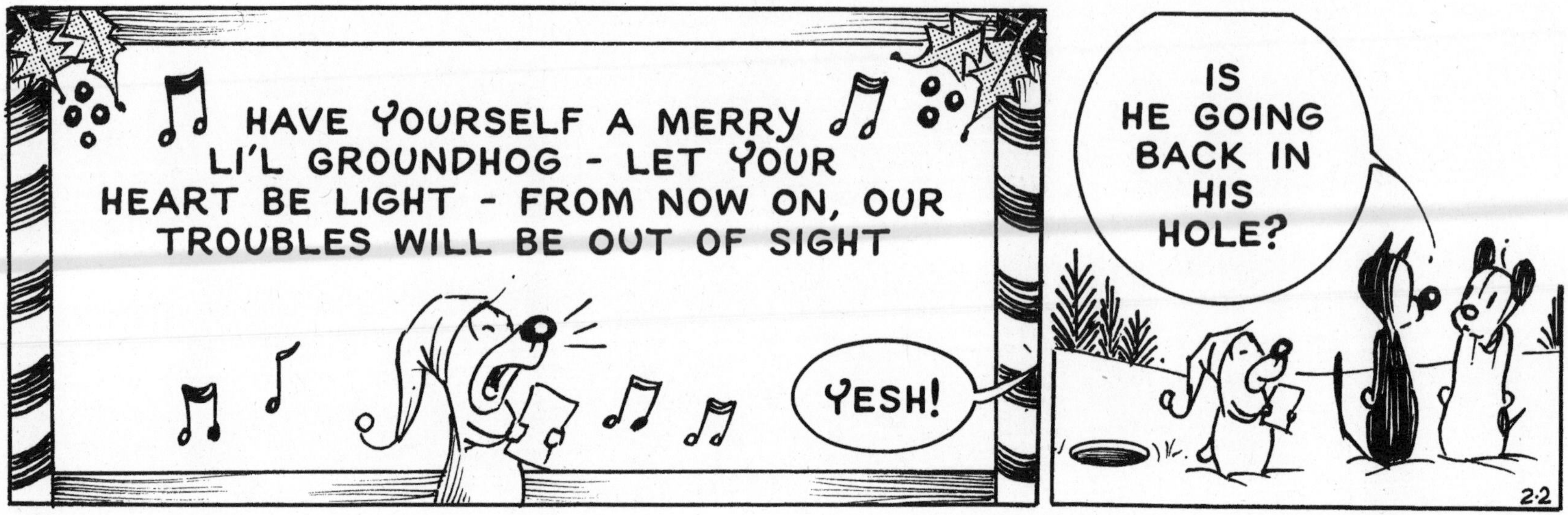
HAVE YOURSELF A MERRY LI'L GROUNDHOG - LET YOUR HEART BE LIGHT - FROM NOW ON, OUR TROUBLES WILL BE OUT OF SIGHT
YESH!
IS HE GOING BACK IN HIS HOLE?
2·2

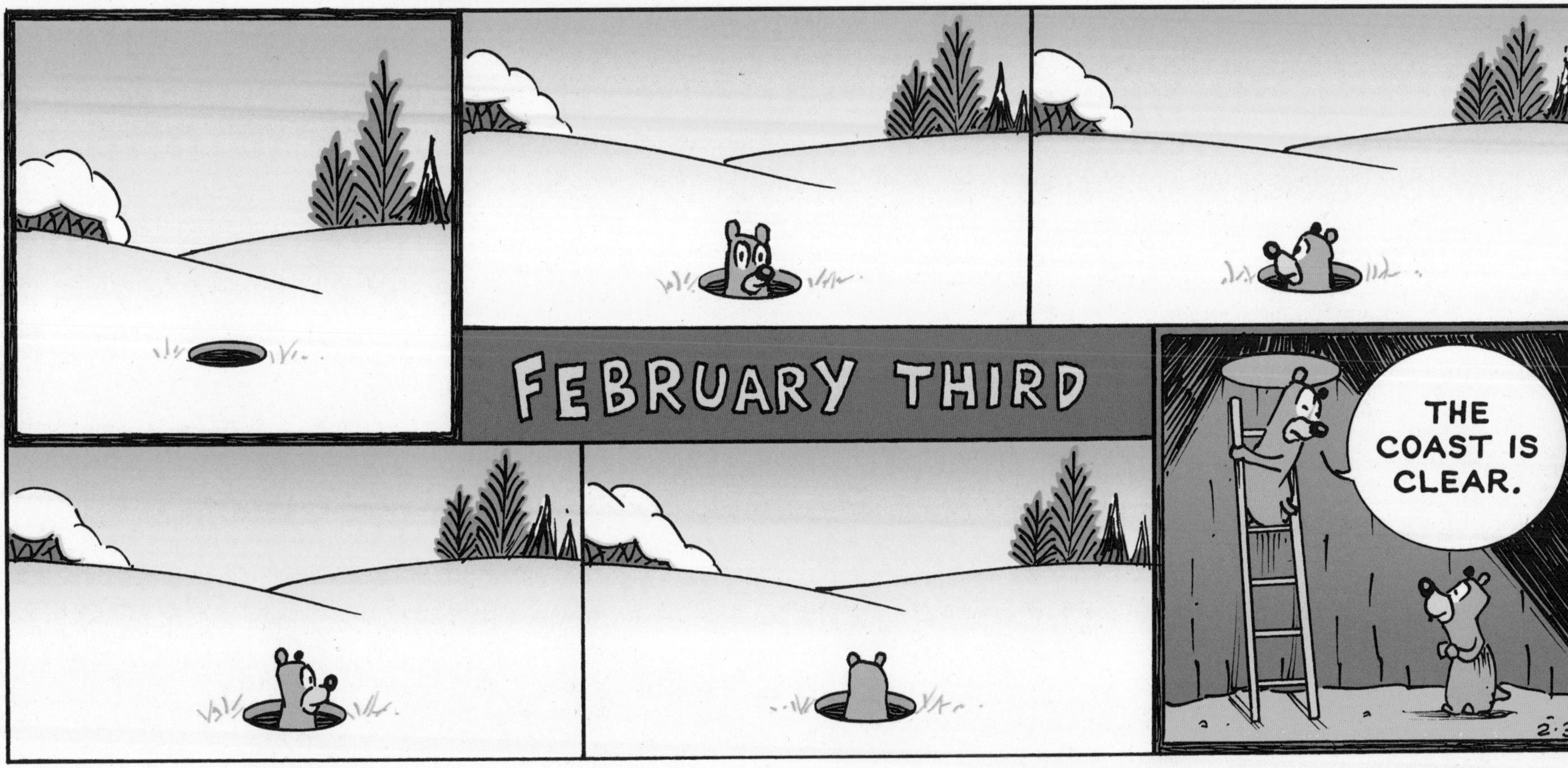
FEBRUARY THIRD
THE COAST IS CLEAR.
2·3

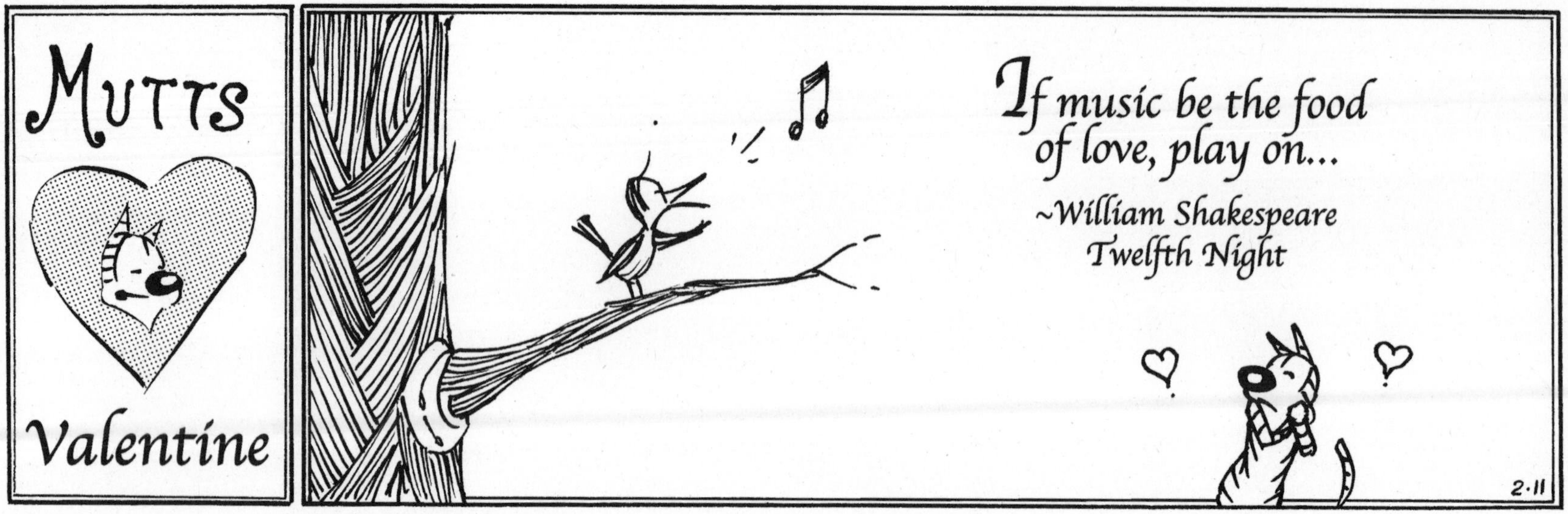
MUTTS
Valentine
If music be the food of love, play on...
~William Shakespeare
Twelfth Night
2·11

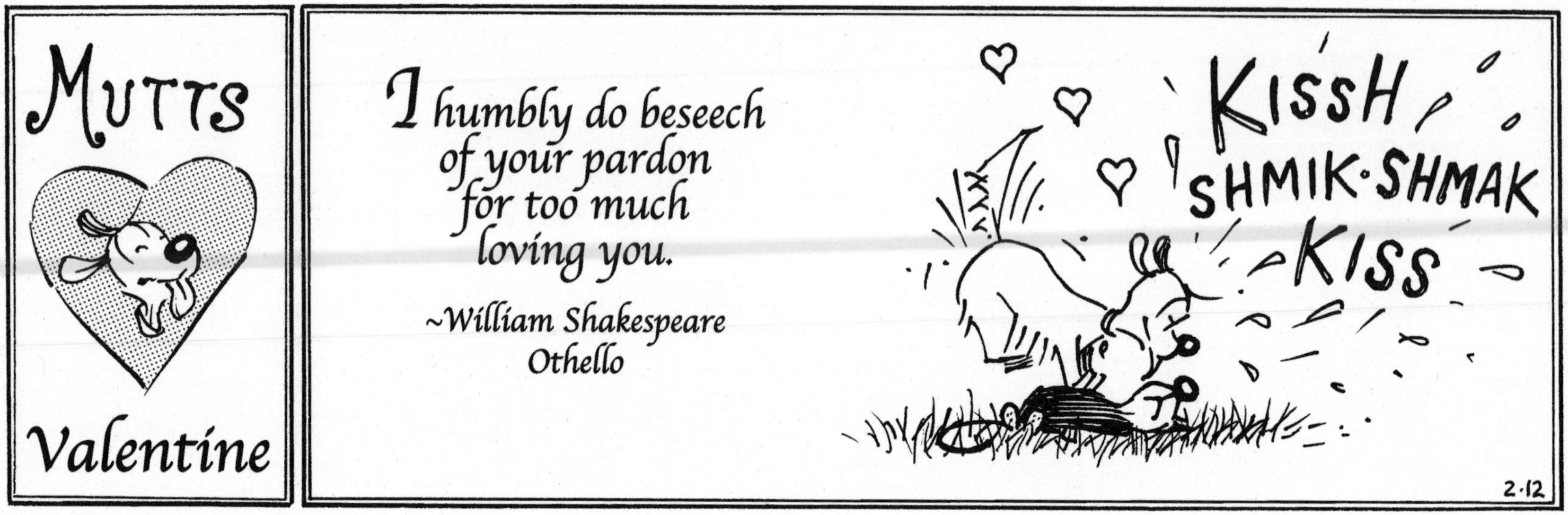
MUTTS
Valentine
I humbly do beseech of your pardon for too much loving you.
~William Shakespeare
Othello
KISSH
SHMIK·SHMAK
KISS
2·12

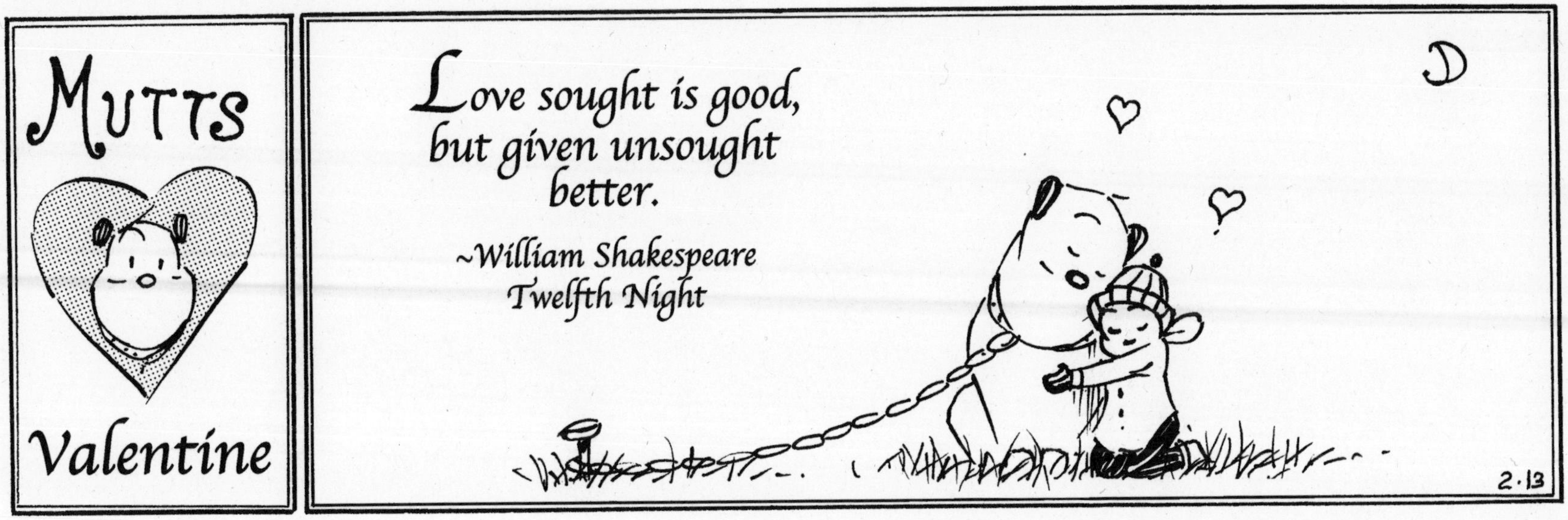
MUTTS
Valentine
Love sought is good, but given unsought better.
~William Shakespeare
Twelfth Night
2.13

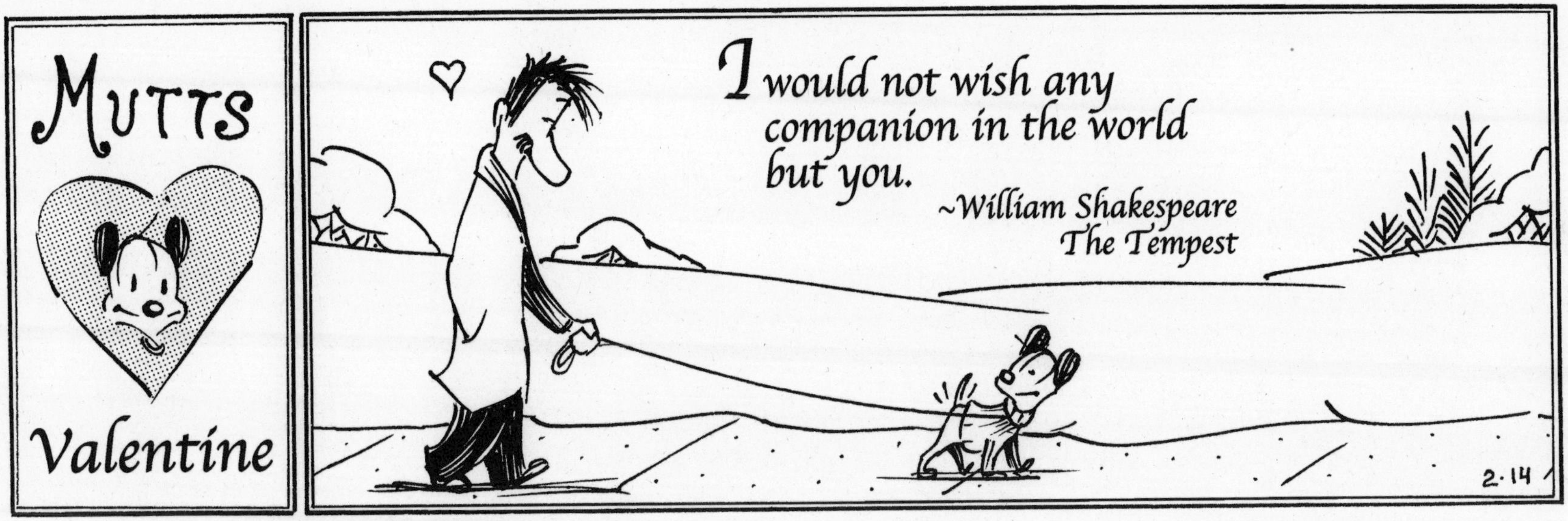
MUTTS
Valentine
I would not wish any companion in the world but you.
~William Shakespeare
The Tempest
2.14

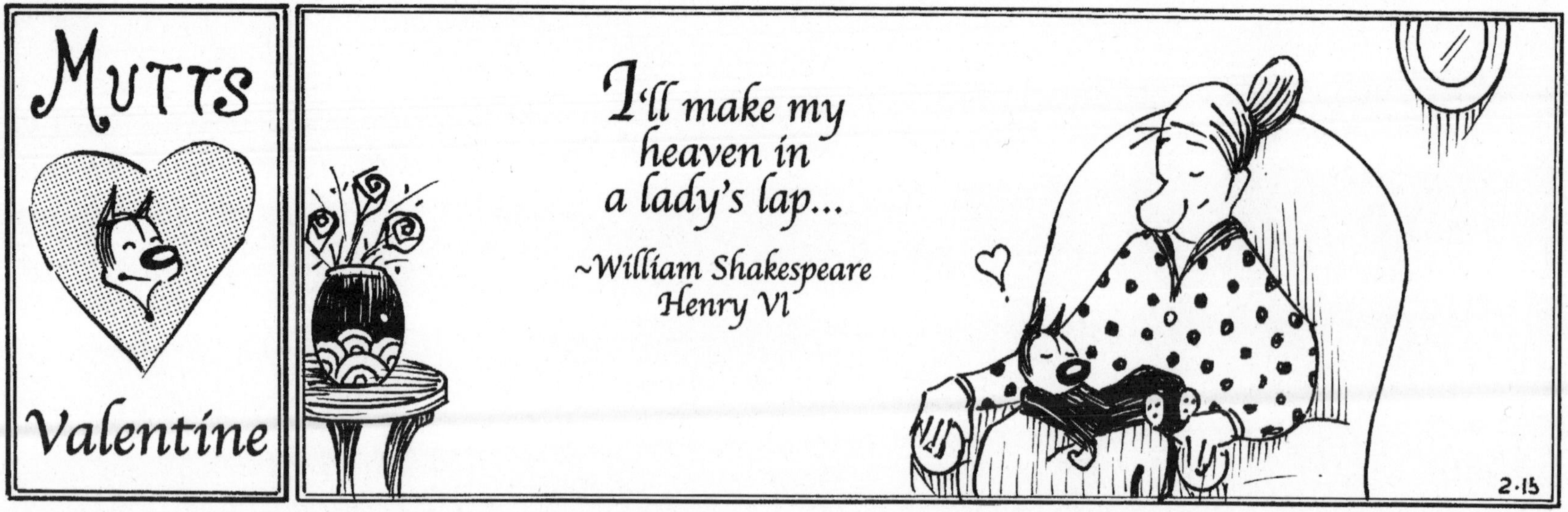
MUTTS
Valentine
I'll make my heaven in a lady's lap...
~William Shakespeare
Henry VI
2.15

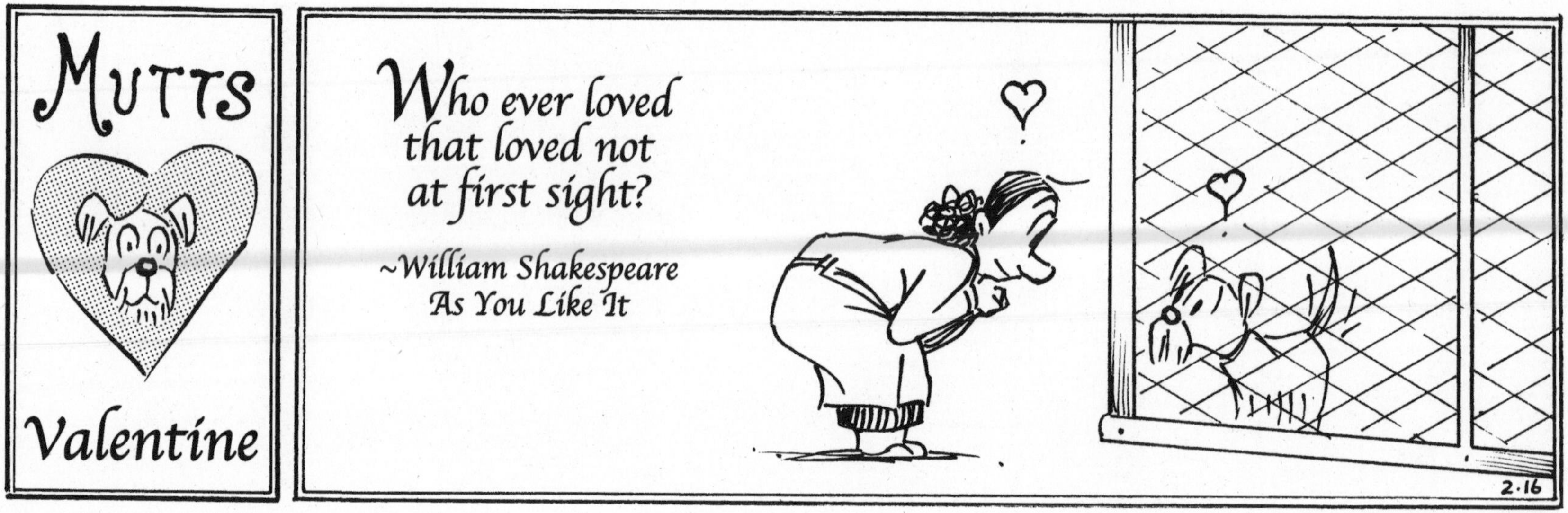
MUTTS
Valentine
Who ever loved that loved not at first sight?
~William Shakespeare
As You Like It
2.16

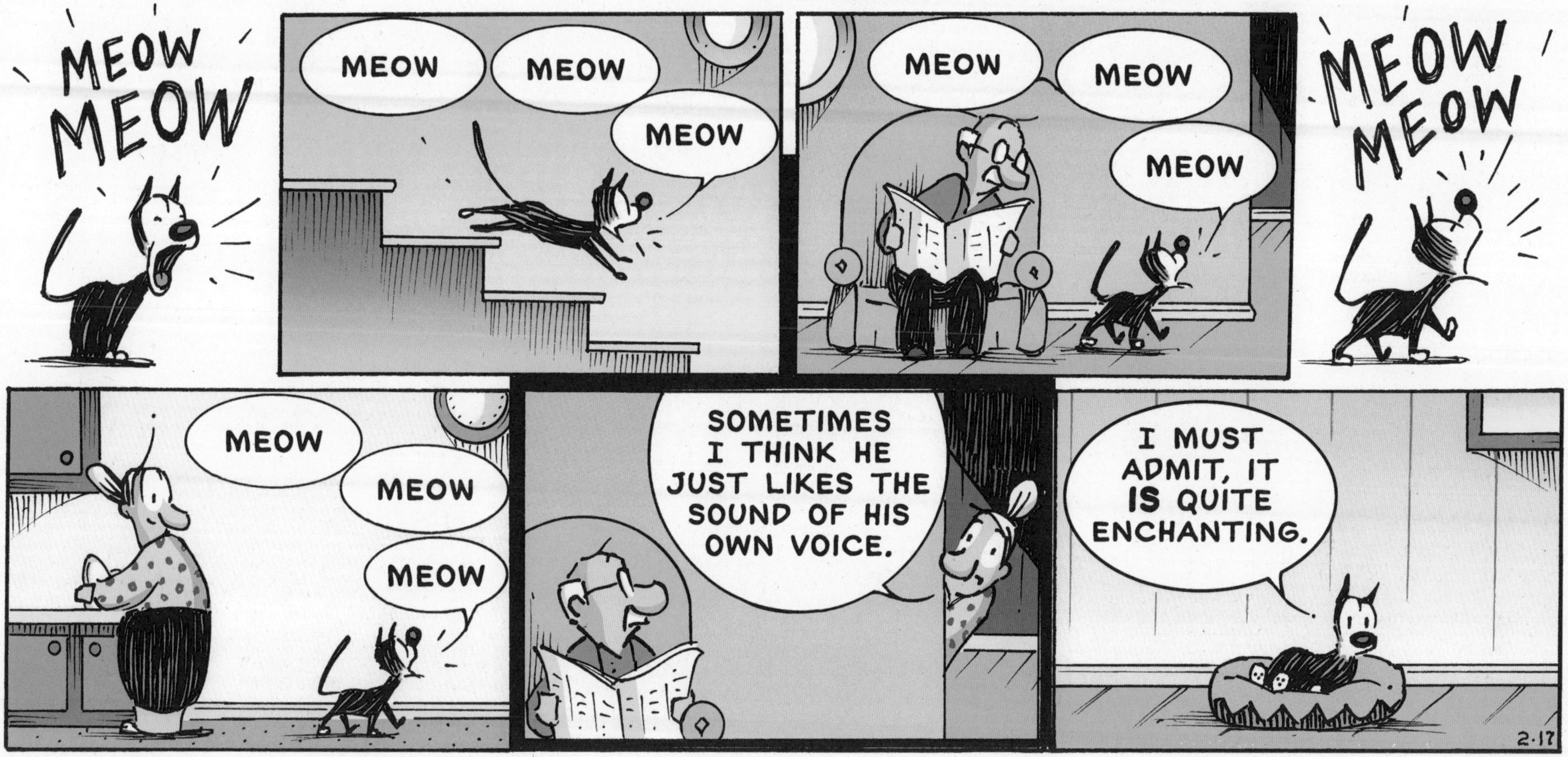
MEOW
MEOW
MEOW
MEOW
MEOW
MEOW
MEOW
MEOW
MEOW
MEOW
MEOW
MEOW
MEOW
MEOW
SOMETIMES I THINK HE JUST LIKES THE SOUND OF HIS OWN VOICE.
I MUST ADMIT, IT **IS** QUITE ENCHANTING.
2·17

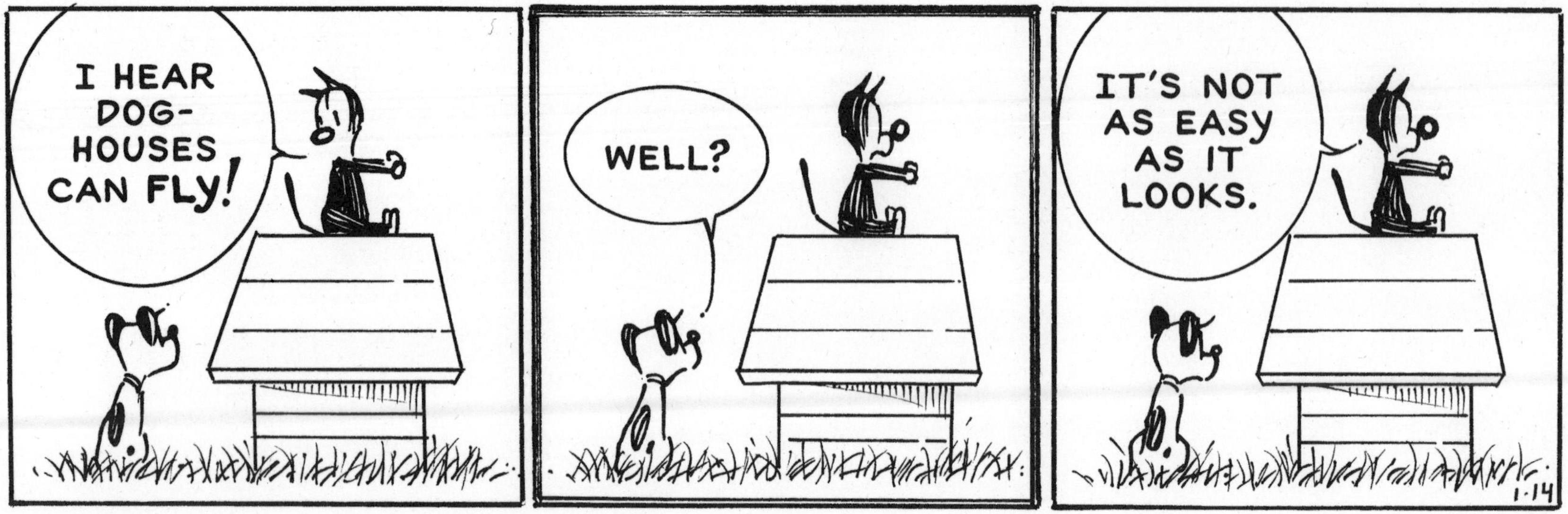
I HEAR DOG-HOUSES CAN FLY!
WELL?
IT'S NOT AS EASY AS IT LOOKS.
1-14

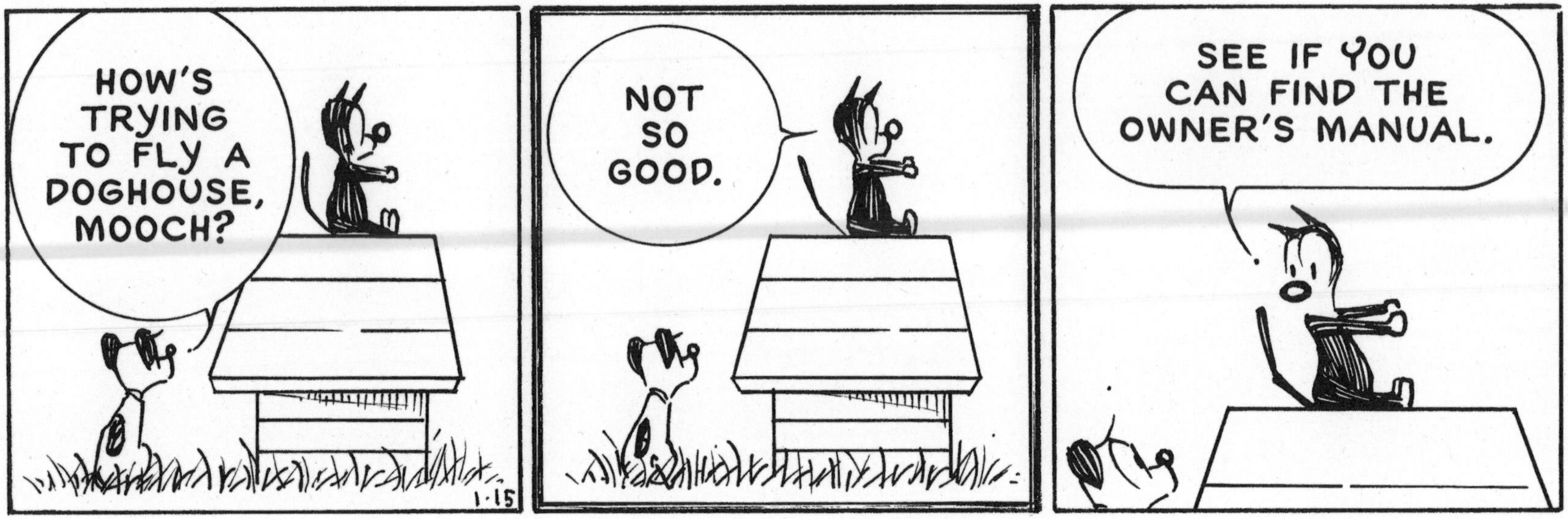
HOW'S TRYING TO FLY A DOGHOUSE, MOOCH?
1-15
NOT SO GOOD.
SEE IF YOU CAN FIND THE OWNER'S MANUAL.

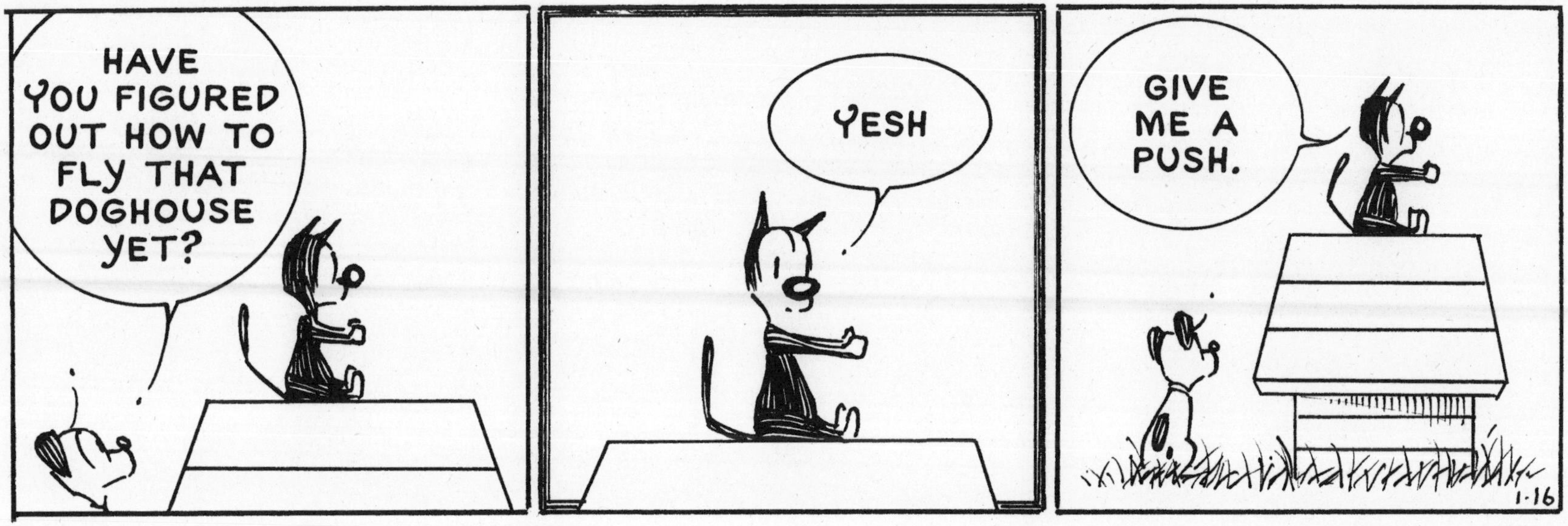
HAVE YOU FIGURED OUT HOW TO FLY THAT DOGHOUSE YET?
YESH
GIVE ME A PUSH.
1·16

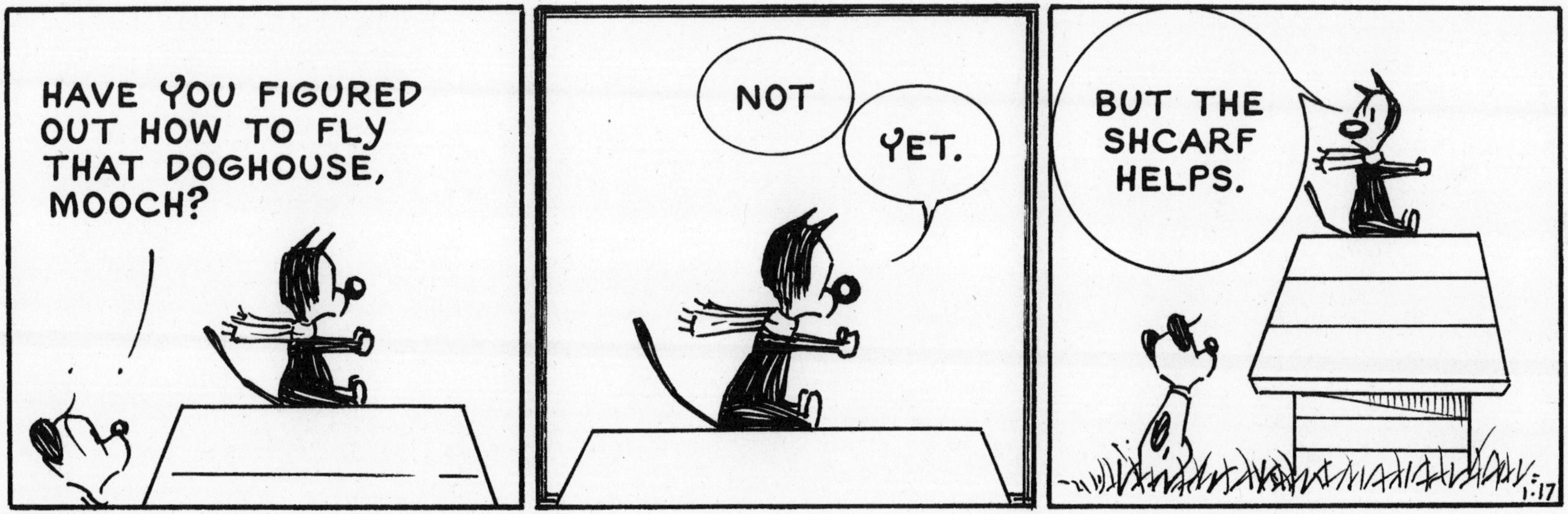
HAVE YOU FIGURED OUT HOW TO FLY THAT DOGHOUSE, MOOCH?
NOT
YET.
BUT THE SHCARF HELPS.
1·17

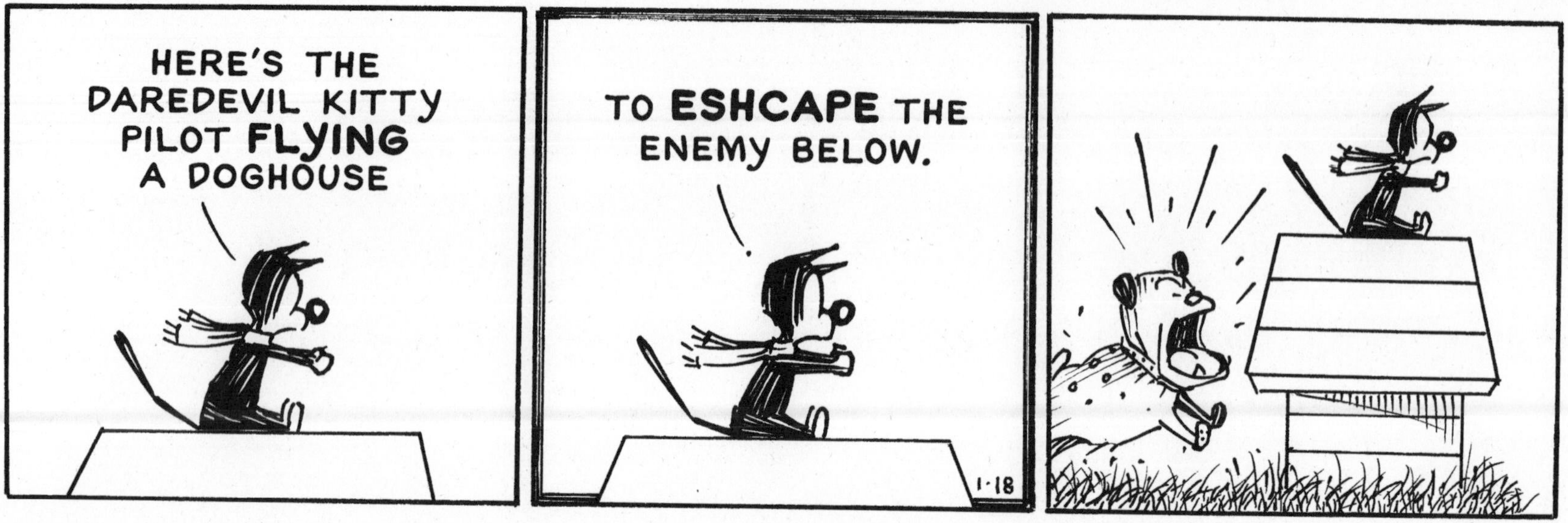
HERE'S THE DAREDEVIL KITTY PILOT FLYING A DOGHOUSE
TO ESHCAPE THE ENEMY BELOW.
1·18

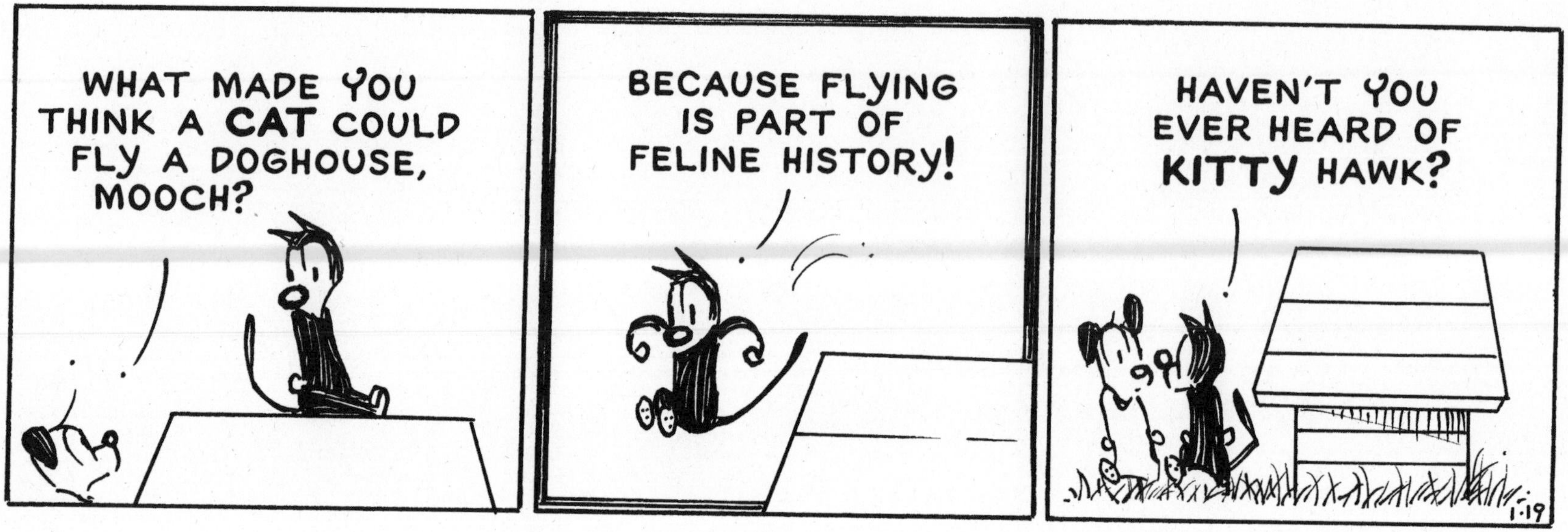
WHAT MADE YOU THINK A CAT COULD FLY A DOGHOUSE, MOOCH?
BECAUSE FLYING IS PART OF FELINE HISTORY!
HAVEN'T YOU EVER HEARD OF KITTY HAWK?
1·19

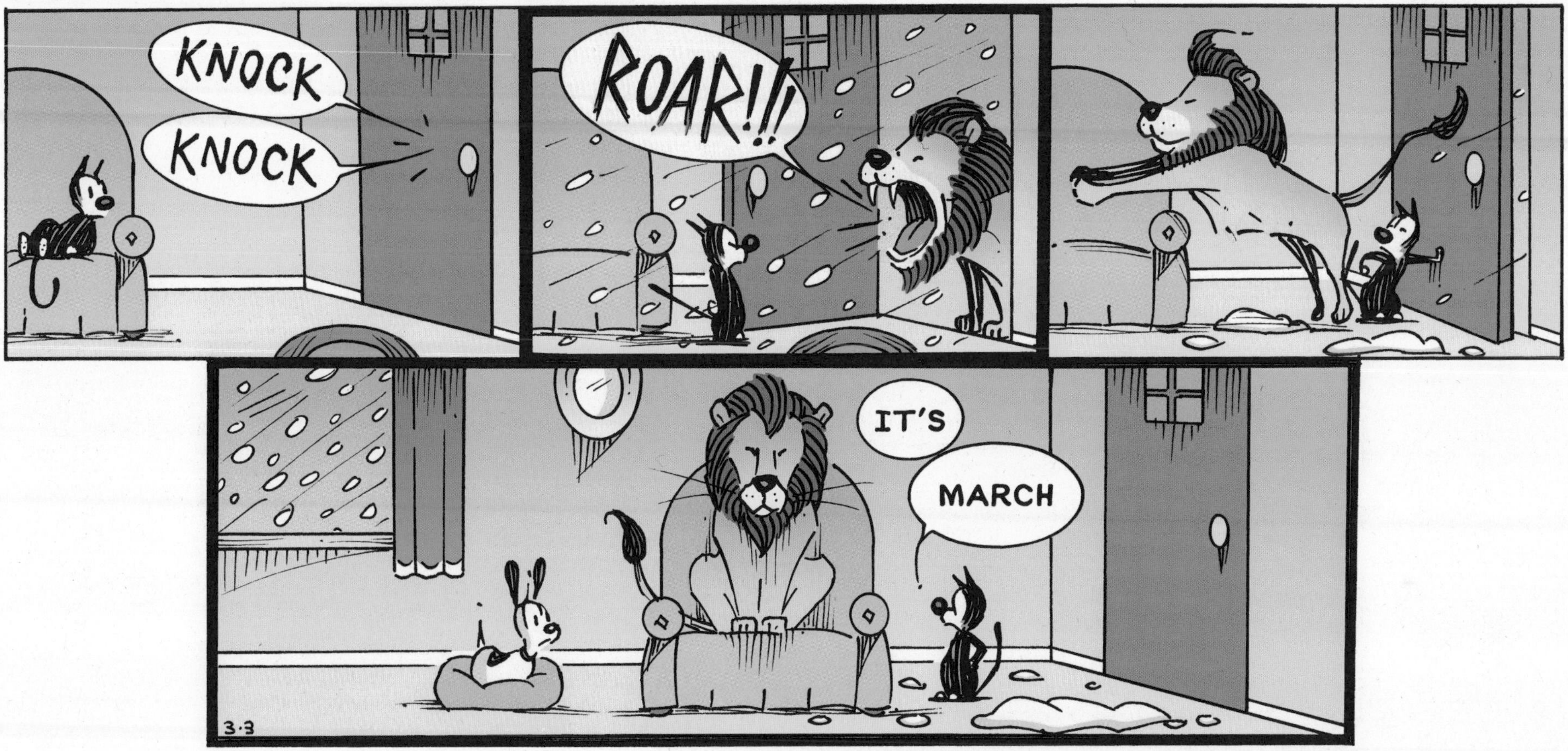
KNOCK
KNOCK
ROAR!!!
IT'S
MARCH
3·3

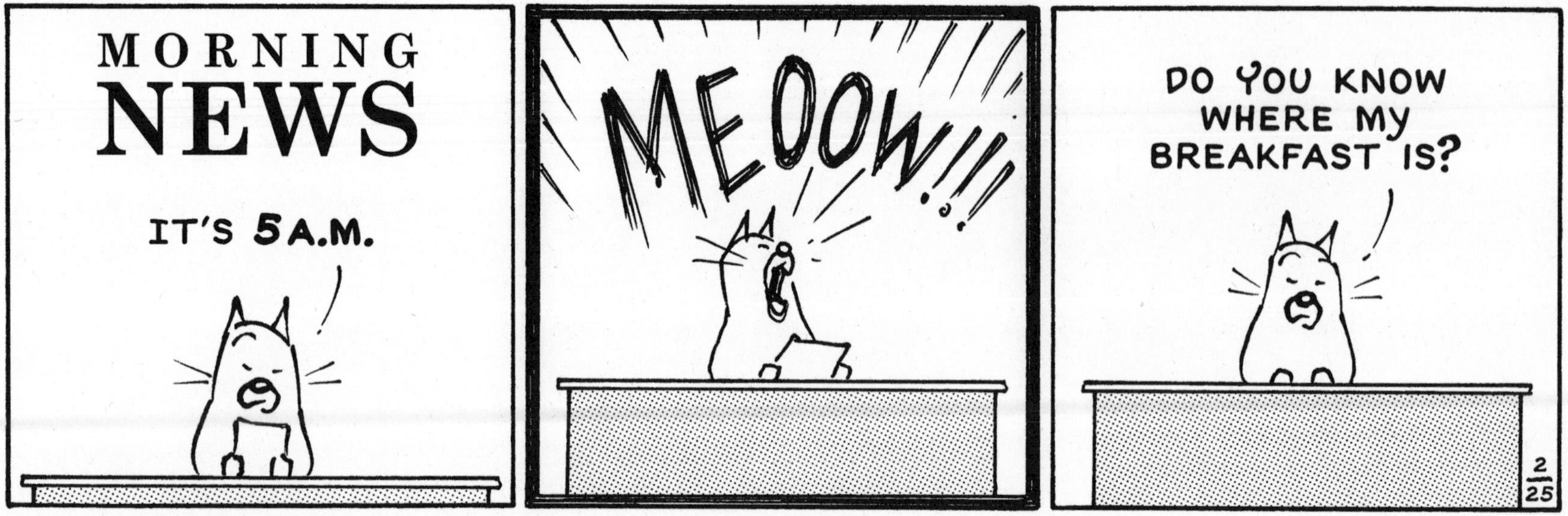
MORNING
NEWS
IT'S 5 A.M.
MEOOW!!!
DO YOU KNOW WHERE MY BREAKFAST IS?
2/25

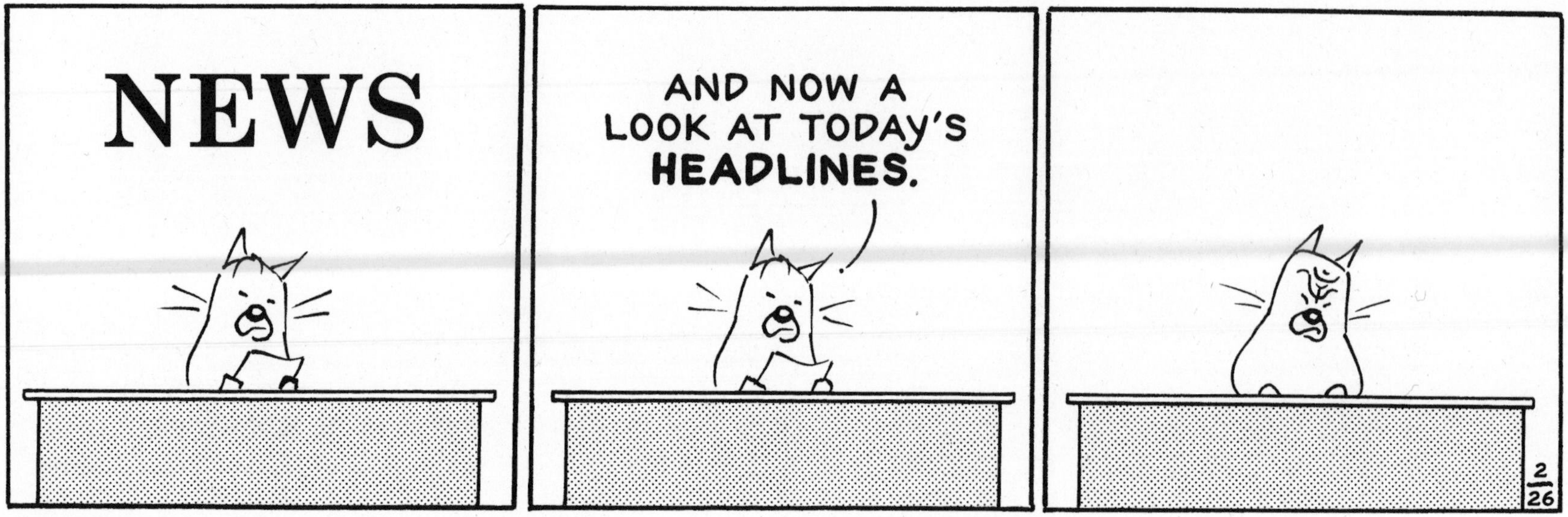
NEWS
AND NOW A LOOK AT TODAY'S HEADLINES.
2/26

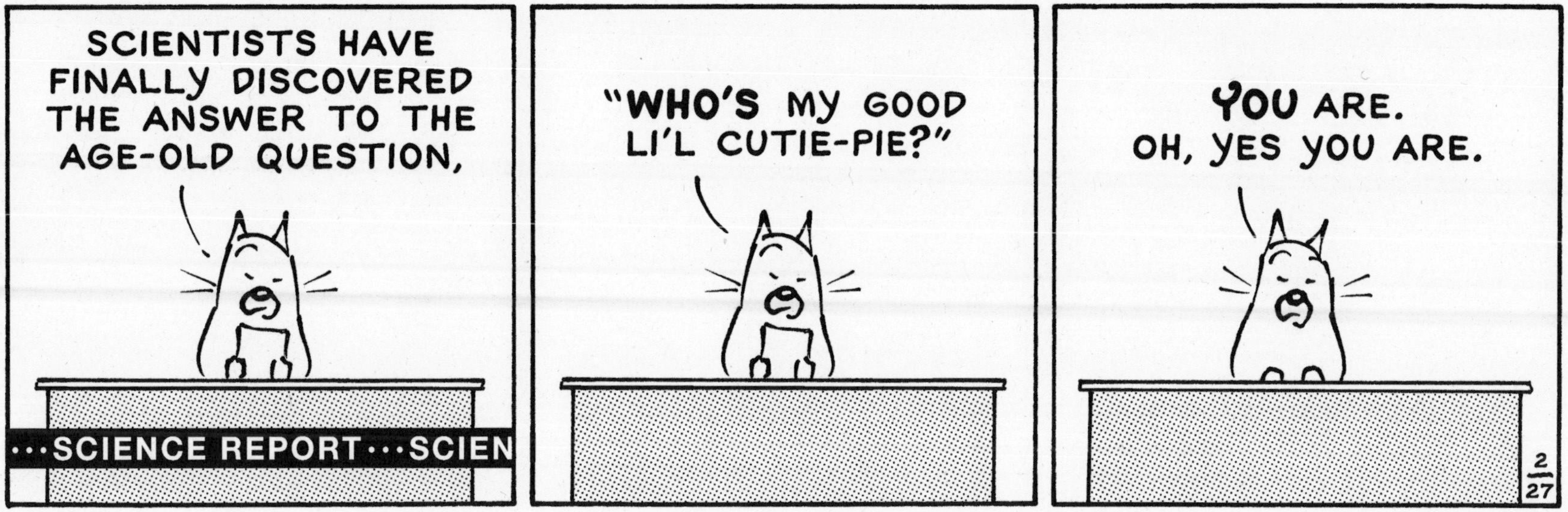
SCIENTISTS HAVE FINALLY DISCOVERED THE ANSWER TO THE AGE-OLD QUESTION,
...SCIENCE REPORT...SCIEN
"WHO'S MY GOOD LI'L CUTIE-PIE?"
YOU ARE. OH, YES YOU ARE.
2/27

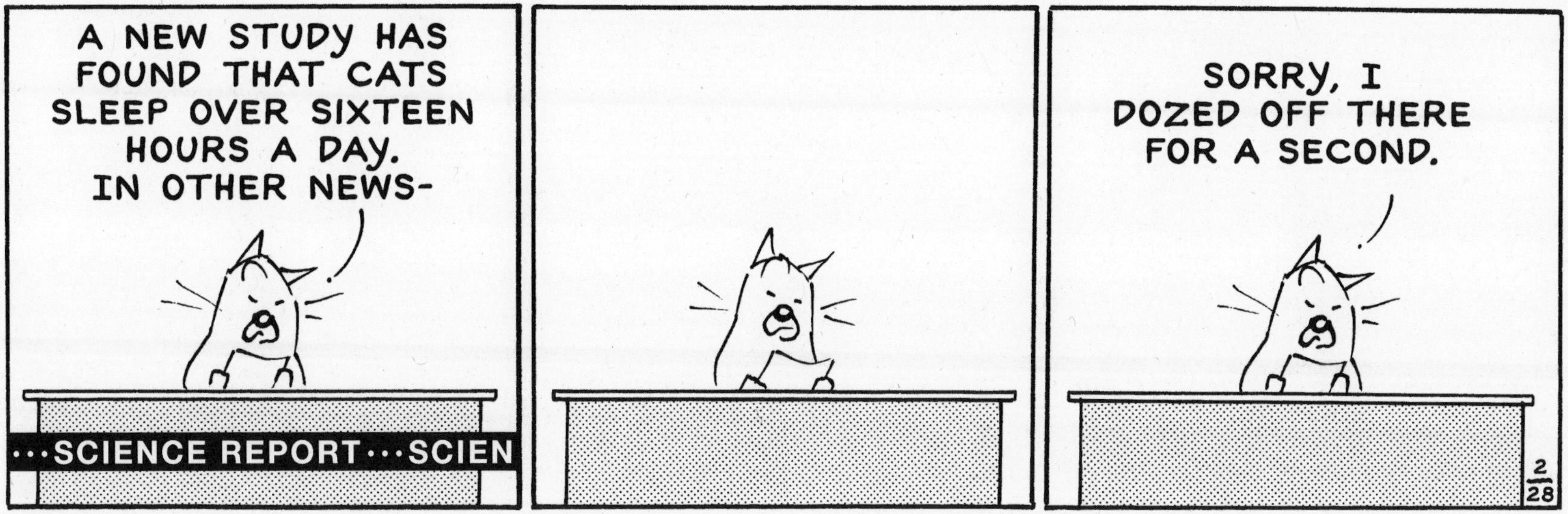
A NEW STUDY HAS FOUND THAT CATS SLEEP OVER SIXTEEN HOURS A DAY. IN OTHER NEWS-
...SCIENCE REPORT...SCIEN
SORRY, I DOZED OFF THERE FOR A SECOND.
2/28

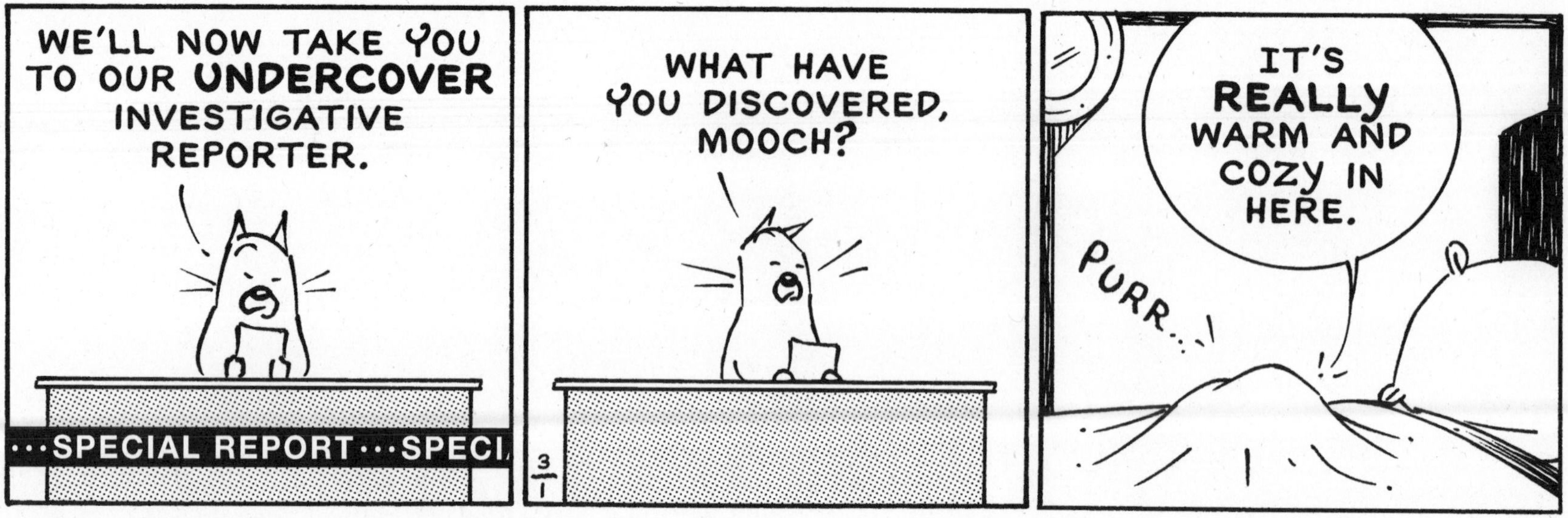
WE'LL NOW TAKE YOU TO OUR **UNDERCOVER** INVESTIGATIVE REPORTER.
···SPECIAL REPORT···SPECI
WHAT HAVE YOU DISCOVERED, MOOCH?
3/1
IT'S **REALLY** WARM AND COZY IN HERE.
PURR...

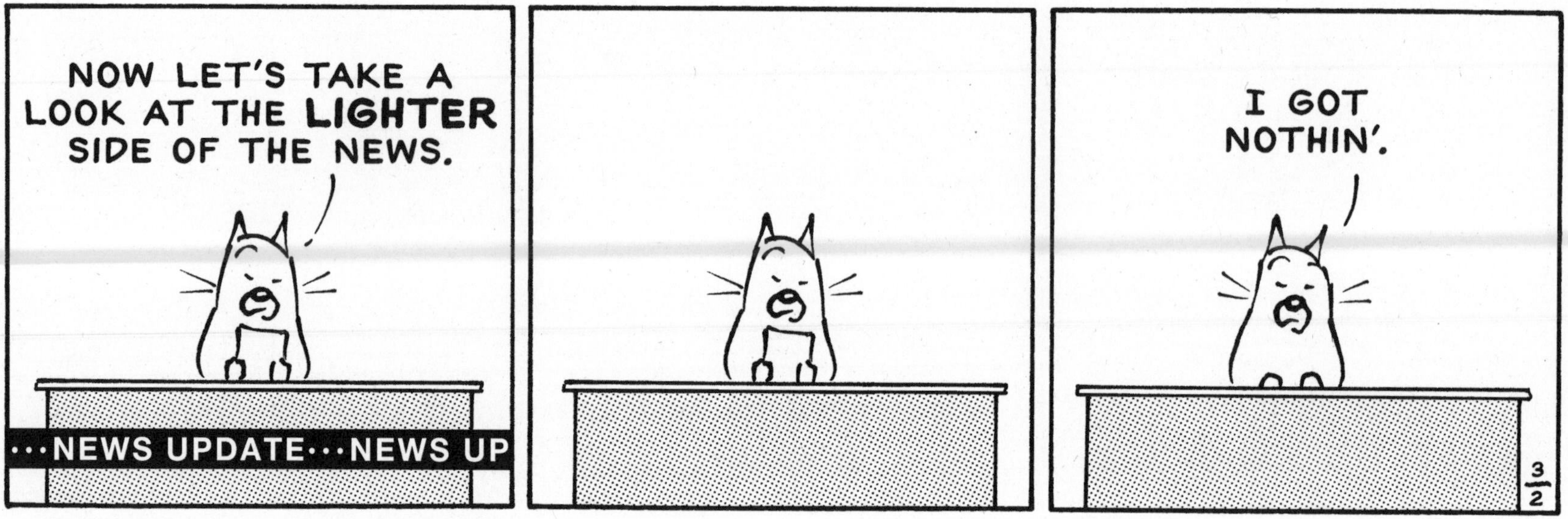
NOW LET'S TAKE A LOOK AT THE **LIGHTER** SIDE OF THE NEWS.
···NEWS UPDATE···NEWS UP
I GOT NOTHIN'.
3/2

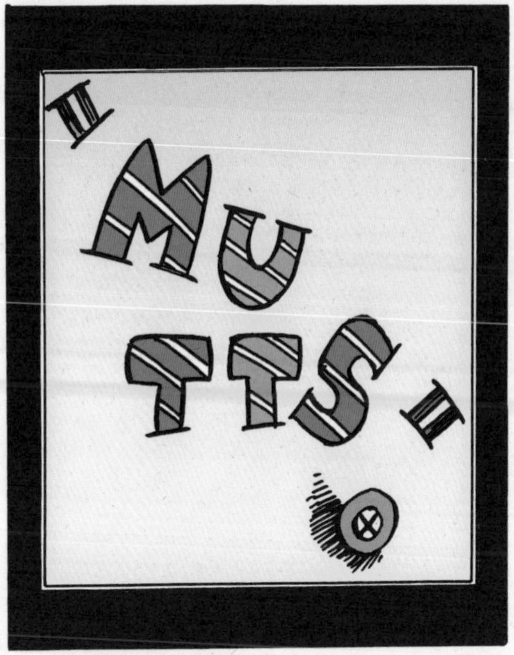
MUTTS

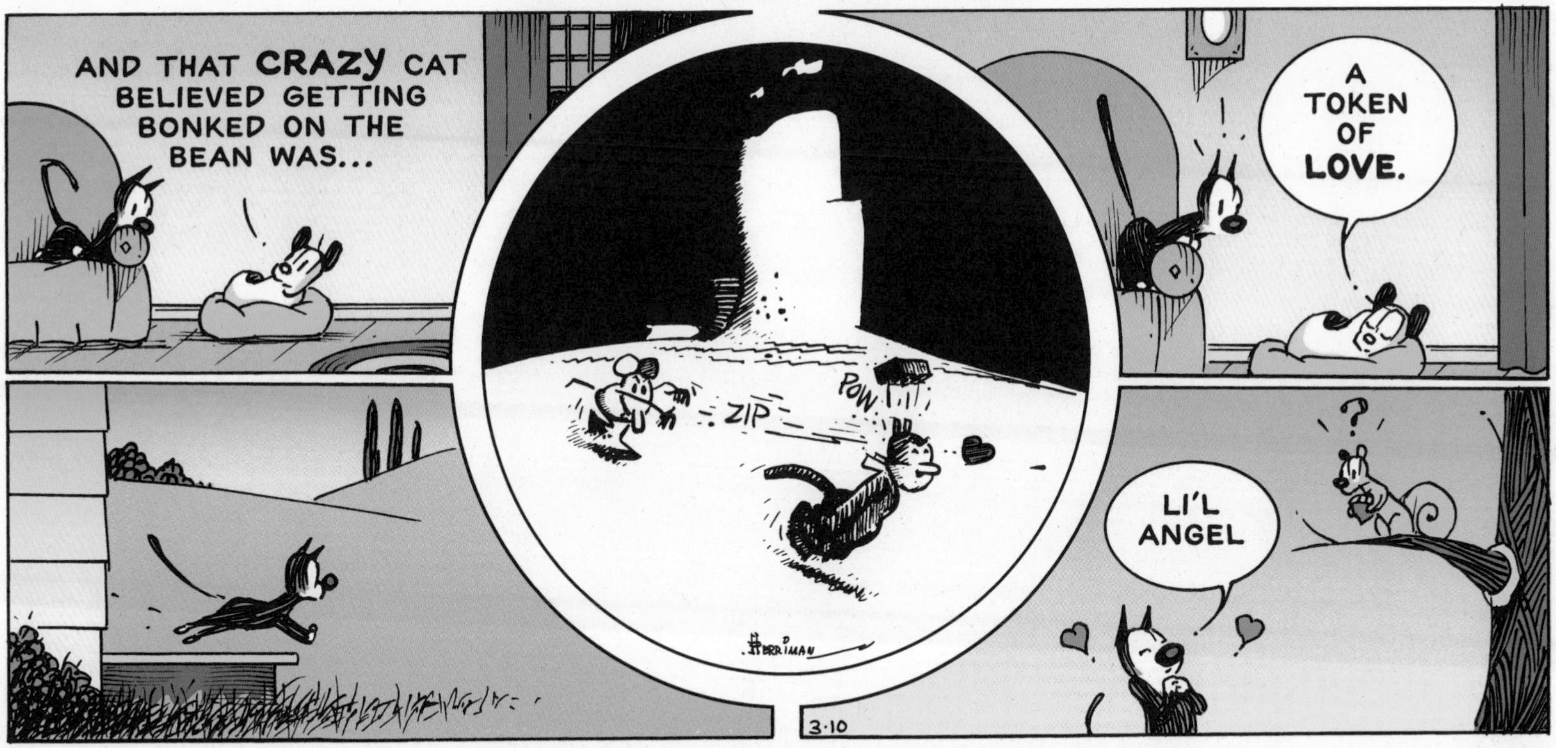
AND THAT CRAZY CAT BELIEVED GETTING BONKED ON THE BEAN WAS...
A TOKEN OF LOVE.
ZIP
POW
HERRIMAN
LI'L ANGEL
3·10

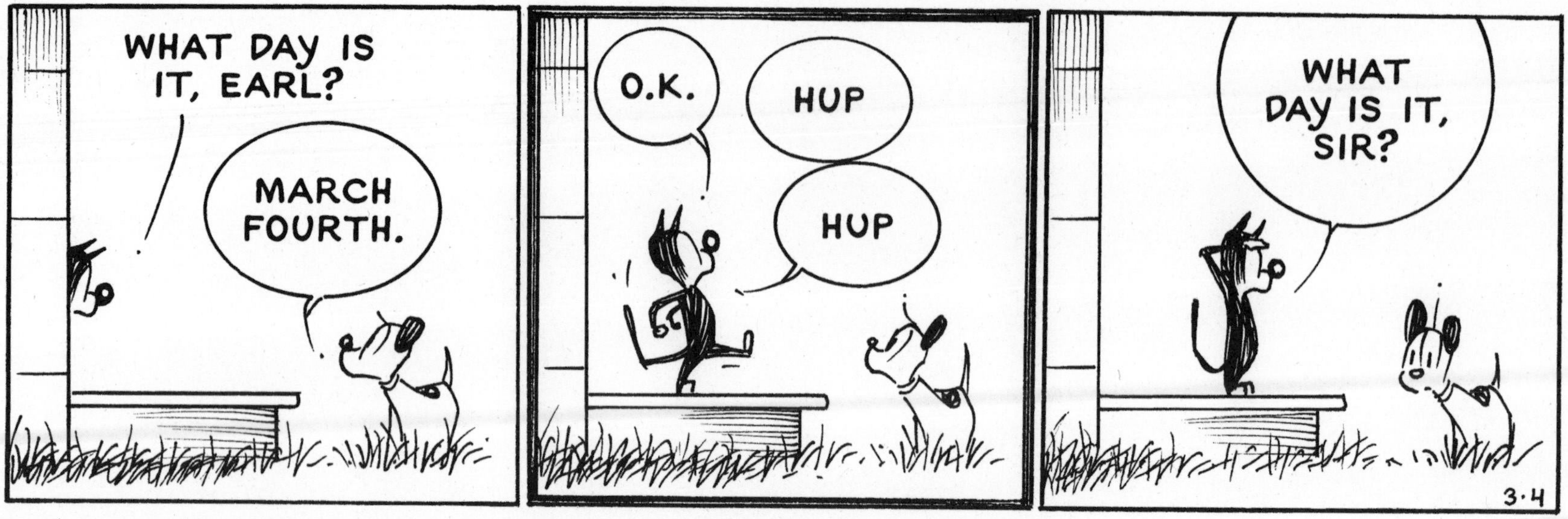
WHAT DAY IS IT, EARL?
MARCH FOURTH.
O.K.
HUP
HUP
WHAT DAY IS IT, SIR?
3·4

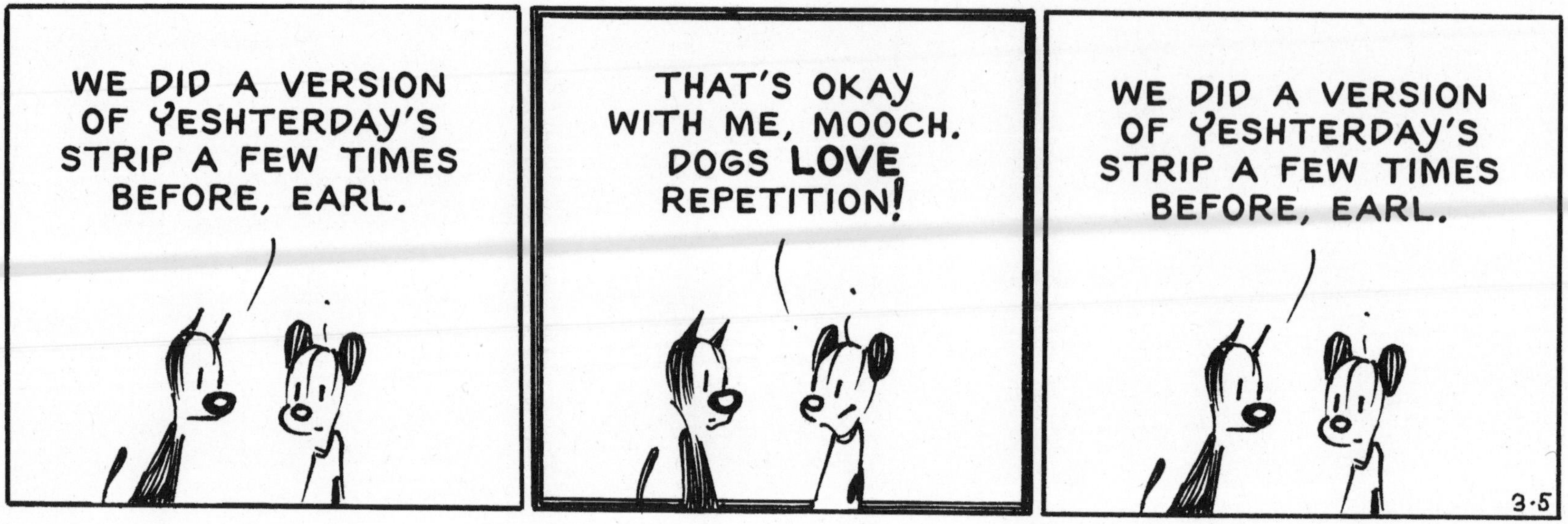
WE DID A VERSION OF YESHTERDAY'S STRIP A FEW TIMES BEFORE, EARL.
THAT'S OKAY WITH ME, MOOCH. DOGS **LOVE** REPETITION!
WE DID A VERSION OF YESHTERDAY'S STRIP A FEW TIMES BEFORE, EARL.
3·5

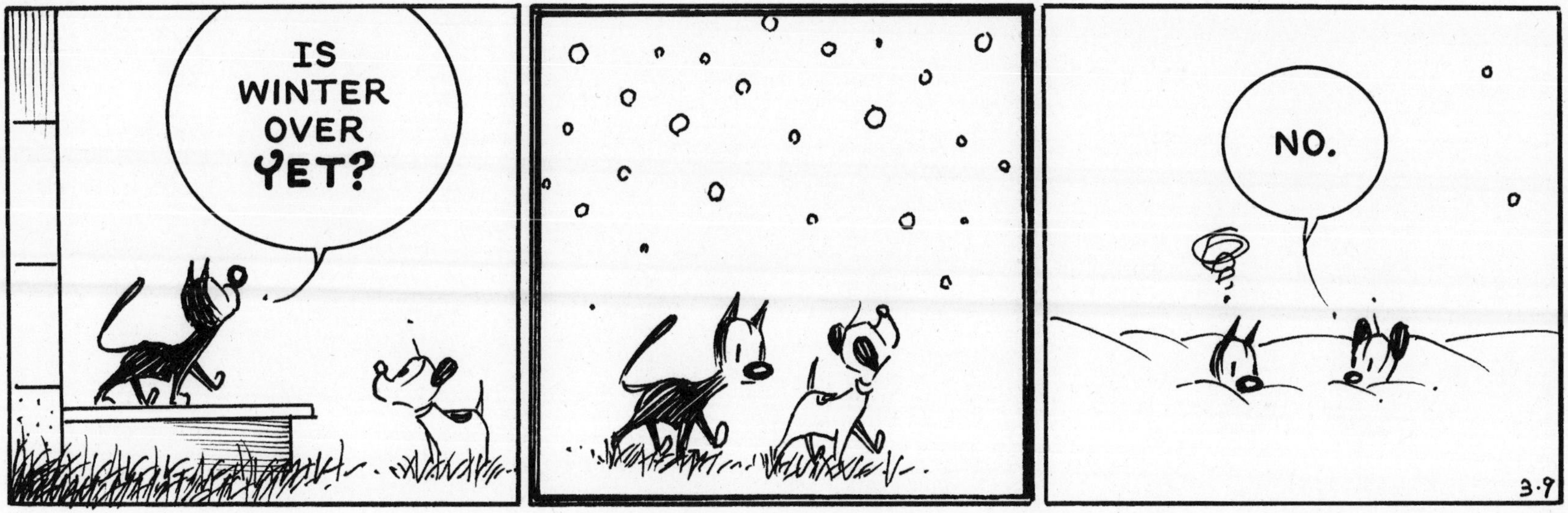
IS WINTER OVER YET?
NO.
3·9

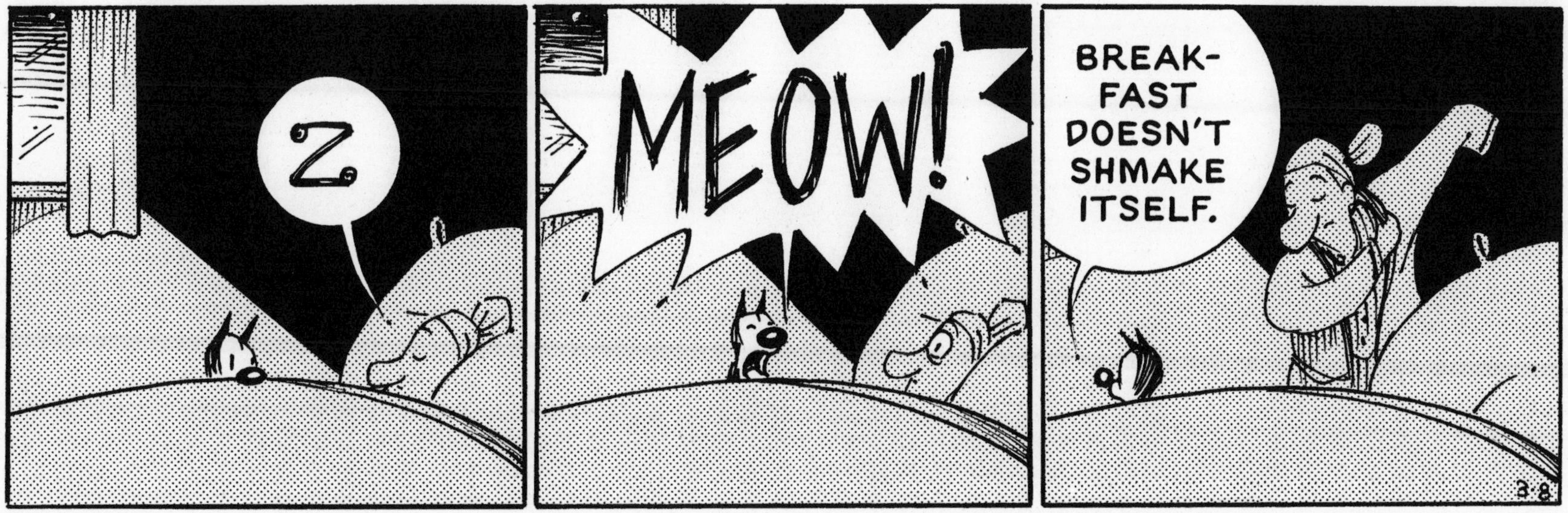
Z
MEOW!
BREAK-FAST DOESN'T SHMAKE ITSELF.
3·8

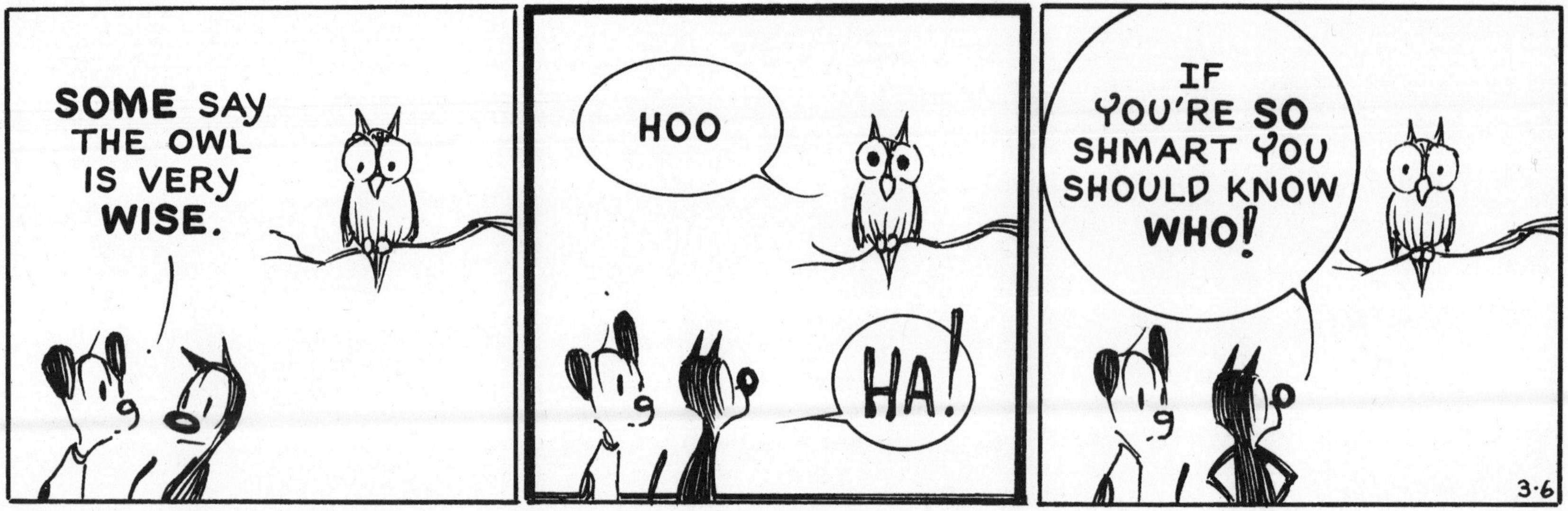
SOME SAY THE OWL IS VERY WISE.
HOO
HA!
IF YOU'RE SO SHMART YOU SHOULD KNOW WHO!
3·6

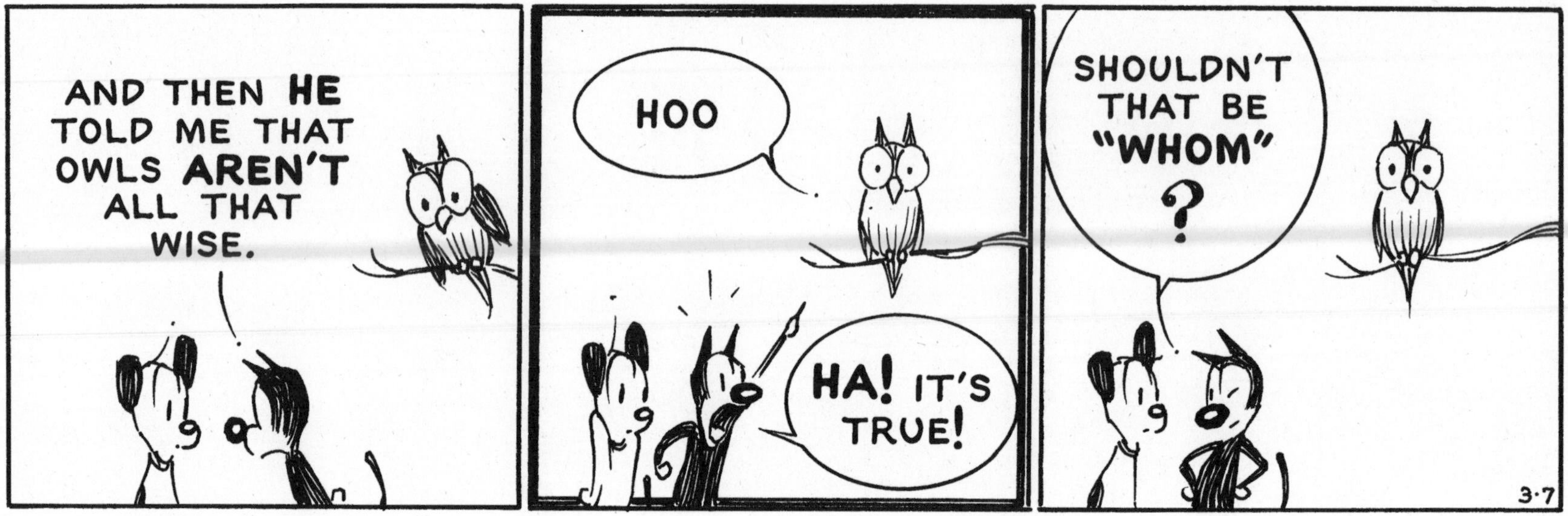
AND THEN HE TOLD ME THAT OWLS AREN'T ALL THAT WISE.
HOO
HA! IT'S TRUE!
SHOULDN'T THAT BE "WHOM" ?
3·7

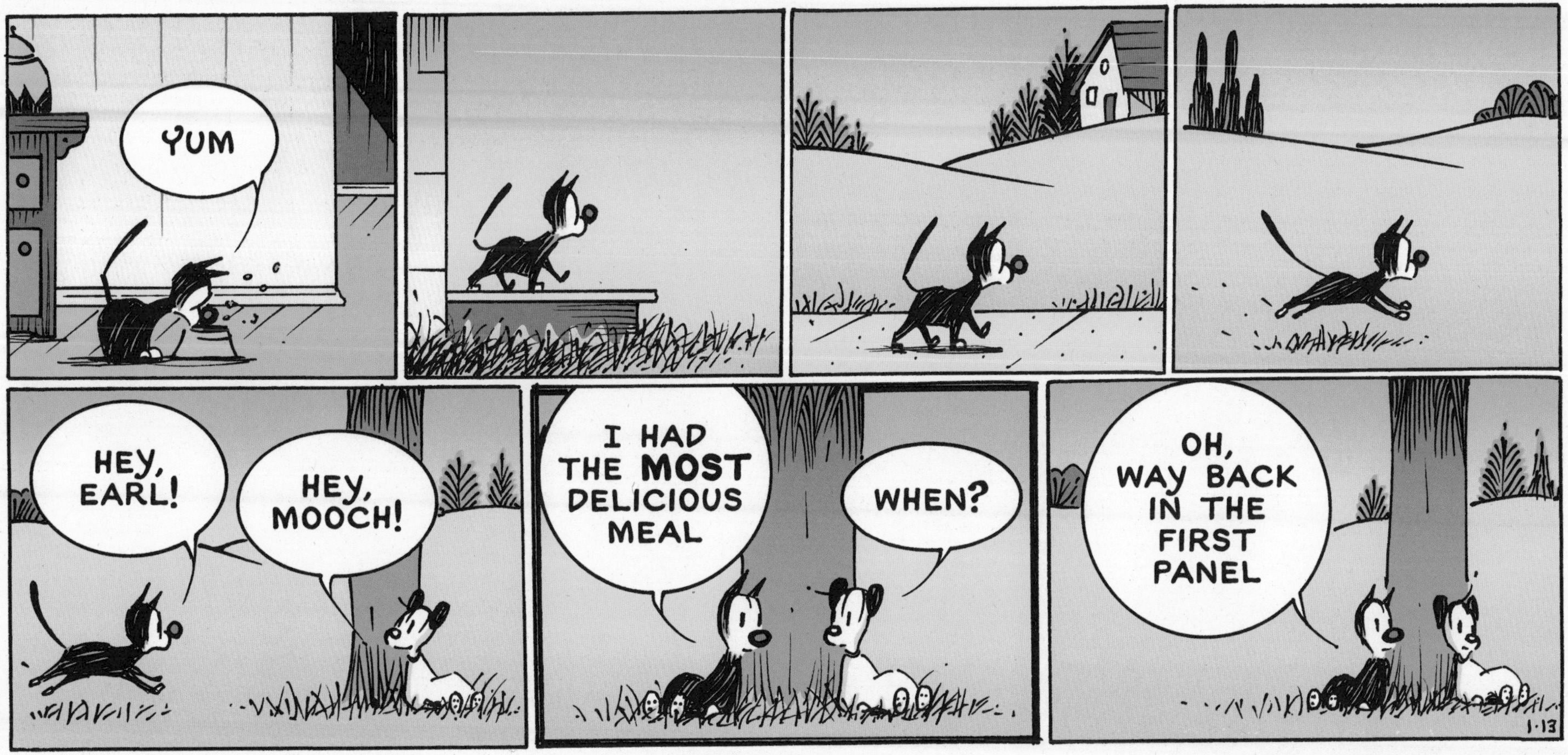
YUM
HEY, EARL!
HEY, MOOCH!
I HAD THE MOST DELICIOUS MEAL
WHEN?
OH, WAY BACK IN THE FIRST PANEL
1·13

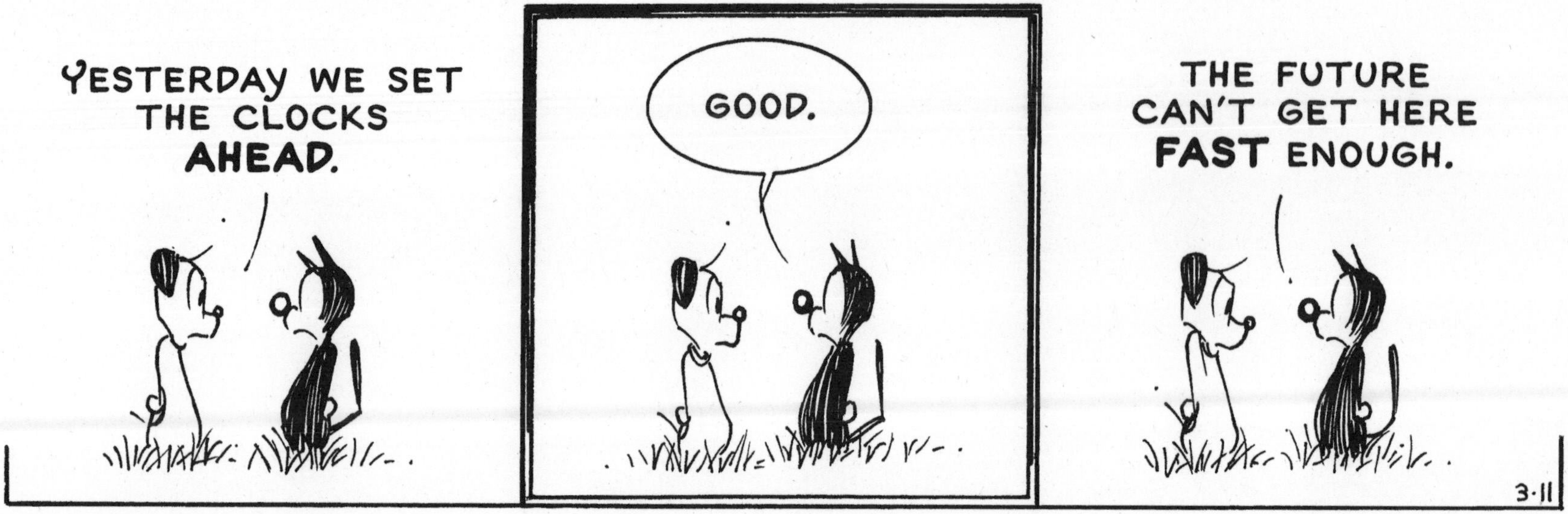
YESTERDAY WE SET THE CLOCKS AHEAD.
GOOD.
THE FUTURE CAN'T GET HERE FAST ENOUGH.
3·11

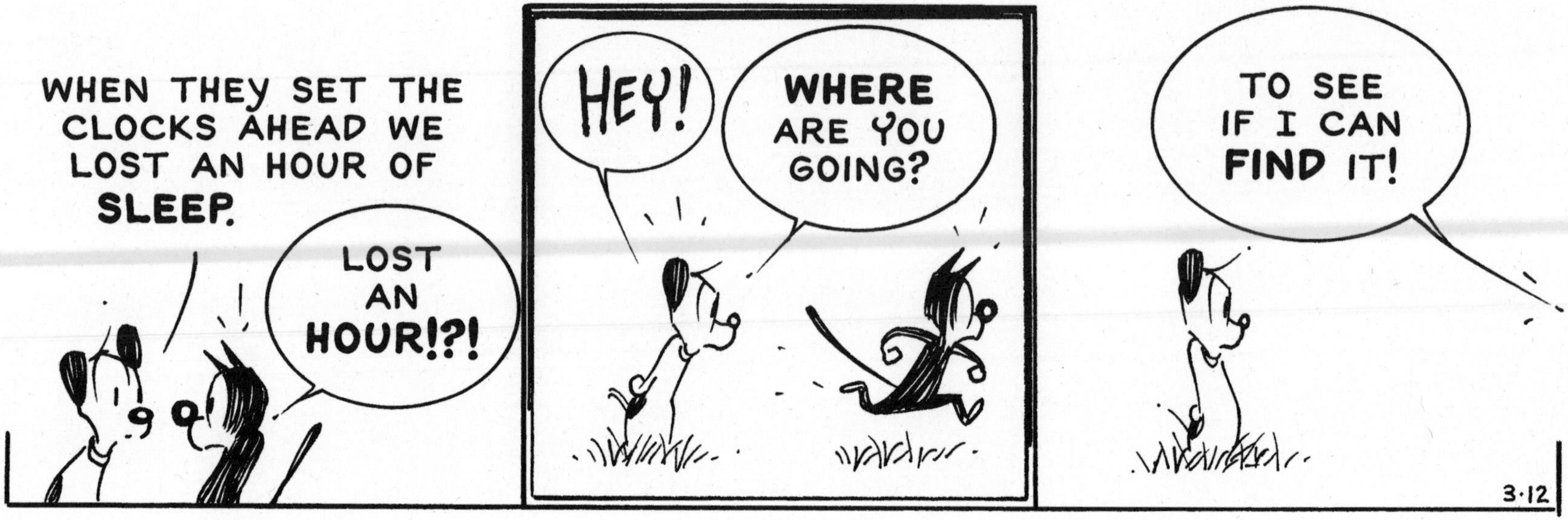
WHEN THEY SET THE CLOCKS AHEAD WE LOST AN HOUR OF SLEEP.
LOST AN HOUR!?!
HEY!
WHERE ARE YOU GOING?
TO SEE IF I CAN FIND IT!
3·12

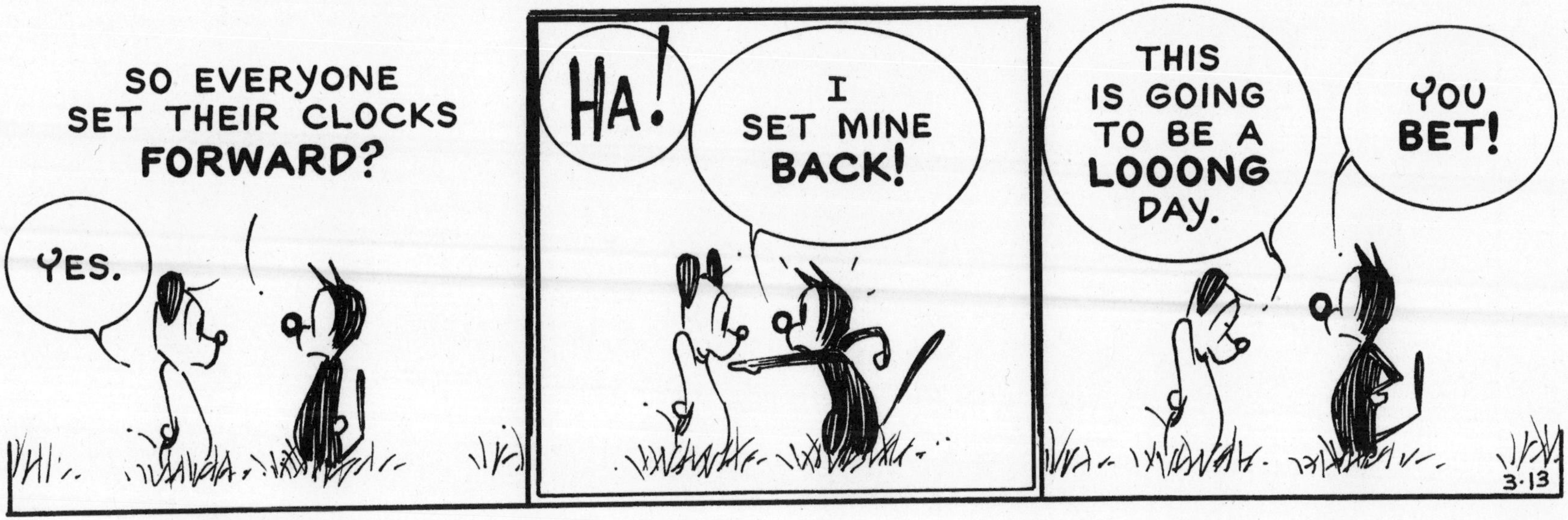
SO EVERYONE SET THEIR CLOCKS FORWARD?
YES.
HA!
I SET MINE BACK!
THIS IS GOING TO BE A LOOONG DAY.
YOU BET!
3·13

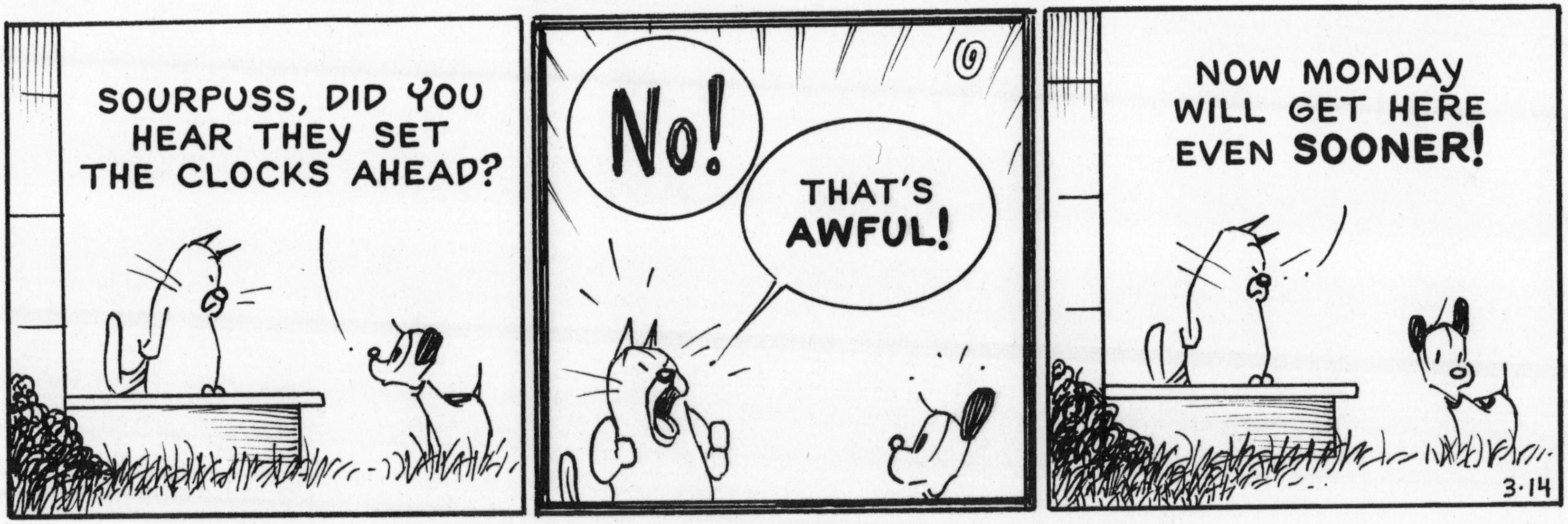
SOURPUSS, DID YOU HEAR THEY SET THE CLOCKS AHEAD?
NO!
THAT'S AWFUL!
NOW MONDAY WILL GET HERE EVEN SOONER!
3·14

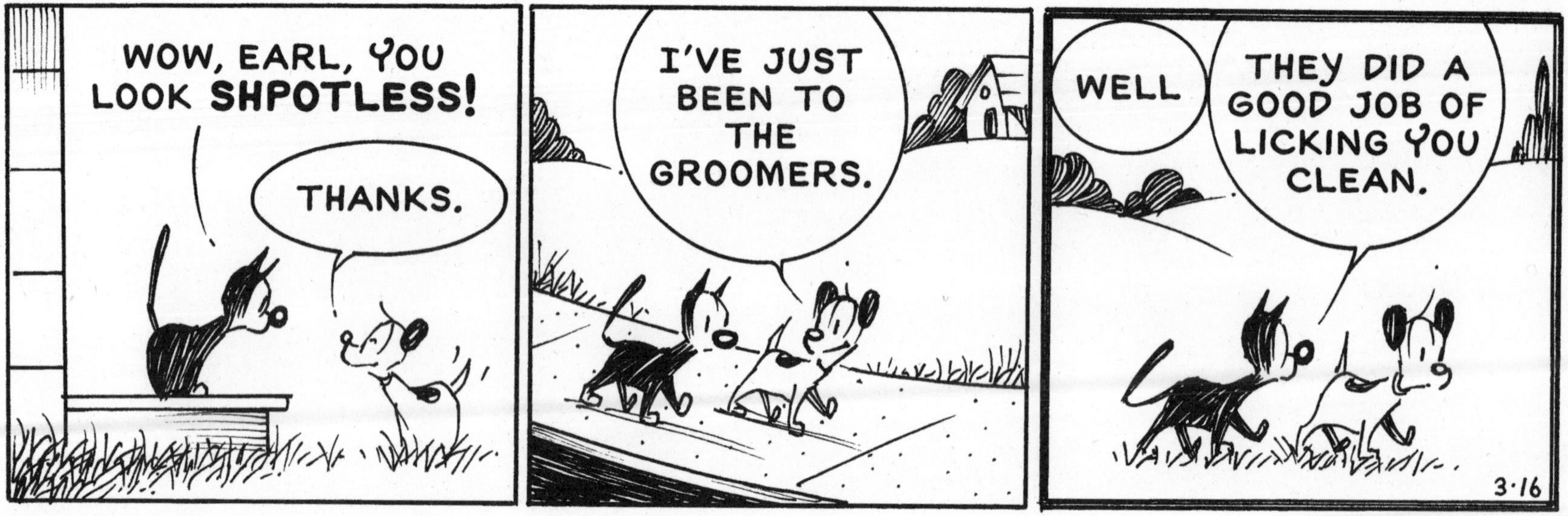
WOW, EARL, YOU LOOK SHPOTLESS!
THANKS.
I'VE JUST BEEN TO THE GROOMERS.
WELL
THEY DID A GOOD JOB OF LICKING YOU CLEAN.
3·16

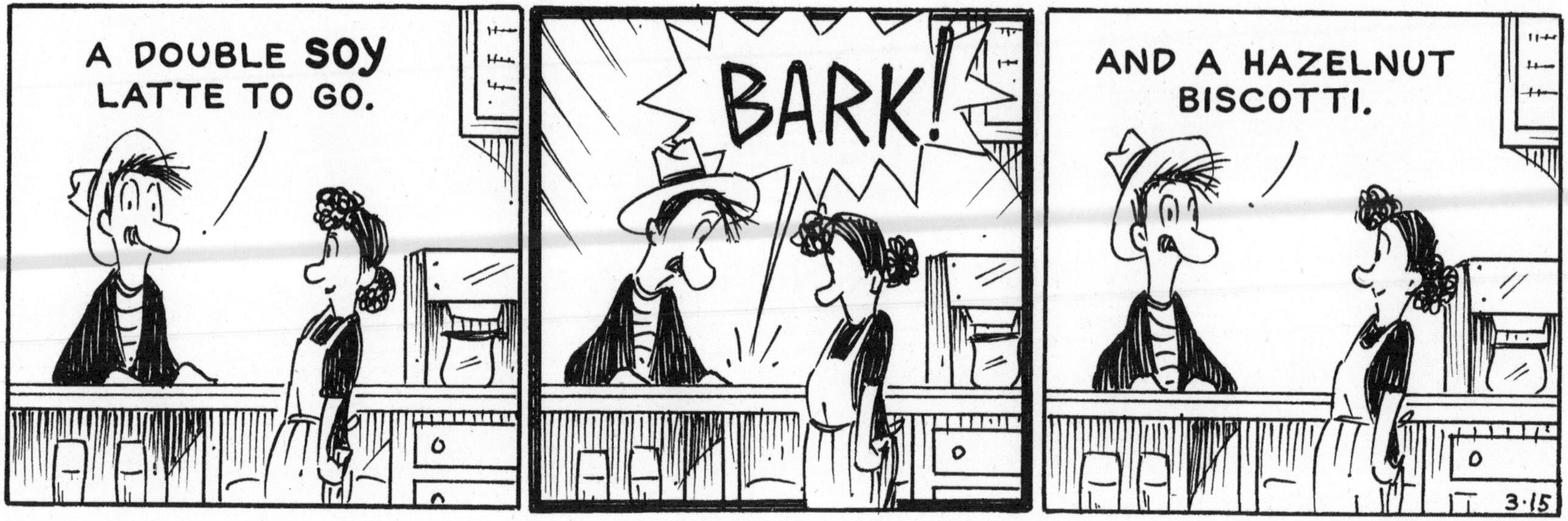
A DOUBLE SOY LATTE TO GO.
BARK!
AND A HAZELNUT BISCOTTI.
3·15

MUTTS

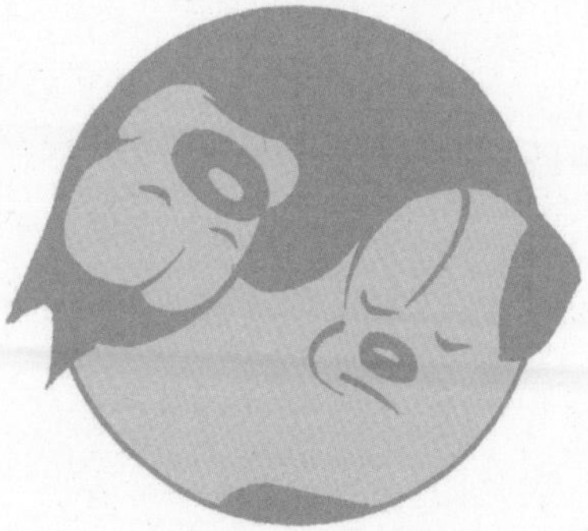

Patrick McDonnell

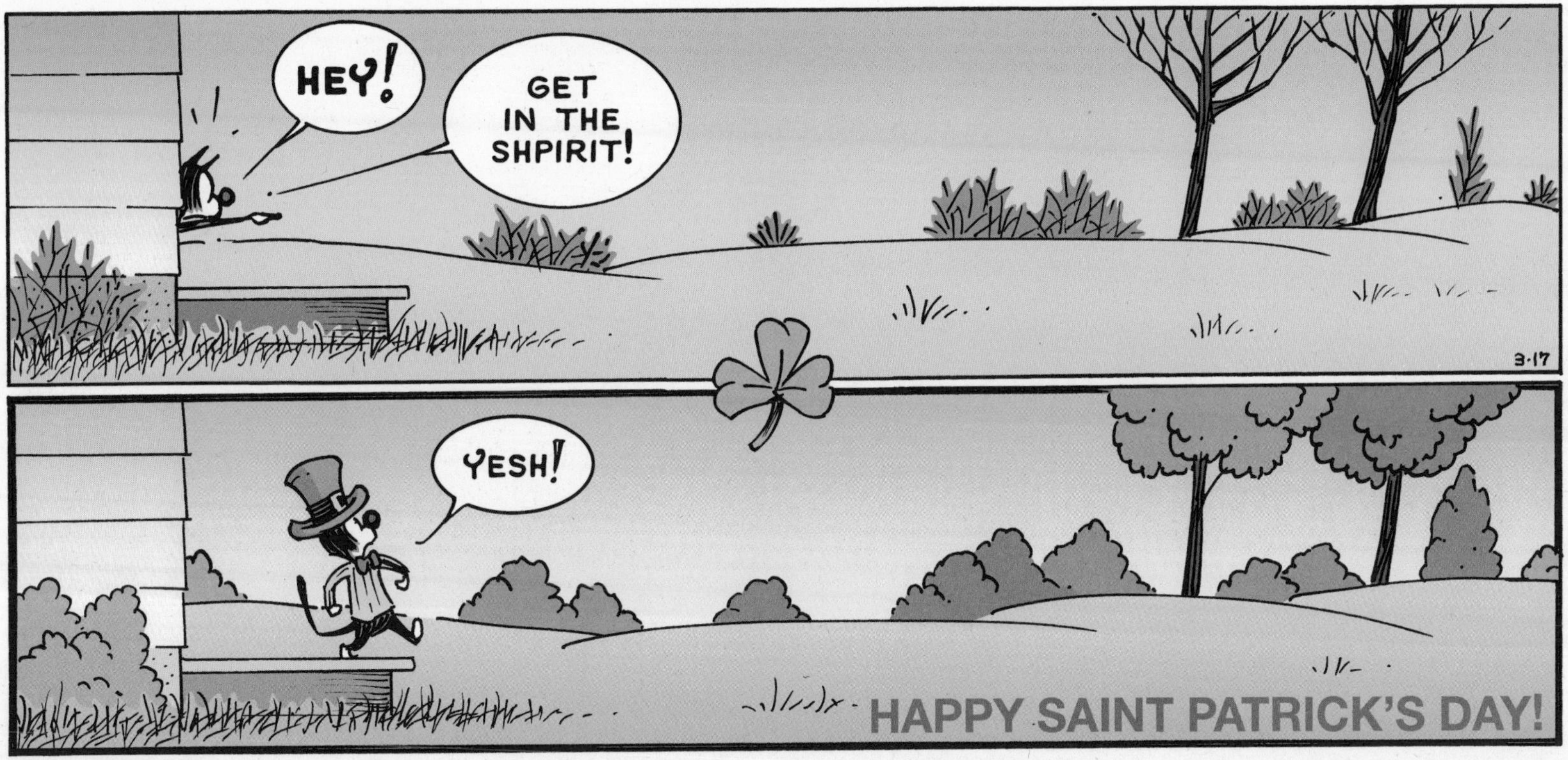
HEY!
GET IN THE SHPIRIT!
3·17
YESH!
HAPPY SAINT PATRICK'S DAY!

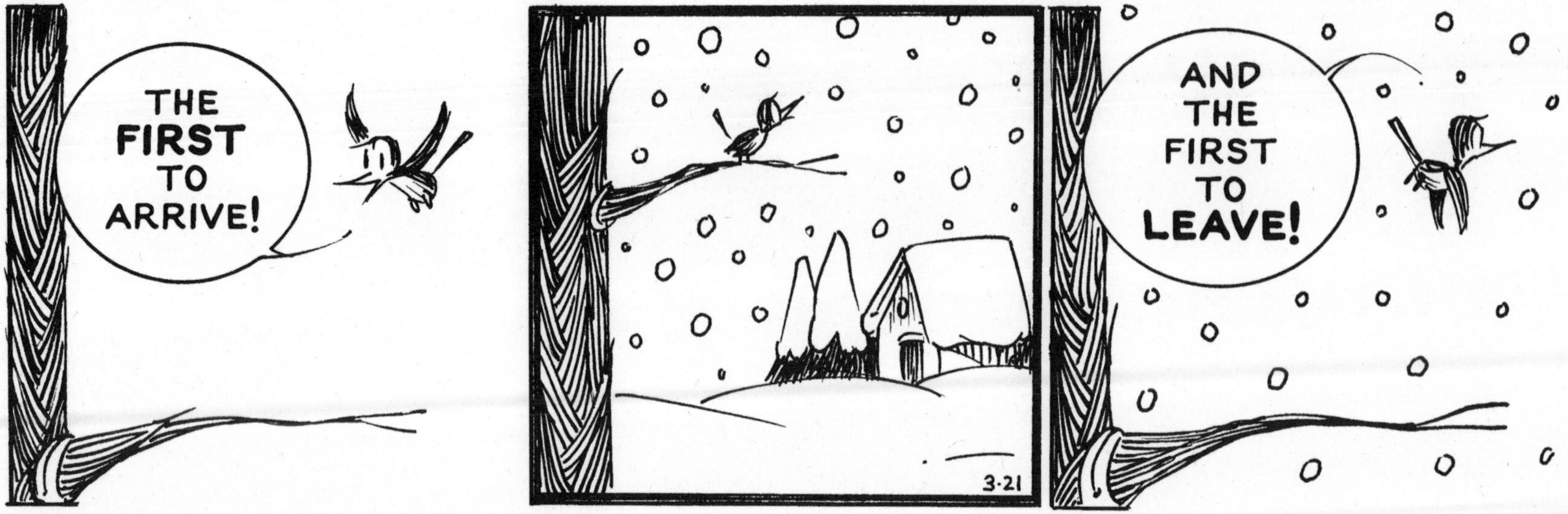
THE FIRST TO ARRIVE!
AND THE FIRST TO LEAVE!
3·21

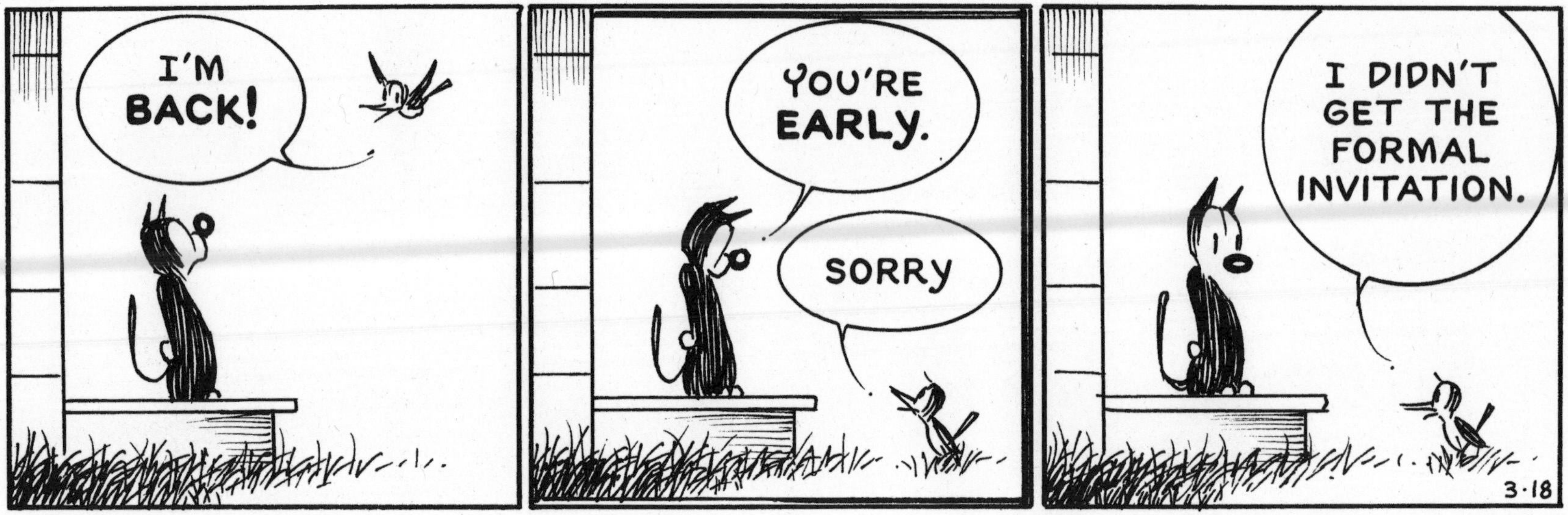
I'M BACK!
YOU'RE EARLY.
SORRY
I DIDN'T GET THE FORMAL INVITATION.
3·18

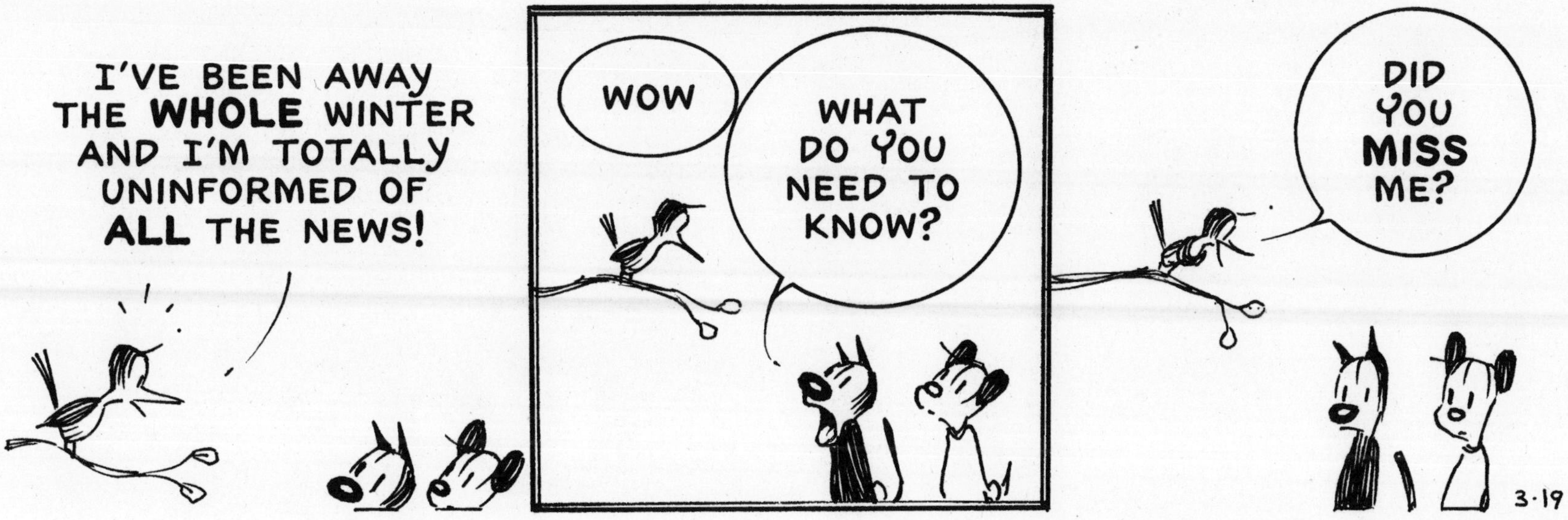
I'VE BEEN AWAY THE **WHOLE** WINTER AND I'M TOTALLY UNINFORMED OF **ALL** THE NEWS!
WOW
WHAT DO YOU NEED TO KNOW?
DID YOU **MISS** ME?
3·19

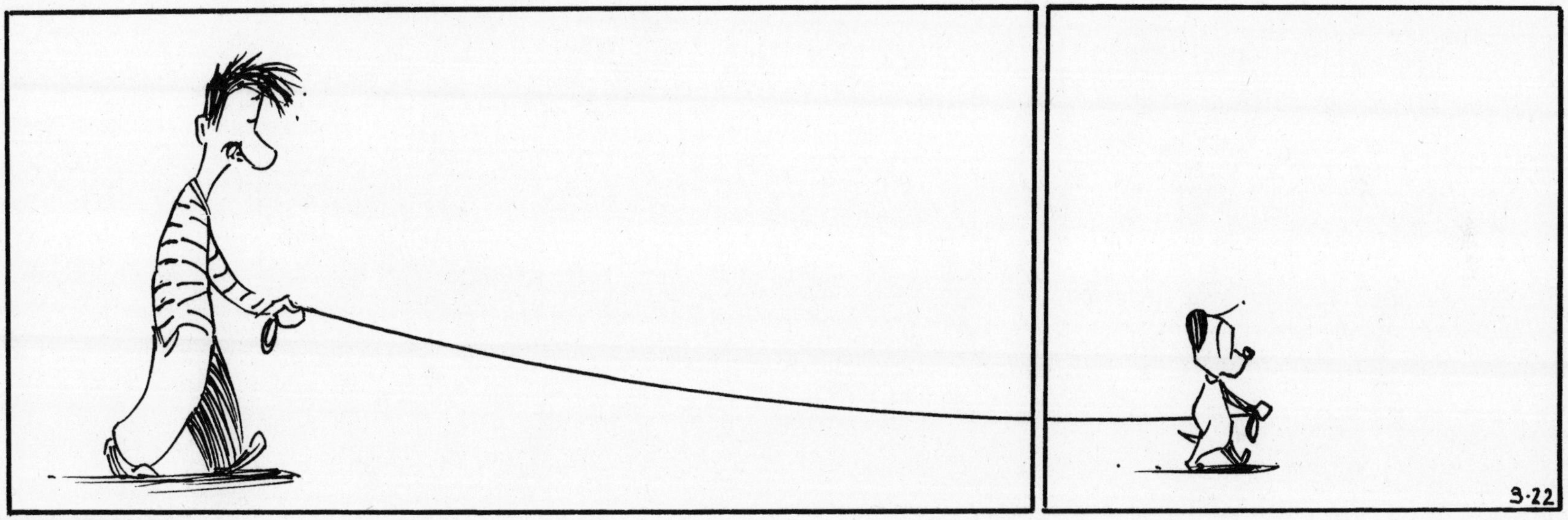
3·22

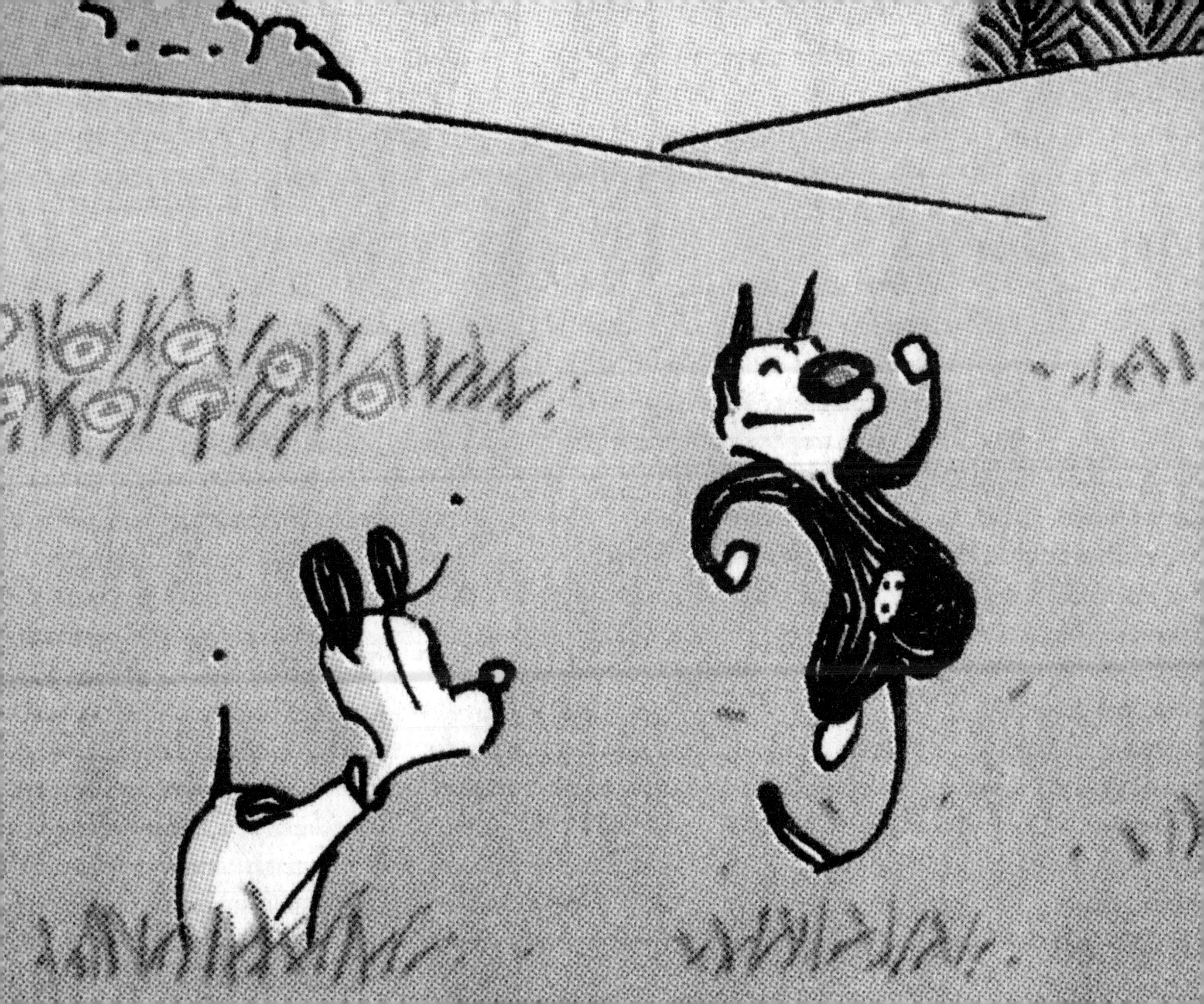

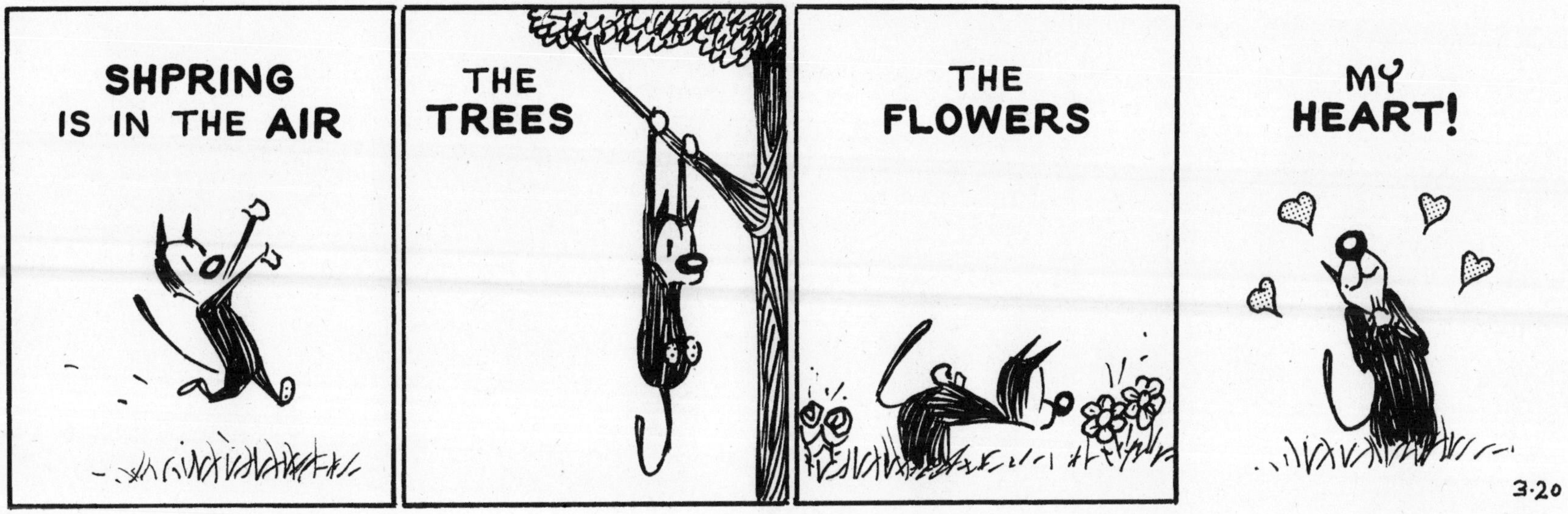
SHPRING IS IN THE AIR
THE TREES
THE FLOWERS
MY HEART!
3·20

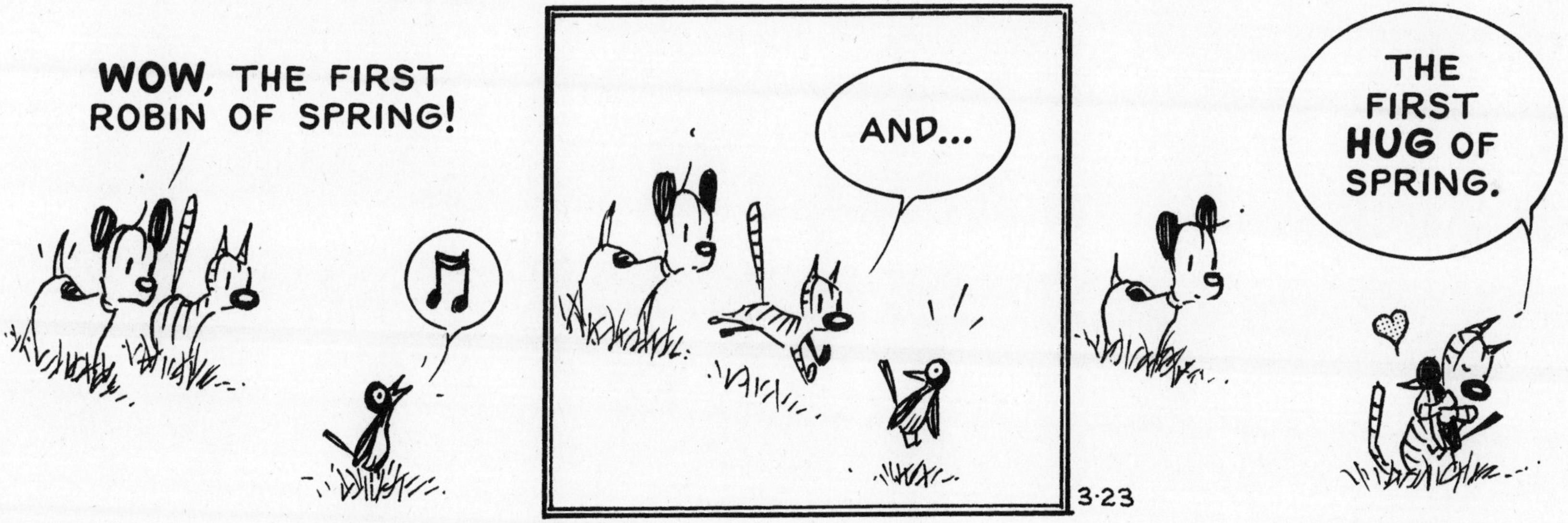
WOW, THE FIRST ROBIN OF SPRING!
AND...
THE FIRST HUG OF SPRING.
3·23

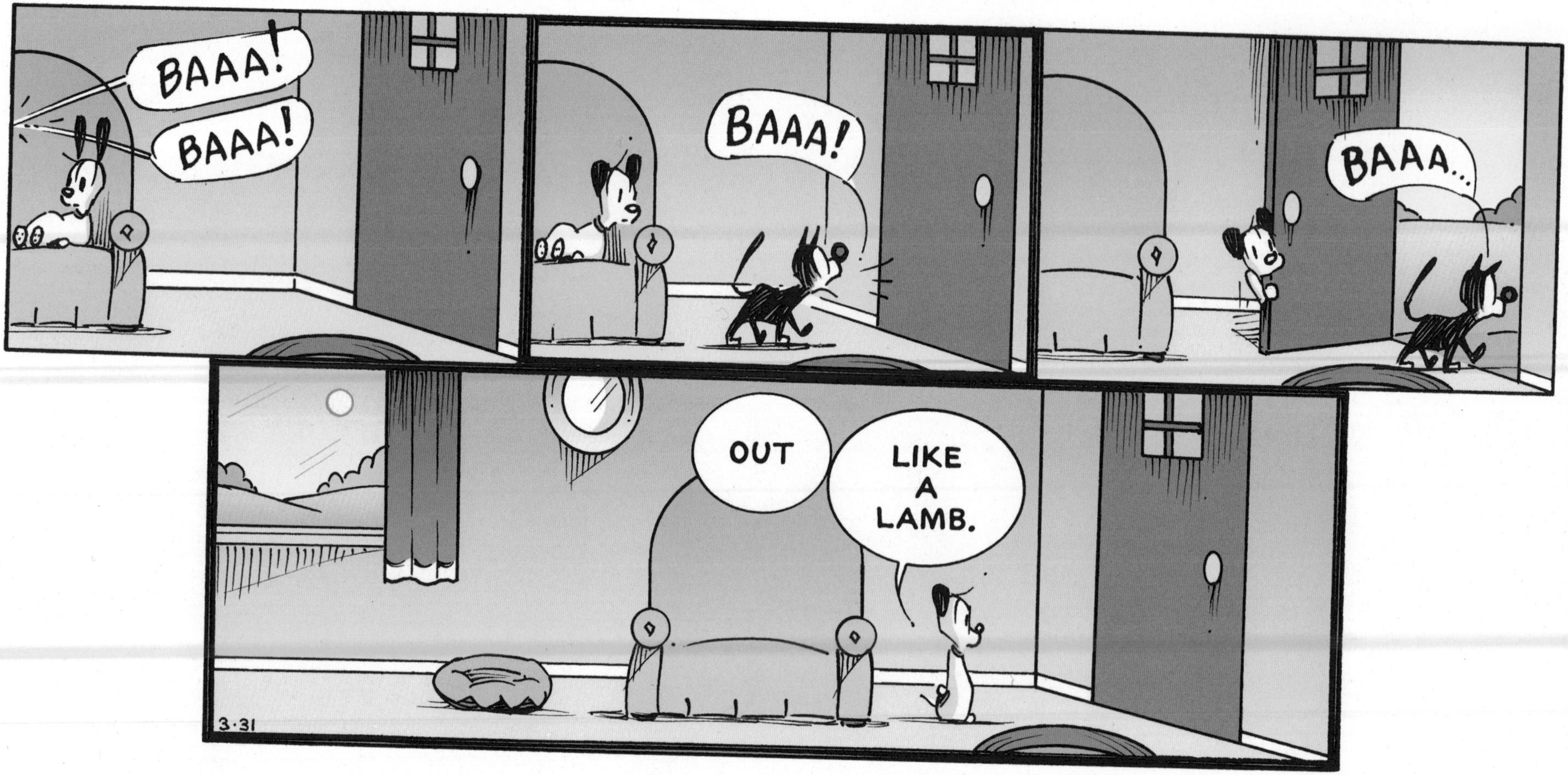
BAAA!
BAAA!
BAAA!
BAAA...
OUT
LIKE A LAMB.
3·31

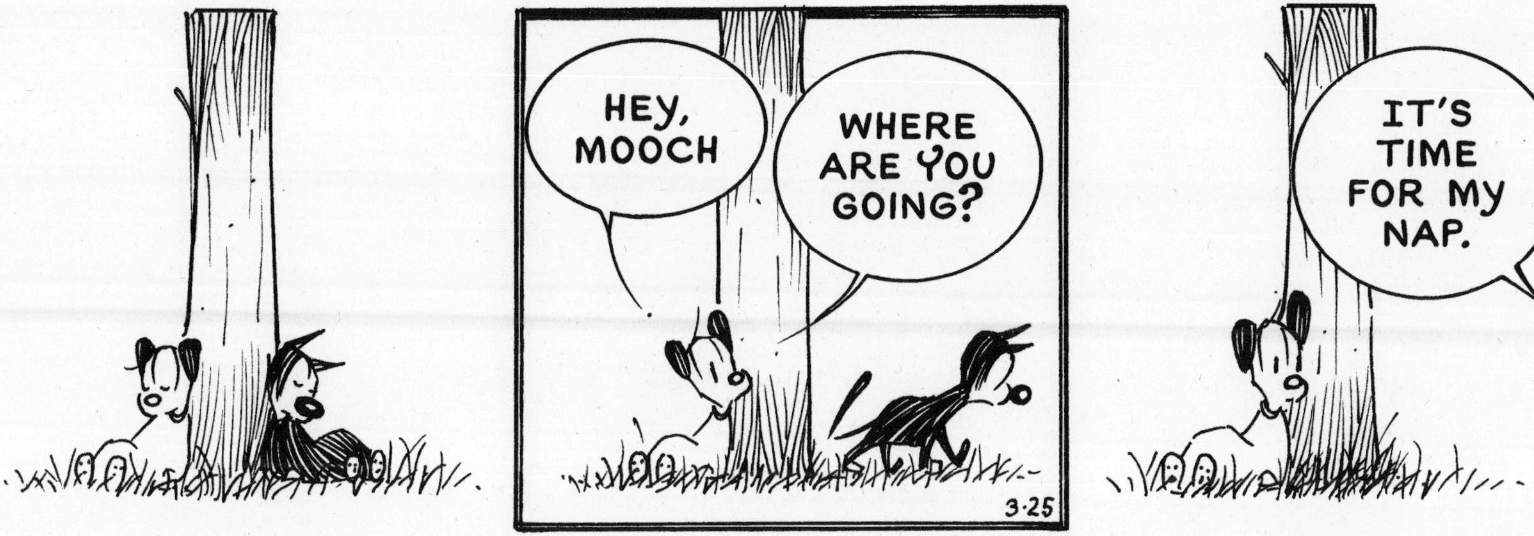
HEY, MOOCH
WHERE ARE YOU GOING?
IT'S TIME FOR MY NAP.
3·25

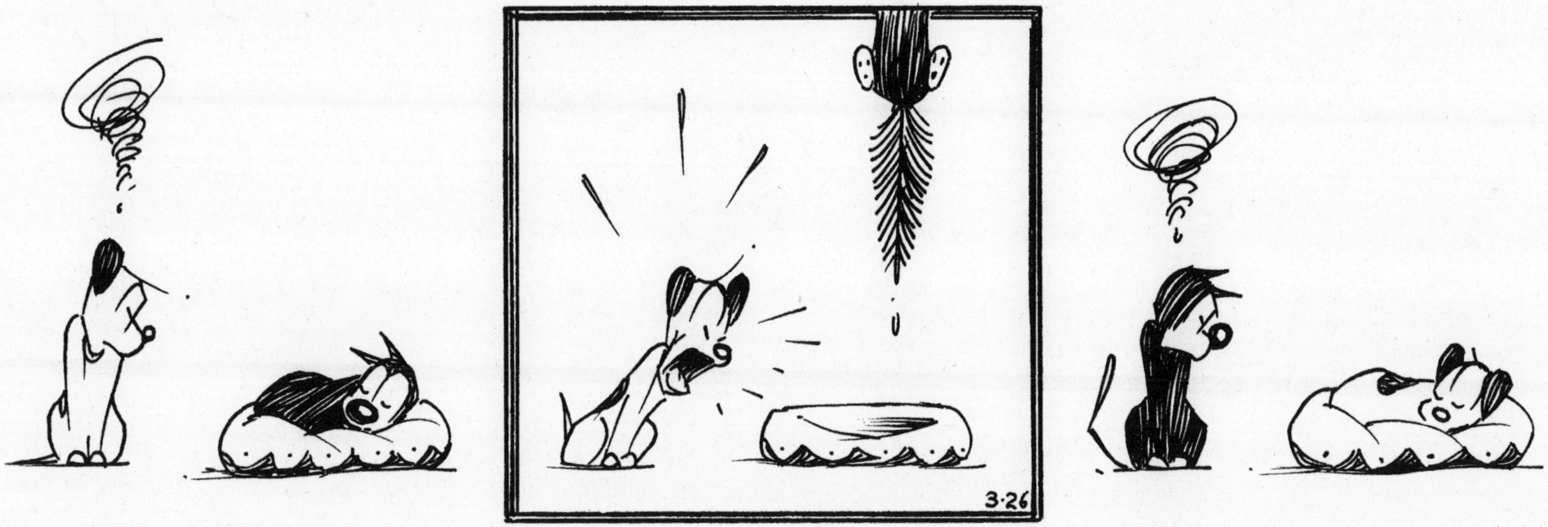
3·26

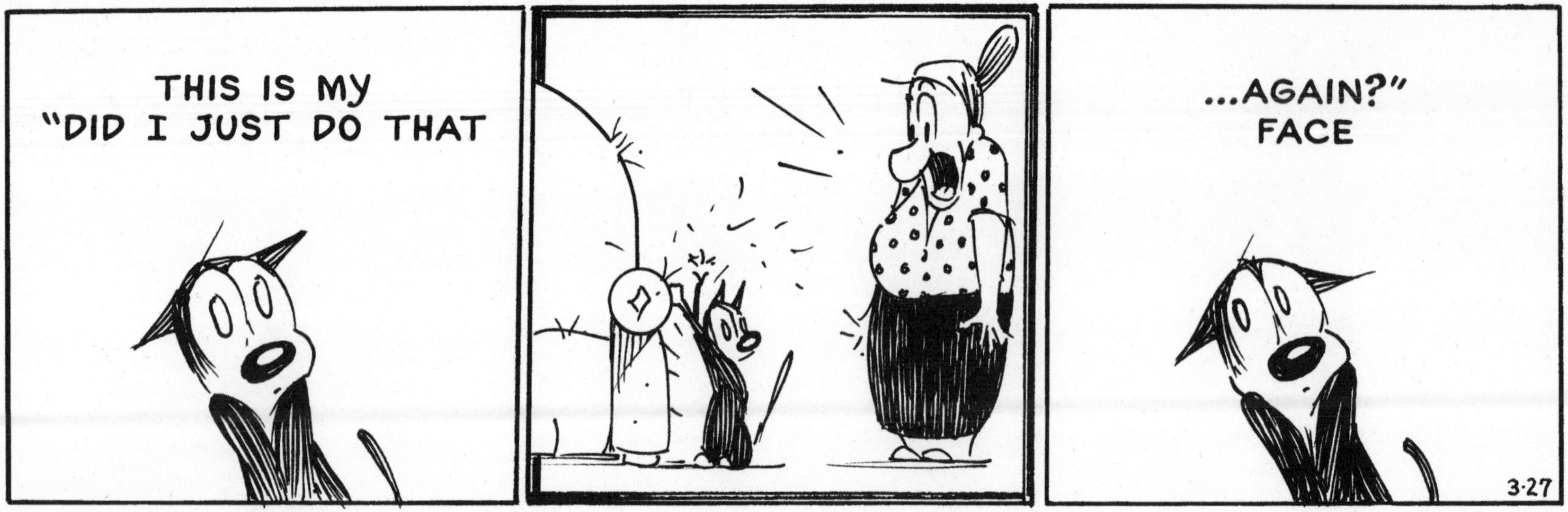
THIS IS MY "DID I JUST DO THAT
...AGAIN?" FACE
3·27

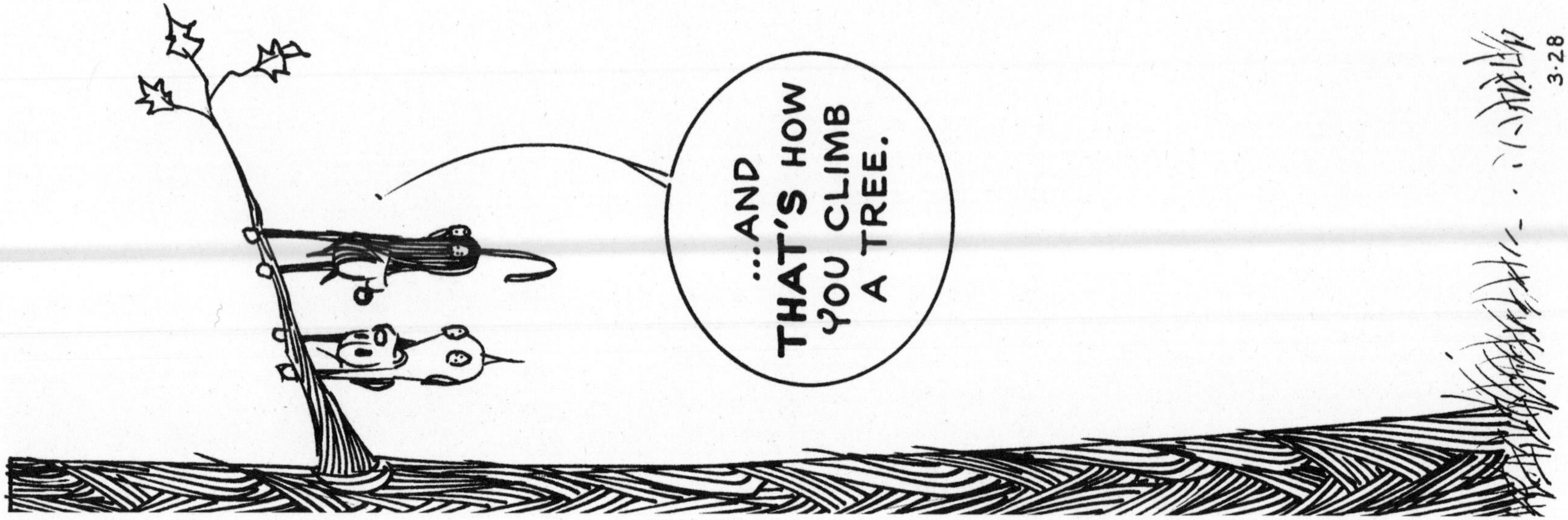
...AND THAT'S HOW YOU CLIMB A TREE.
3·28

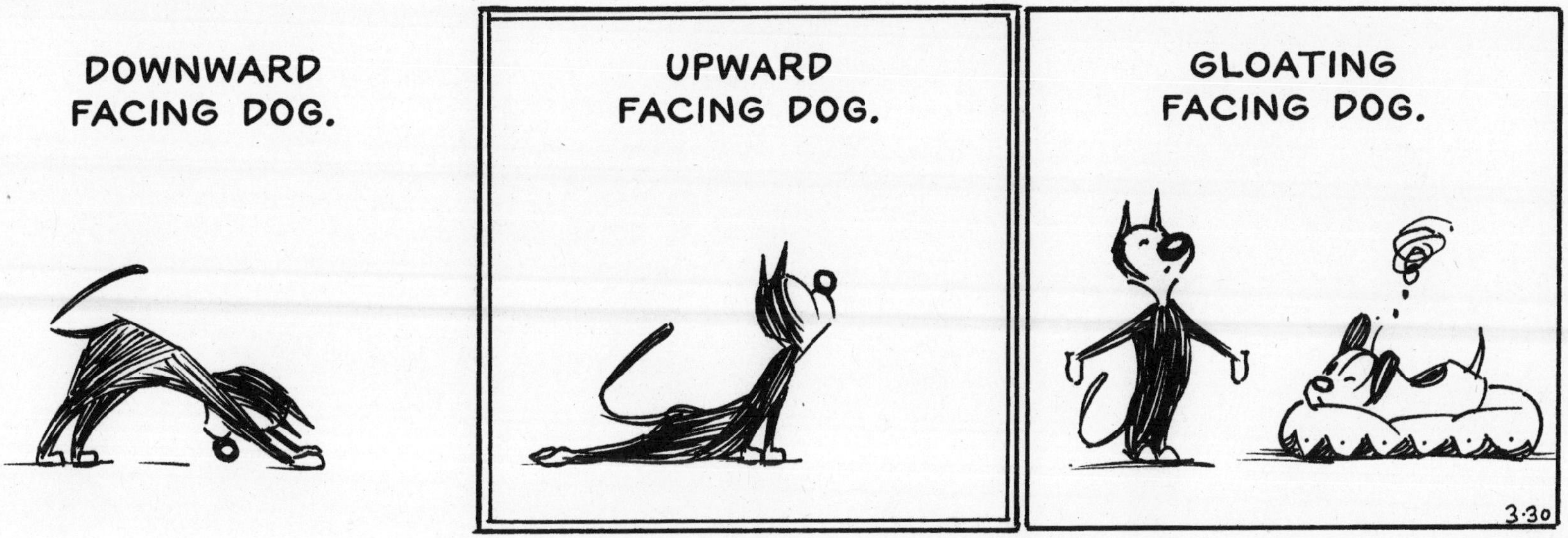
DOWNWARD FACING DOG.
UPWARD FACING DOG.
GLOATING FACING DOG.
3·30

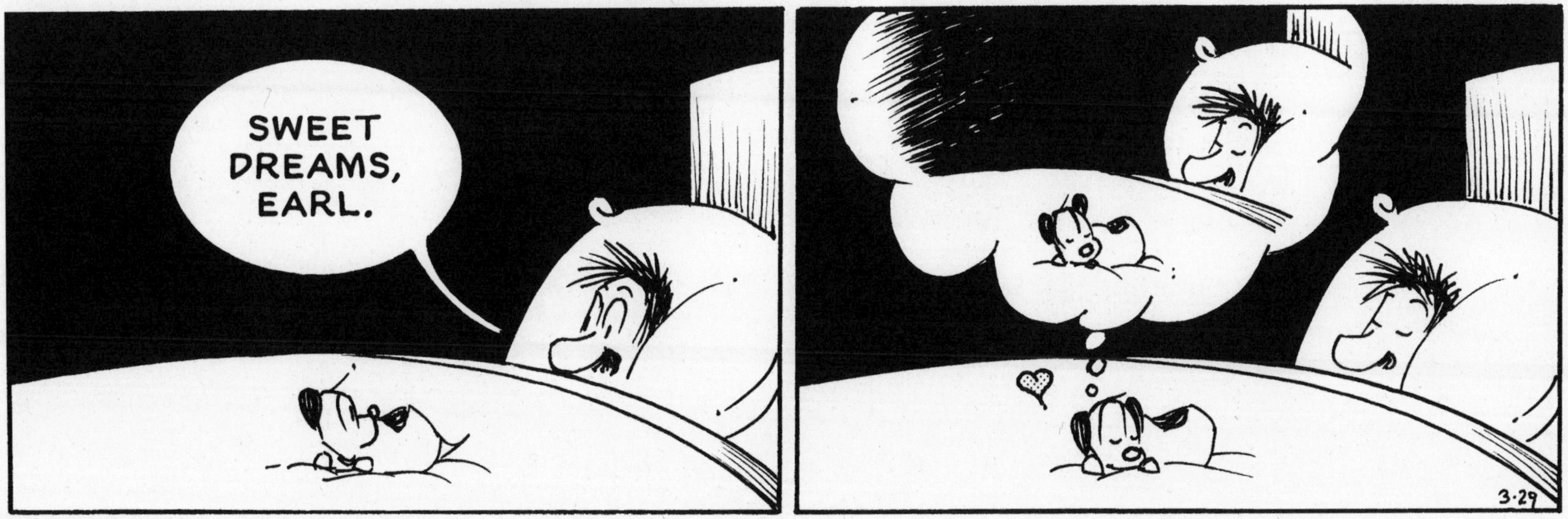
SWEET DREAMS, EARL.
3·29

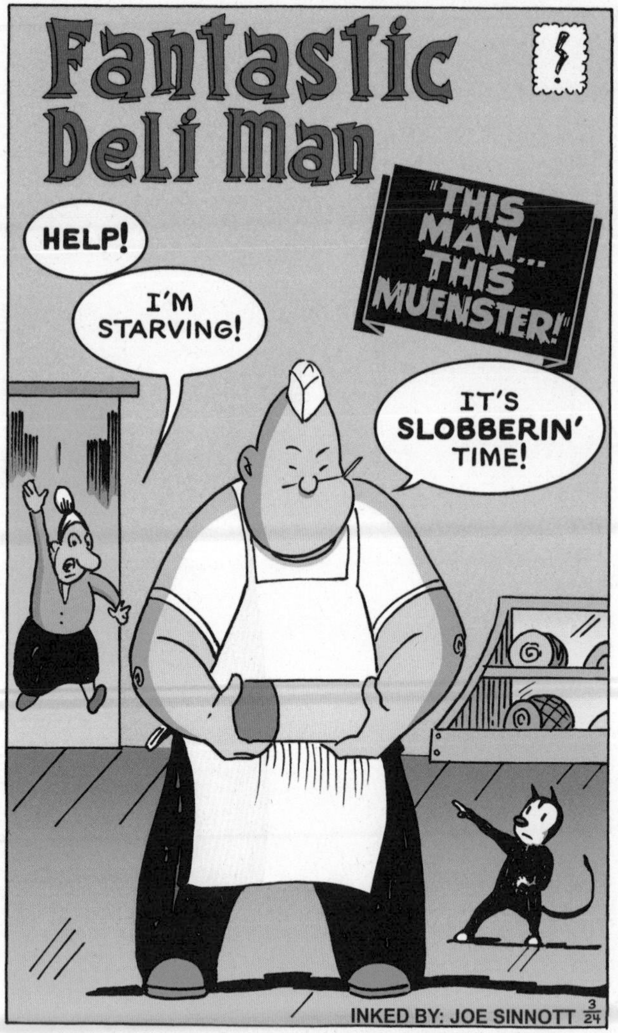
Fantastic Deli Man
HELP!
I'M STARVING!
"THIS MAN... THIS MUENSTER!"
IT'S SLOBBERIN' TIME!
INKED BY: JOE SINNOTT 3/24

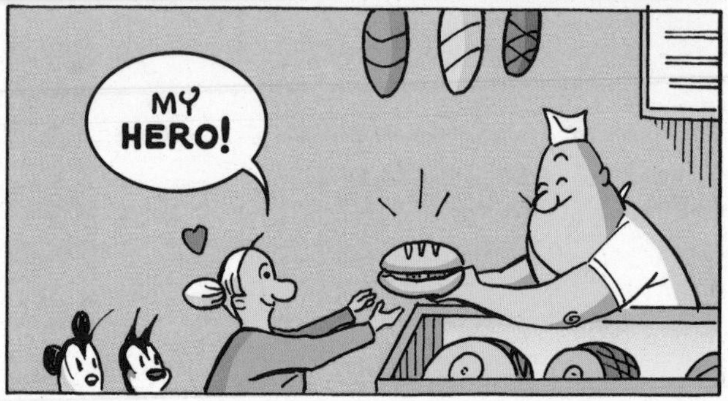
MY HERO!

AT LAST YOU WILL LEARN WHAT LIVES... WITHIN THE COCOON!
INKED BY: JOE SINNOTT
4-14
HIM!?!

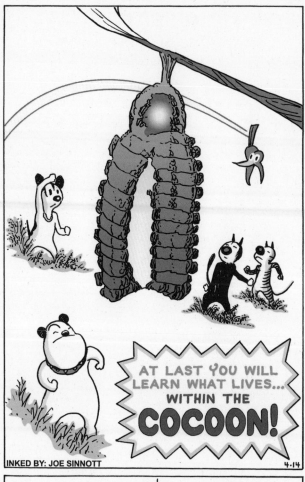

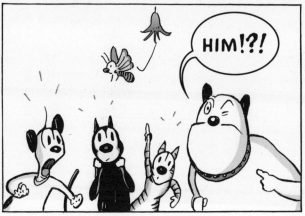

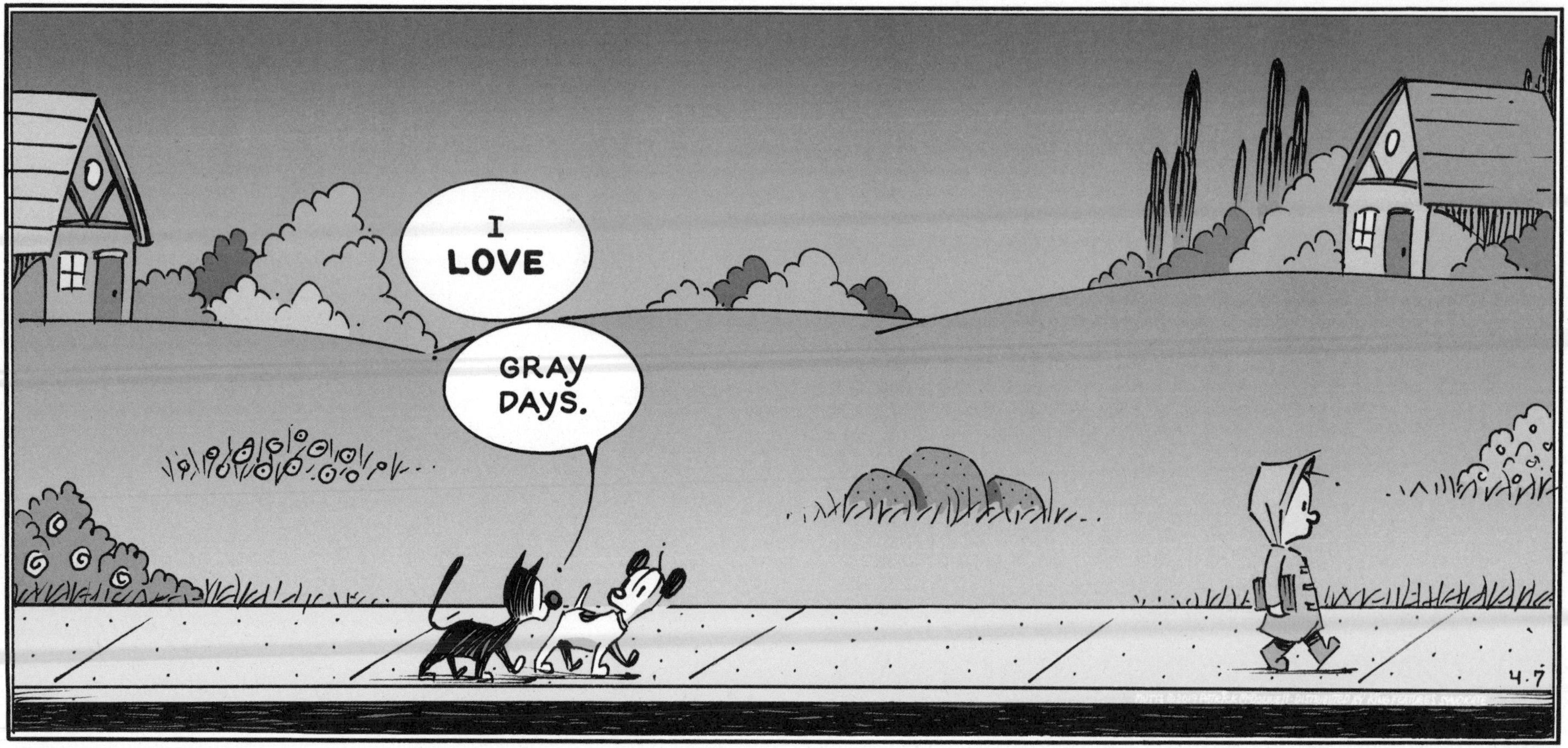
I LOVE
GRAY DAYS.
4.7

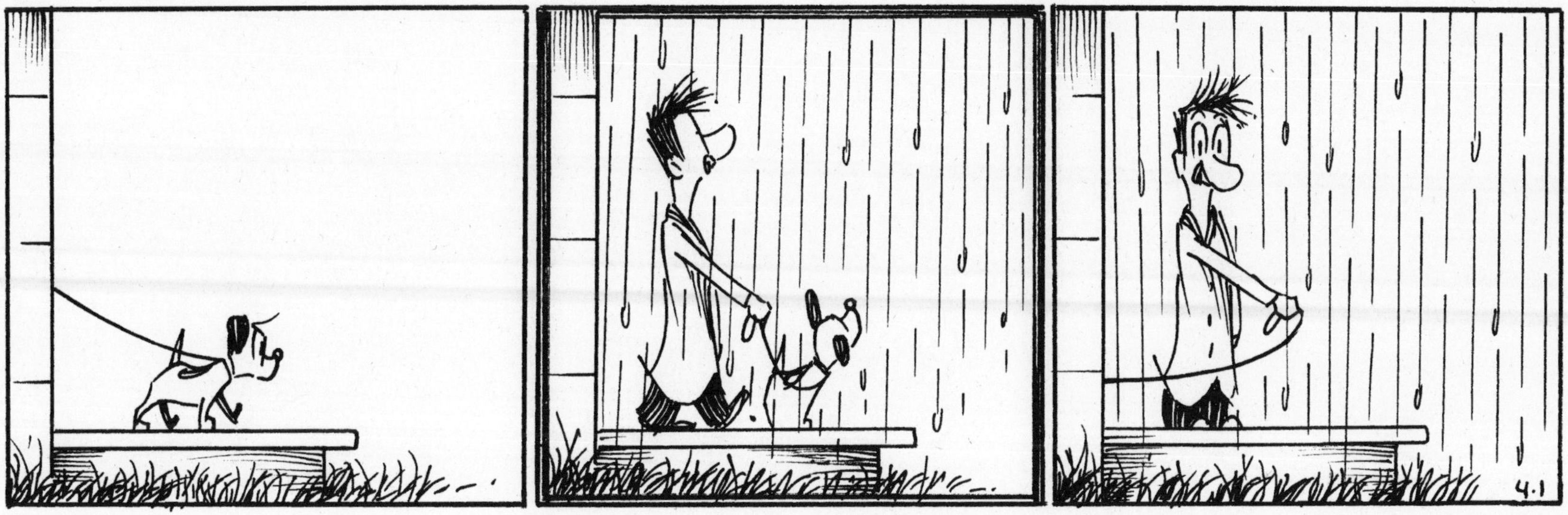
4.1

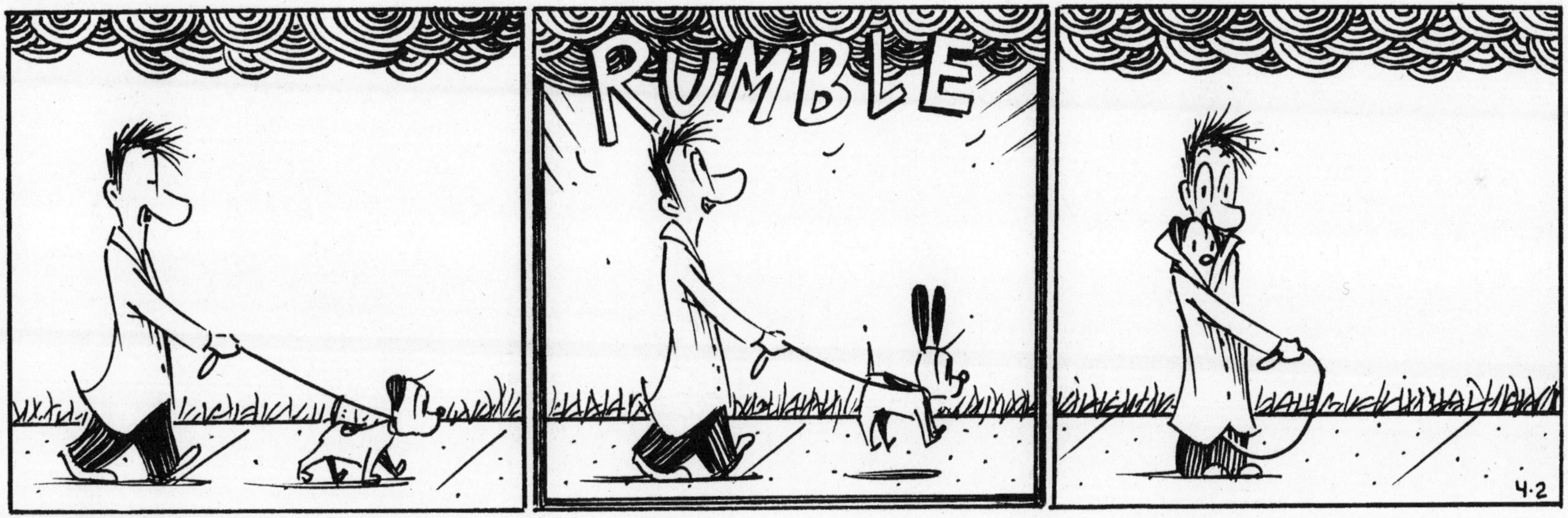
RUMBLE
4.2

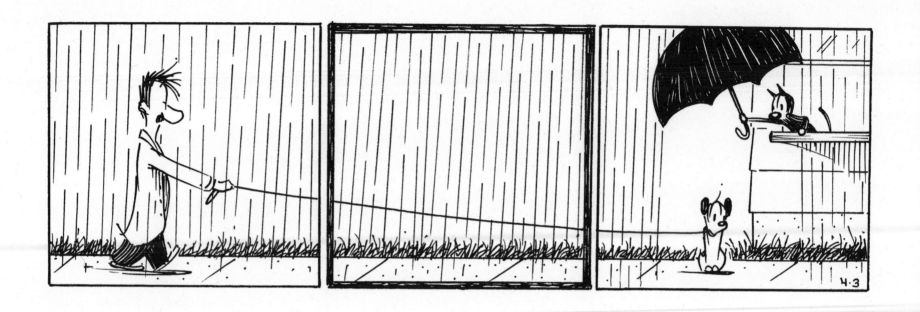

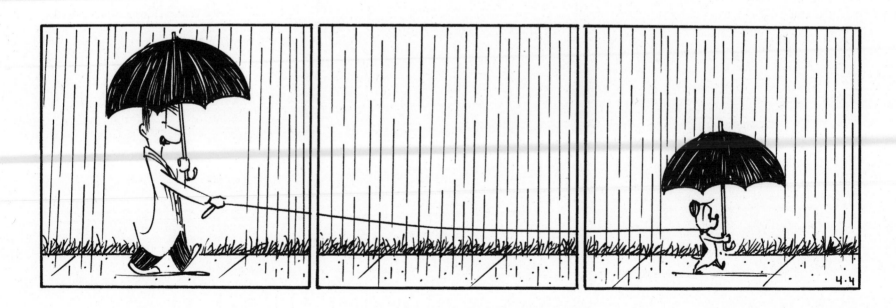

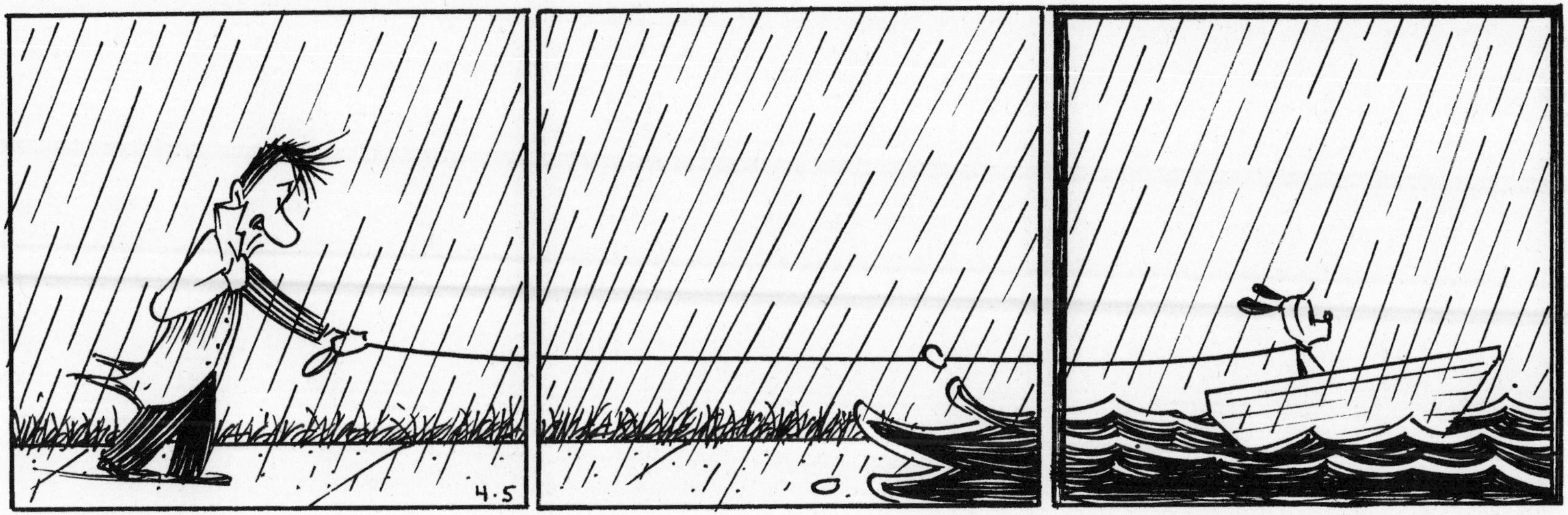
4.5

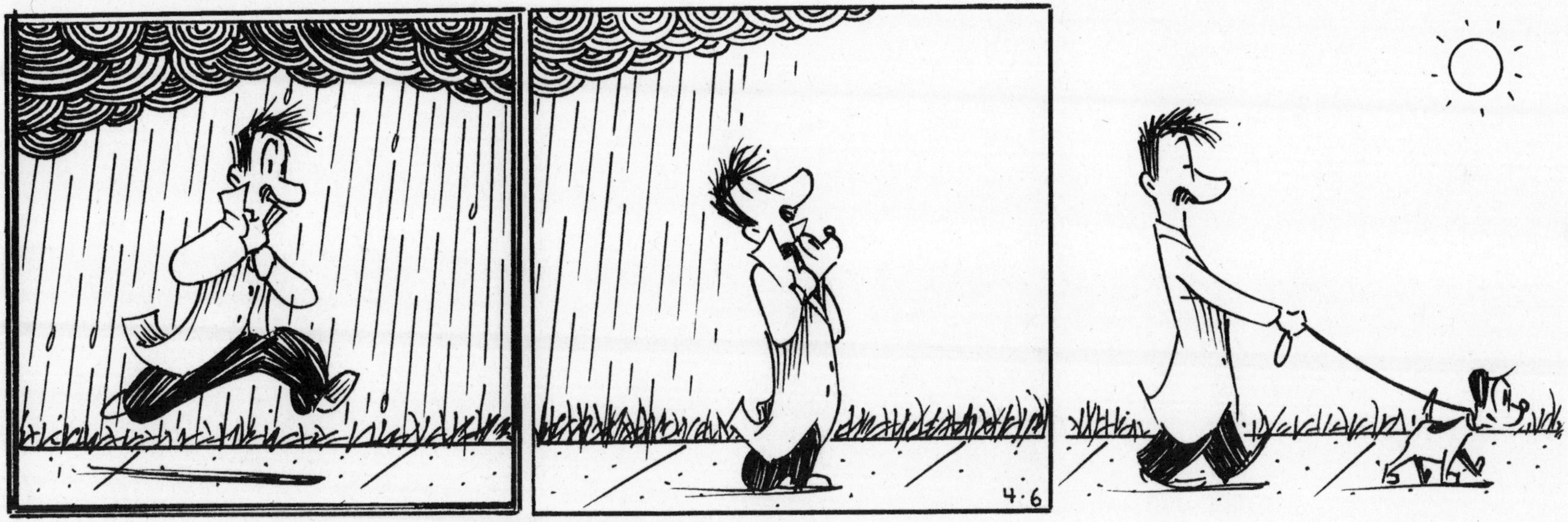
4.6

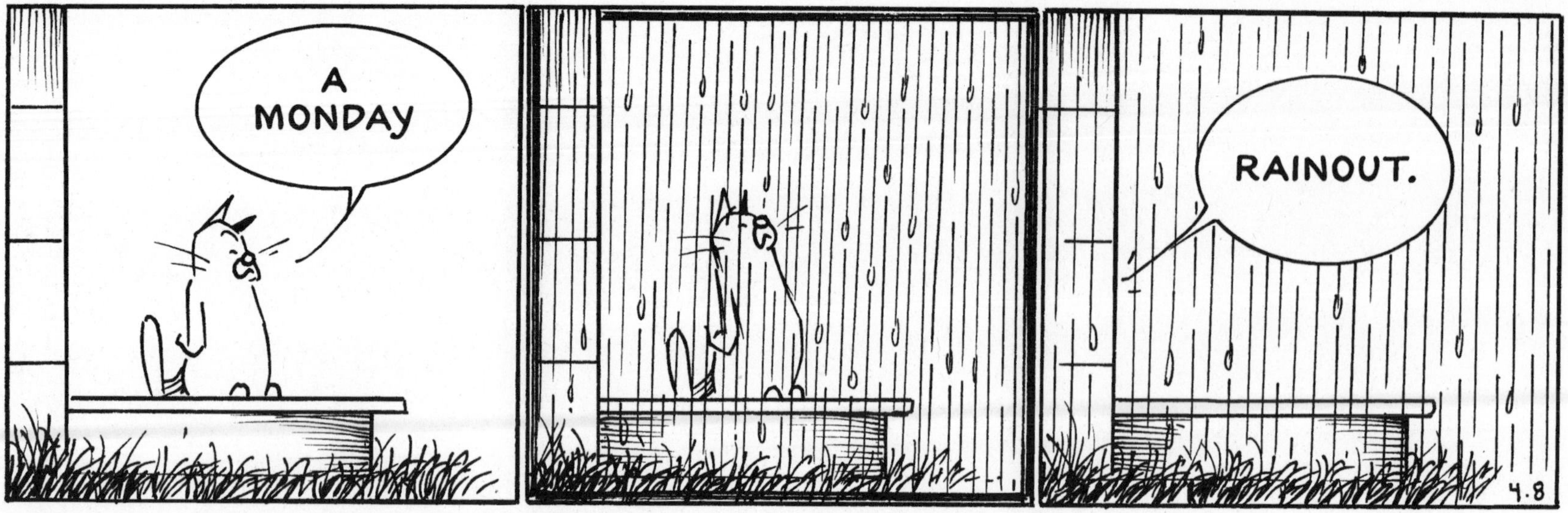
A MONDAY
RAINOUT.
4·8

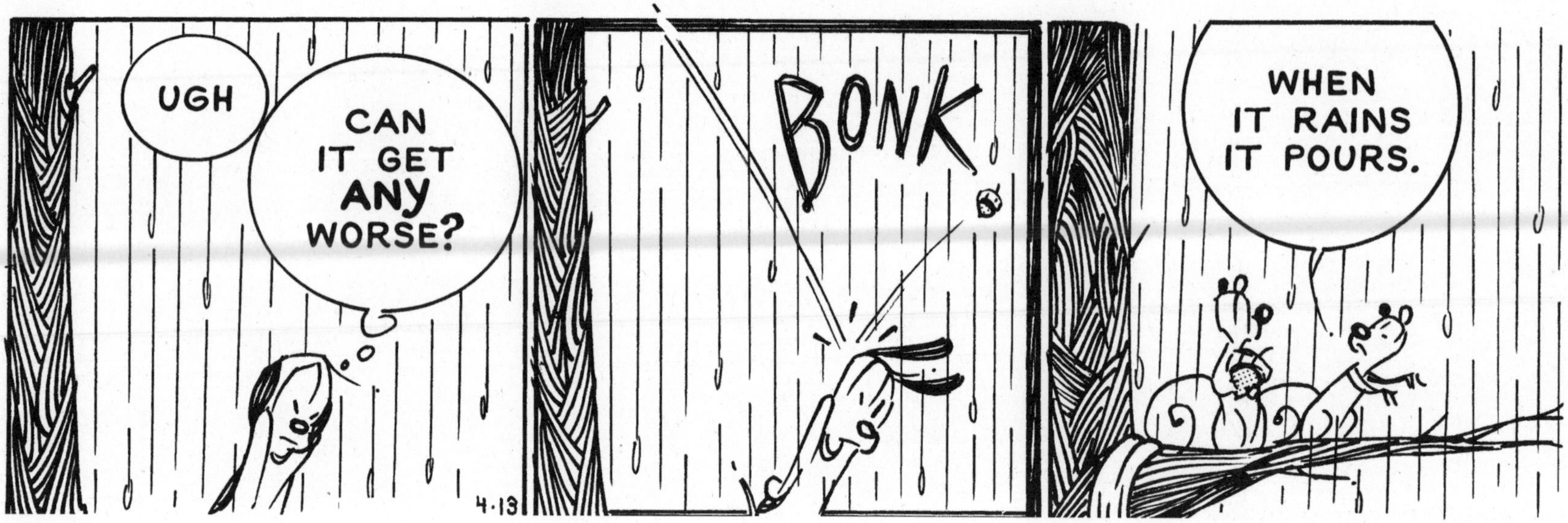
UGH
CAN IT GET ANY WORSE?
4·13
BONK
WHEN IT RAINS IT POURS.

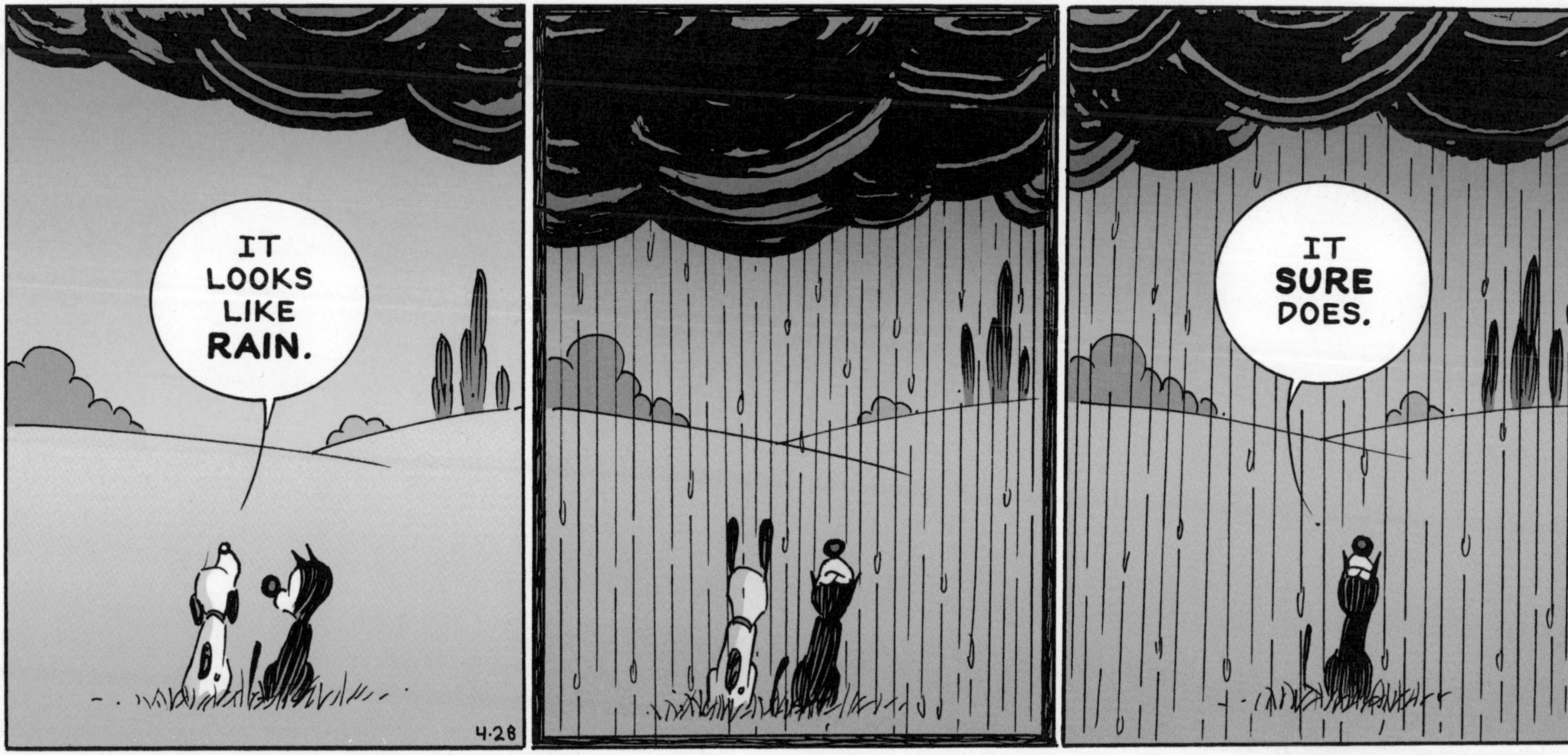
IT LOOKS LIKE RAIN.
4·28
IT SURE DOES.

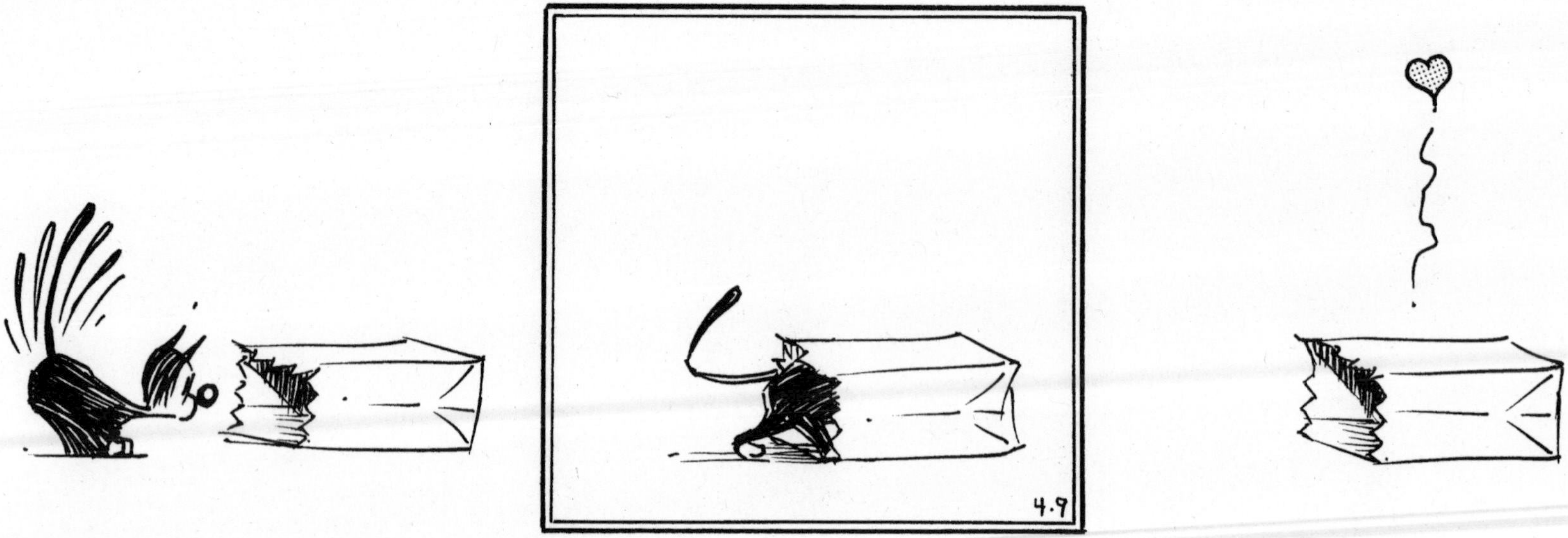
4·9

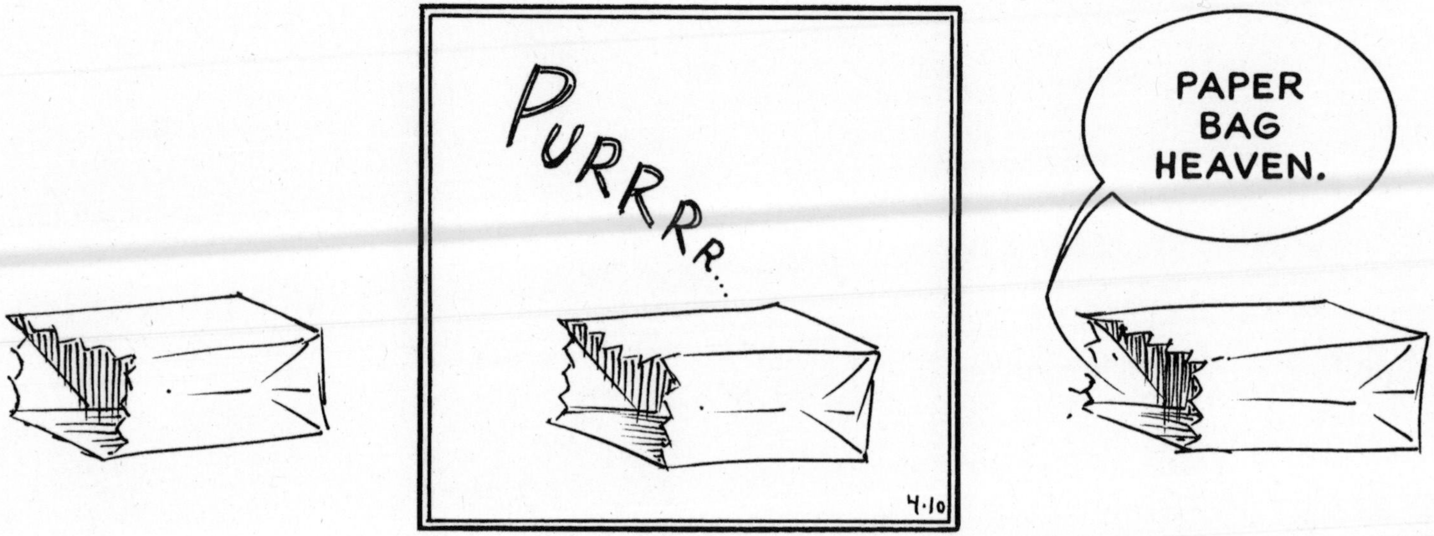
PURRRRR...
4·10
PAPER BAG HEAVEN.

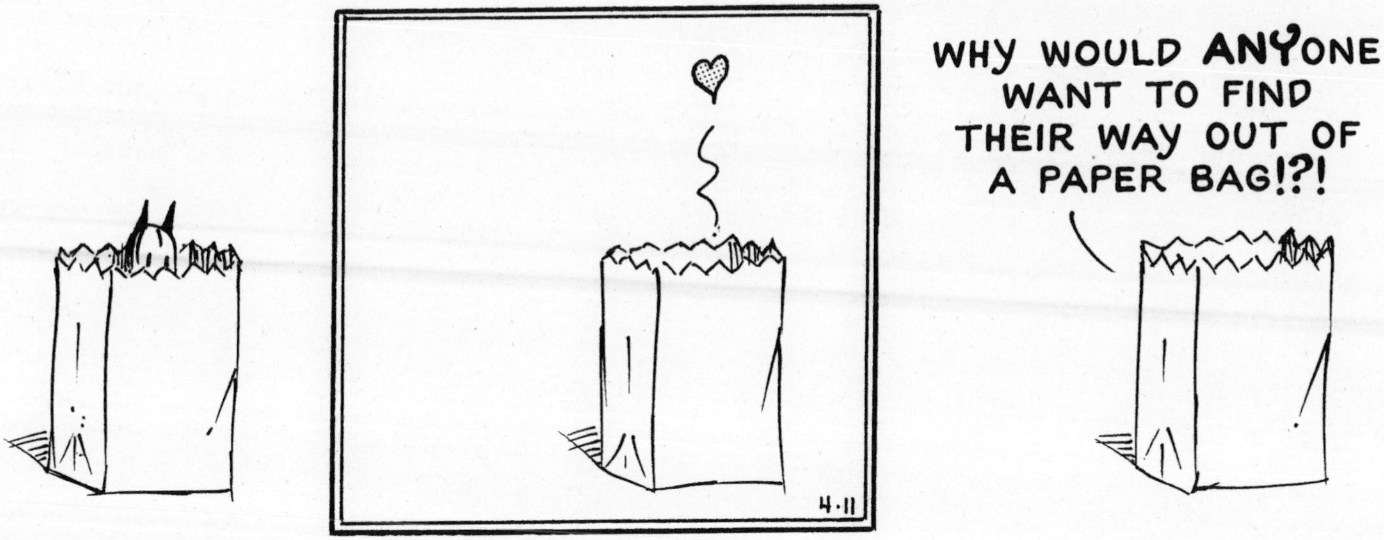
WHY WOULD ANYONE WANT TO FIND THEIR WAY OUT OF A PAPER BAG!?!
4·11

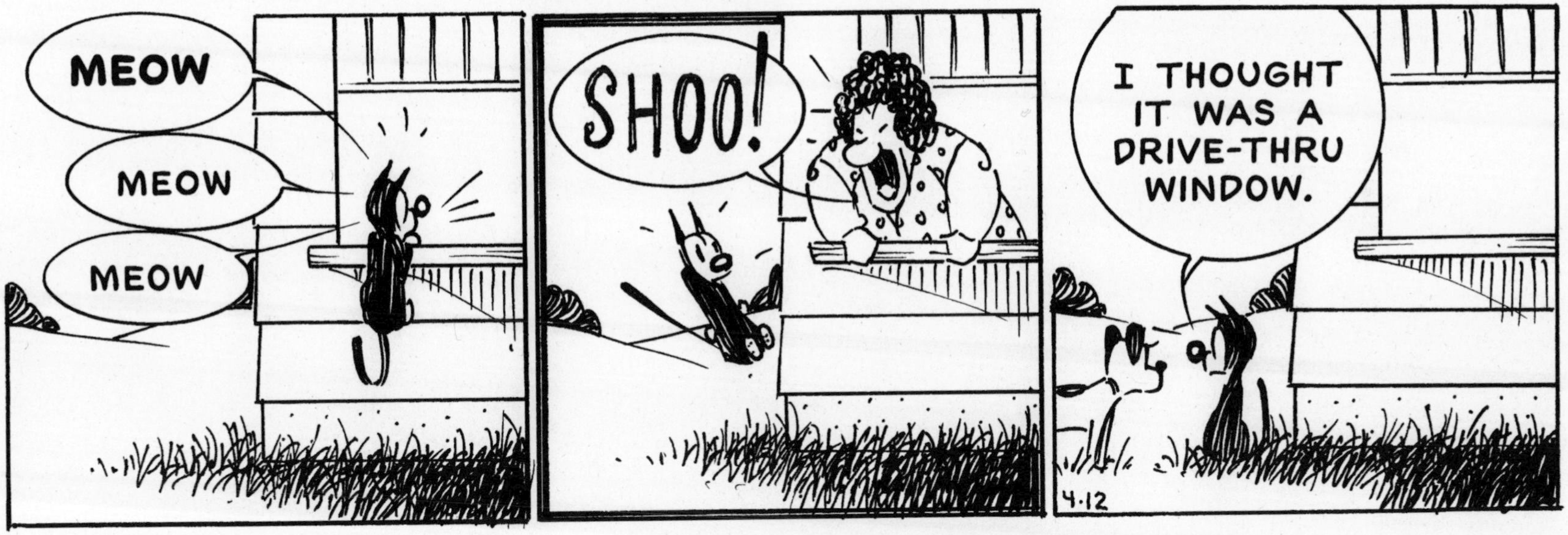
MEOW
MEOW
MEOW
SHOO!
I THOUGHT IT WAS A DRIVE-THRU WINDOW.
4·12

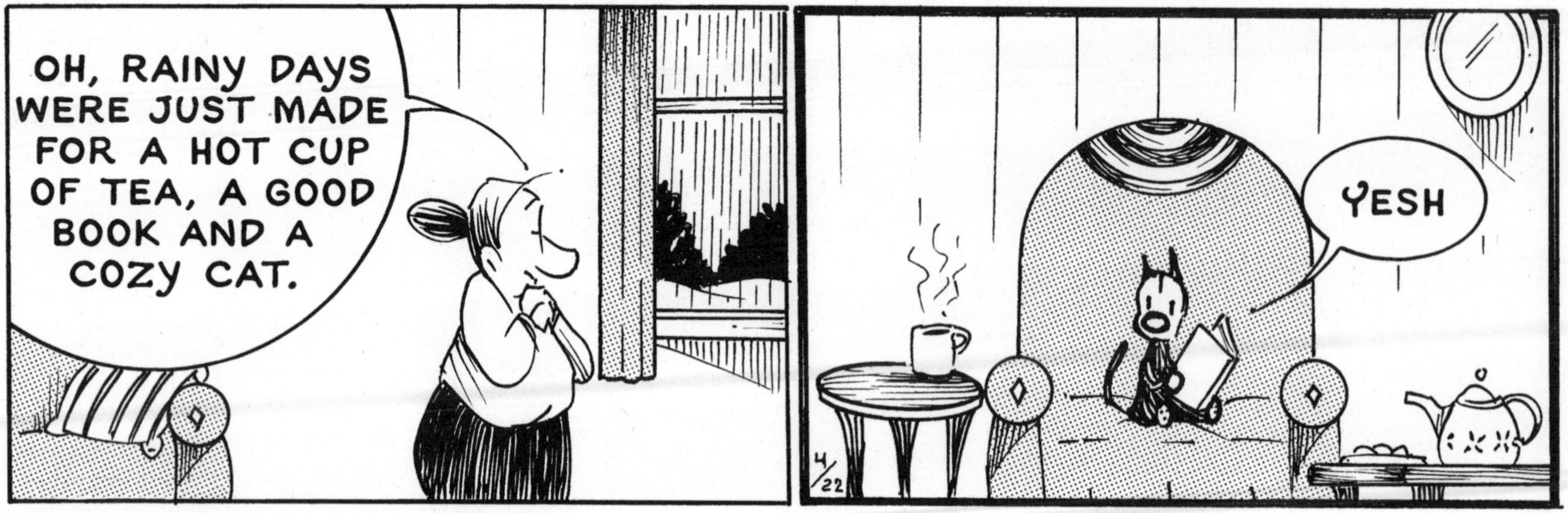
OH, RAINY DAYS WERE JUST MADE FOR A HOT CUP OF TEA, A GOOD BOOK AND A COZY CAT.
YESH
4/22

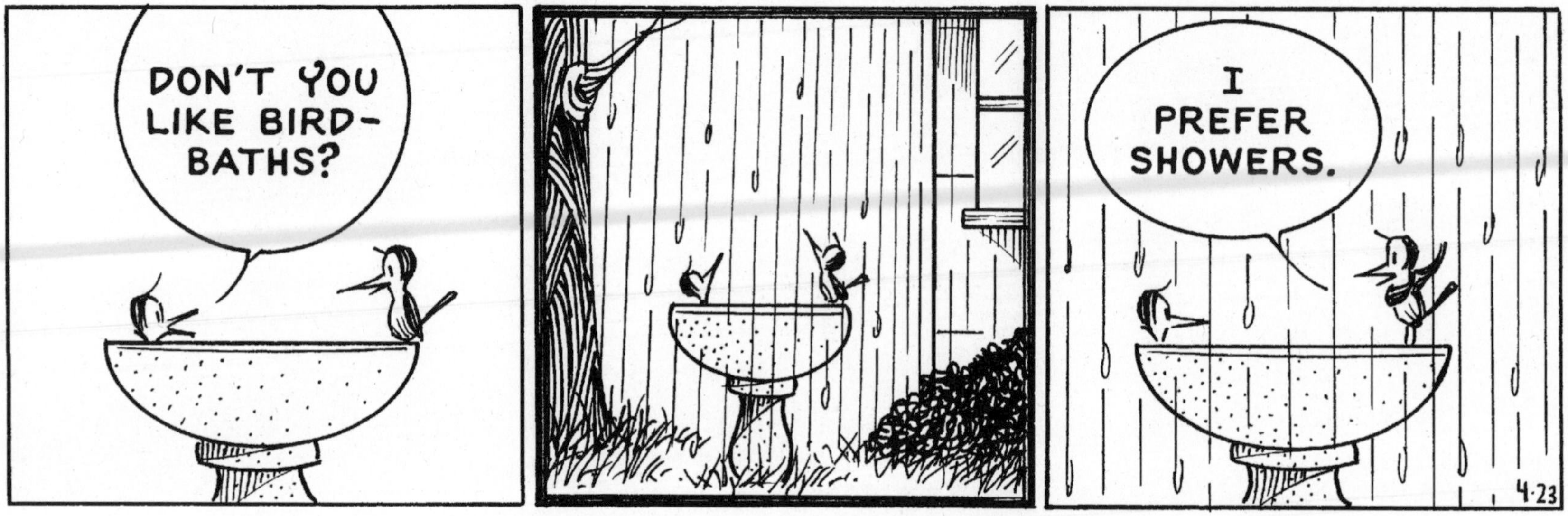
DON'T YOU LIKE BIRD-BATHS?
I PREFER SHOWERS.
4·23

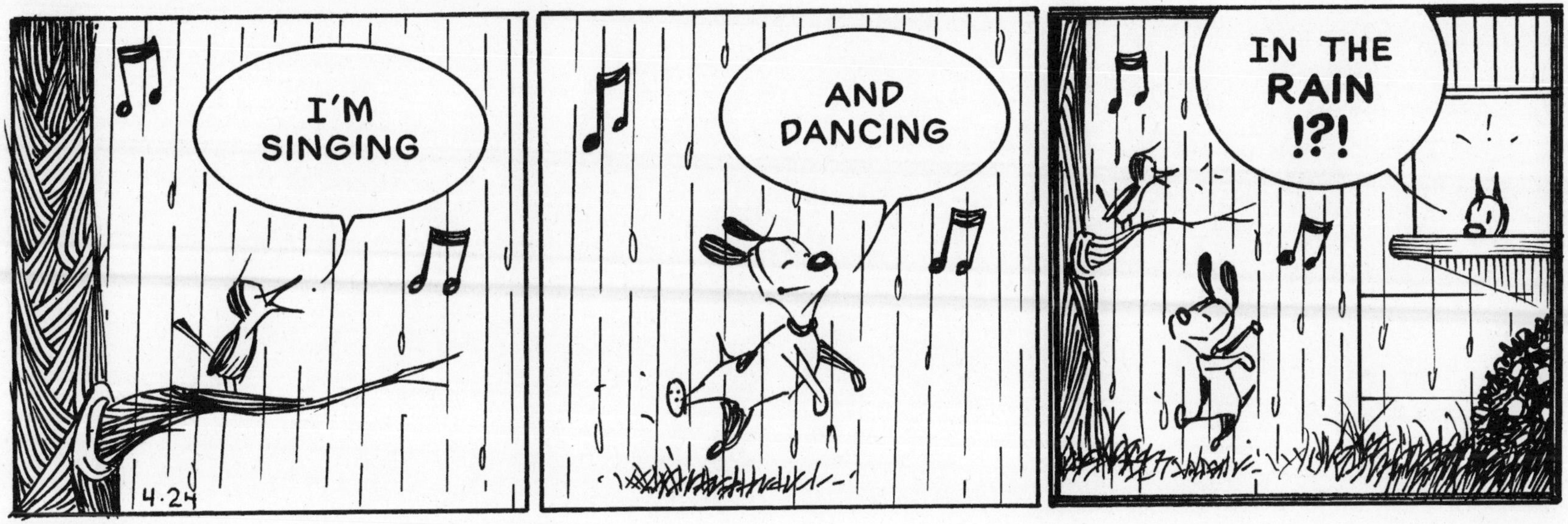
I'M SINGING
AND DANCING
IN THE RAIN !?!
4·24

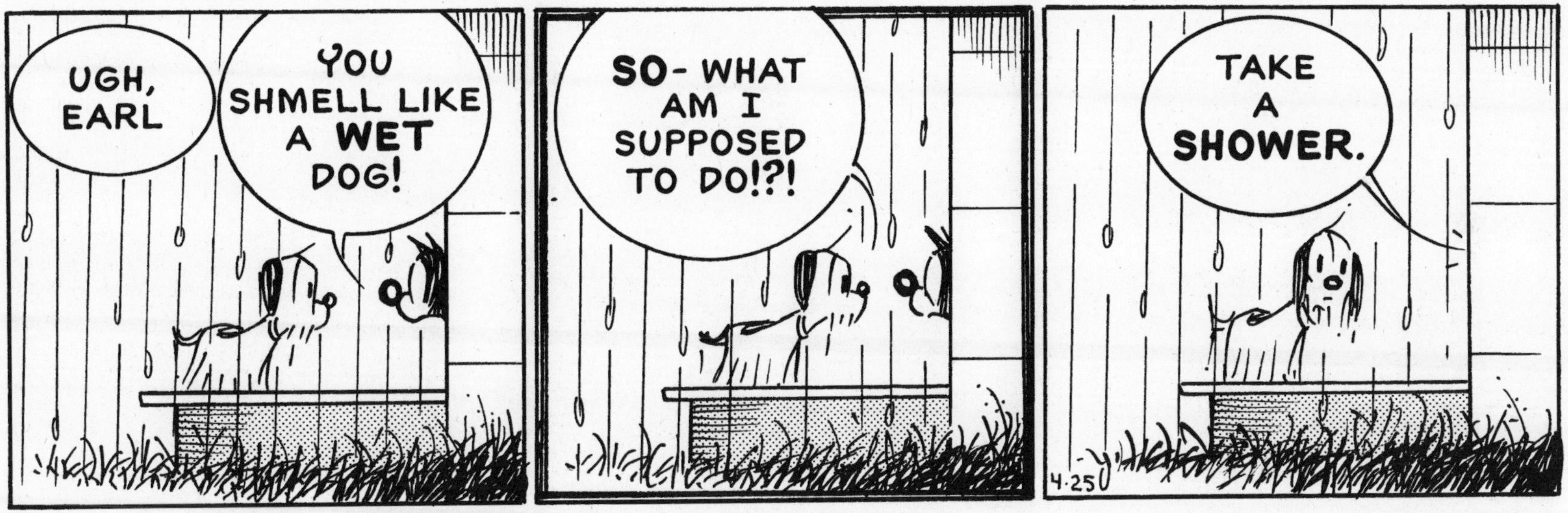
UGH, EARL
YOU SHMELL LIKE A WET DOG!
SO- WHAT AM I SUPPOSED TO DO!?!
TAKE A SHOWER.
4·25

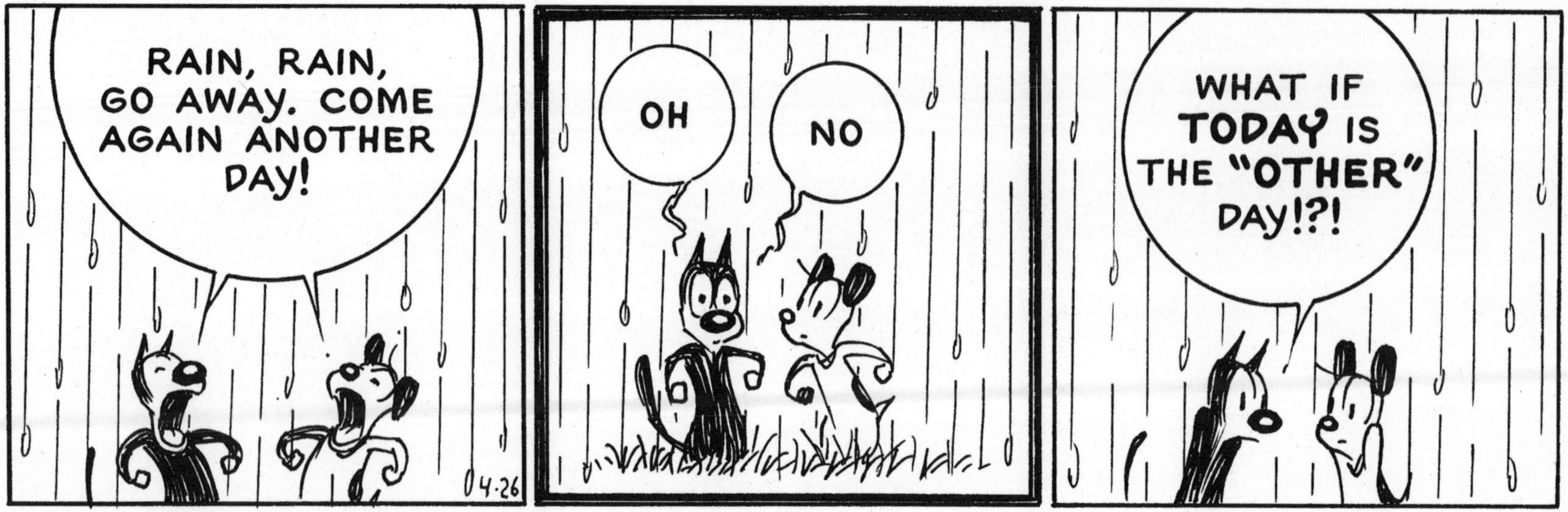
RAIN, RAIN, GO AWAY. COME AGAIN ANOTHER DAY!
4·26
OH
NO
WHAT IF TODAY IS THE "OTHER" DAY!?!

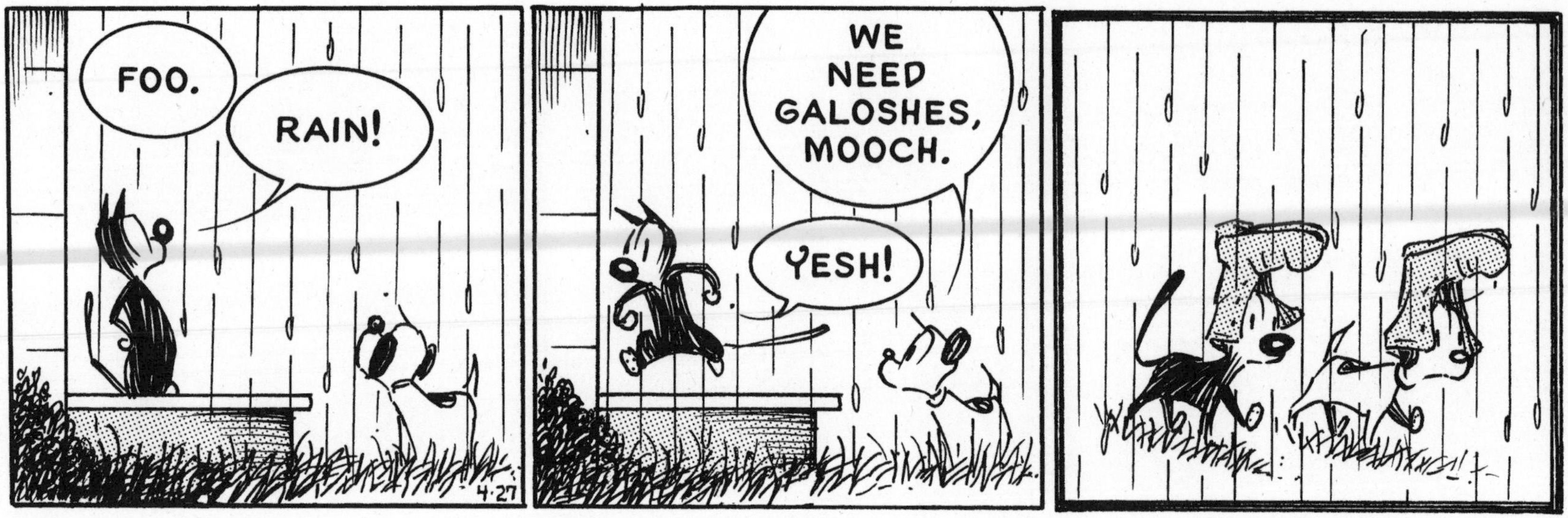
FOO.
RAIN!
4·27
WE NEED GALOSHES, MOOCH.
YESH!

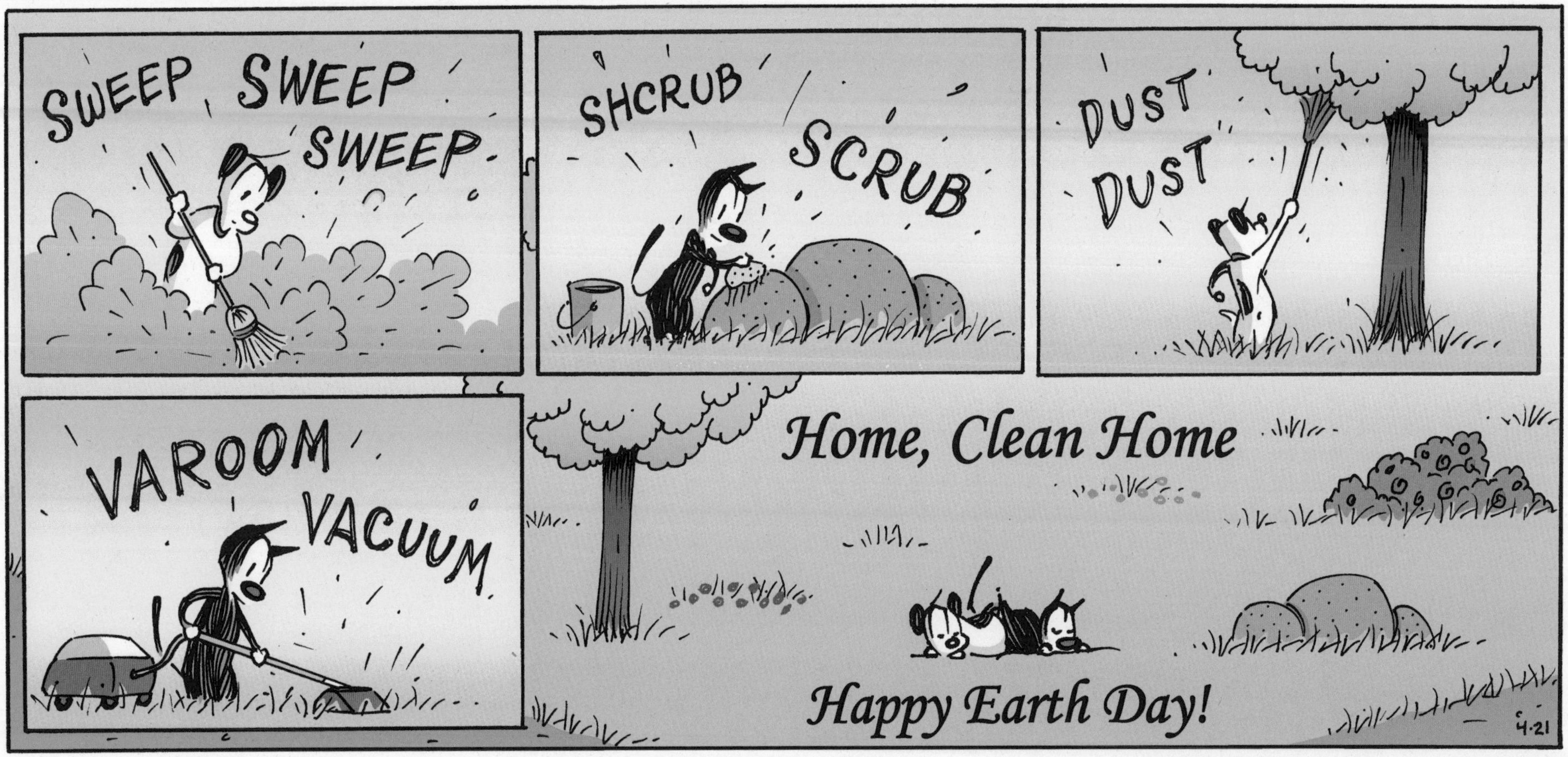
SWEEP SWEEP
SWEEP
SHCRUB
SCRUB
DUST
DUST
VAROOM
VACUUM
Home, Clean Home
Happy Earth Day!
4·21

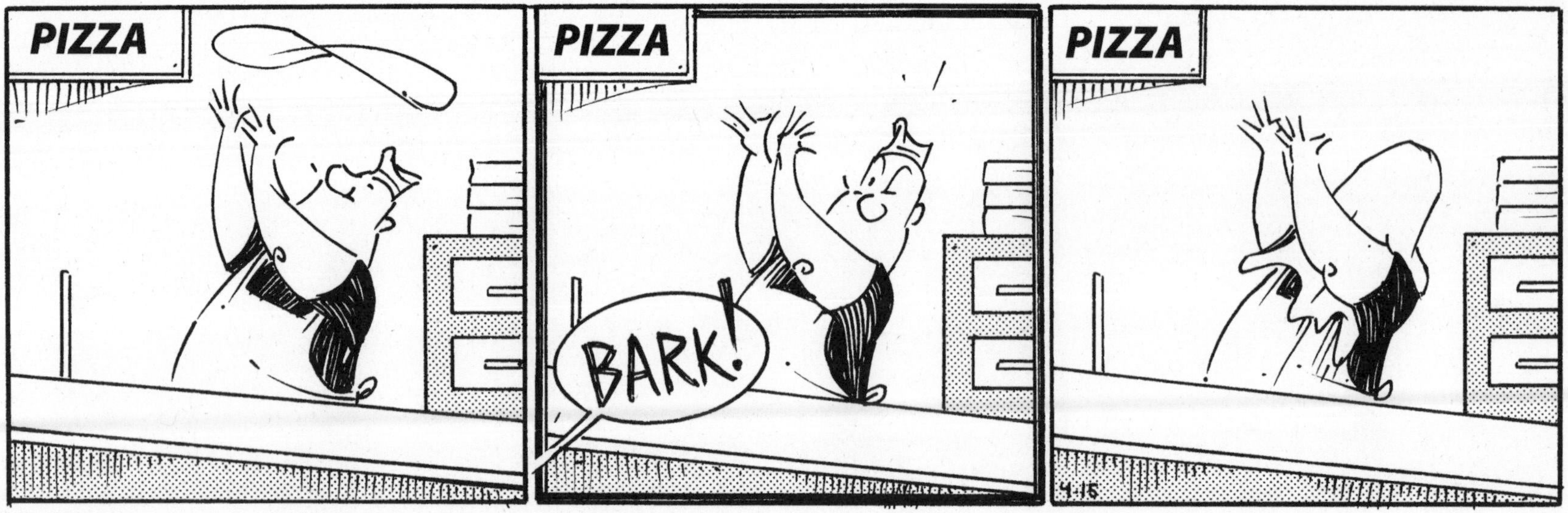
PIZZA
PIZZA
BARK!
PIZZA
4.15

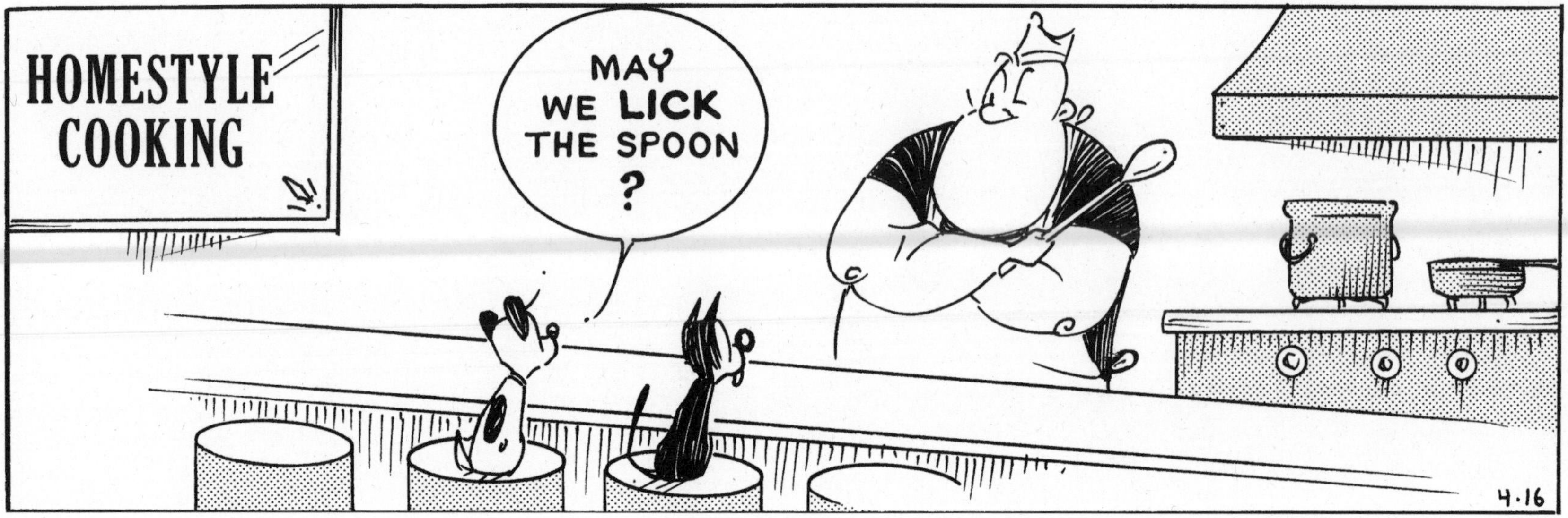
HOMESTYLE COOKING
MAY WE LICK THE SPOON ?
4.16

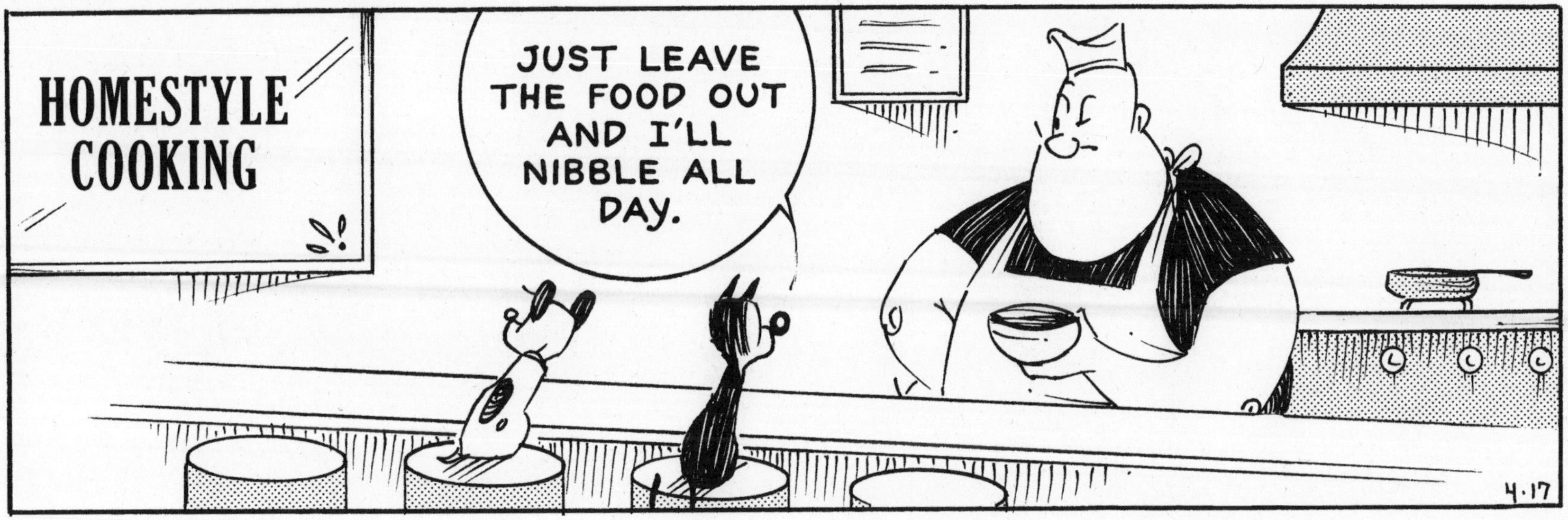
HOMESTYLE COOKING
JUST LEAVE THE FOOD OUT AND I'LL NIBBLE ALL DAY.
4·17

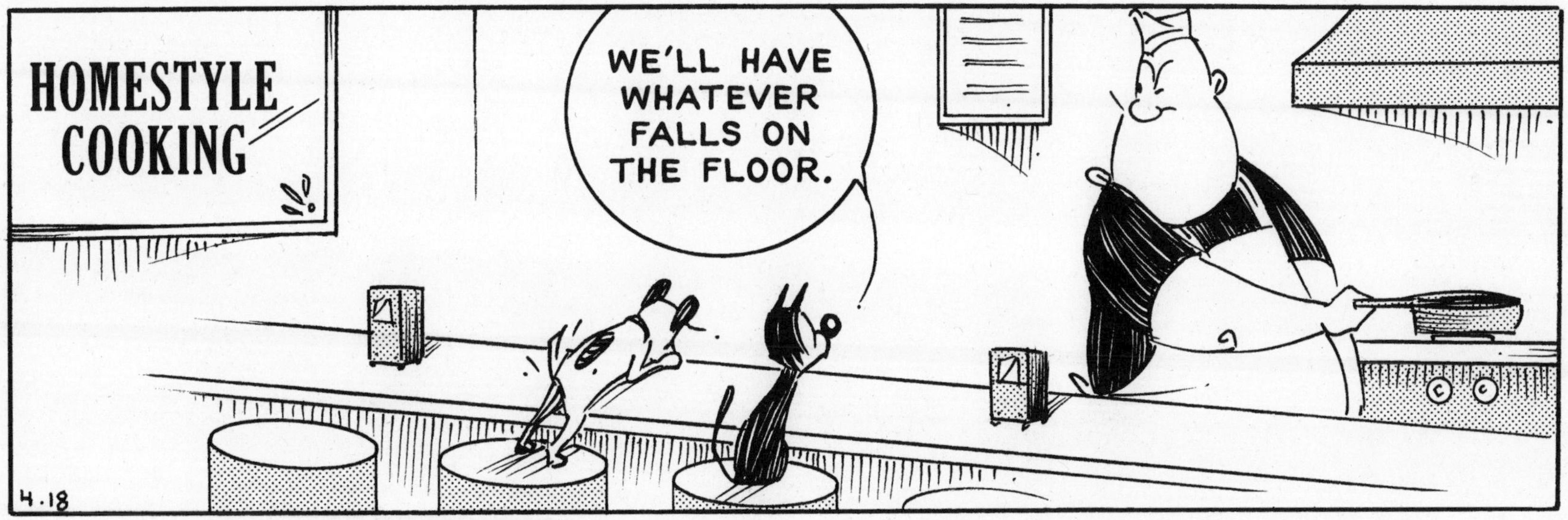
HOMESTYLE COOKING
WE'LL HAVE WHATEVER FALLS ON THE FLOOR.
4.18

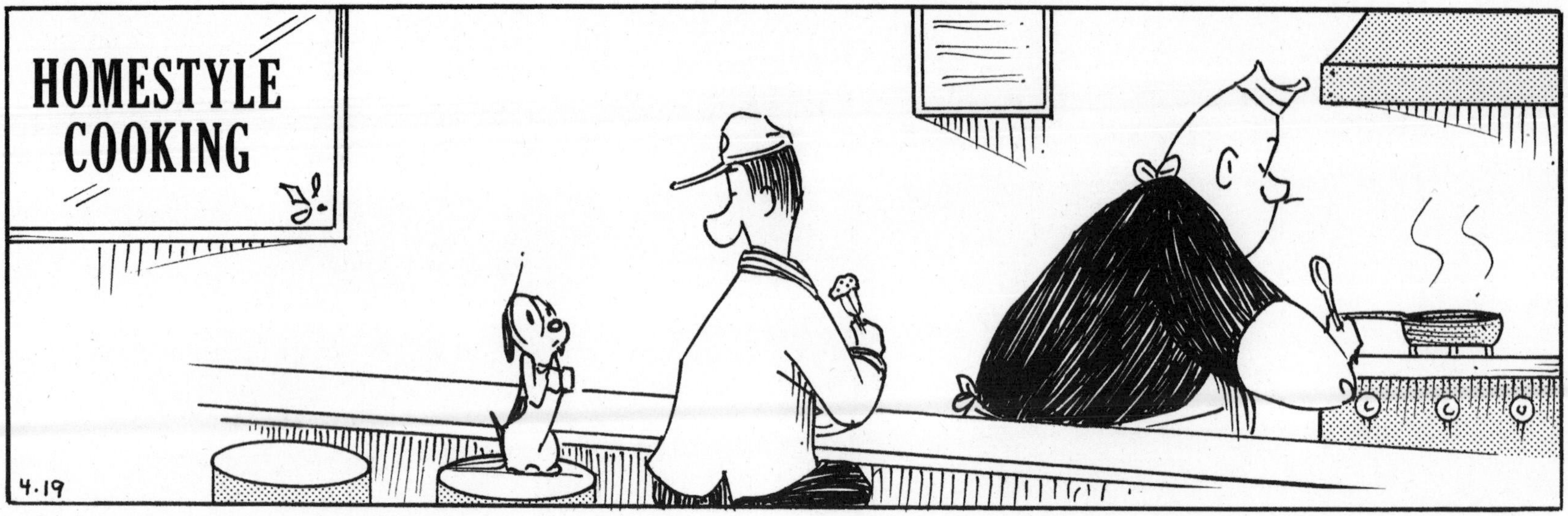
HOMESTYLE
COOKING
4.19

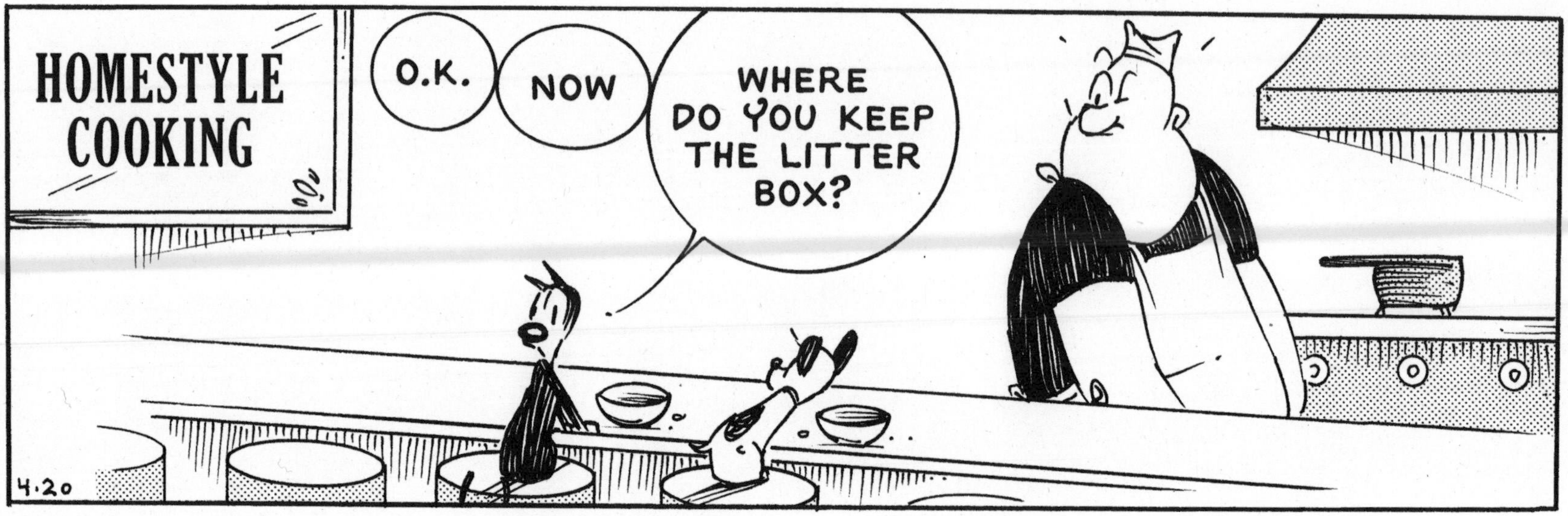
HOMESTYLE
COOKING
O.K.
NOW
WHERE DO YOU KEEP THE LITTER BOX?
4.20

MUTTS

Patrick McDonnell

RED NOSE DAY
WELCOME TO THE CLUB.
5·19

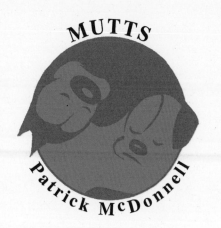

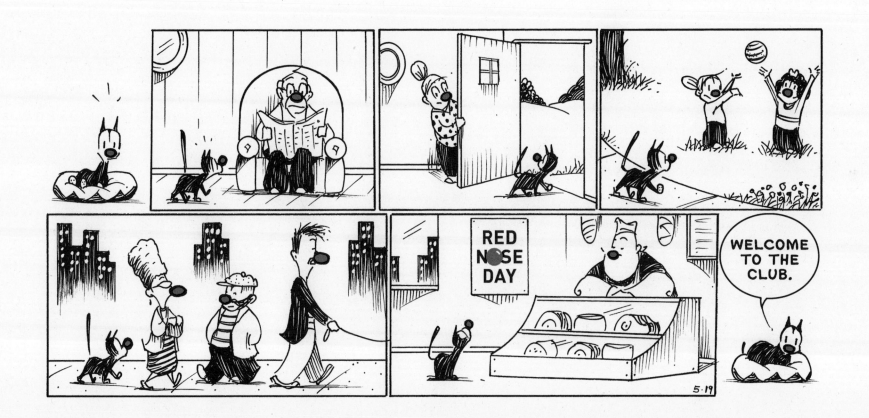

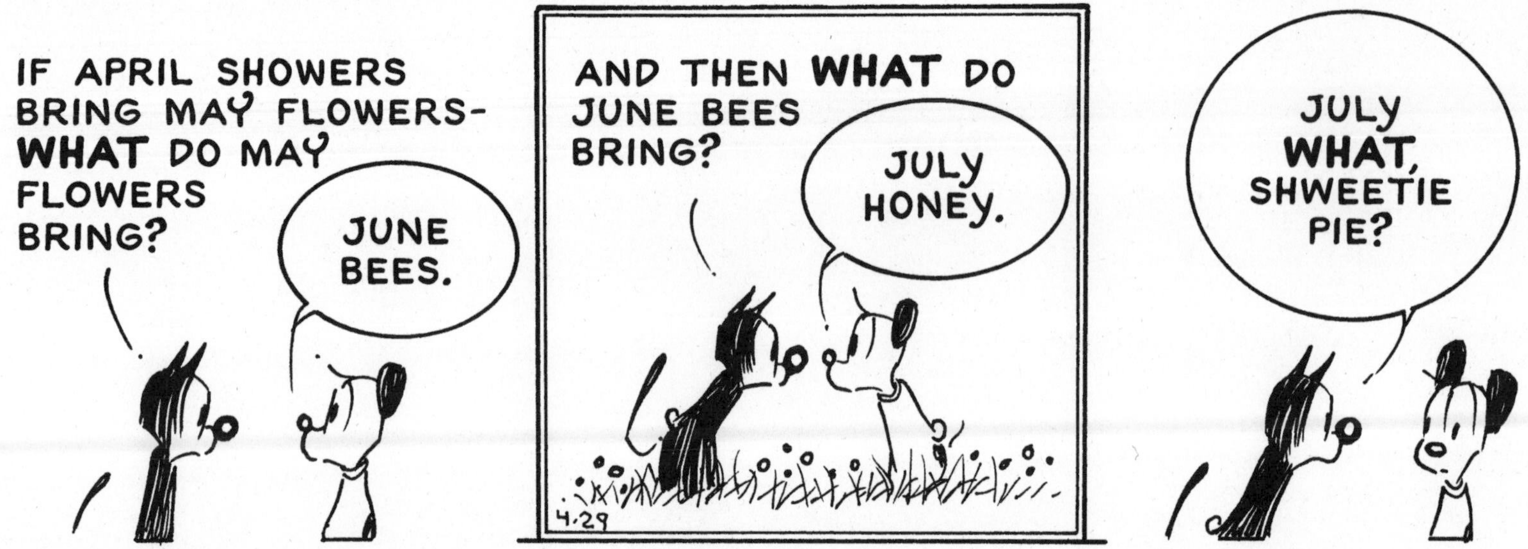
IF APRIL SHOWERS BRING MAY FLOWERS- **WHAT** DO MAY FLOWERS BRING?
JUNE BEES.
AND THEN **WHAT** DO JUNE BEES BRING?
JULY HONEY.
JULY **WHAT**, SHWEETIE PIE?
4·29

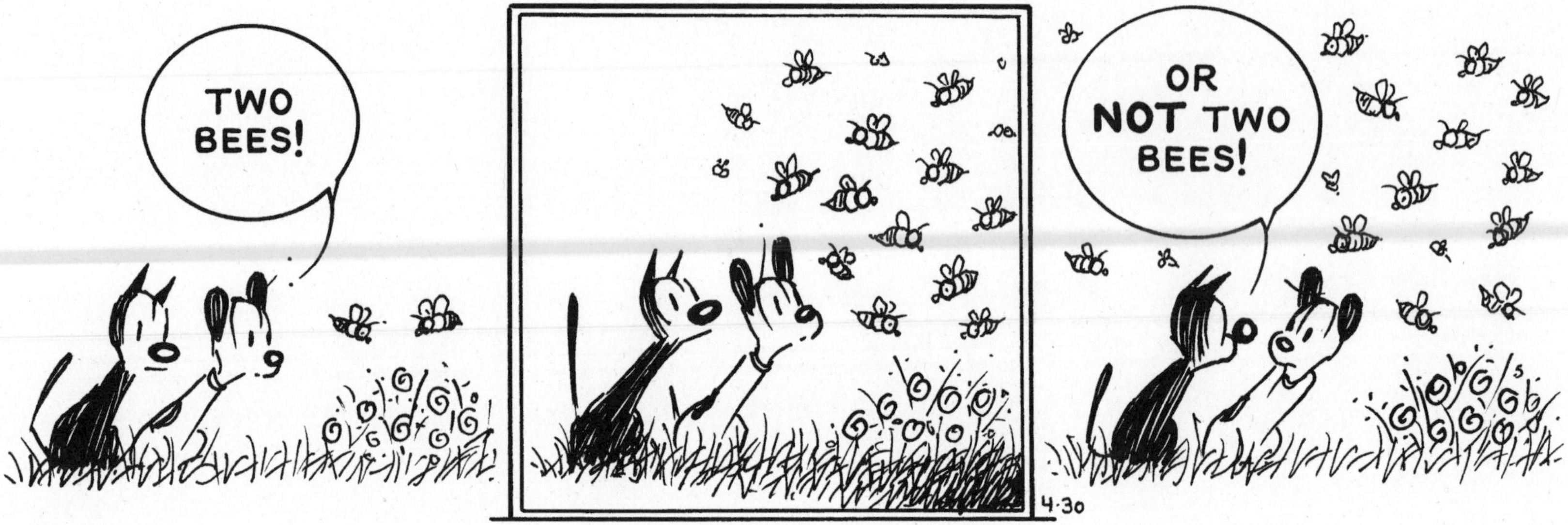
TWO BEES!
OR **NOT** TWO BEES!
4·30

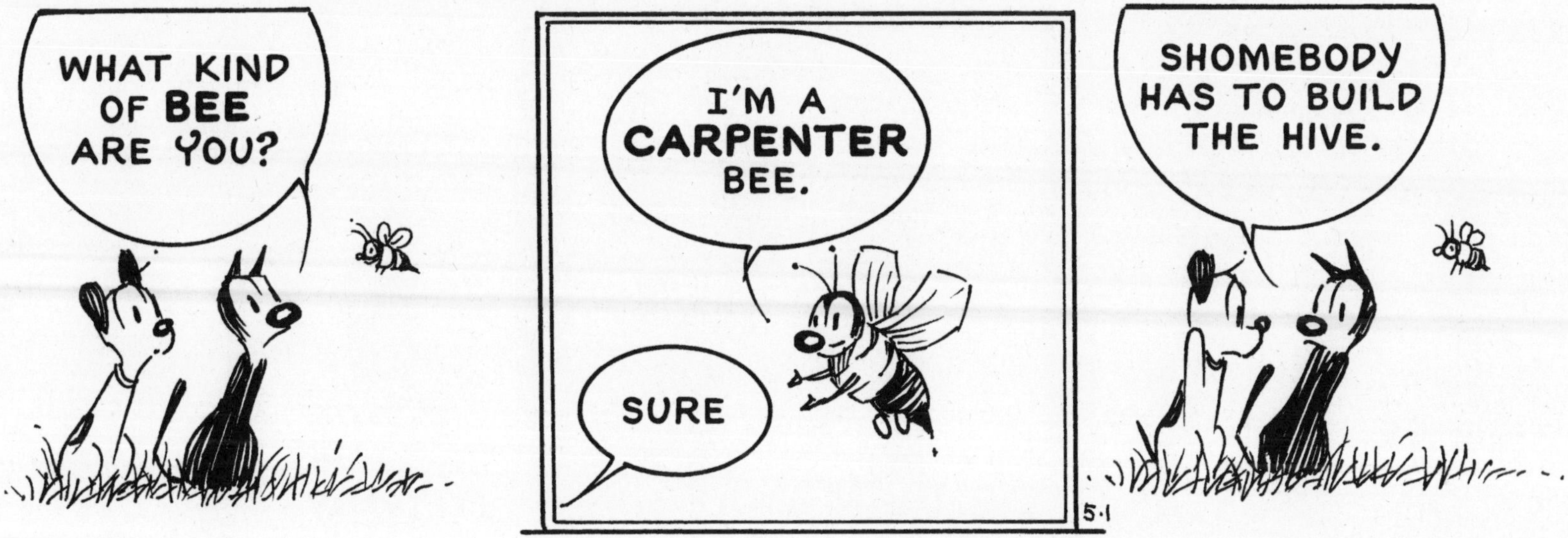
WHAT KIND OF **BEE** ARE YOU?
I'M A **CARPENTER** BEE.
SURE
SHOMEBODY HAS TO BUILD THE HIVE.
5.1

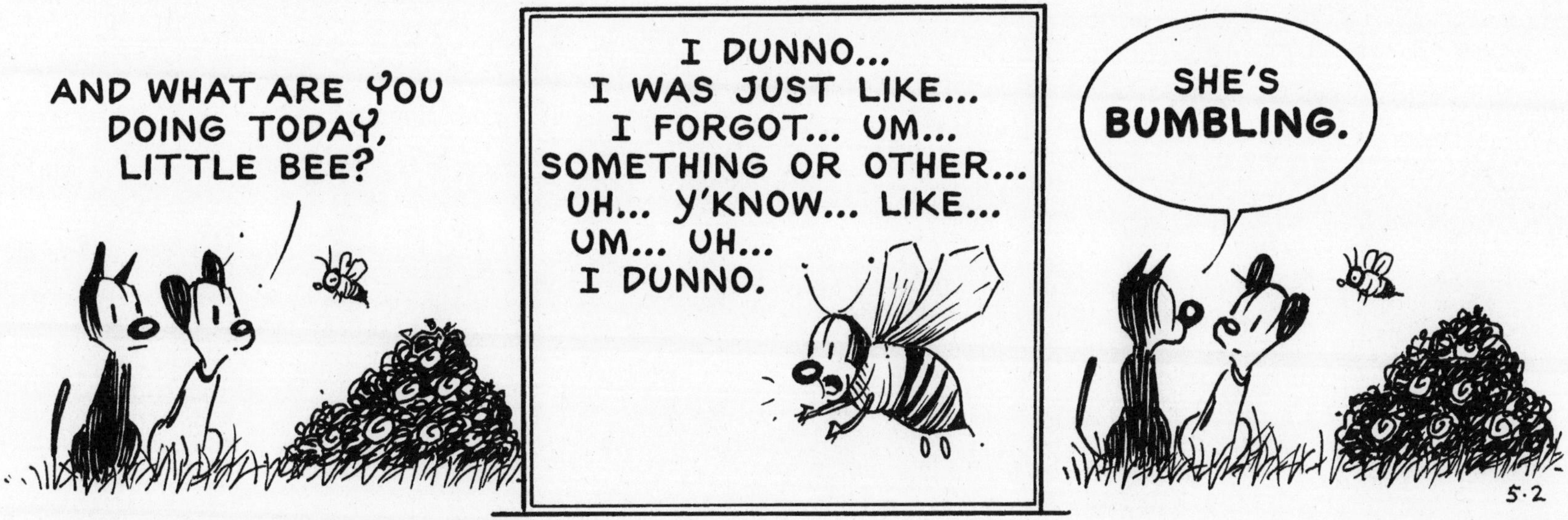
AND WHAT ARE YOU DOING TODAY, LITTLE BEE?
I DUNNO... I WAS JUST LIKE... I FORGOT... UM... SOMETHING OR OTHER... UH... Y'KNOW... LIKE... UM... UH... I DUNNO.
SHE'S **BUMBLING.**
5.2

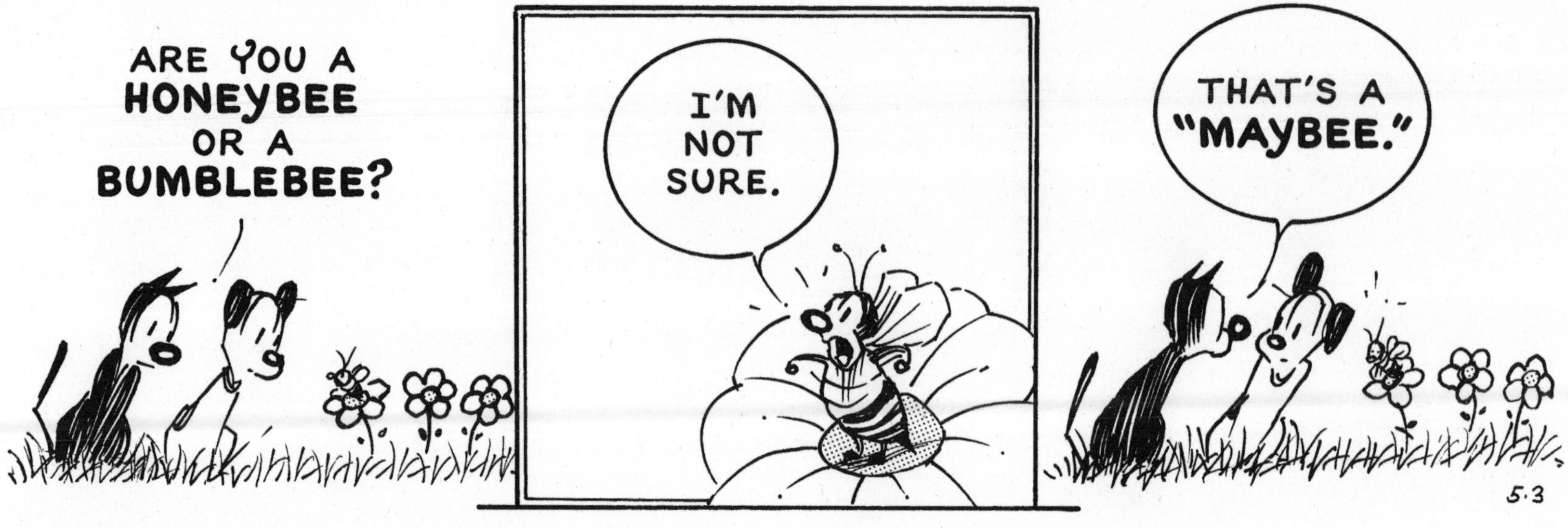
ARE YOU A HONEYBEE OR A BUMBLEBEE?
I'M NOT SURE.
THAT'S A "MAYBEE."
5·3

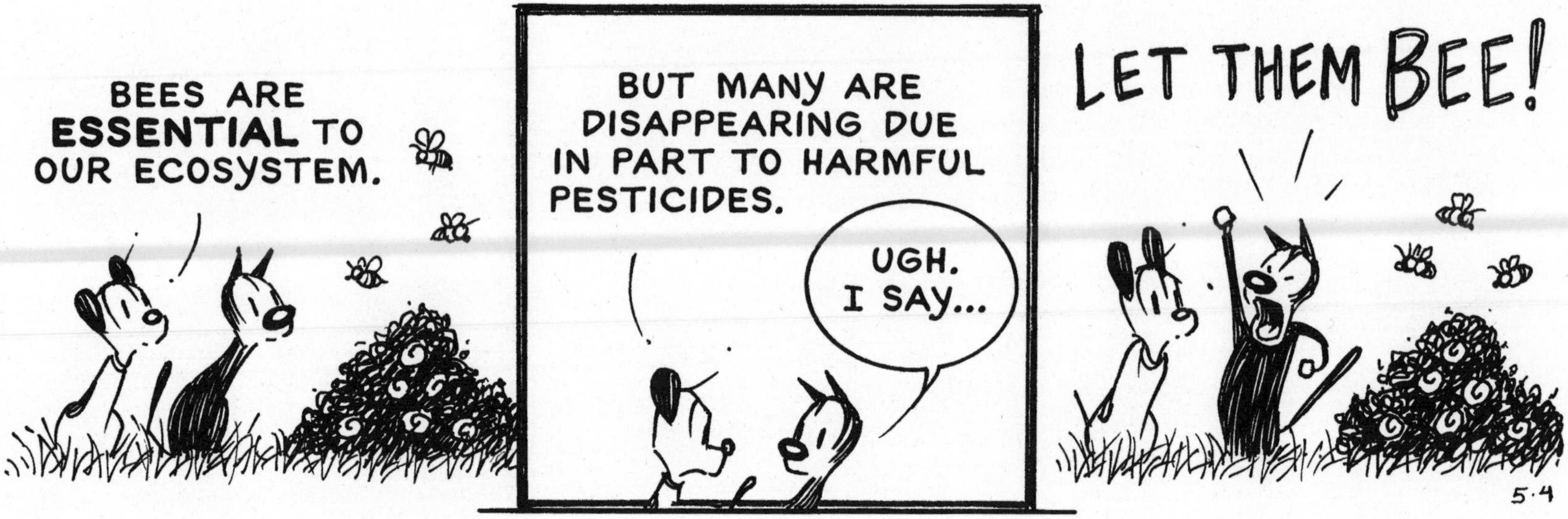
BEES ARE ESSENTIAL TO OUR ECOSYSTEM.
BUT MANY ARE DISAPPEARING DUE IN PART TO HARMFUL PESTICIDES.
UGH. I SAY...
LET THEM BEE!
5·4

MUTTS BY PATRICK McDONNELL

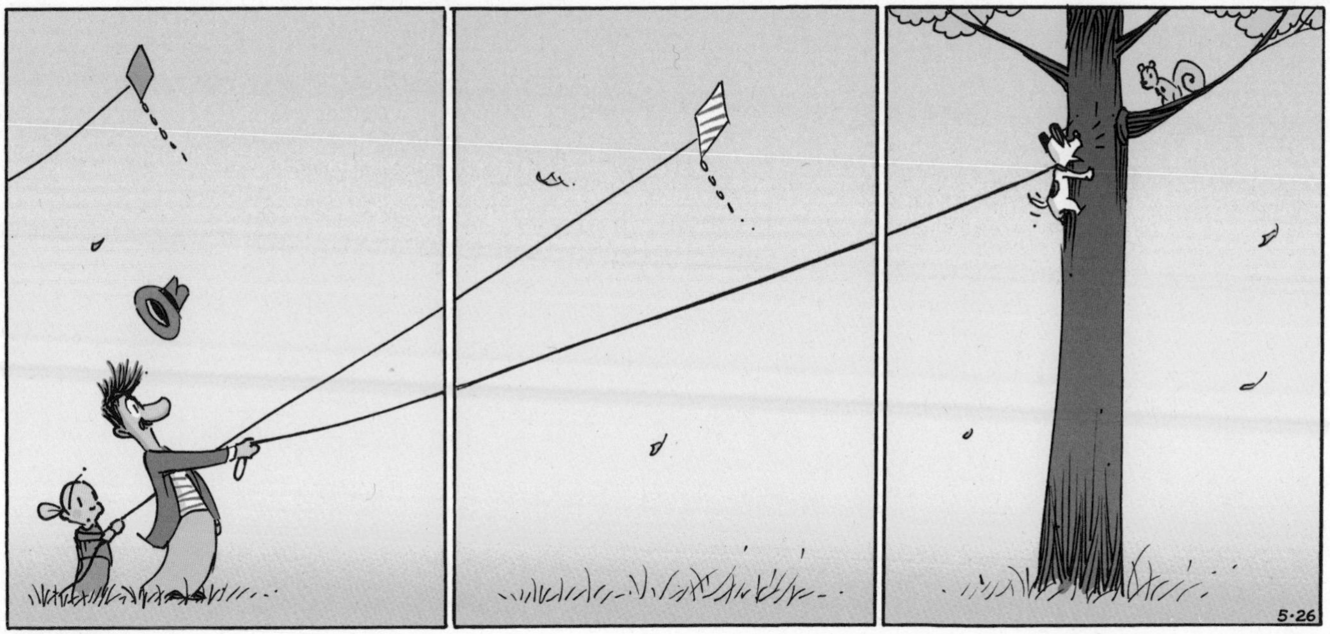
5·26

MUTTS
Patrick McDonnell

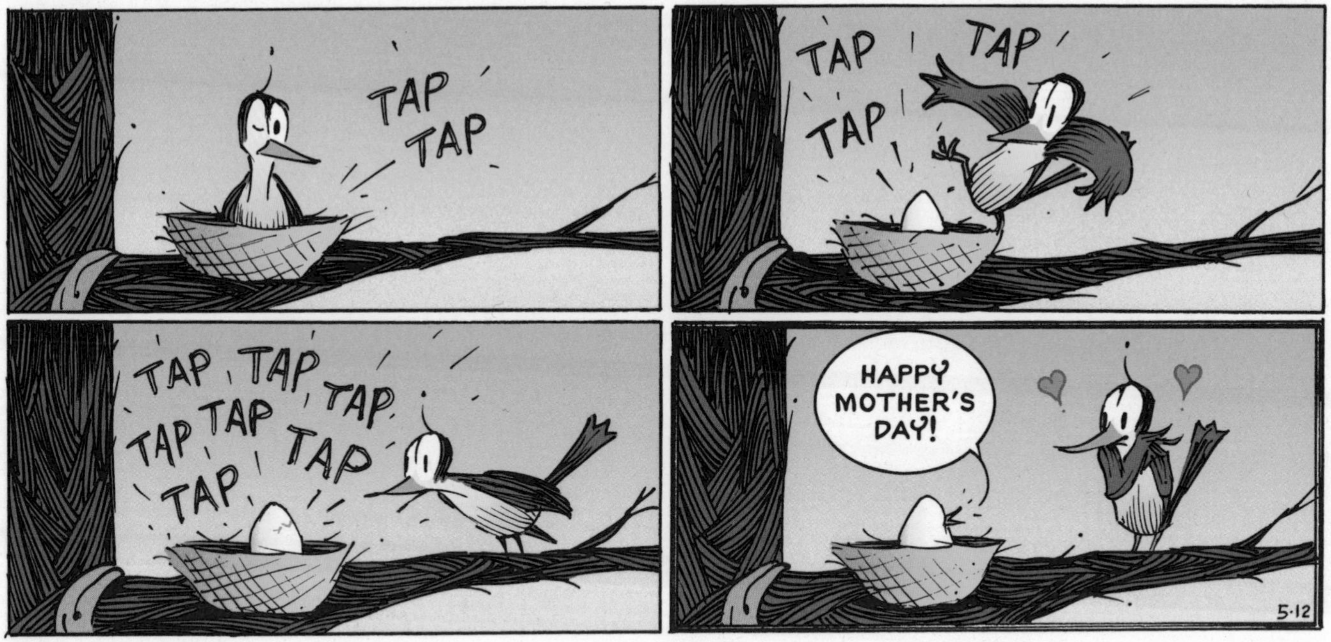
TAP
TAP
TAP
TAP
TAP
TAP TAP TAP
TAP TAP TAP
TAP
HAPPY MOTHER'S DAY!
5·12

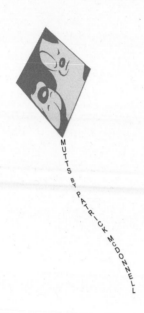

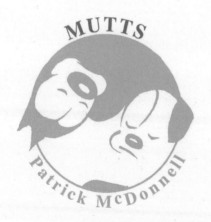

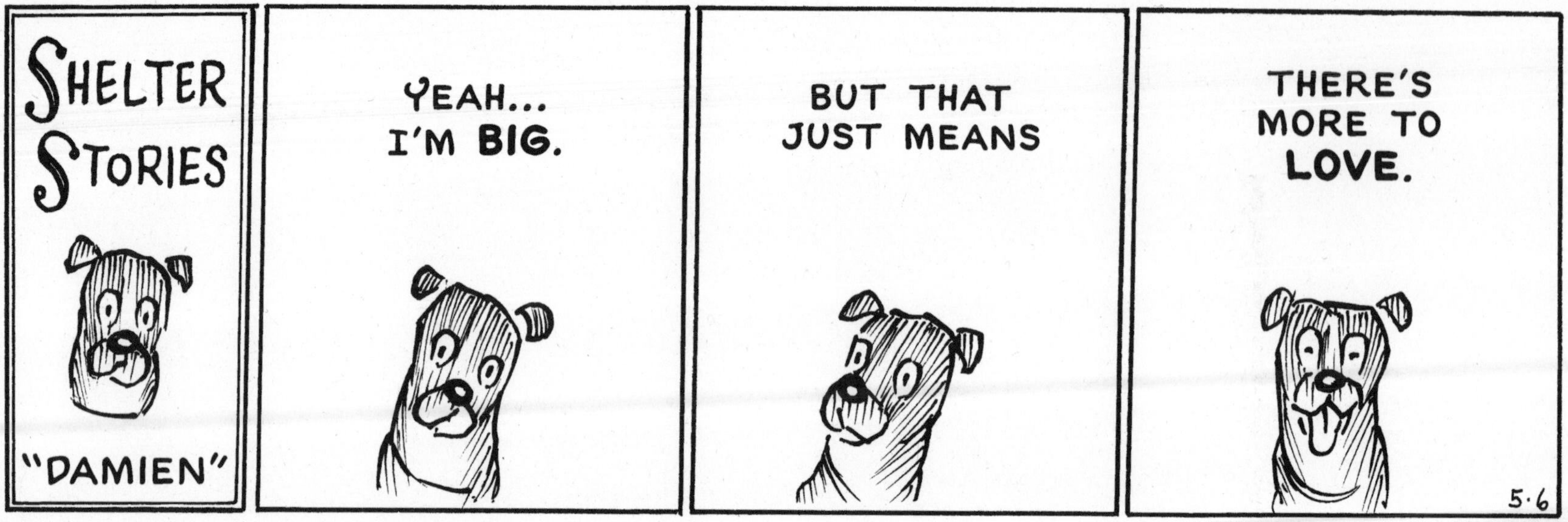
SHELTER STORIES
"DAMIEN"
YEAH... I'M **BIG**.
BUT THAT JUST MEANS
THERE'S MORE TO **LOVE**.
5·6

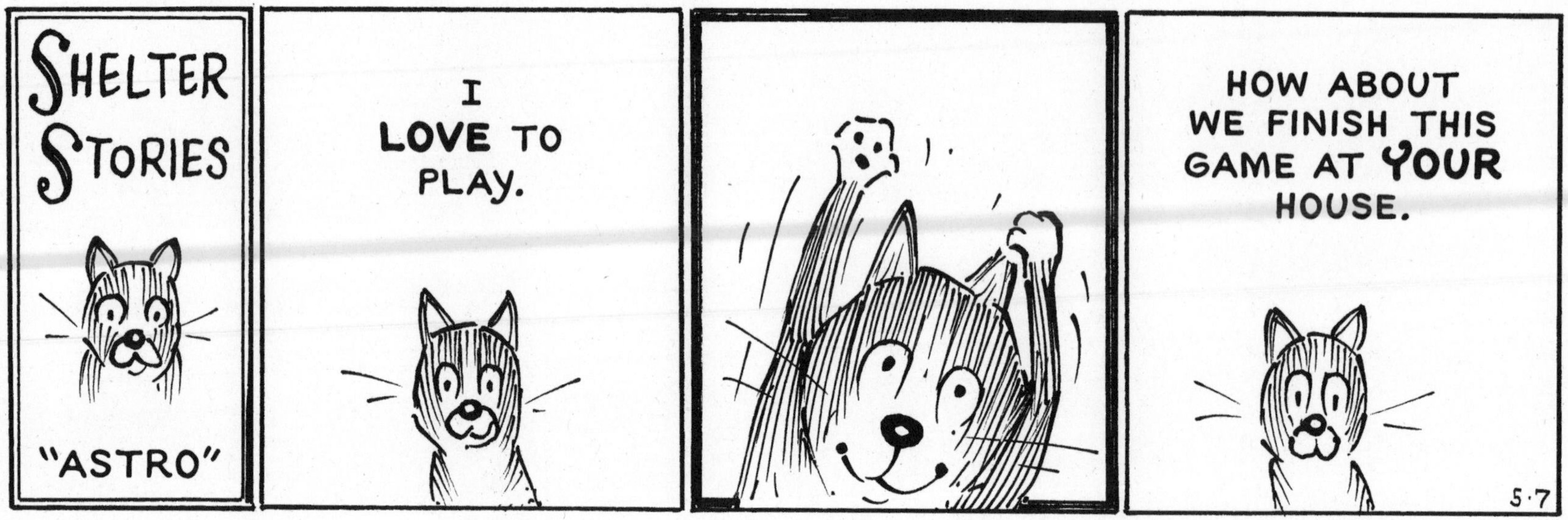
SHELTER STORIES
"ASTRO"
I **LOVE** TO PLAY.
HOW ABOUT WE FINISH THIS GAME AT **YOUR** HOUSE.
5·7

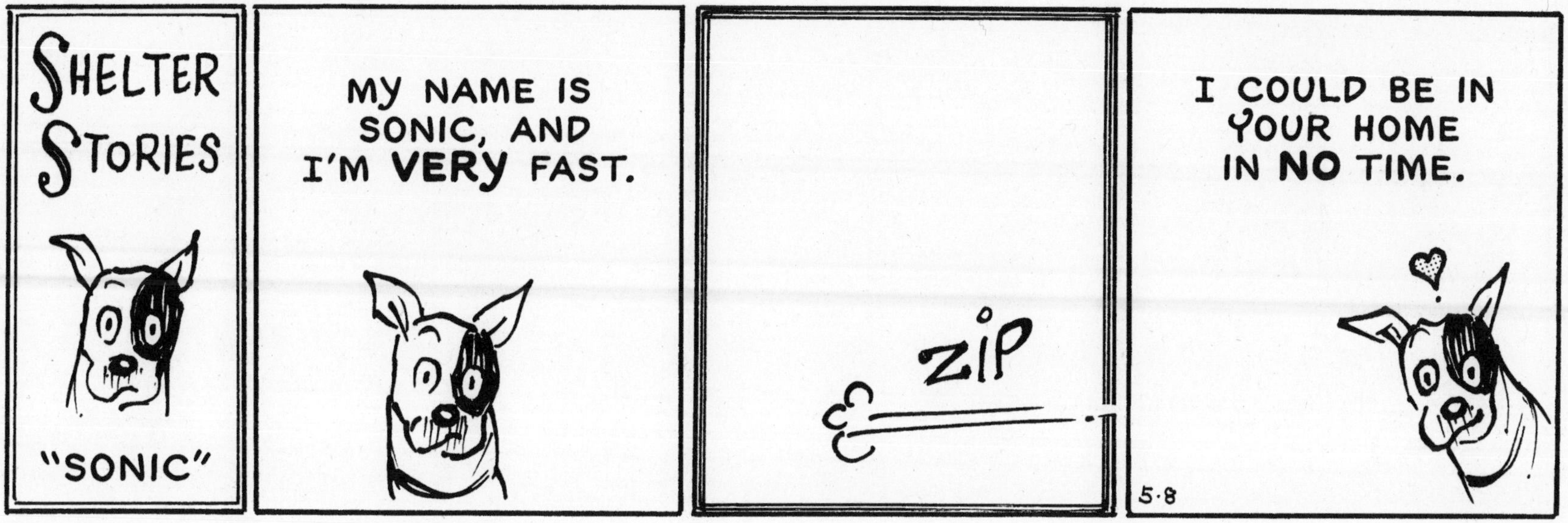
SHELTER STORIES
"SONIC"
MY NAME IS SONIC, AND I'M VERY FAST.
ZIP
I COULD BE IN YOUR HOME IN NO TIME.
5·8

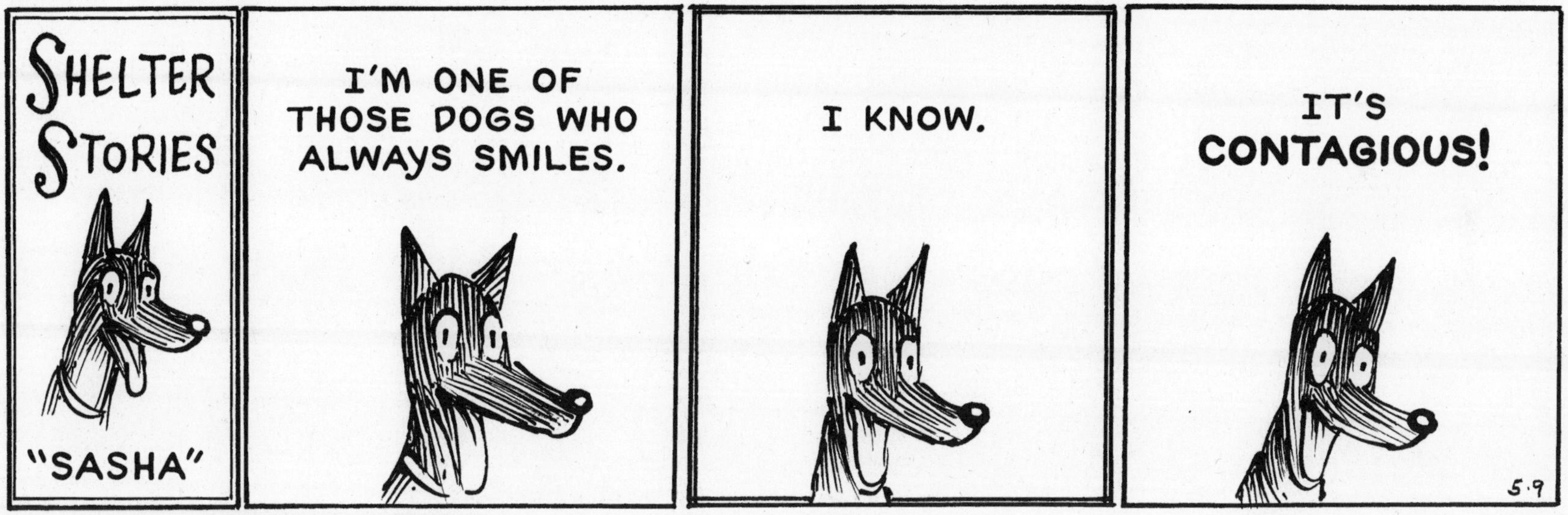
SHELTER STORIES
"SASHA"
I'M ONE OF THOSE DOGS WHO ALWAYS SMILES.
I KNOW.
IT'S CONTAGIOUS!
5·9

Panel 1 (top row)

SHELTER STORIES

"GATOR"

Panel 2

MY NAME'S **GATOR.**

Panel 3

I SUPPOSE YOU COULD CHANGE IT IF YOU'D LIKE,

Panel 4

AS LONG AS YOU CALL ME **"YOURS."**

5·10

Panel 1 (bottom row)

SHELTER STORIES

"MACINTOSH"

Panel 2

I'M NAMED AFTER A POPULAR APPLE.

Panel 3

Panel 4

PICK ME.

5·11

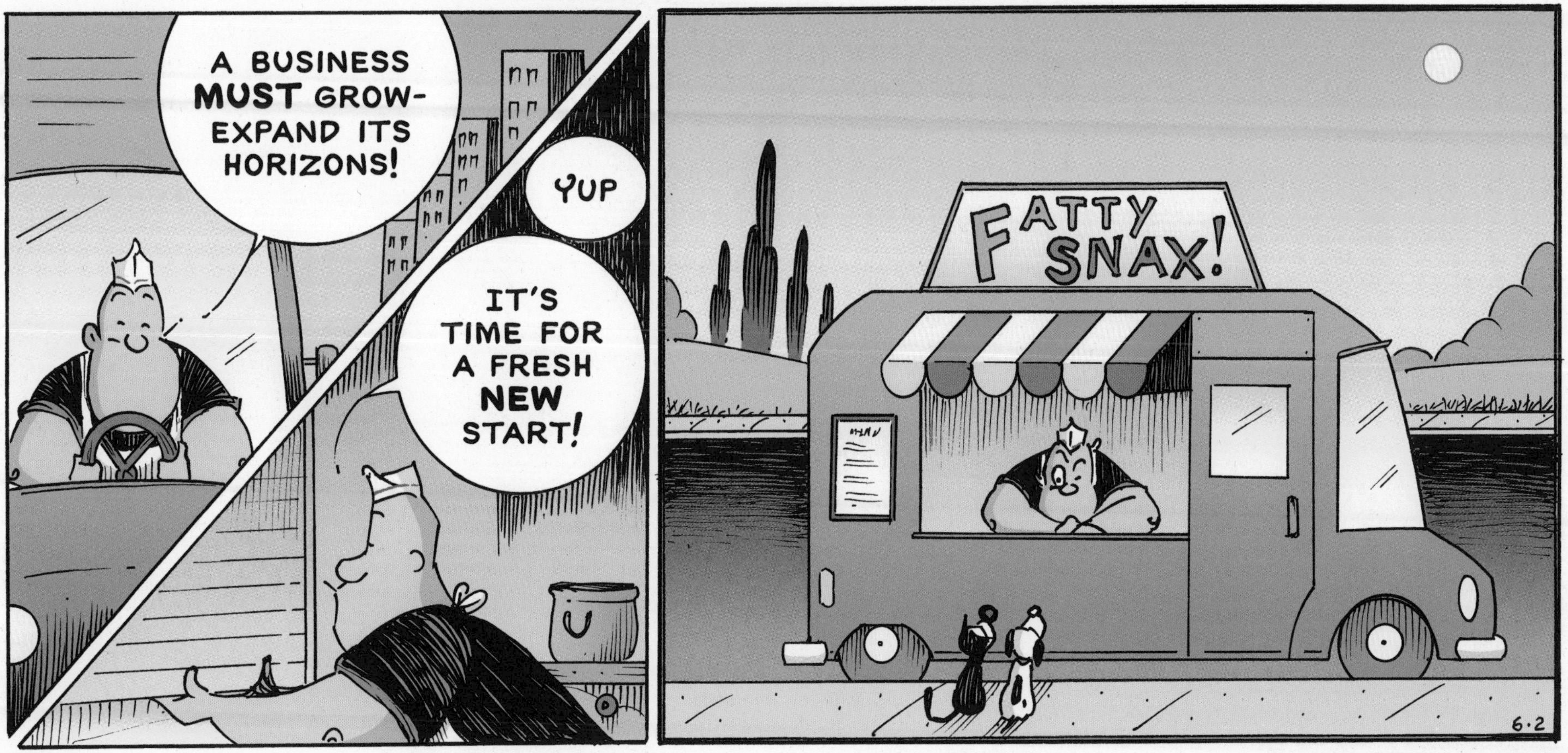
A BUSINESS MUST GROW-
EXPAND ITS HORIZONS!
YUP
IT'S TIME FOR A FRESH NEW START!
FATTY SNAX!
6·2

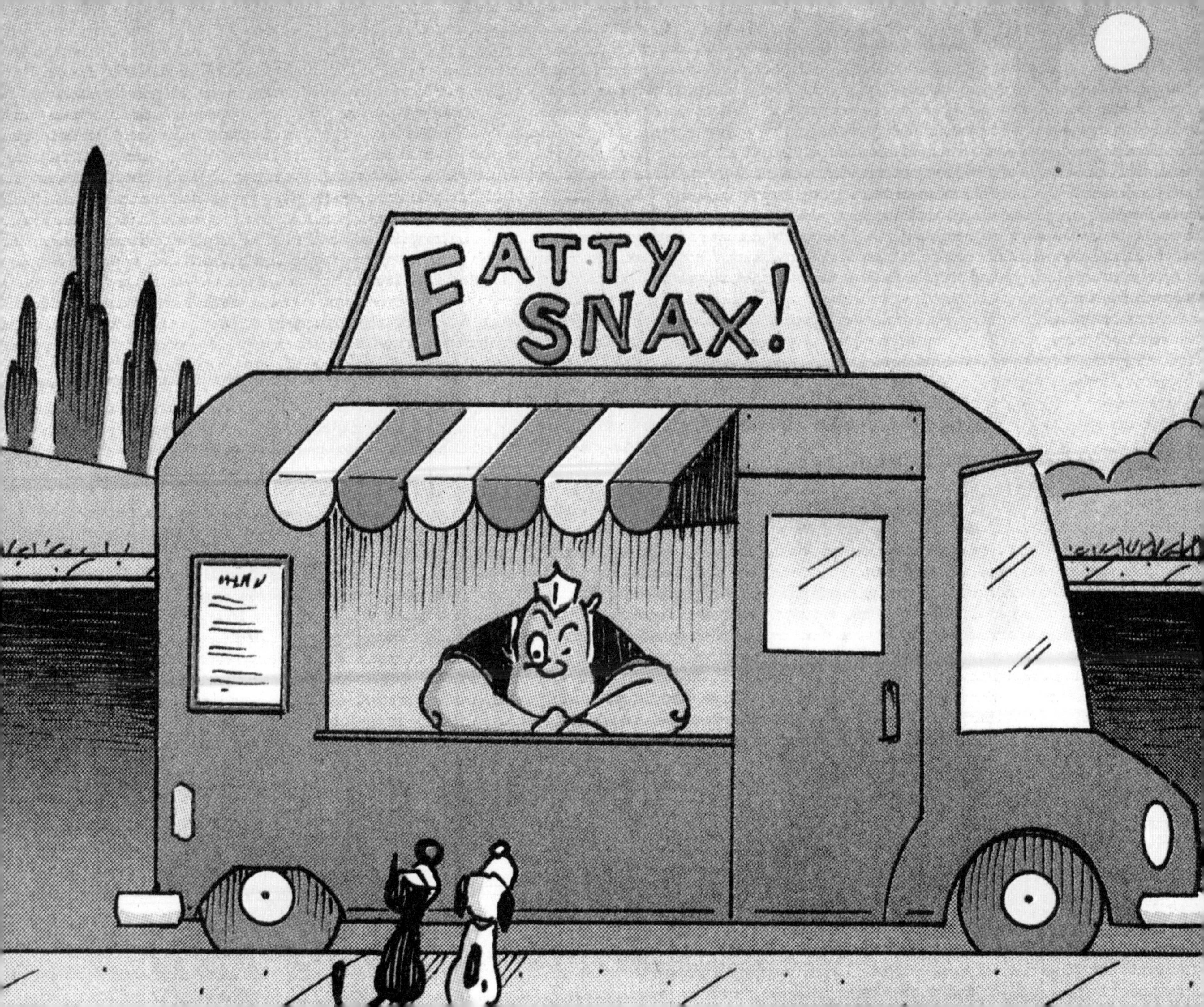
FATTY SNAX!

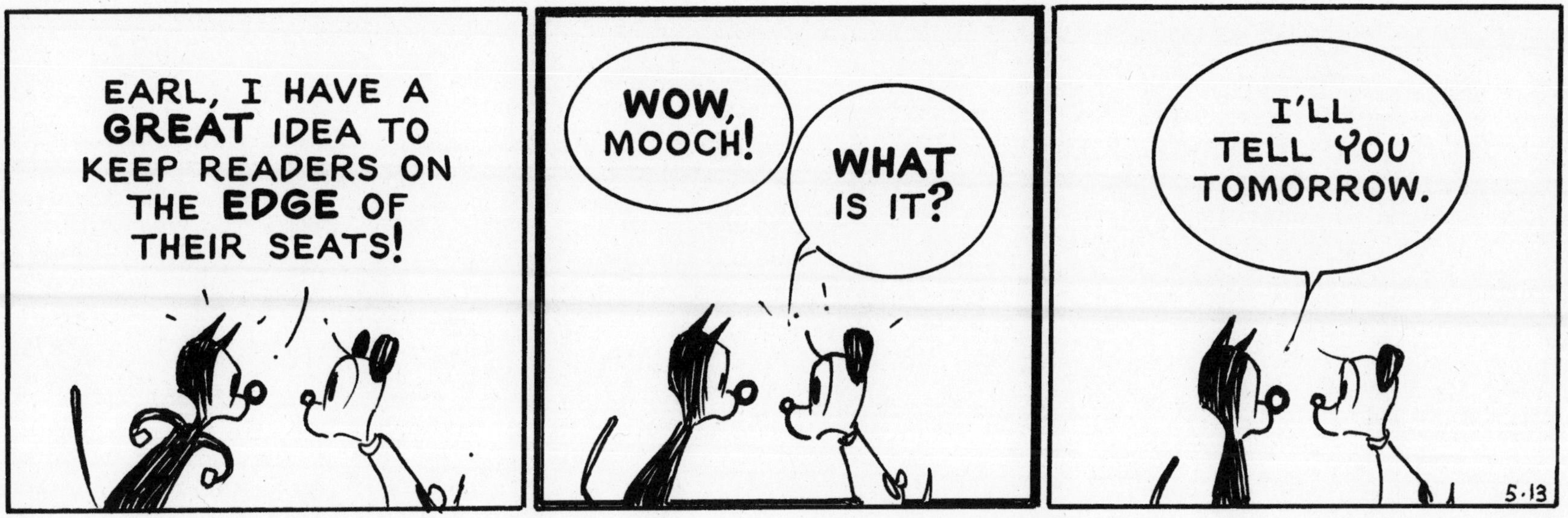
EARL, I HAVE A GREAT IDEA TO KEEP READERS ON THE EDGE OF THEIR SEATS!
WOW, MOOCH!
WHAT IS IT?
I'LL TELL YOU TOMORROW.
5·13

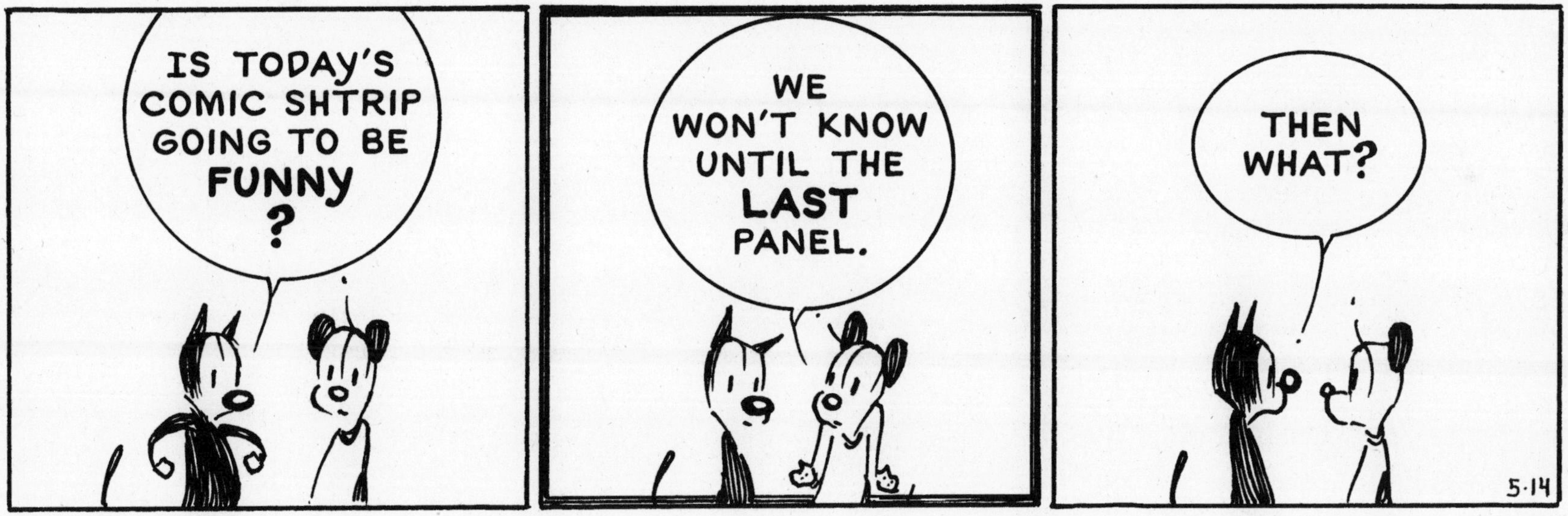
IS TODAY'S COMIC SHTRIP GOING TO BE FUNNY ?
WE WON'T KNOW UNTIL THE LAST PANEL.
THEN WHAT?
5·14

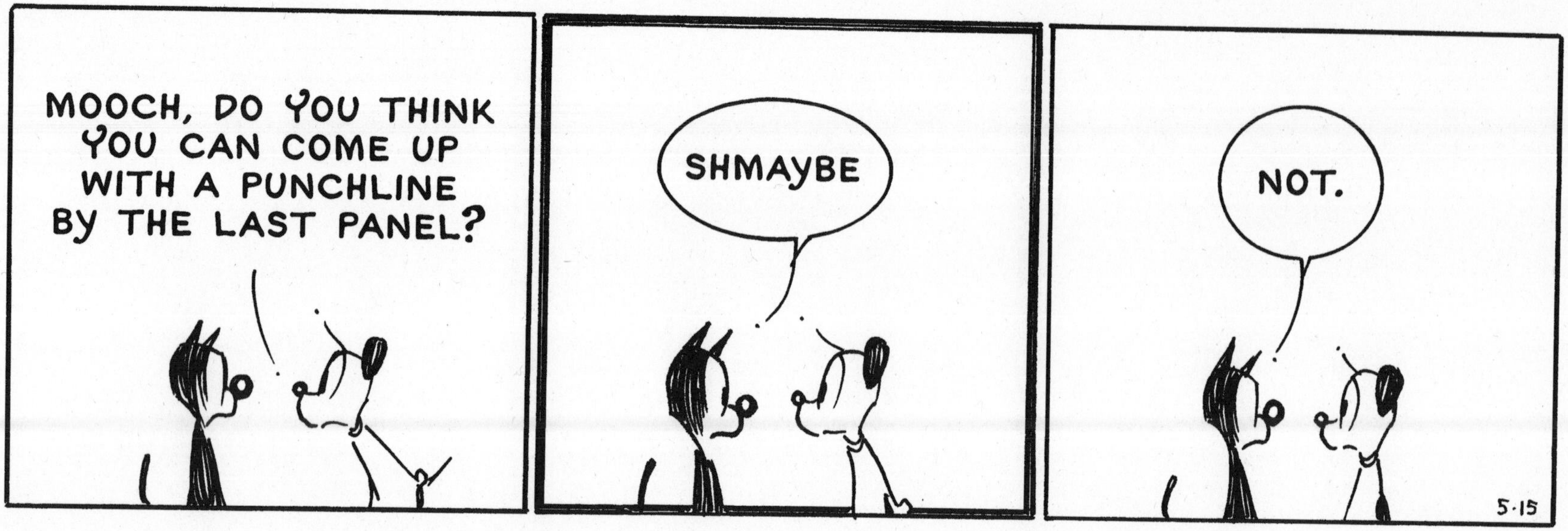
MOOCH, DO YOU THINK YOU CAN COME UP WITH A PUNCHLINE BY THE LAST PANEL?
SHMAYBE
NOT.
5·15

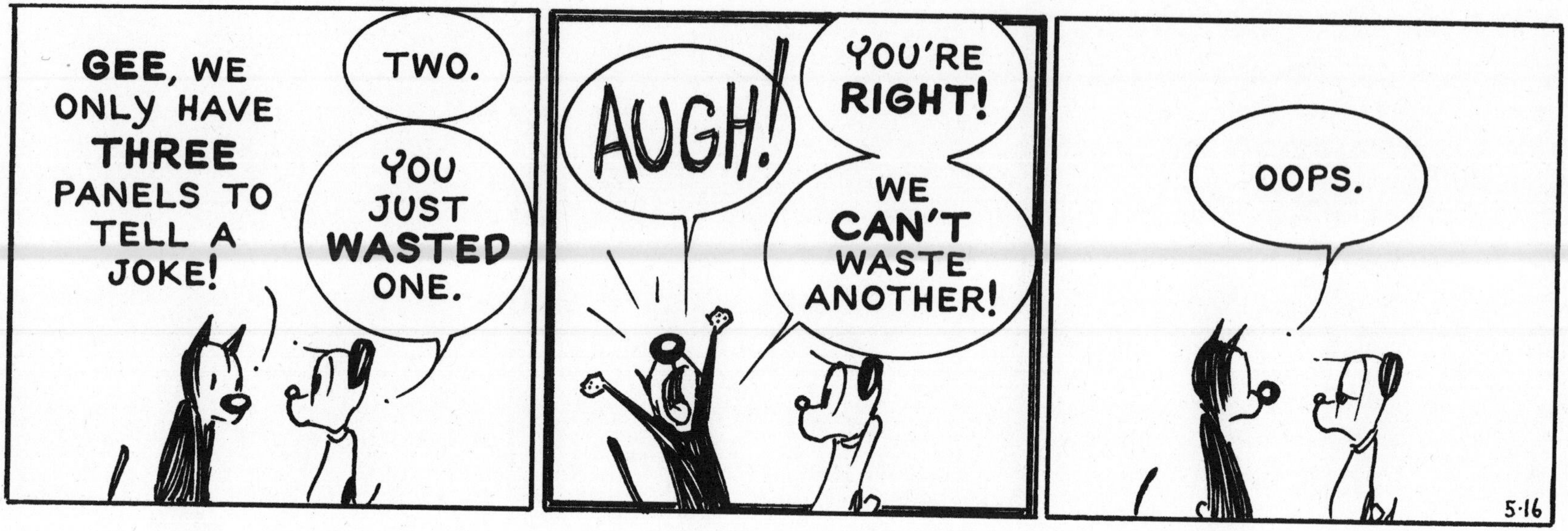
GEE, WE ONLY HAVE THREE PANELS TO TELL A JOKE!
TWO.
YOU JUST WASTED ONE.
AUGH!
YOU'RE RIGHT!
WE CAN'T WASTE ANOTHER!
OOPS.
5·16

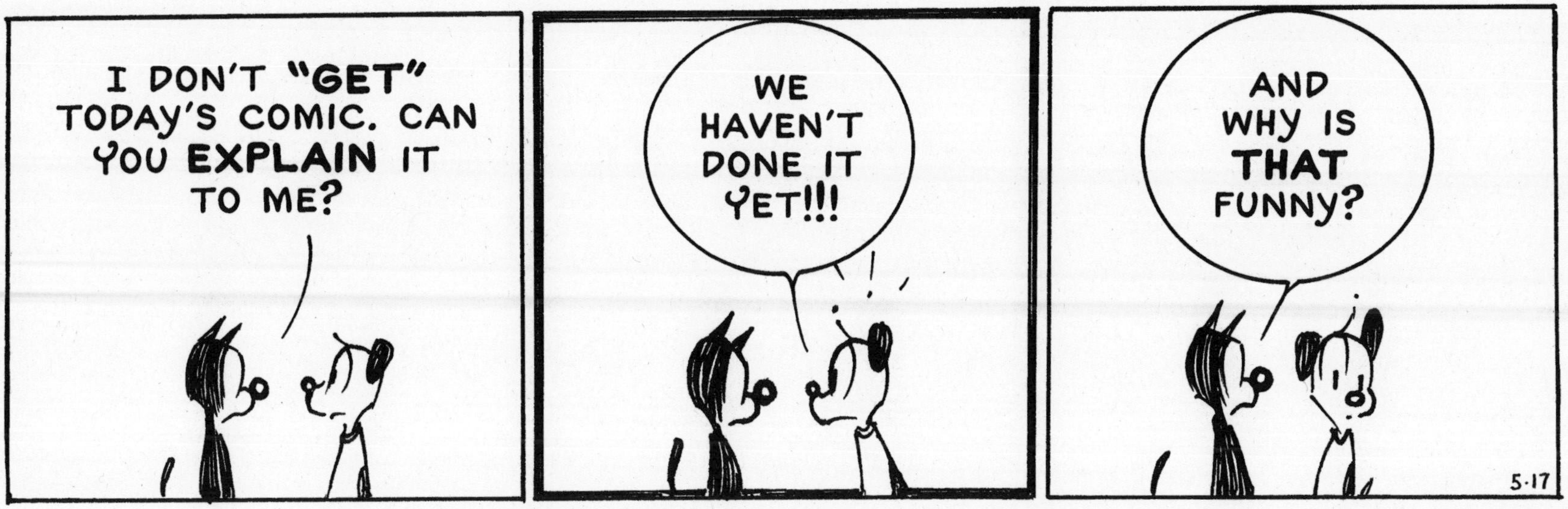
I DON'T "GET" TODAY'S COMIC. CAN YOU EXPLAIN IT TO ME?
WE HAVEN'T DONE IT YET!!!
AND WHY IS THAT FUNNY?
5·17

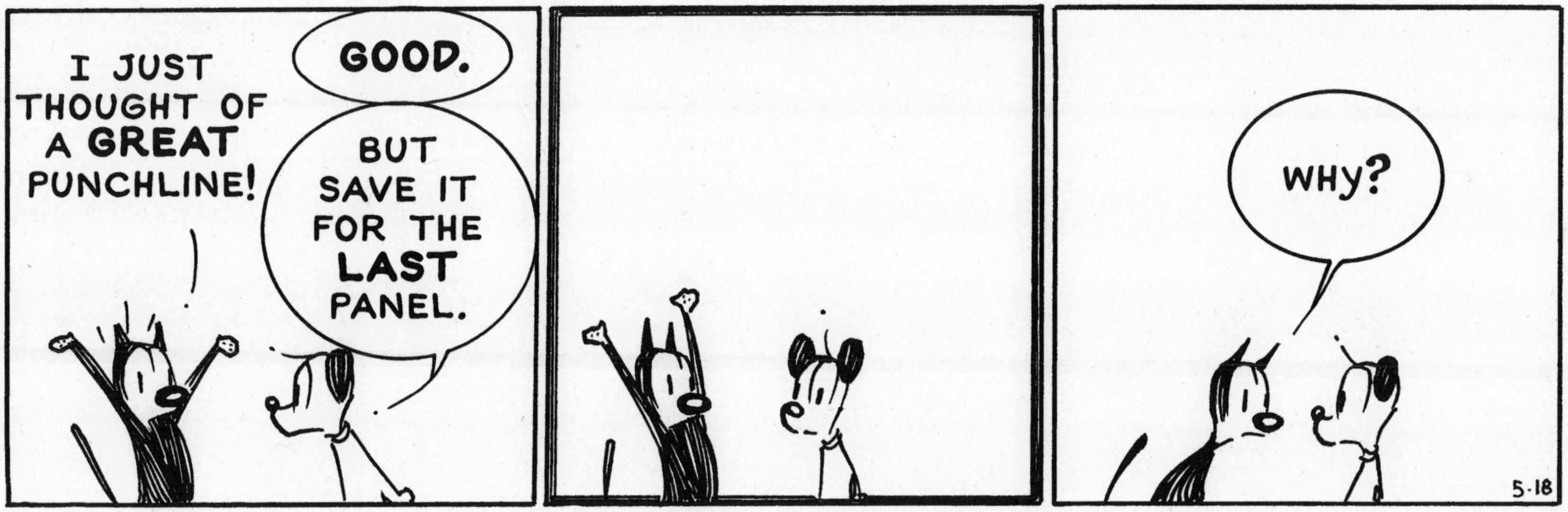
I JUST THOUGHT OF A GREAT PUNCHLINE!
GOOD.
BUT SAVE IT FOR THE LAST PANEL.
WHY?
5·18

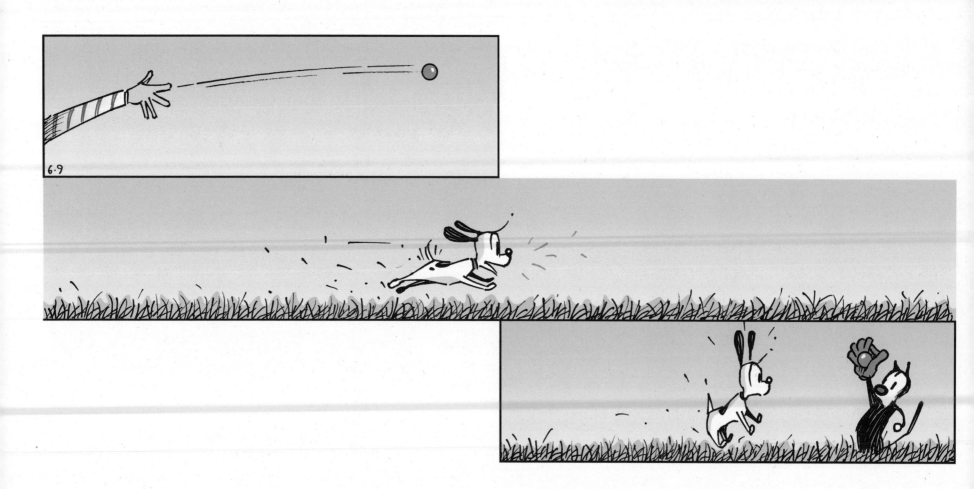

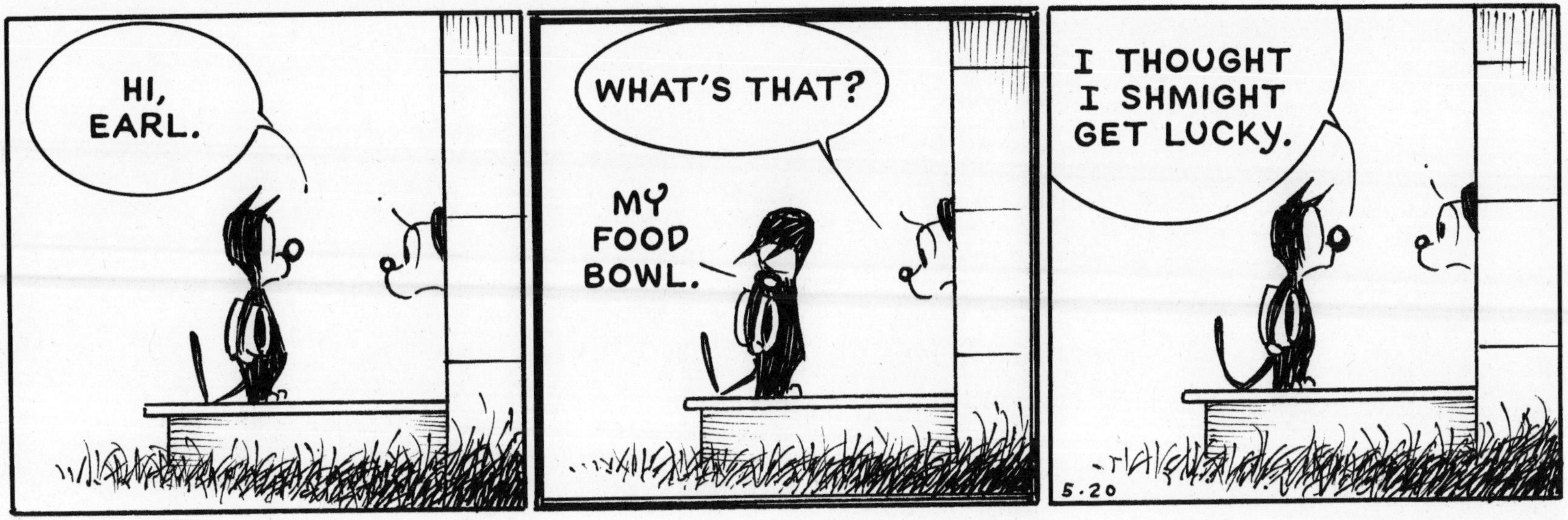
HI, EARL.
WHAT'S THAT?
MY FOOD BOWL.
I THOUGHT I SHMIGHT GET LUCKY.
5·20

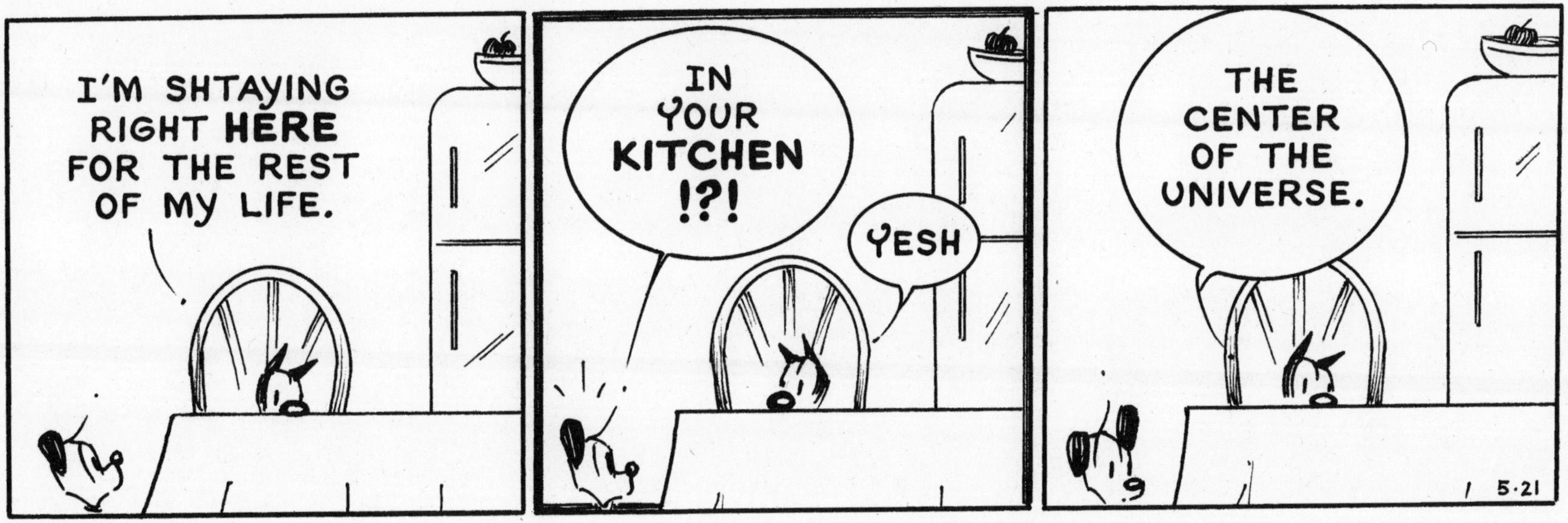
I'M SHTAYING RIGHT **HERE** FOR THE REST OF MY LIFE.
IN YOUR **KITCHEN** !?!
YESH
THE CENTER OF THE UNIVERSE.
5·21

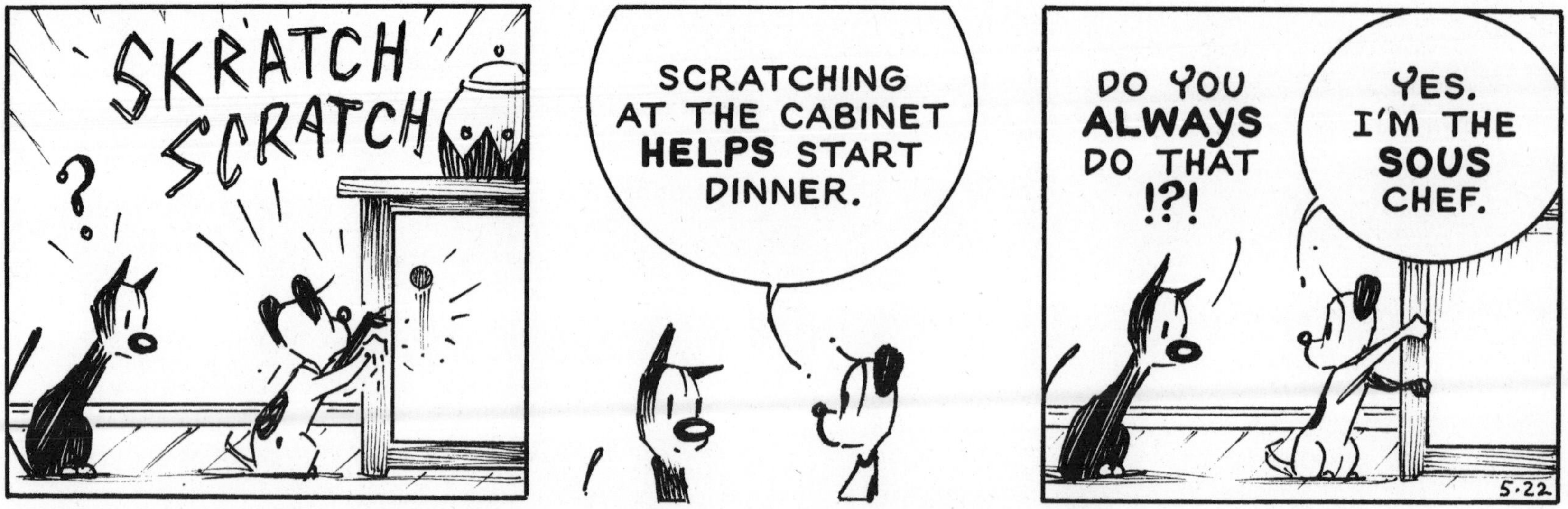
SKRATCH SCRATCH
?
SCRATCHING AT THE CABINET **HELPS** START DINNER.
DO YOU **ALWAYS** DO THAT !?!
YES. I'M THE **SOUS** CHEF.
5·22

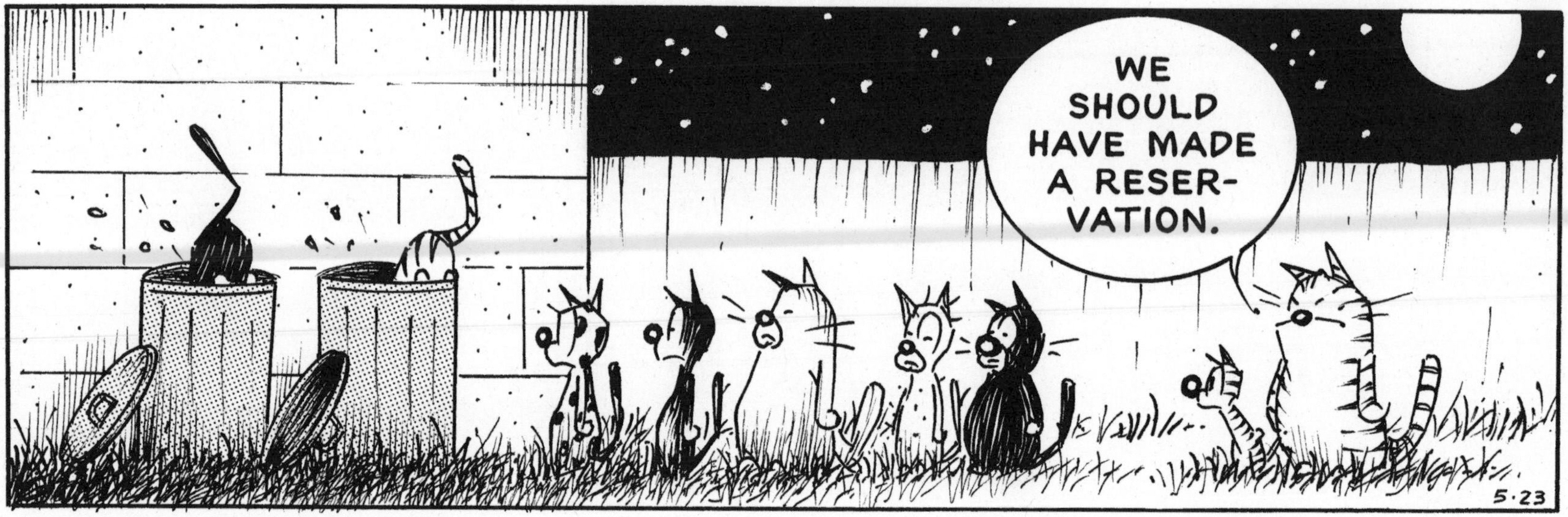
WE SHOULD HAVE MADE A RESER-VATION.
5·23

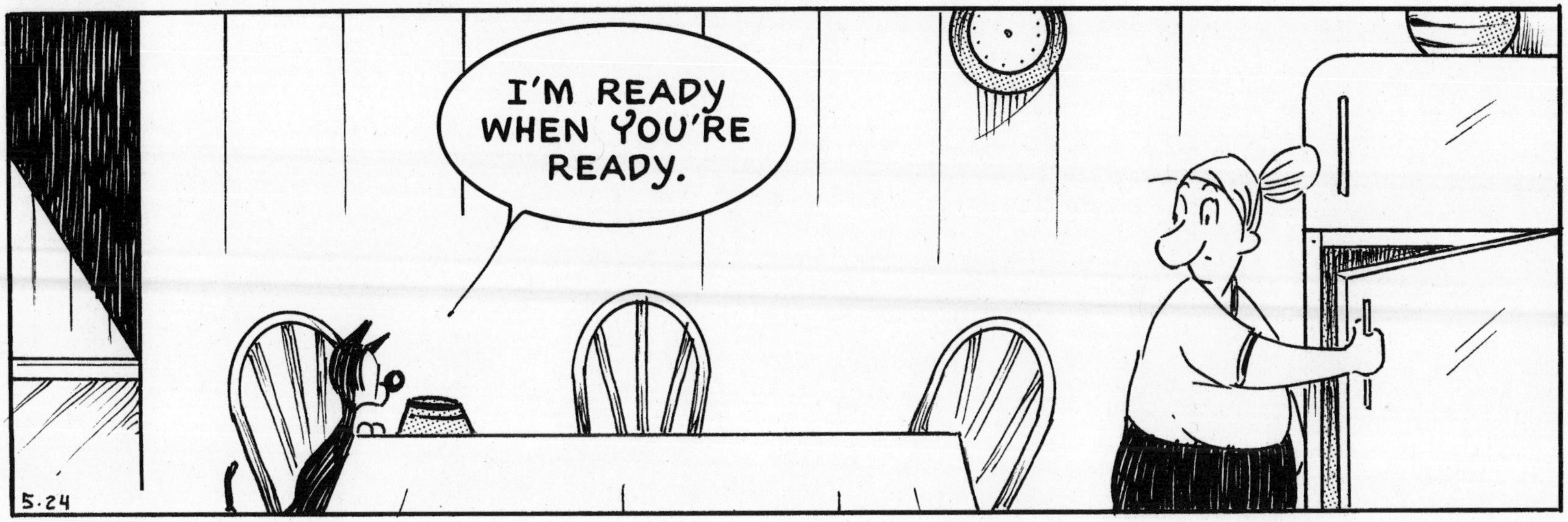
I'M READY WHEN YOU'RE READY.
5·24

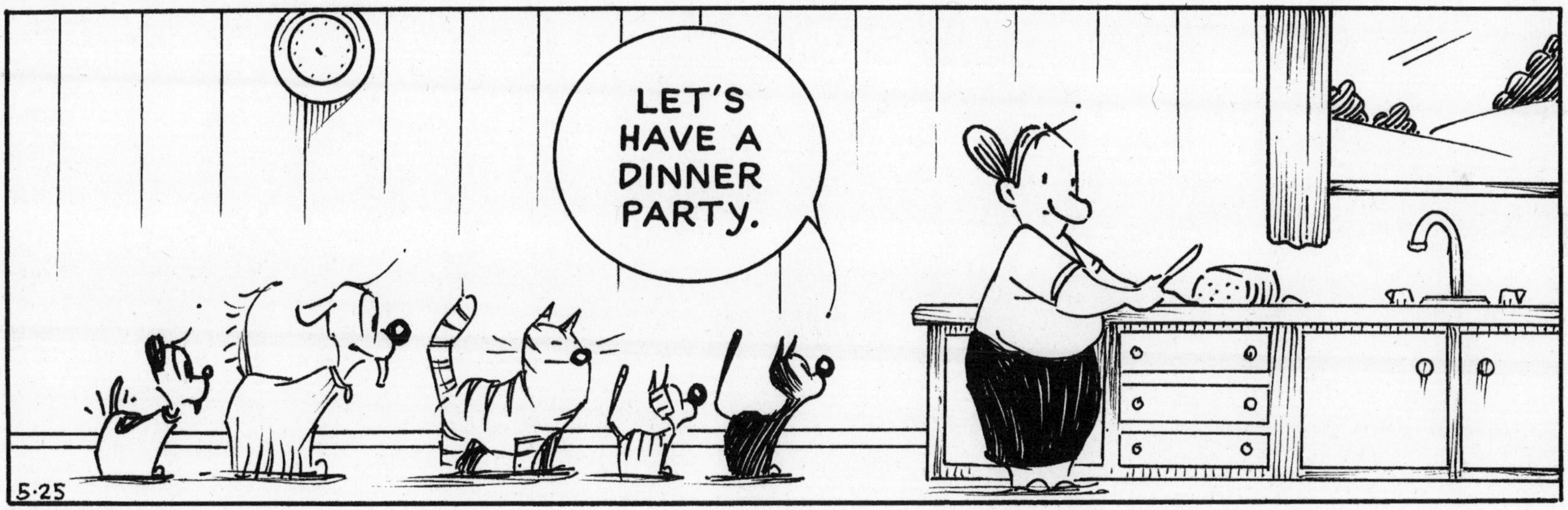
LET'S HAVE A DINNER PARTY.
5·25

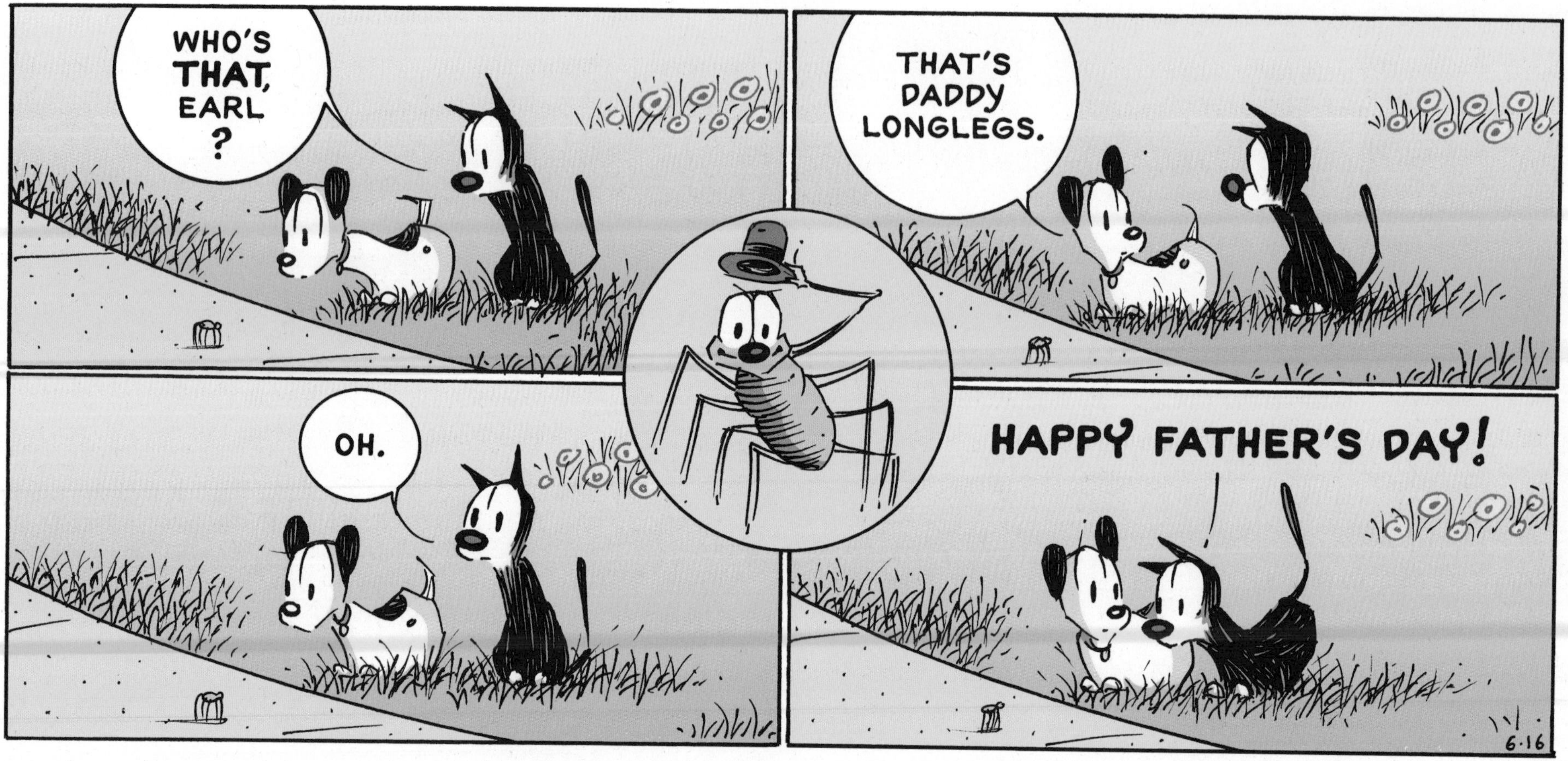
WHO'S THAT, EARL ?
THAT'S DADDY LONGLEGS.
OH.
HAPPY FATHER'S DAY!
6·16

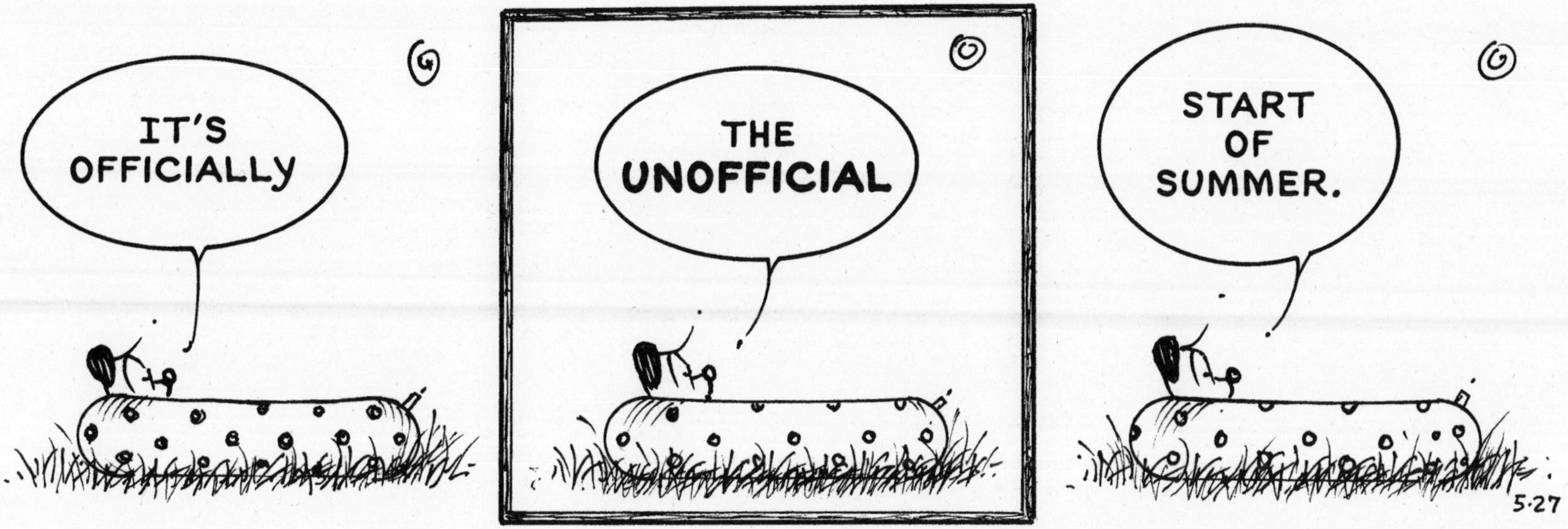
IT'S OFFICIALLY
THE UNOFFICIAL
START OF SUMMER.
5·27

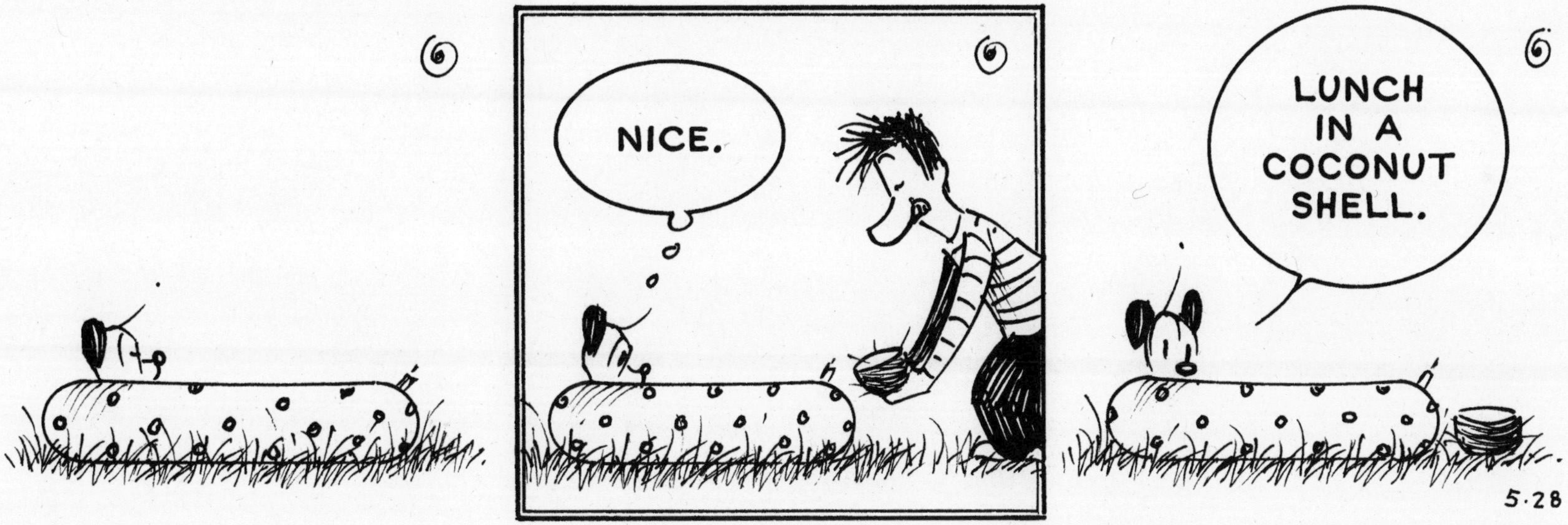
NICE.
LUNCH IN A COCONUT SHELL.
5·28

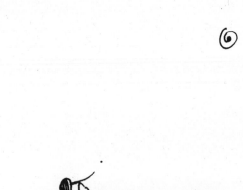

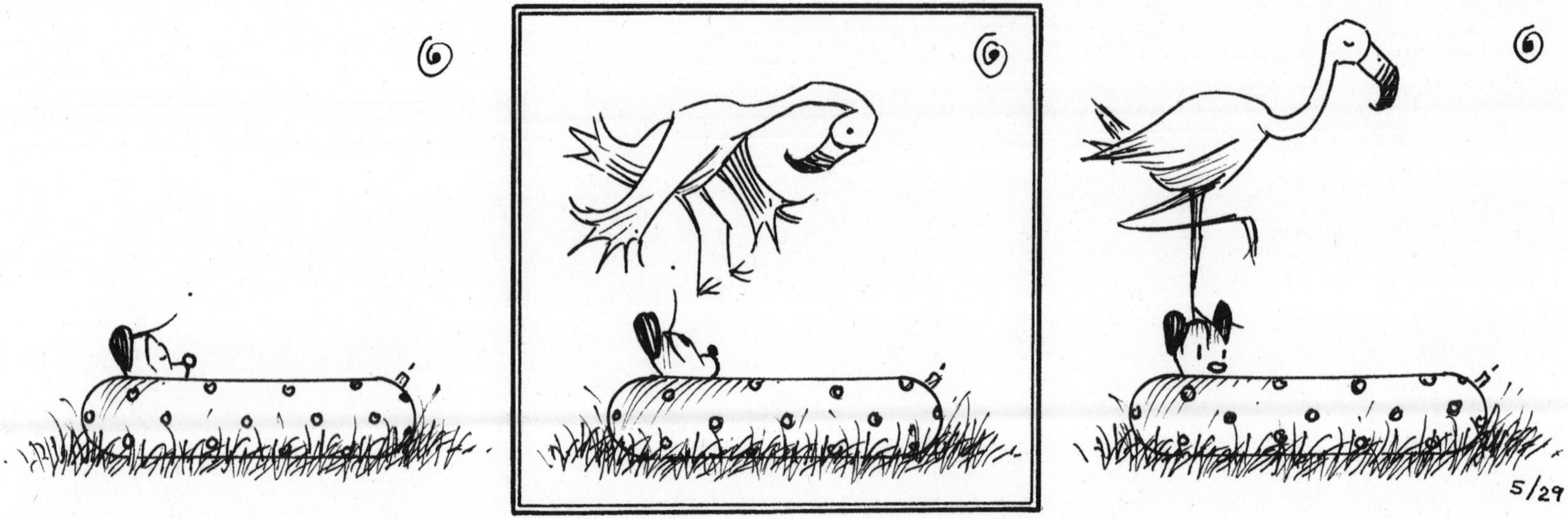
5/29

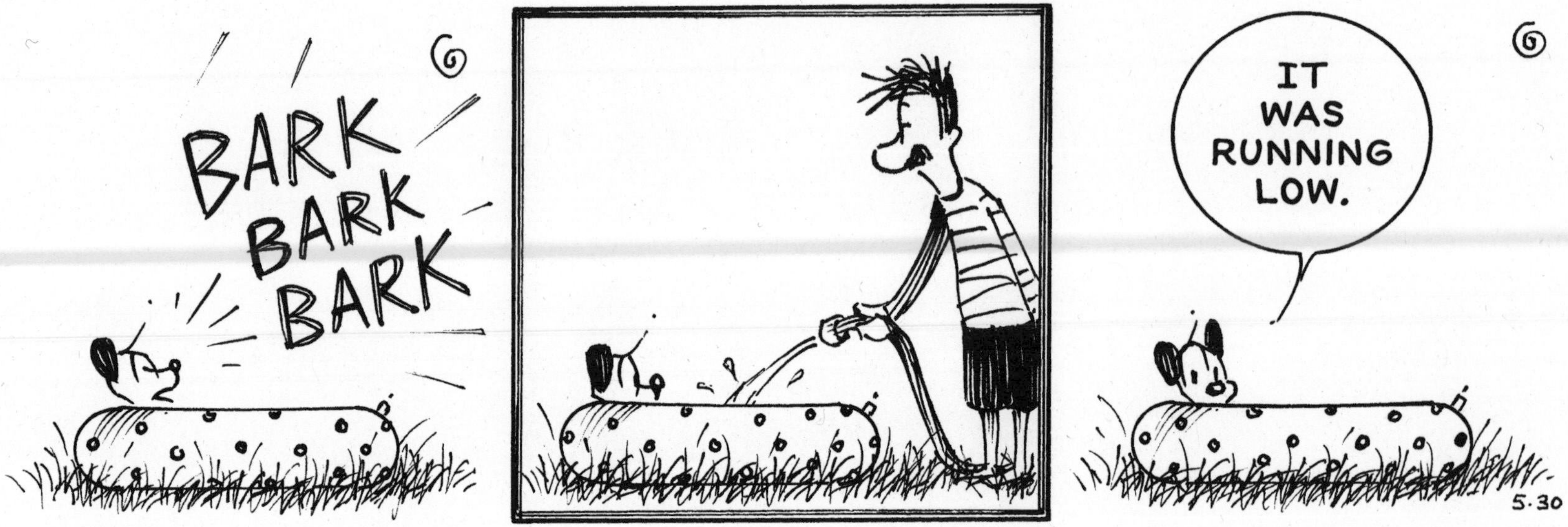
BARK
BARK
BARK
IT WAS RUNNING LOW.
5.30

WHY DON'T YOU
JOIN ME, MOOCH.
OKAY.
6·23

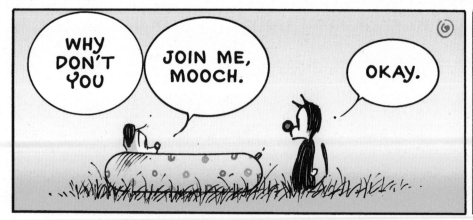

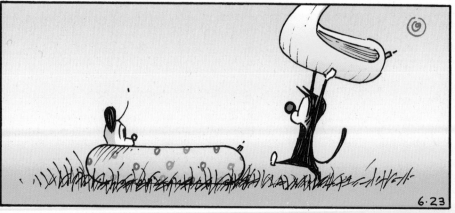

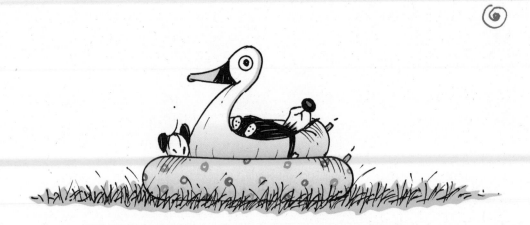

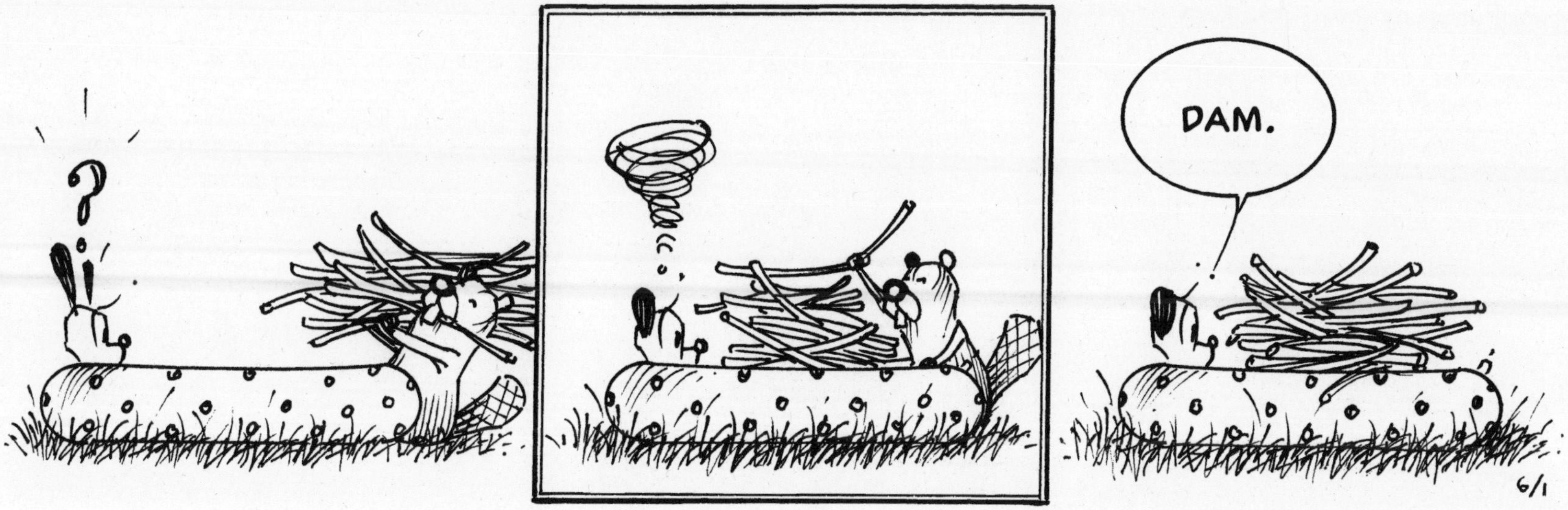
DAM.
6/1

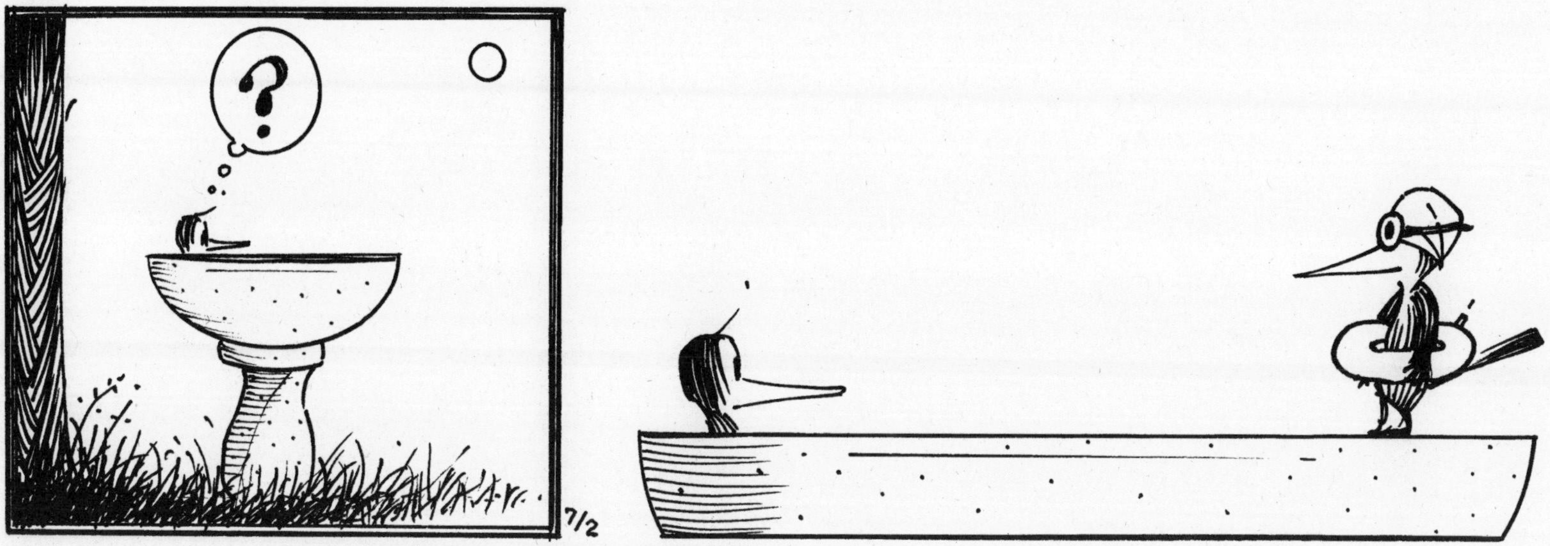
7/2

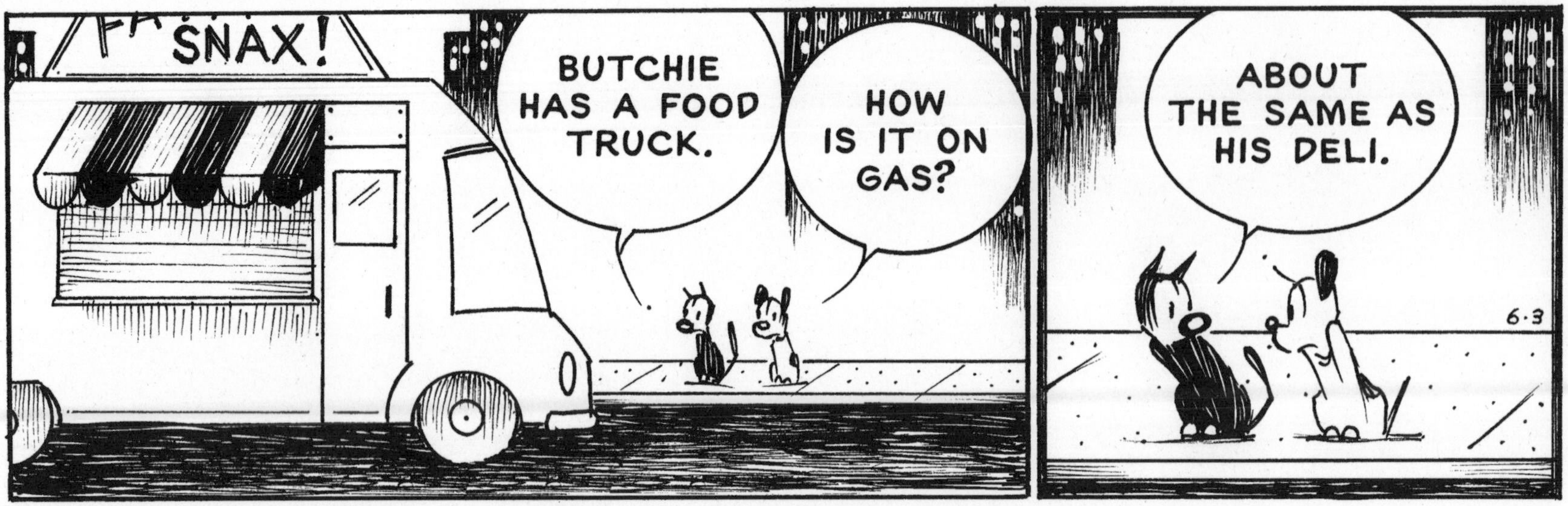
SNAX!
BUTCHIE HAS A FOOD TRUCK.
HOW IS IT ON GAS?
ABOUT THE SAME AS HIS DELI.
6·3

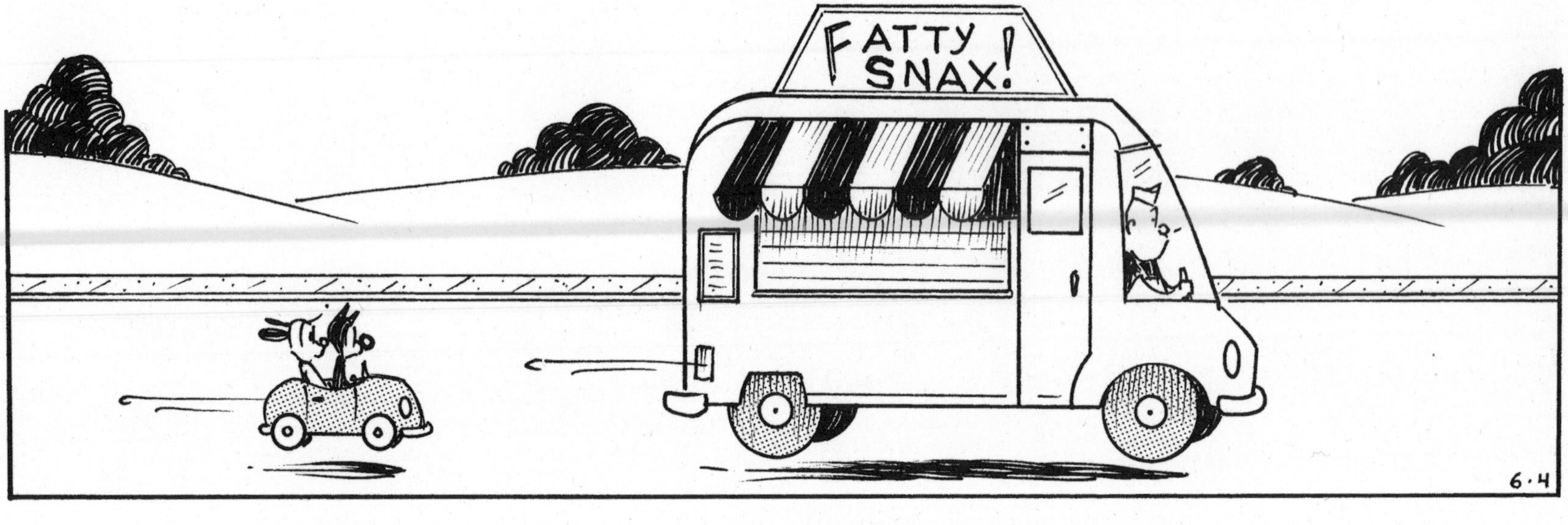
FATTY SNAX!
6·4

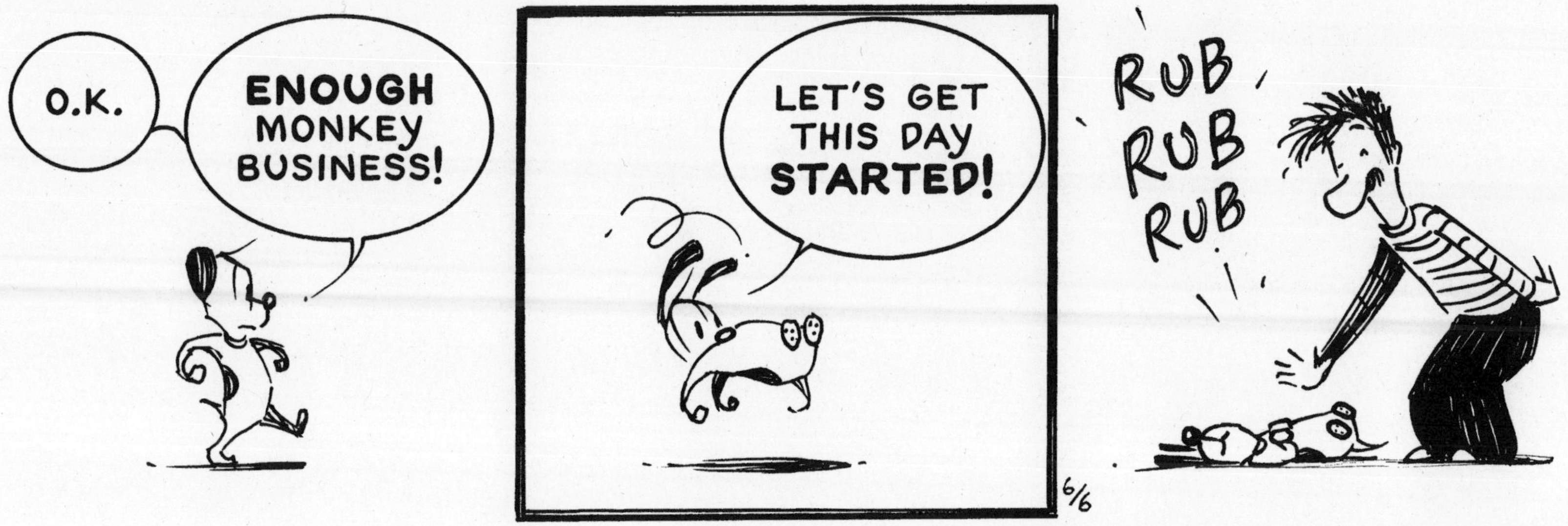
O.K.
ENOUGH MONKEY BUSINESS!
LET'S GET THIS DAY STARTED!
RUB RUB RUB
6/6

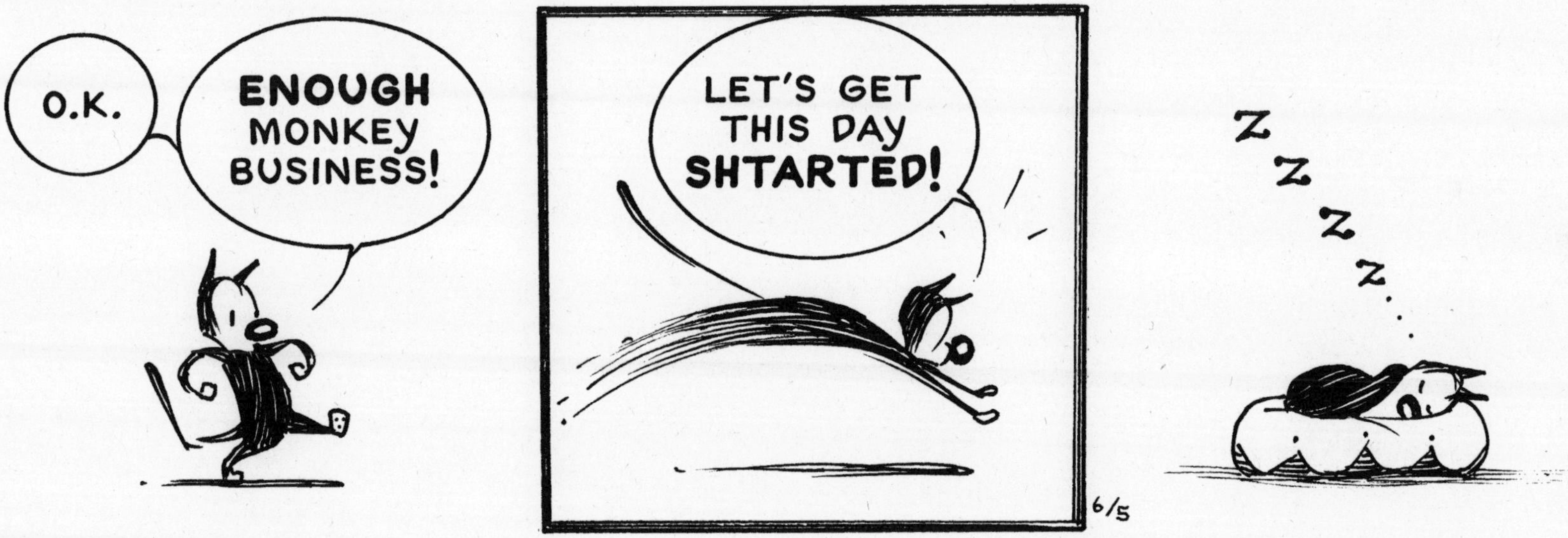
O.K.
ENOUGH MONKEY BUSINESS!
LET'S GET THIS DAY SHTARTED!
Z Z Z Z...
6/5

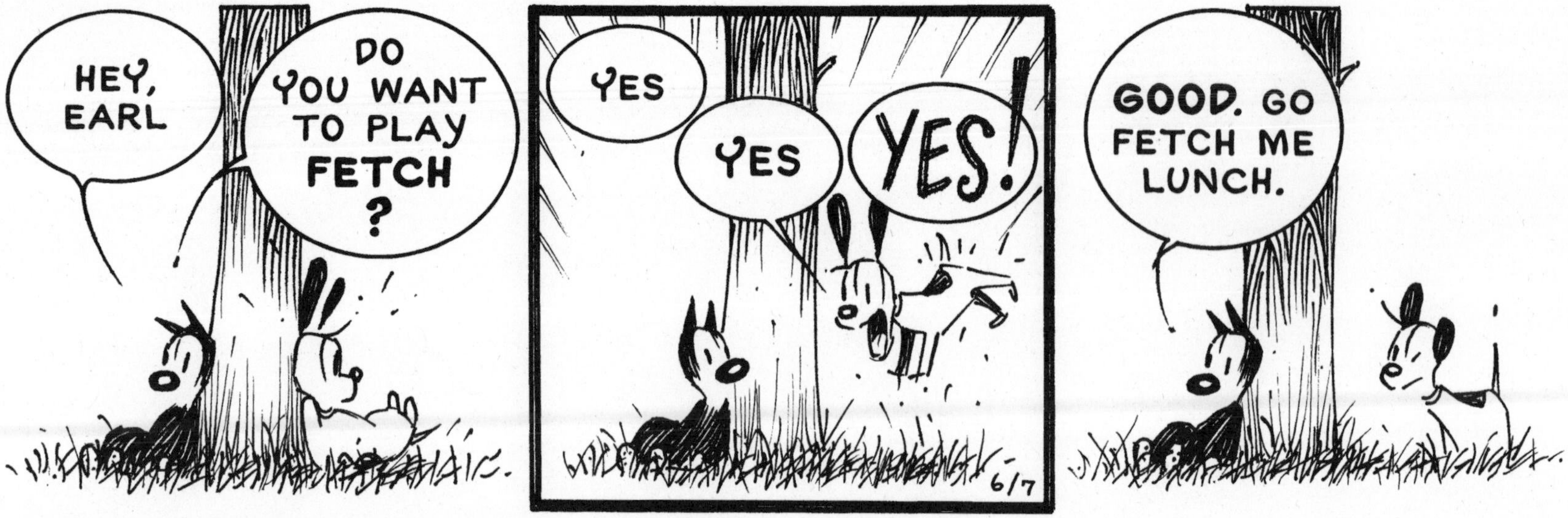
HEY, EARL
DO YOU WANT TO PLAY FETCH ?
YES
YES
YES!
GOOD. GO FETCH ME LUNCH.
6/7

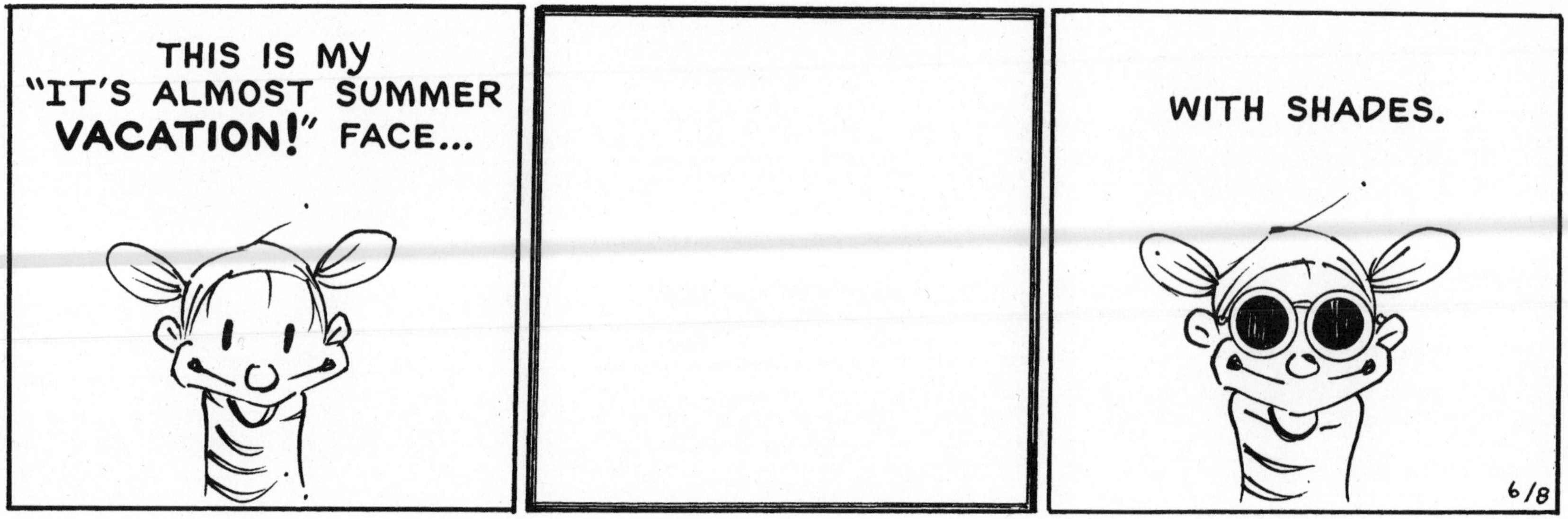
THIS IS MY "IT'S ALMOST SUMMER VACATION!" FACE...
WITH SHADES.
6/8

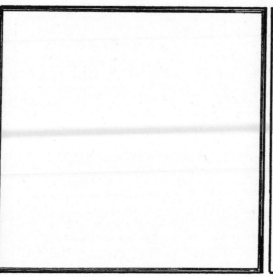

MUTTS
MUTTS
by PATRICK McDONNELL
by PATRICK McDONNELL

WHO'S THAT !?!
HE'S A COPY-CAT!
HE'S A COPY-CAT!
NOT ME- YOU!
NOT ME- YOU!
HE'S BEEN FOLLOWING ME ALL DAY, DRIVING ME NUTS!!!
HE'S BEEN FOLLOWING ME ALL DAY, DRIVING ME NUTS!!!
SHTOP THAT!
SHTOP THAT!
WHY DON'T YOU JUST STAY AWAY FROM HIM ?
WELL...
WELL...
I DO AGREE WITH EVERY-THING HE SAYS.
I DO AGREE WITH EVERY-THING HE SAYS.
7-14

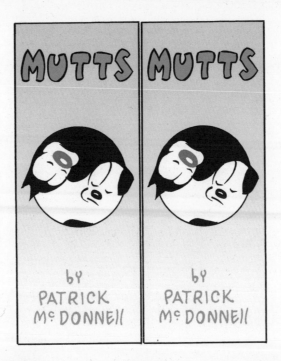

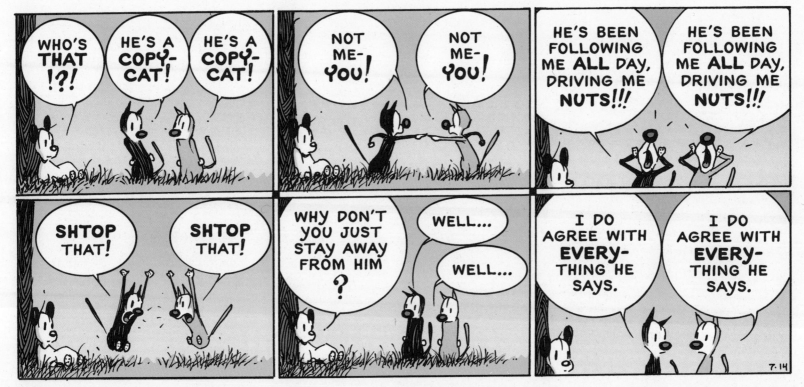

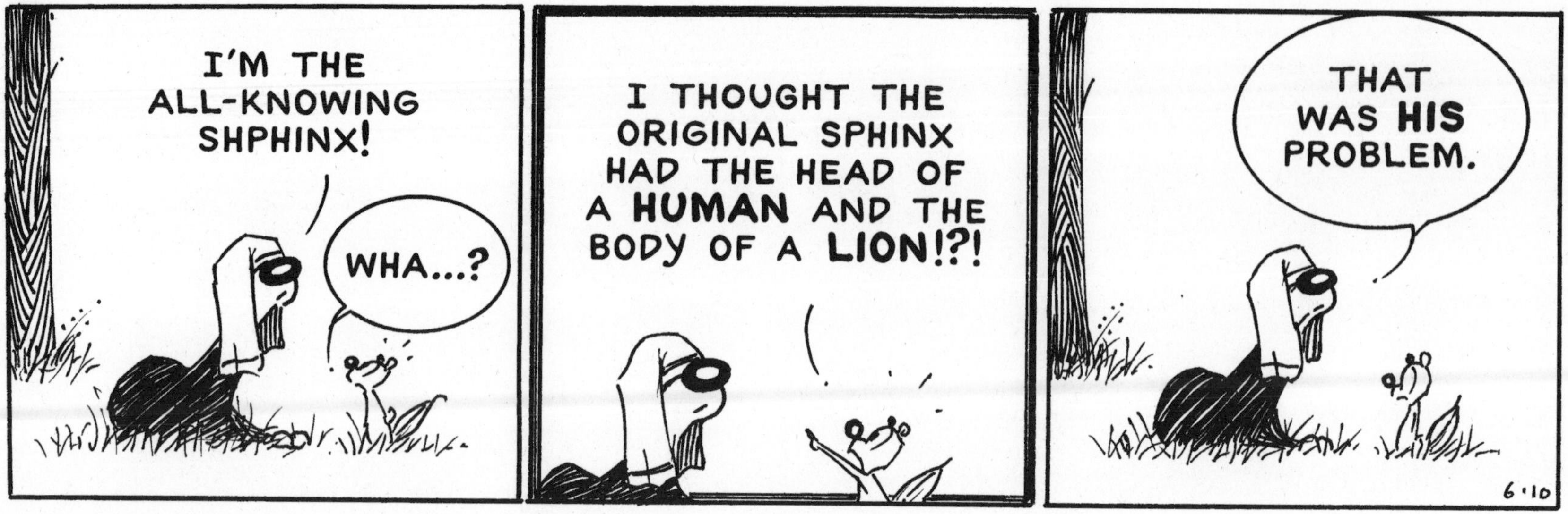
I'M THE ALL-KNOWING SHPHINX!
WHA...?
I THOUGHT THE ORIGINAL SPHINX HAD THE HEAD OF A **HUMAN** AND THE BODY OF A **LION**!?!
THAT WAS **HIS** PROBLEM.
6·10

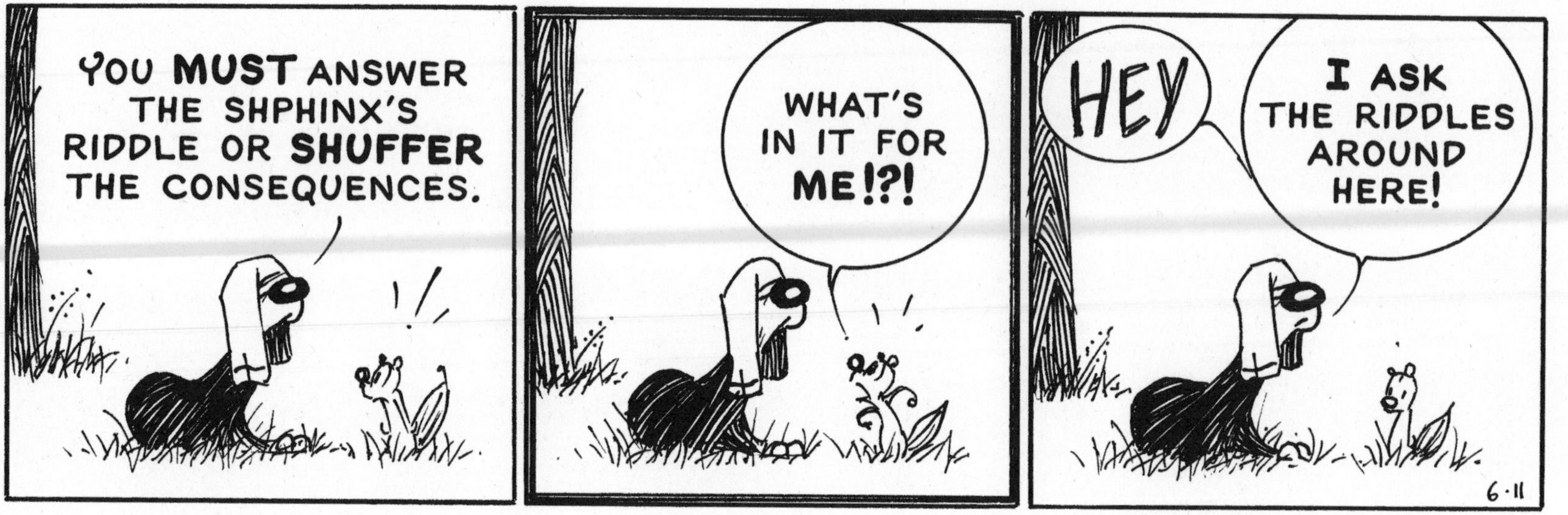
YOU **MUST** ANSWER THE SHPHINX'S RIDDLE OR **SHUFFER** THE CONSEQUENCES.
WHAT'S IN IT FOR **ME**!?!
HEY
I ASK THE RIDDLES AROUND HERE!
6·11

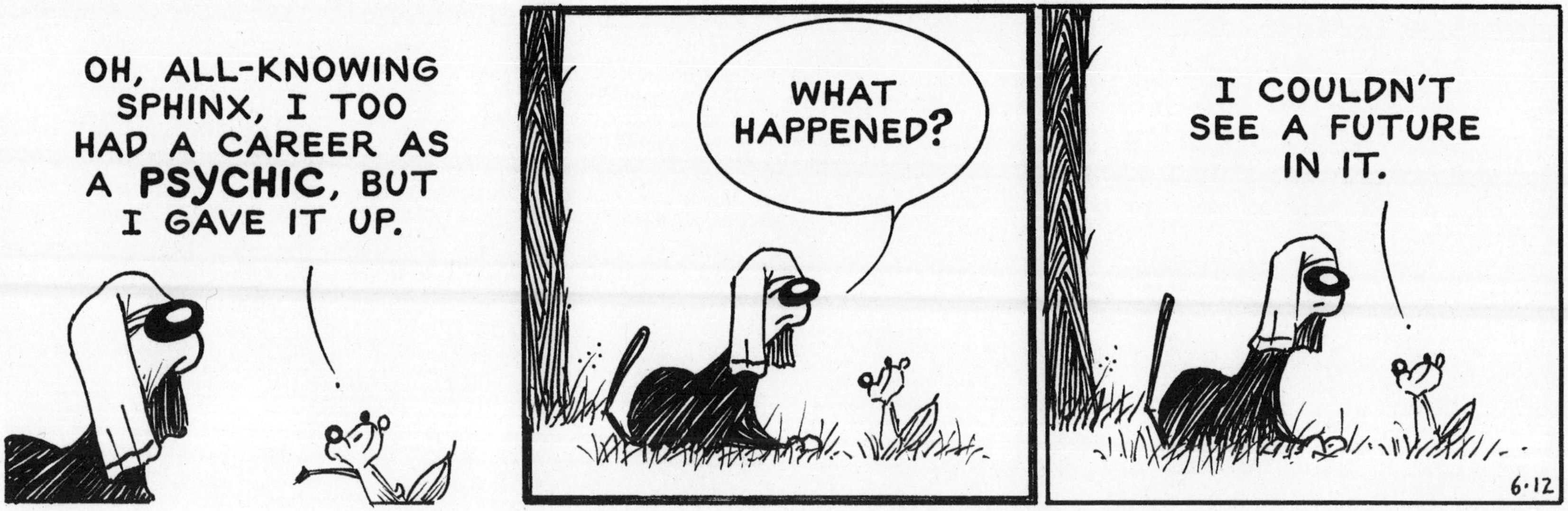
OH, ALL-KNOWING SPHINX, I TOO HAD A CAREER AS A **PSYCHIC**, BUT I GAVE IT UP.
WHAT HAPPENED?
I COULDN'T SEE A FUTURE IN IT.
6·12

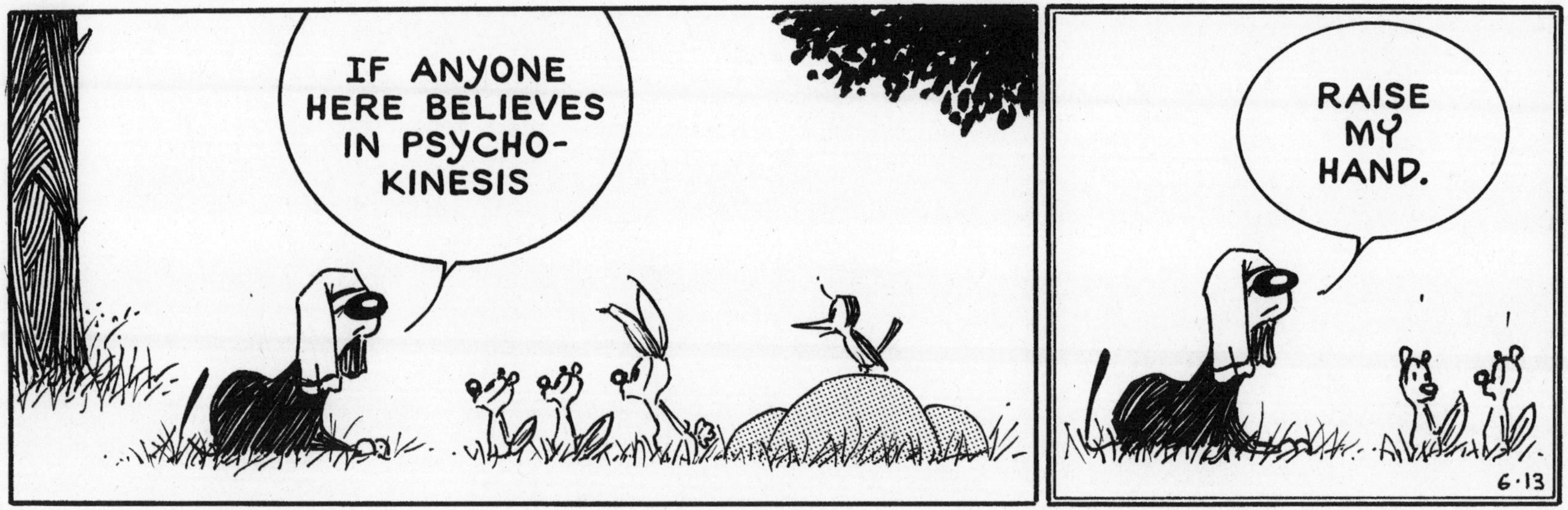
IF ANYONE HERE BELIEVES IN PSYCHO-KINESIS
RAISE MY HAND.
6·13

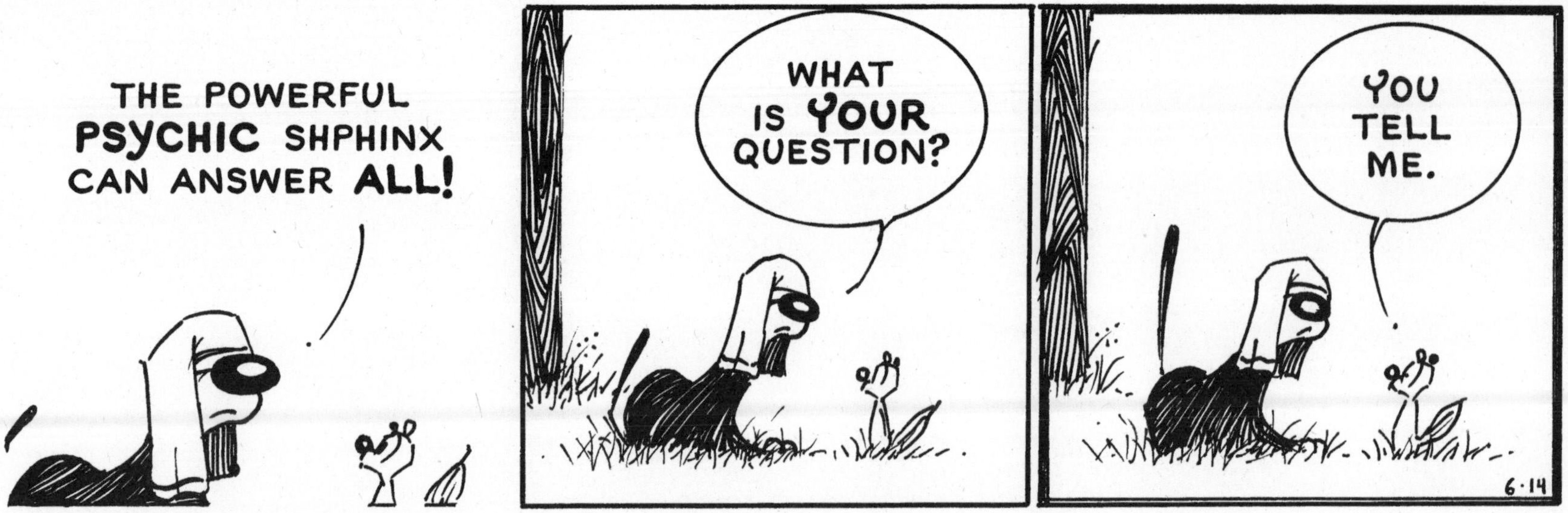
THE POWERFUL PSYCHIC SHPHINX CAN ANSWER ALL!
WHAT IS YOUR QUESTION?
YOU TELL ME.
6·14

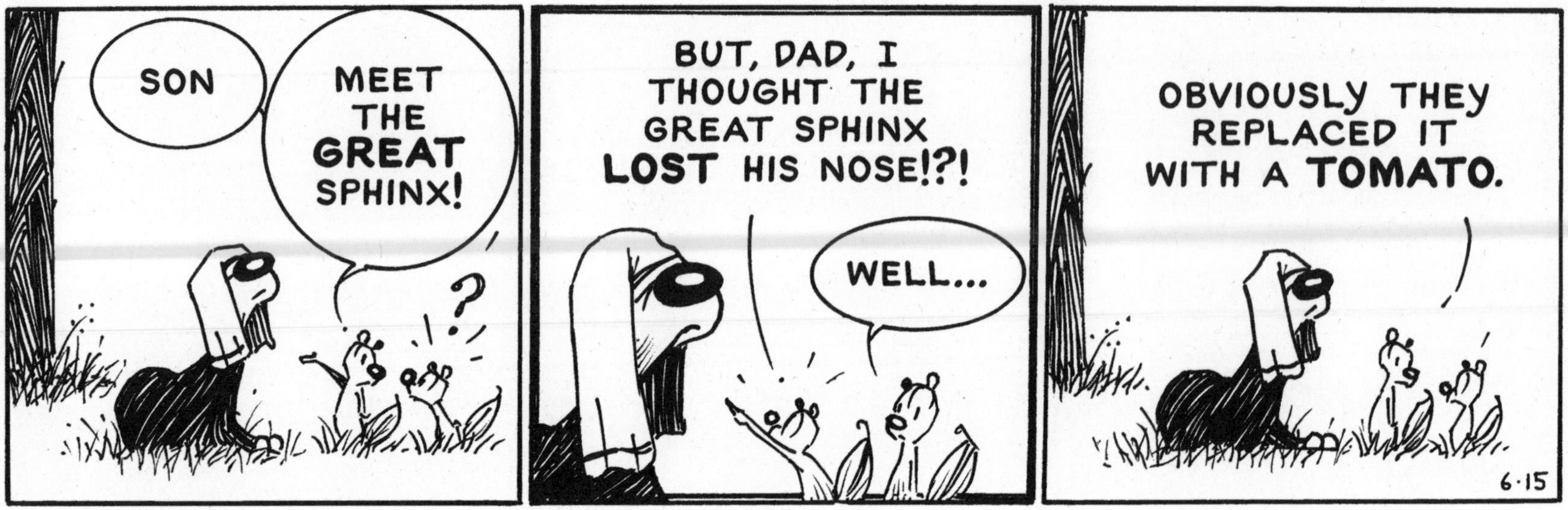
SON
MEET THE GREAT SPHINX!
?
BUT, DAD, I THOUGHT THE GREAT SPHINX LOST HIS NOSE!?!
WELL...
OBVIOUSLY THEY REPLACED IT WITH A TOMATO.
6·15

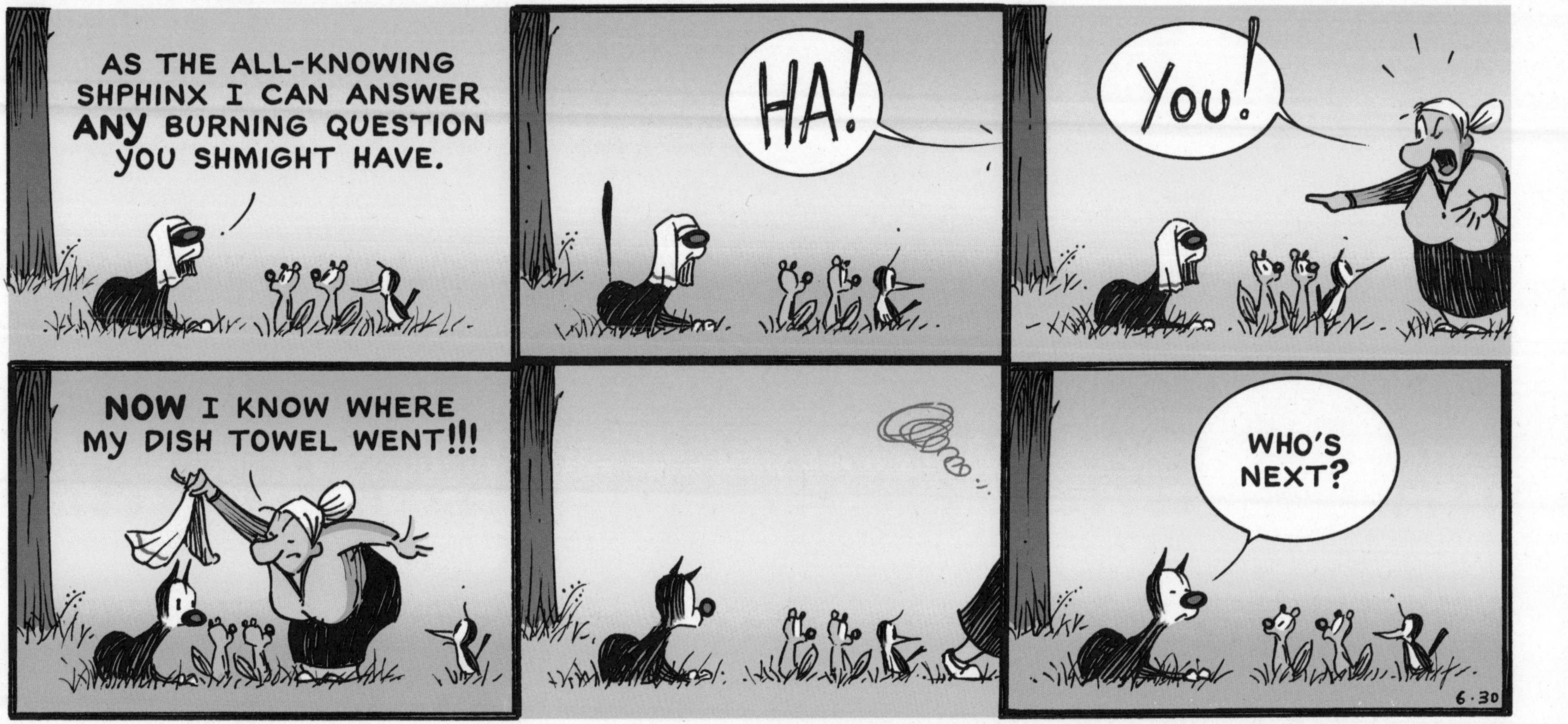
AS THE ALL-KNOWING SHPHINX I CAN ANSWER ANY BURNING QUESTION YOU SHMIGHT HAVE.
HA!
YOU!
NOW I KNOW WHERE MY DISH TOWEL WENT!!!
WHO'S NEXT?
6·30

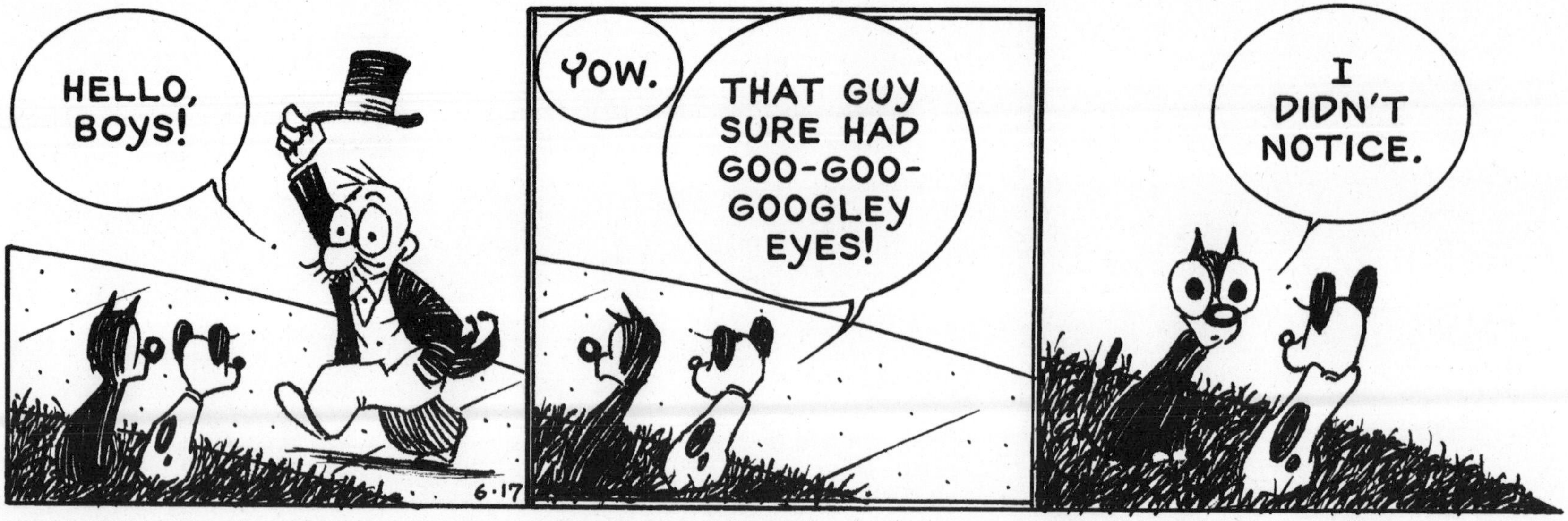
HELLO, BOYS!
6·17
YOW.
THAT GUY SURE HAD GOO-GOO-GOOGLEY EYES!
I DIDN'T NOTICE.

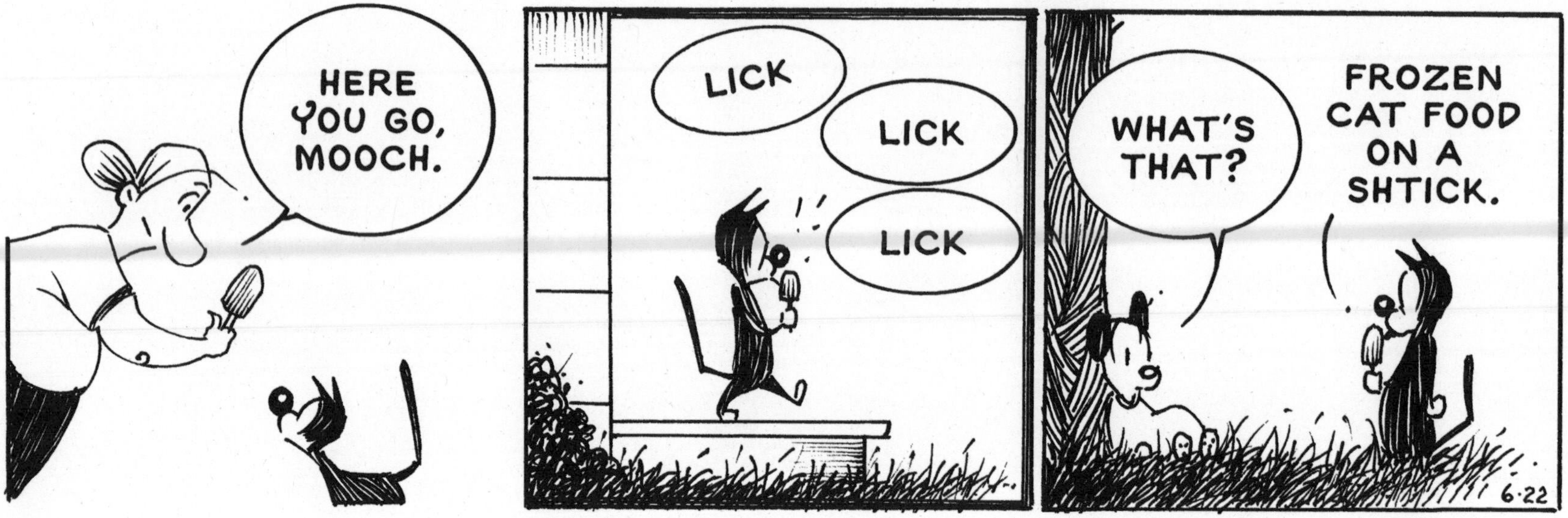
HERE YOU GO, MOOCH.
LICK
LICK
LICK
WHAT'S THAT?
FROZEN CAT FOOD ON A SHTICK.
6·22

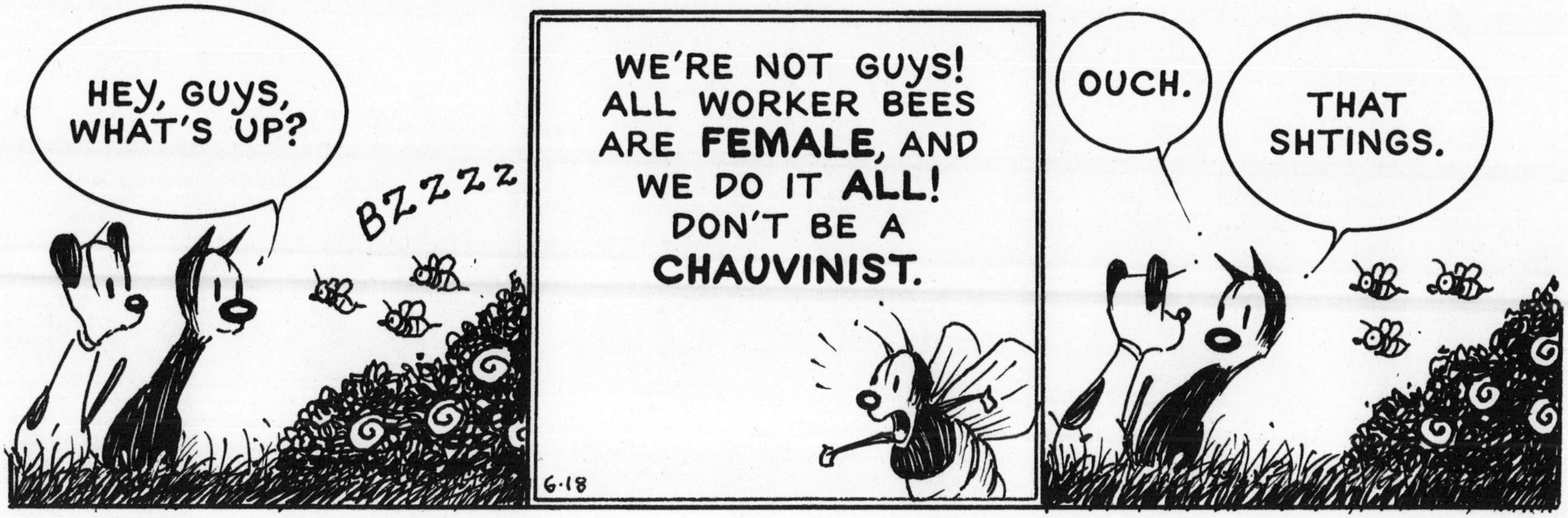
HEY, GUYS, WHAT'S UP?
BZZZZ
WE'RE NOT GUYS! ALL WORKER BEES ARE FEMALE, AND WE DO IT ALL! DON'T BE A CHAUVINIST.
6·18
OUCH.
THAT SHTINGS.

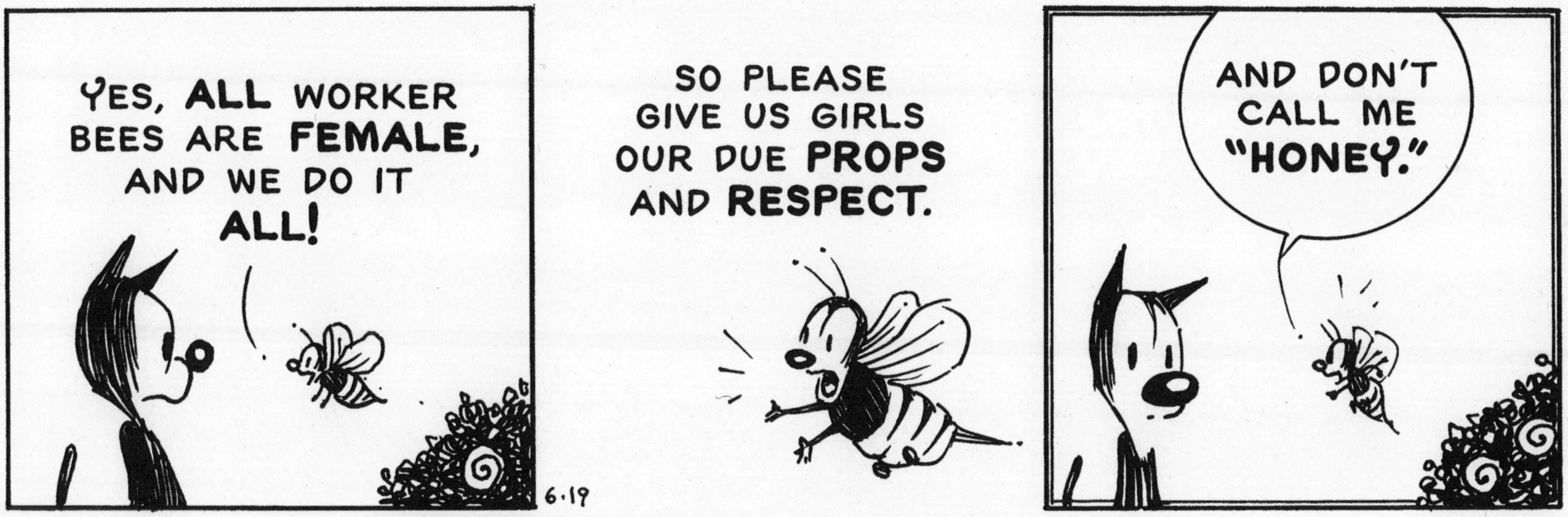
YES, ALL WORKER BEES ARE FEMALE, AND WE DO IT ALL!
6·19
SO PLEASE GIVE US GIRLS OUR DUE PROPS AND RESPECT.
AND DON'T CALL ME "HONEY."

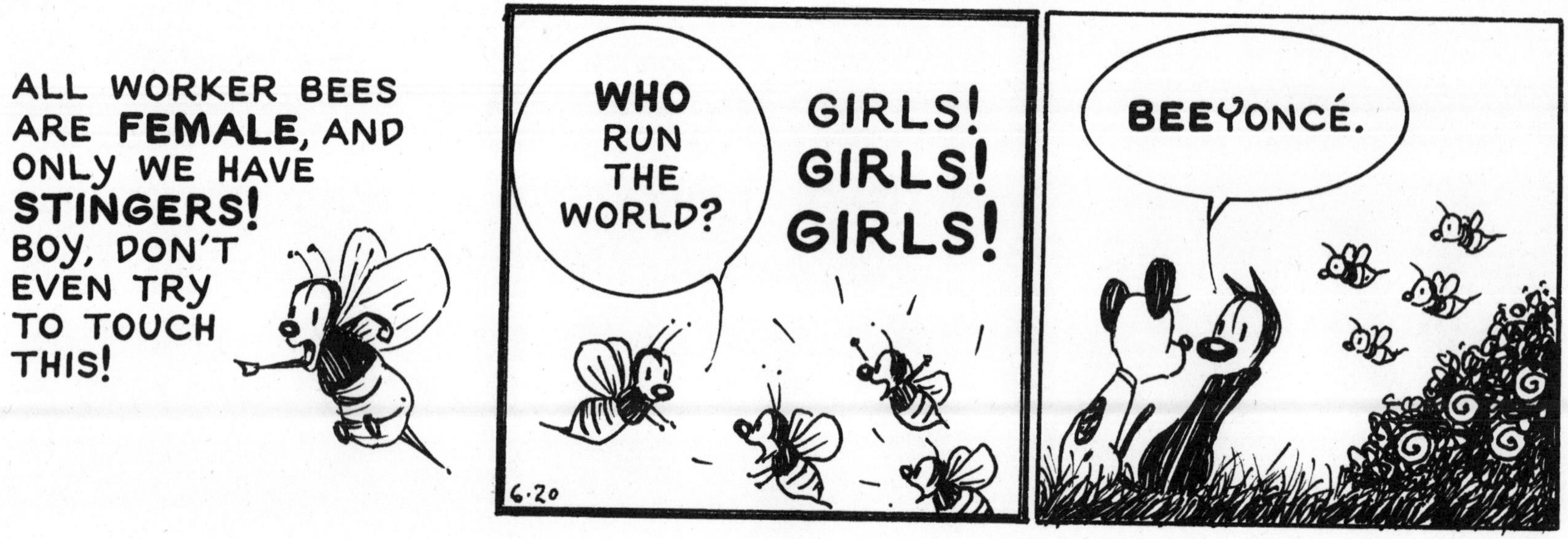
ALL WORKER BEES ARE FEMALE, AND ONLY WE HAVE STINGERS! BOY, DON'T EVEN TRY TO TOUCH THIS!
WHO RUN THE WORLD?
GIRLS! GIRLS! GIRLS!
6·20
BEEYONCÉ.

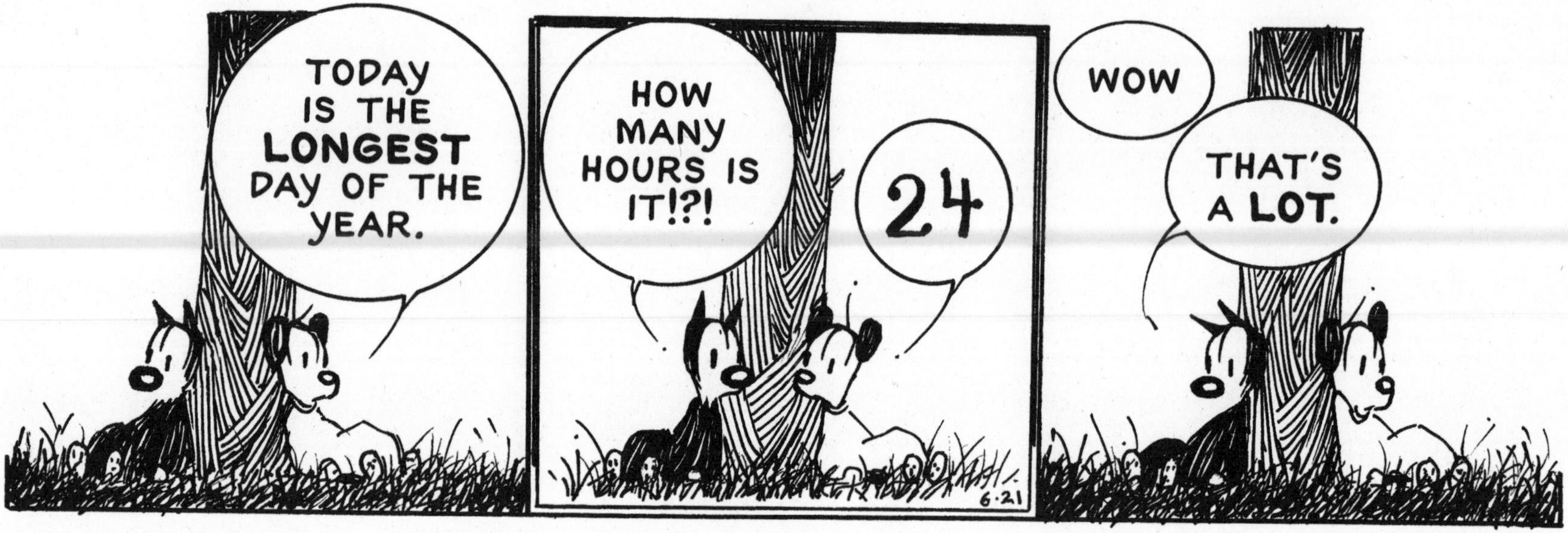
TODAY IS THE LONGEST DAY OF THE YEAR.
HOW MANY HOURS IS IT!?!
24
6·21
WOW
THAT'S A LOT.

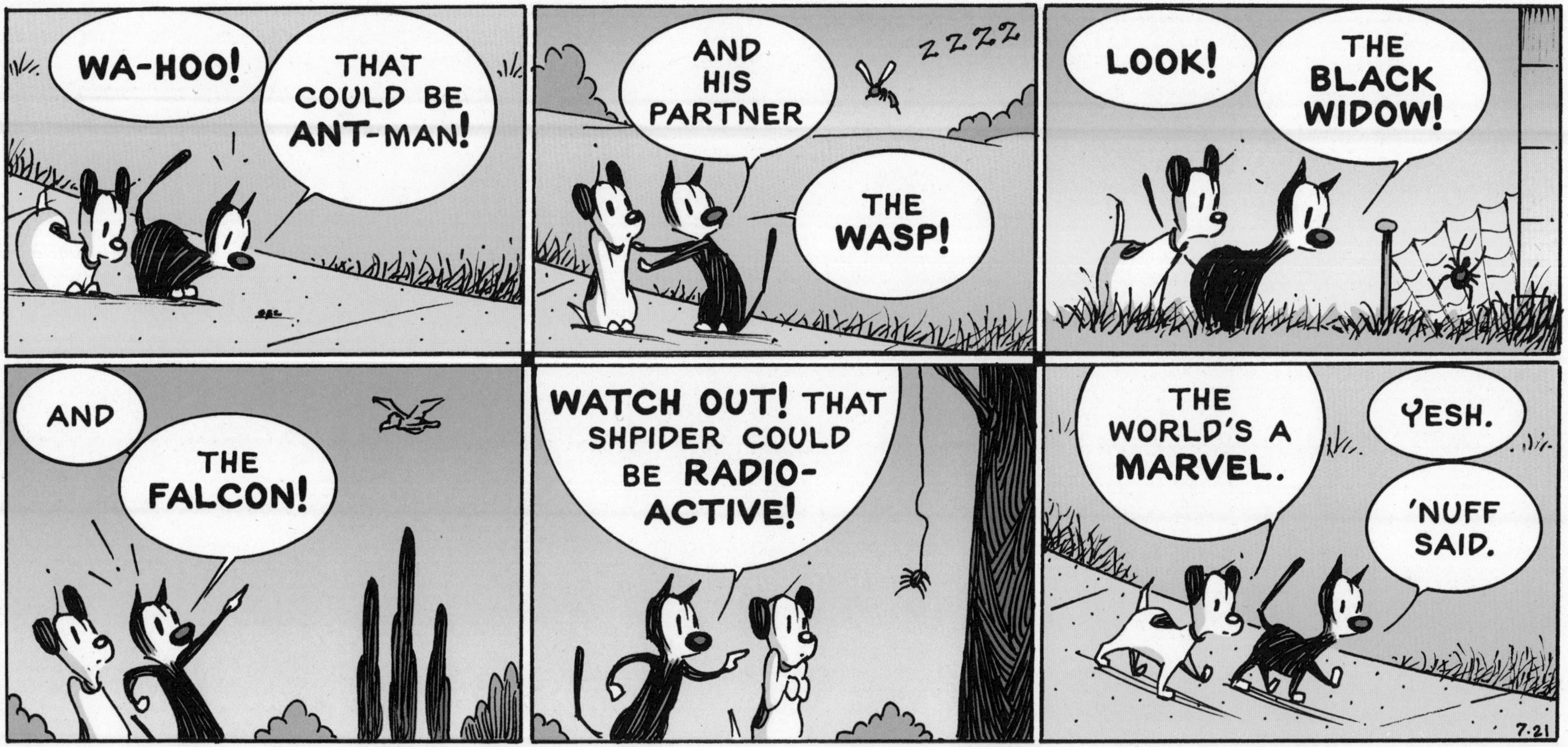
WA-HOO!
THAT COULD BE ANT-MAN!
AND HIS PARTNER
ZZZZ
THE WASP!
LOOK!
THE BLACK WIDOW!
AND
THE FALCON!
WATCH OUT! THAT SHPIDER COULD BE RADIO-ACTIVE!
THE WORLD'S A MARVEL.
YESH.
'NUFF SAID.
7-21

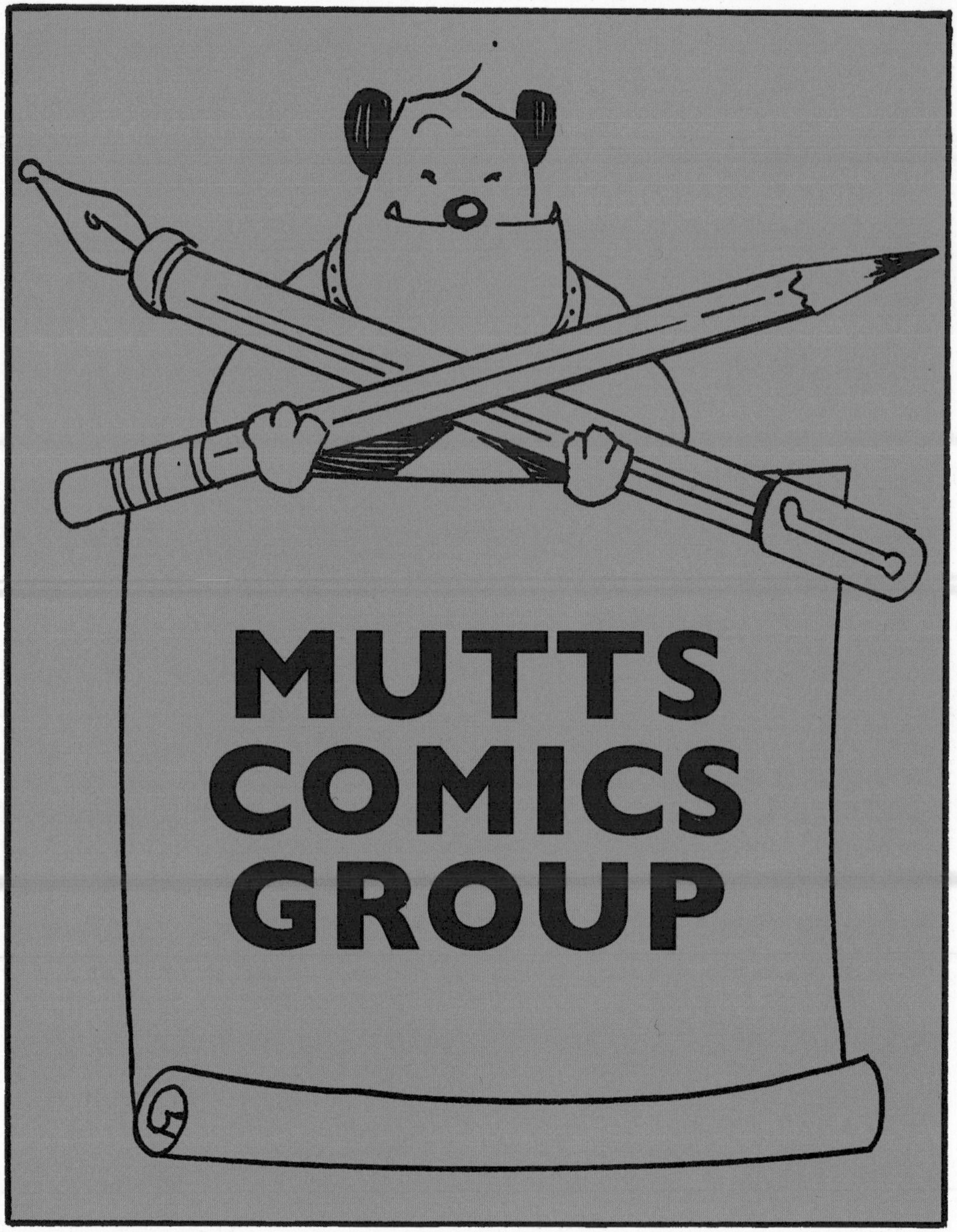
MUTTS
COMICS
GROUP

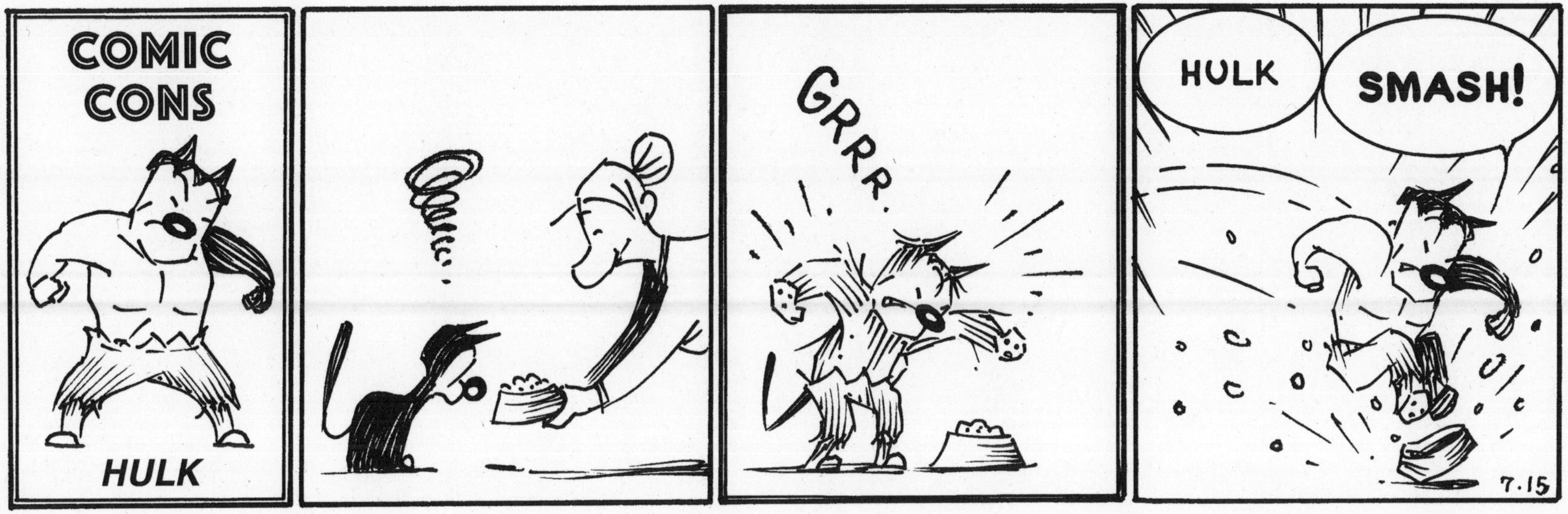
COMIC
CONS
HULK
GRRR.
HULK
SMASH!
7.15

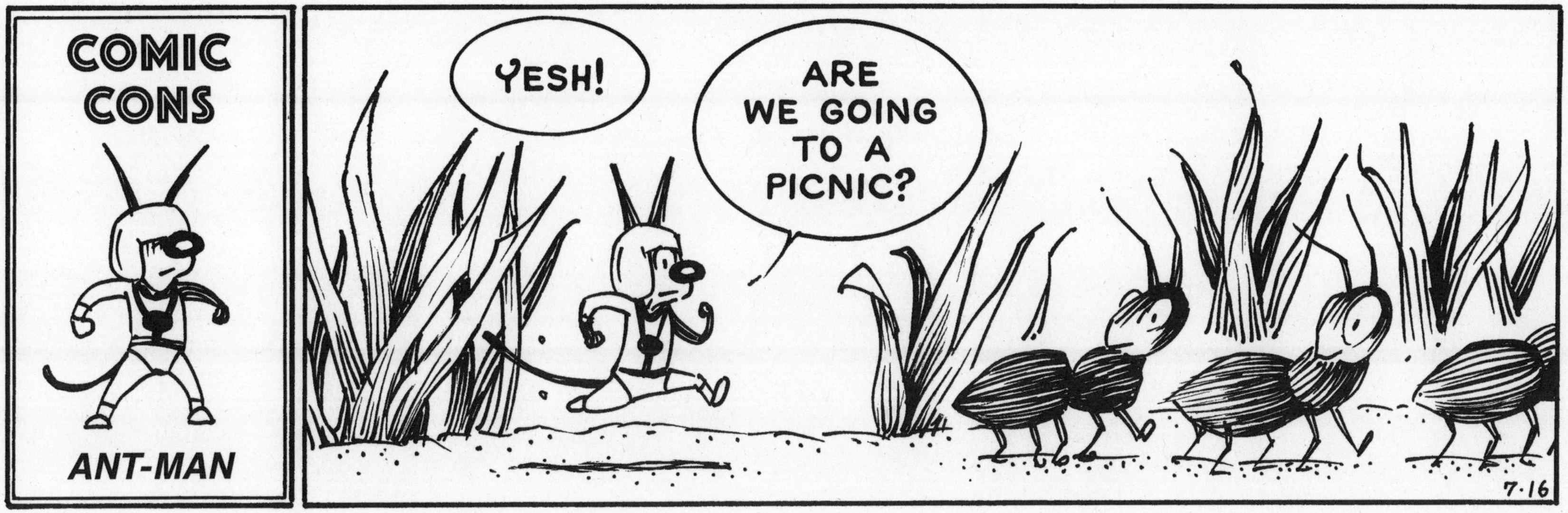
COMIC
CONS
ANT-MAN
YESH!
ARE WE GOING TO A PICNIC?
7.16

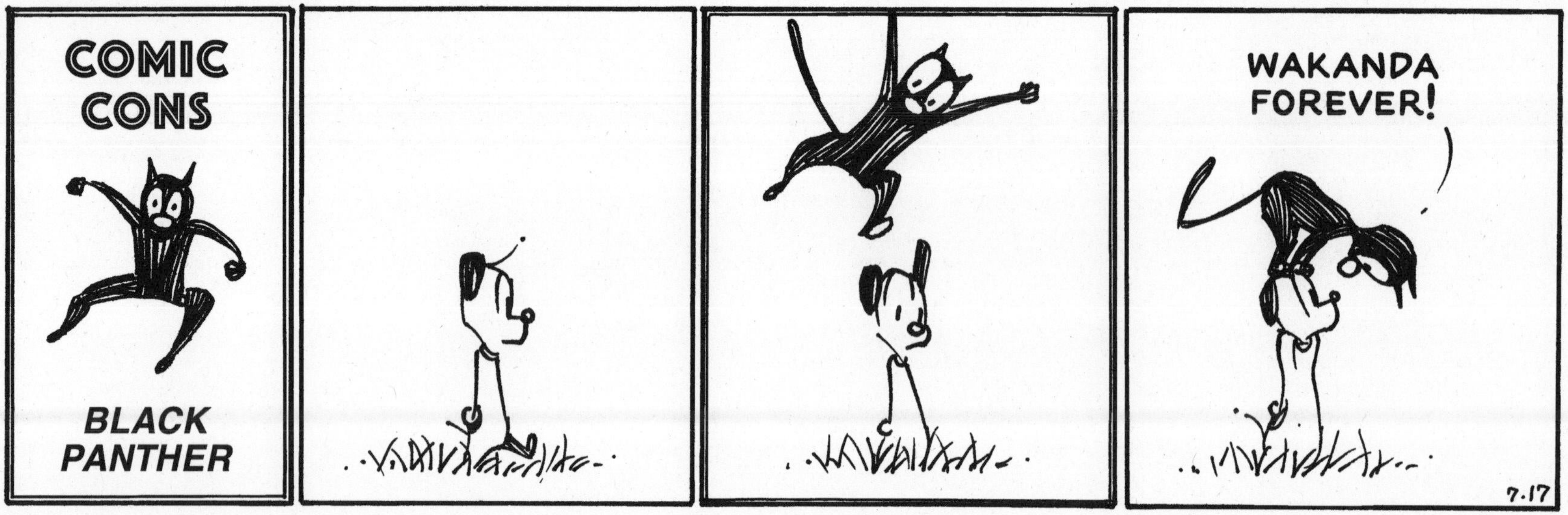
COMIC CONS
BLACK PANTHER
WAKANDA FOREVER!
7.17

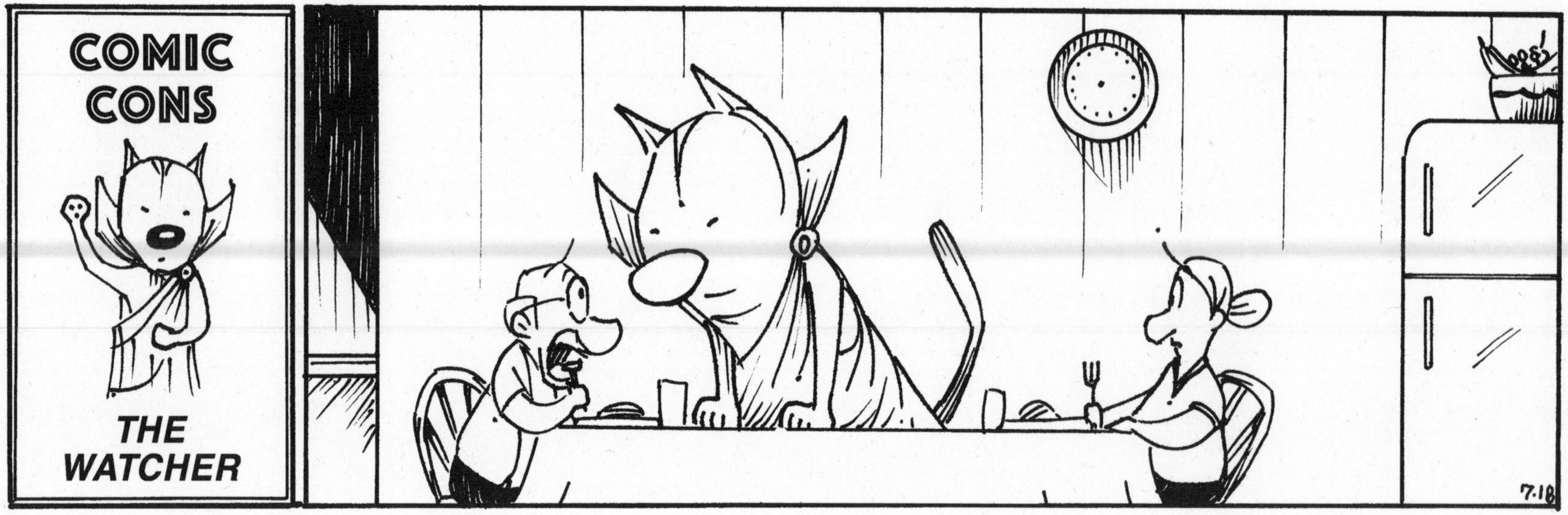
COMIC CONS
THE WATCHER
7.18

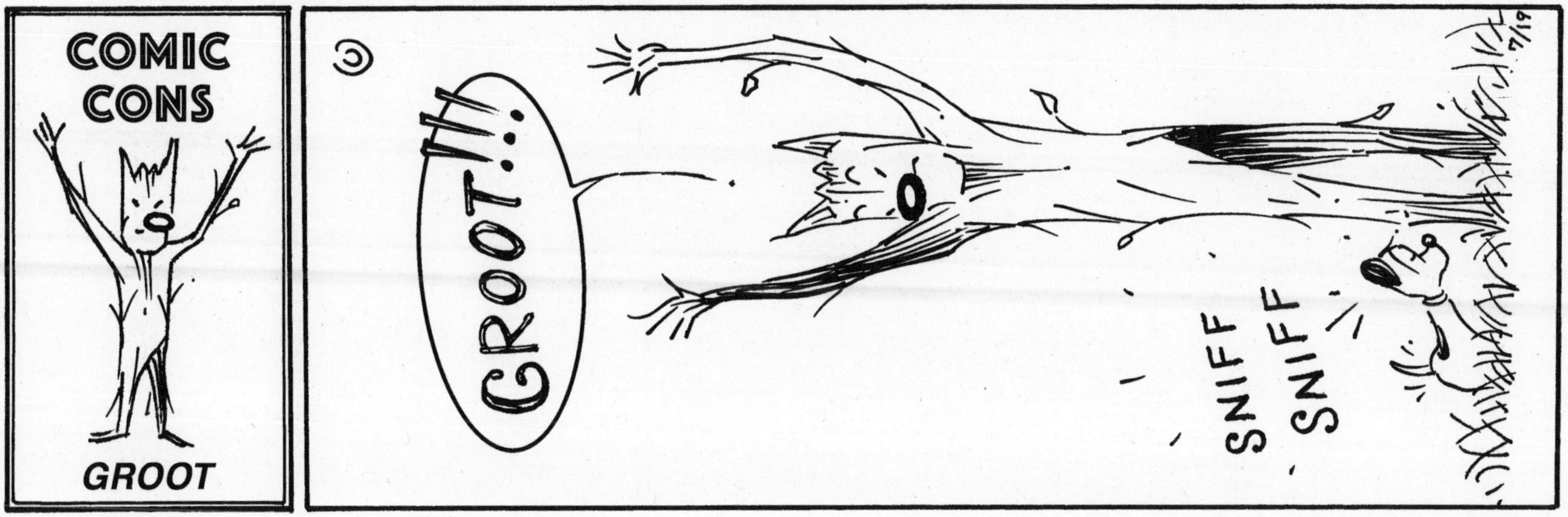
COMIC CONS
GROOT
GROOT!!...
SNIFF
SNIFF
7/19

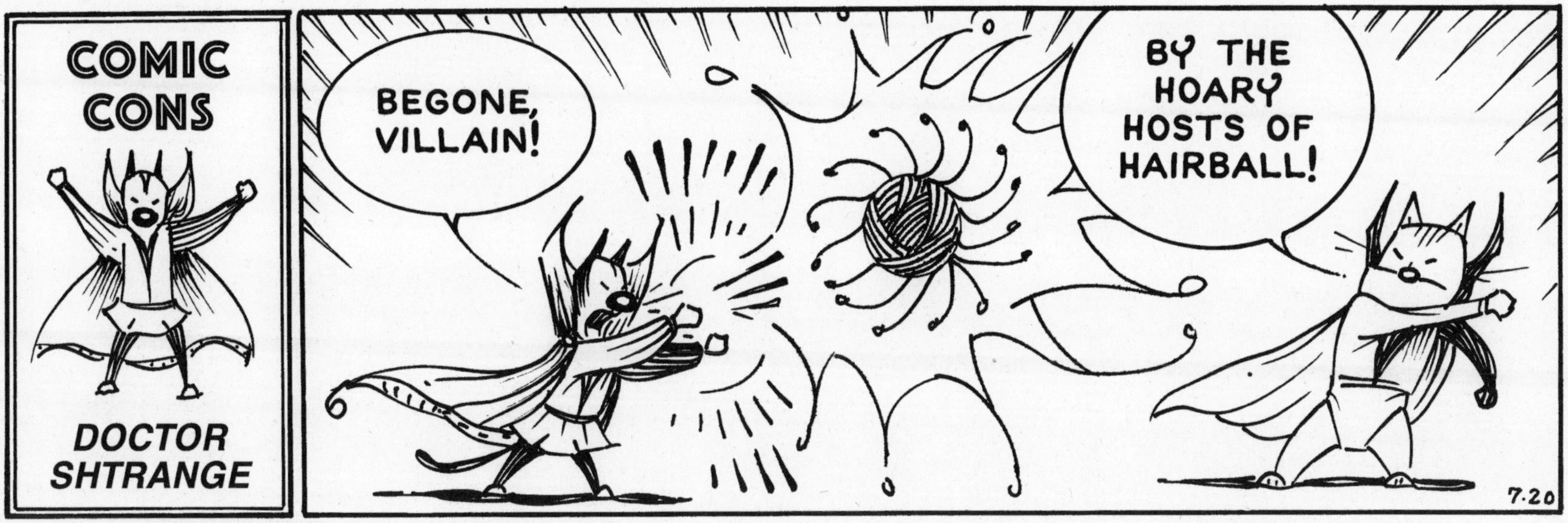
COMIC CONS
DOCTOR SHTRANGE
BEGONE, VILLAIN!
BY THE HOARY HOSTS OF HAIRBALL!
7·20

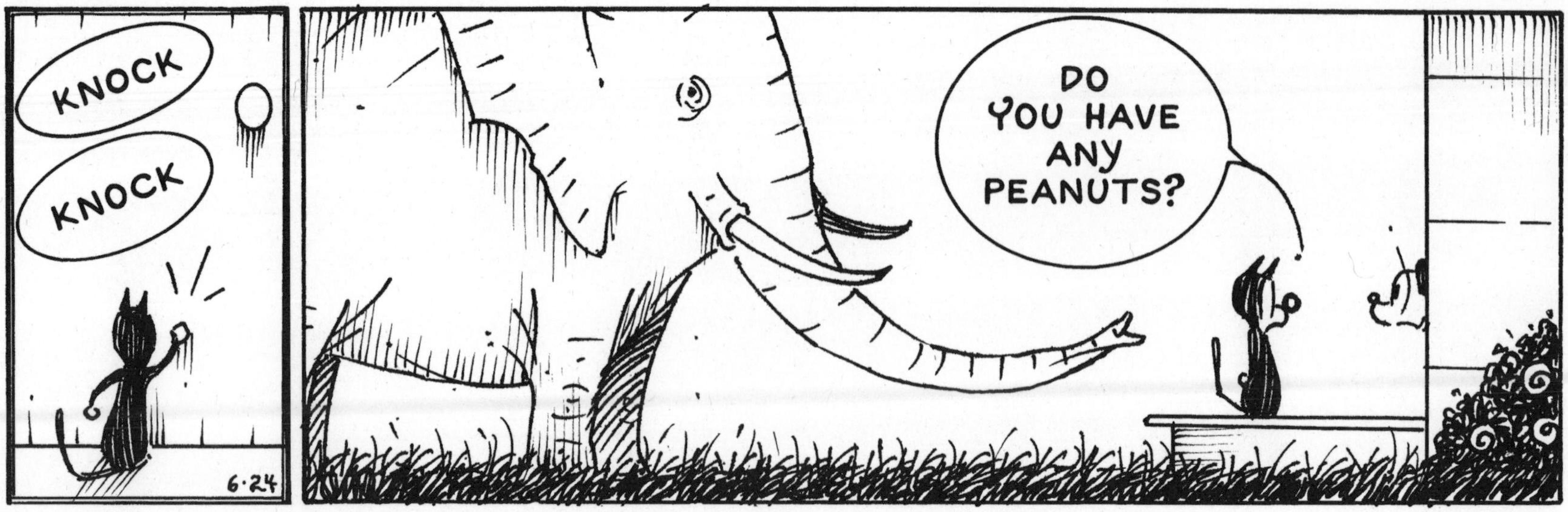
KNOCK
KNOCK
DO YOU HAVE ANY PEANUTS?
6·24

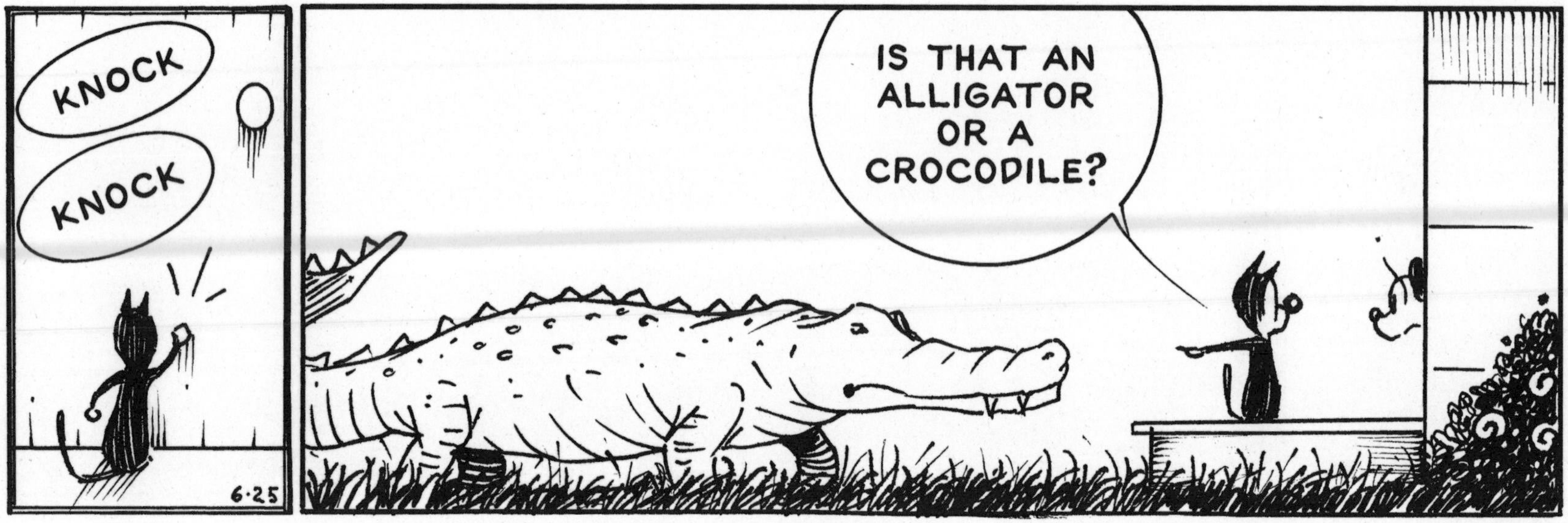
KNOCK
KNOCK
IS THAT AN ALLIGATOR OR A CROCODILE?
6·25

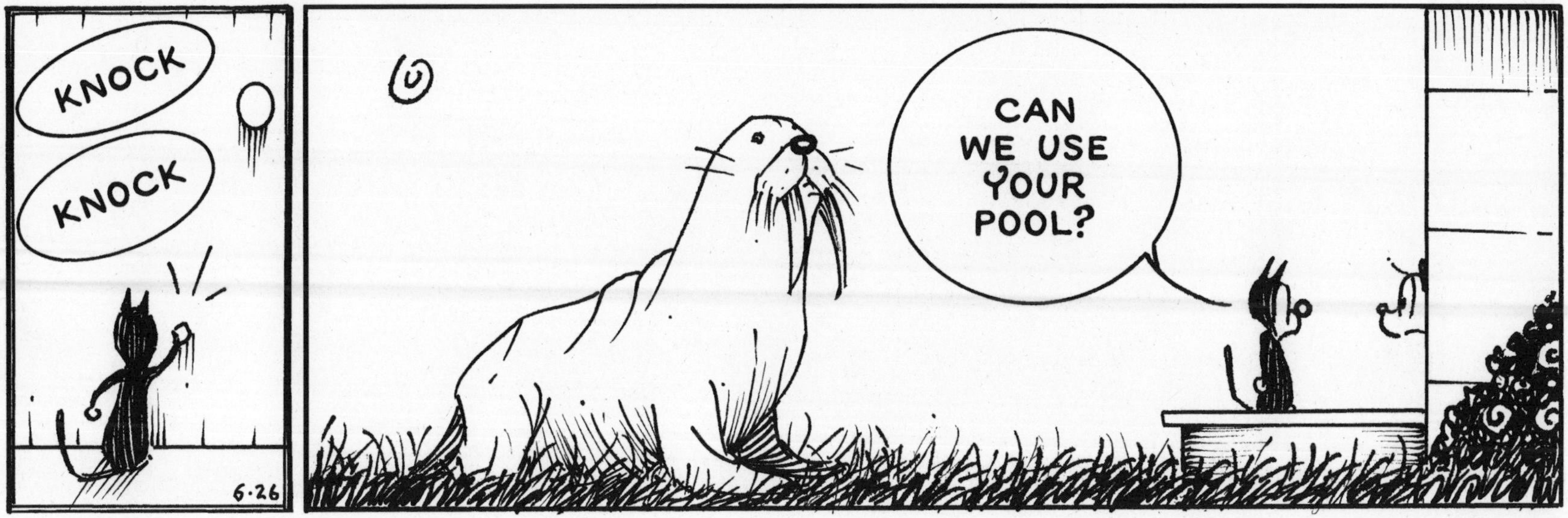
KNOCK
KNOCK
6·26
CAN WE USE YOUR POOL?

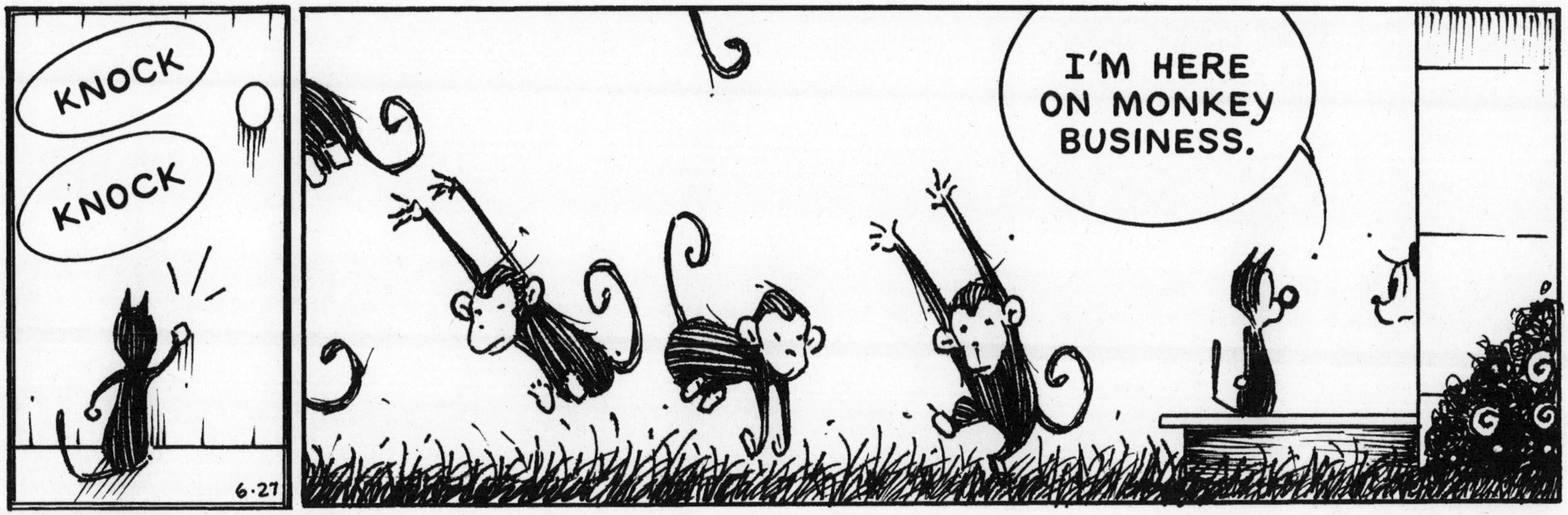
KNOCK
KNOCK
6·27
I'M HERE ON MONKEY BUSINESS.

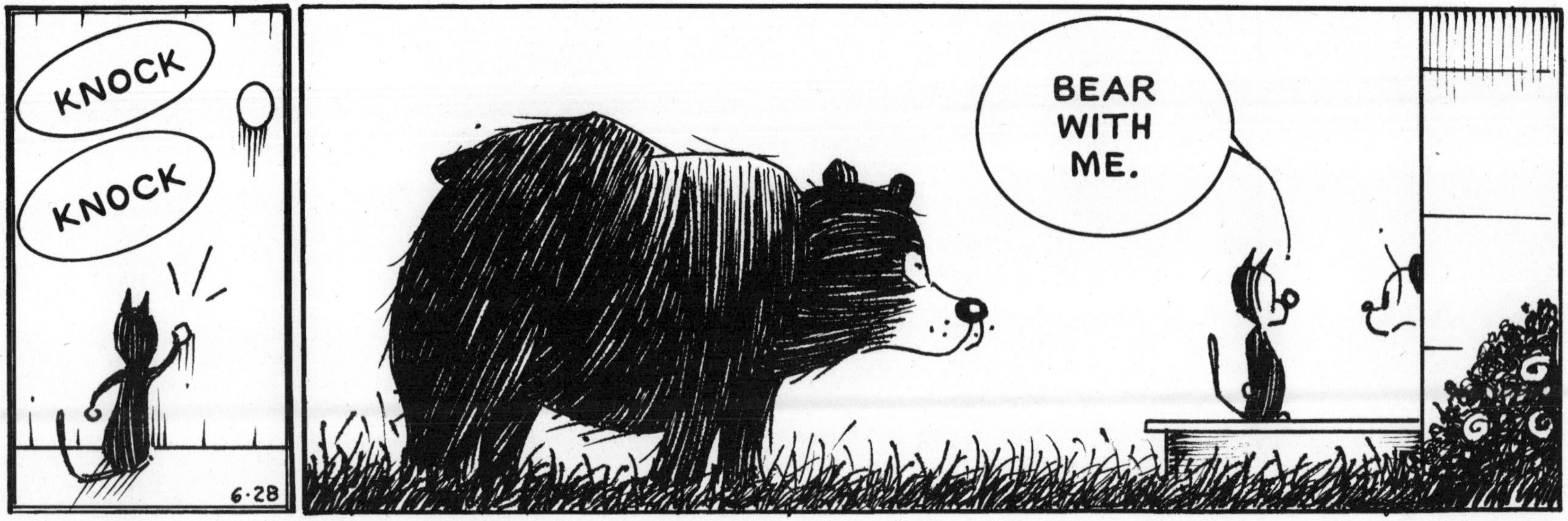
KNOCK
KNOCK
6·28
BEAR WITH ME.

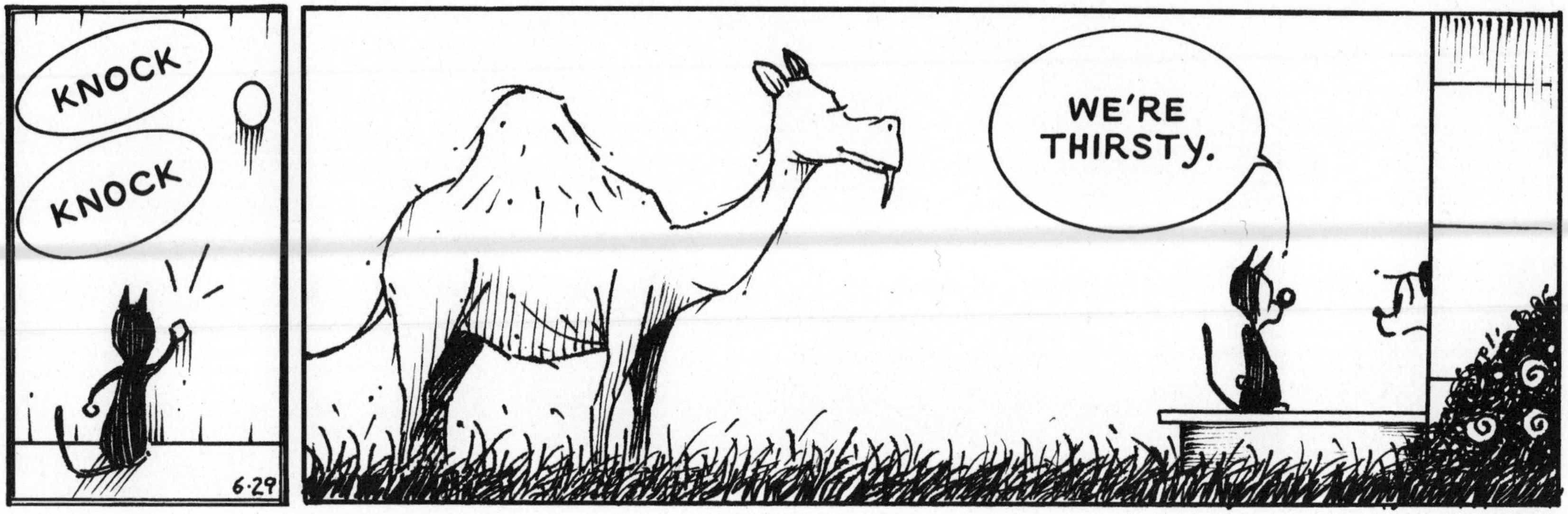
KNOCK
KNOCK
6·29
WE'RE THIRSTY.

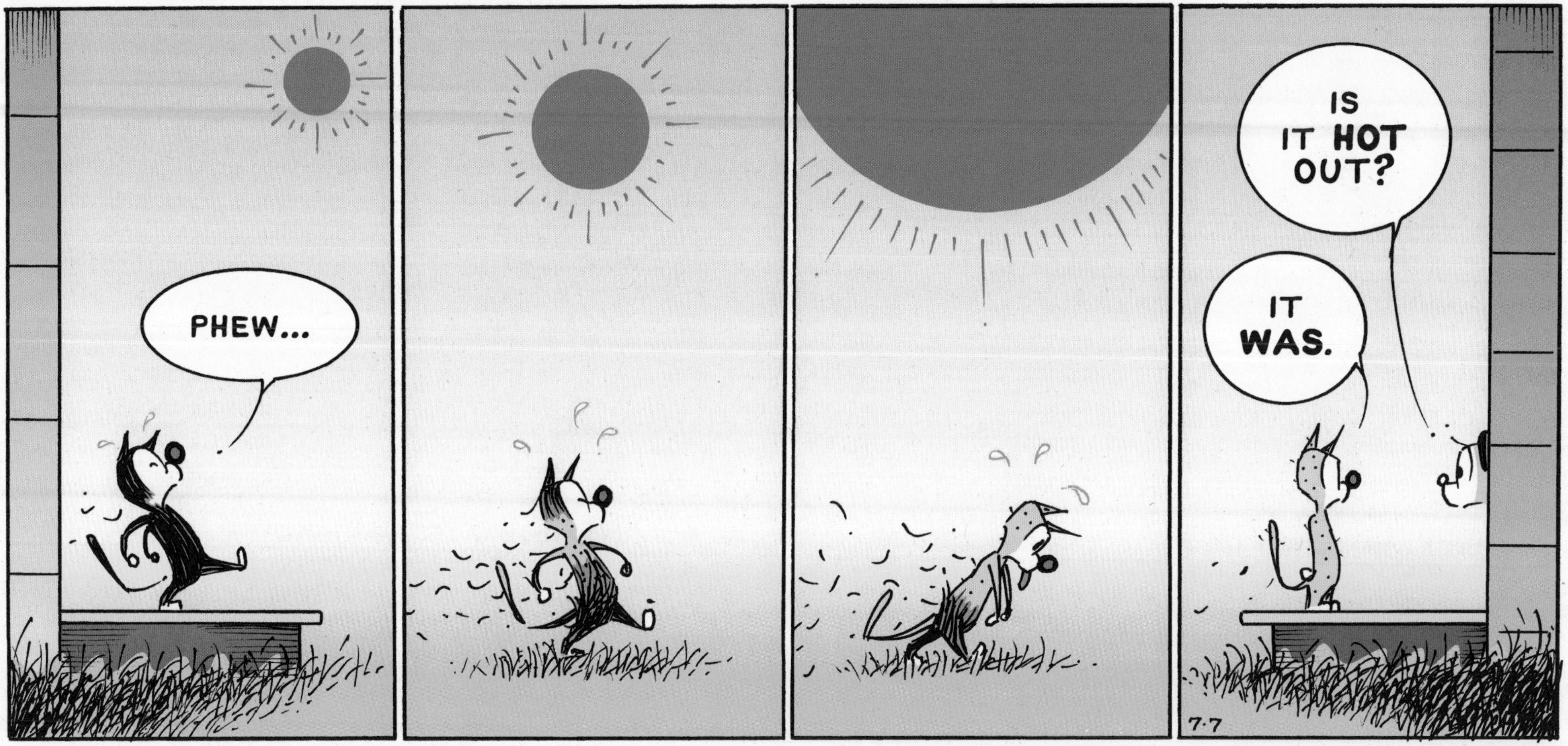

PHEW...
IS IT HOT OUT?
IT WAS.
7·7

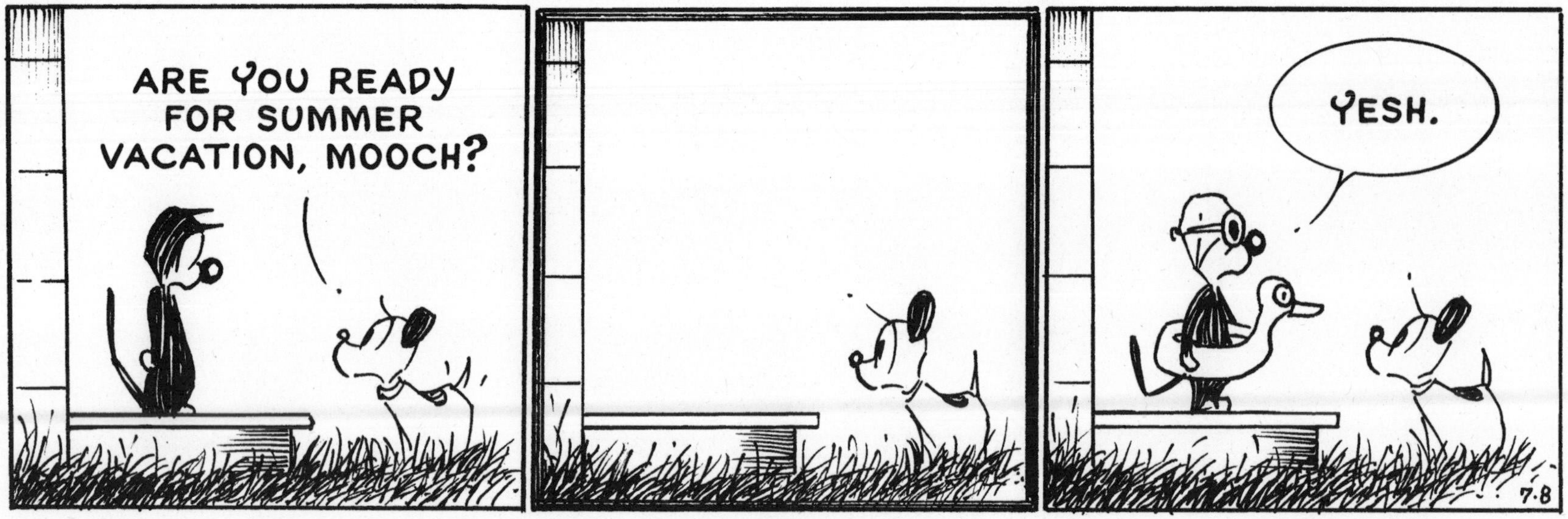
ARE YOU READY FOR SUMMER VACATION, MOOCH?
YESH.
7.8

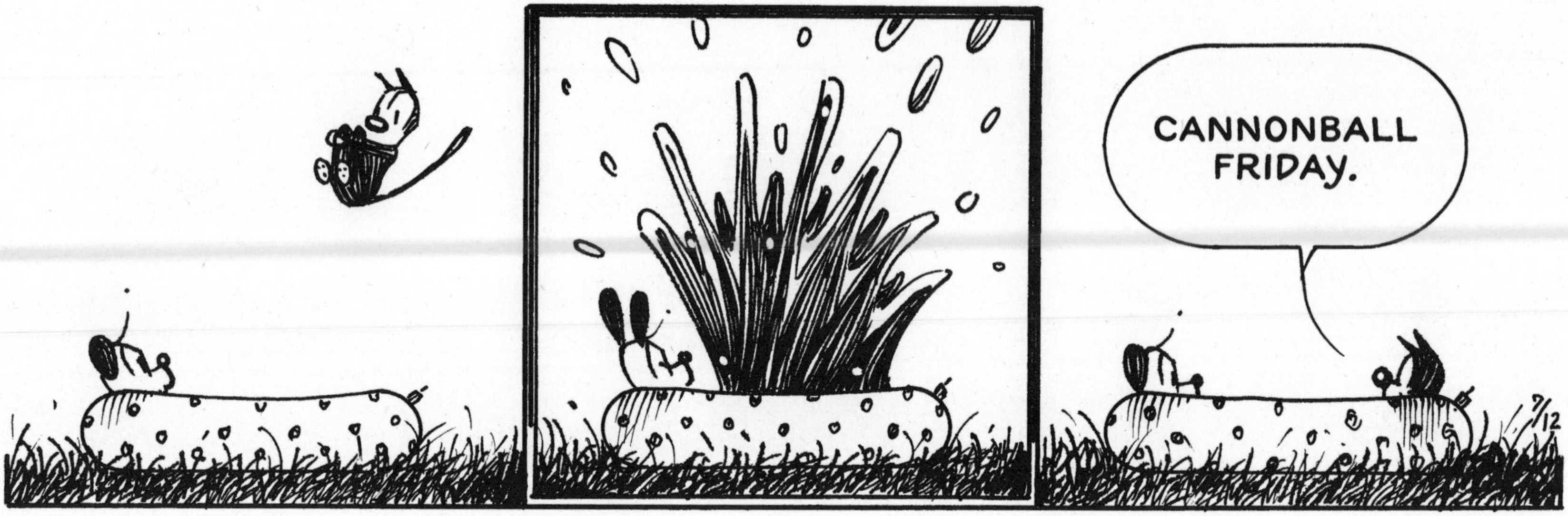
CANNONBALL FRIDAY.
9/12

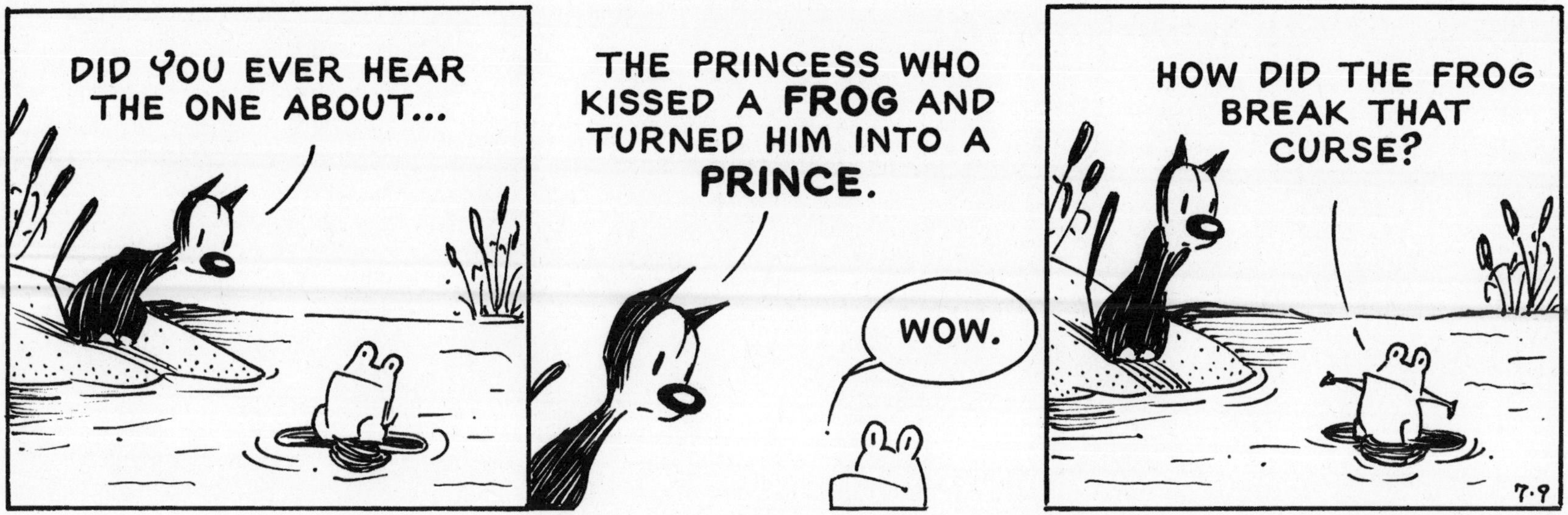
DID YOU EVER HEAR THE ONE ABOUT...
THE PRINCESS WHO KISSED A FROG AND TURNED HIM INTO A PRINCE.
WOW.
HOW DID THE FROG BREAK THAT CURSE?
7.9

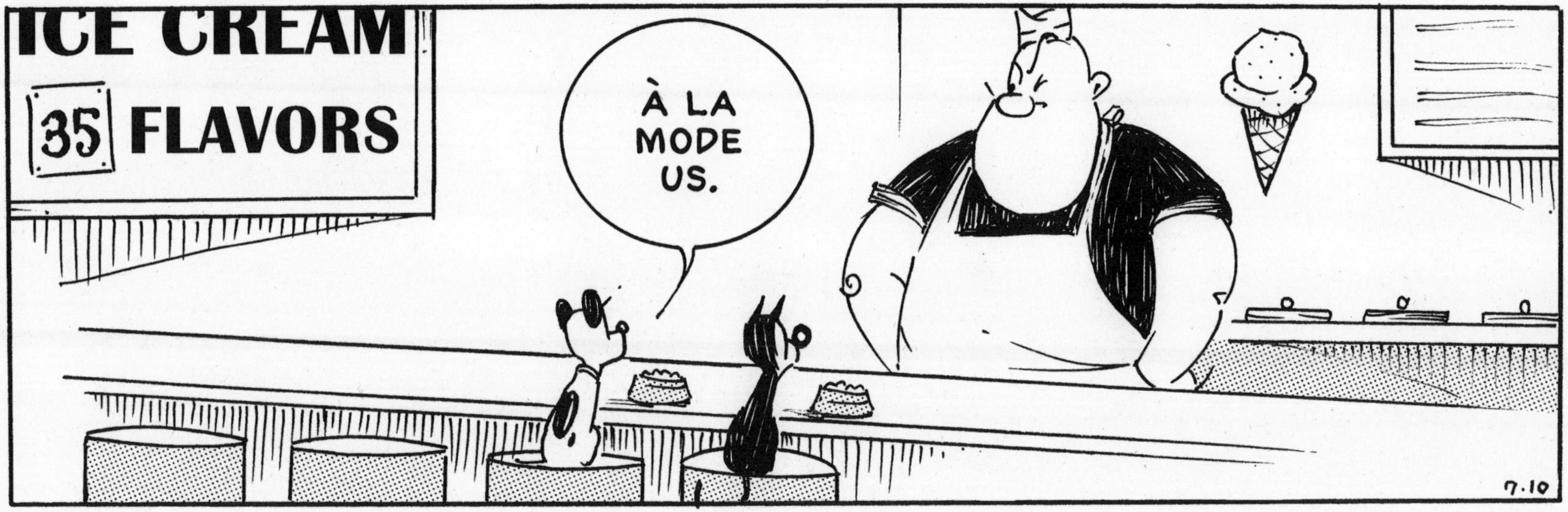
ICE CREAM
35 FLAVORS
À LA MODE US.
7.10

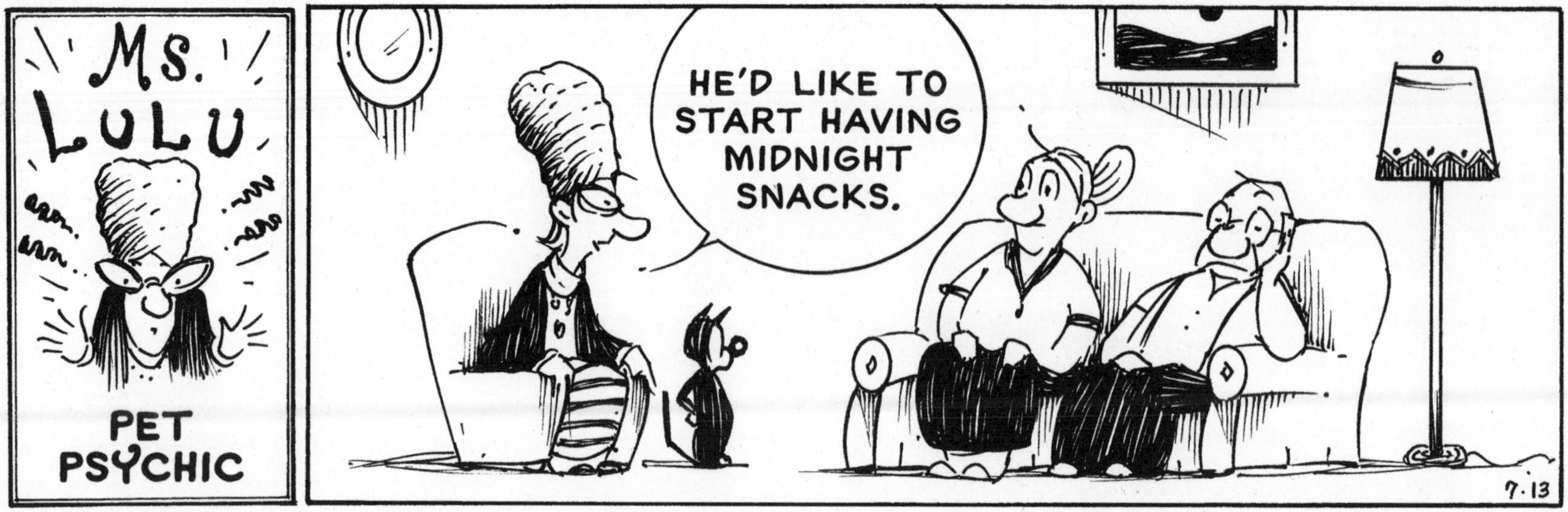
MS. LULU
PET PSYCHIC
HE'D LIKE TO START HAVING MIDNIGHT SNACKS.
7.13

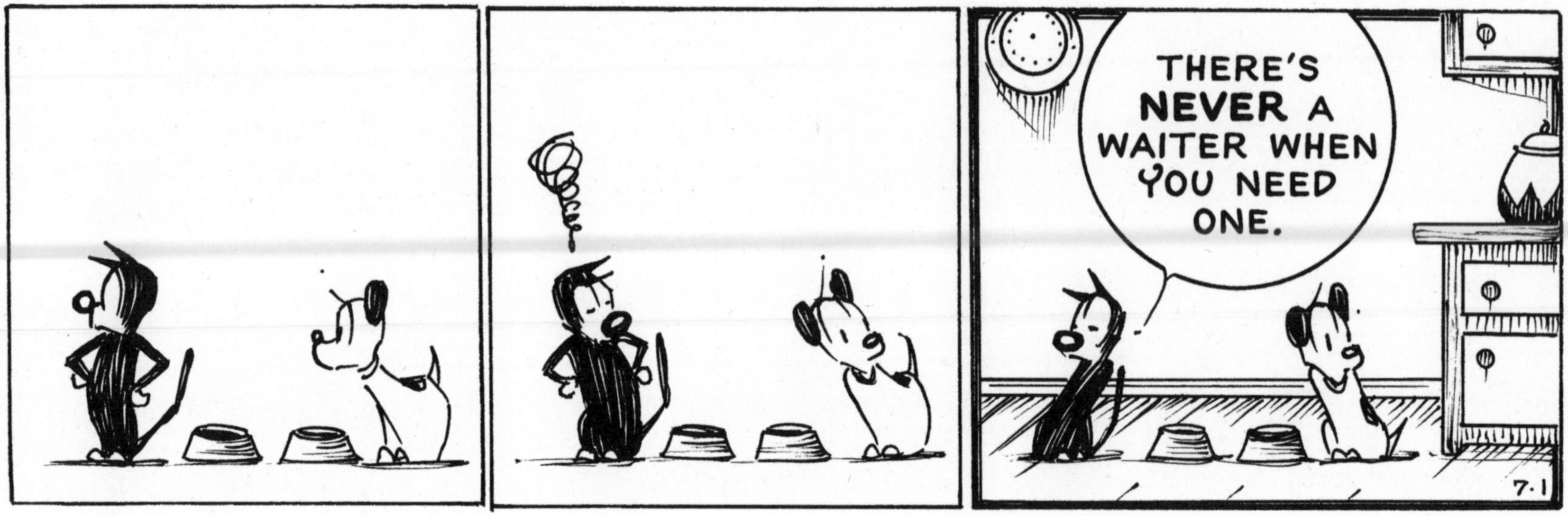
THERE'S **NEVER** A WAITER WHEN YOU NEED ONE.
7.1

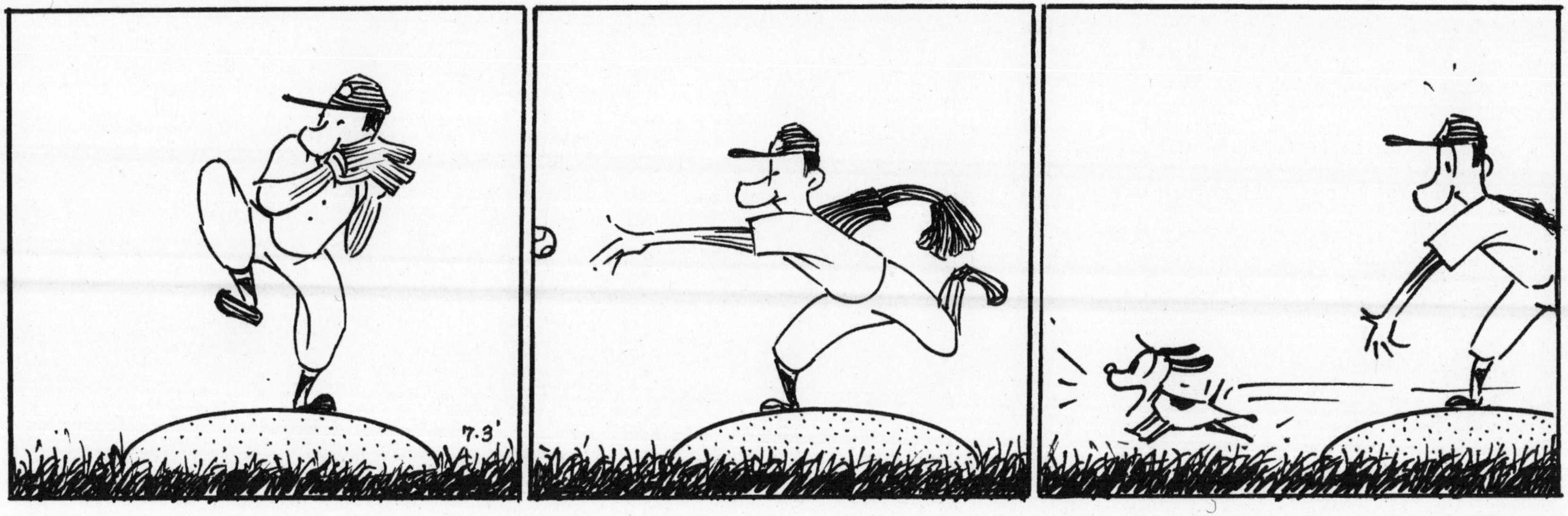
7.3

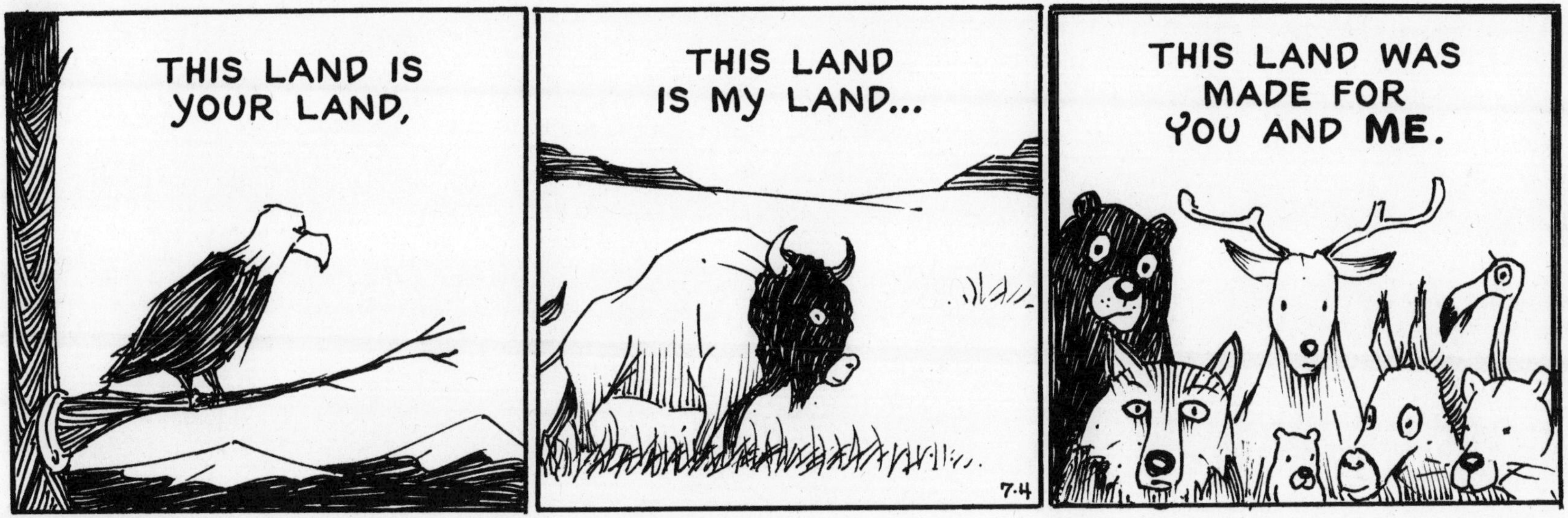
THIS LAND IS YOUR LAND,
THIS LAND IS MY LAND...
7.4
THIS LAND WAS MADE FOR YOU AND **ME**.

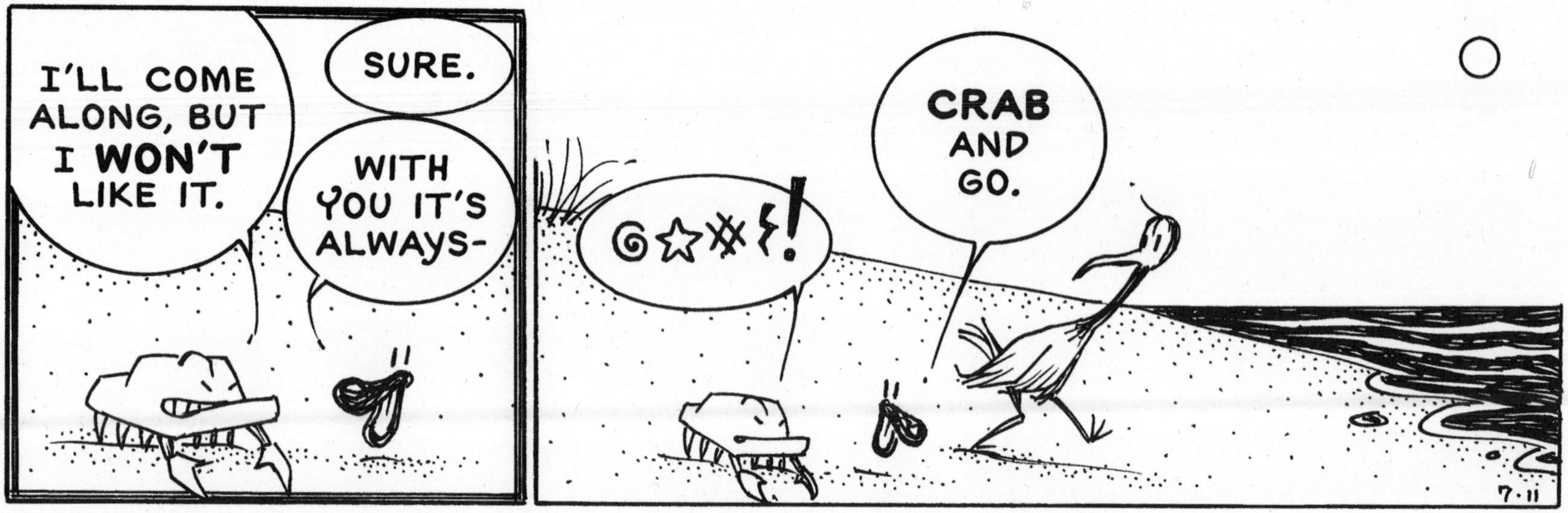
I'LL COME ALONG, BUT I **WON'T** LIKE IT.
SURE.
WITH YOU IT'S ALWAYS-
CRAB AND GO.
7·11

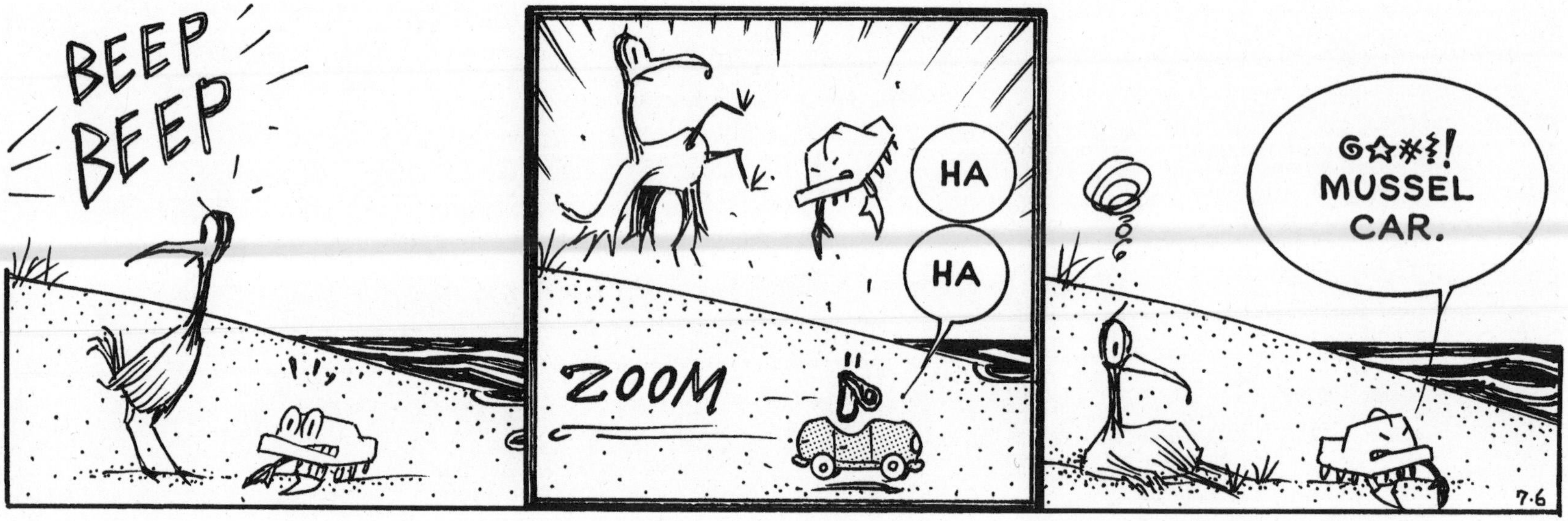
BEEP BEEP
ZOOM
HA
HA
MUSSEL CAR.
7·6

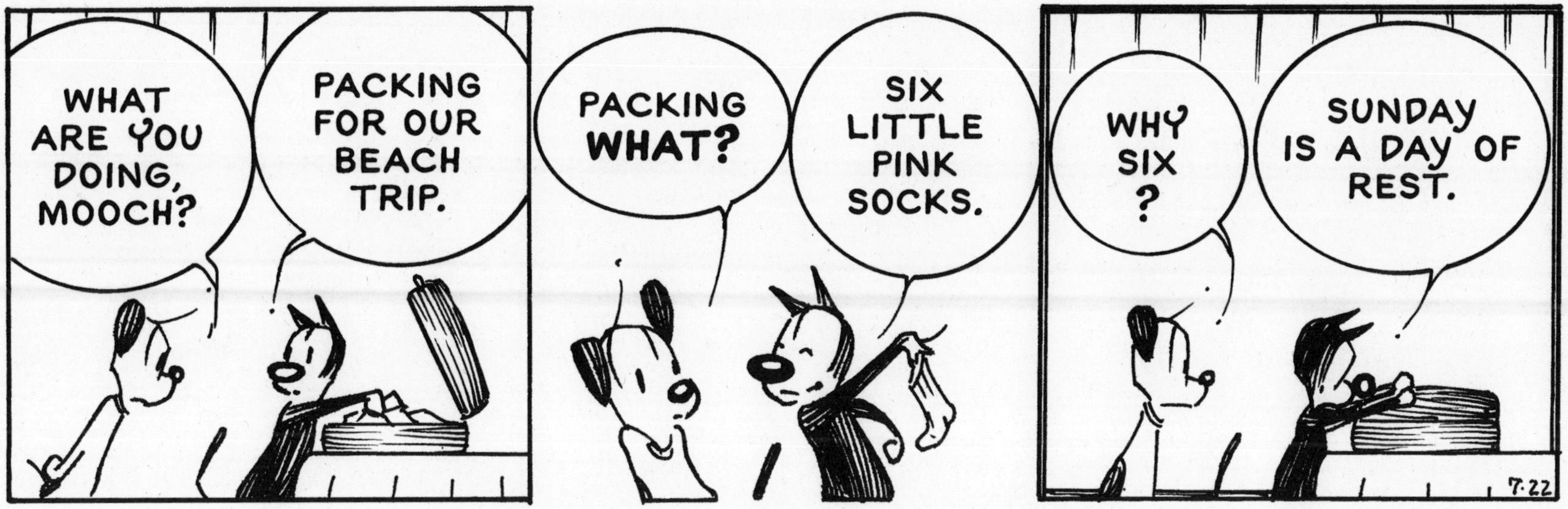
WHAT ARE YOU DOING, MOOCH?
PACKING FOR OUR BEACH TRIP.
PACKING WHAT?
SIX LITTLE PINK SOCKS.
WHY SIX ?
SUNDAY IS A DAY OF REST.
7·22

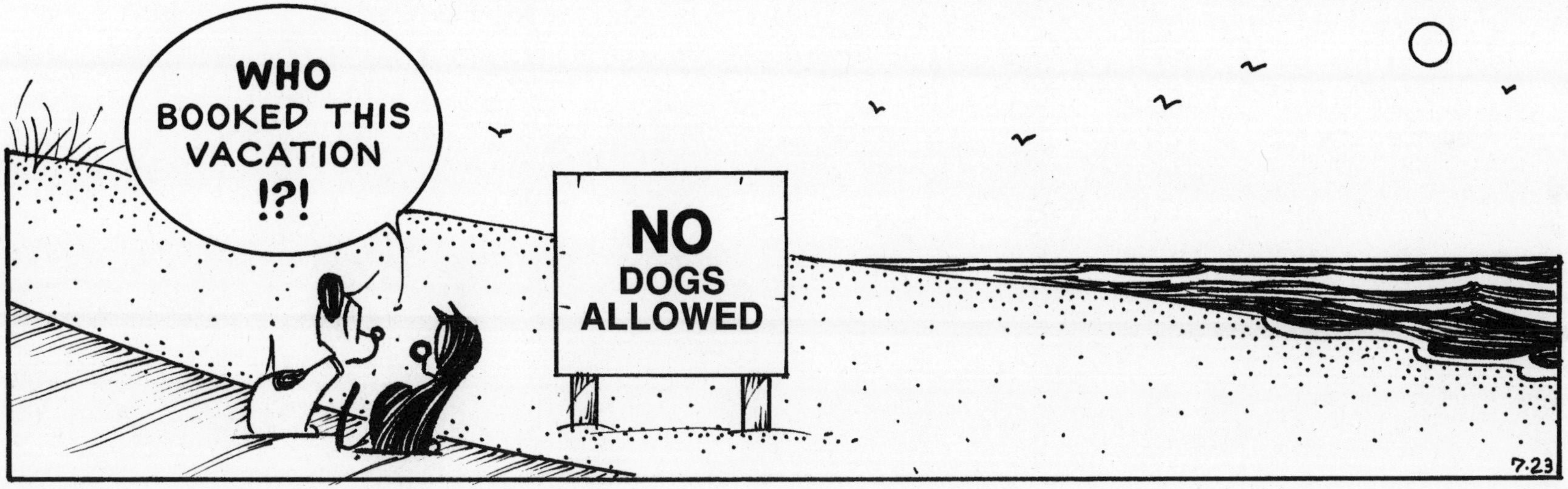
WHO BOOKED THIS VACATION !?!
NO DOGS ALLOWED
7·23

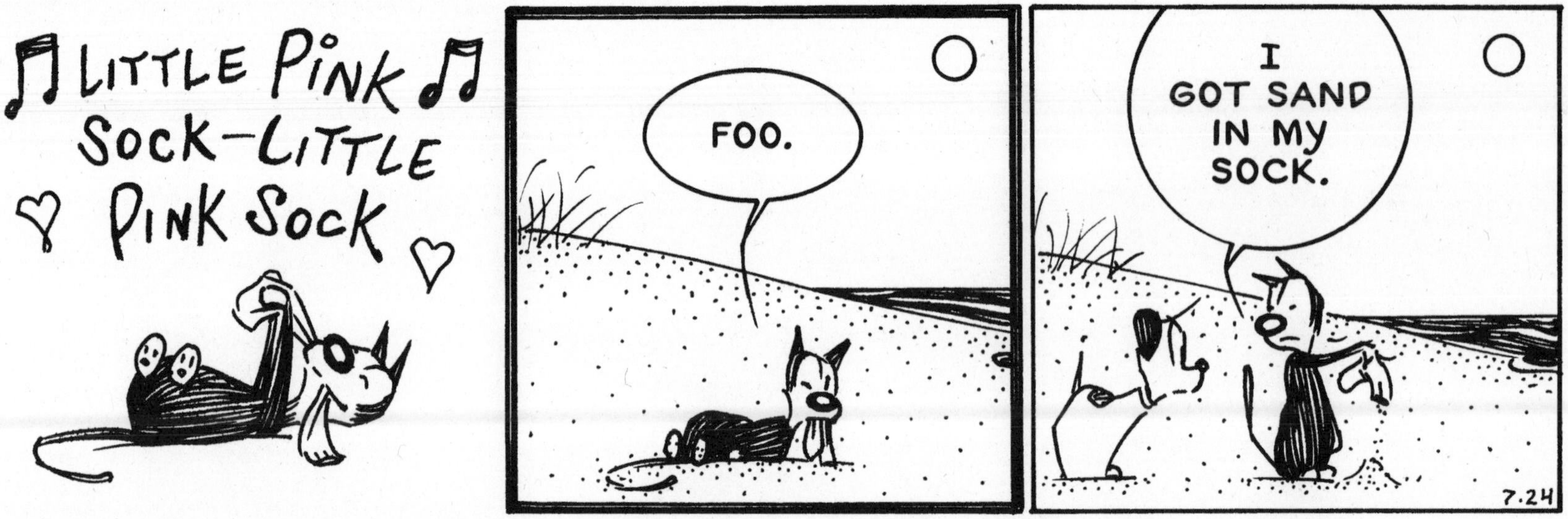
LITTLE PINK SOCK–LITTLE PINK SOCK
FOO.
I GOT SAND IN MY SOCK.
7.24

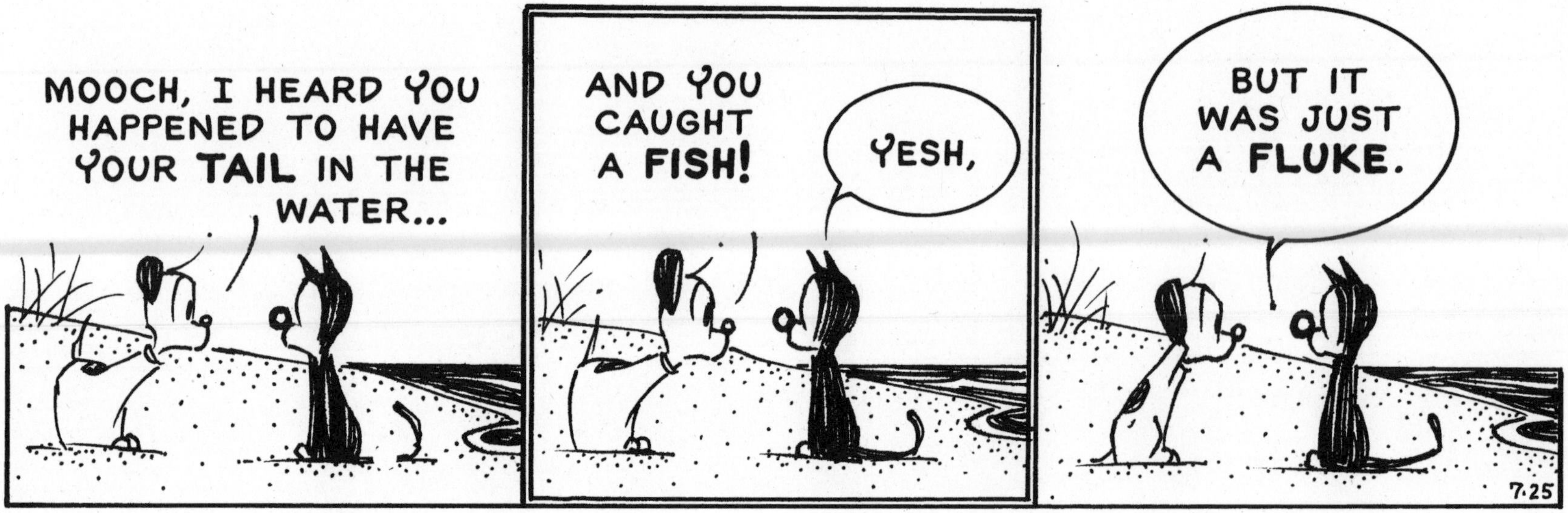
MOOCH, I HEARD YOU HAPPENED TO HAVE YOUR TAIL IN THE WATER...
AND YOU CAUGHT A FISH!
YESH,
BUT IT WAS JUST A FLUKE.
7.25

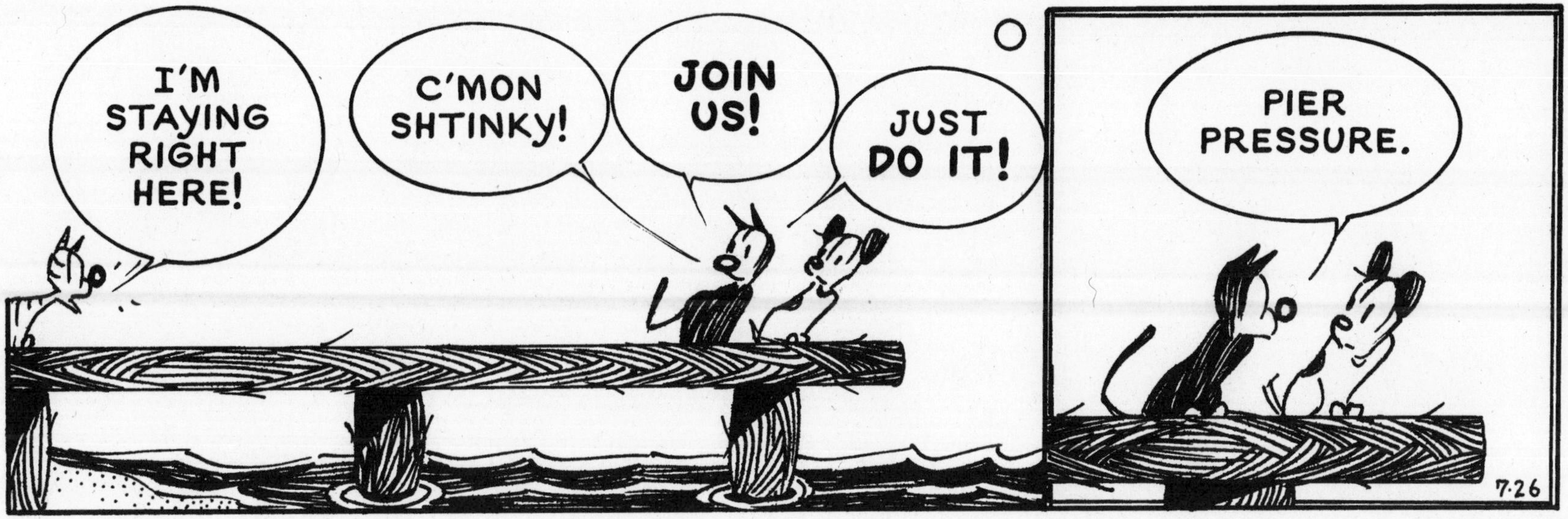
I'M STAYING RIGHT HERE!
C'MON SHTINKY!
JOIN US!
JUST DO IT!
PIER PRESSURE.
7·26

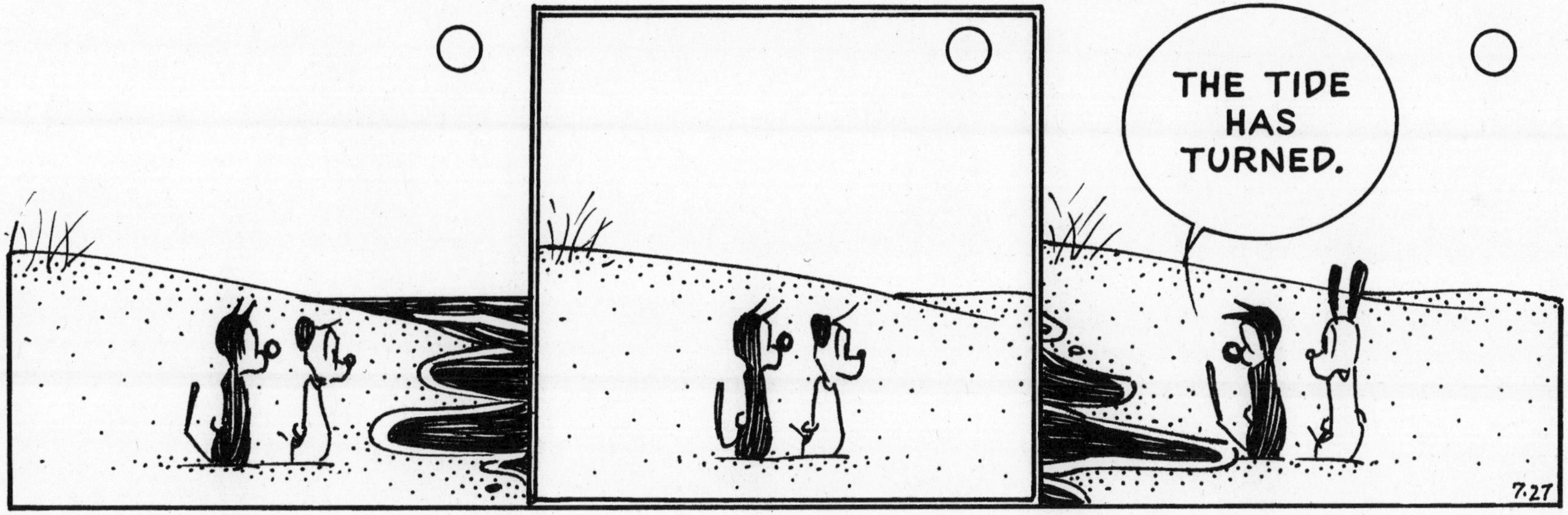
THE TIDE HAS TURNED.
7·27

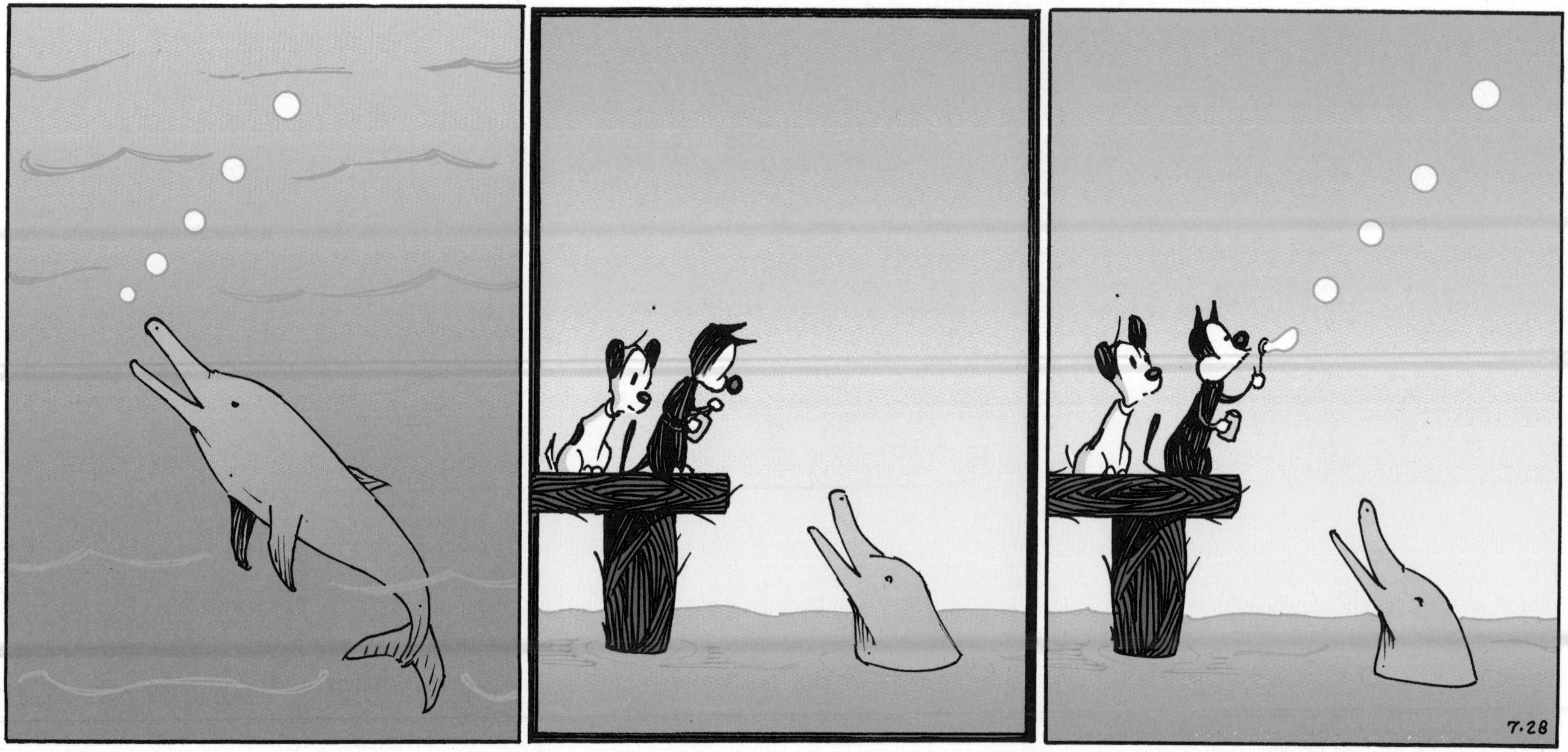
7.28

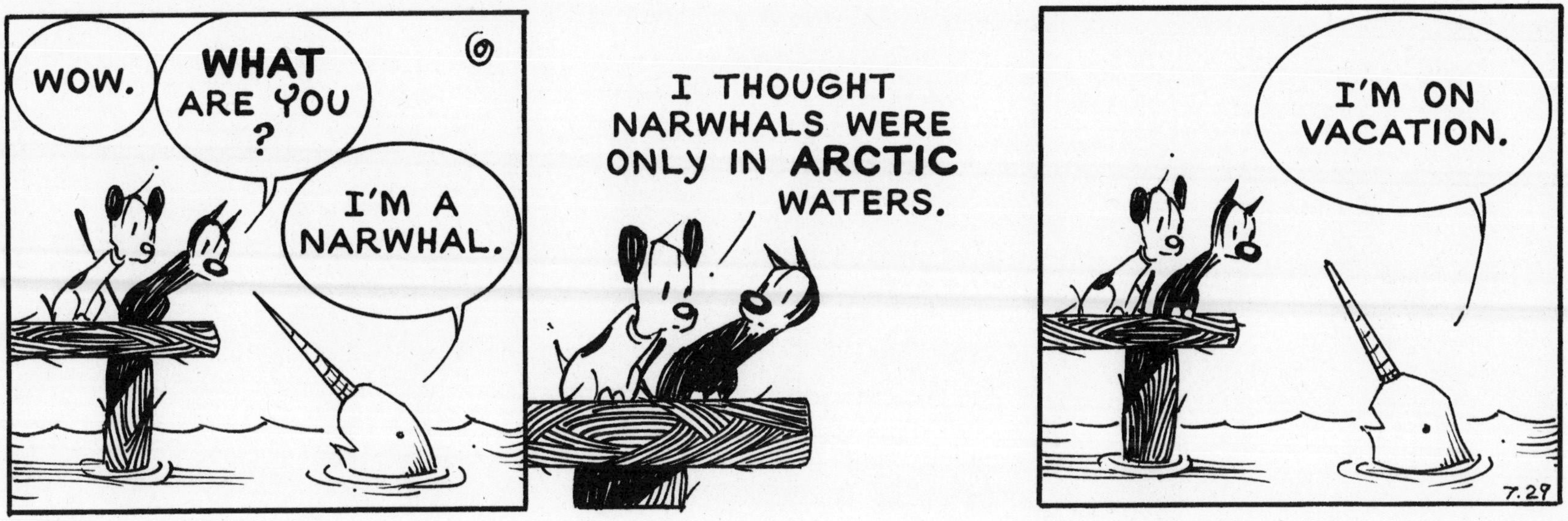
WOW.
WHAT ARE YOU ?
I'M A NARWHAL.
I THOUGHT NARWHALS WERE ONLY IN ARCTIC WATERS.
I'M ON VACATION.
7.29

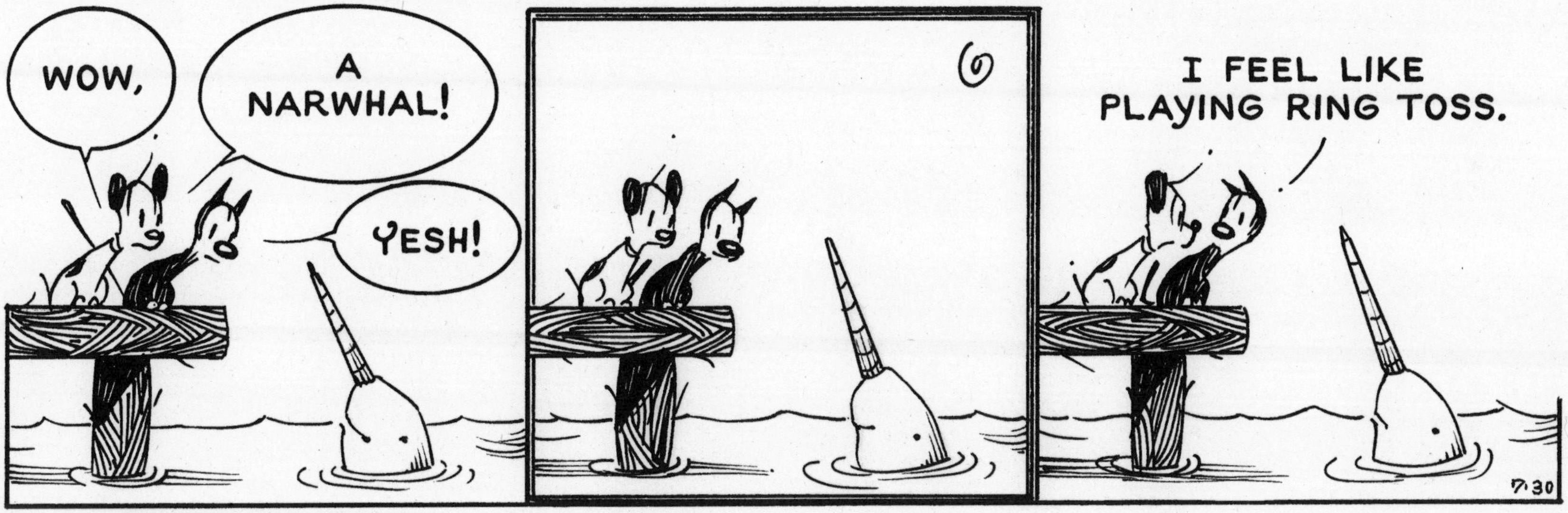
WOW,
A NARWHAL!
YESH!
I FEEL LIKE PLAYING RING TOSS.
7.30

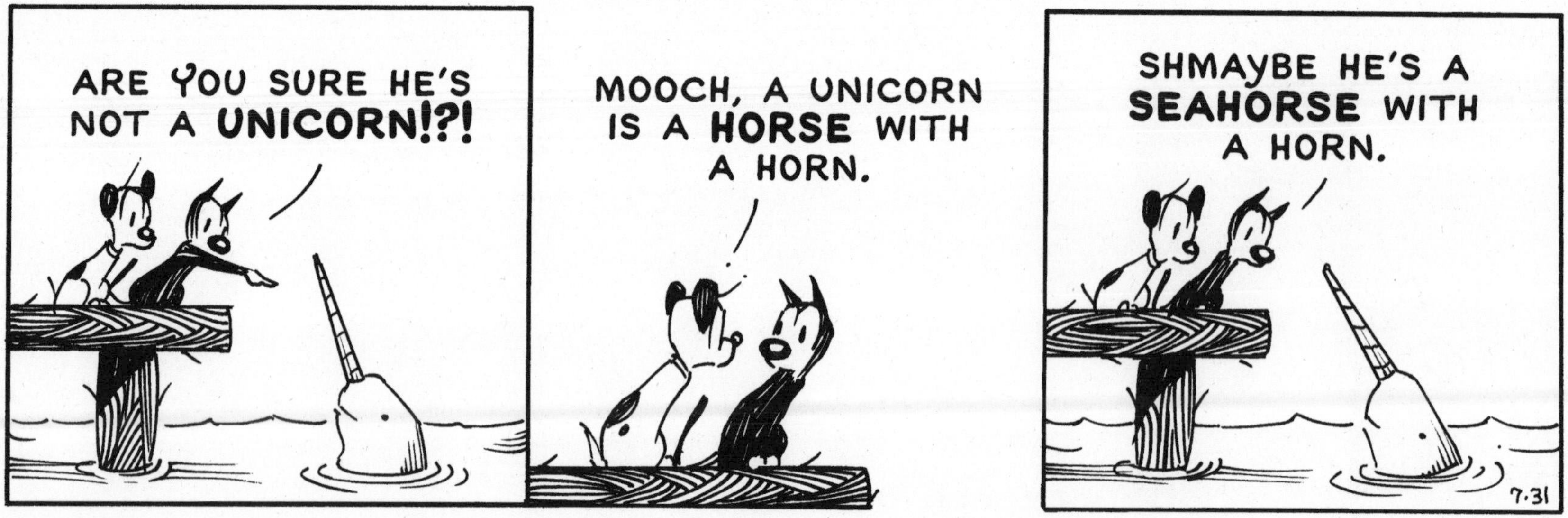
ARE YOU SURE HE'S NOT A **UNICORN!?!**
MOOCH, A UNICORN IS A **HORSE** WITH A HORN.
SHMAYBE HE'S A **SEAHORSE** WITH A HORN.
7·31

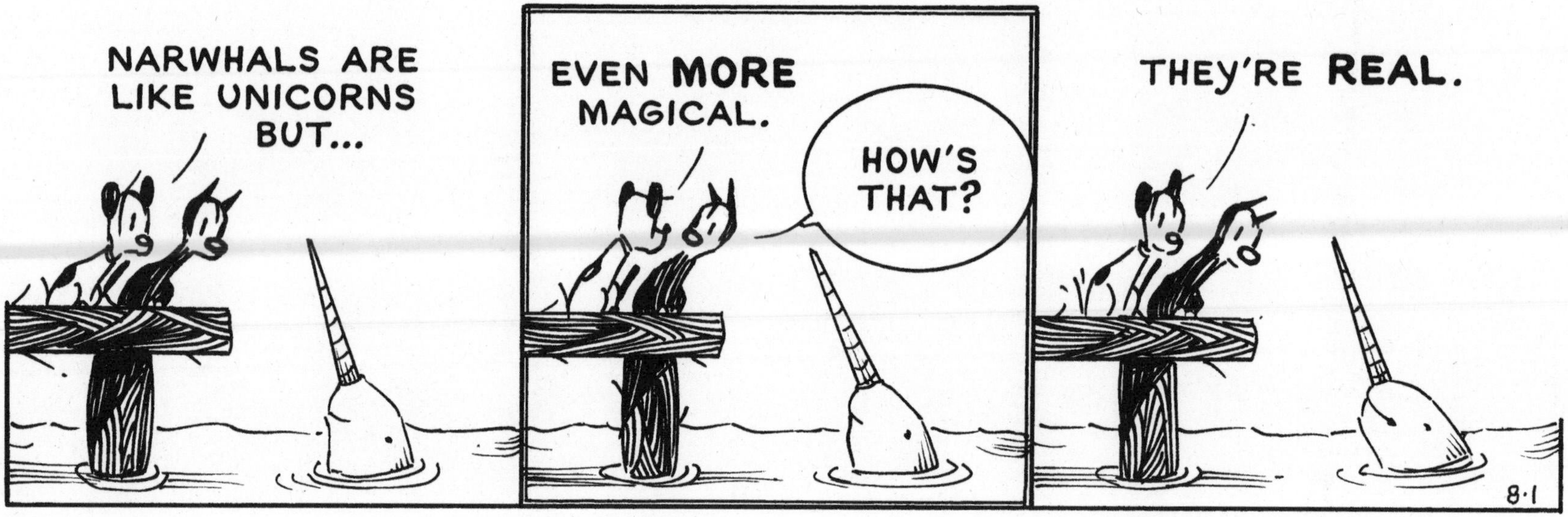
NARWHALS ARE LIKE UNICORNS BUT...
EVEN **MORE** MAGICAL.
HOW'S THAT?
THEY'RE **REAL**.
8·1

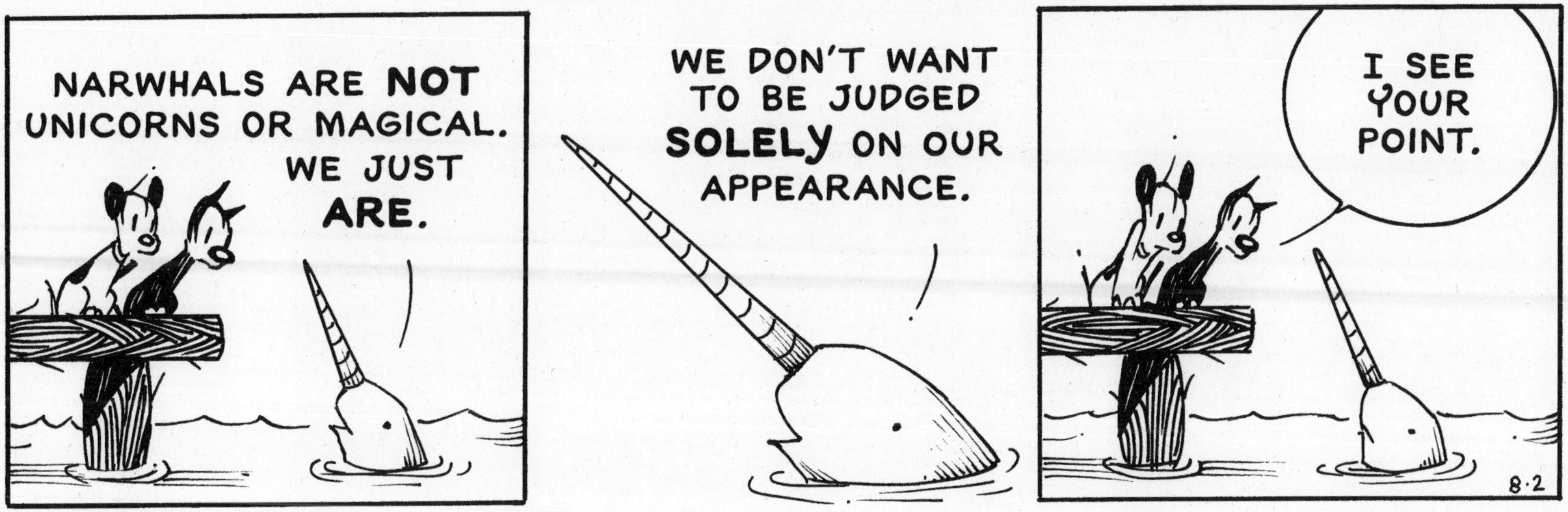
NARWHALS ARE NOT UNICORNS OR MAGICAL.
WE JUST ARE.
WE DON'T WANT TO BE JUDGED SOLELY ON OUR APPEARANCE.
I SEE YOUR POINT.
8·2

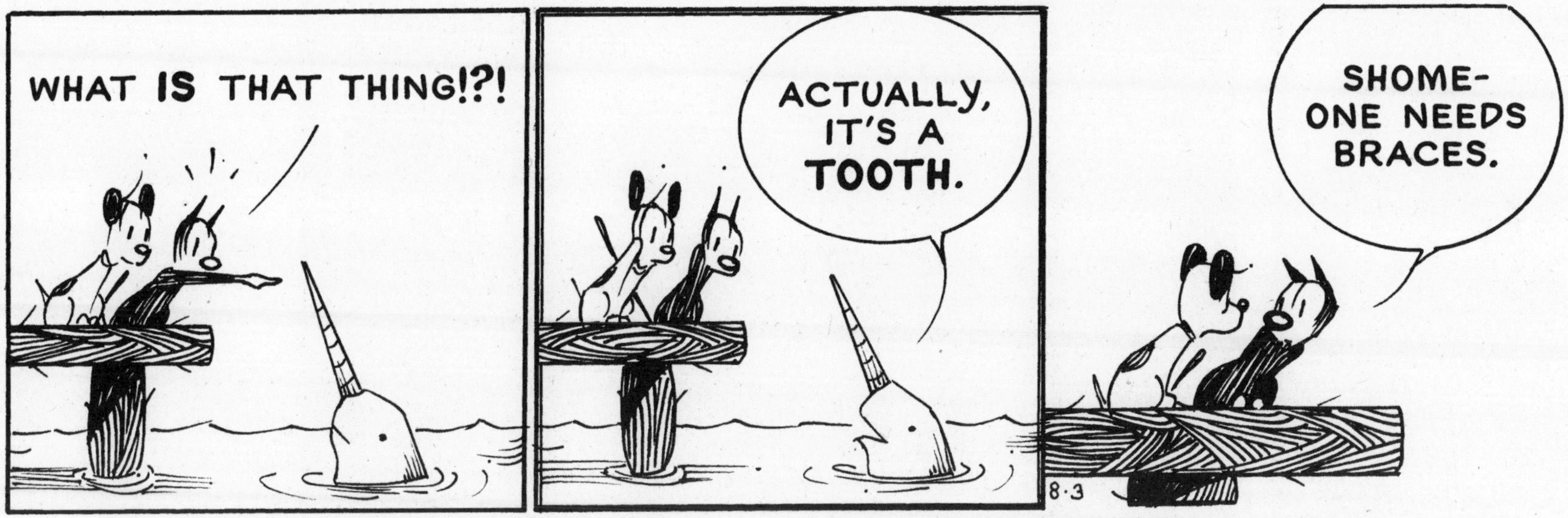
WHAT IS THAT THING!?!
ACTUALLY, IT'S A TOOTH.
SHOME-ONE NEEDS BRACES.
8·3

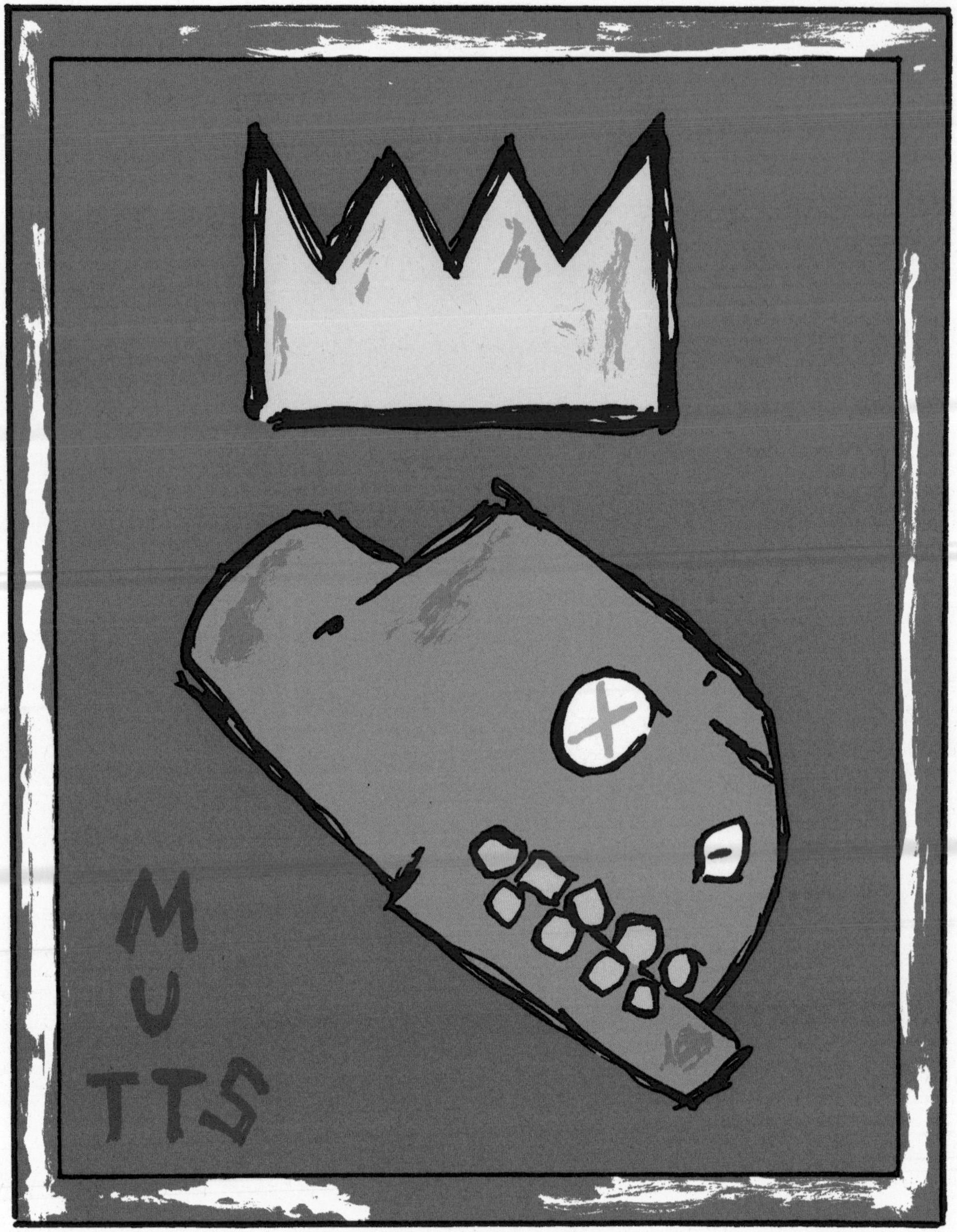
MUTTS

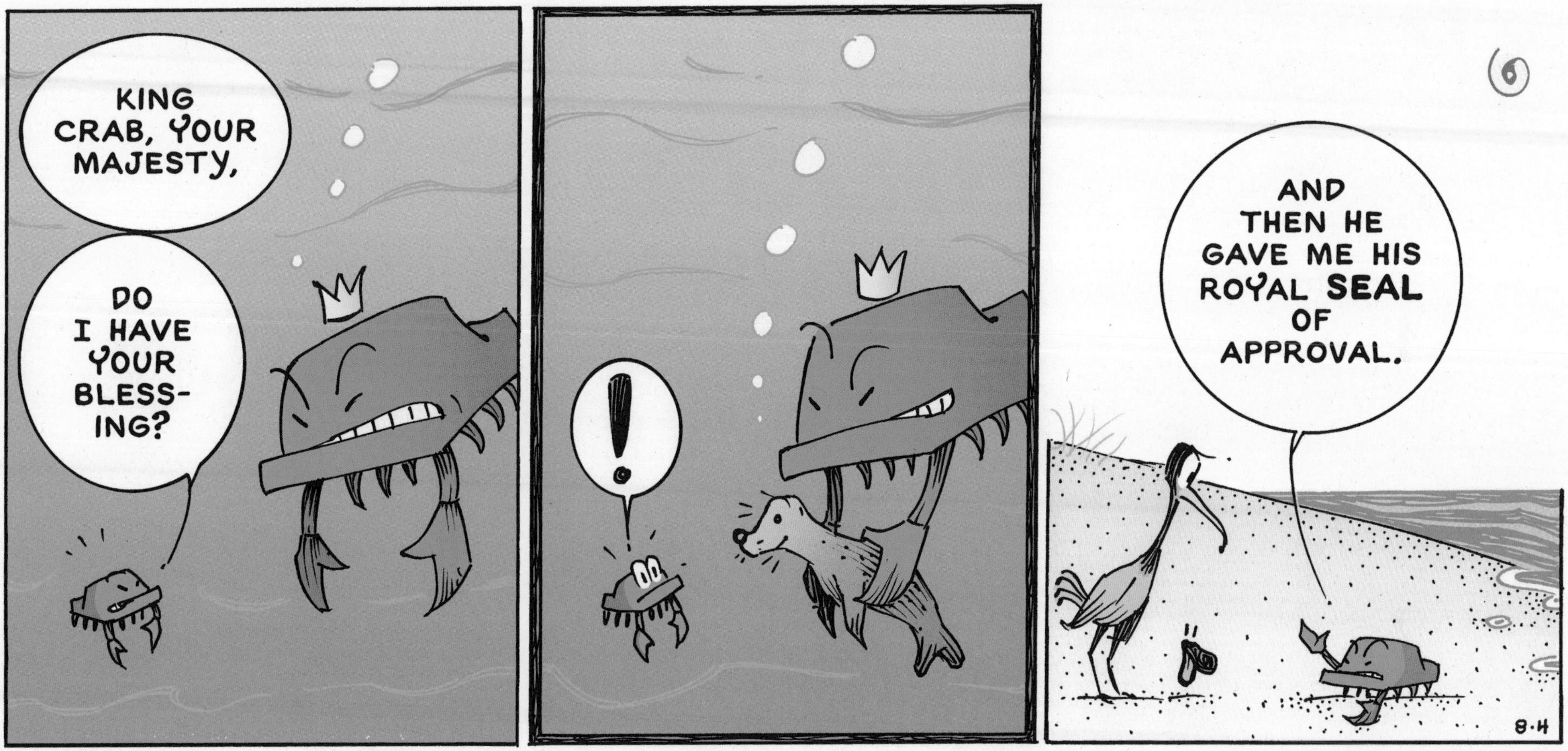
KING CRAB, YOUR MAJESTY,
DO I HAVE YOUR BLESS-ING?
!
AND THEN HE GAVE ME HIS ROYAL **SEAL** OF APPROVAL.
8·H

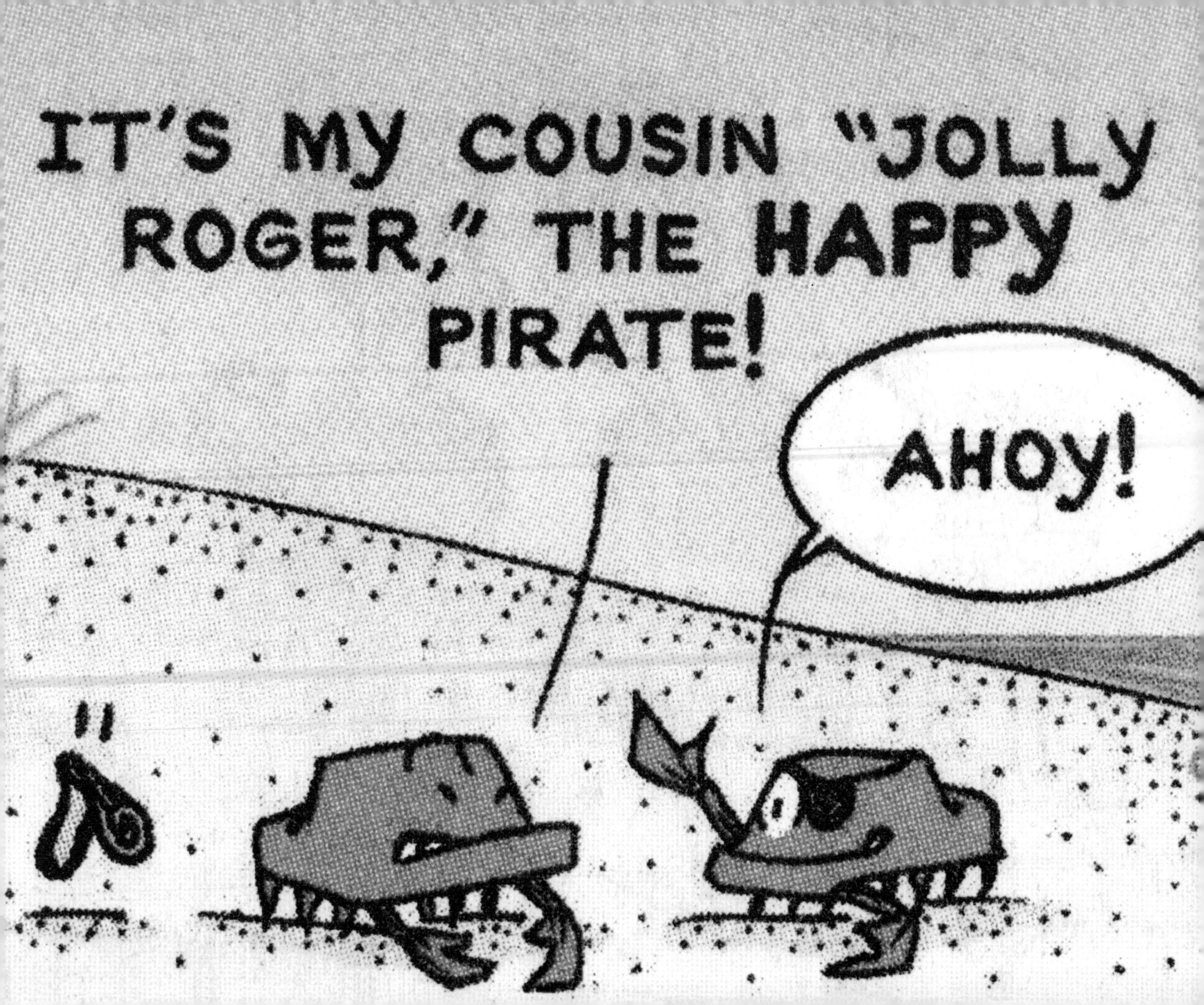
IT'S MY COUSIN "JOLLY ROGER," THE HAPPY PIRATE!
AHOY!

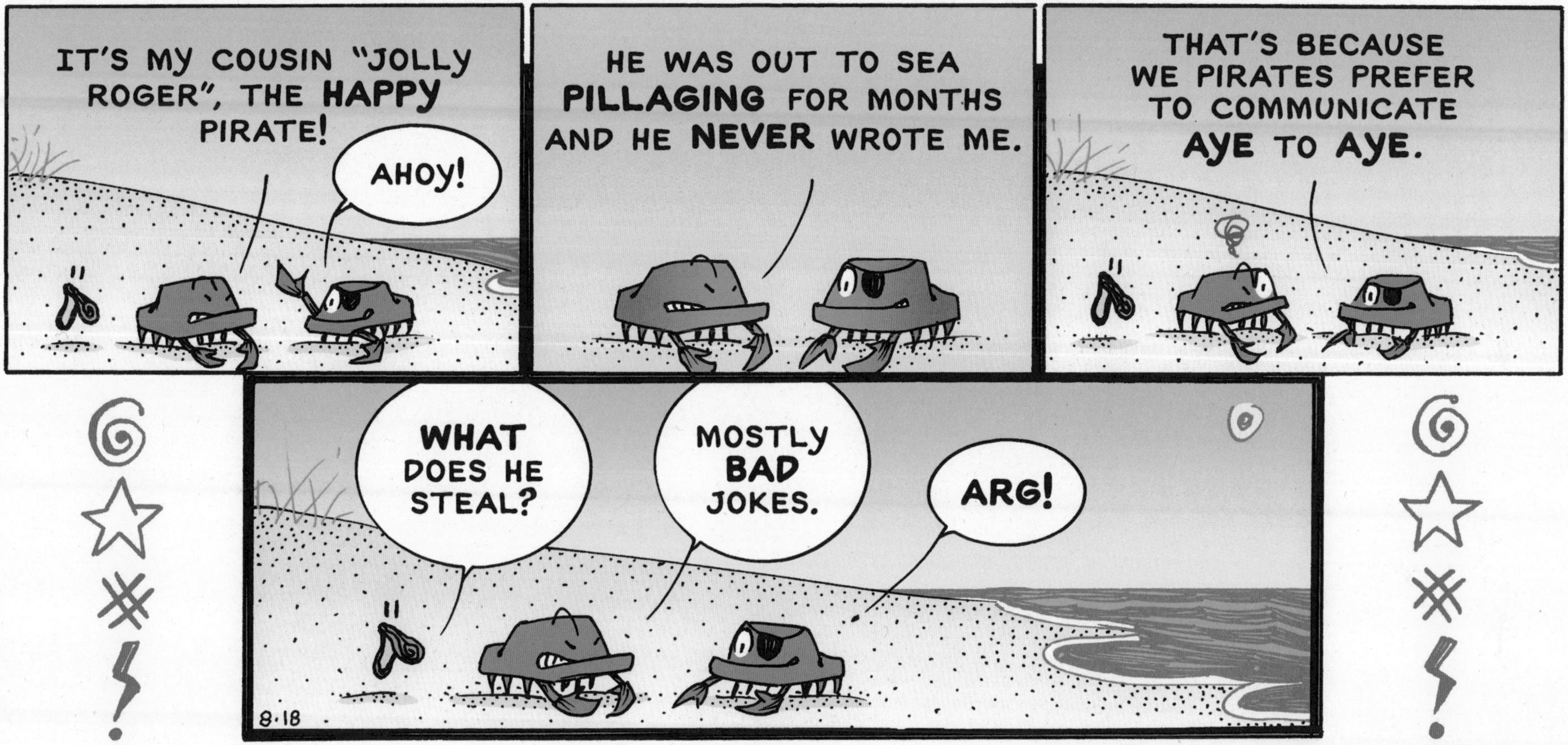
IT'S MY COUSIN "JOLLY ROGER", THE HAPPY PIRATE!
AHOY!
HE WAS OUT TO SEA PILLAGING FOR MONTHS AND HE NEVER WROTE ME.
THAT'S BECAUSE WE PIRATES PREFER TO COMMUNICATE AYE TO AYE.
WHAT DOES HE STEAL?
MOSTLY BAD JOKES.
ARG!
8·18

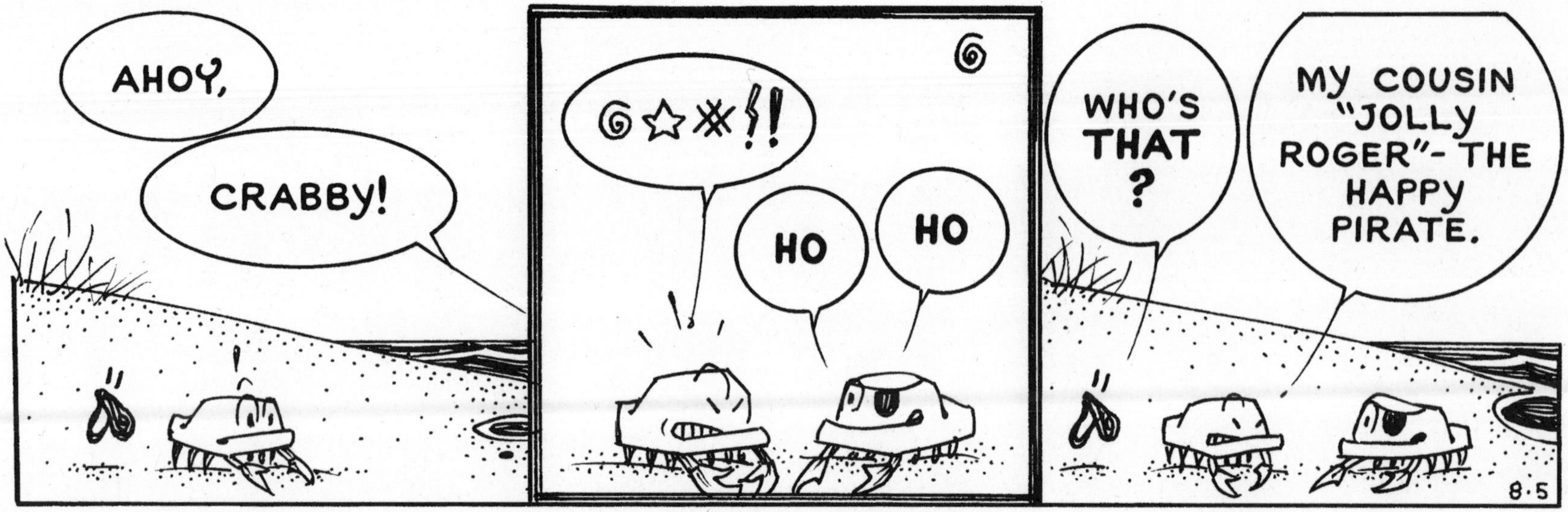
AHOY,
CRABBY!
@☆#!!
HO
HO
WHO'S THAT ?
MY COUSIN "JOLLY ROGER"- THE HAPPY PIRATE.
8·5

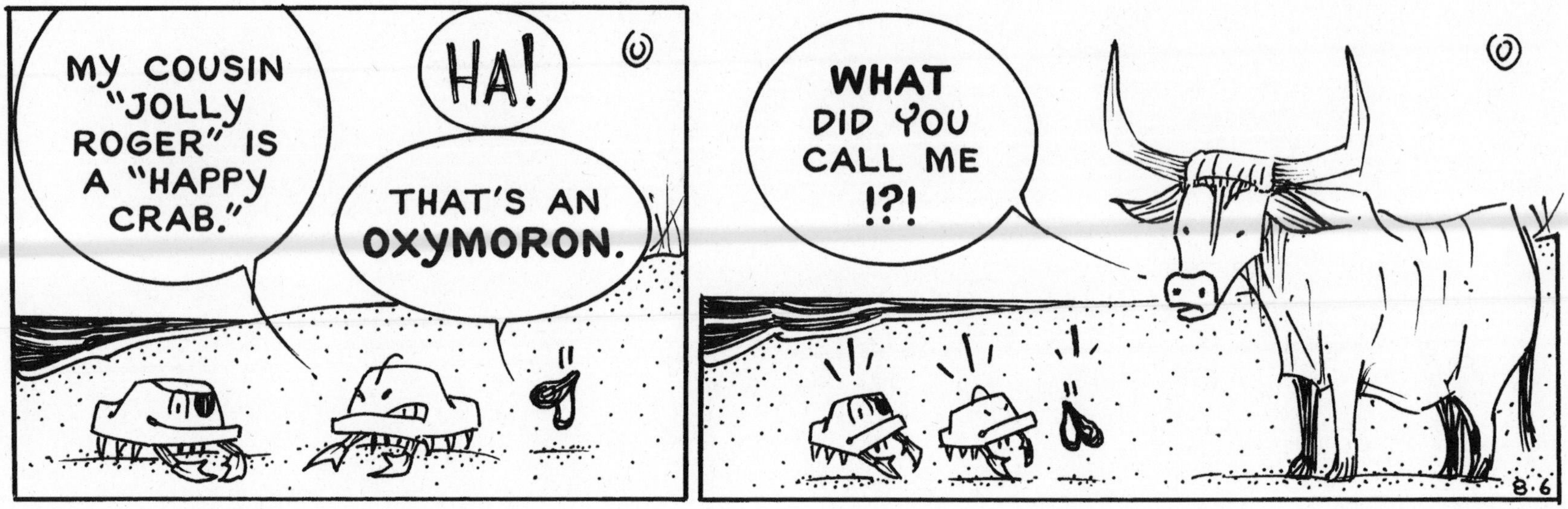
MY COUSIN "JOLLY ROGER" IS A "HAPPY CRAB."
HA!
THAT'S AN OXYMORON.
WHAT DID YOU CALL ME !?!
8·6

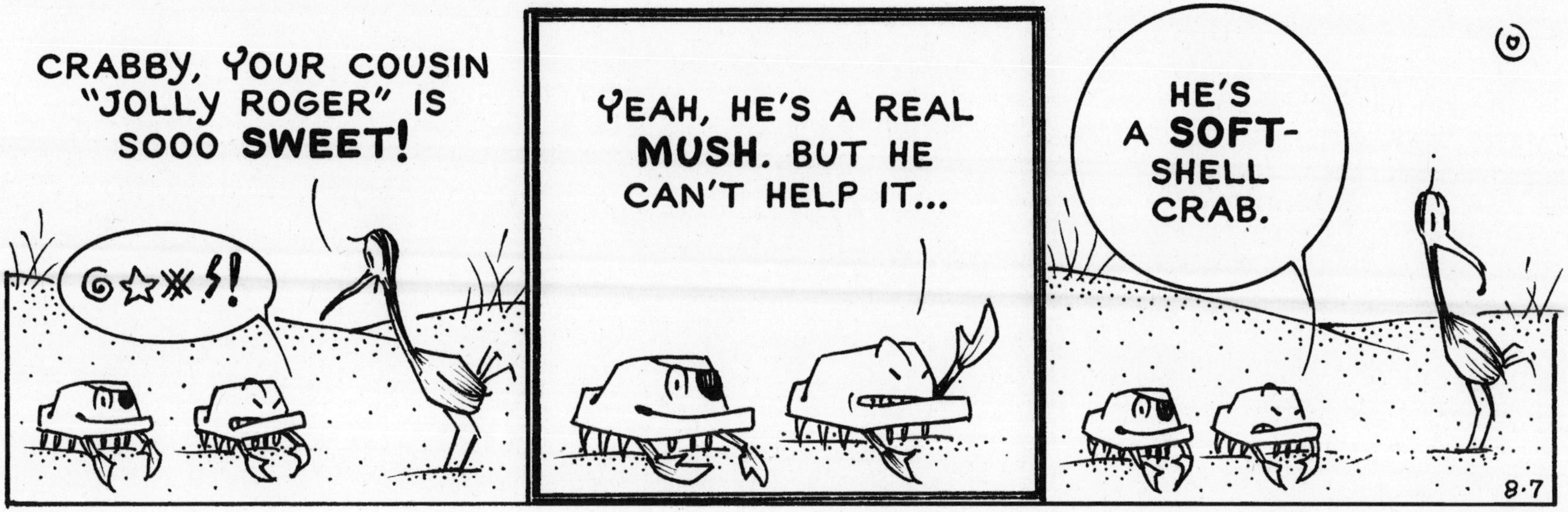
CRABBY, YOUR COUSIN "JOLLY ROGER" IS SOOO **SWEET!**
@☆※ϟ!
YEAH, HE'S A REAL **MUSH**. BUT HE CAN'T HELP IT...
HE'S A **SOFT**-SHELL CRAB.
8·7

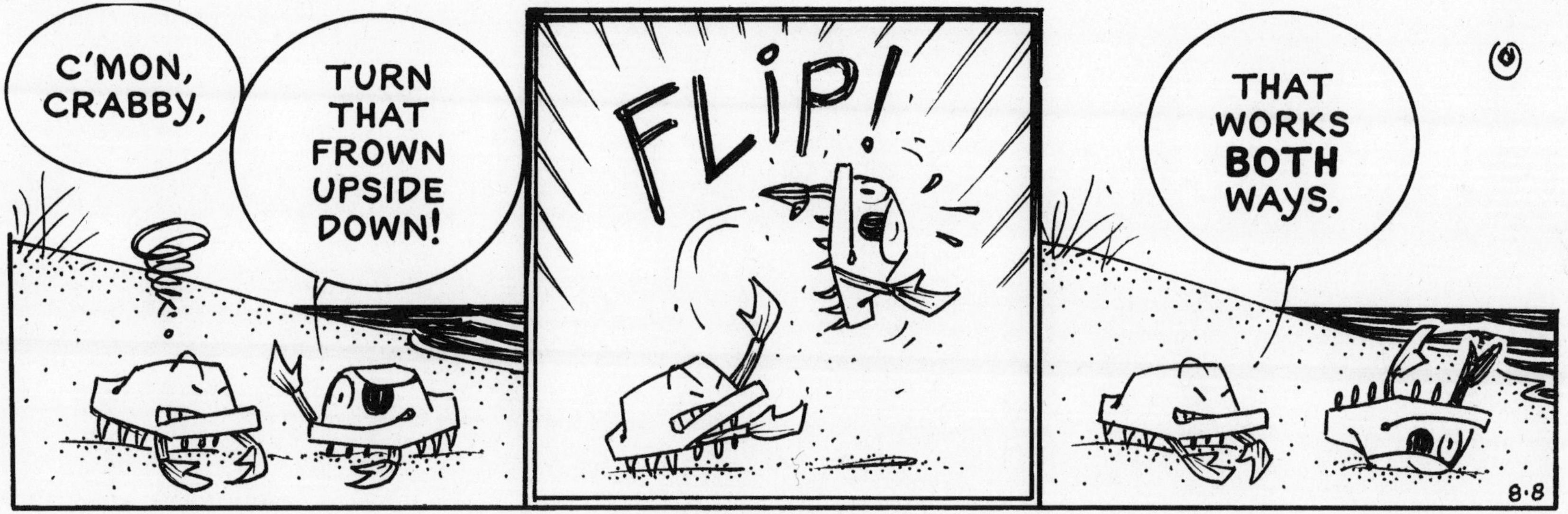
C'MON, CRABBY,
TURN THAT FROWN UPSIDE DOWN!
FLIP!
THAT WORKS **BOTH** WAYS.
8·8

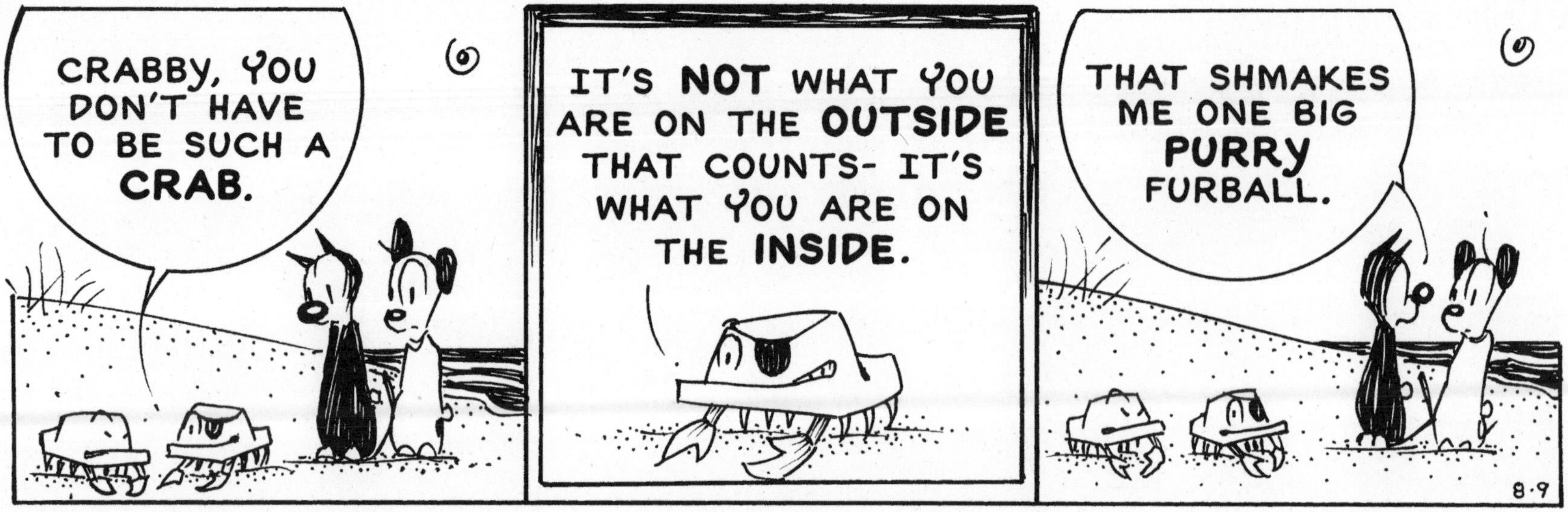
CRABBY, YOU DON'T HAVE TO BE SUCH A CRAB.
IT'S NOT WHAT YOU ARE ON THE OUTSIDE THAT COUNTS- IT'S WHAT YOU ARE ON THE INSIDE.
THAT SHMAKES ME ONE BIG PURRY FURBALL.
8·9

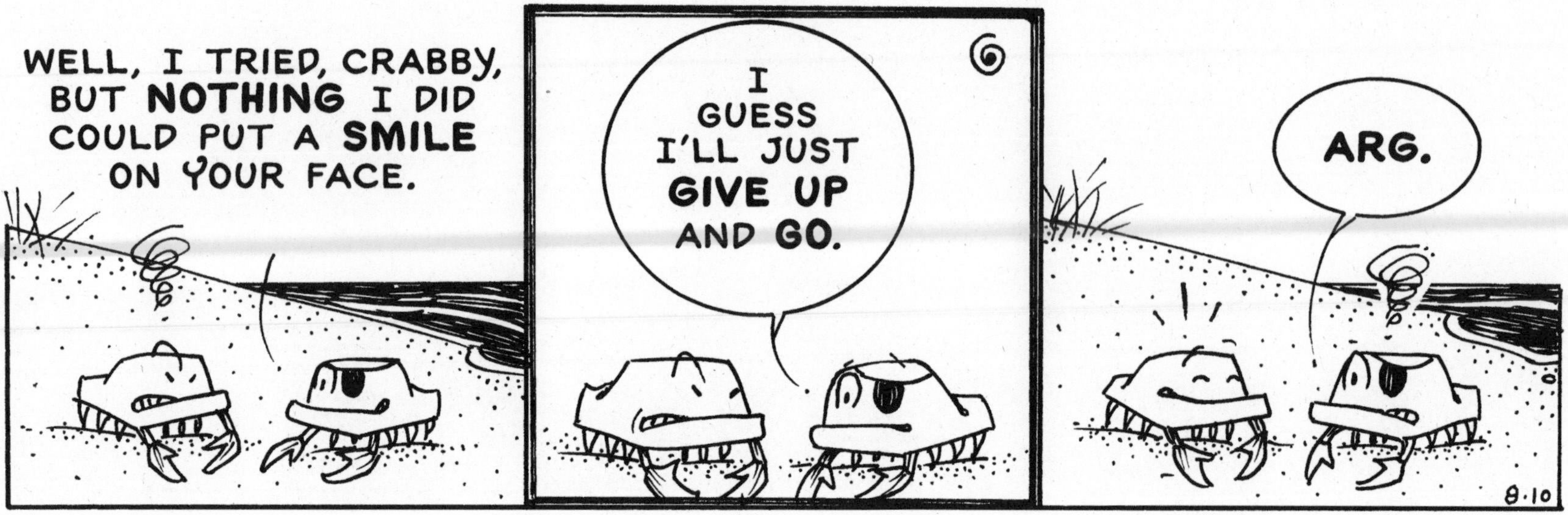
WELL, I TRIED, CRABBY, BUT NOTHING I DID COULD PUT A SMILE ON YOUR FACE.
I GUESS I'LL JUST GIVE UP AND GO.
ARG.
8·10

Mutts

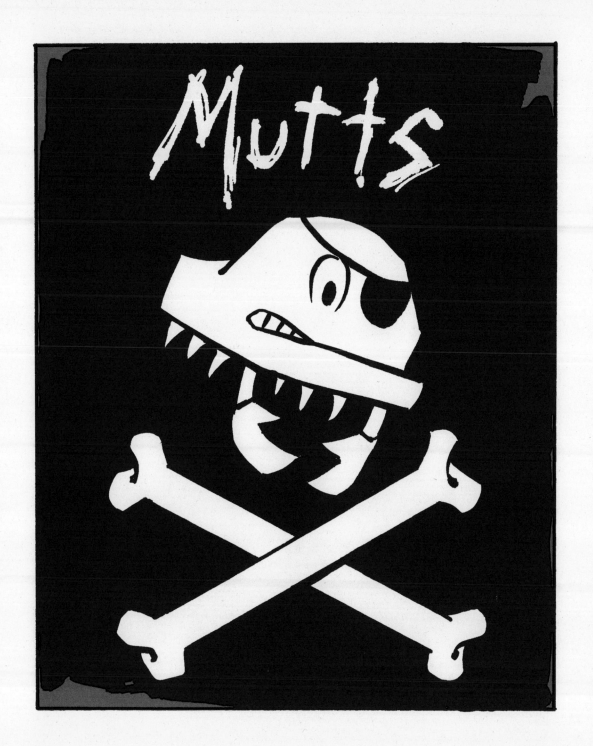

MUTTS

Patrick McDonnell

LIFE
IS
A BALL.
8·25

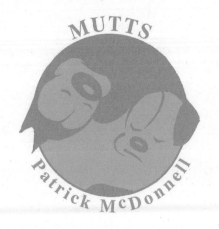

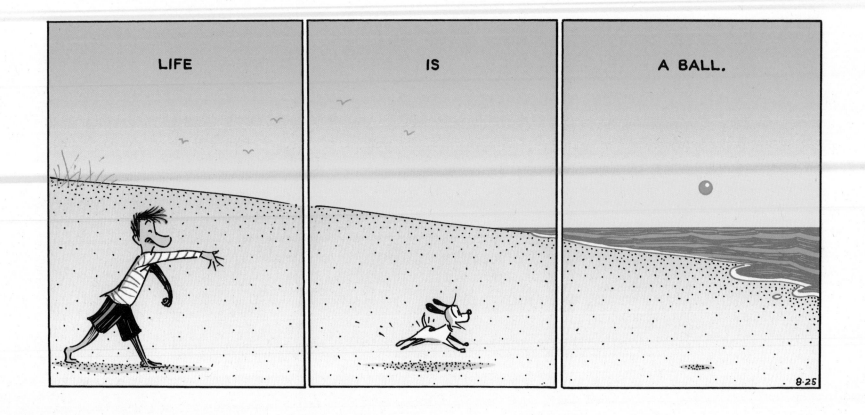

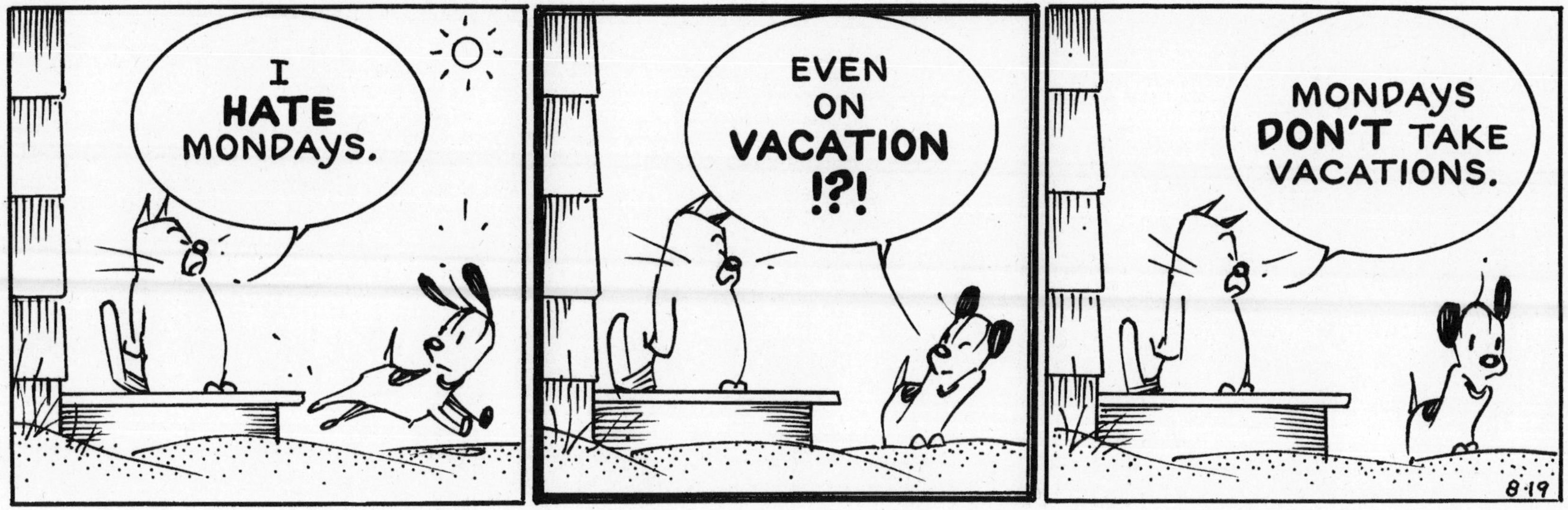
I **HATE** MONDAYS.
EVEN ON **VACATION** **!?!**
MONDAYS **DON'T** TAKE VACATIONS.
8·19

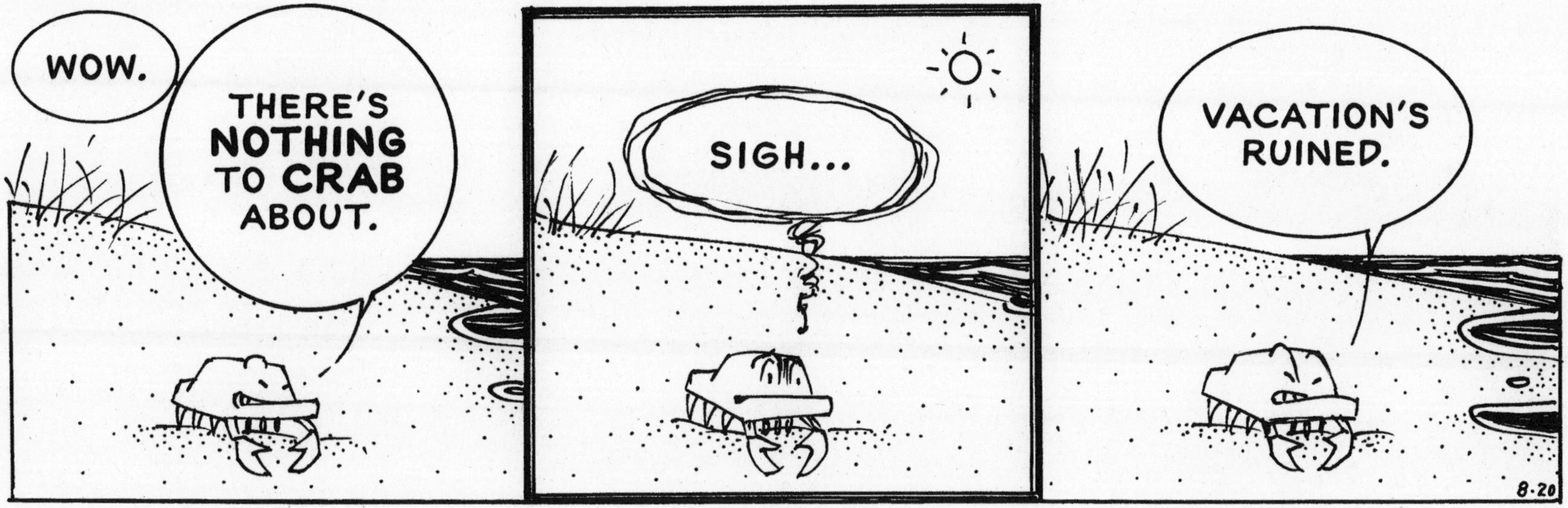
WOW.
THERE'S **NOTHING** TO **CRAB** ABOUT.
SIGH...
VACATION'S RUINED.
8·20

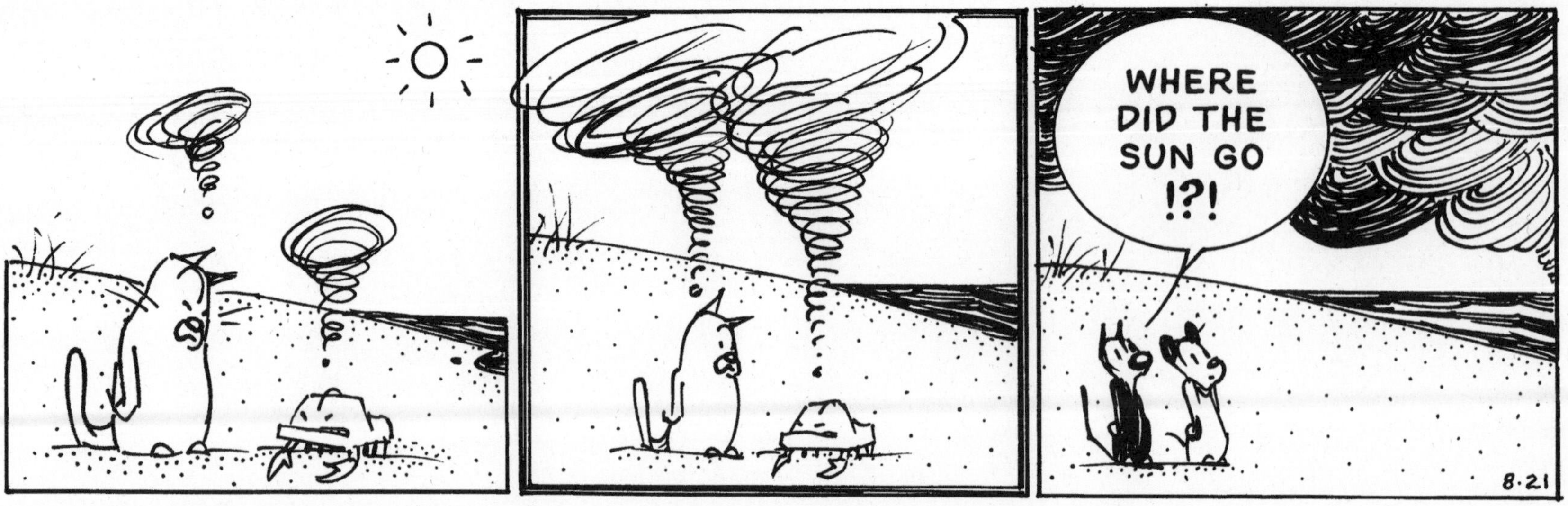
WHERE DID THE SUN GO !?!
8·21

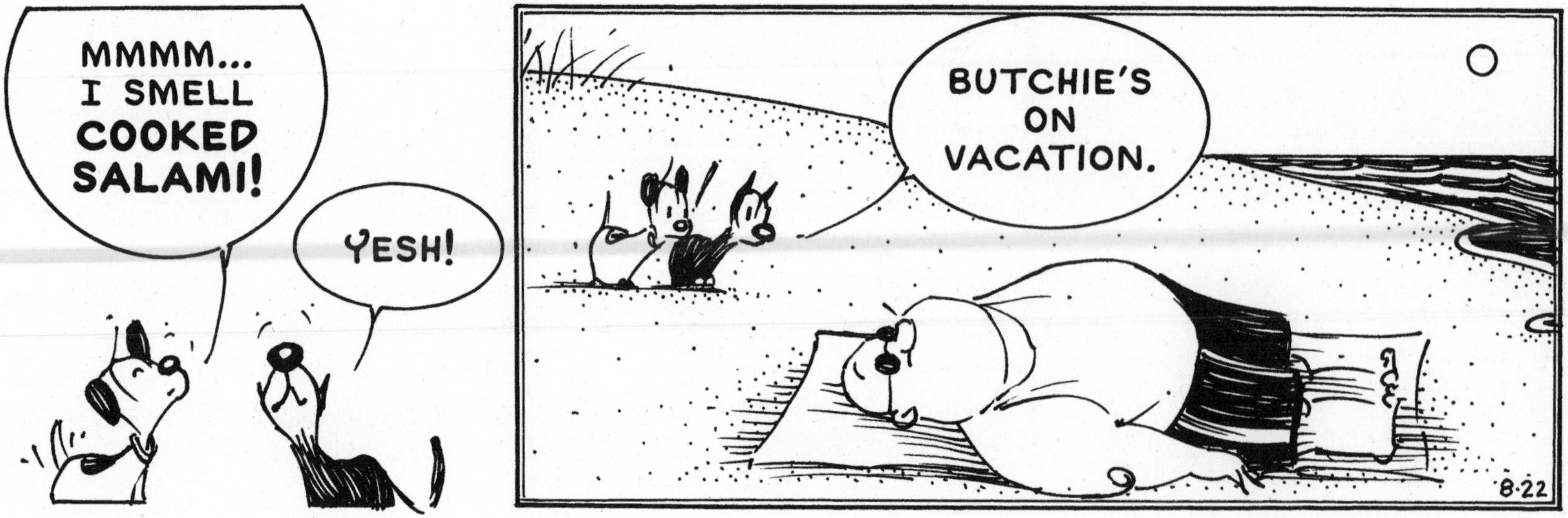
MMMM... I SMELL COOKED SALAMI!
YESH!
BUTCHIE'S ON VACATION.
8·22

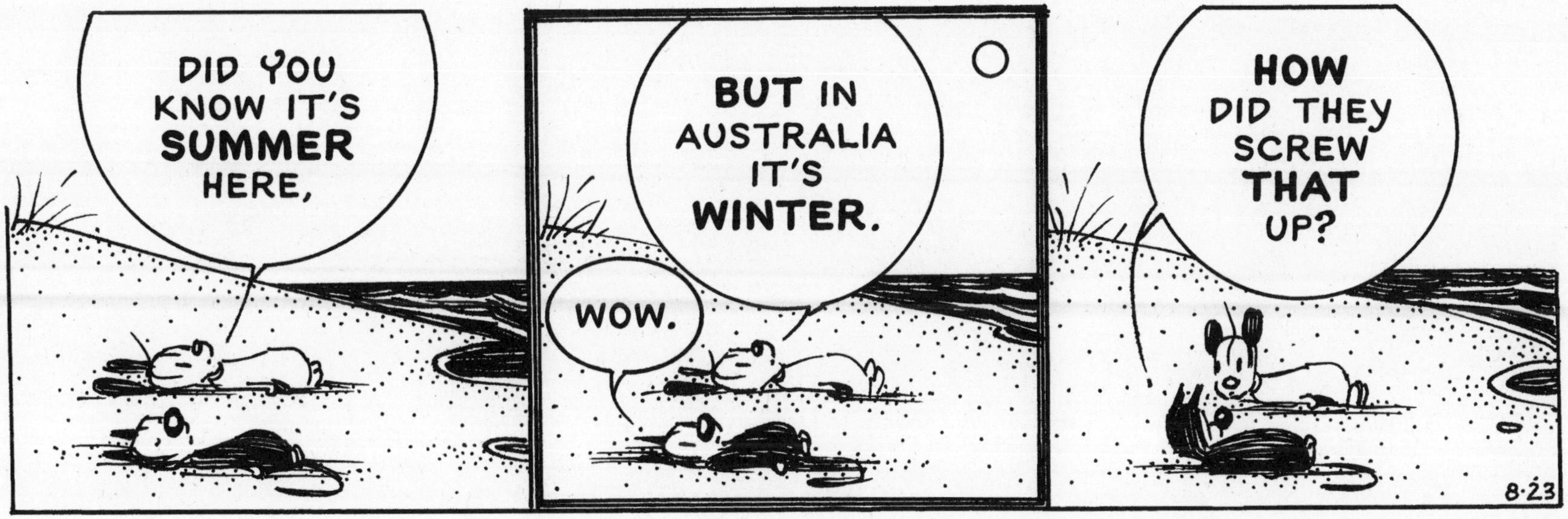
DID YOU KNOW IT'S **SUMMER** HERE,
BUT IN AUSTRALIA IT'S **WINTER.**
WOW.
HOW DID THEY SCREW **THAT** UP?
8·23

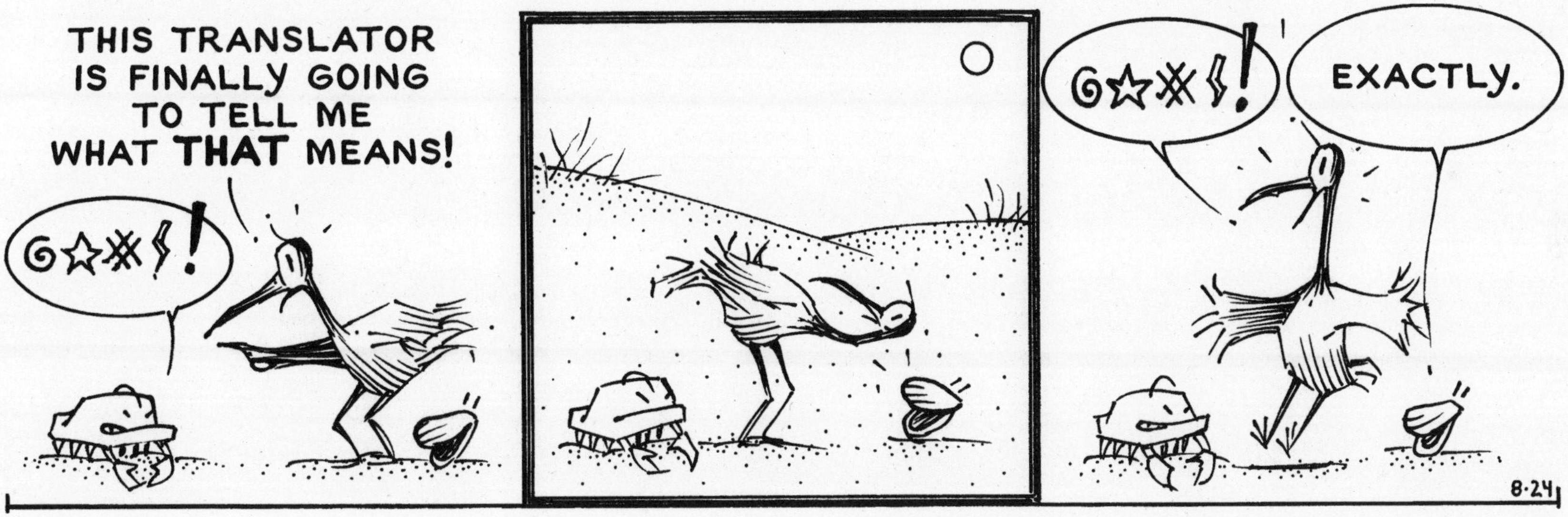
THIS TRANSLATOR IS FINALLY GOING TO TELL ME WHAT **THAT** MEANS!
EXACTLY.
8·24

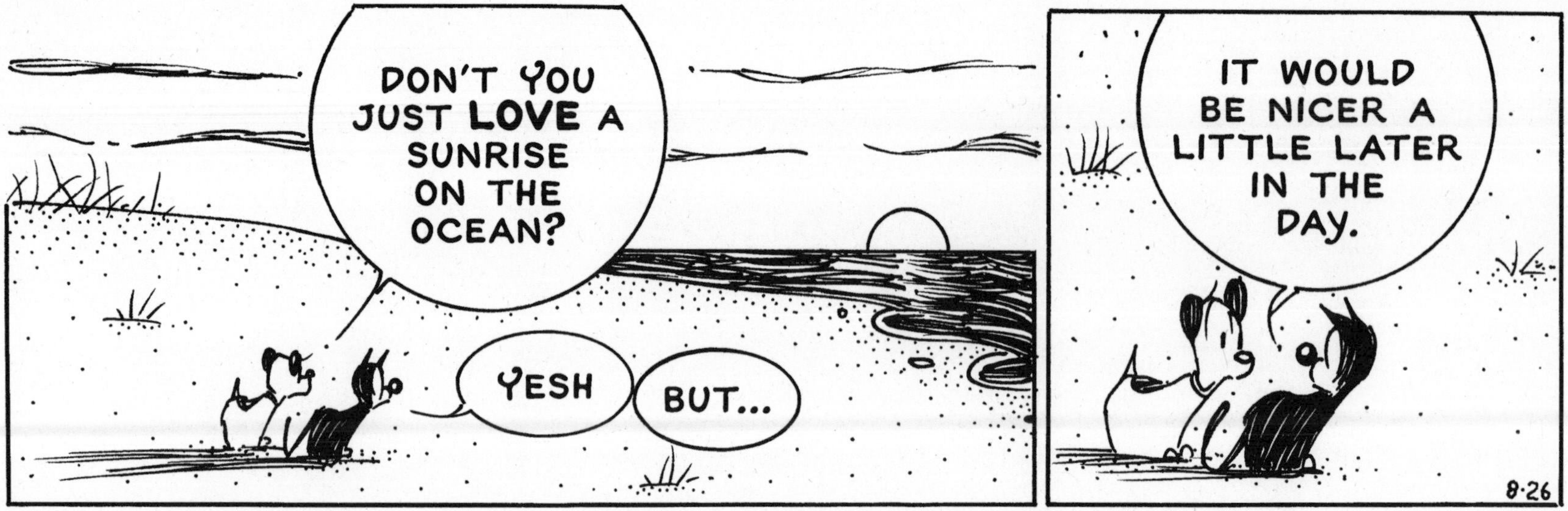
DON'T YOU JUST **LOVE** A SUNRISE ON THE OCEAN?
YESH
BUT...
IT WOULD BE NICER A LITTLE LATER IN THE DAY.
8·26

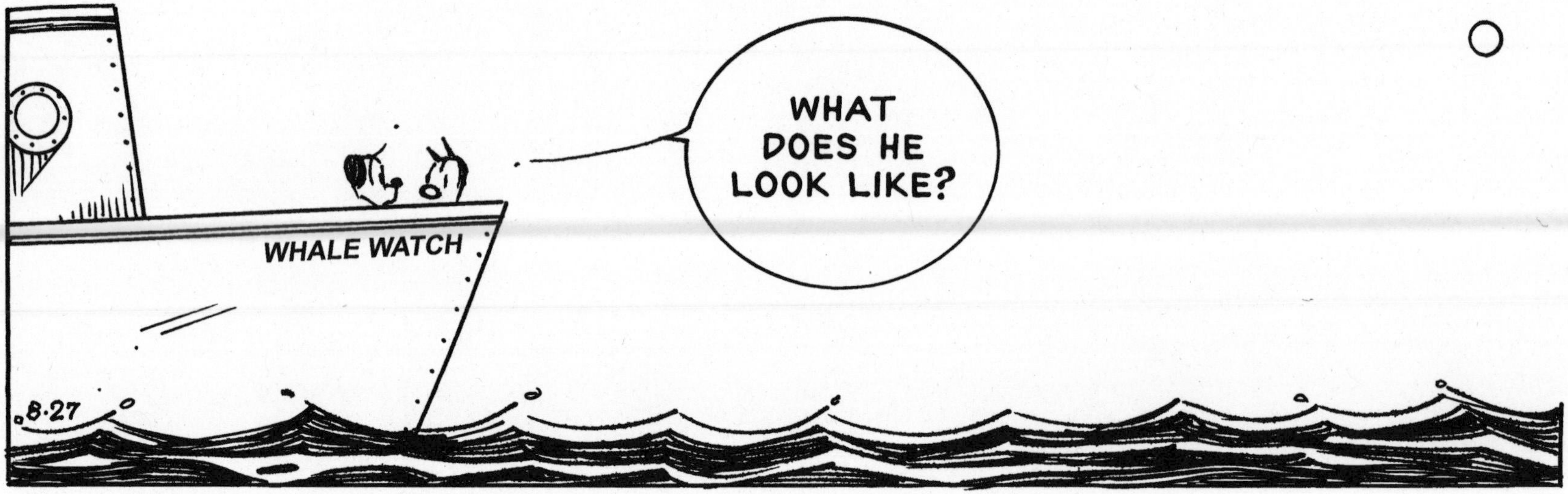
WHAT DOES HE LOOK LIKE?
WHALE WATCH
8·27

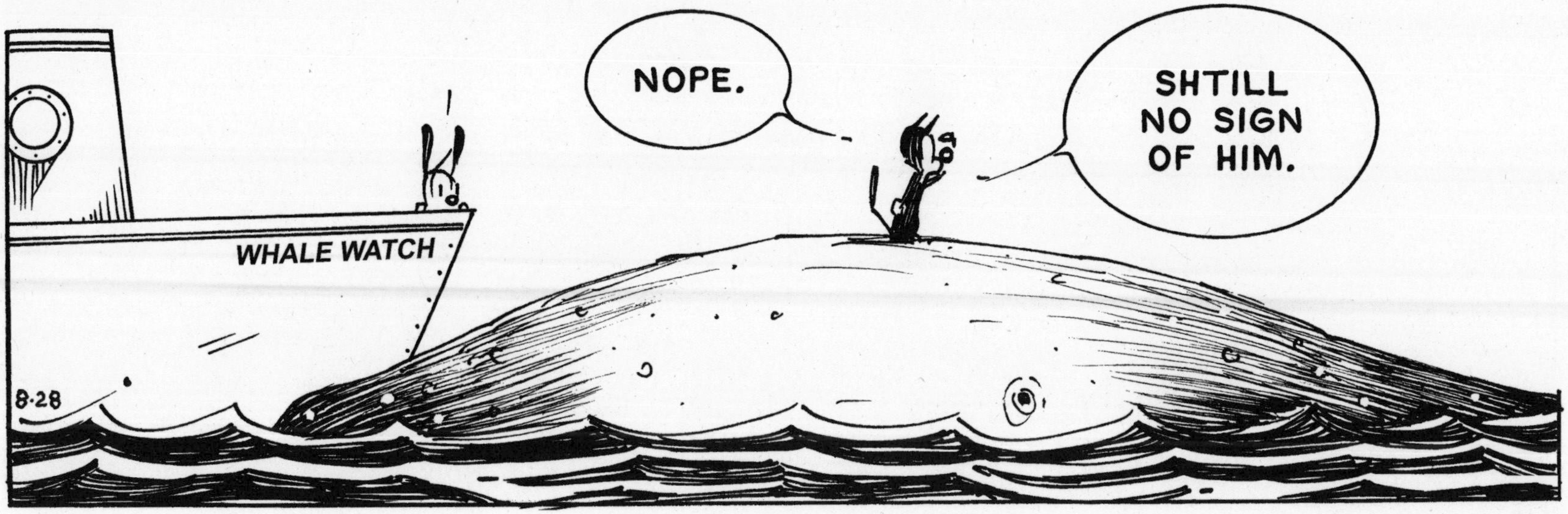
WHALE WATCH
NOPE.
SHTILL NO SIGN OF HIM.
8·28

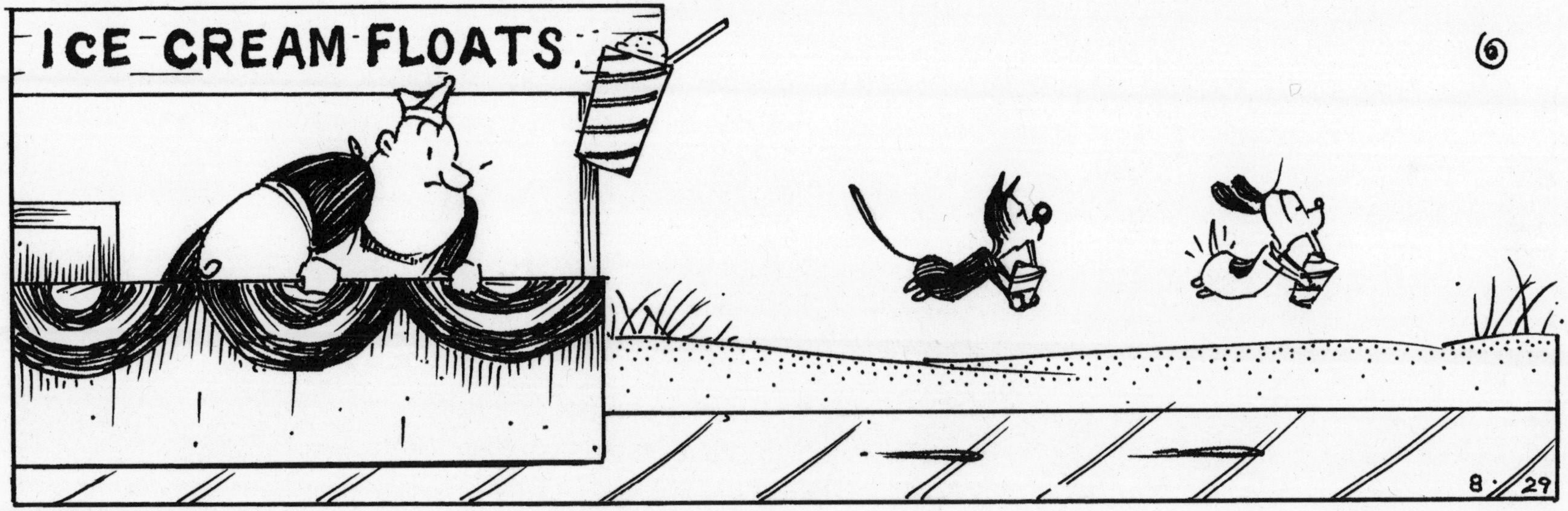
ICE CREAM FLOATS
8·29

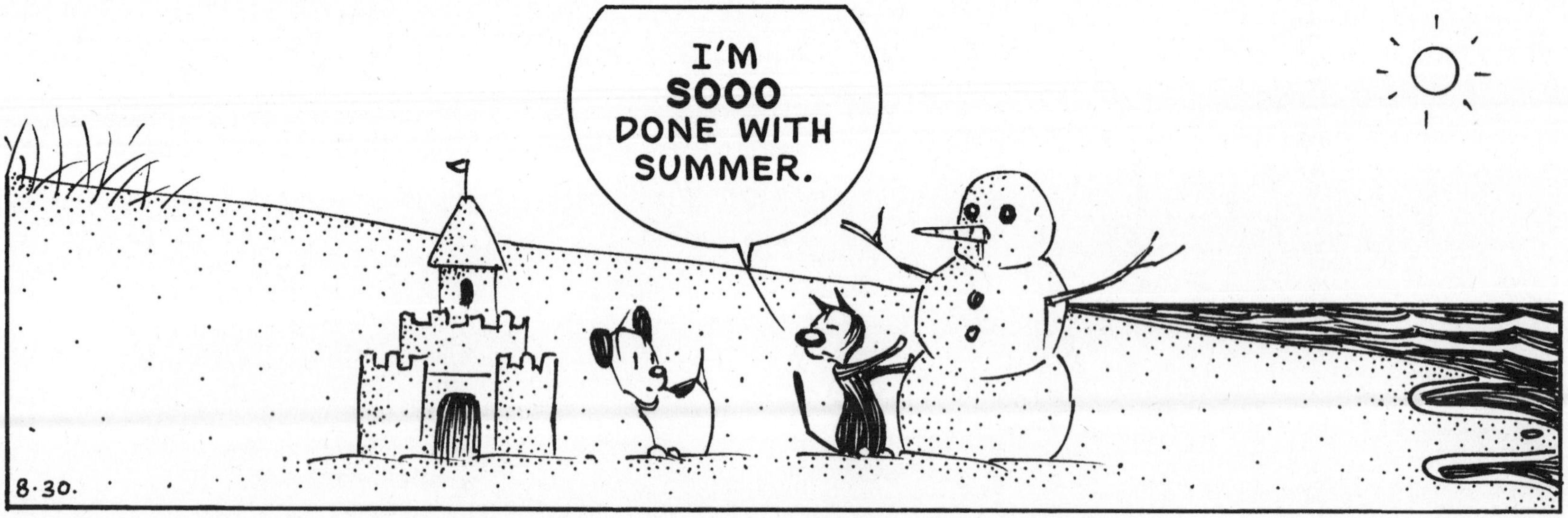
I'M SOOO DONE WITH SUMMER.
8·30.

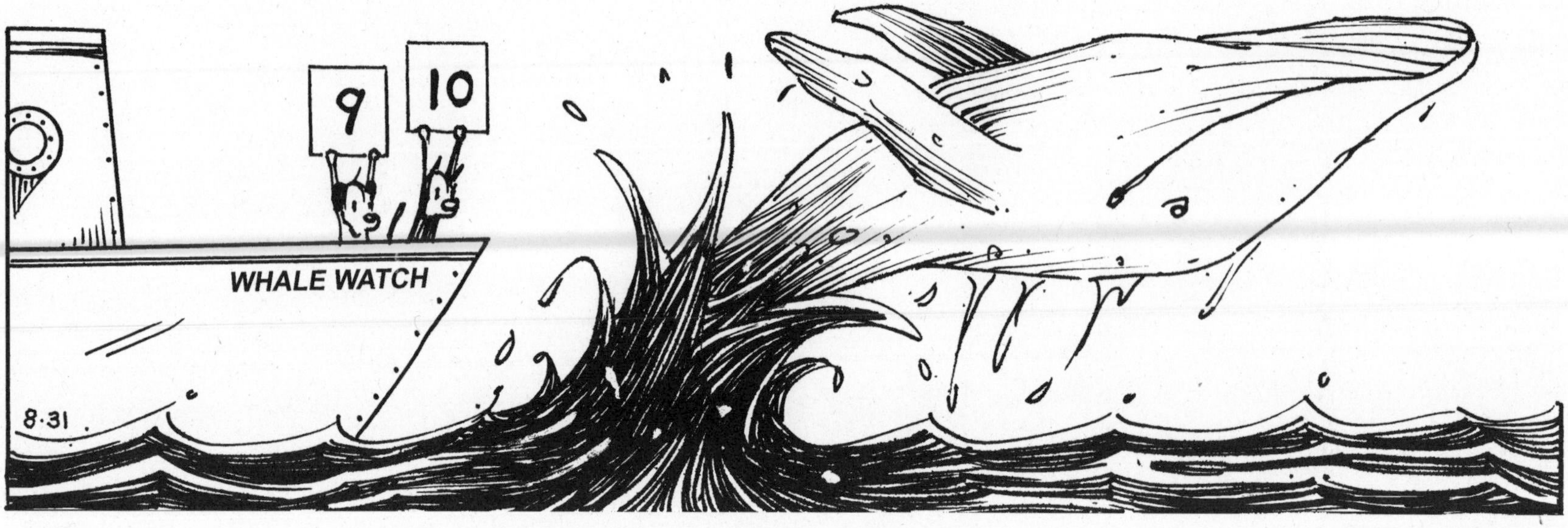
9
10
WHALE WATCH
8·31

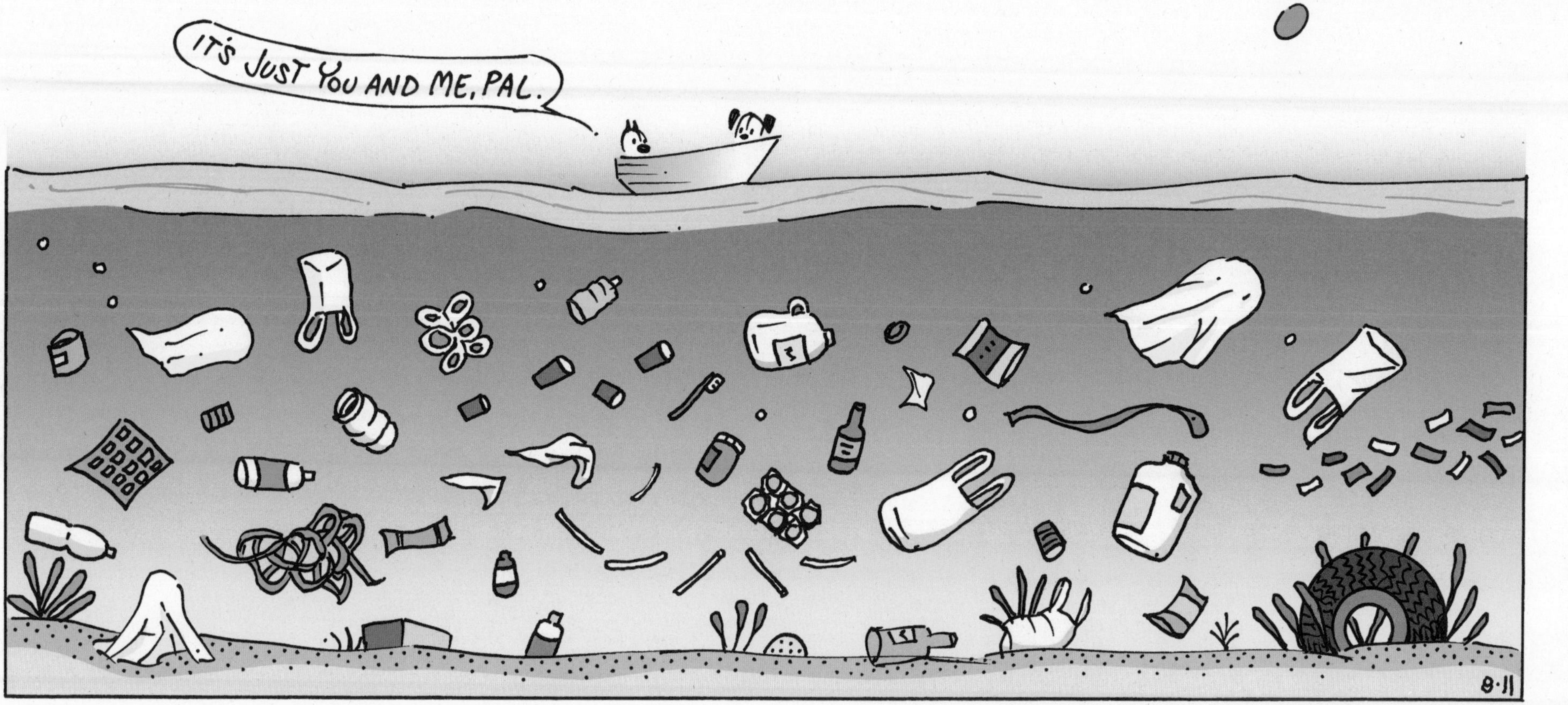
IT'S JUST YOU AND ME, PAL.
8·11

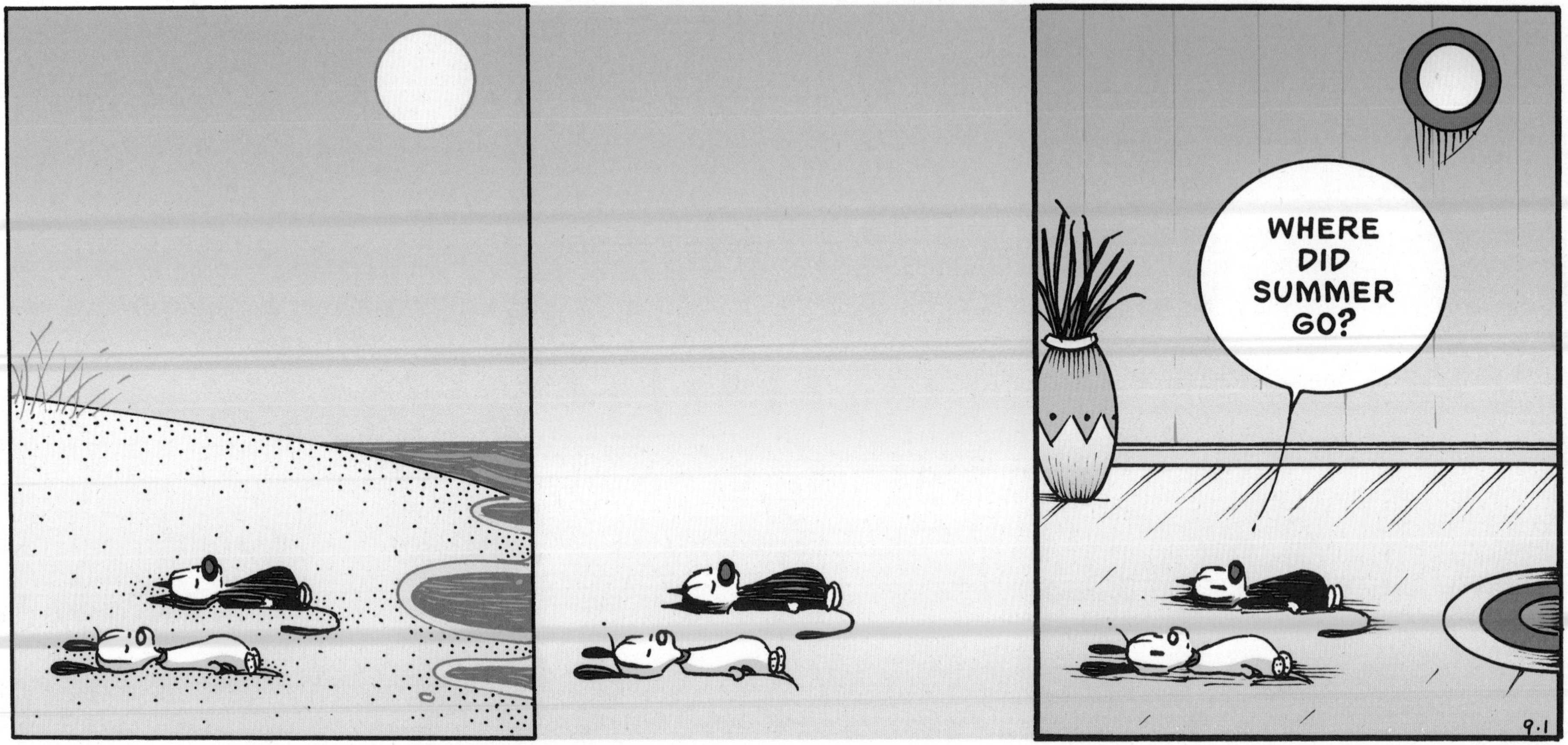
WHERE DID SUMMER GO?
9.1

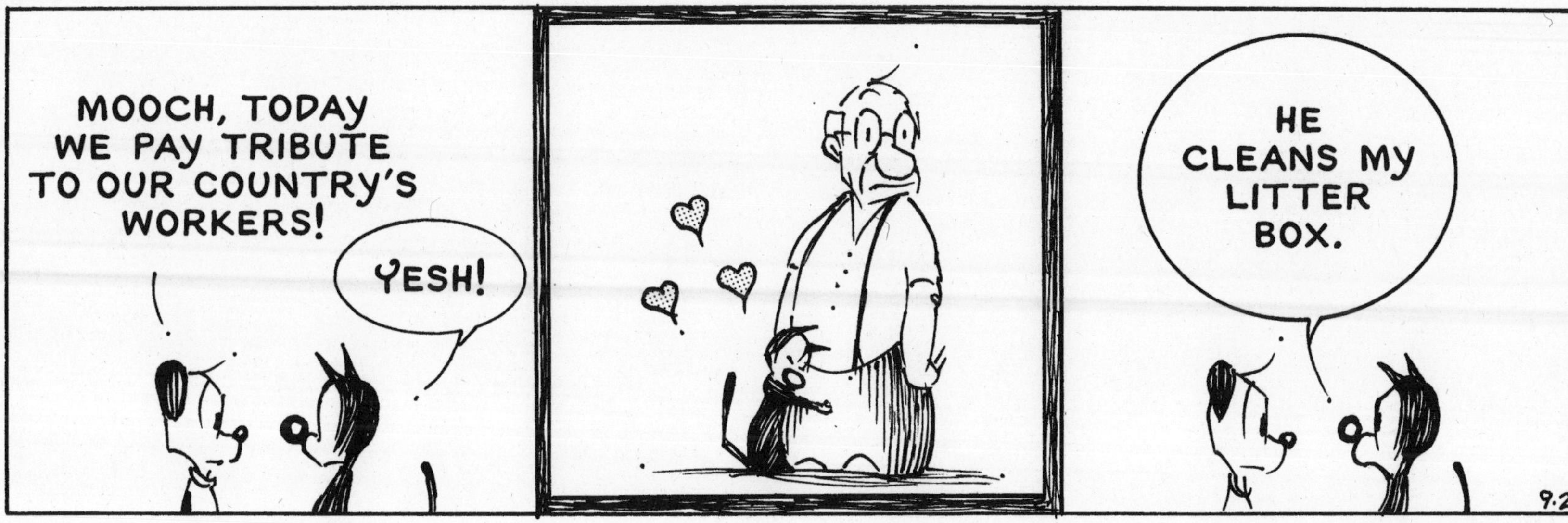
MOOCH, TODAY WE PAY TRIBUTE TO OUR COUNTRY'S WORKERS!
YESH!
HE CLEANS MY LITTER BOX.
9·2

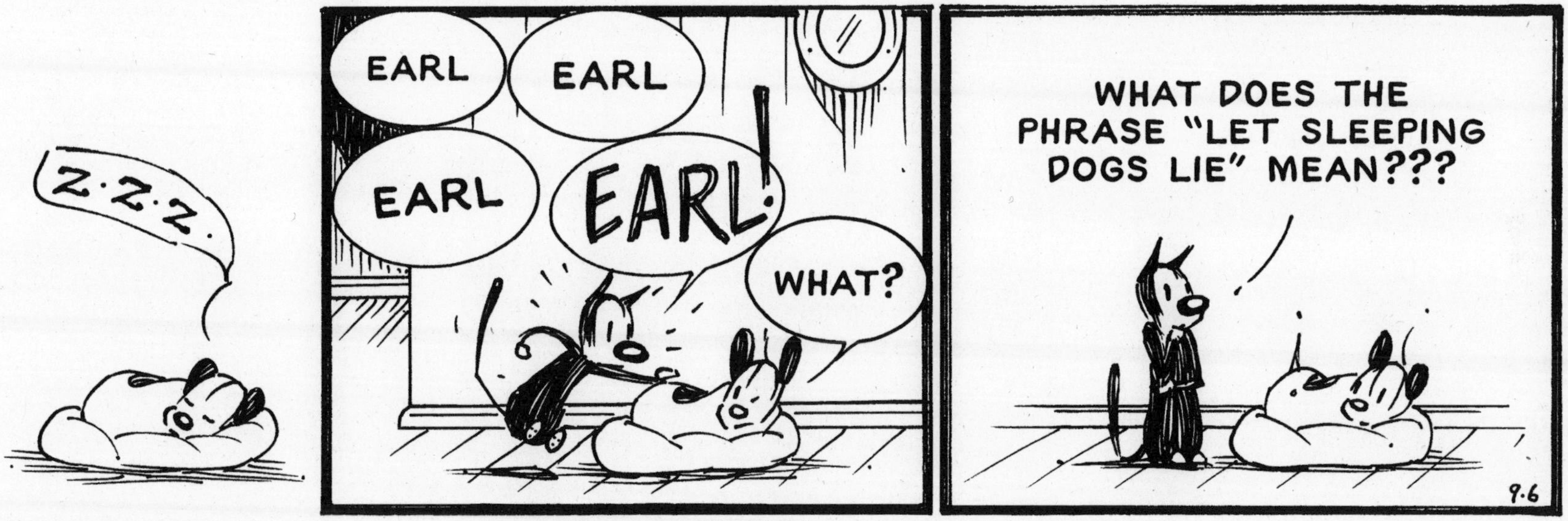
Z·Z·Z·
EARL
EARL
EARL
EARL!
WHAT?
WHAT DOES THE PHRASE "LET SLEEPING DOGS LIE" MEAN???
9·6

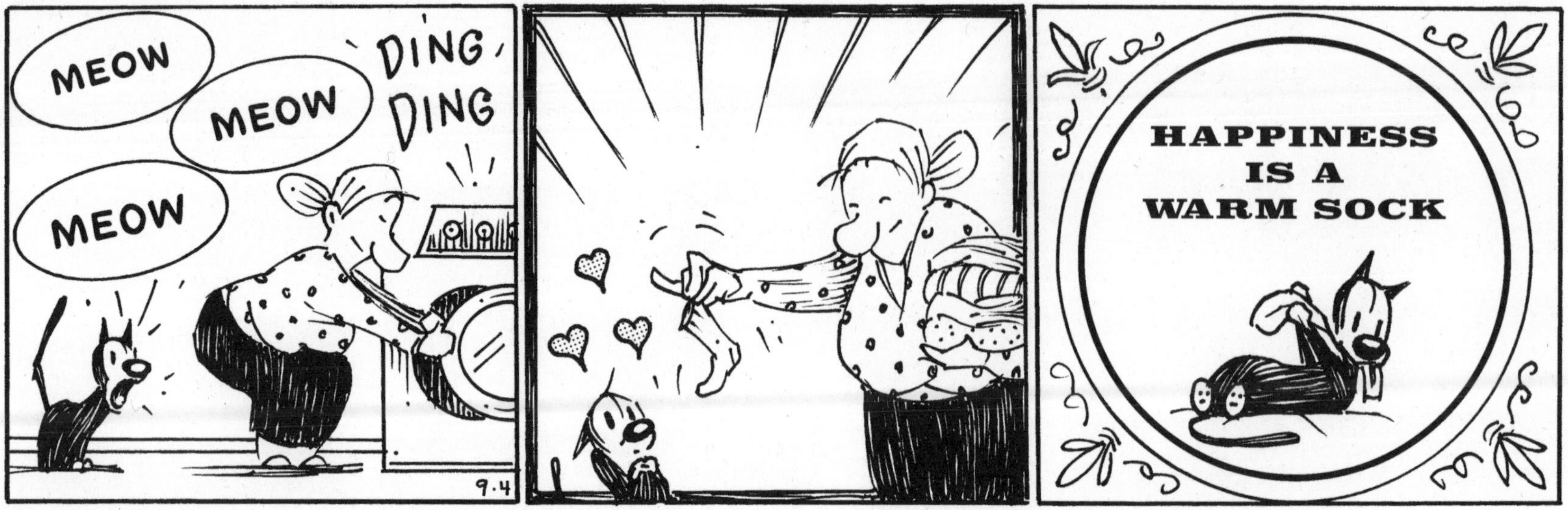
MEOW
MEOW
MEOW
DING
DING
9.4
HAPPINESS
IS A
WARM SOCK

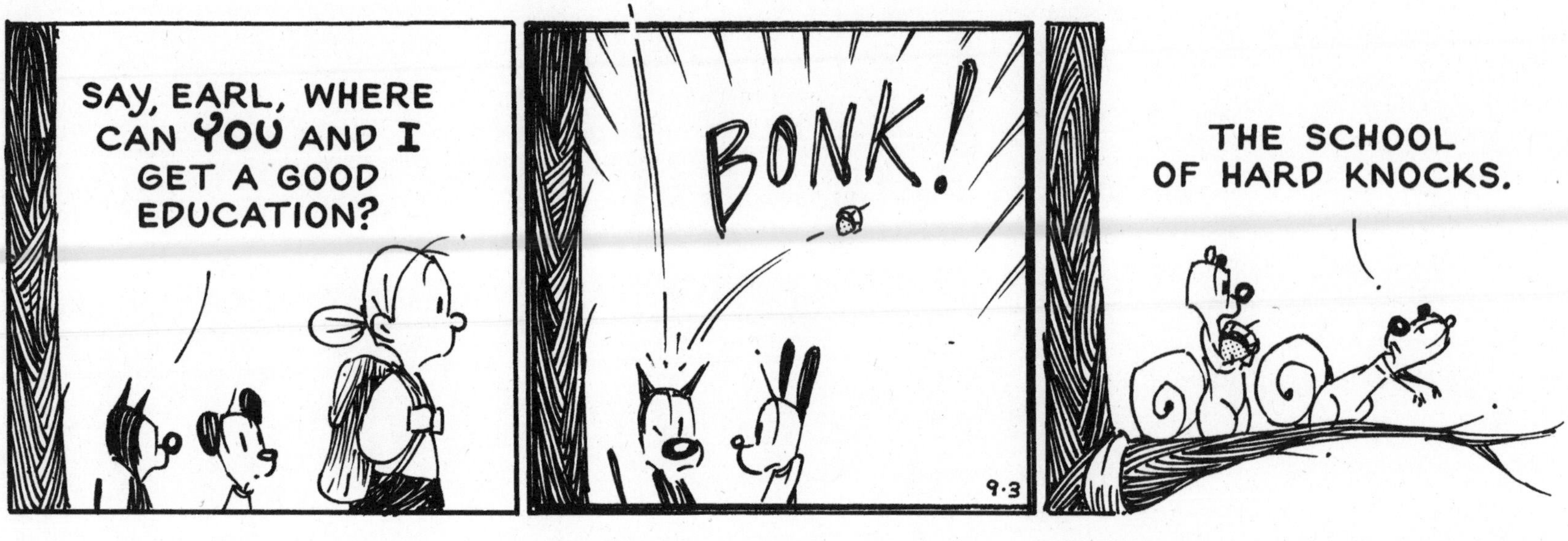
SAY, EARL, WHERE CAN YOU AND I GET A GOOD EDUCATION?
BONK!
9.3
THE SCHOOL OF HARD KNOCKS.

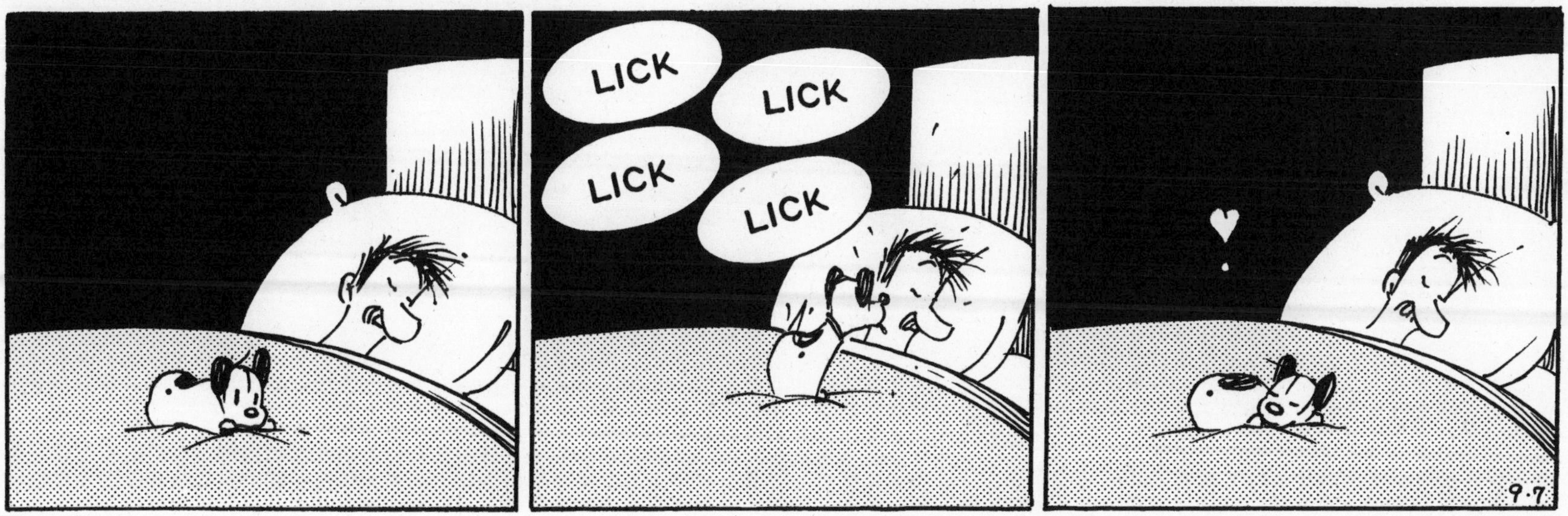
LICK
LICK
LICK
LICK
9·7

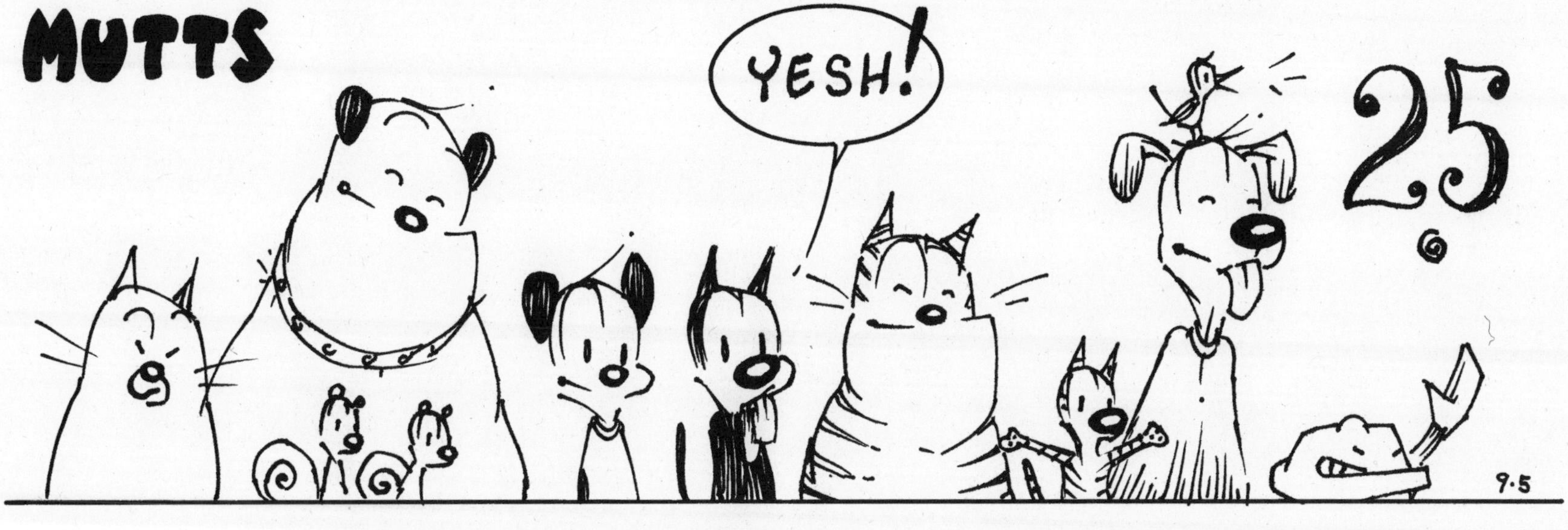
MUTTS
YESH!
25
9·5

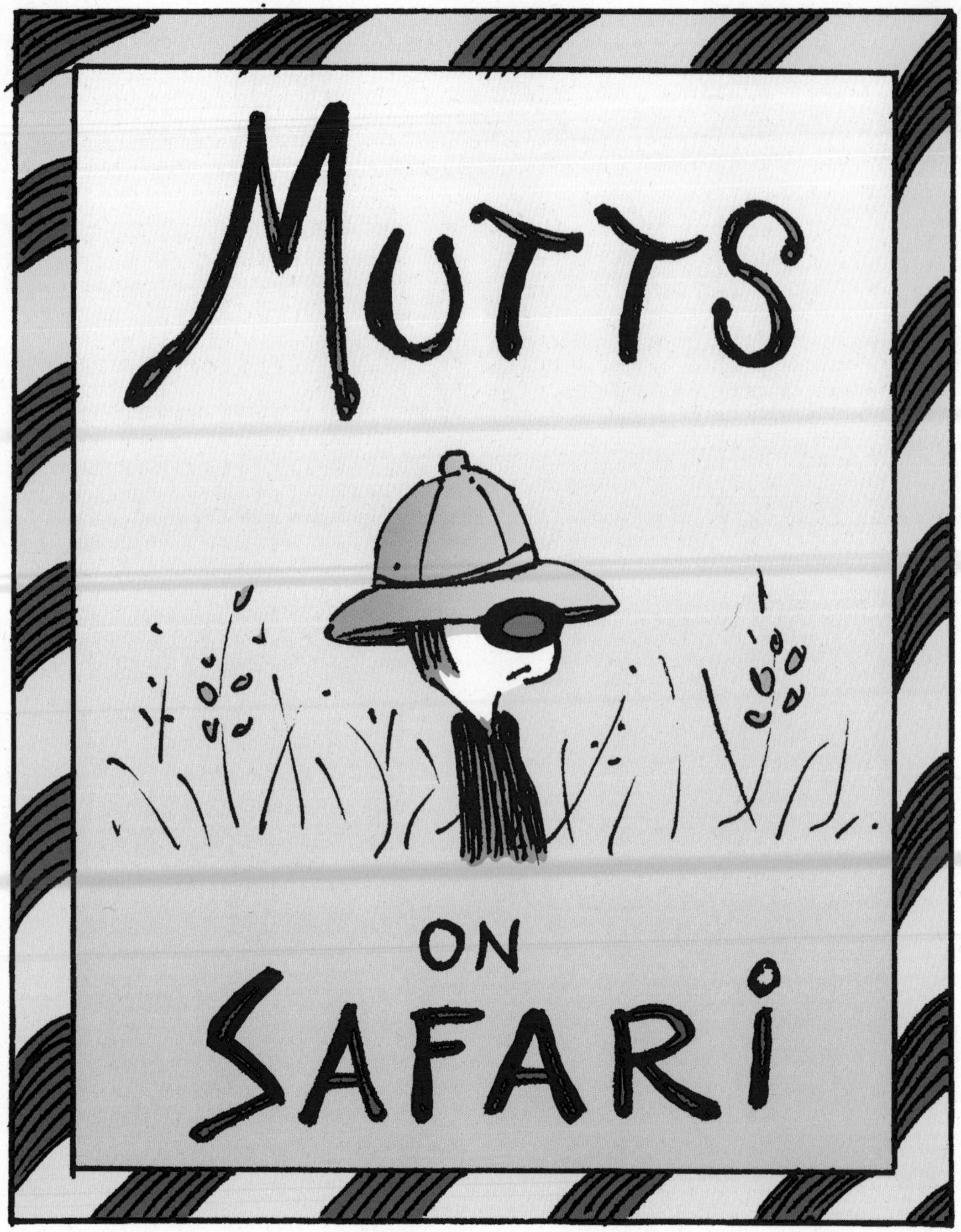
MUTTS
ON
SAFARI

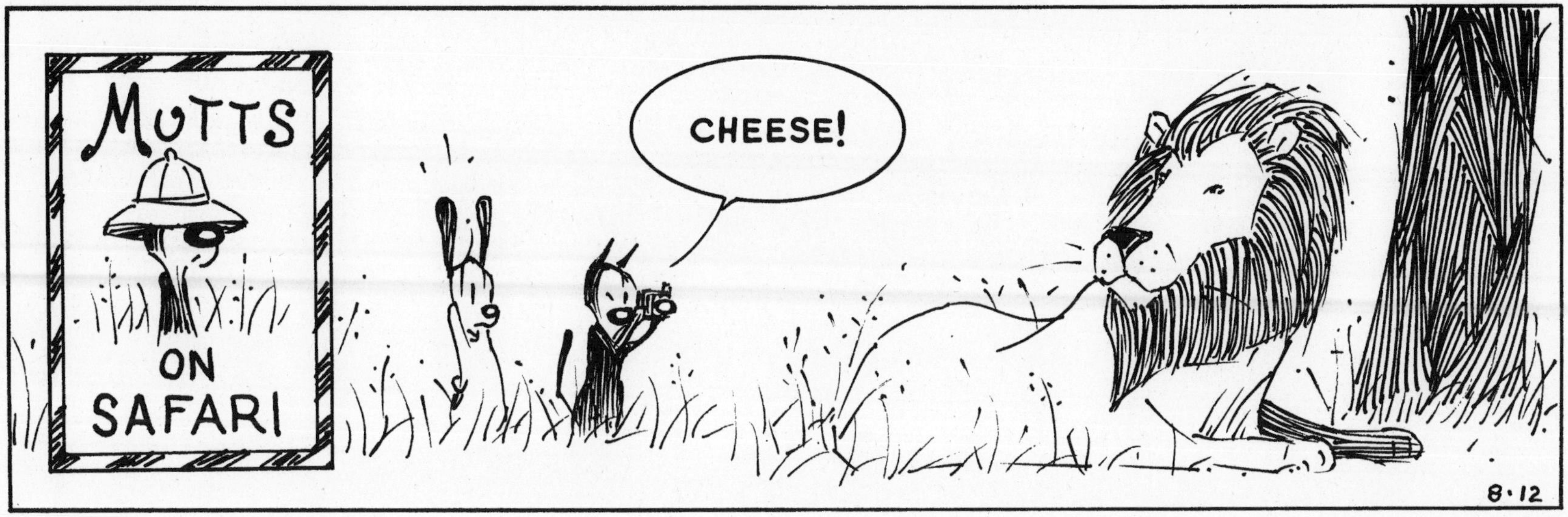
MUTTS
ON
SAFARI
CHEESE!
8·12

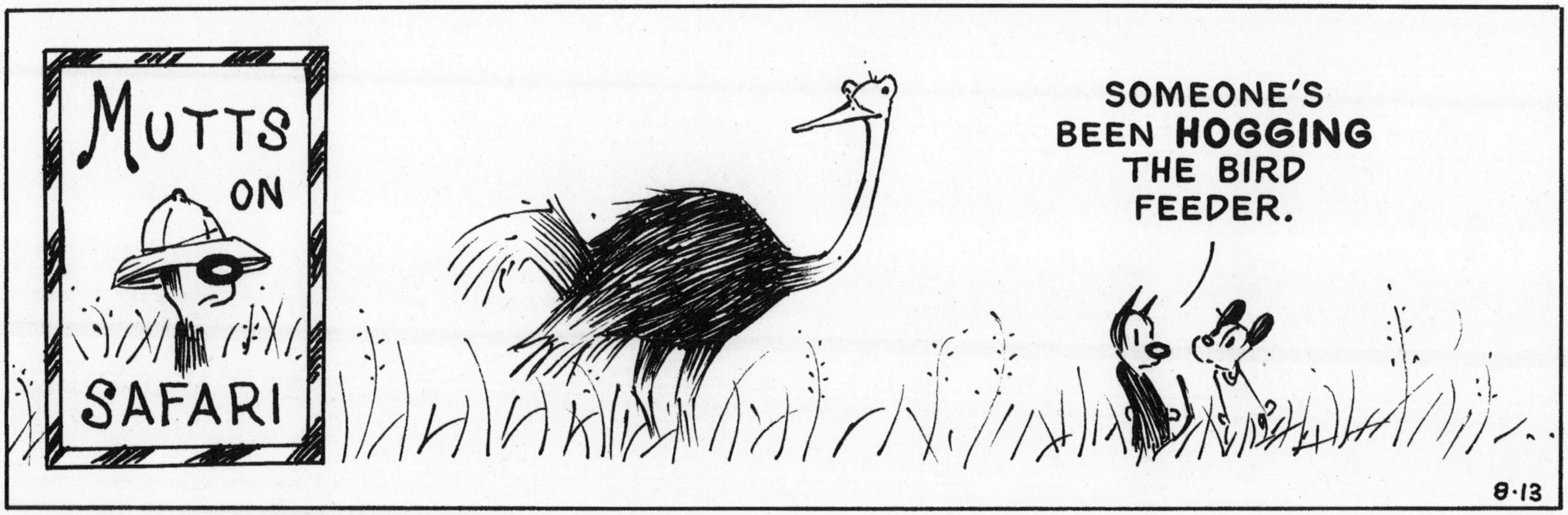
MUTTS
ON
SAFARI
SOMEONE'S BEEN HOGGING THE BIRD FEEDER.
8·13

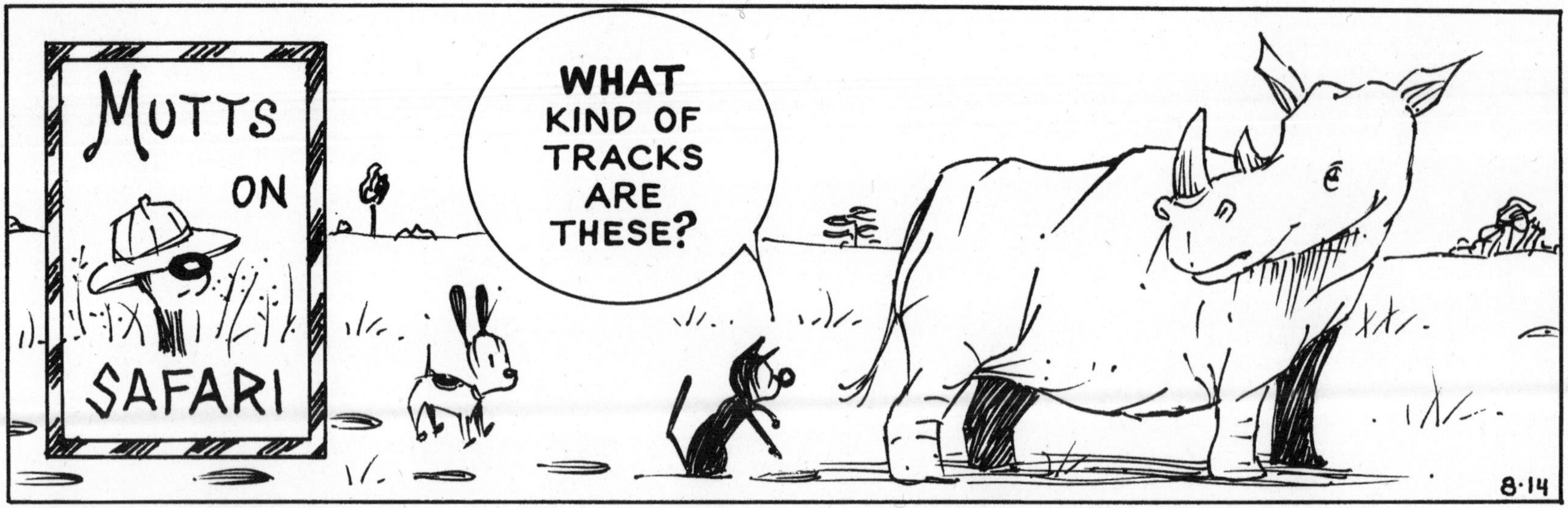
MUTTS ON SAFARI
WHAT KIND OF TRACKS ARE THESE?
8·14

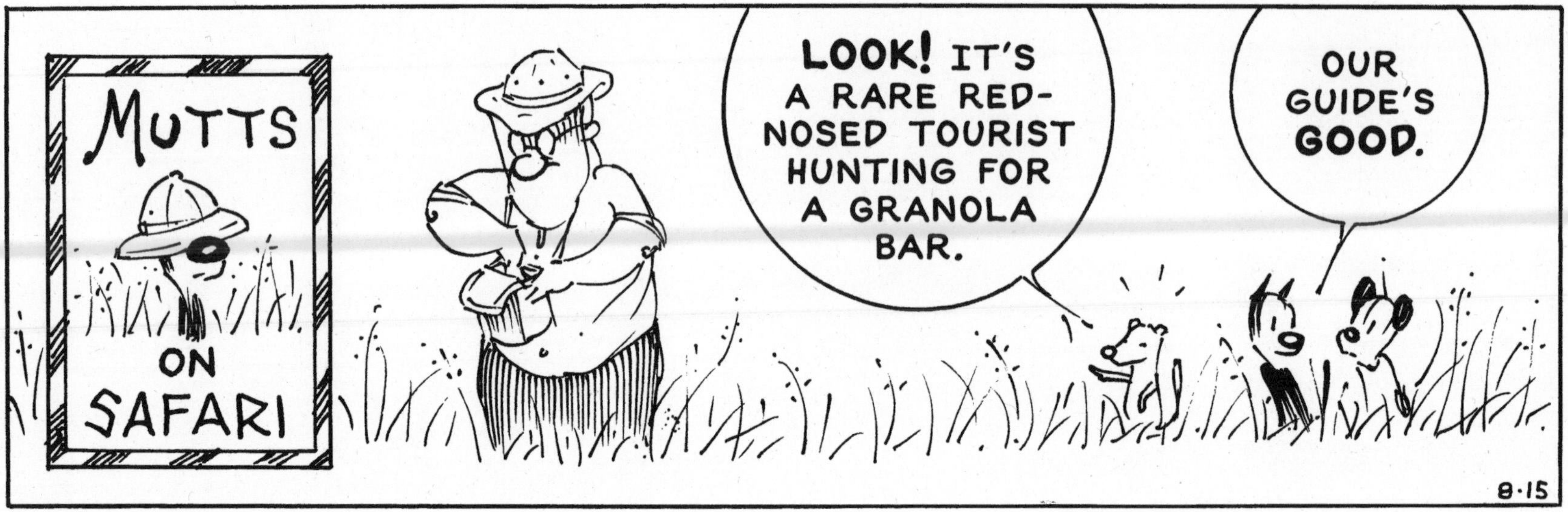
MUTTS ON SAFARI
LOOK! IT'S A RARE RED-NOSED TOURIST HUNTING FOR A GRANOLA BAR.
OUR GUIDE'S GOOD.
8·15

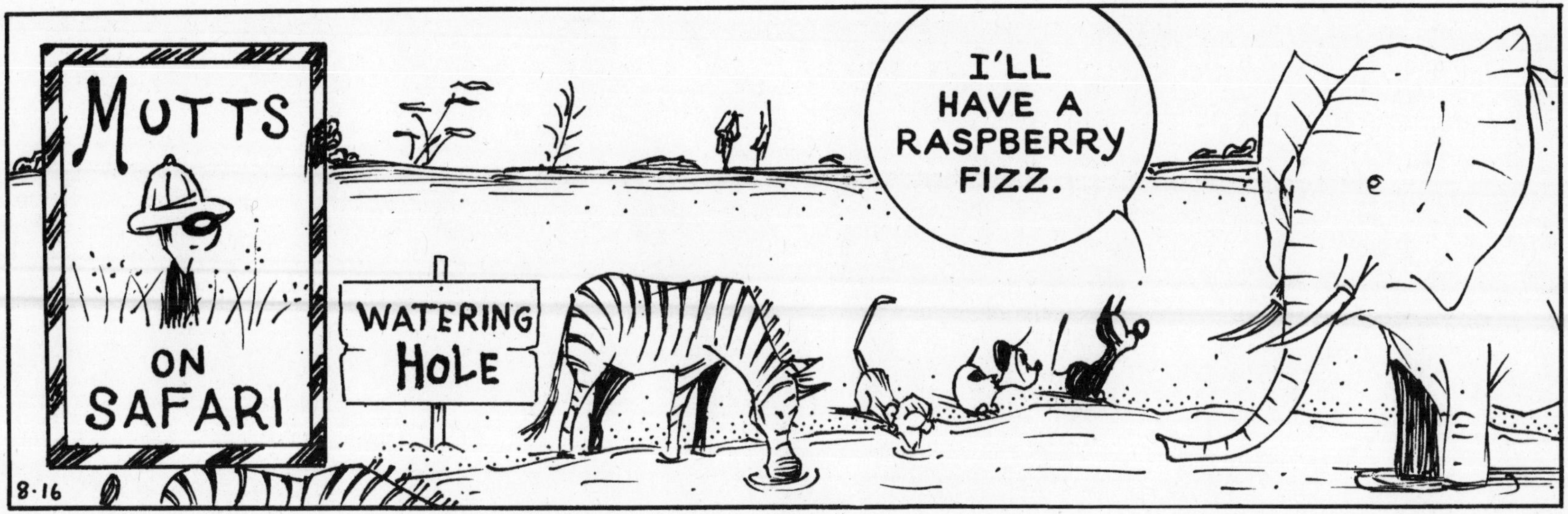
MUTTS
ON SAFARI
WATERING HOLE
I'LL HAVE A RASPBERRY FIZZ.
8·16

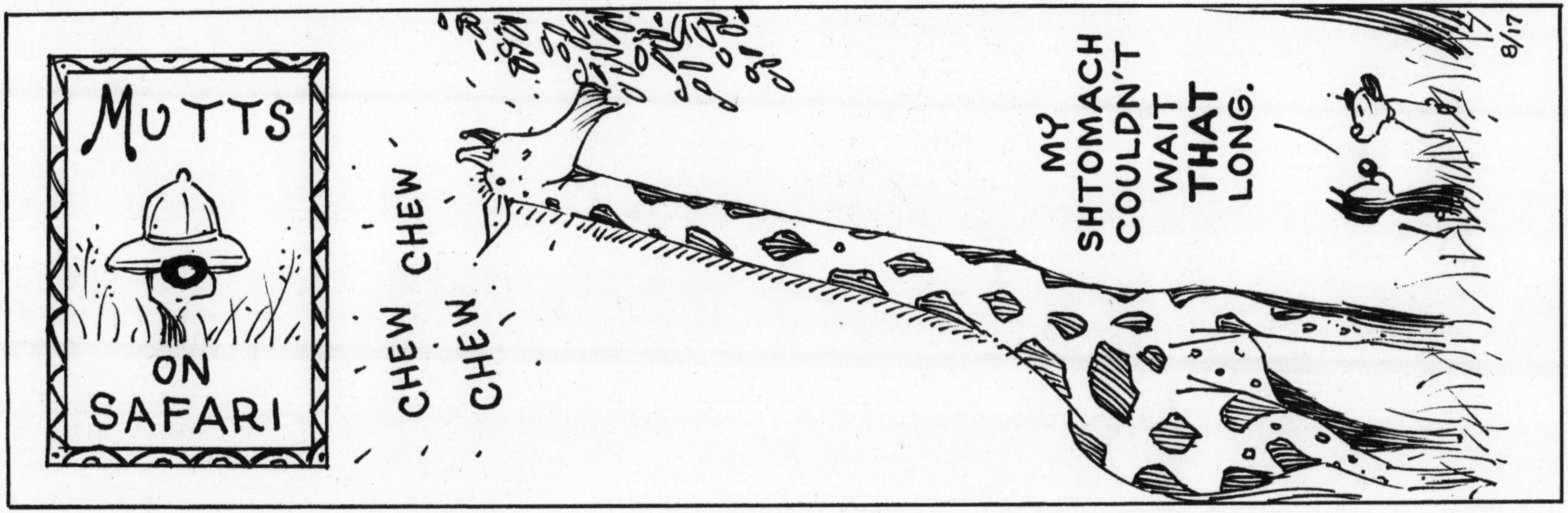
MUTTS
ON SAFARI
CHEW CHEW
CHEW CHEW
MY SHTOMACH COULDN'T WAIT THAT LONG.
8/17

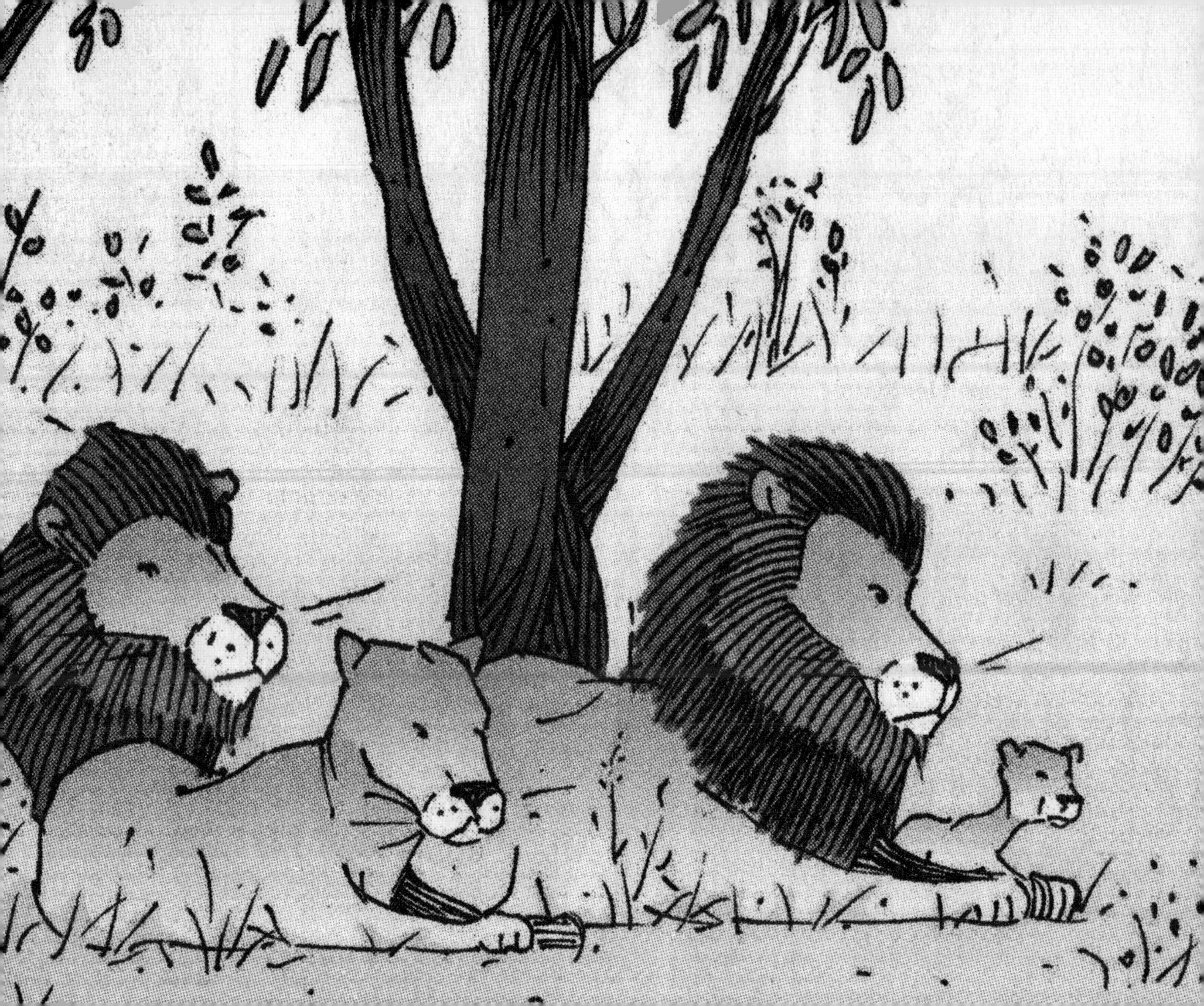

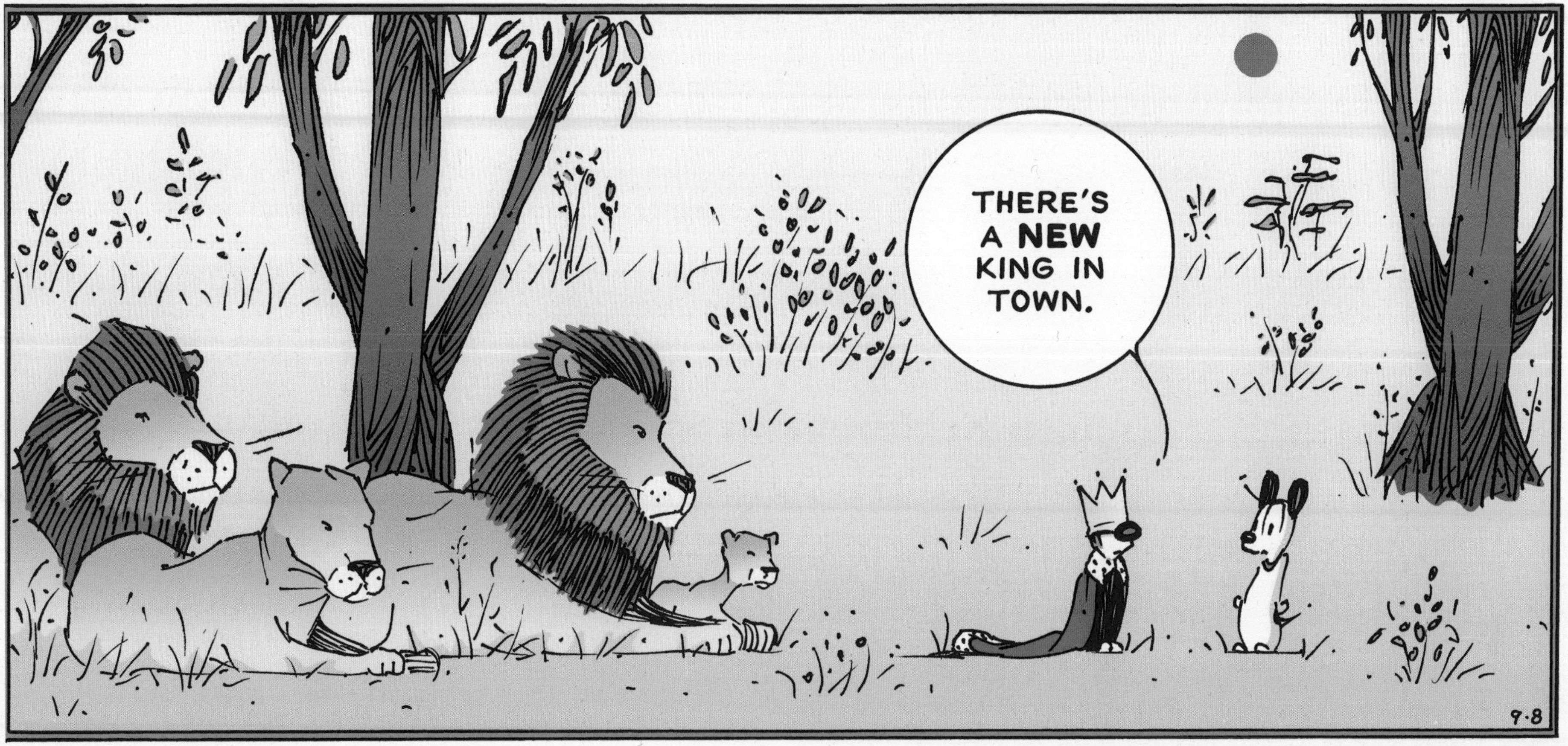
THERE'S A **NEW** KING IN TOWN.
9·8

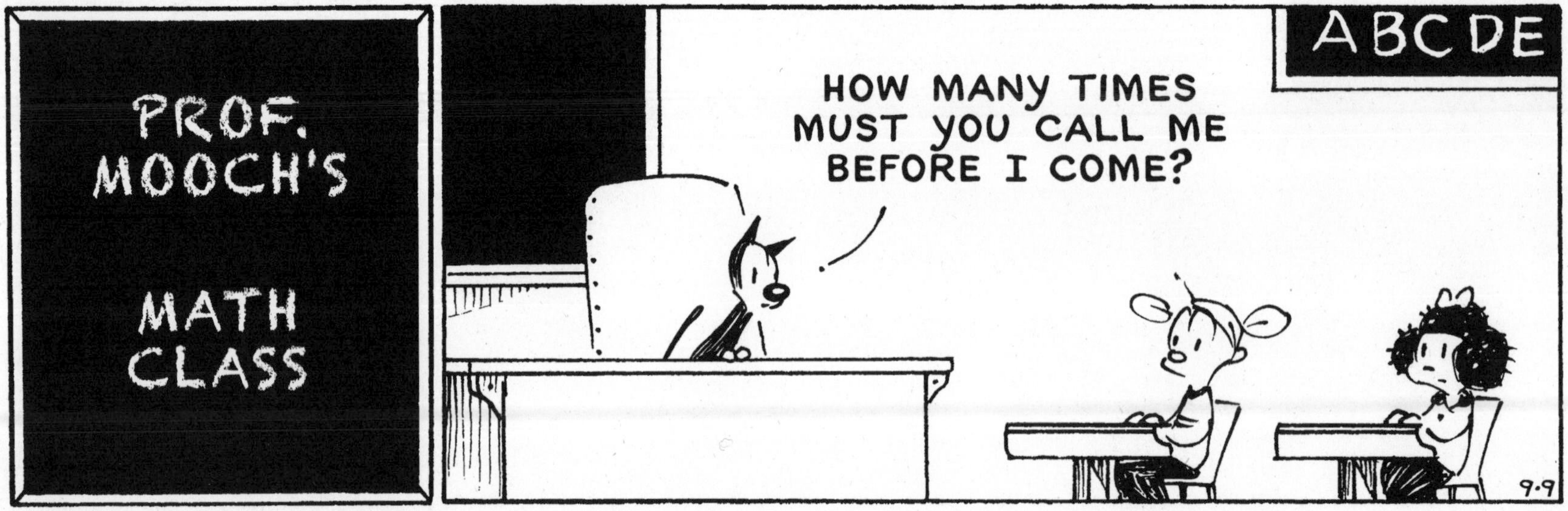
PROF. MOOCH'S
MATH CLASS
ABCDE
HOW MANY TIMES MUST YOU CALL ME BEFORE I COME?
9·9

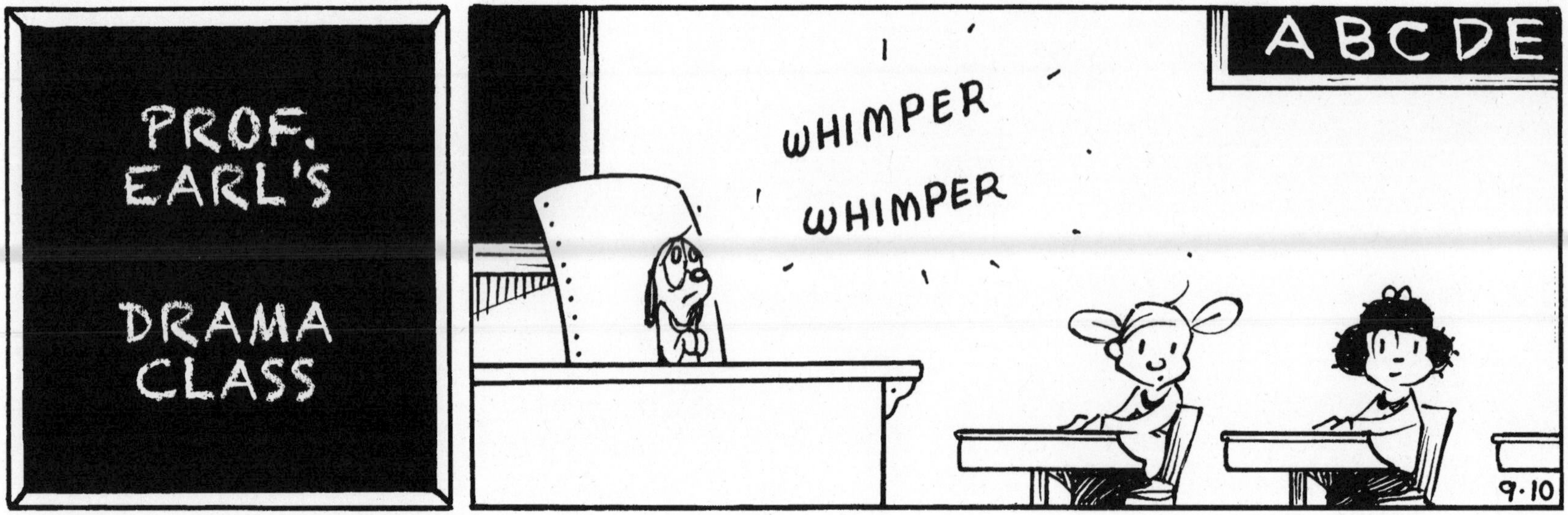
PROF. EARL'S
DRAMA CLASS
ABCDE
WHIMPER
WHIMPER
9·10

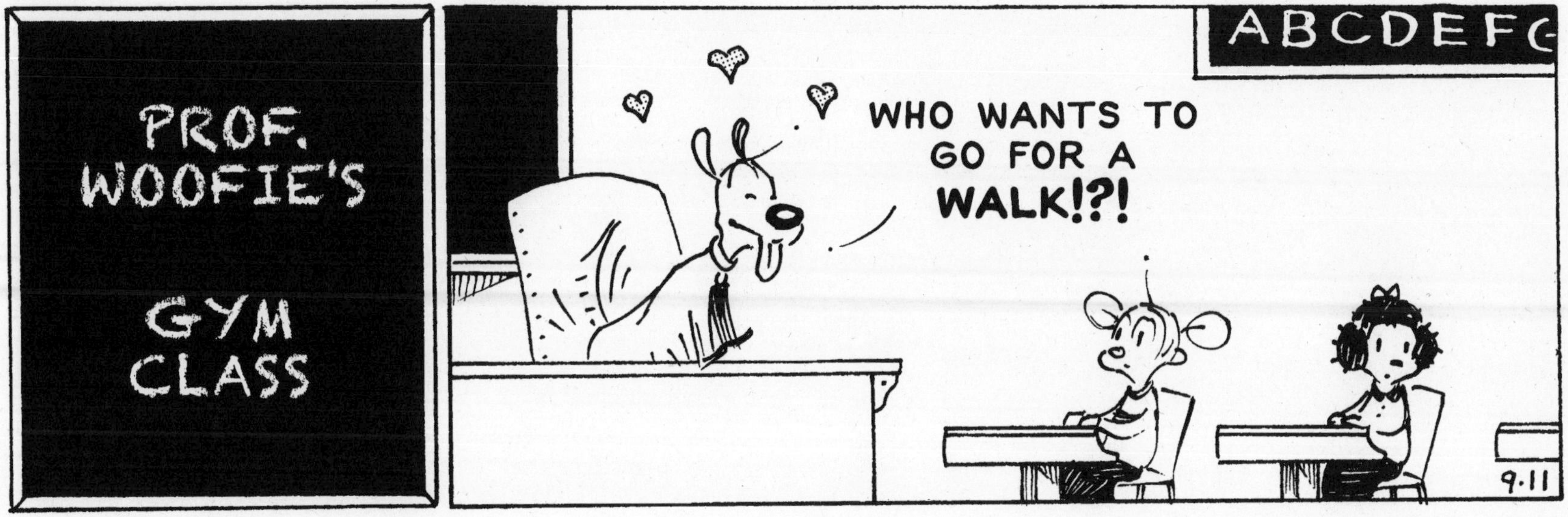
PROF. WOOFIE'S
GYM CLASS
ABCDEFG
WHO WANTS TO GO FOR A WALK!?!
9·11

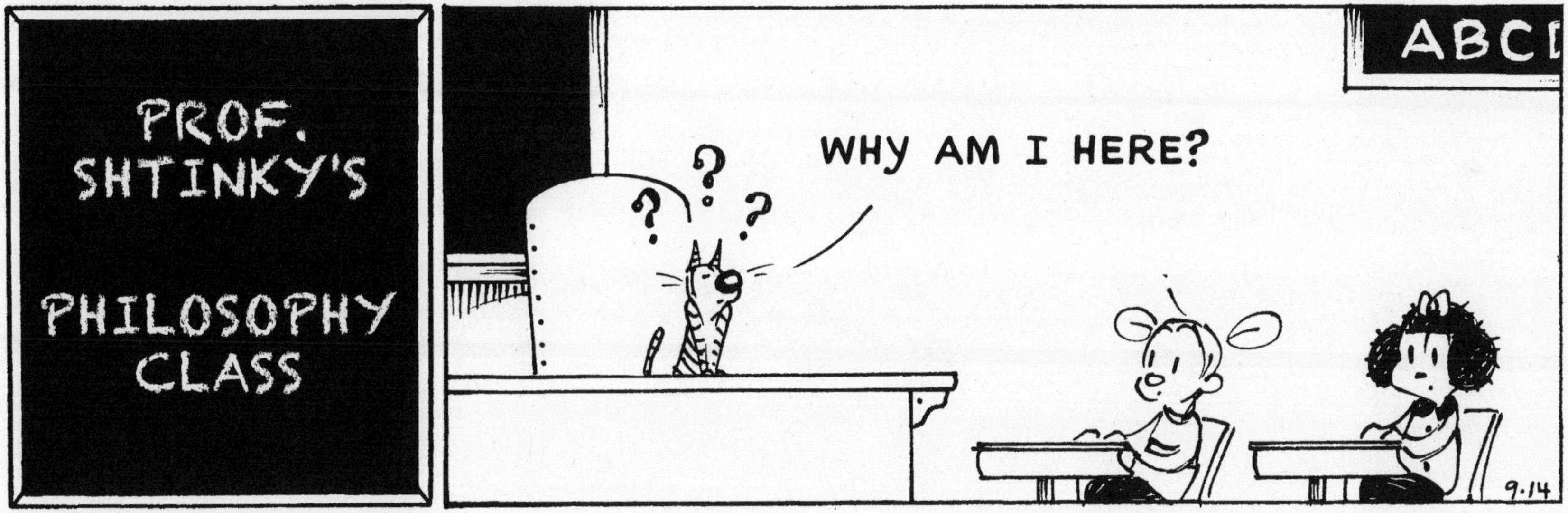
PROF. SHTINKY'S
PHILOSOPHY CLASS
ABCD
WHY AM I HERE?
9·14

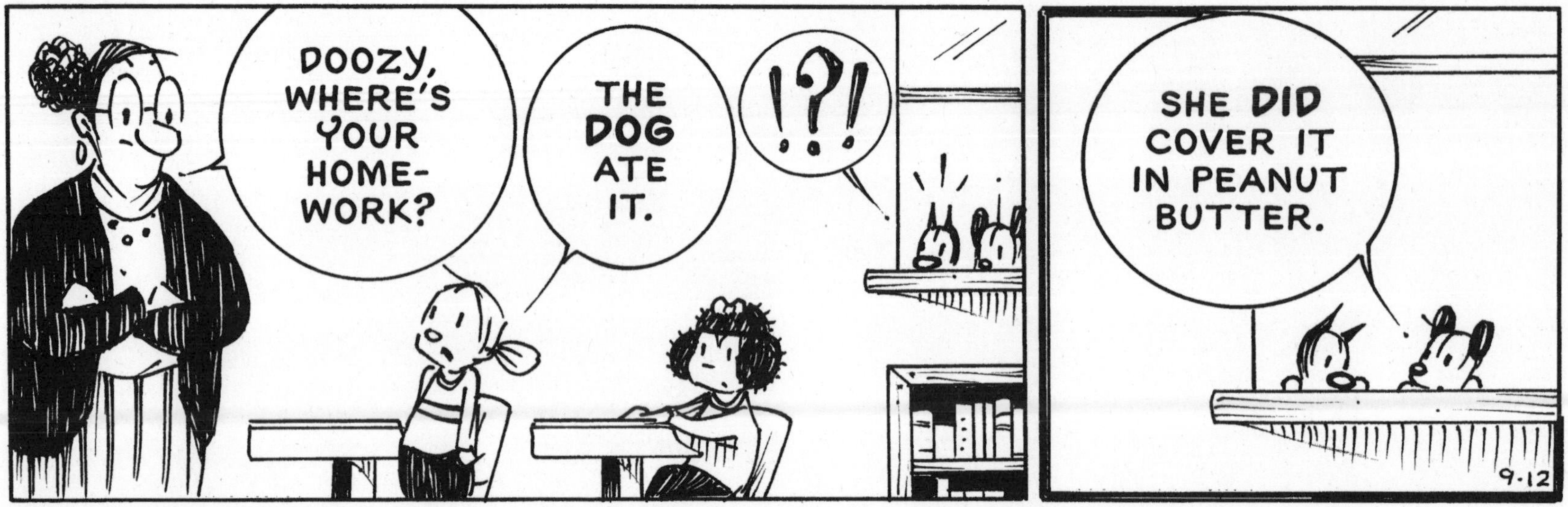
DOOZY, WHERE'S YOUR HOME-WORK?
THE DOG ATE IT.
!?!
SHE DID COVER IT IN PEANUT BUTTER.
9-12

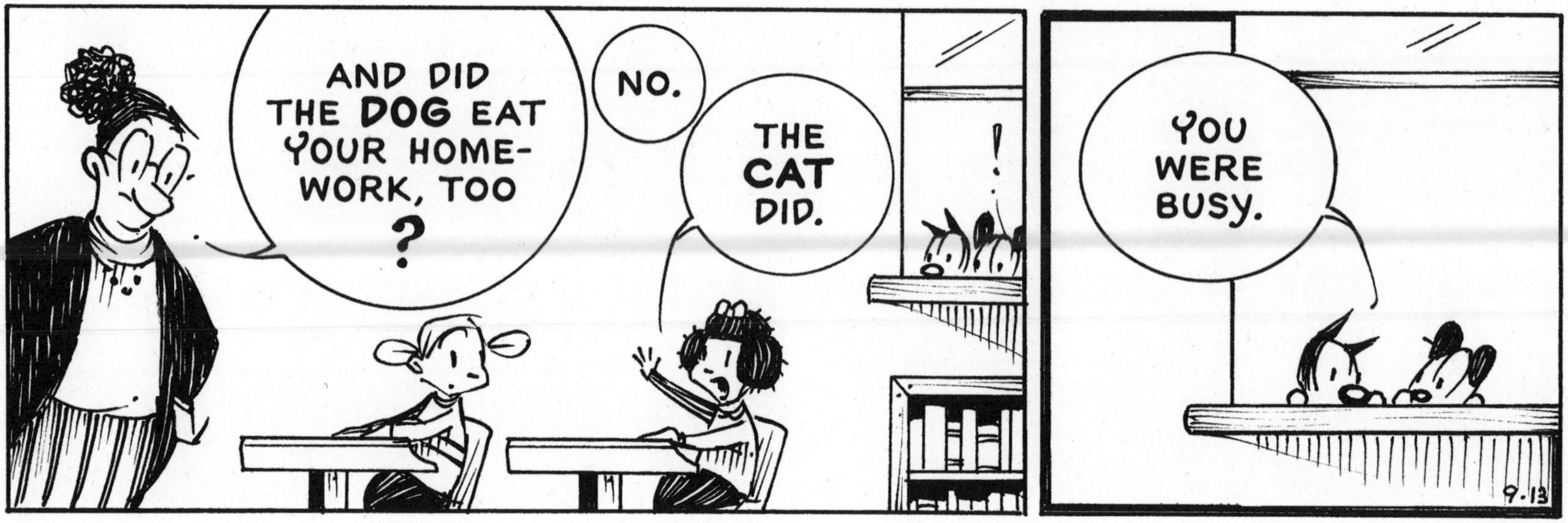
AND DID THE DOG EAT YOUR HOME-WORK, TOO ?
NO.
THE CAT DID.
!
YOU WERE BUSY.
9-13

HOWL

MUTTS

by
Patrick McDonnell

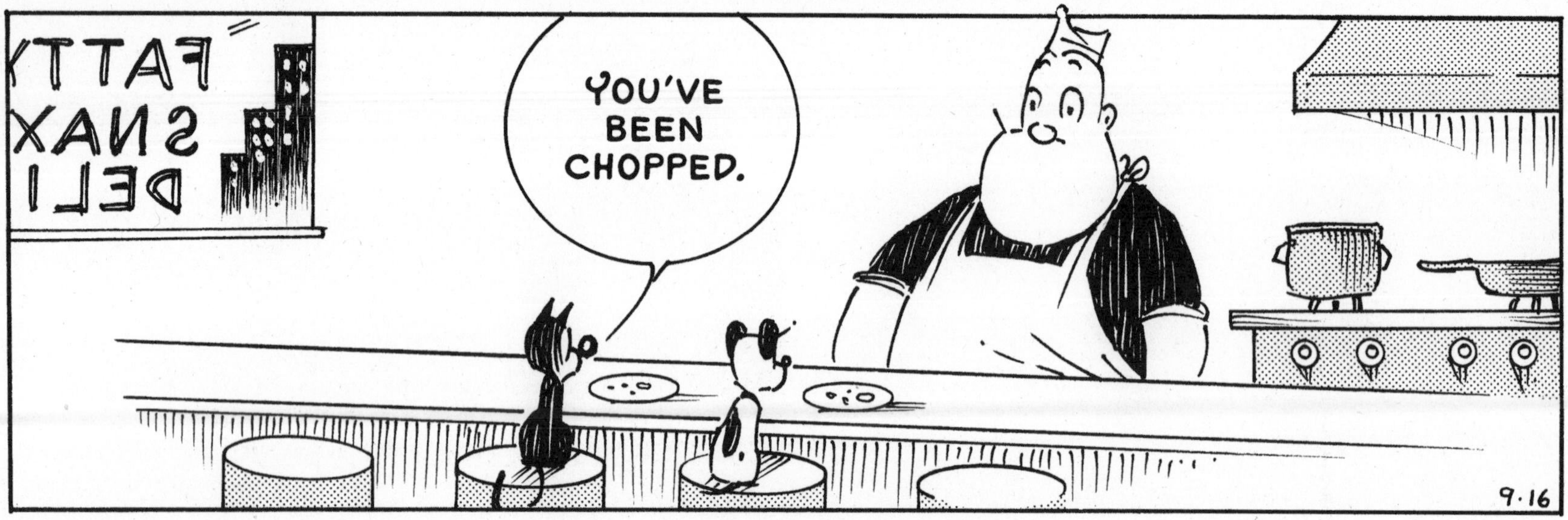
FATTY SNAX DELI
YOU'VE BEEN CHOPPED.
9·16

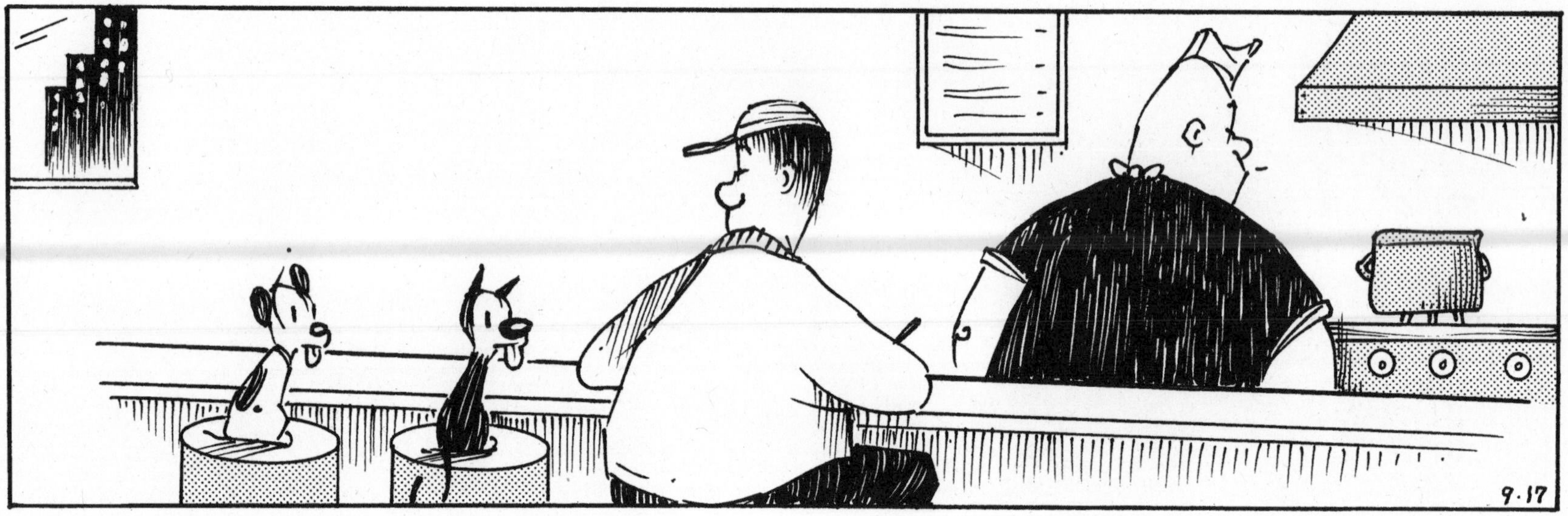
9·17

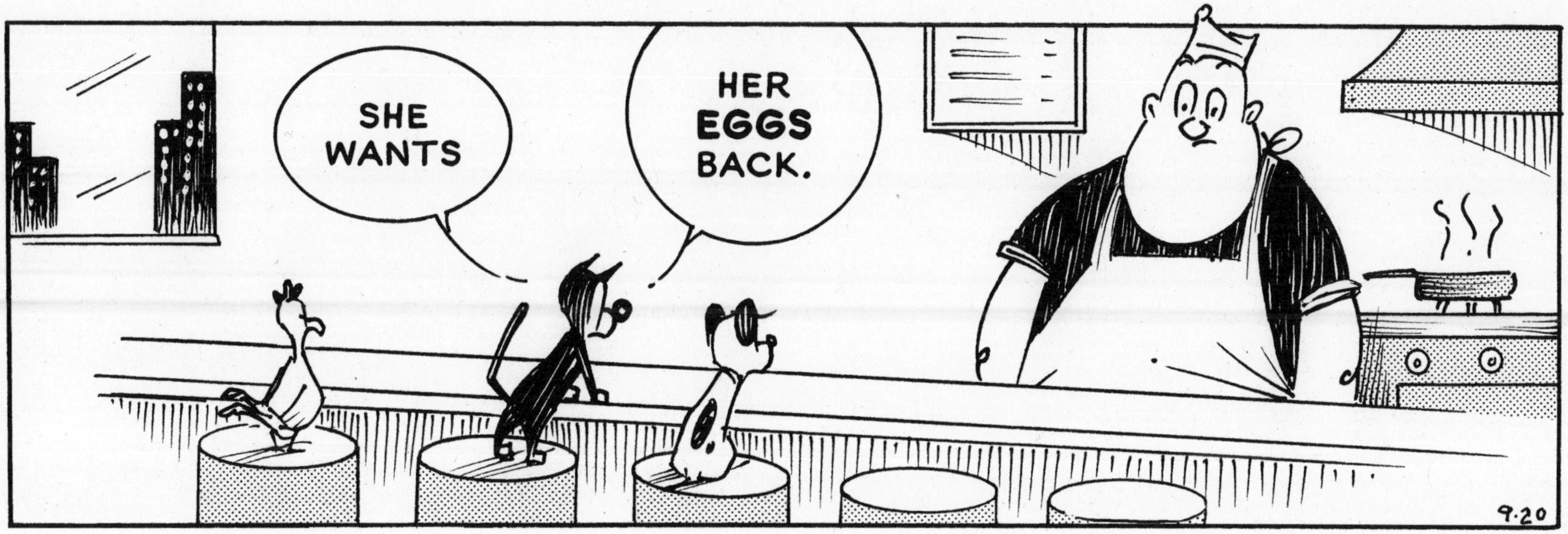
SHE WANTS
HER EGGS BACK.
9·20

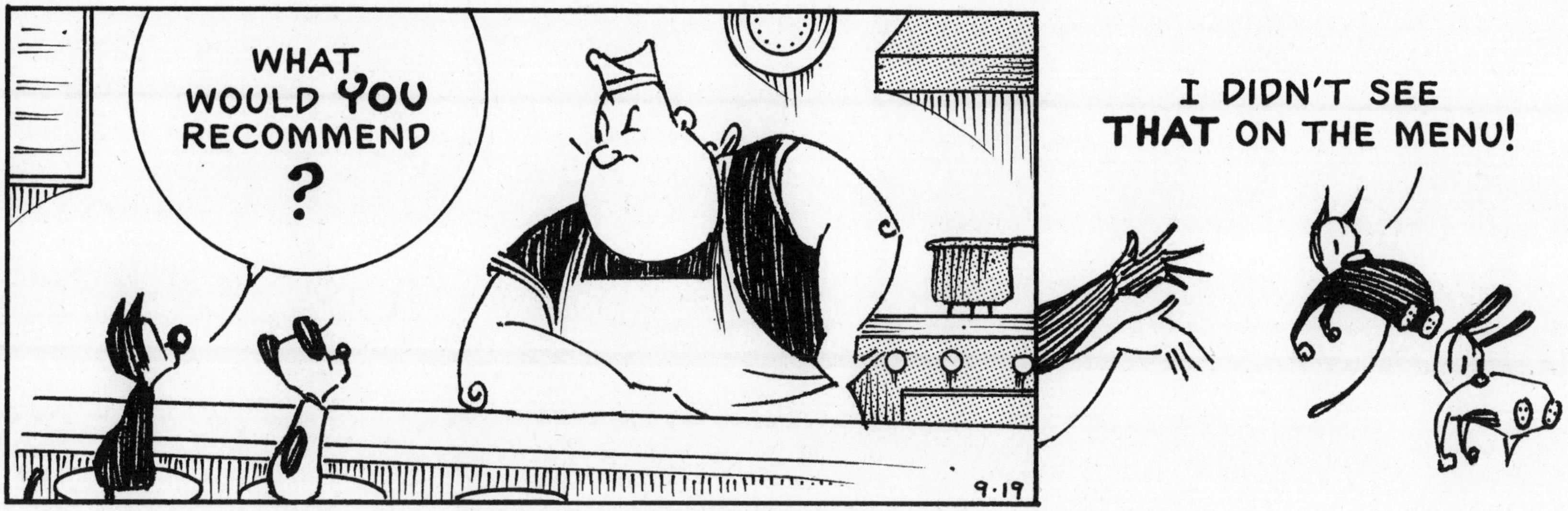
WHAT WOULD YOU RECOMMEND ?
9·19
I DIDN'T SEE THAT ON THE MENU!

MUTTS
by PATRICK McDONNELL

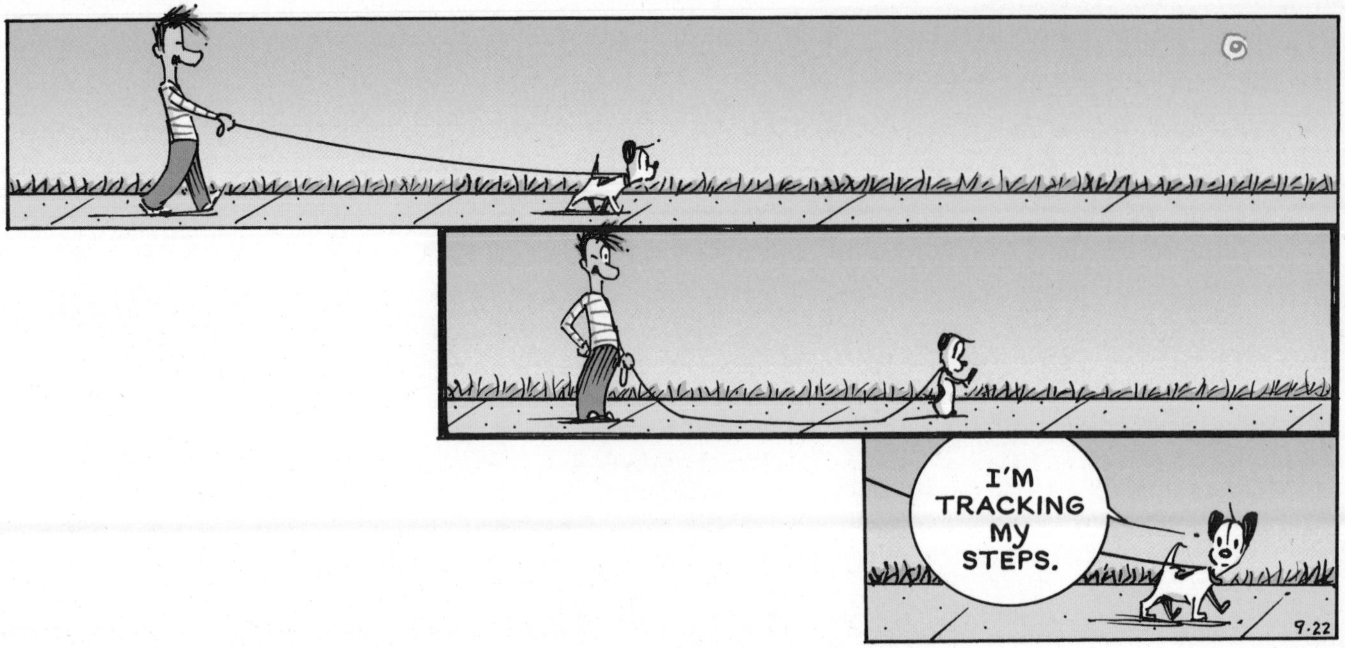
I'M TRACKING MY STEPS.
9.22

MUTTS
Patrick McDonnell

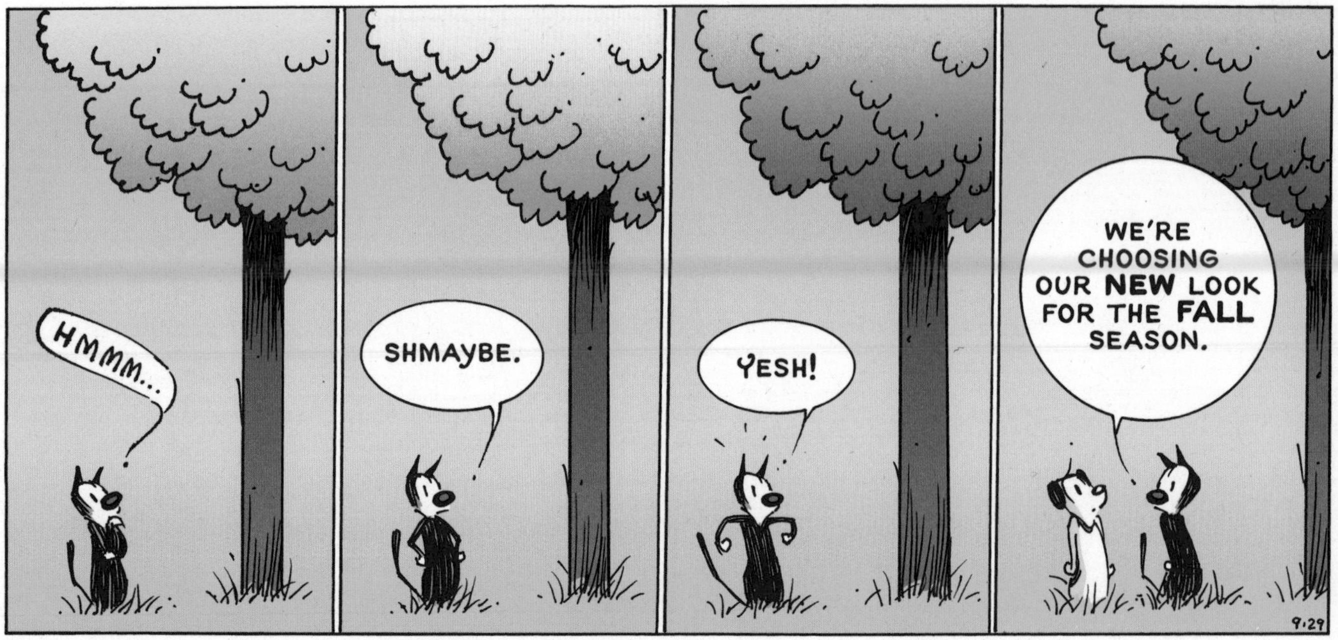
HMMM...
SHMAYBE.
YESH!
WE'RE CHOOSING OUR NEW LOOK FOR THE FALL SEASON.
9.29

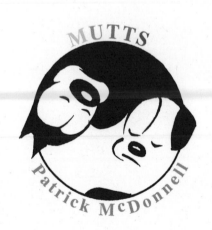

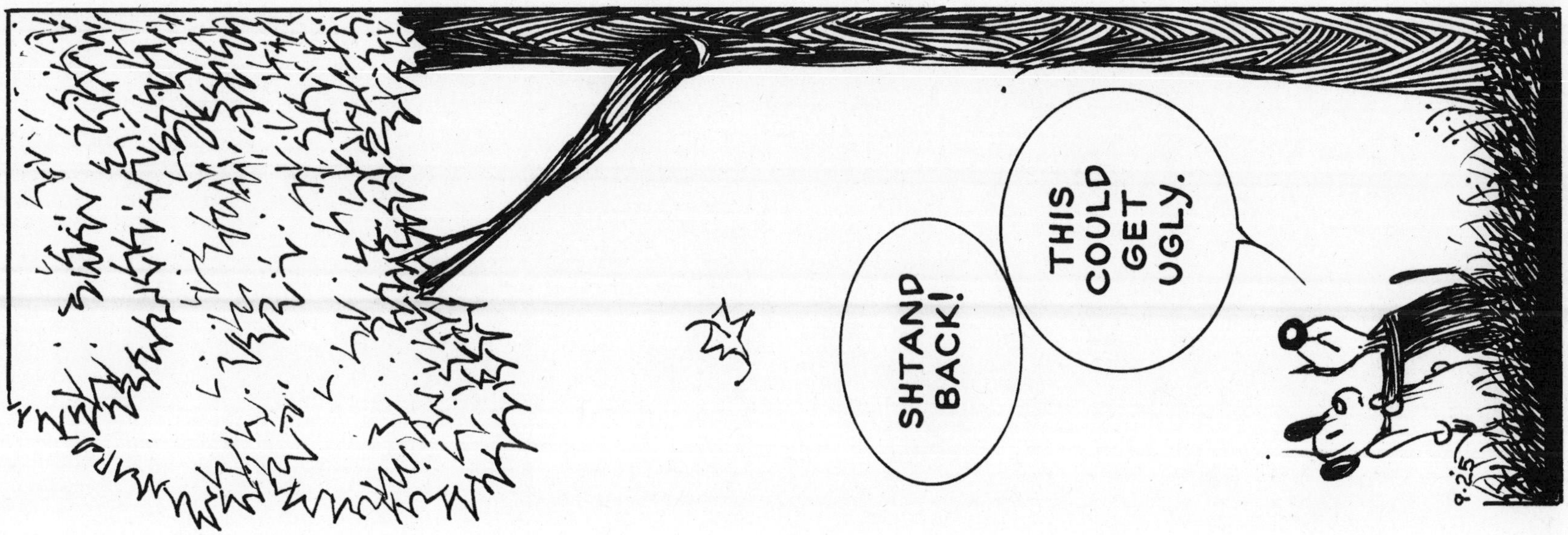
SHTAND BACK!
THIS COULD GET UGLY.
9-25

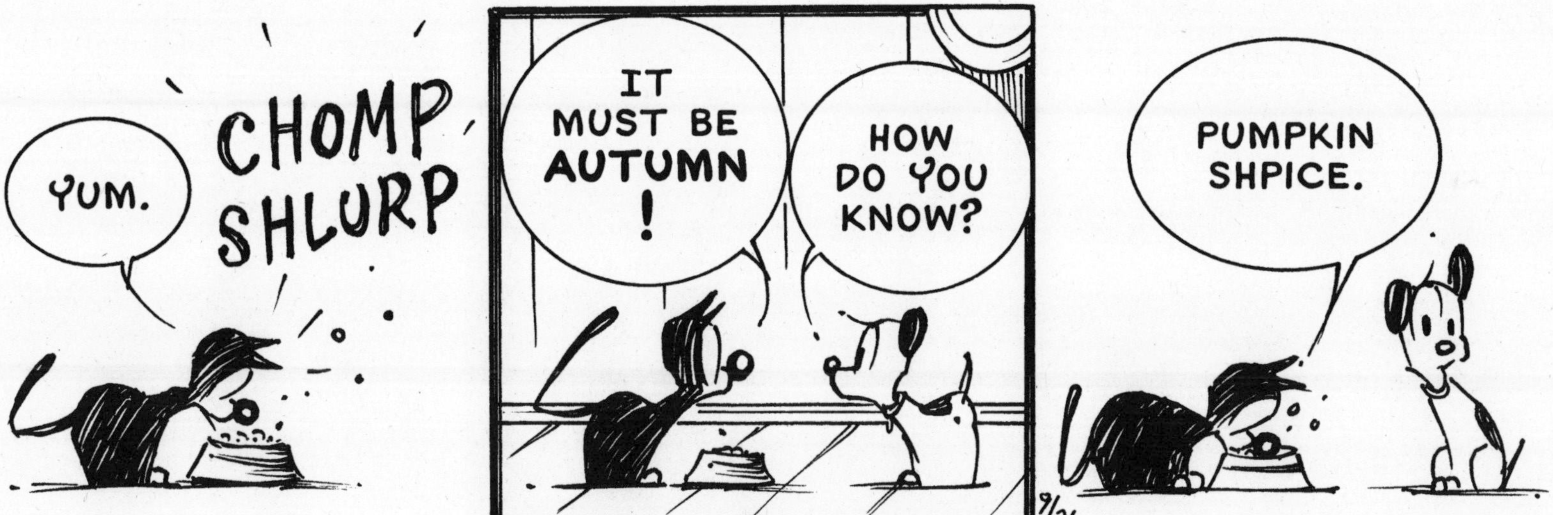
YUM.
CHOMP SHLURP
IT MUST BE AUTUMN !
HOW DO YOU KNOW?
PUMPKIN SHPICE.
9/26

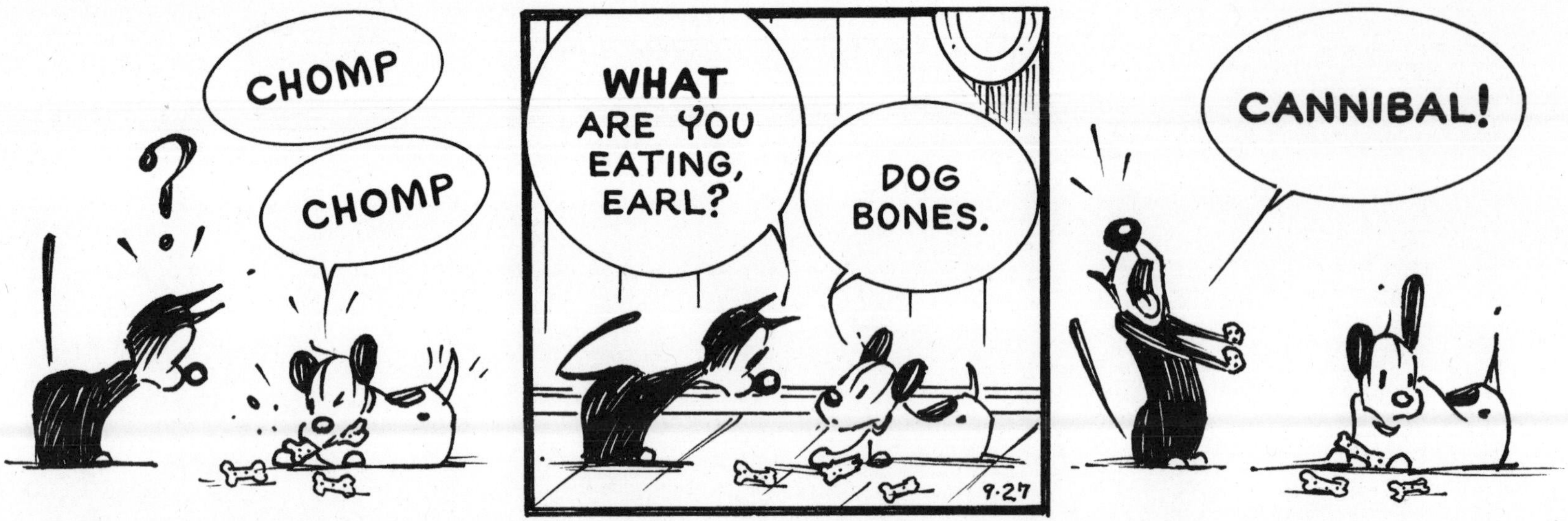
CHOMP
CHOMP
WHAT ARE YOU EATING, EARL?
DOG BONES.
9·27
CANNIBAL!

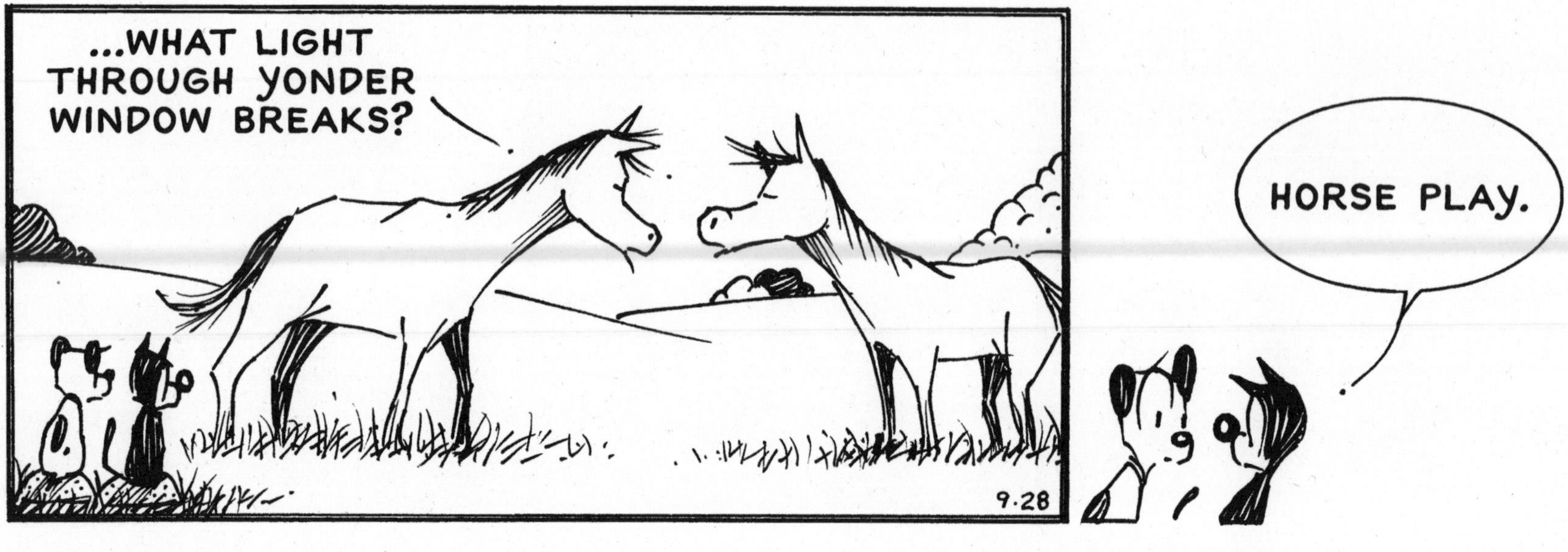
...WHAT LIGHT THROUGH YONDER WINDOW BREAKS?
9·28
HORSE PLAY.

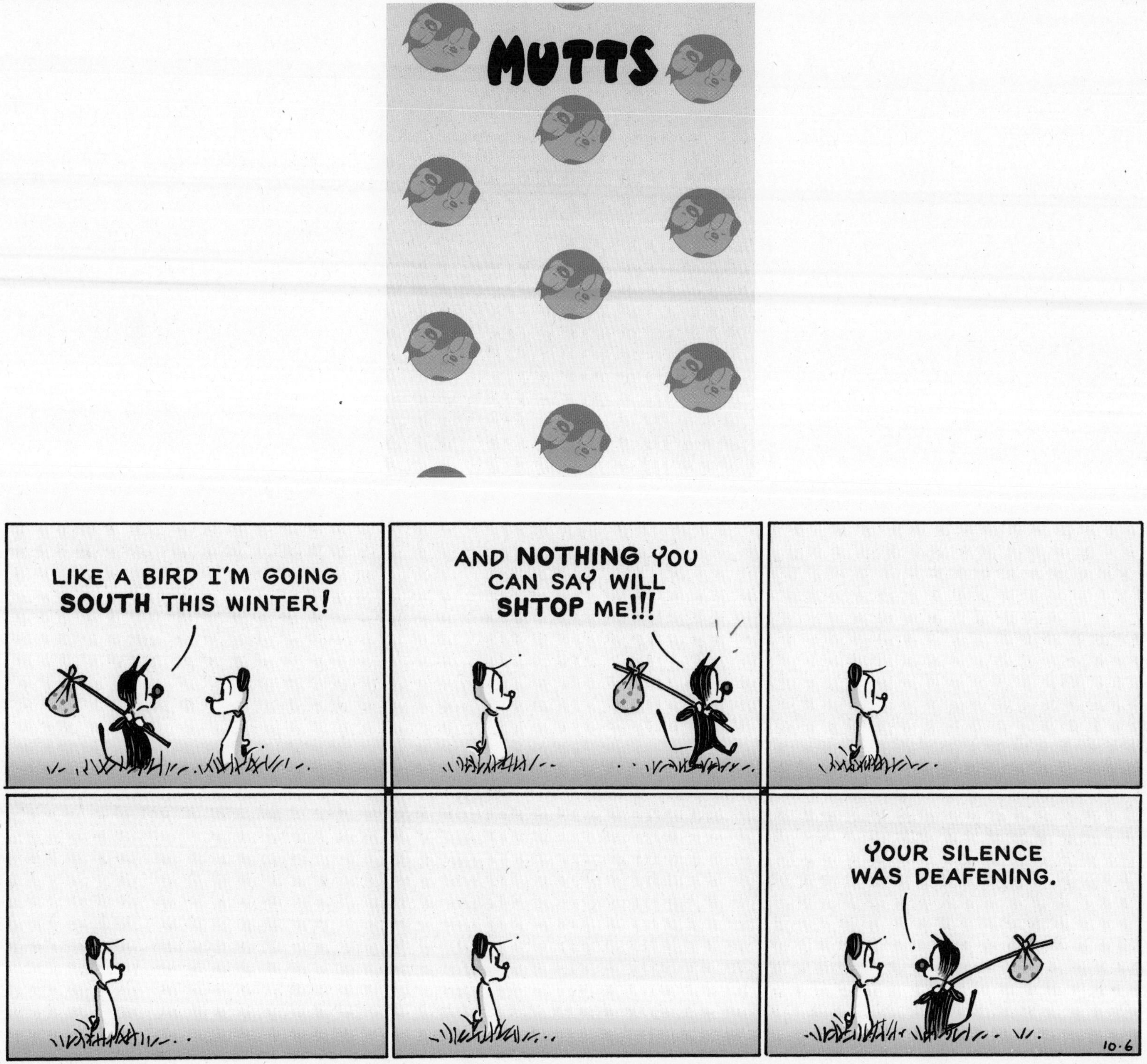
MUTTS
LIKE A BIRD I'M GOING SOUTH THIS WINTER!
AND NOTHING YOU CAN SAY WILL SHTOP ME!!!
YOUR SILENCE WAS DEAFENING.
10·6

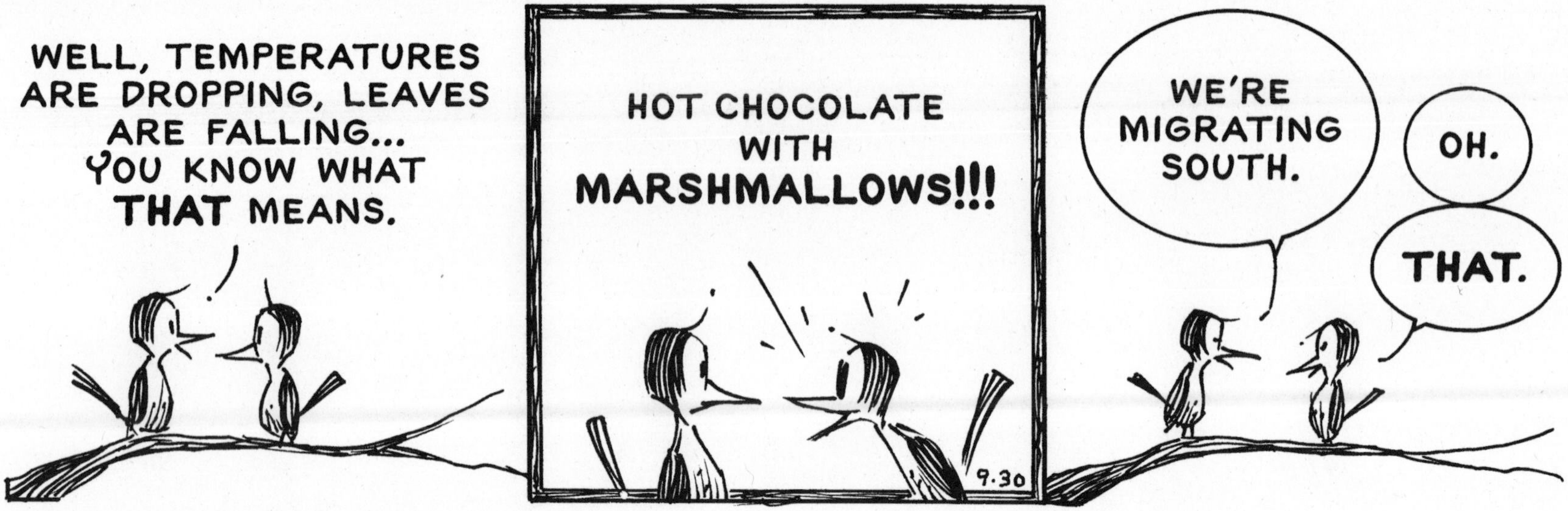
WELL, TEMPERATURES ARE DROPPING, LEAVES ARE FALLING... YOU KNOW WHAT **THAT** MEANS.
HOT CHOCOLATE WITH **MARSHMALLOWS!!!**
WE'RE MIGRATING SOUTH.
OH.
THAT.
9·30

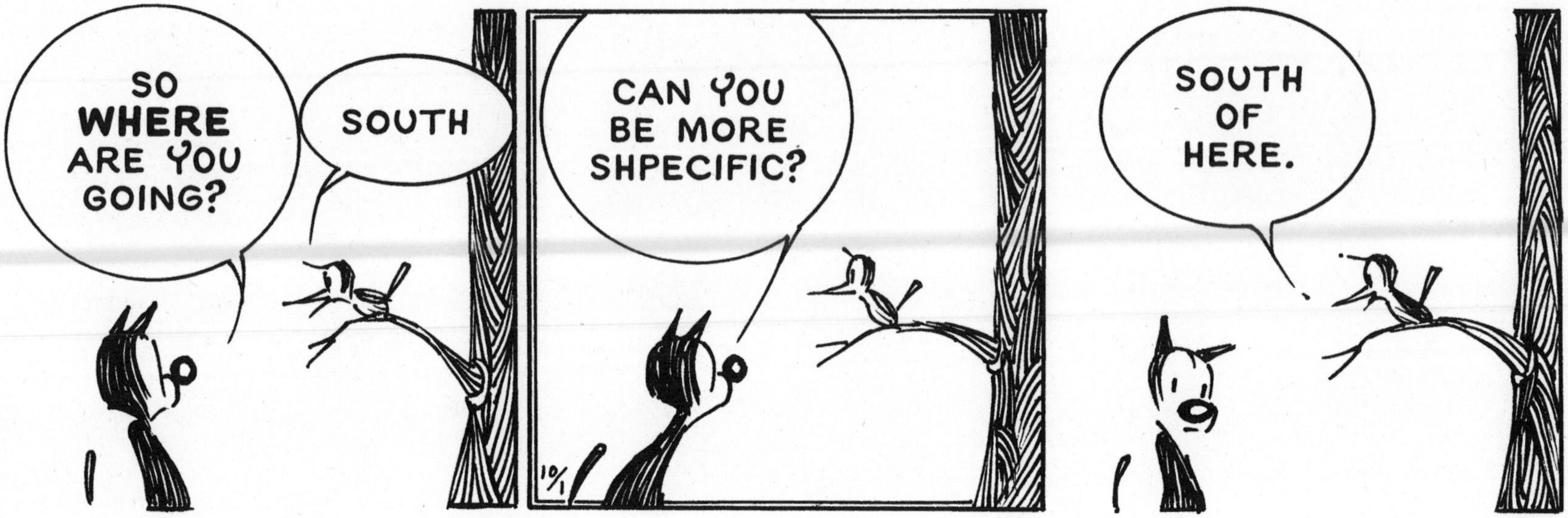
SO **WHERE** ARE YOU GOING?
SOUTH
CAN YOU BE MORE SHPECIFIC?
10/1
SOUTH OF HERE.

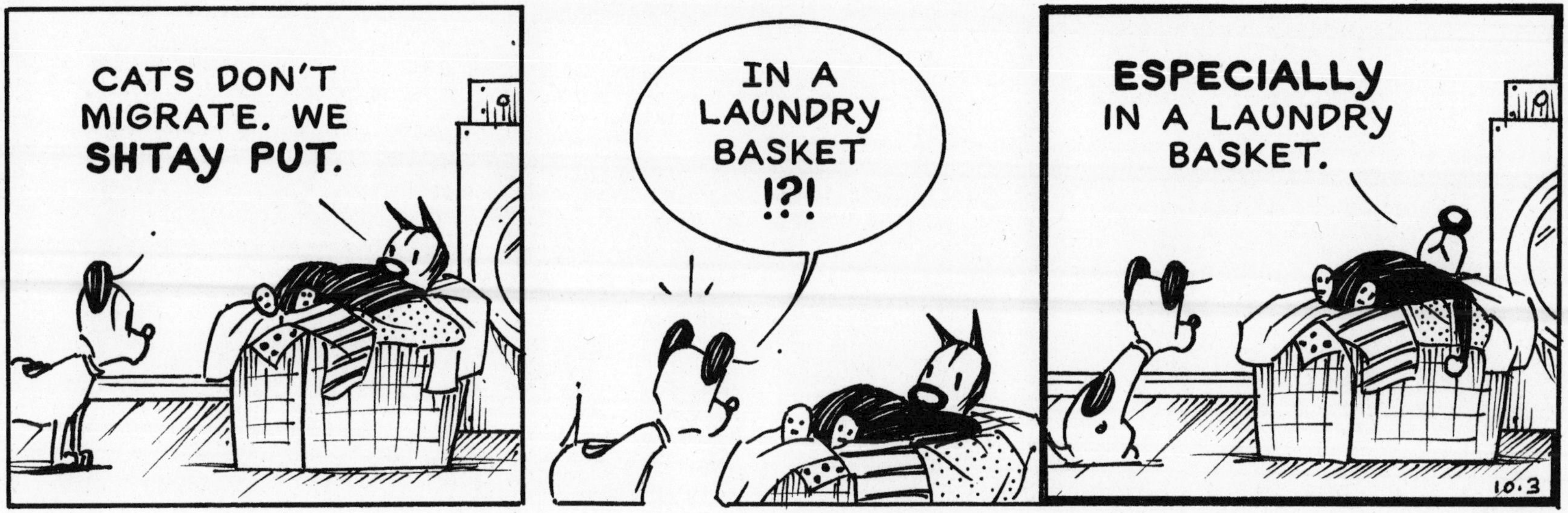
CATS DON'T MIGRATE. WE SHTAY PUT.
IN A LAUNDRY BASKET !?!
ESPECIALLY IN A LAUNDRY BASKET.
10.3

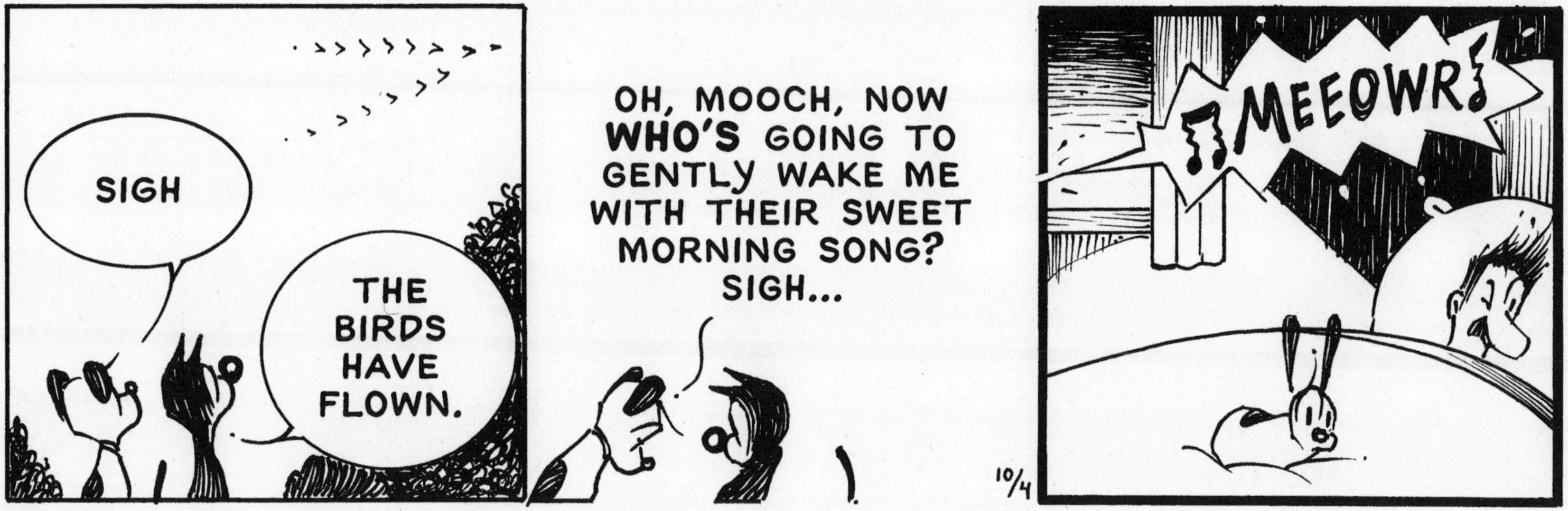
SIGH
THE BIRDS HAVE FLOWN.
OH, MOOCH, NOW WHO'S GOING TO GENTLY WAKE ME WITH THEIR SWEET MORNING SONG? SIGH...
10/4
MEEOWR

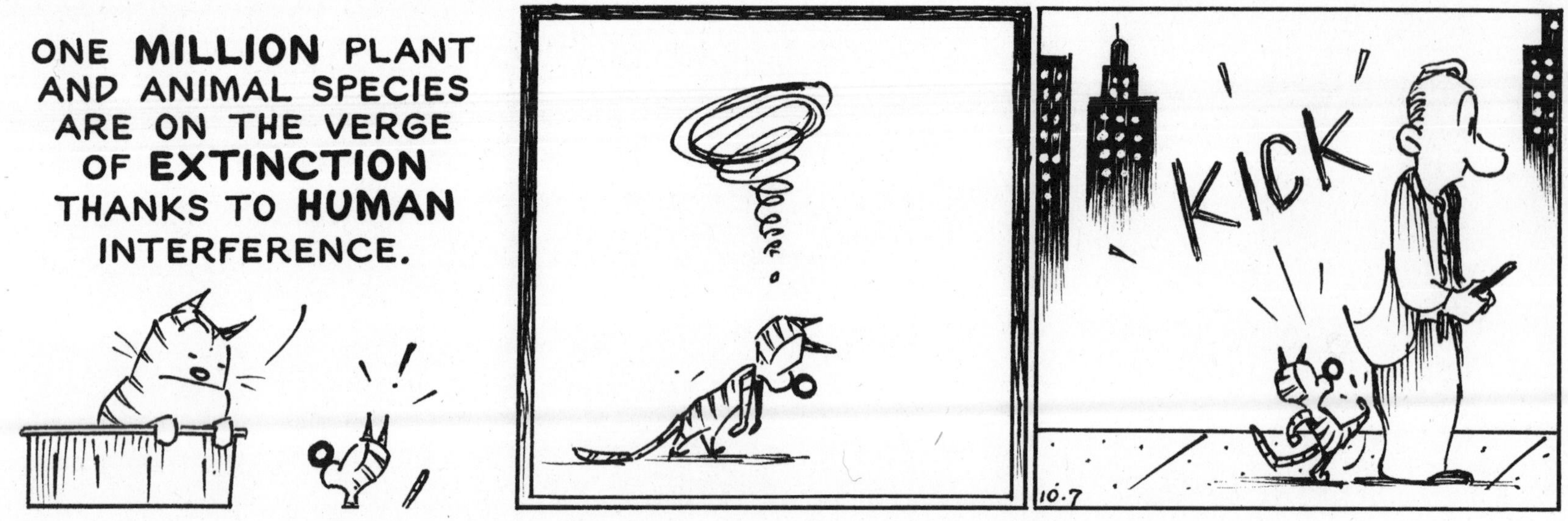
ONE MILLION PLANT AND ANIMAL SPECIES ARE ON THE VERGE OF EXTINCTION THANKS TO HUMAN INTERFERENCE.
KICK
10·7

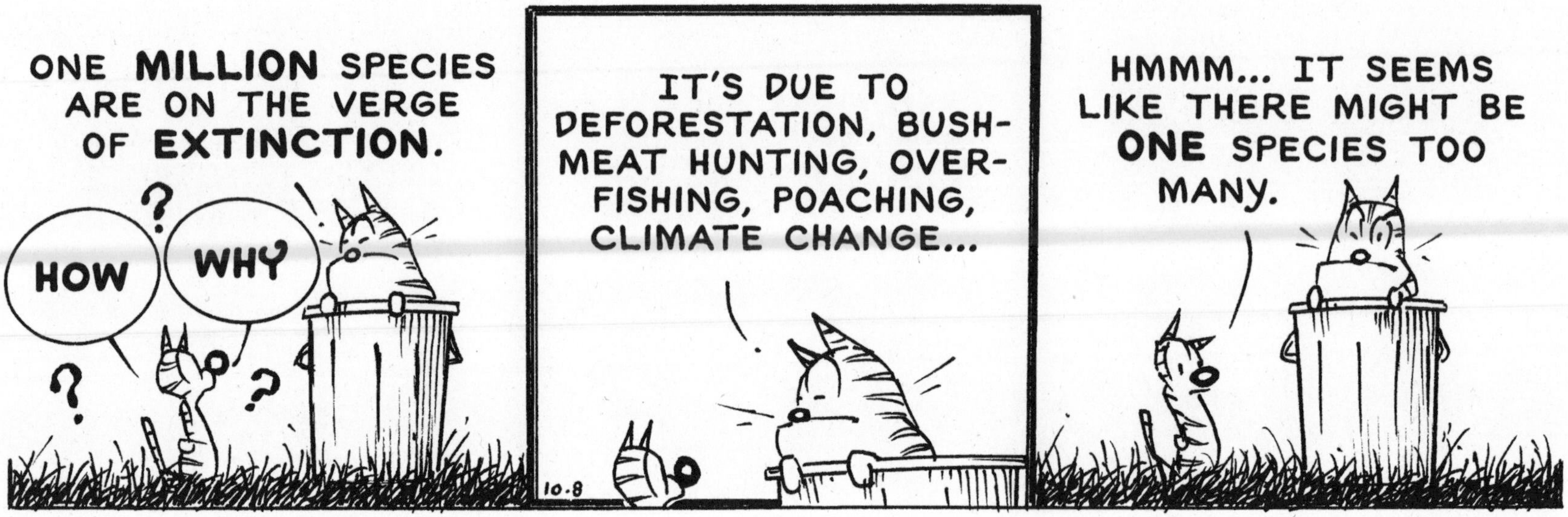
ONE MILLION SPECIES ARE ON THE VERGE OF EXTINCTION.
HOW
WHY
IT'S DUE TO DEFORESTATION, BUSH-MEAT HUNTING, OVER-FISHING, POACHING, CLIMATE CHANGE...
10·8
HMMM... IT SEEMS LIKE THERE MIGHT BE ONE SPECIES TOO MANY.

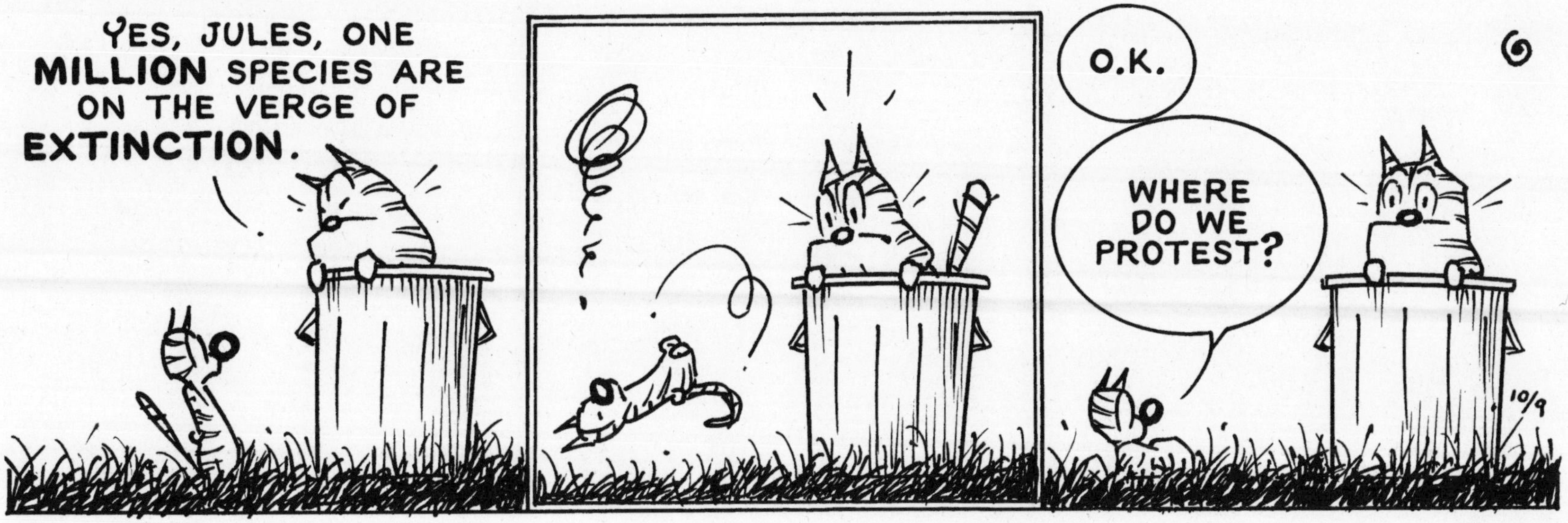

YES, JULES, ONE MILLION SPECIES ARE ON THE VERGE OF EXTINCTION.
O.K.
WHERE DO WE PROTEST?
10/9

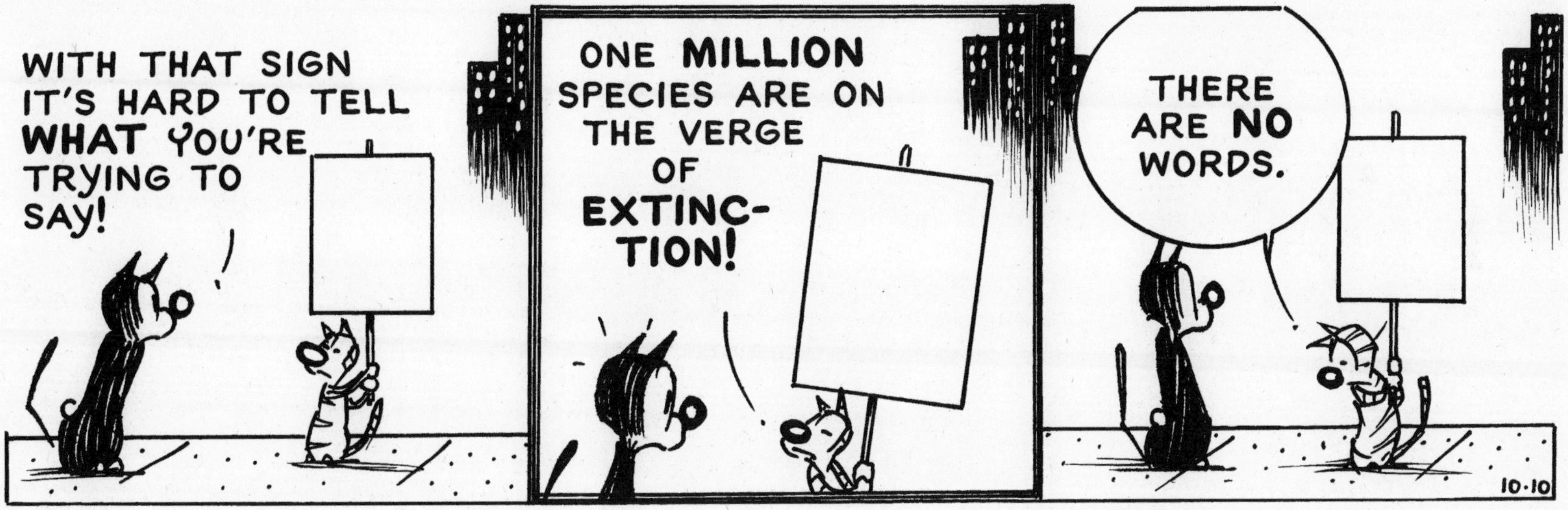

WITH THAT SIGN IT'S HARD TO TELL WHAT YOU'RE TRYING TO SAY!
ONE MILLION SPECIES ARE ON THE VERGE OF EXTINC-TION!
THERE ARE NO WORDS.
10·10

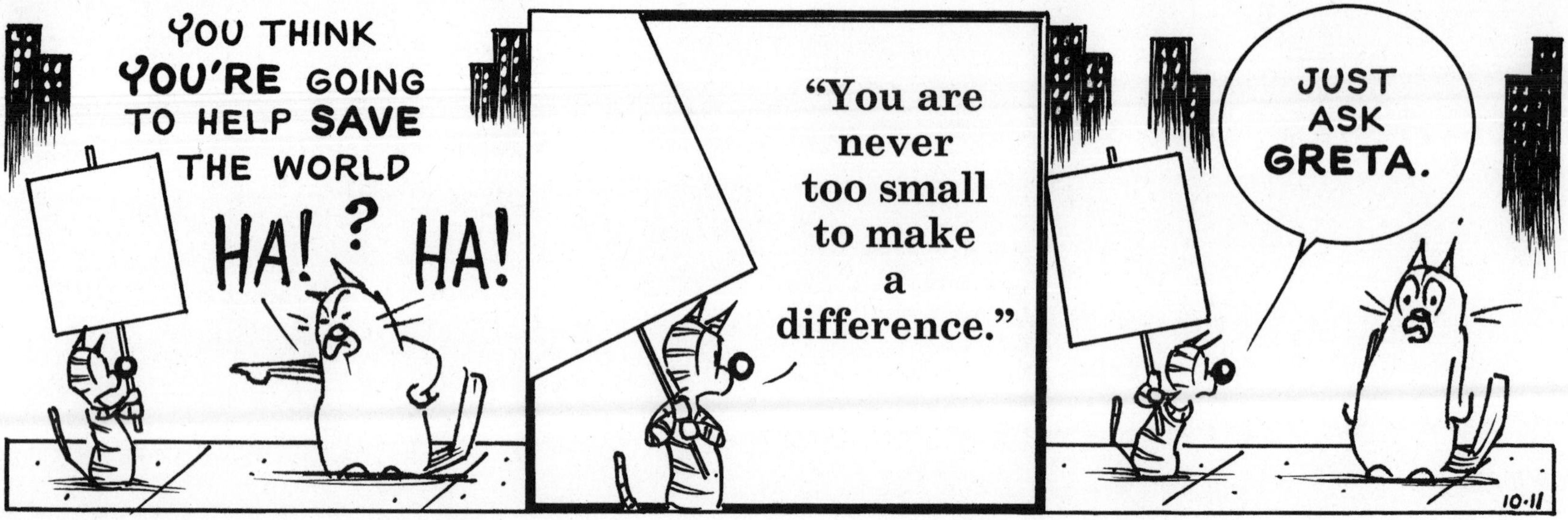
YOU THINK YOU'RE GOING TO HELP SAVE THE WORLD
HA! ? HA!
"You are never too small to make a difference."
JUST ASK GRETA.
10·11

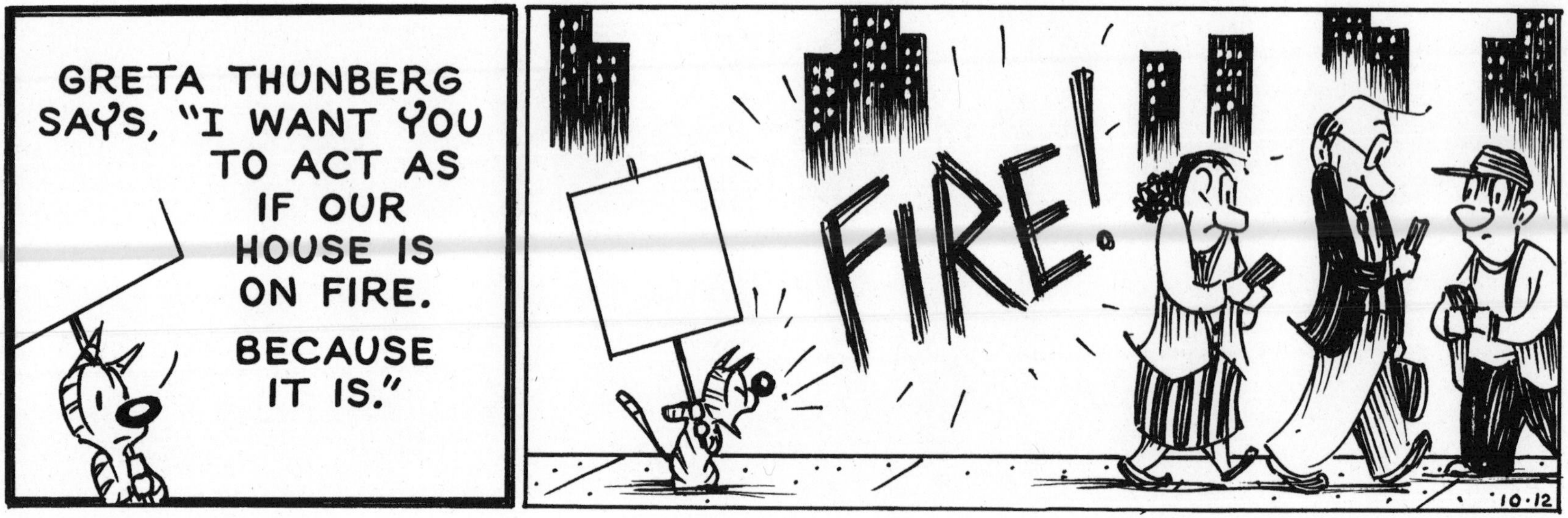
GRETA THUNBERG SAYS, "I WANT YOU TO ACT AS IF OUR HOUSE IS ON FIRE.
BECAUSE IT IS."
FIRE!
10·12

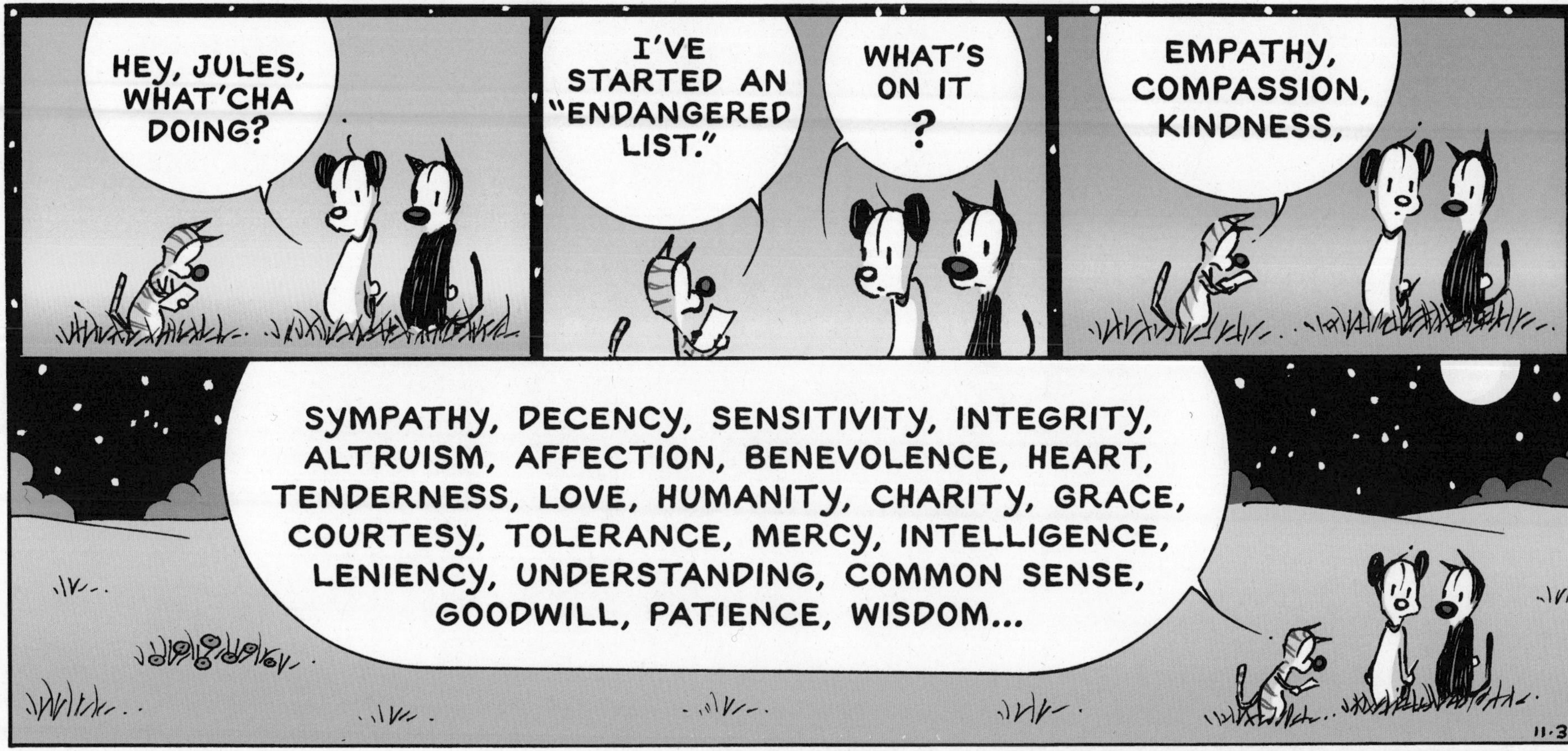
HEY, JULES, WHAT'CHA DOING?
I'VE STARTED AN "ENDANGERED LIST."
WHAT'S ON IT ?
EMPATHY, COMPASSION, KINDNESS,
SYMPATHY, DECENCY, SENSITIVITY, INTEGRITY, ALTRUISM, AFFECTION, BENEVOLENCE, HEART, TENDERNESS, LOVE, HUMANITY, CHARITY, GRACE, COURTESY, TOLERANCE, MERCY, INTELLIGENCE, LENIENCY, UNDERSTANDING, COMMON SENSE, GOODWILL, PATIENCE, WISDOM...
11·3

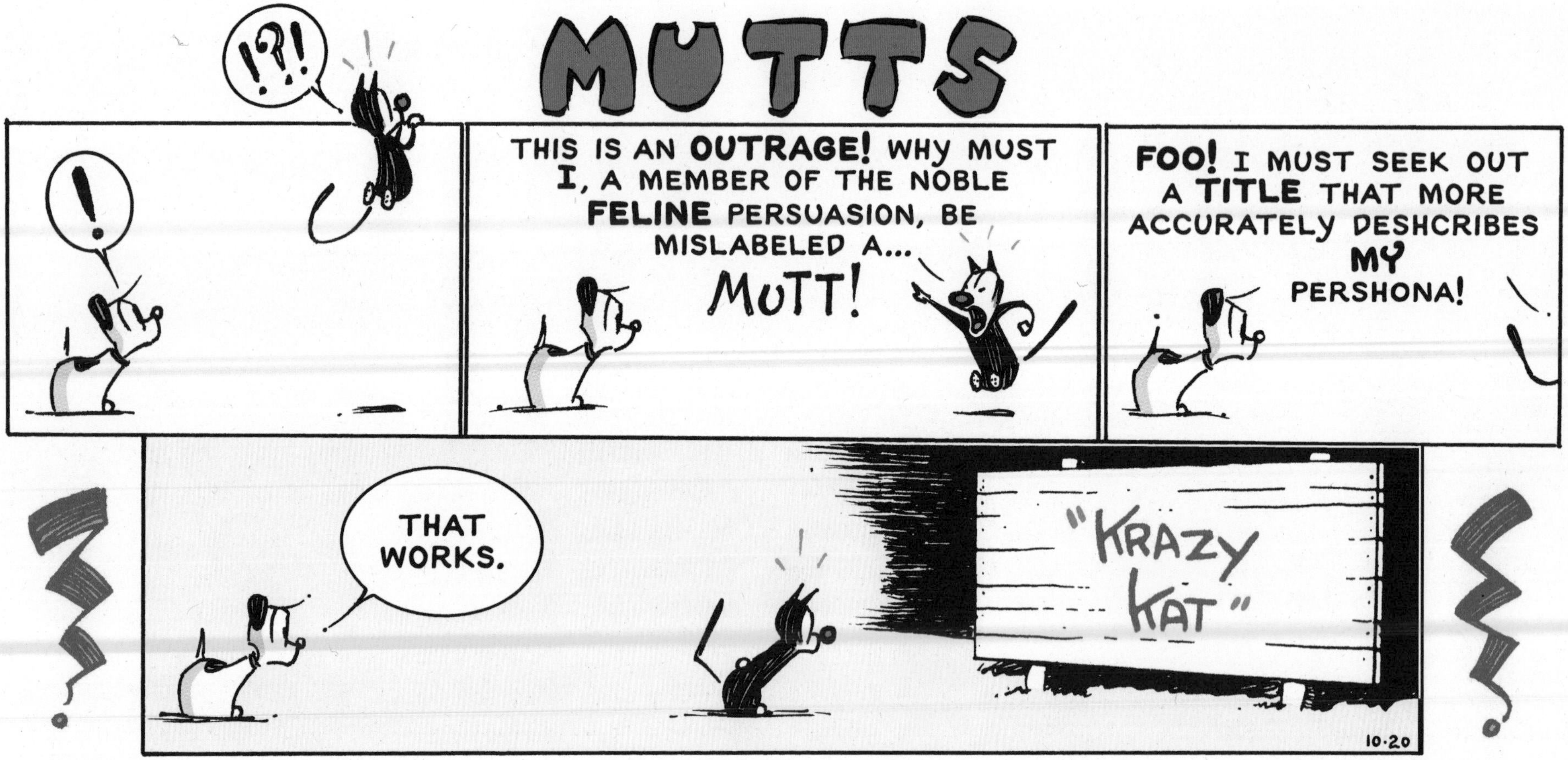

MUTTS
!?!
!
THIS IS AN OUTRAGE! WHY MUST I, A MEMBER OF THE NOBLE FELINE PERSUASION, BE MISLABELED A... MUTT!
FOO! I MUST SEEK OUT A TITLE THAT MORE ACCURATELY DESHCRIBES MY PERSHONA!
THAT WORKS.
"KRAZY KAT"
10·20

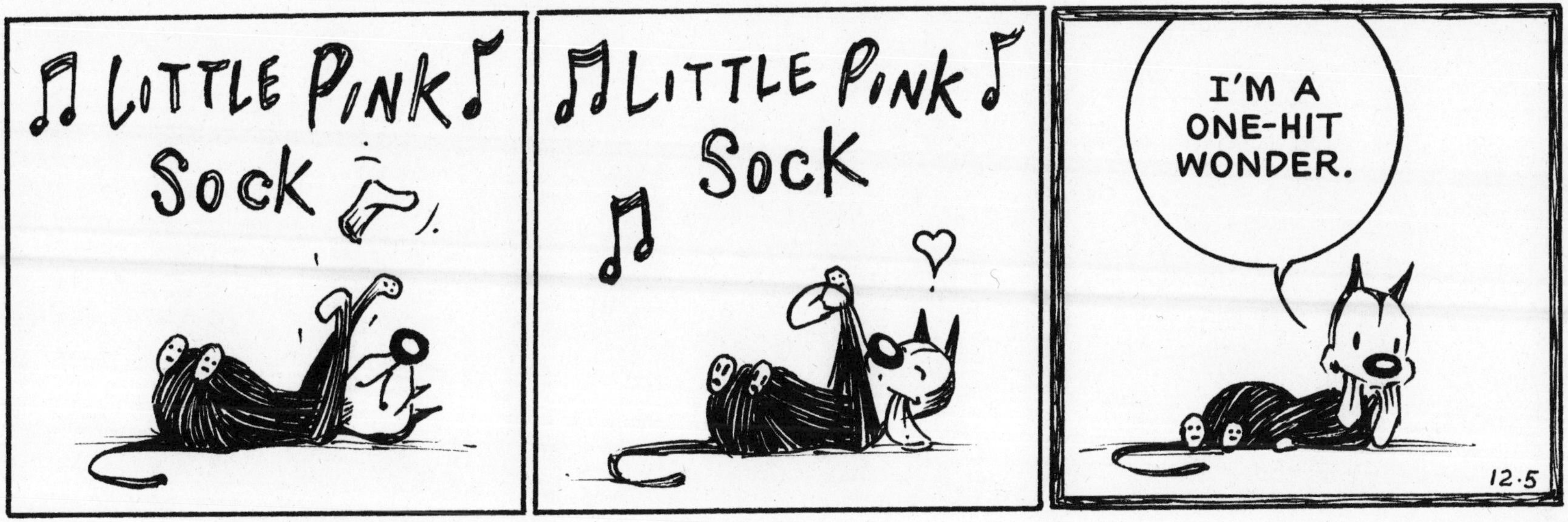
♫ LITTLE PINK ♪ SOCK
♫ LITTLE PINK ♪ SOCK ♫
I'M A ONE-HIT WONDER.
12.5

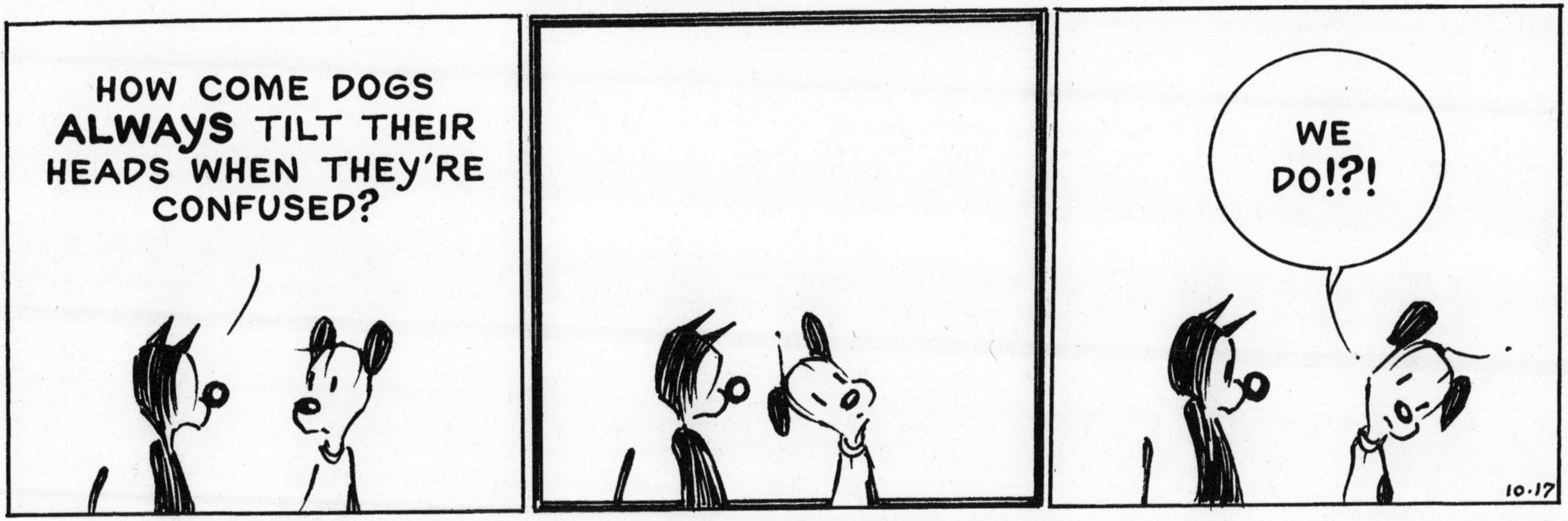
HOW COME DOGS **ALWAYS** TILT THEIR HEADS WHEN THEY'RE CONFUSED?
WE DO!?!
10.17

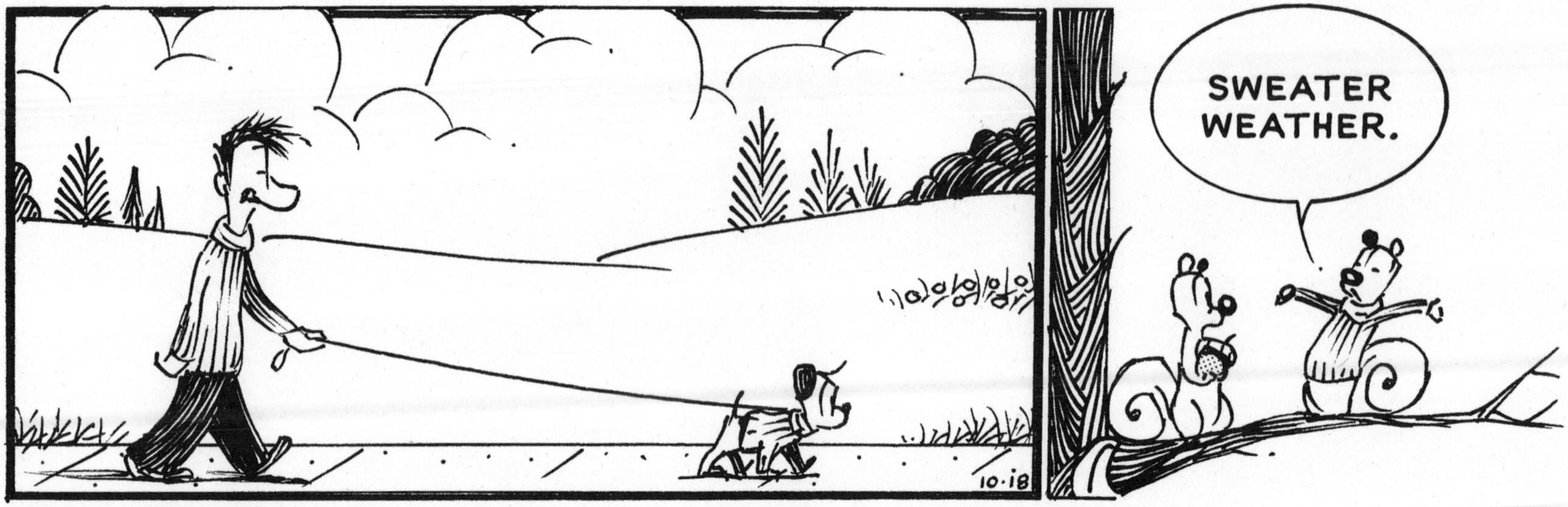
10·18
SWEATER WEATHER.

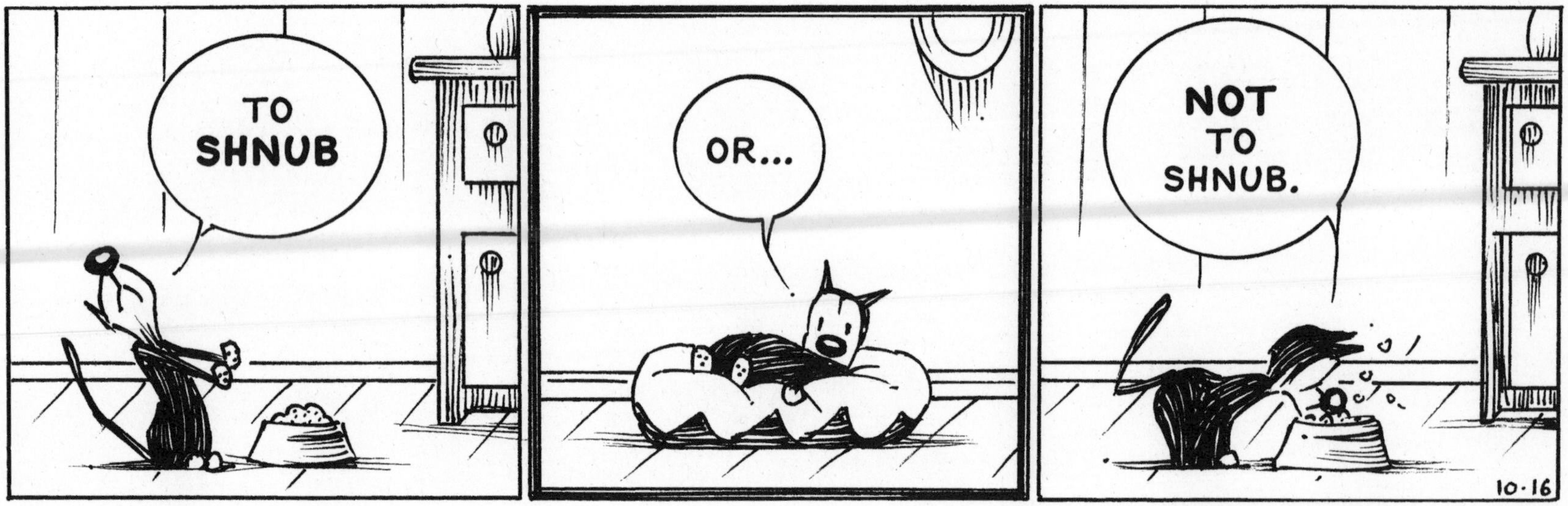
TO SHNUB
OR...
NOT TO SHNUB.
10·16

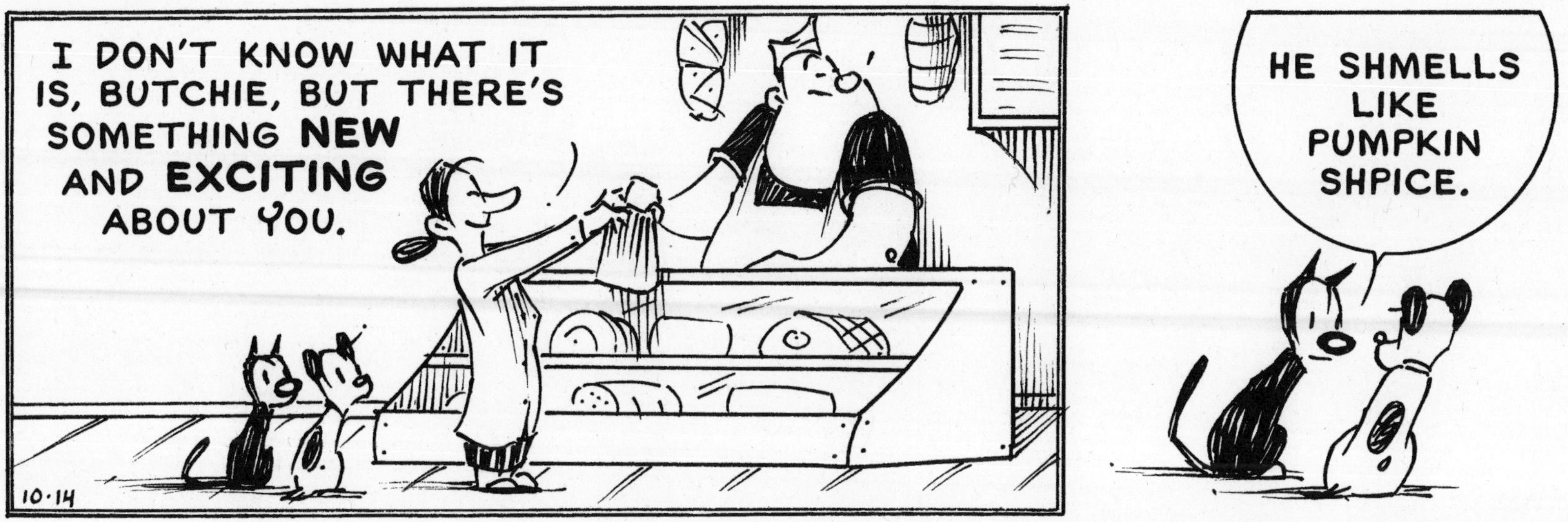
I DON'T KNOW WHAT IT IS, BUTCHIE, BUT THERE'S SOMETHING NEW AND EXCITING ABOUT YOU.
10·14
HE SHMELLS LIKE PUMPKIN SHPICE.

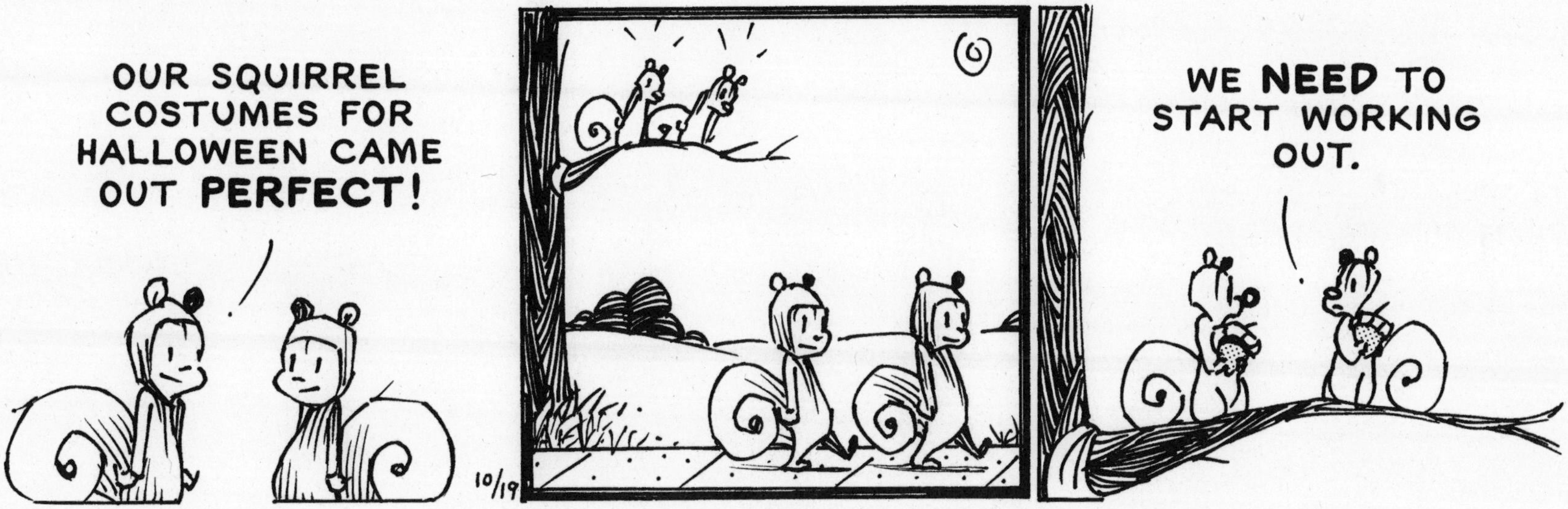
OUR SQUIRREL COSTUMES FOR HALLOWEEN CAME OUT PERFECT!
10/19
WE NEED TO START WORKING OUT.

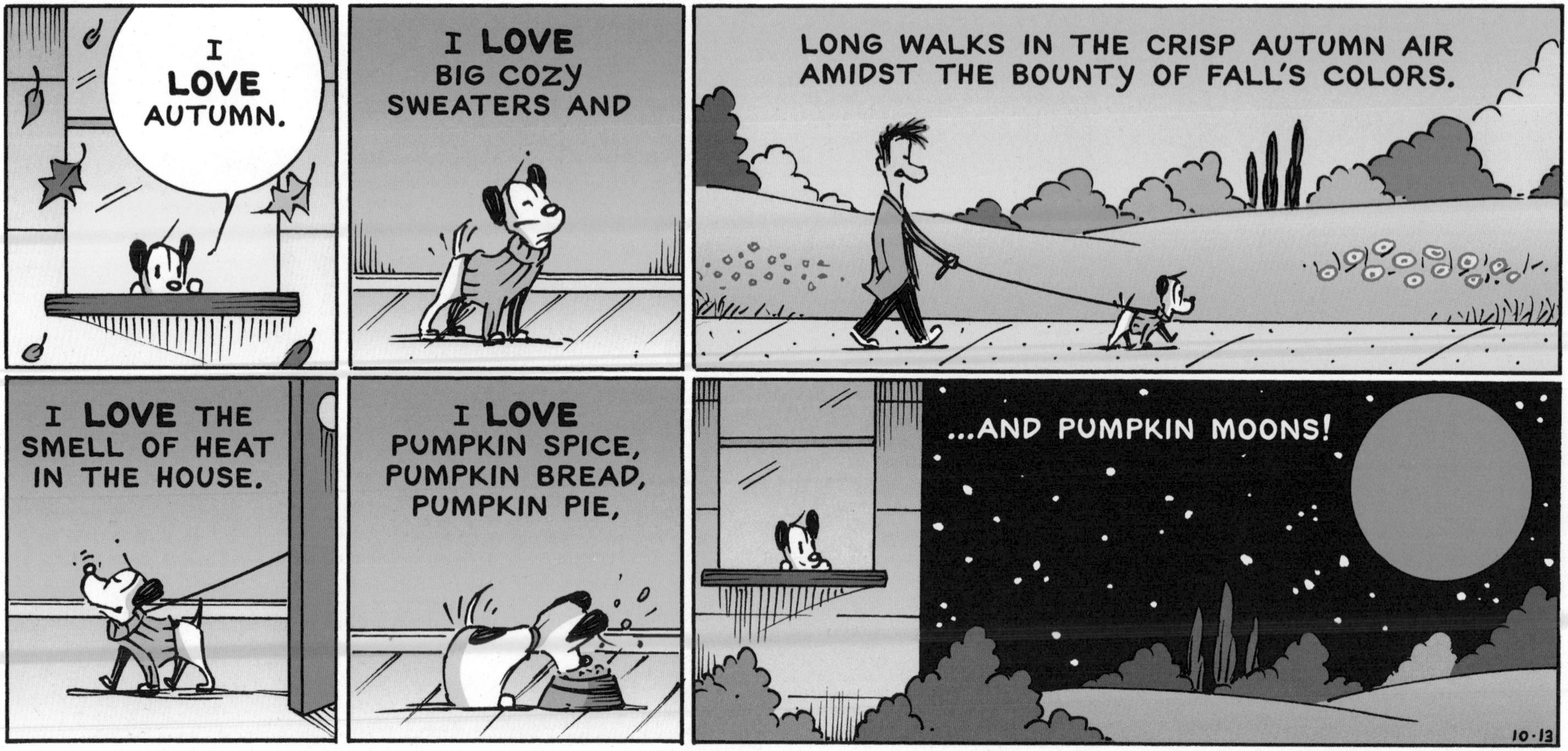
I LOVE AUTUMN.
I LOVE BIG COZY SWEATERS AND
LONG WALKS IN THE CRISP AUTUMN AIR AMIDST THE BOUNTY OF FALL'S COLORS.
I LOVE THE SMELL OF HEAT IN THE HOUSE.
I LOVE PUMPKIN SPICE, PUMPKIN BREAD, PUMPKIN PIE,
...AND PUMPKIN MOONS!
10·13

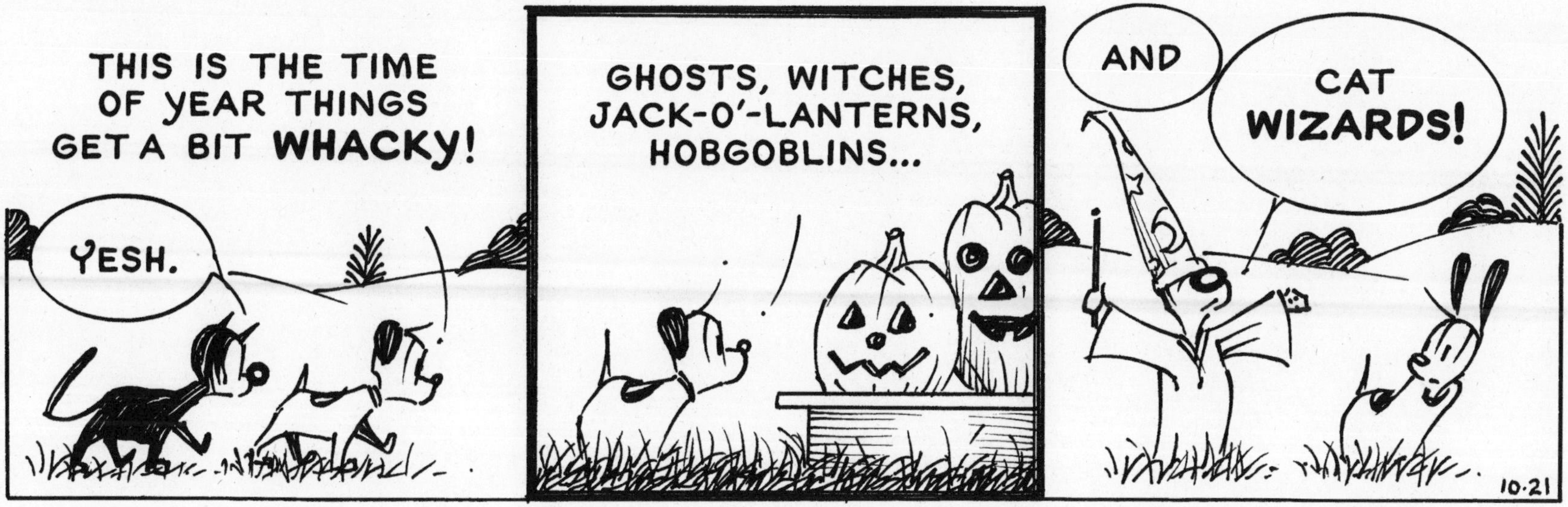
THIS IS THE TIME OF YEAR THINGS GET A BIT WHACKY!
YESH.
GHOSTS, WITCHES, JACK-O'-LANTERNS, HOBGOBLINS...
AND
CAT WIZARDS!
10·21

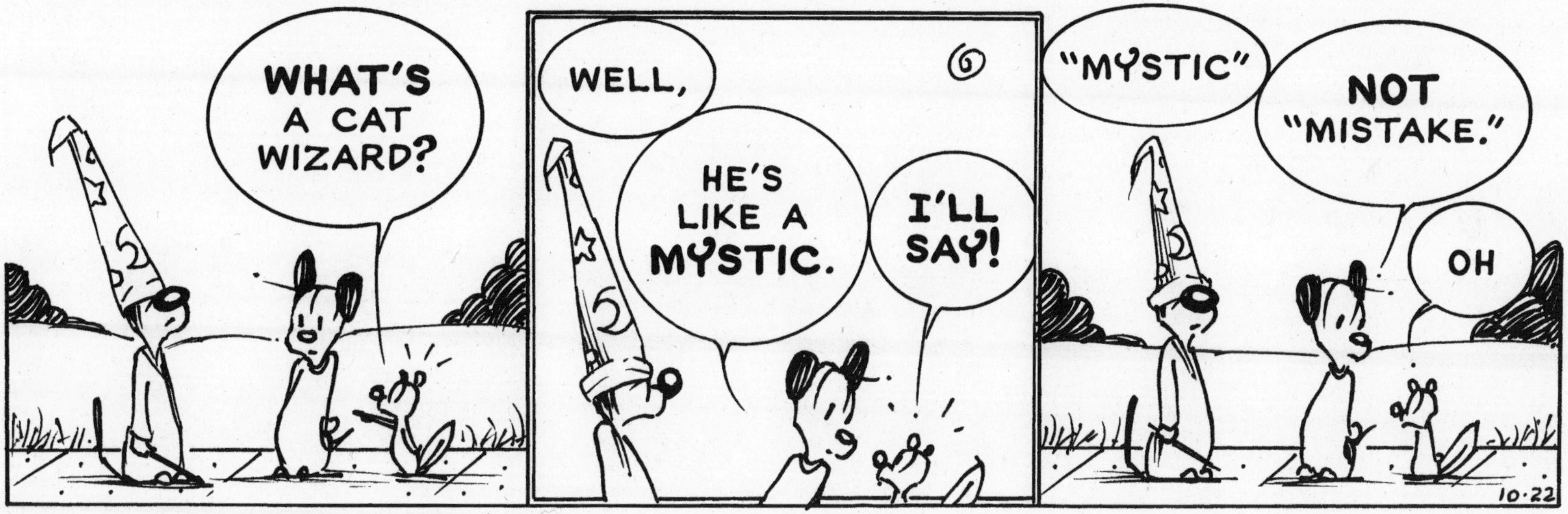
WHAT'S A CAT WIZARD?
WELL,
HE'S LIKE A MYSTIC.
I'LL SAY!
"MYSTIC"
NOT "MISTAKE."
OH
10·22

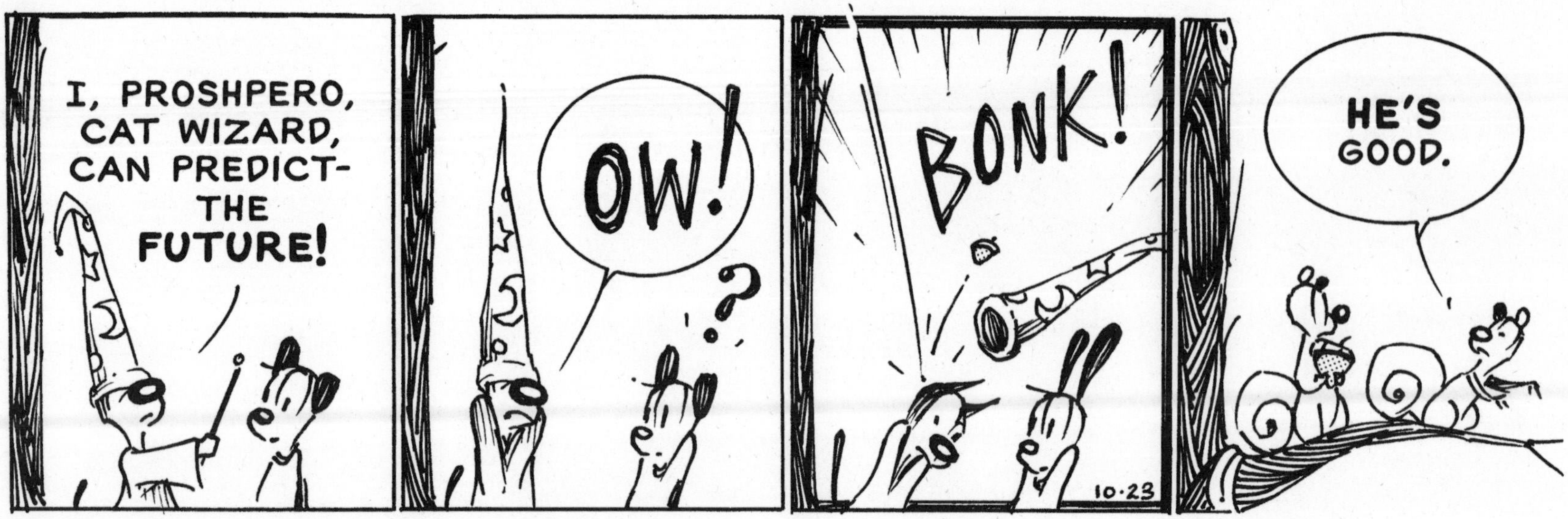
I, PROSHPERO, CAT WIZARD, CAN PREDICT- THE FUTURE!
OW!
?
BONK!
10·23
HE'S GOOD.

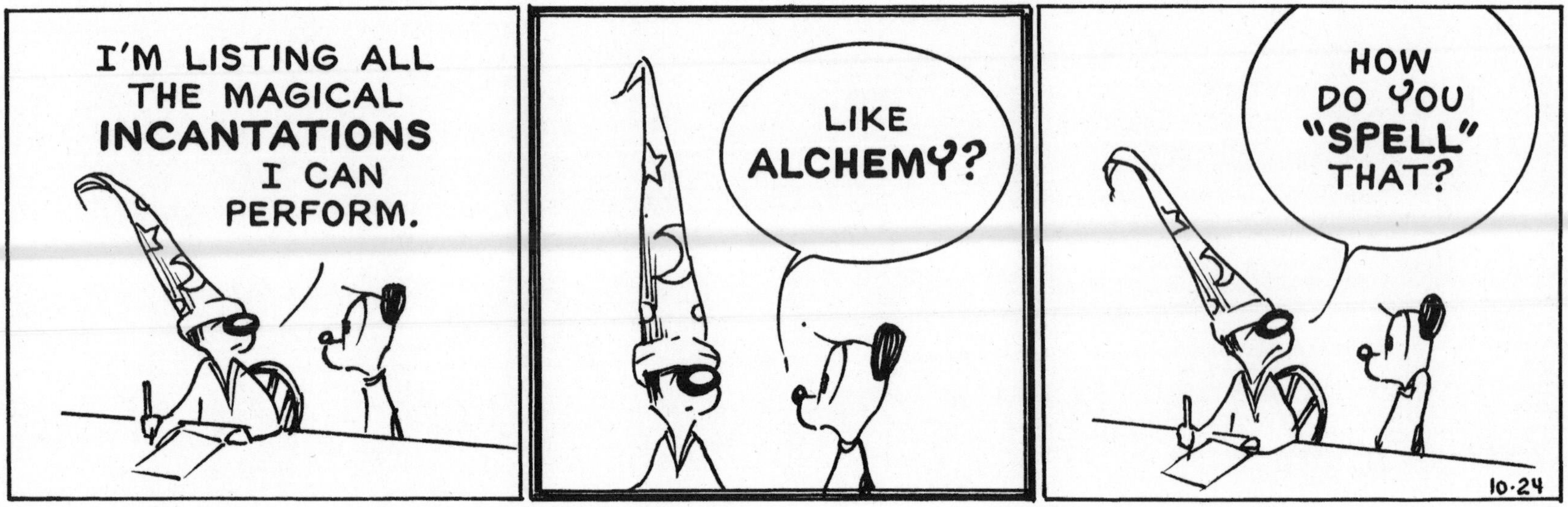
I'M LISTING ALL THE MAGICAL INCANTATIONS I CAN PERFORM.
LIKE ALCHEMY?
HOW DO YOU "SPELL" THAT?
10·24

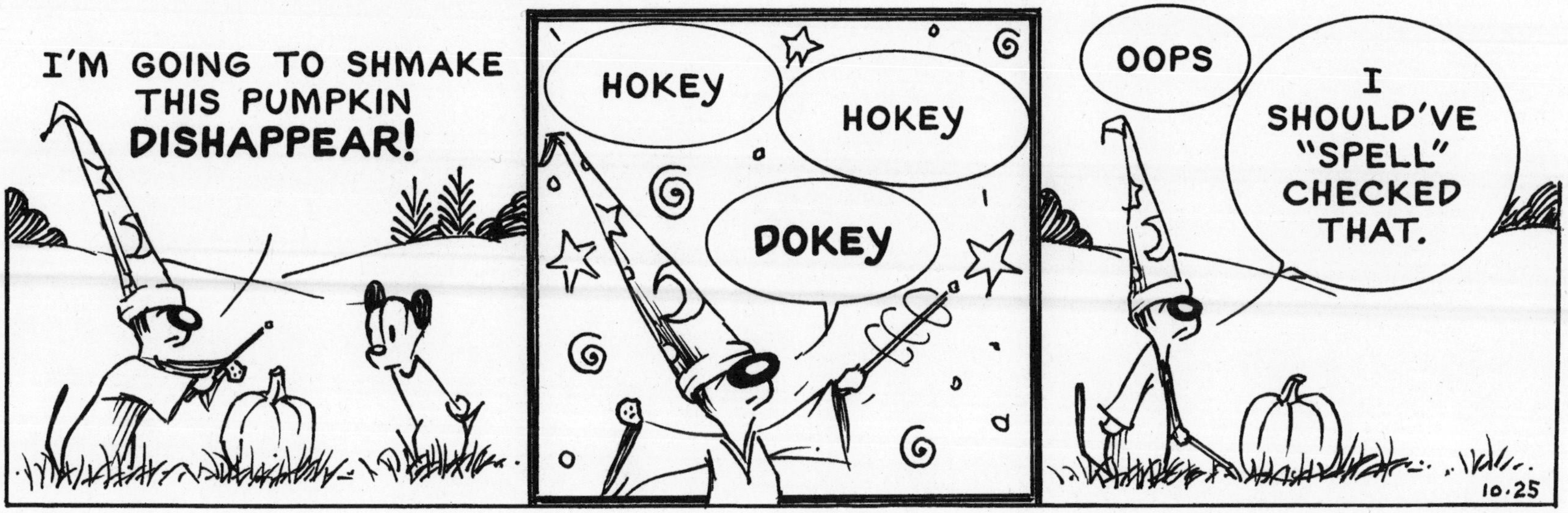
I'M GOING TO SHMAKE THIS PUMPKIN DISHAPPEAR!
HOKEY
HOKEY
DOKEY
OOPS
I SHOULD'VE "SPELL" CHECKED THAT.
10·25

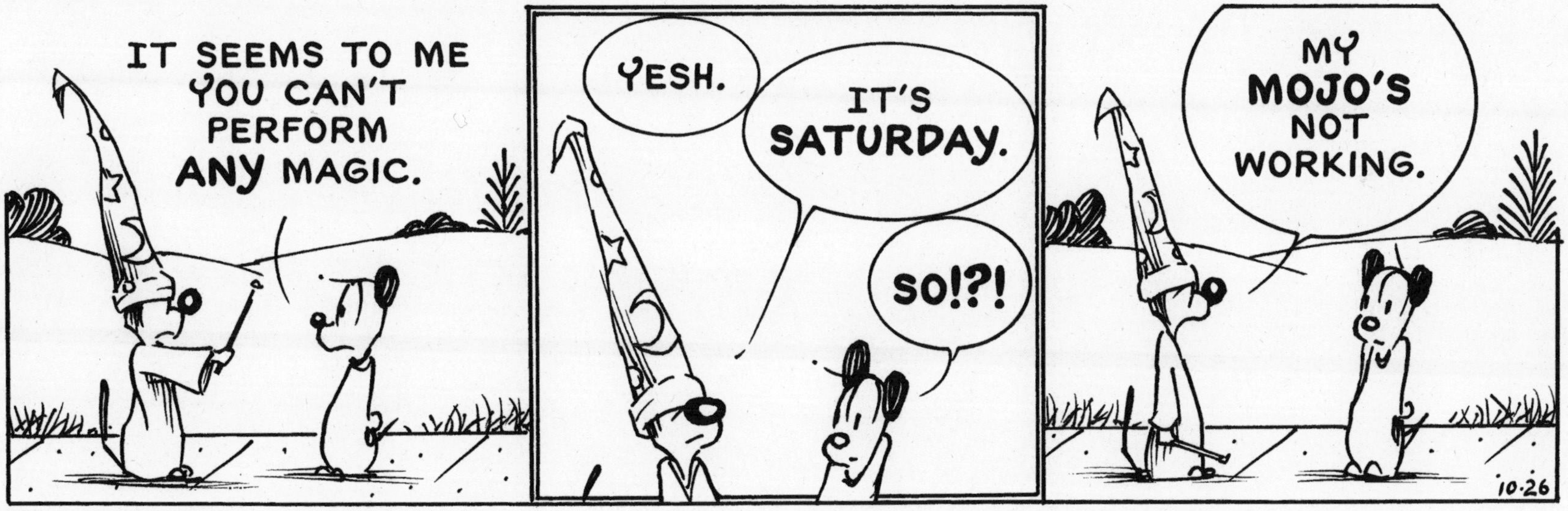
IT SEEMS TO ME YOU CAN'T PERFORM ANY MAGIC.
YESH.
IT'S SATURDAY.
SO!?!
MY MOJO'S NOT WORKING.
10·26

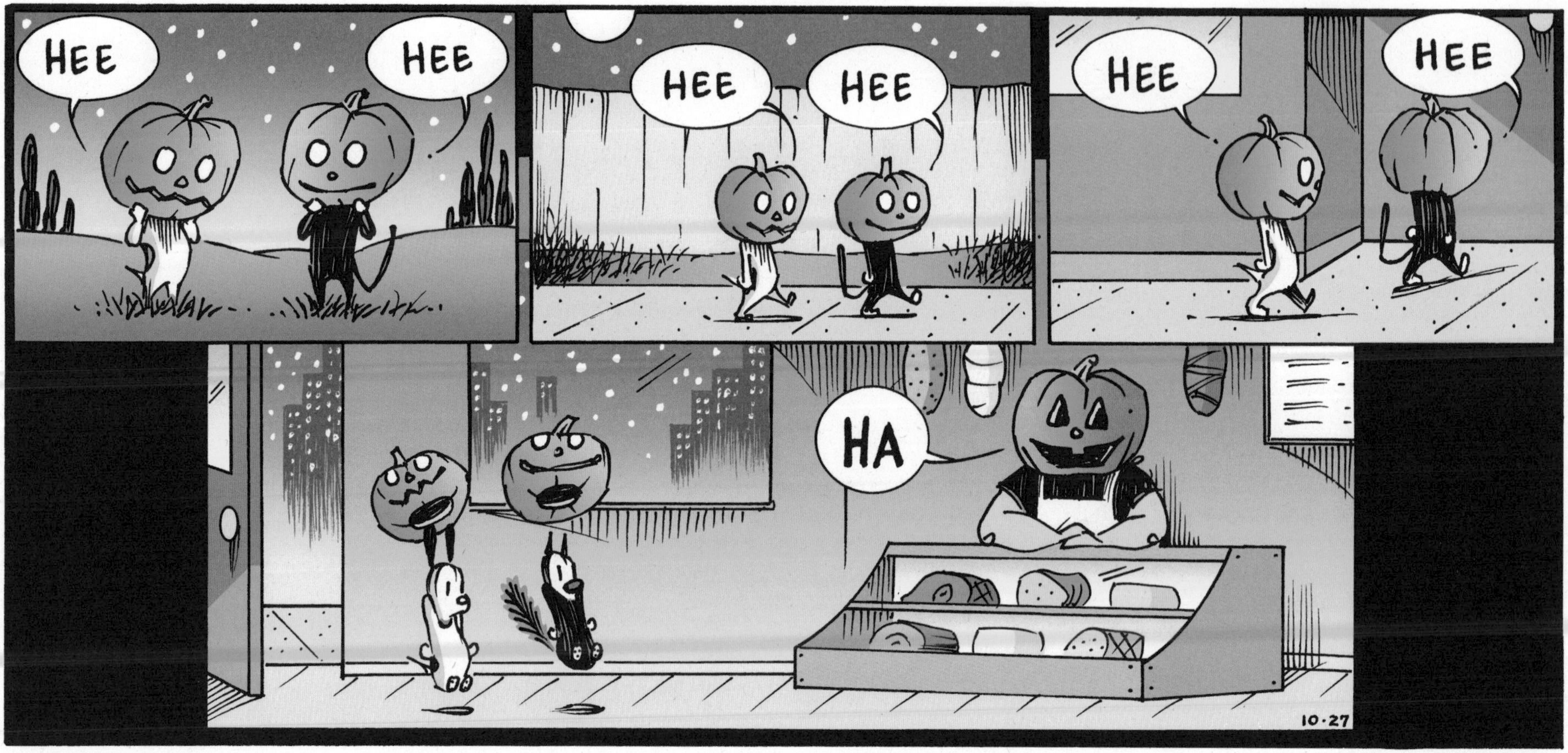
HEE
HEE
HEE
HEE
HEE
HEE
HA
10·27

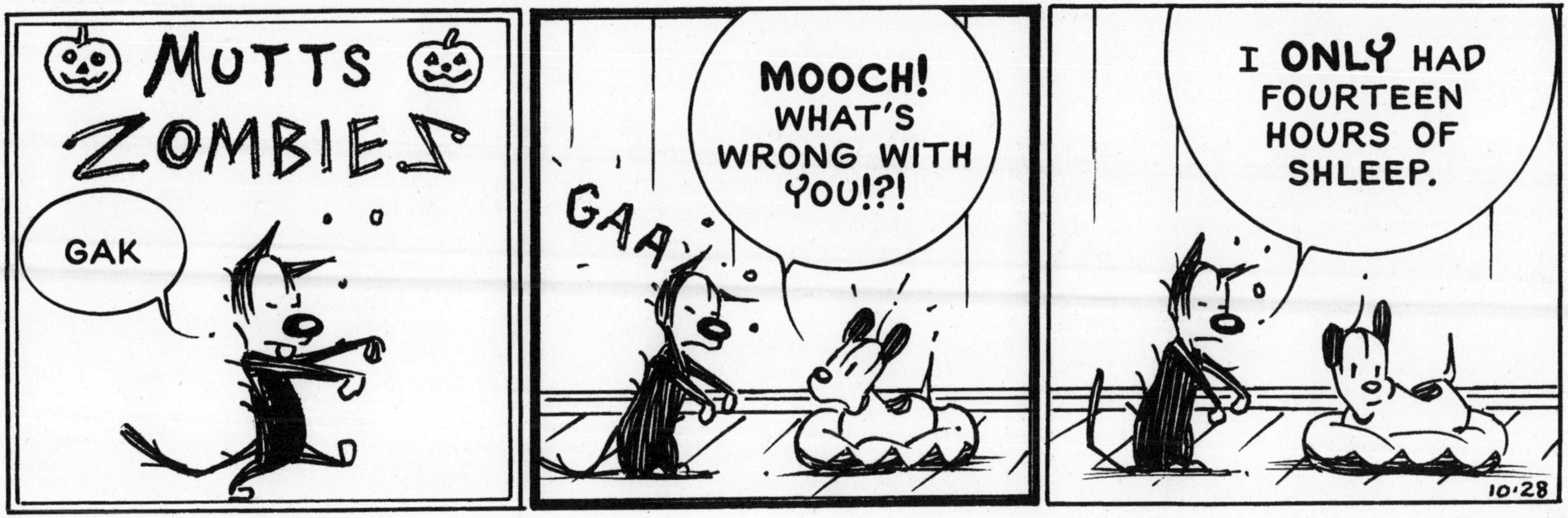
MUTTS ZOMBIES
GAK
GAA
MOOCH! WHAT'S WRONG WITH YOU!?!
I ONLY HAD FOURTEEN HOURS OF SHLEEP.
10·28

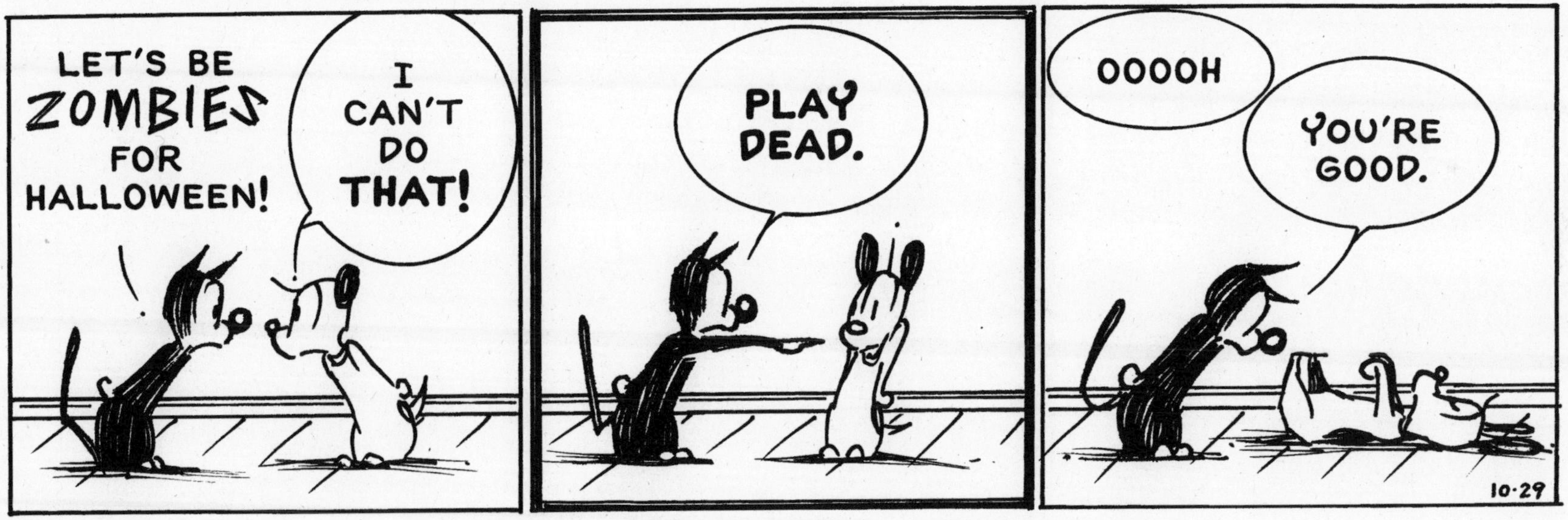
LET'S BE ZOMBIES FOR HALLOWEEN!
I CAN'T DO THAT!
PLAY DEAD.
OOOOH
YOU'RE GOOD.
10·29

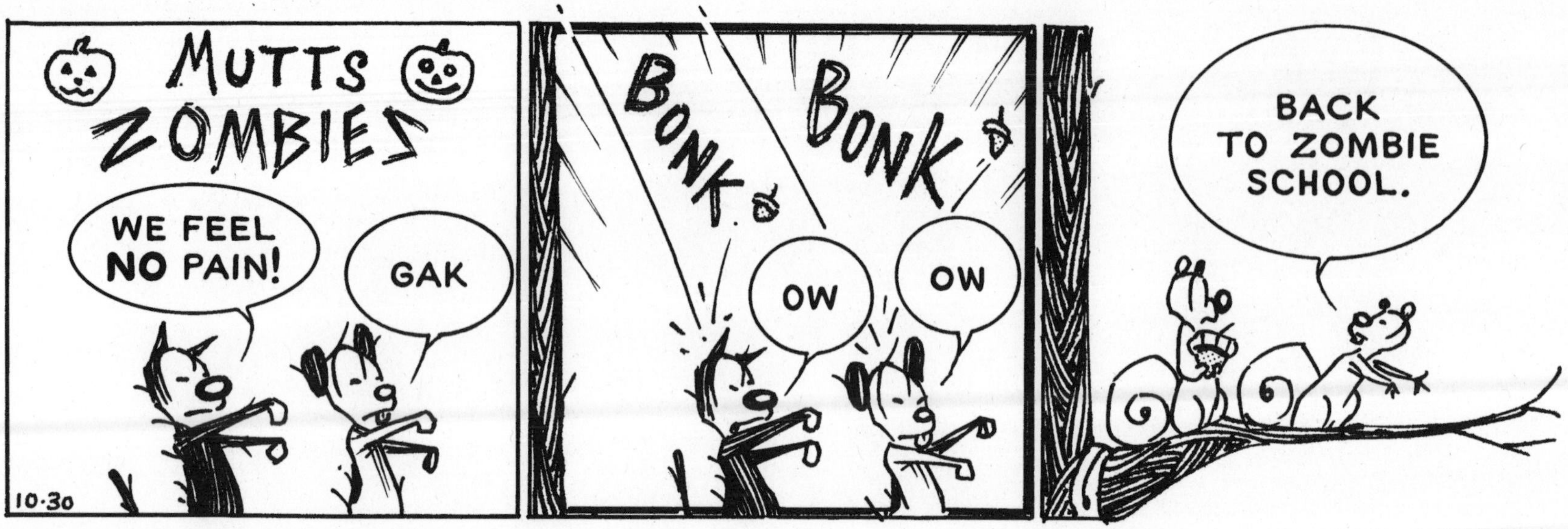
MUTTS ZOMBIES
WE FEEL NO PAIN!
GAK
10·30
BONK
BONK
OW
OW
BACK TO ZOMBIE SCHOOL.

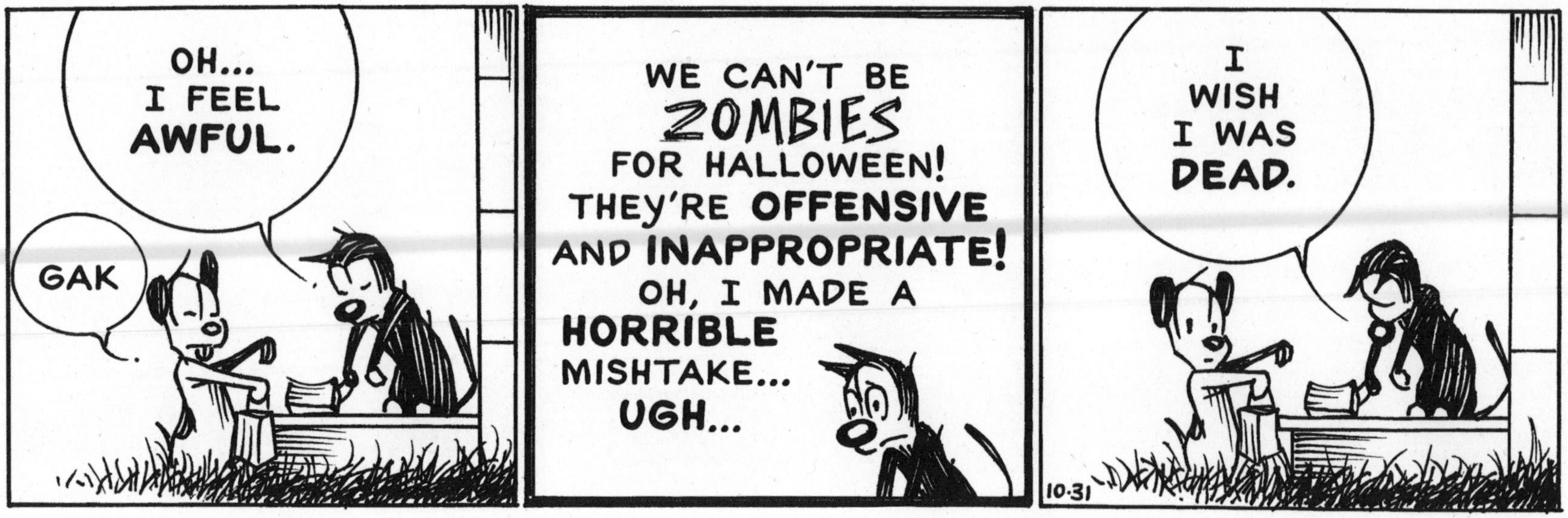
OH... I FEEL AWFUL.
GAK
WE CAN'T BE ZOMBIES FOR HALLOWEEN! THEY'RE OFFENSIVE AND INAPPROPRIATE! OH, I MADE A HORRIBLE MISHTAKE... UGH...
I WISH I WAS DEAD.
10·31

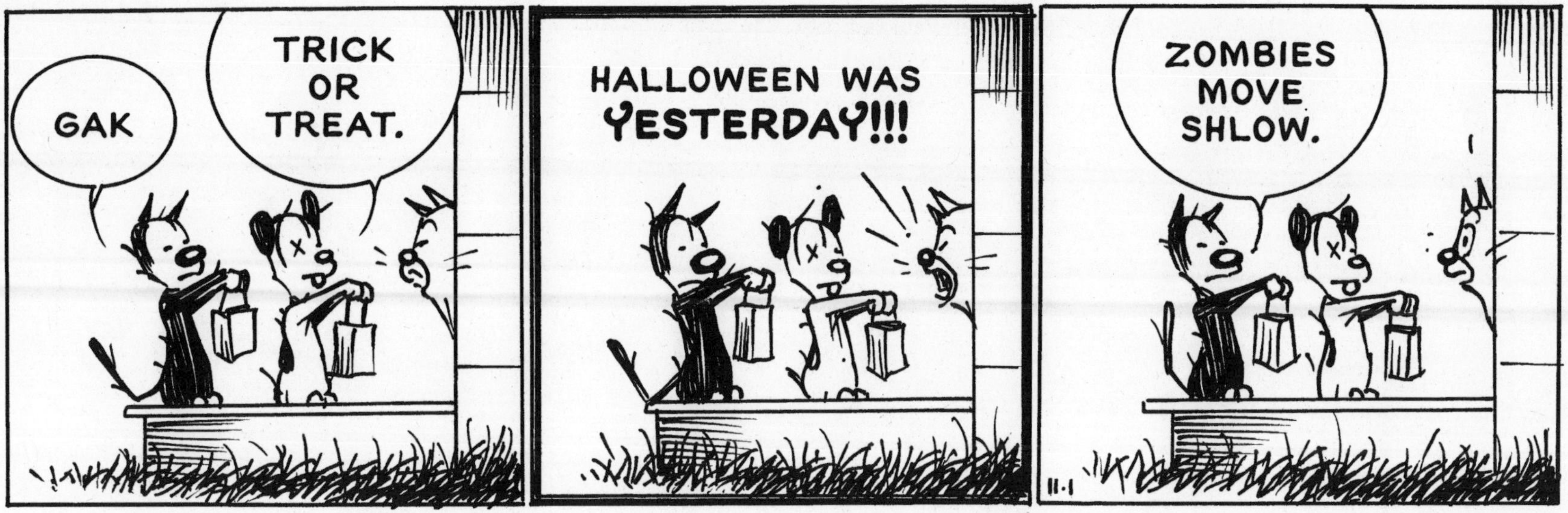
GAK
TRICK OR TREAT.
HALLOWEEN WAS YESTERDAY!!!
ZOMBIES MOVE SHLOW.
11·1

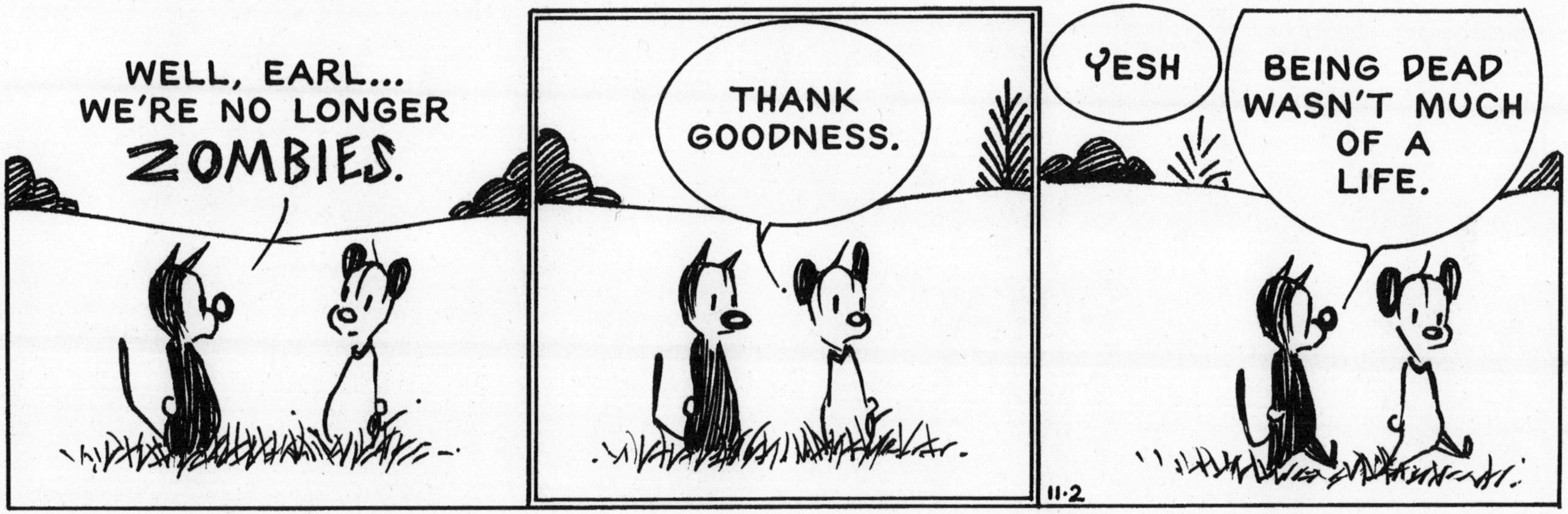
WELL, EARL... WE'RE NO LONGER ZOMBIES.
THANK GOODNESS.
YESH
BEING DEAD WASN'T MUCH OF A LIFE.
11·2

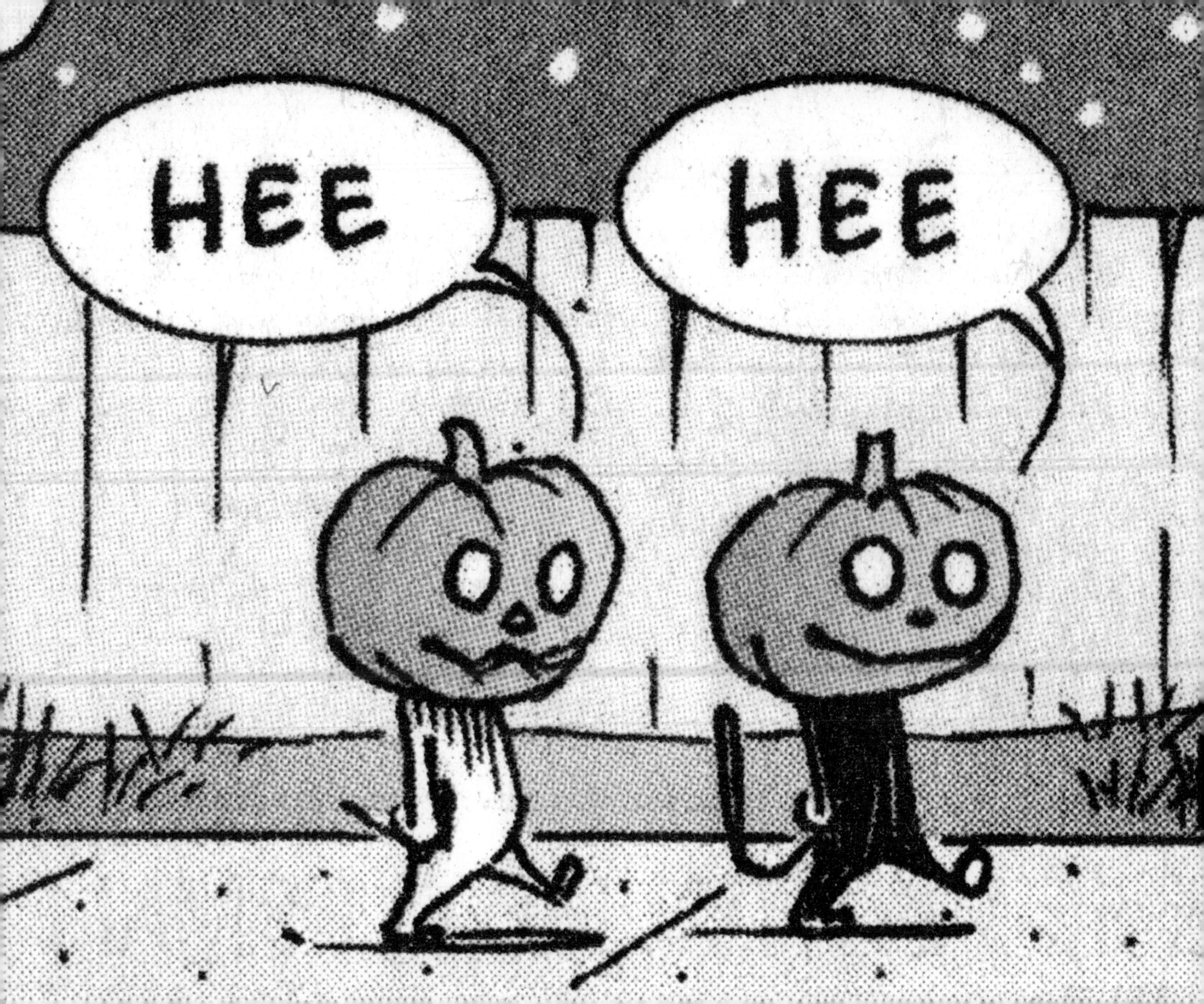
HEE
HEE

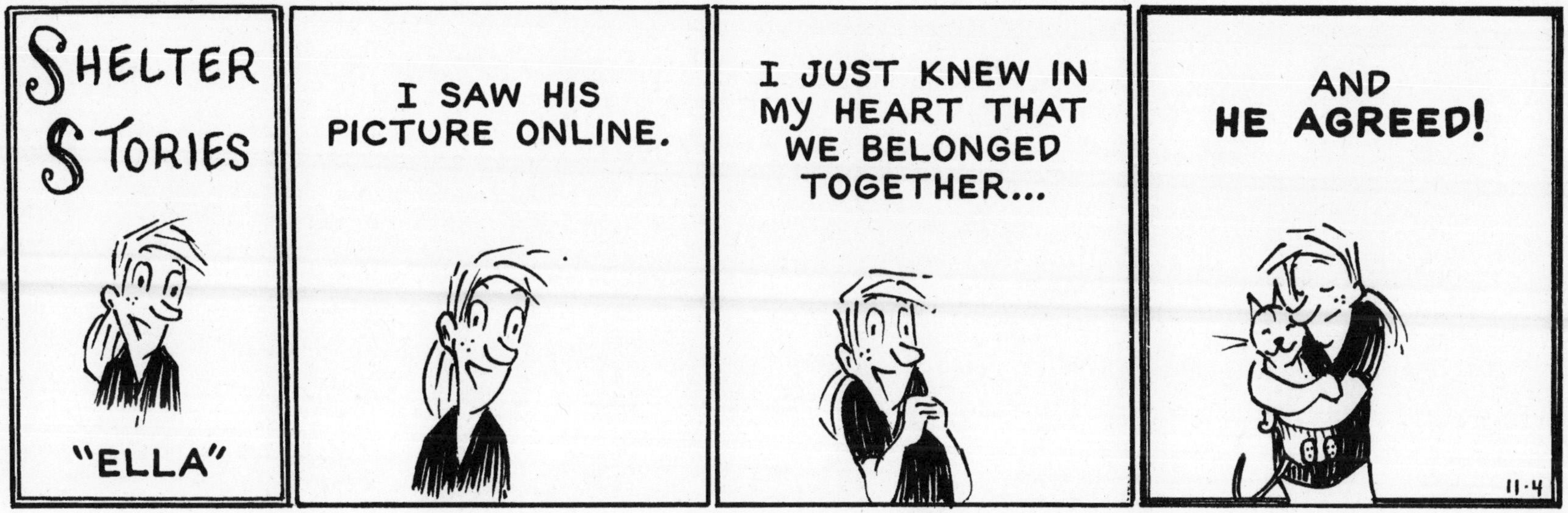
SHELTER STORIES
"ELLA"
I SAW HIS PICTURE ONLINE.
I JUST KNEW IN MY HEART THAT WE BELONGED TOGETHER...
AND HE AGREED!
11·4

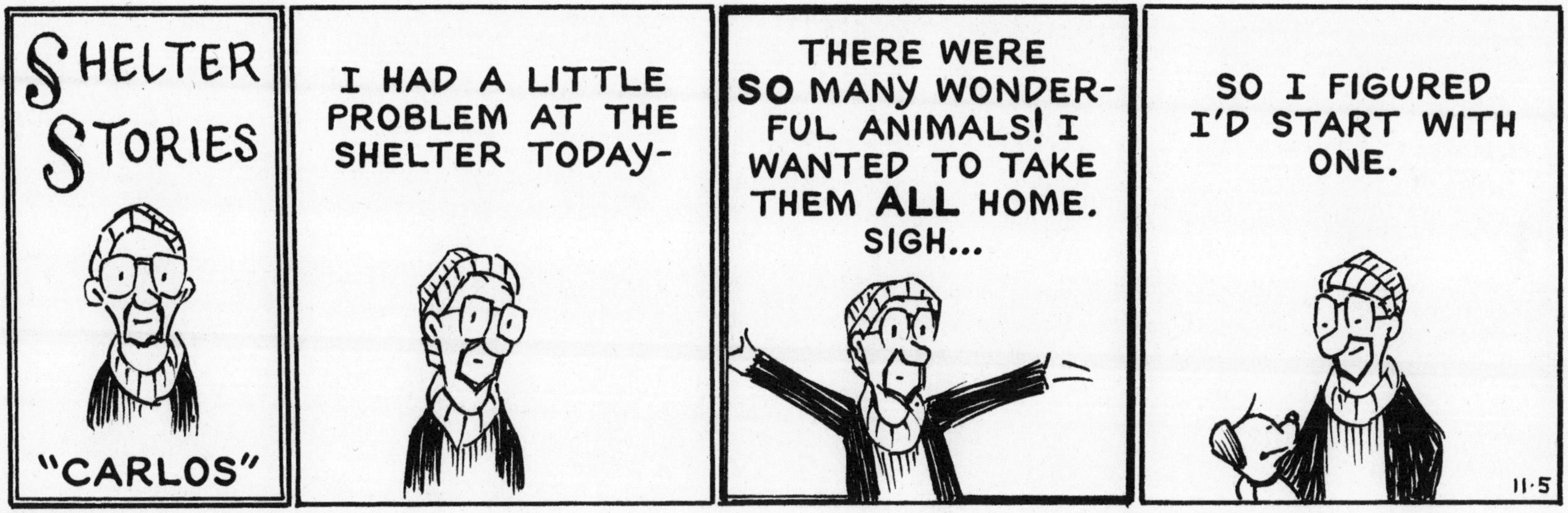
SHELTER STORIES
"CARLOS"
I HAD A LITTLE PROBLEM AT THE SHELTER TODAY-
THERE WERE SO MANY WONDERFUL ANIMALS! I WANTED TO TAKE THEM ALL HOME. SIGH...
SO I FIGURED I'D START WITH ONE.
11·5

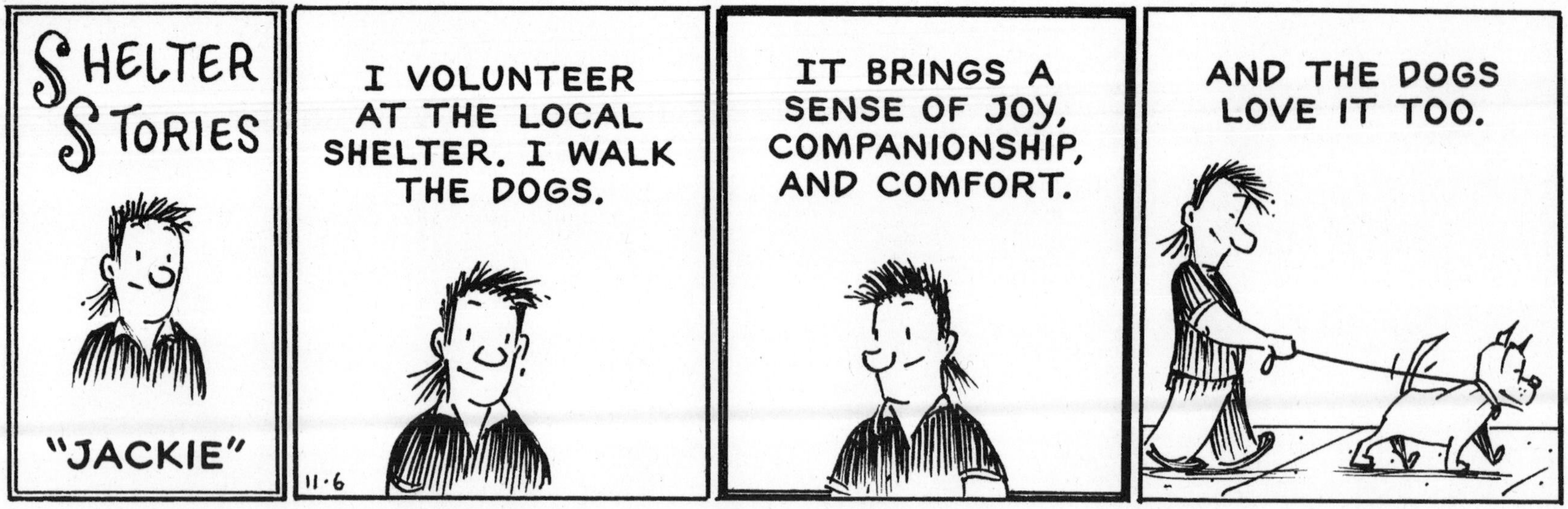
SHELTER STORIES
"JACKIE"
I VOLUNTEER AT THE LOCAL SHELTER. I WALK THE DOGS.
11·6
IT BRINGS A SENSE OF JOY, COMPANIONSHIP, AND COMFORT.
AND THE DOGS LOVE IT TOO.

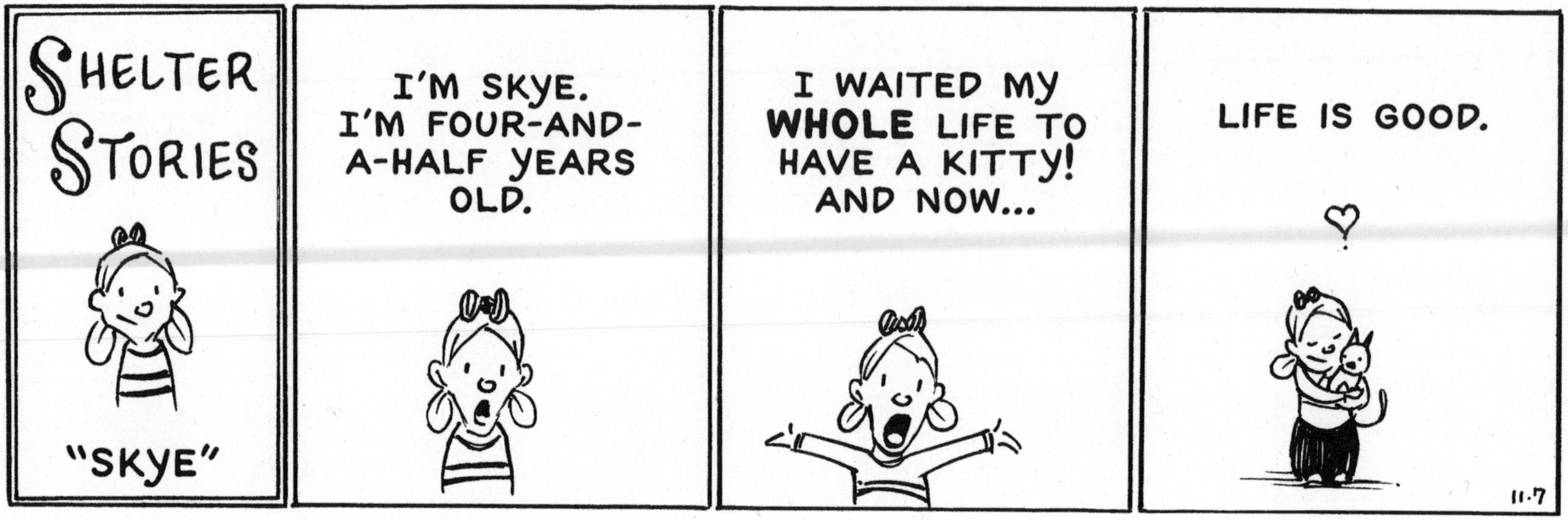
SHELTER STORIES
"SKYE"
I'M SKYE. I'M FOUR-AND-A-HALF YEARS OLD.
I WAITED MY **WHOLE** LIFE TO HAVE A KITTY! AND NOW...
LIFE IS GOOD.
11·7

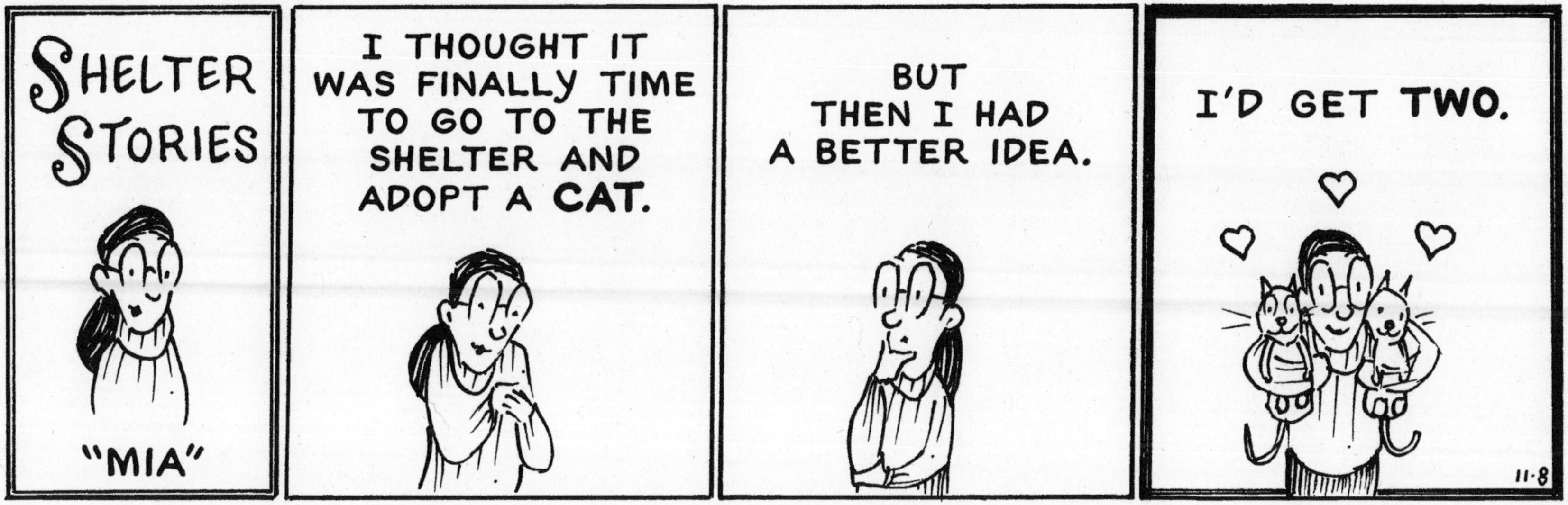
SHELTER STORIES
"MIA"
I THOUGHT IT WAS FINALLY TIME TO GO TO THE SHELTER AND ADOPT A CAT.
BUT THEN I HAD A BETTER IDEA.
I'D GET TWO.
11·8

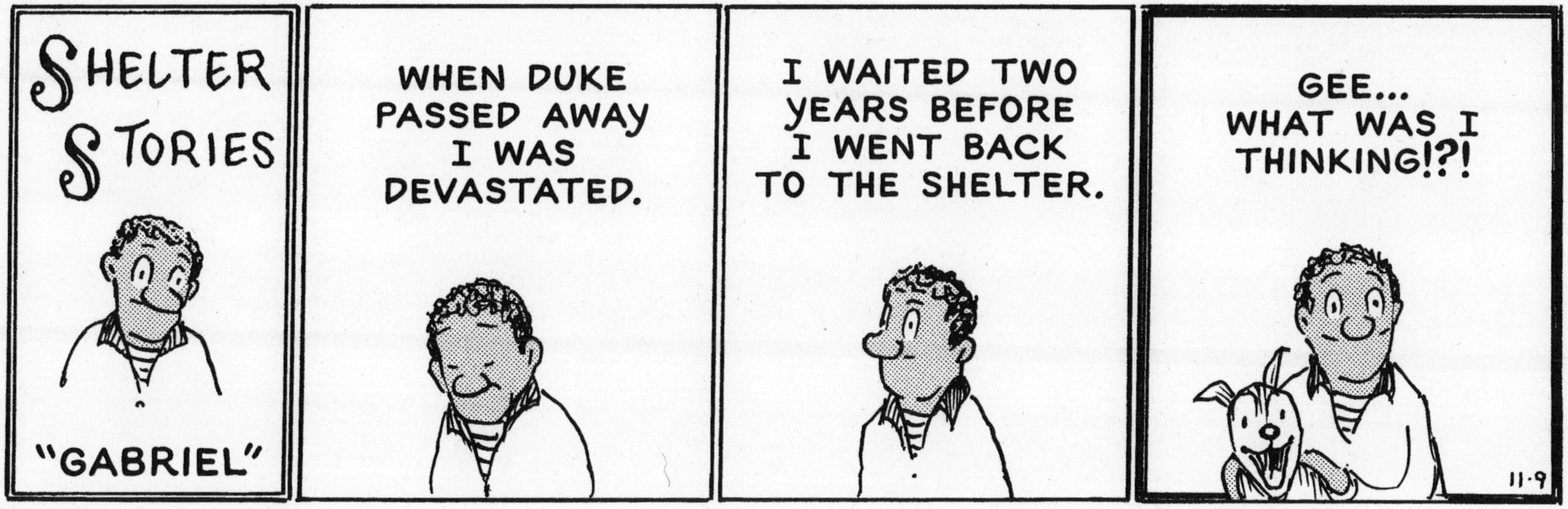
SHELTER STORIES
"GABRIEL"
WHEN DUKE PASSED AWAY I WAS DEVASTATED.
I WAITED TWO YEARS BEFORE I WENT BACK TO THE SHELTER.
GEE... WHAT WAS I THINKING!?!
11·9

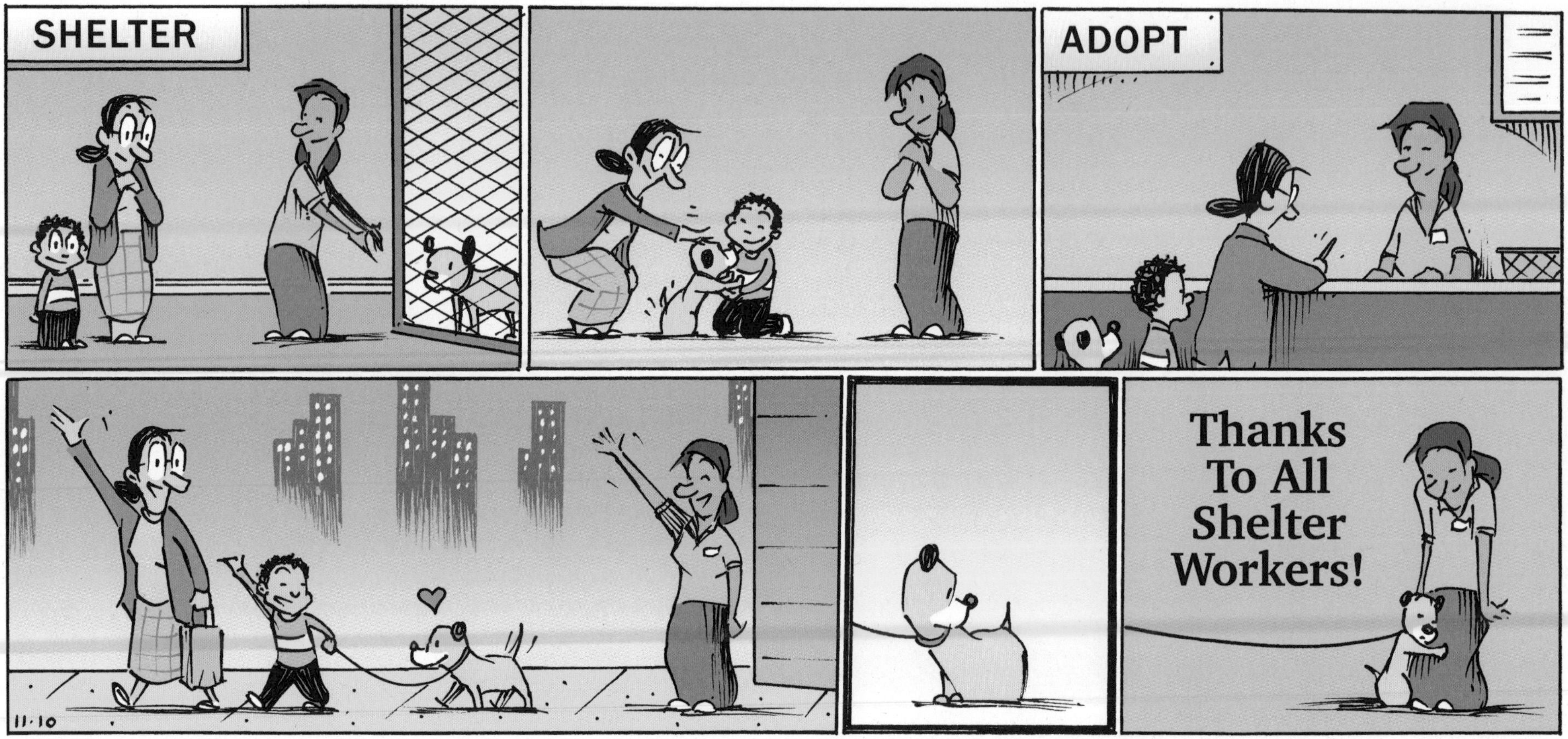
SHELTER
ADOPT
11·10
Thanks To All Shelter Workers!

MUTTS

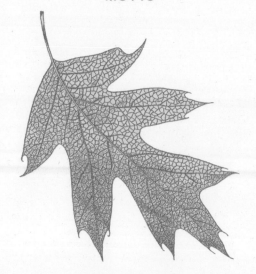

Patrick McDonnell

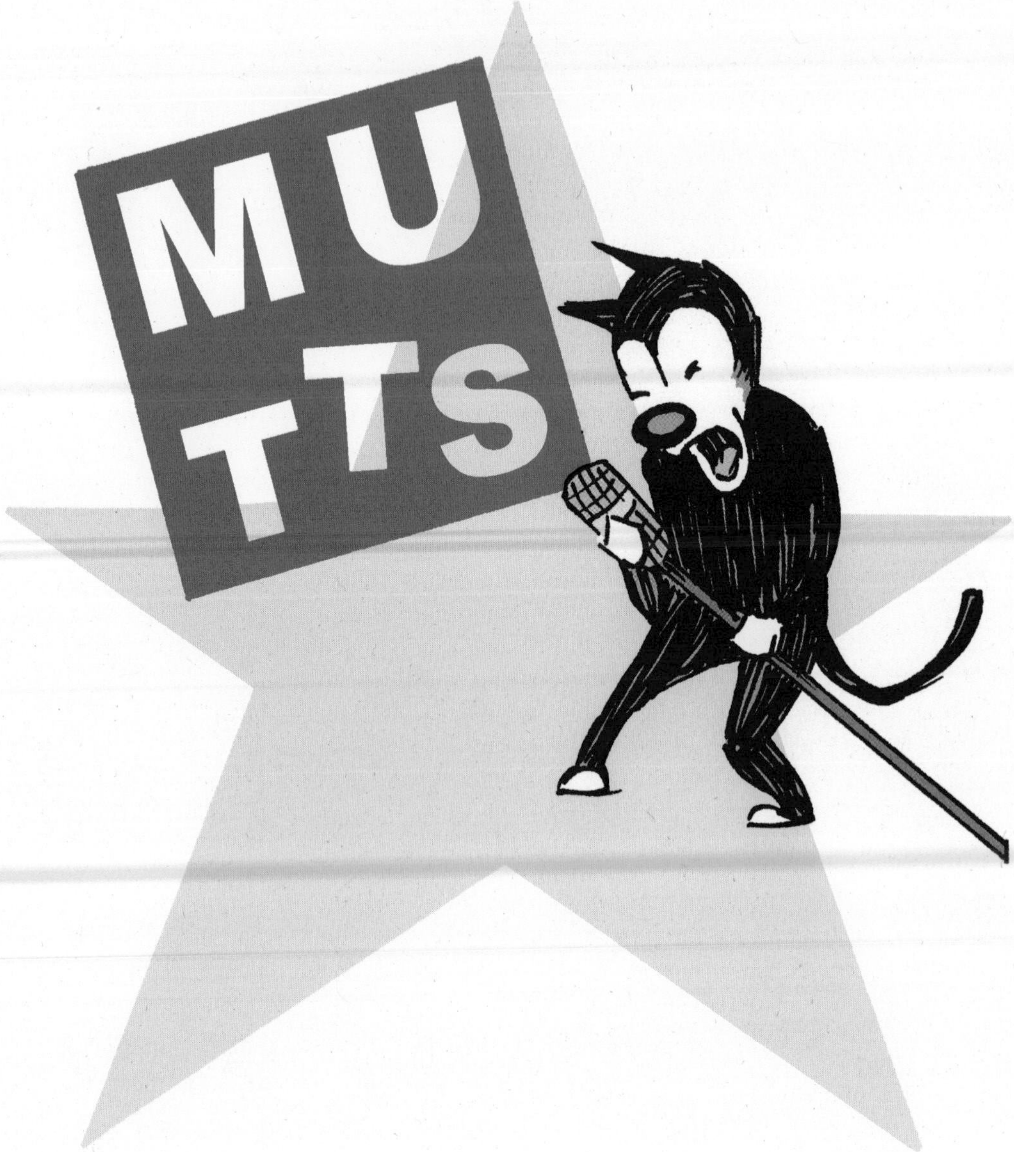
MUTTS

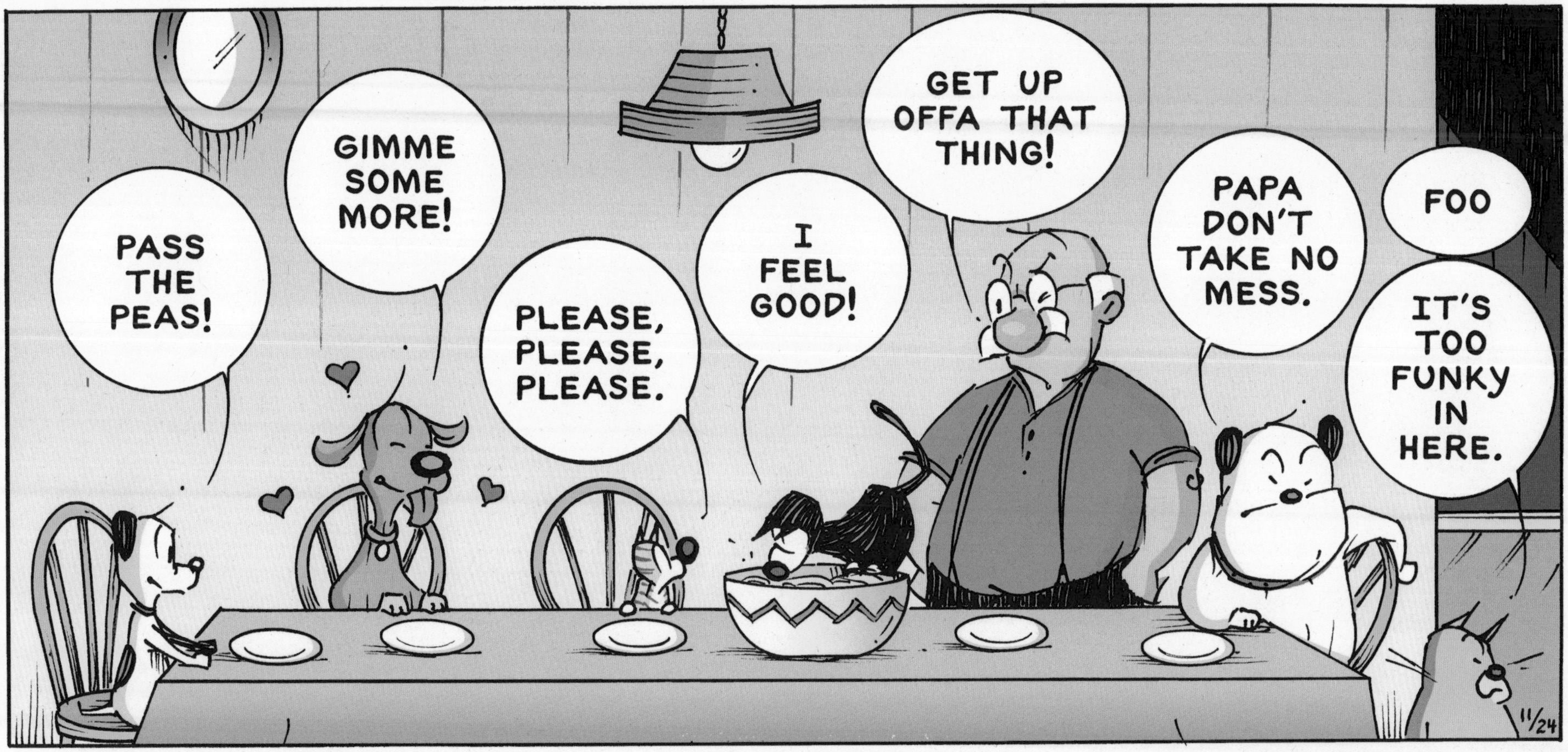
PASS THE PEAS!
GIMME SOME MORE!
PLEASE, PLEASE, PLEASE.
I FEEL GOOD!
GET UP OFFA THAT THING!
PAPA DON'T TAKE NO MESS.
FOO
IT'S TOO FUNKY IN HERE.
11/24

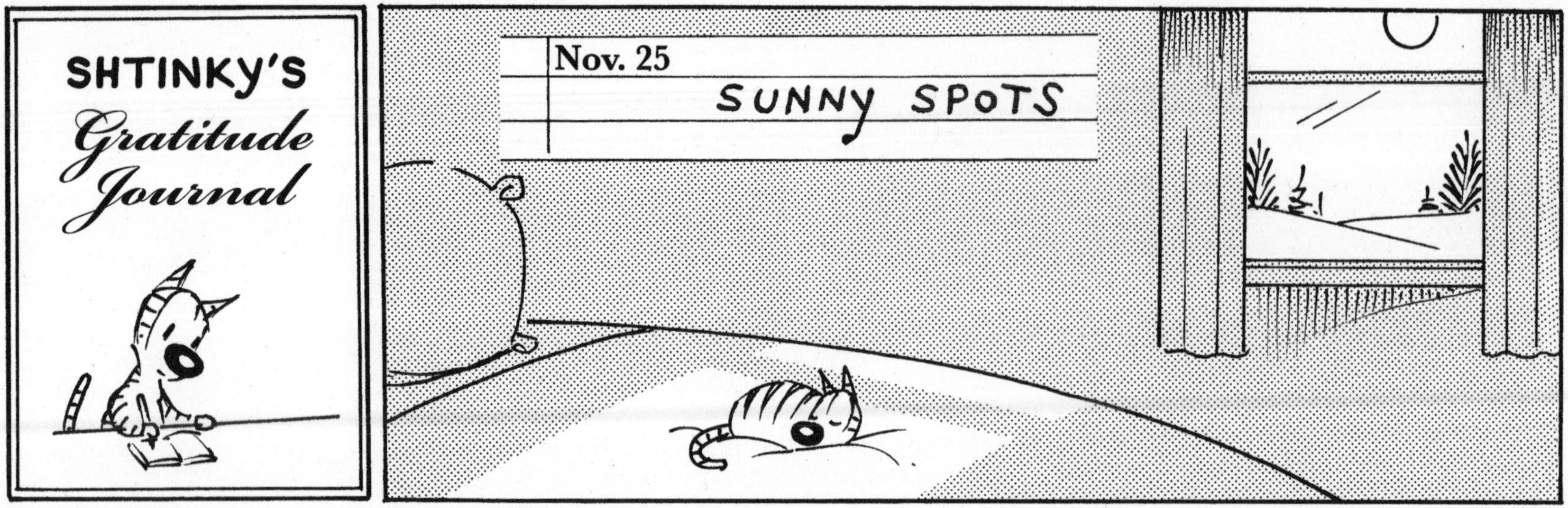
SHTINKY'S
Gratitude
Journal
Nov. 25
SUNNY SPOTS

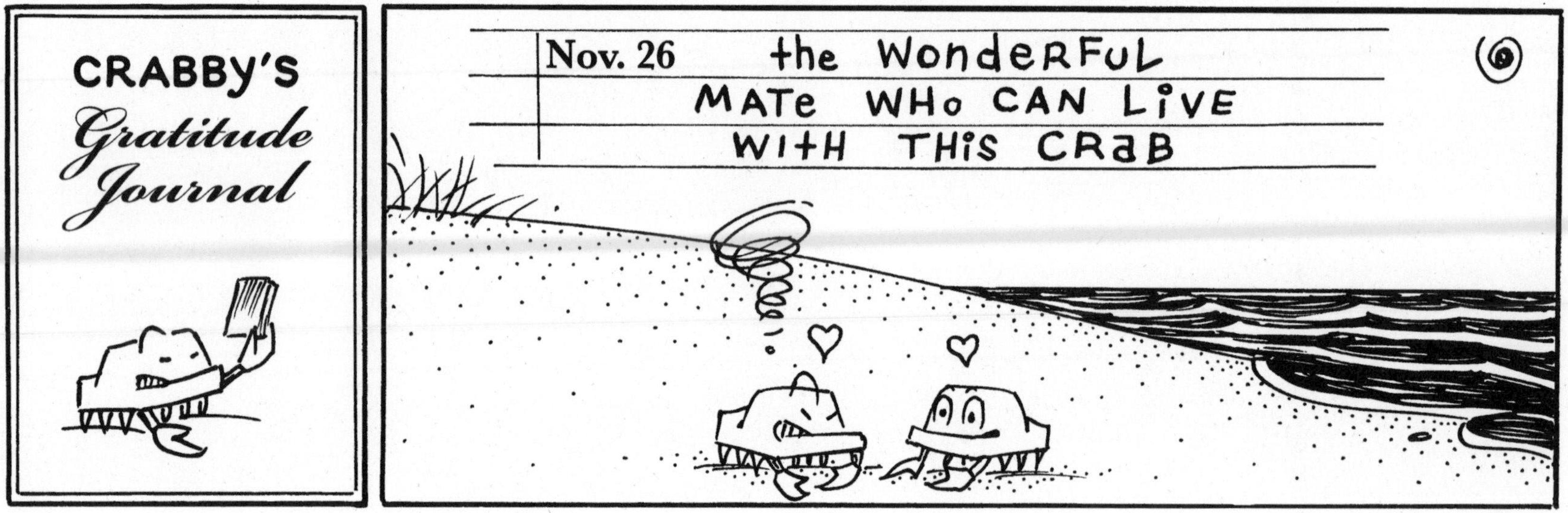
CRABBY'S
Gratitude
Journal
Nov. 26
the WONdeRFuL
MATe WHo CAN LiVE
WitH THiS CRaB

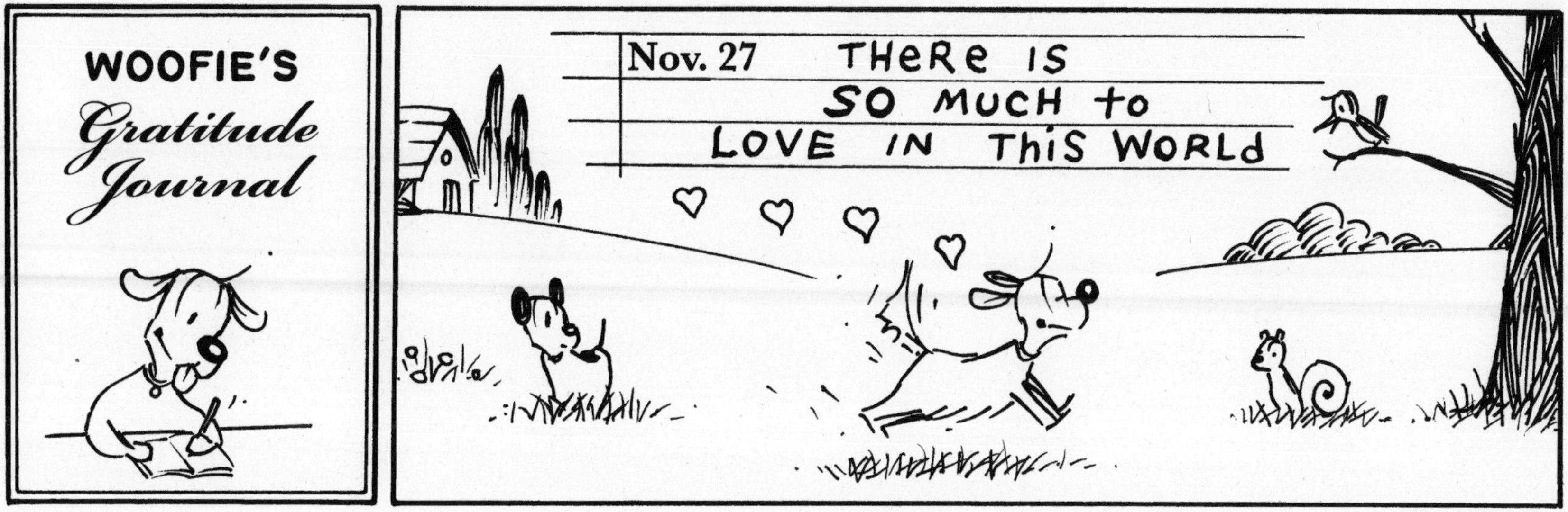
WOOFIE'S
Gratitude Journal
Nov. 27 THERE IS SO MUCH to LOVE IN THIS WORLD

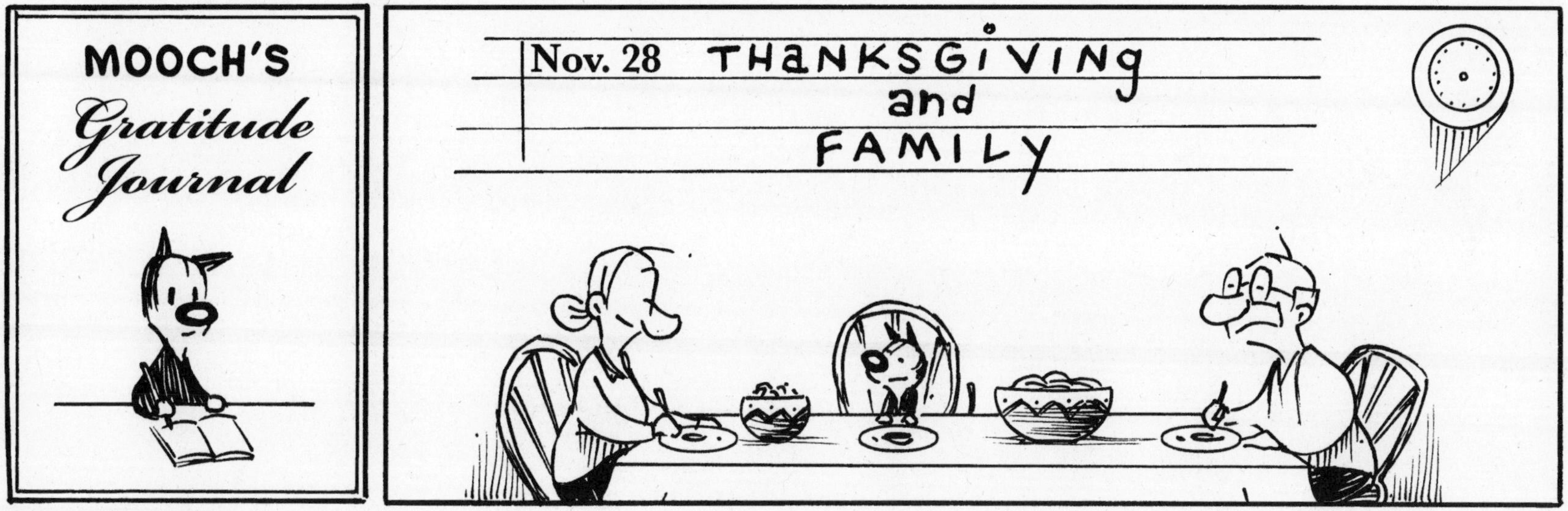
MOOCH'S
Gratitude Journal
Nov. 28 THANKSGIVING and FAMILY

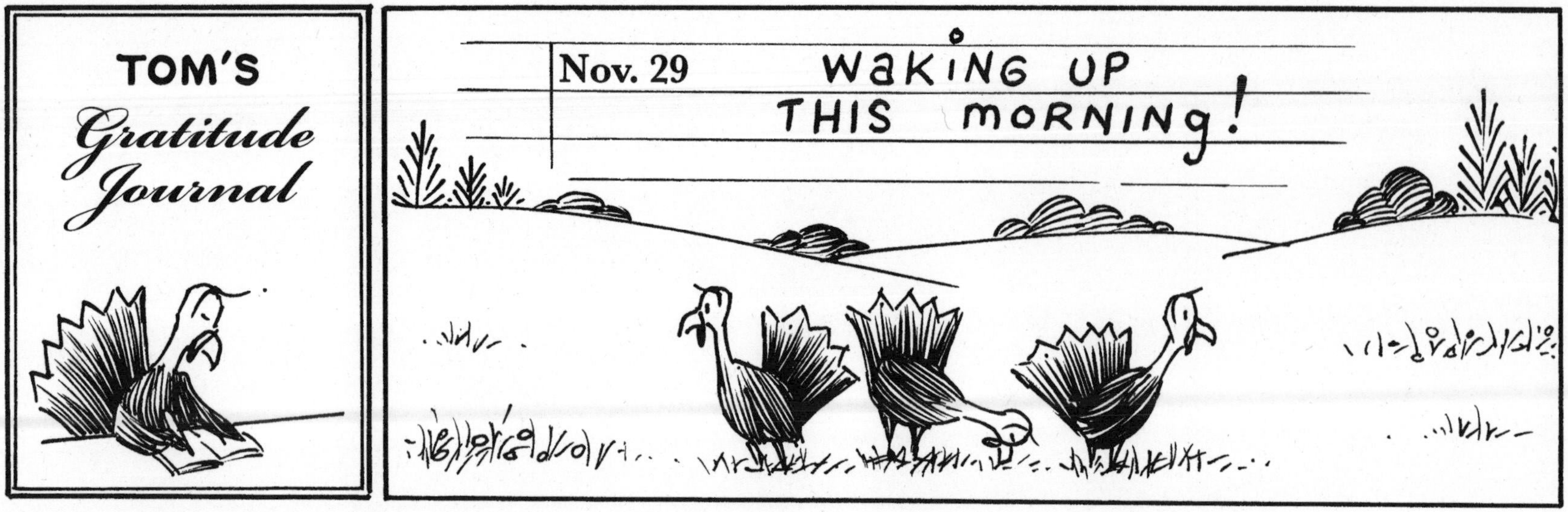
TOM'S
Gratitude
Journal
Nov. 29
WAKING UP
THIS MORNING!

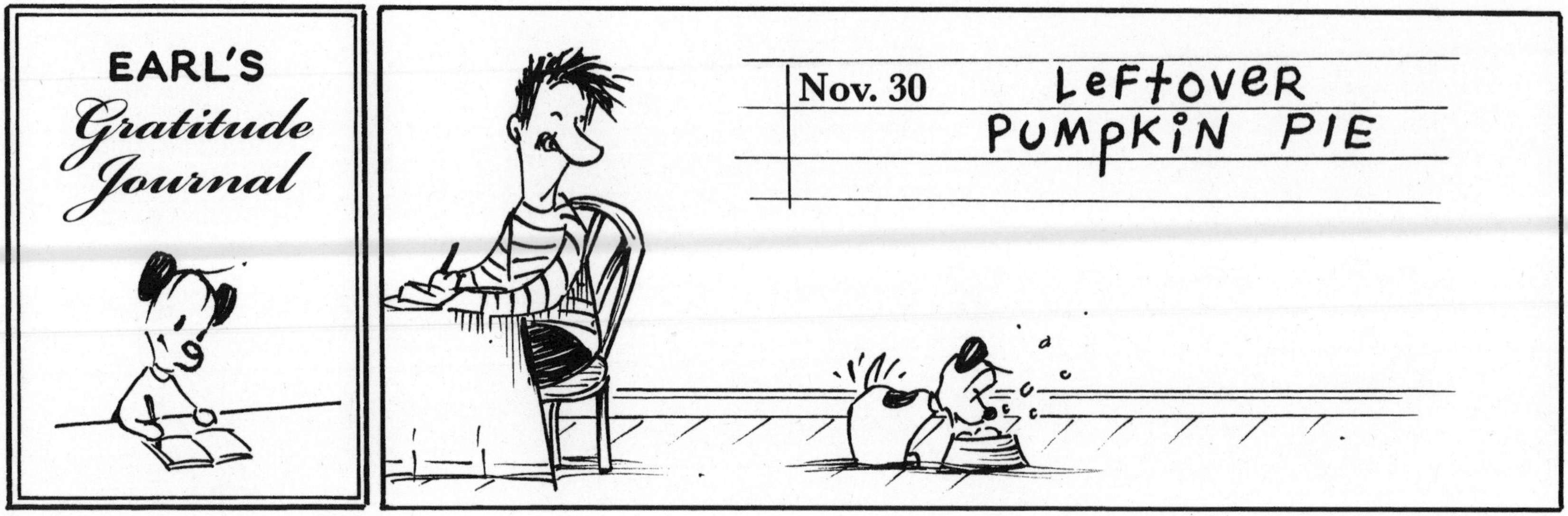
EARL'S
Gratitude
Journal
Nov. 30
LEFTOVER
PUMPKIN PIE

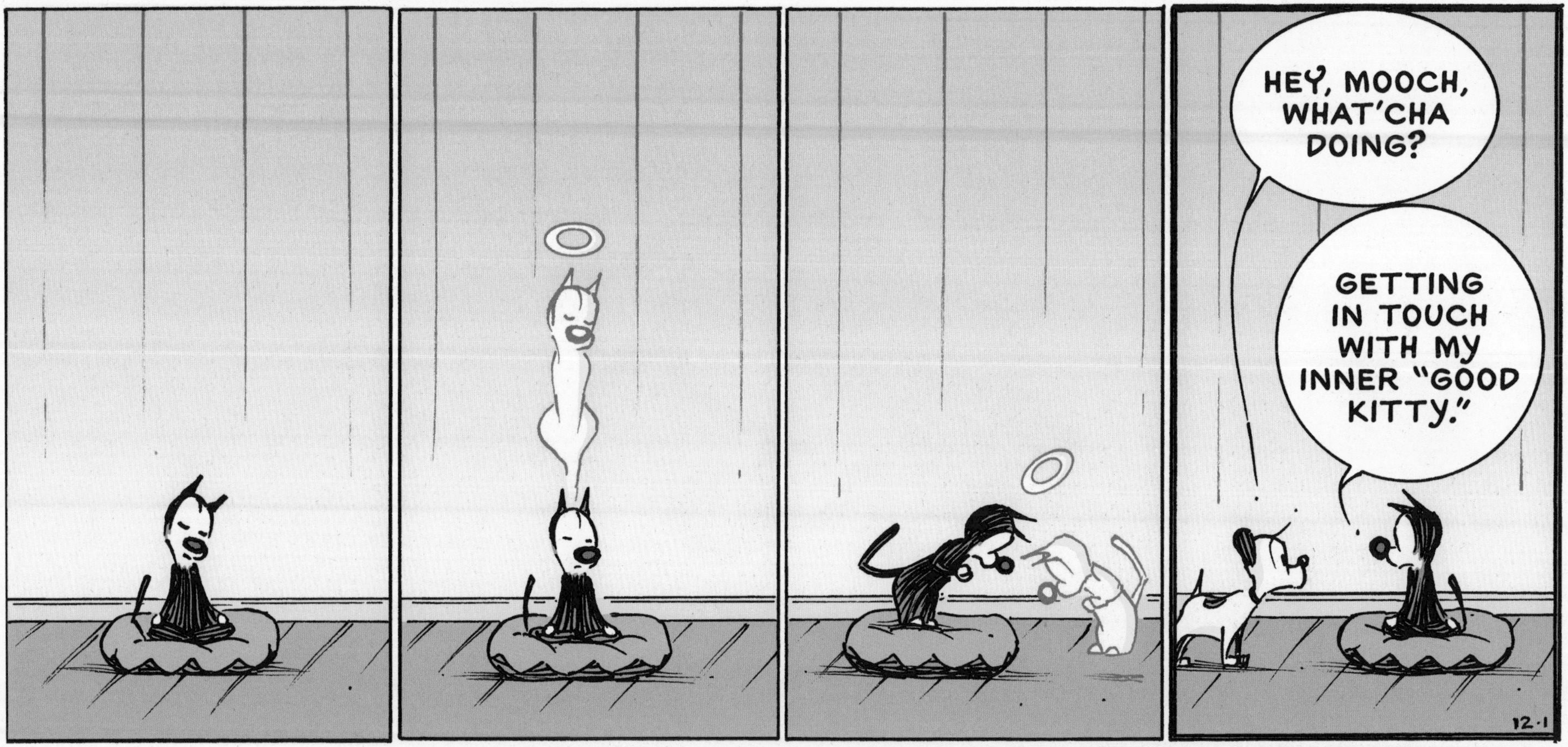
HEY, MOOCH, WHAT'CHA DOING?
GETTING IN TOUCH WITH MY INNER "GOOD KITTY."
12-1

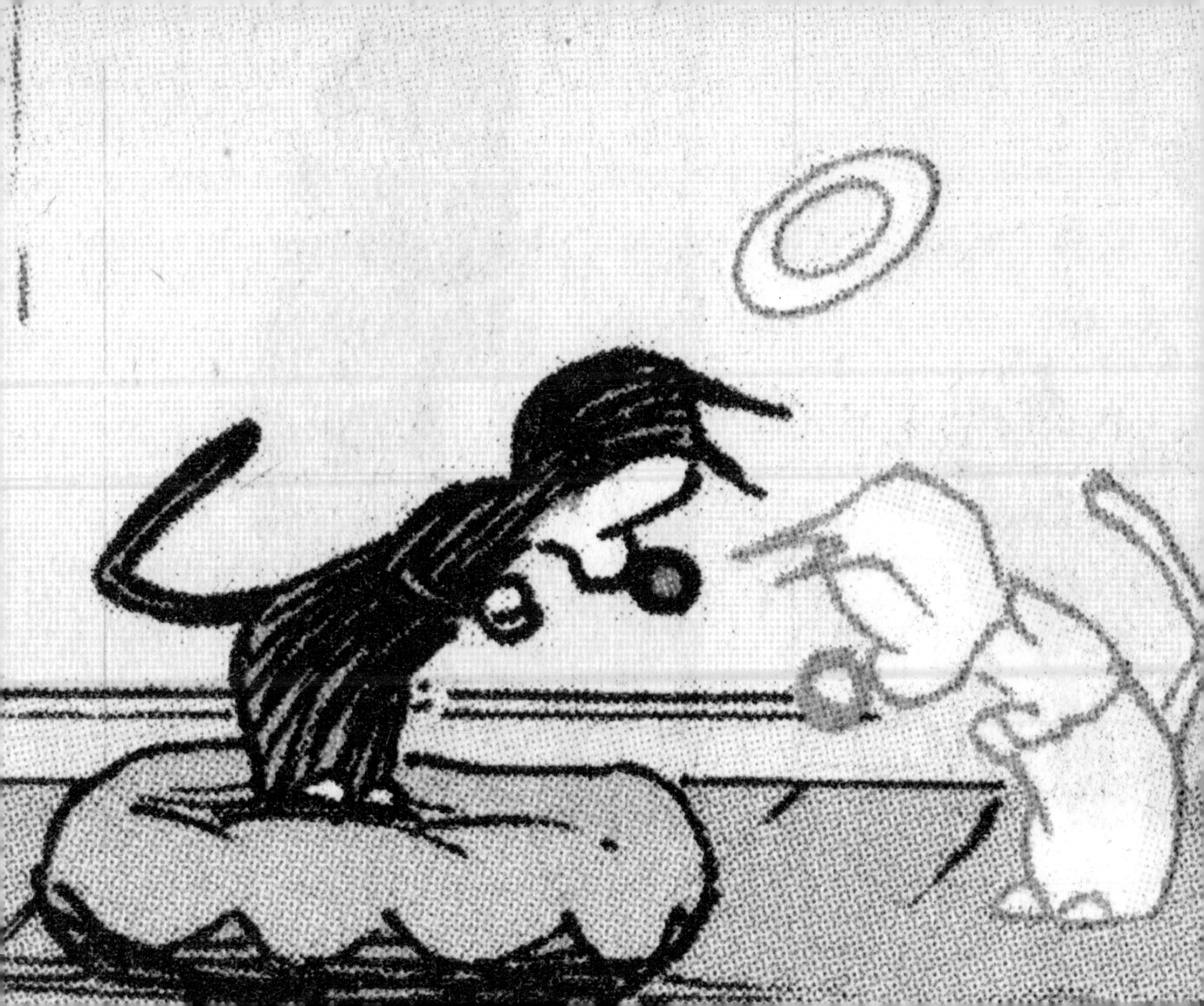

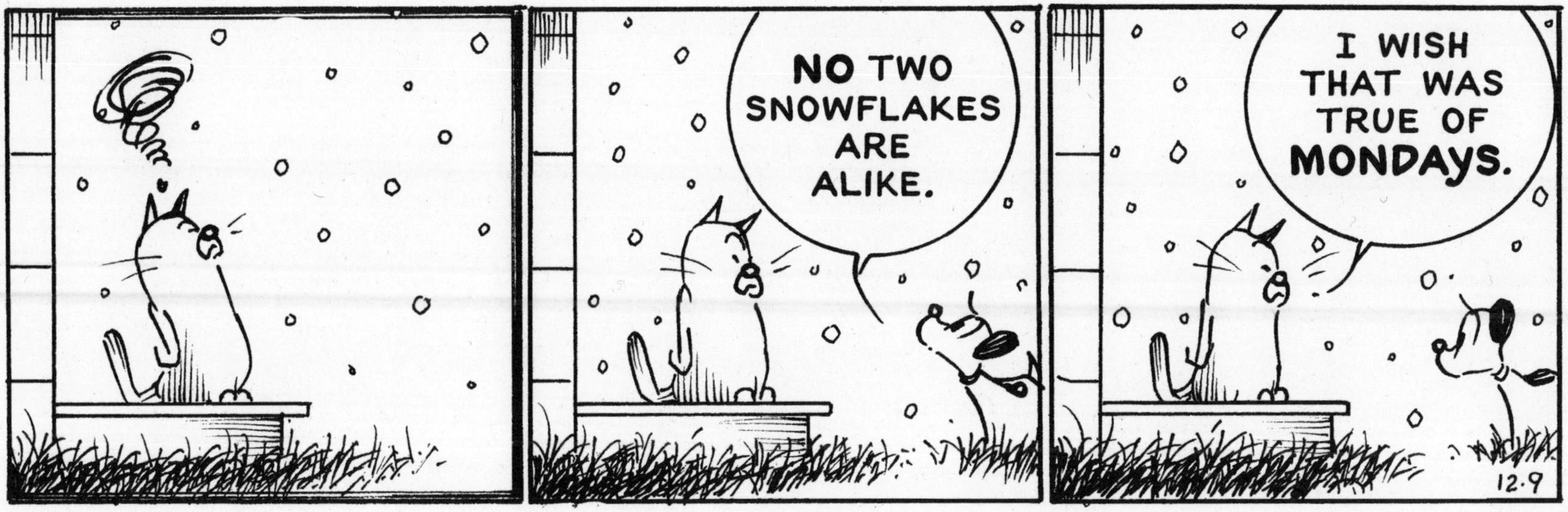
NO TWO SNOWFLAKES ARE ALIKE.
I WISH THAT WAS TRUE OF MONDAYS.
12·9

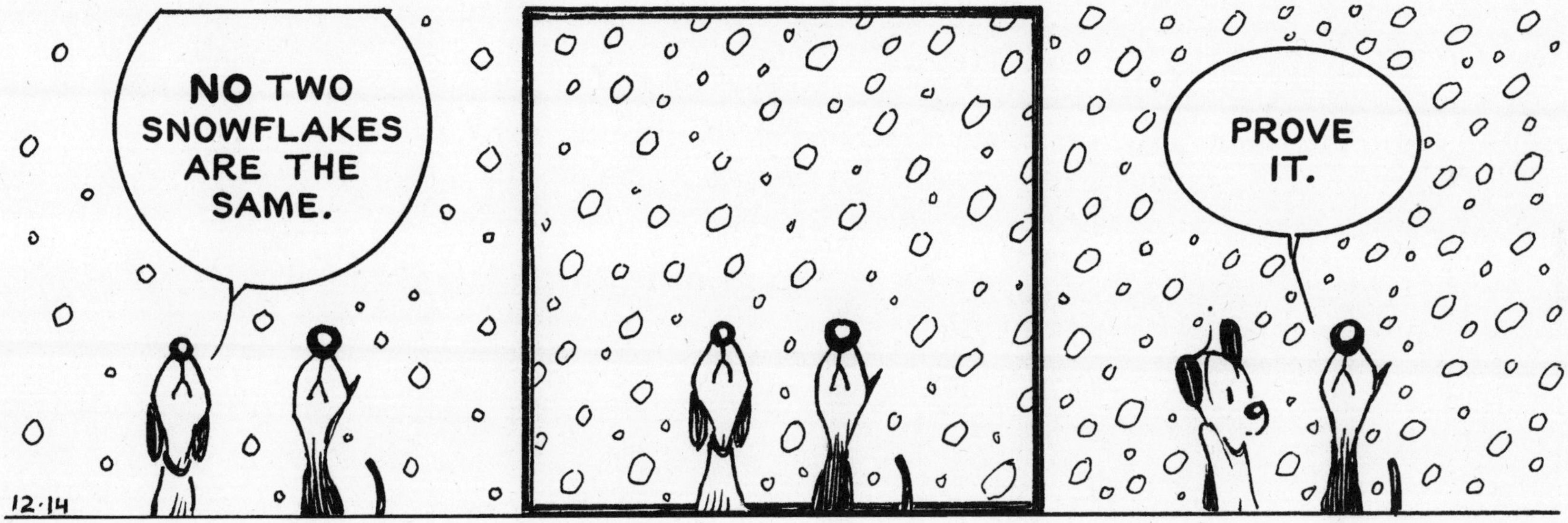
NO TWO SNOWFLAKES ARE THE SAME.
PROVE IT.
12·14

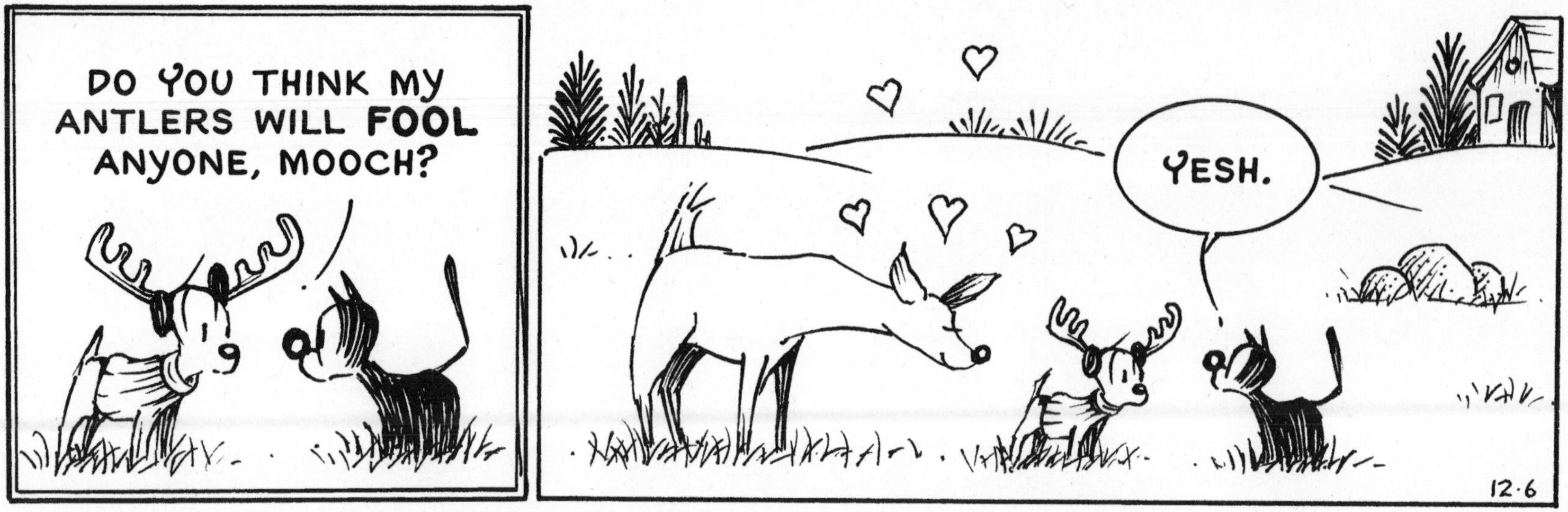
DO YOU THINK MY ANTLERS WILL FOOL ANYONE, MOOCH?
YESH.
12·6

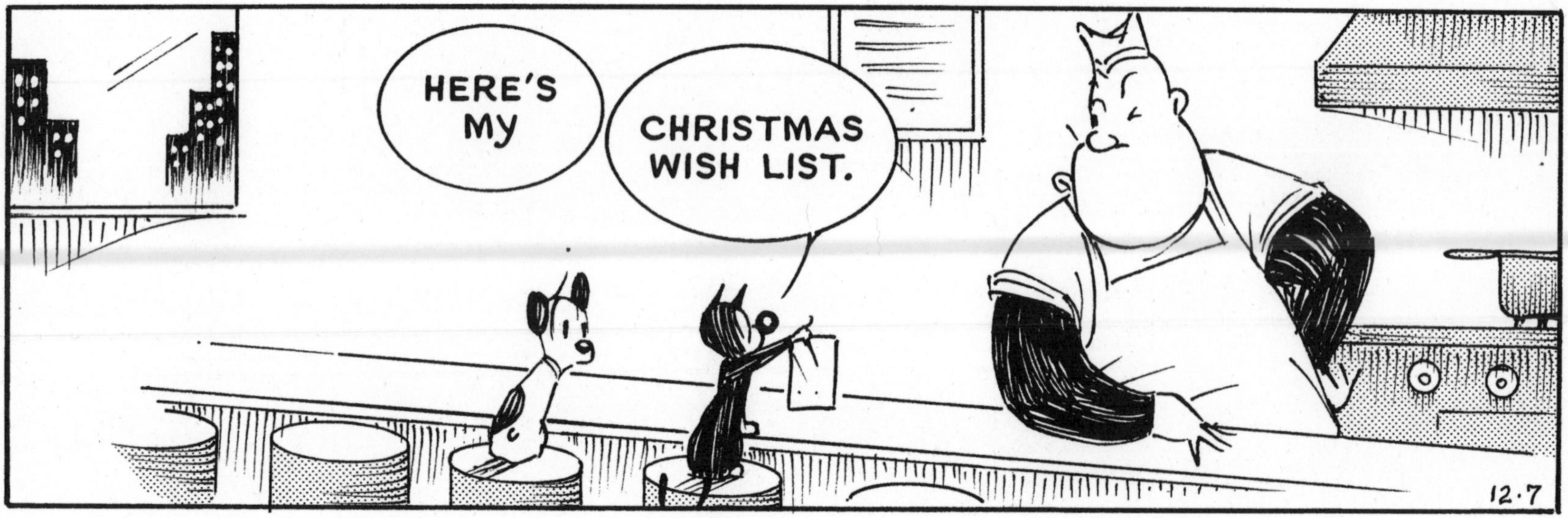
HERE'S MY
CHRISTMAS WISH LIST.
12·7

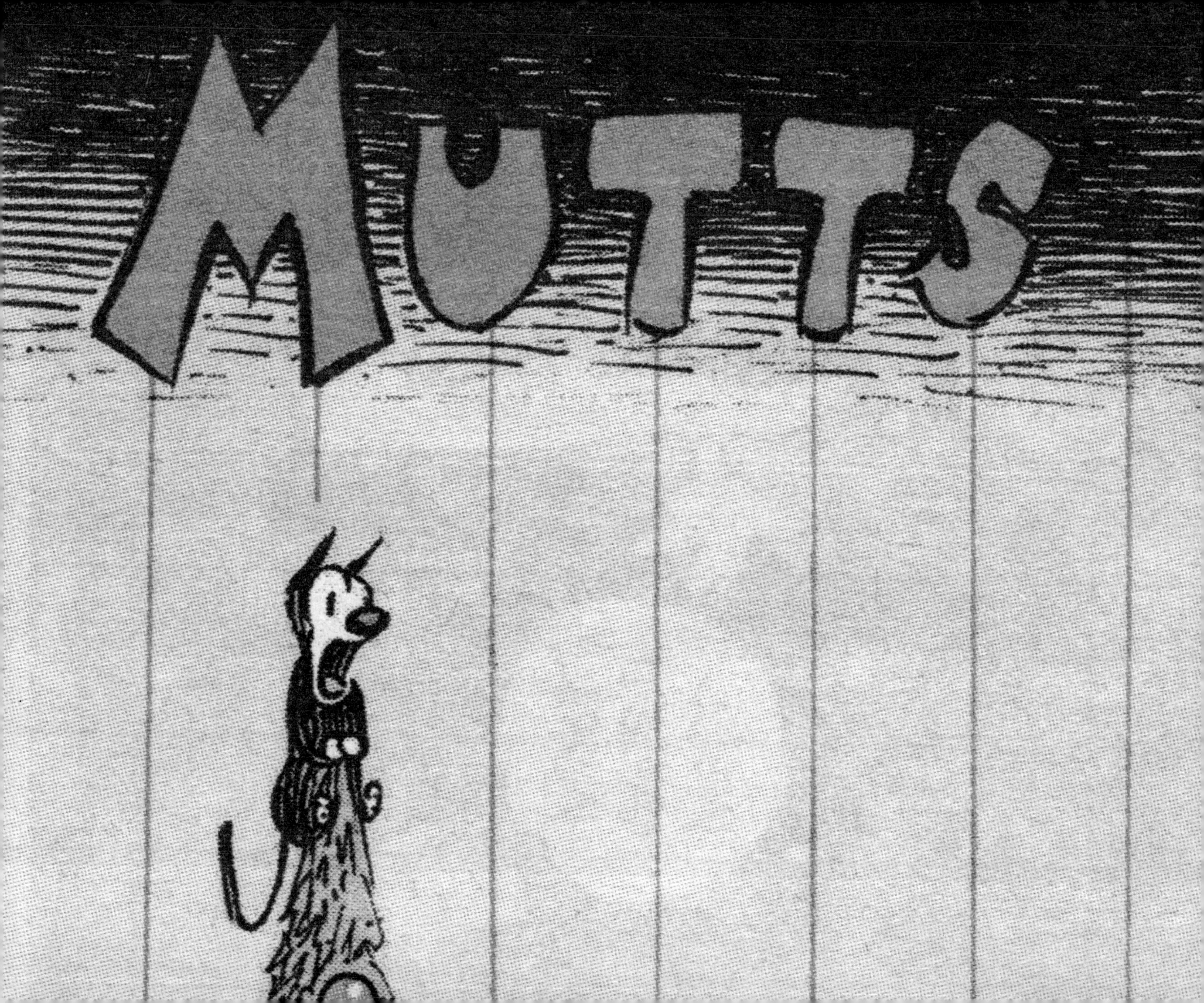
MUTTS

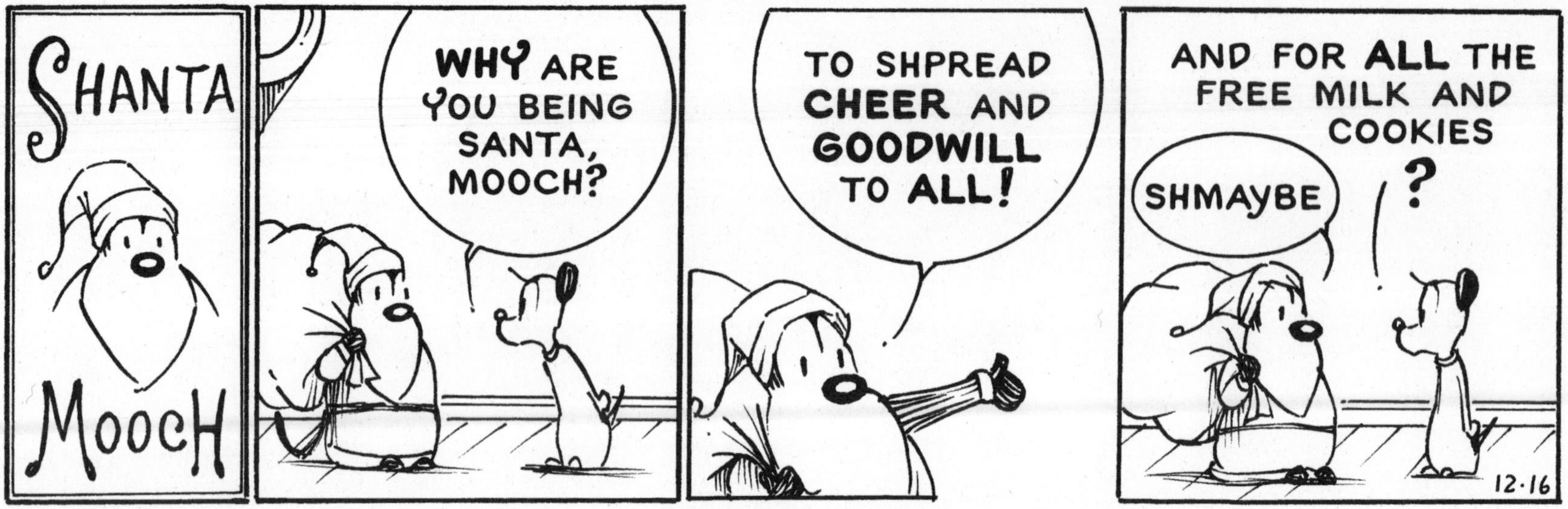
SHANTA MOOCH
WHY ARE YOU BEING SANTA, MOOCH?
TO SHPREAD CHEER AND GOODWILL TO ALL!
AND FOR ALL THE FREE MILK AND COOKIES
?
SHMAYBE
12·16

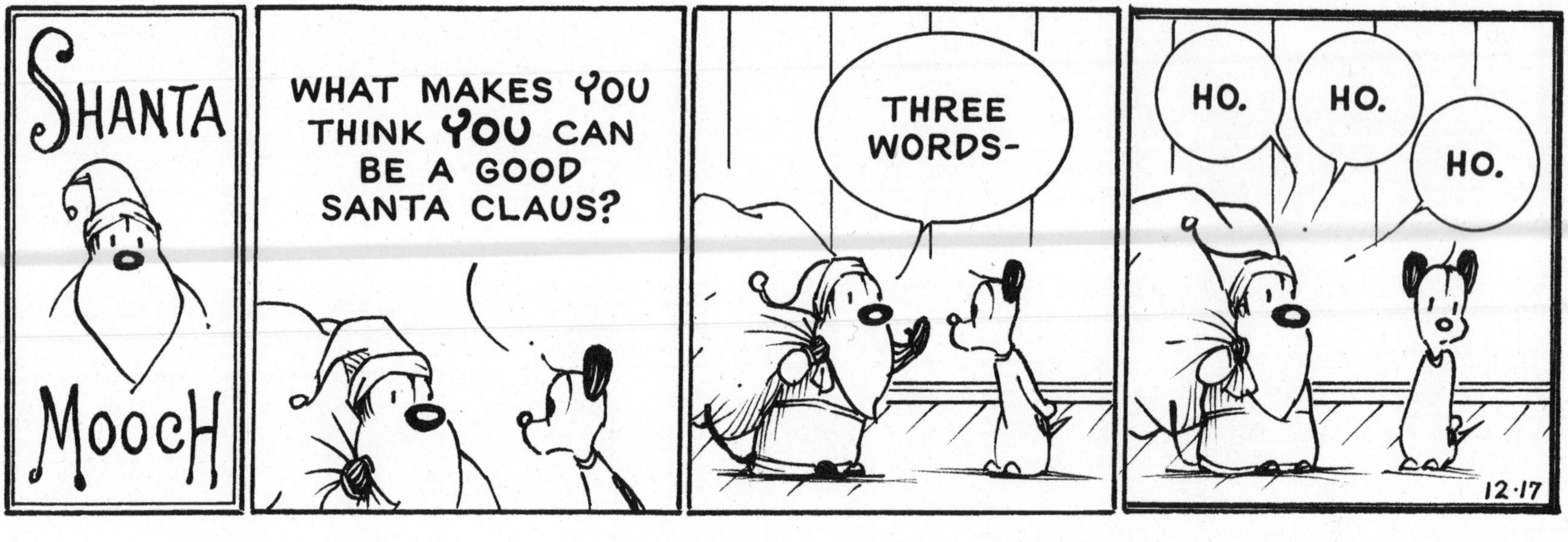
SHANTA MOOCH
WHAT MAKES YOU THINK YOU CAN BE A GOOD SANTA CLAUS?
THREE WORDS-
HO.
HO.
HO.
12·17

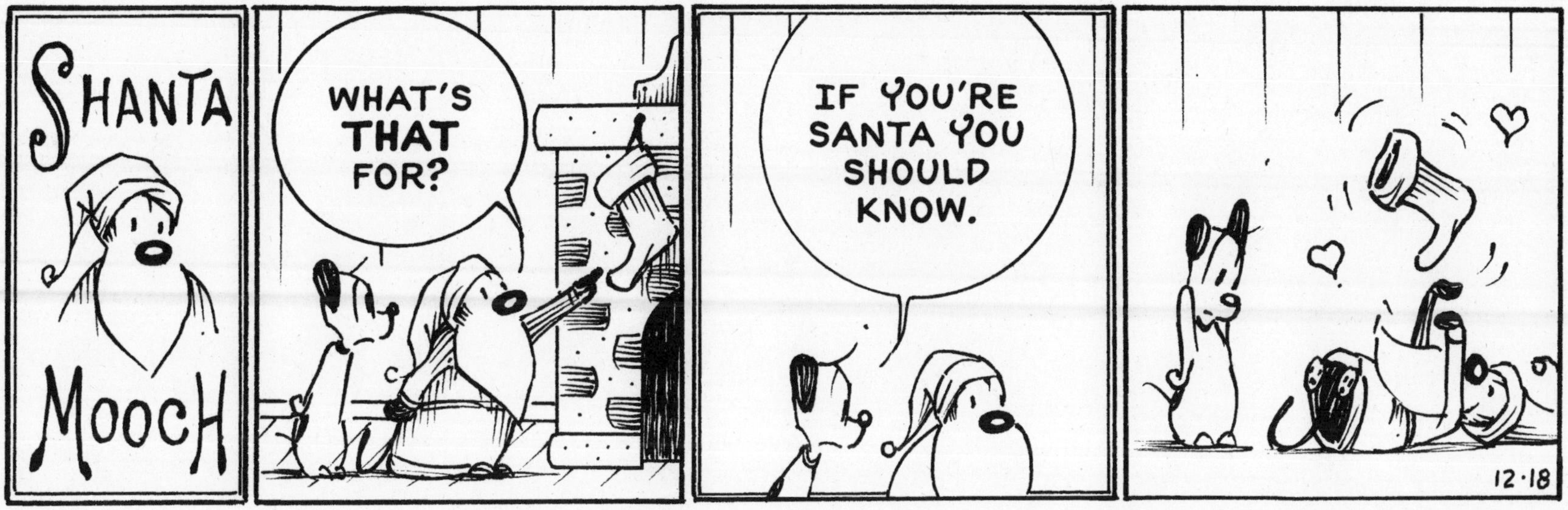
SHANTA MOOCH
WHAT'S THAT FOR?
IF YOU'RE SANTA YOU SHOULD KNOW.
12·18

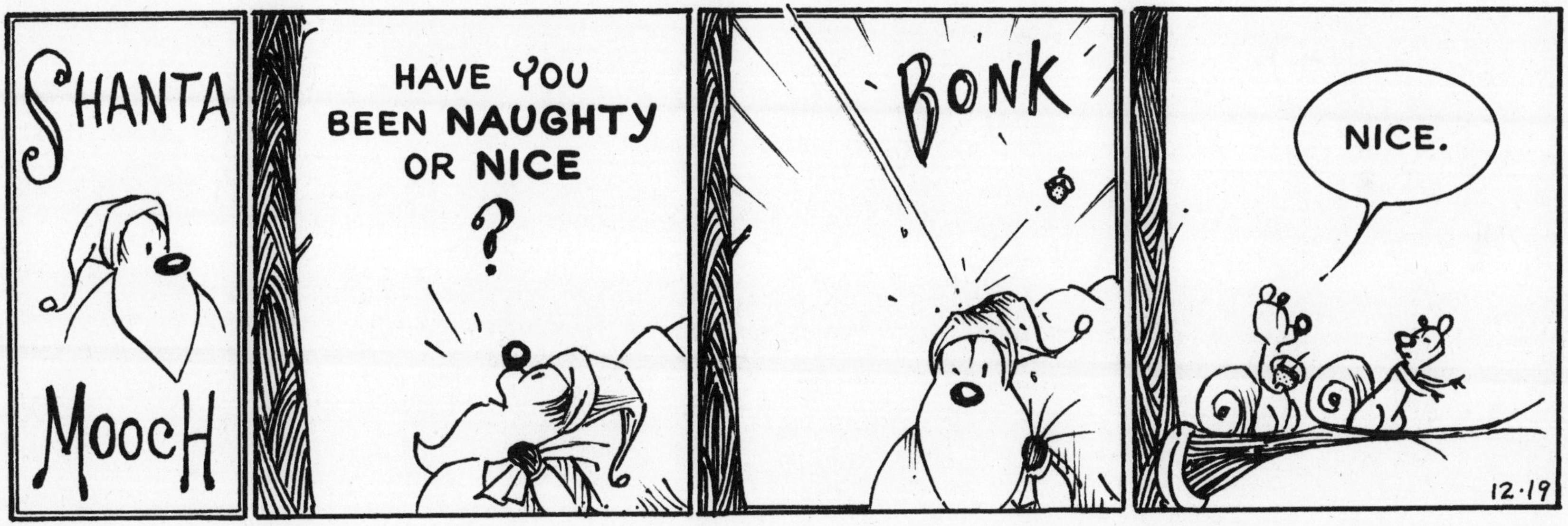
SHANTA MOOCH
HAVE YOU BEEN NAUGHTY OR NICE ?
BONK
NICE.
12·19

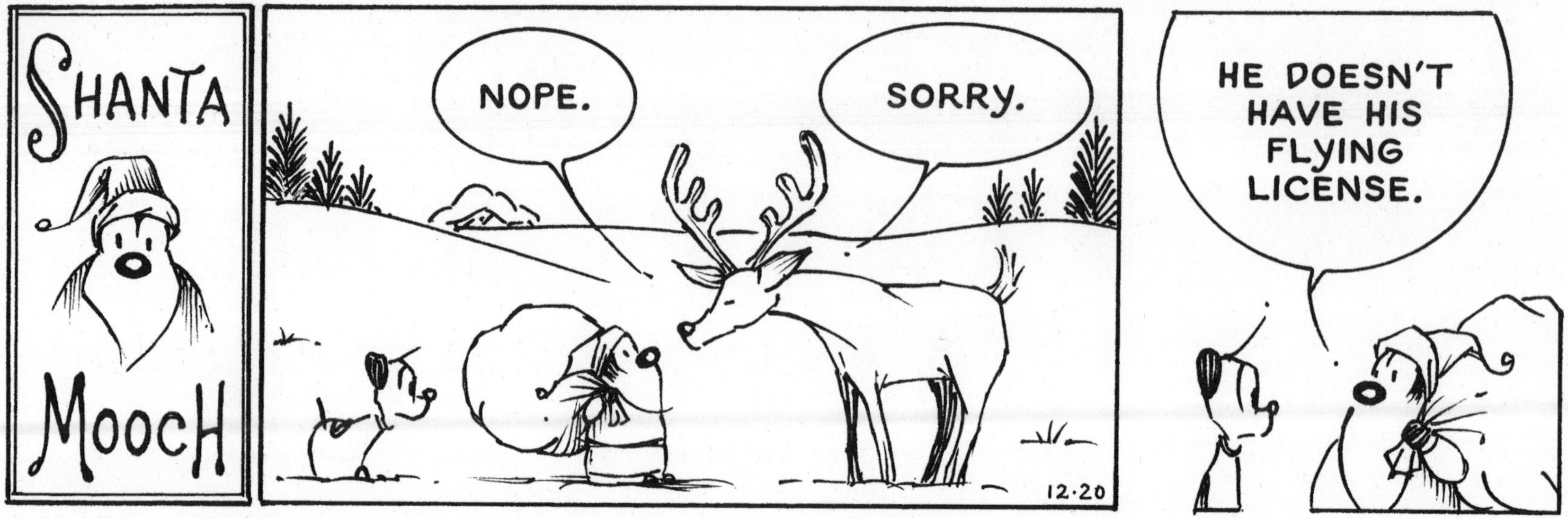
SHANTA MOOCH
NOPE.
SORRY.
12·20
HE DOESN'T HAVE HIS FLYING LICENSE.

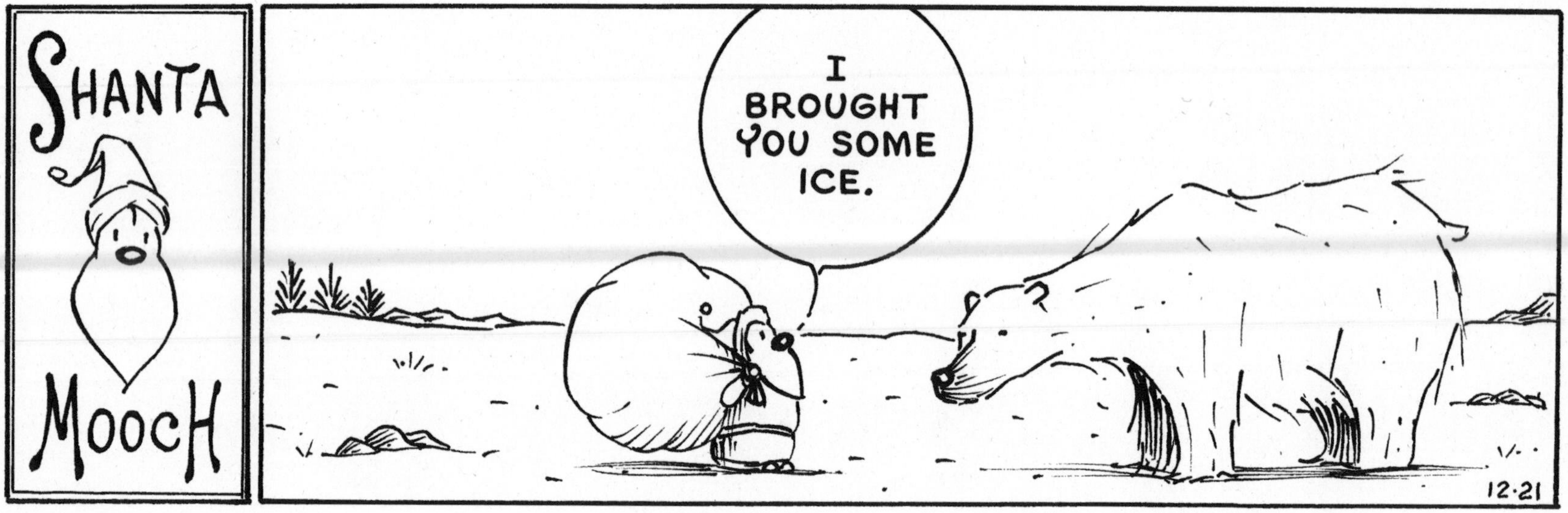
SHANTA MOOCH
I BROUGHT YOU SOME ICE.
12·21

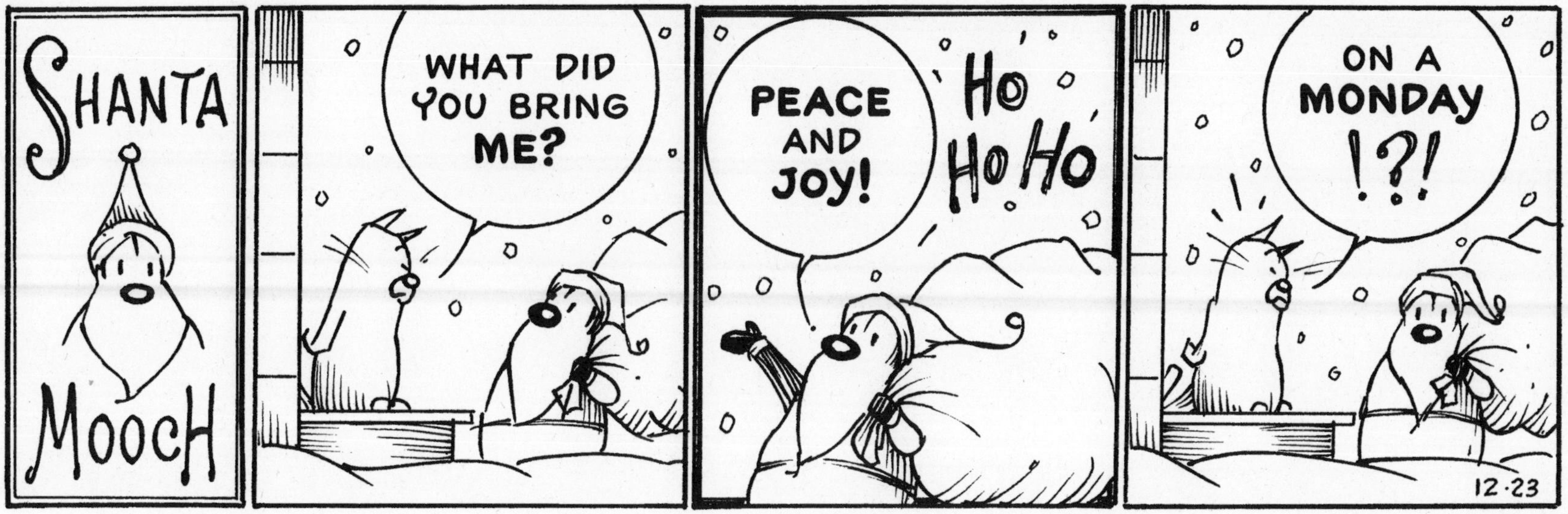
SHANTA MOOCH
WHAT DID YOU BRING ME?
PEACE AND JOY!
HO HO HO
ON A MONDAY !?!
12·23

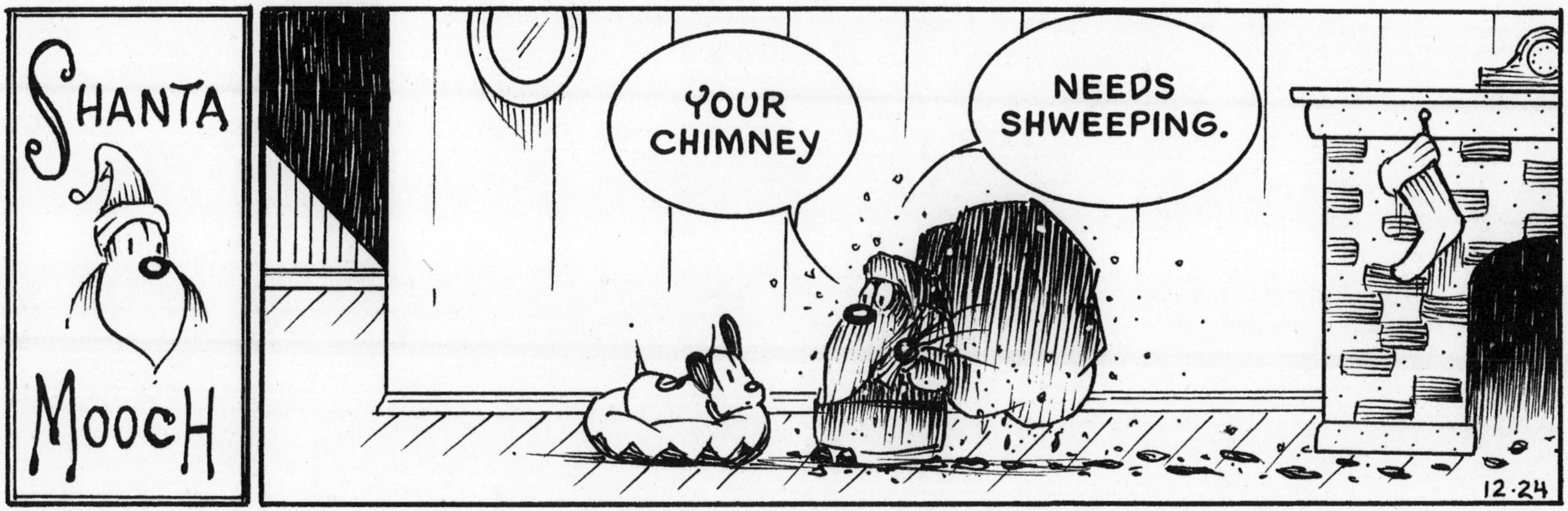
SHANTA MOOCH
YOUR CHIMNEY
NEEDS SHWEEPING.
12·24

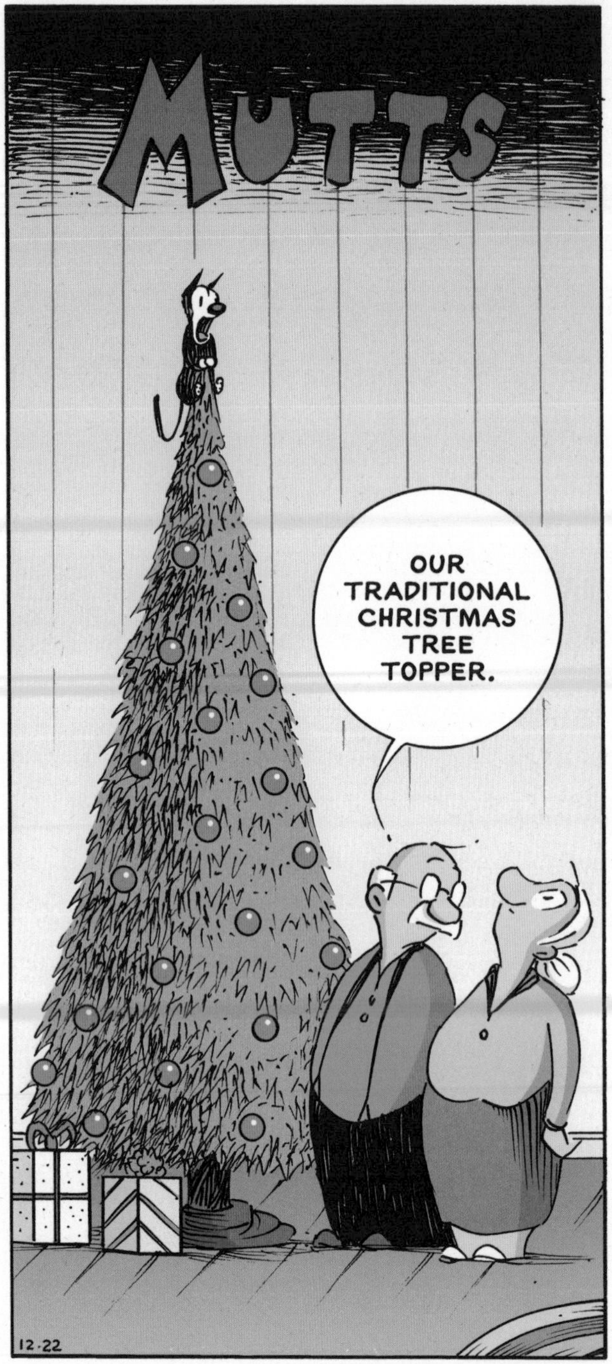
MUTTS
OUR TRADITIONAL CHRISTMAS TREE TOPPER.
12-22

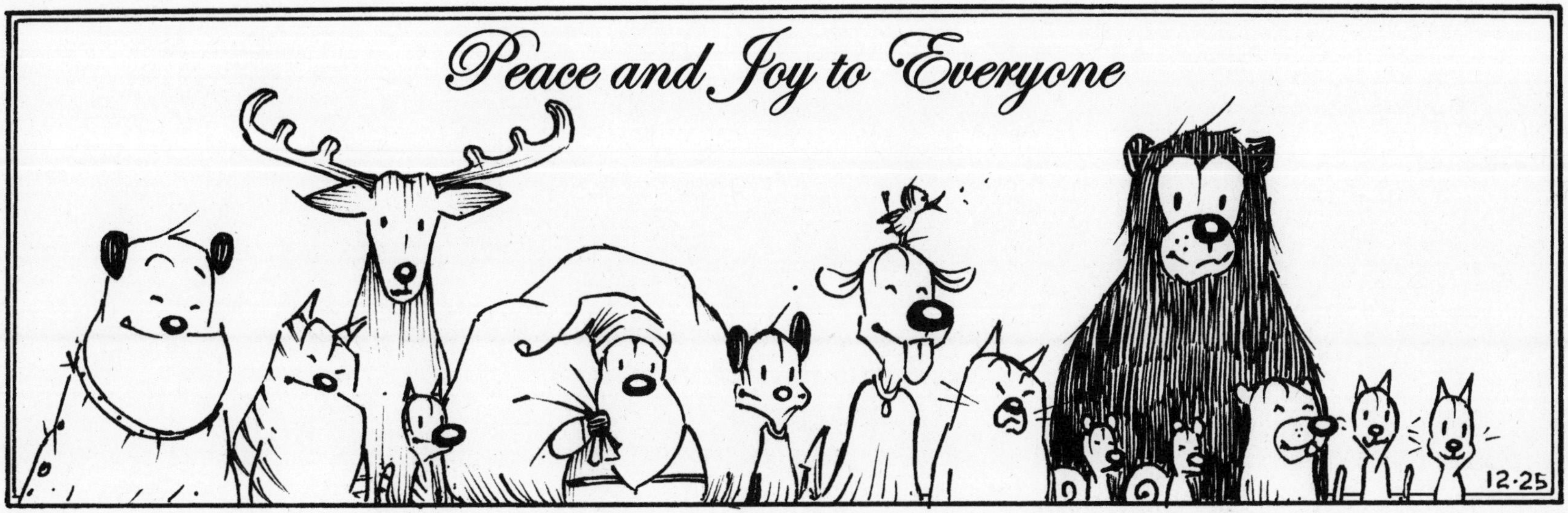
Peace and Joy to Everyone
12·25

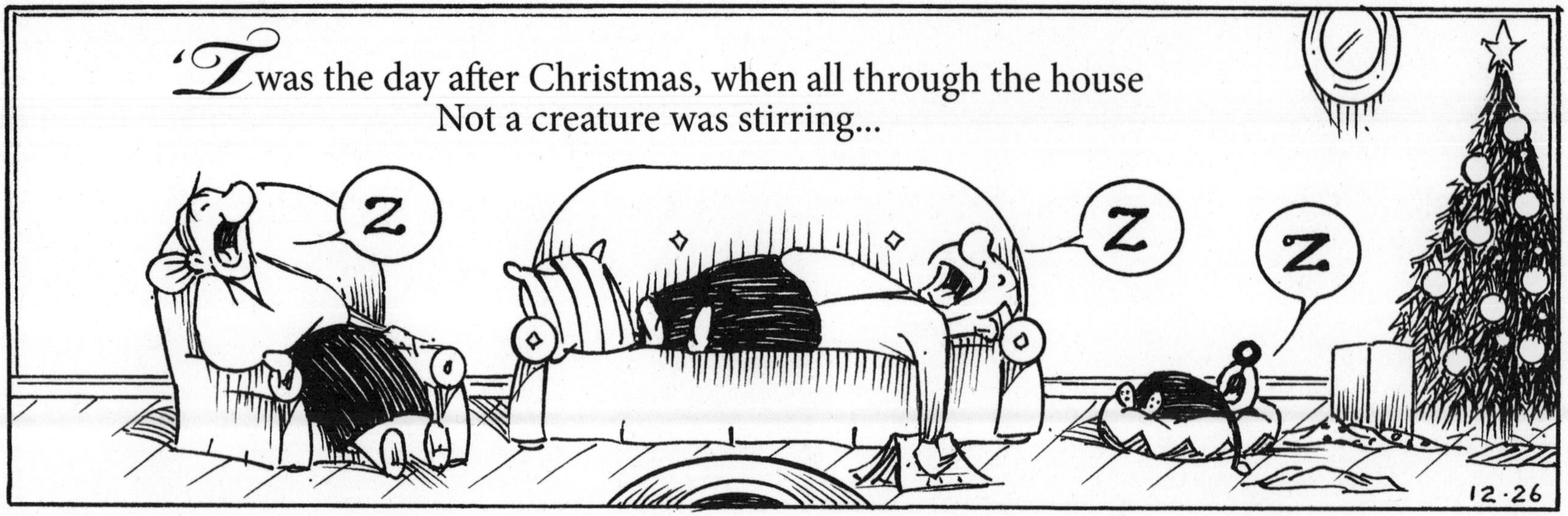
'Twas the day after Christmas, when all through the house
Not a creature was stirring...
Z
Z
Z
12·26

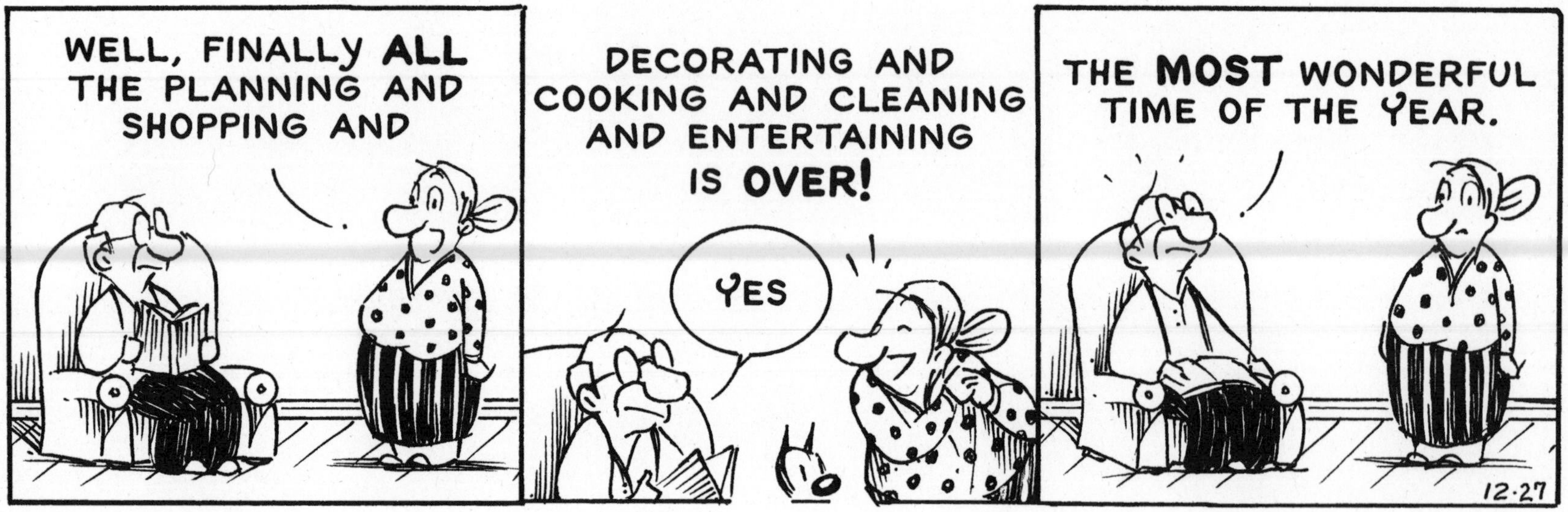
WELL, FINALLY ALL THE PLANNING AND SHOPPING AND
DECORATING AND COOKING AND CLEANING AND ENTERTAINING IS OVER!
YES
THE MOST WONDERFUL TIME OF THE YEAR.
12·27

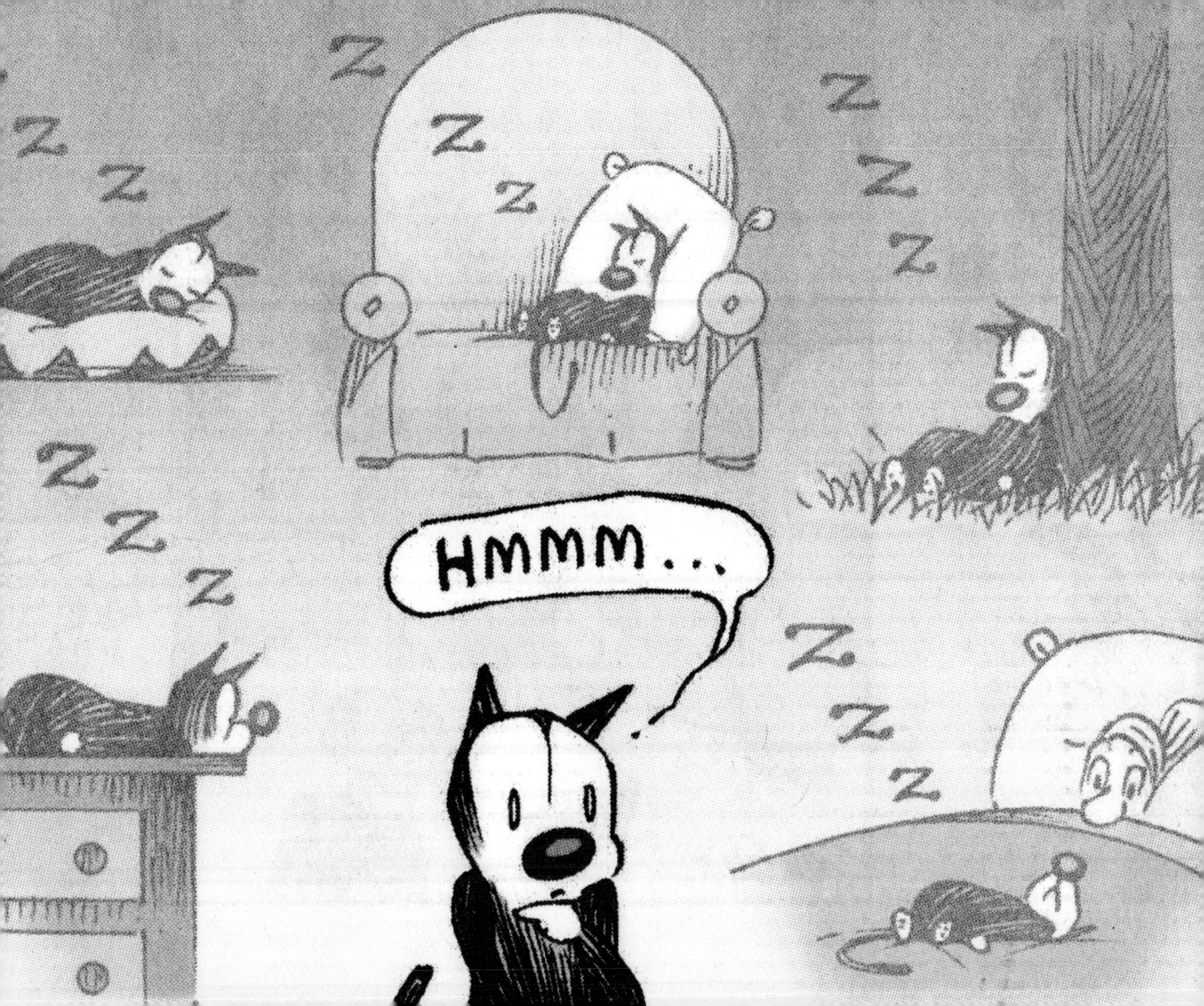
Z
Z
Z
Z
Z
Z
Z
Z
Z
Z
Z
Z
Z
Z
Z
HMMM...

MOOCH, THIS IS A GOOD TIME FOR YOUR ANNUAL REVIEW.
HMMM...
YESH!
ANOTHER GREAT YEAR.
12·29